HUNT EMERSON

T0269782

KNOCKABOUT

Cover painting for Fortean Times issue 29.

Phenomenomix ©2022 by Hunt Emerson
Published by Knockabout Comics 42c Lancaster Road, London, W11 1QR, United Kingdom.
Hunt Emerson has asserted their rights under the Copyright, Designs and Patents Act 1988
to be identified as the author of this work.
ISBN 9780861662906
Printed in Lithuania
10 9 8 7 6 5 4 3 2 1

INTRODUCTION

by Bob Rickard

t is my very great pleasure and privilege to introduce this wonderful collection of comic trips created by Hunt Emerson for Fortean Times (FT), the magazine of strange phenomena that I founded in 1973.

n those early days, the text was bashed out on my old Olivetti Leterra 22 typewriter, in columns. Under the skylight of my attic flat in he Moseley district of Birmingham, I would ut out the columns ready to paste onto he layout sheets. For graphics, I'd cut items rom newspapers, make up headings with etraset, and then head down to the nearest nstaprint' shop/ store to rush off some copes. It was a genuine kitchen-table top punk anzine of that era. But it was also rather dullooking and text heavy. I needed to improve he graphics and add some humour.

had known of Hunt earlier but not yet met im. On my way into the Art College at Gosa Green, I would often stop in at the Japeus bookshop, to browse the comix and SF. unt was working from a local arts centre nd would bring his latest Large Cow comics the shop. I must have mentioned my need or an illustrator to Carol and Nick Moore, the wners, and they arranged for us to meet.

was, at the time, living in an upturned boat . well that's what my attic flat looked like. It as the location of the momentous encouner between Hunt and myself. I had almost rgotten that first meeting, but crazily Hunt id not, and his comic account of it opens this ntology. A short time later, when I left Biringham to live in London, Hunt took over is same attic flat of fond memory.

At that early meeting, I was immediately struck by Hunt's style. It seemed to me to belong to same genre as Bill Elder and Wally Wood, whose strips I adored from the old Mad Magazine. Even more appealing was the surrealism that Hunt's art shared with one of the 'greats' of American newspaper cartooning, George Herriman, whose Krazy Kat was one of the delights of my teens.

It was not difficult to see why Hunt's involvement was so right for FT. Fortean phenomena encompasses such weird happenings as falls of frogs, human combustion, UFOs, religious visions, encounters with fairies and ghosts, teleporting people and mystery animals, etc. FT is named after Charles Fort (1874-1932), the American who pioneered collecting such news stories and writing them up.

To an everyday view these topics are strangely absurd and yet interesting; to the orthodox and closed-minded they are outrageously impossible. Hunt's own remarkable style of illustration, so dream-like, seemed to encompass, precisely, the sort of chaotic, funny, and yet wonderful surrealism of these often unexplained phenomena.

Asking Hunt to join the young FT was one of the best decisions I've ever made. We were a good fit with his own innate sense of absurdity, and our subject matter provided him endless inspiration. His first art for FT appeared in the following year, 1974. I had commissioned a set of banner headings for around 30 of our major headings; the first in FT8 (February 1975). Hunt's contributions have since become an essential visual component of FT – complementing how we are carrying out

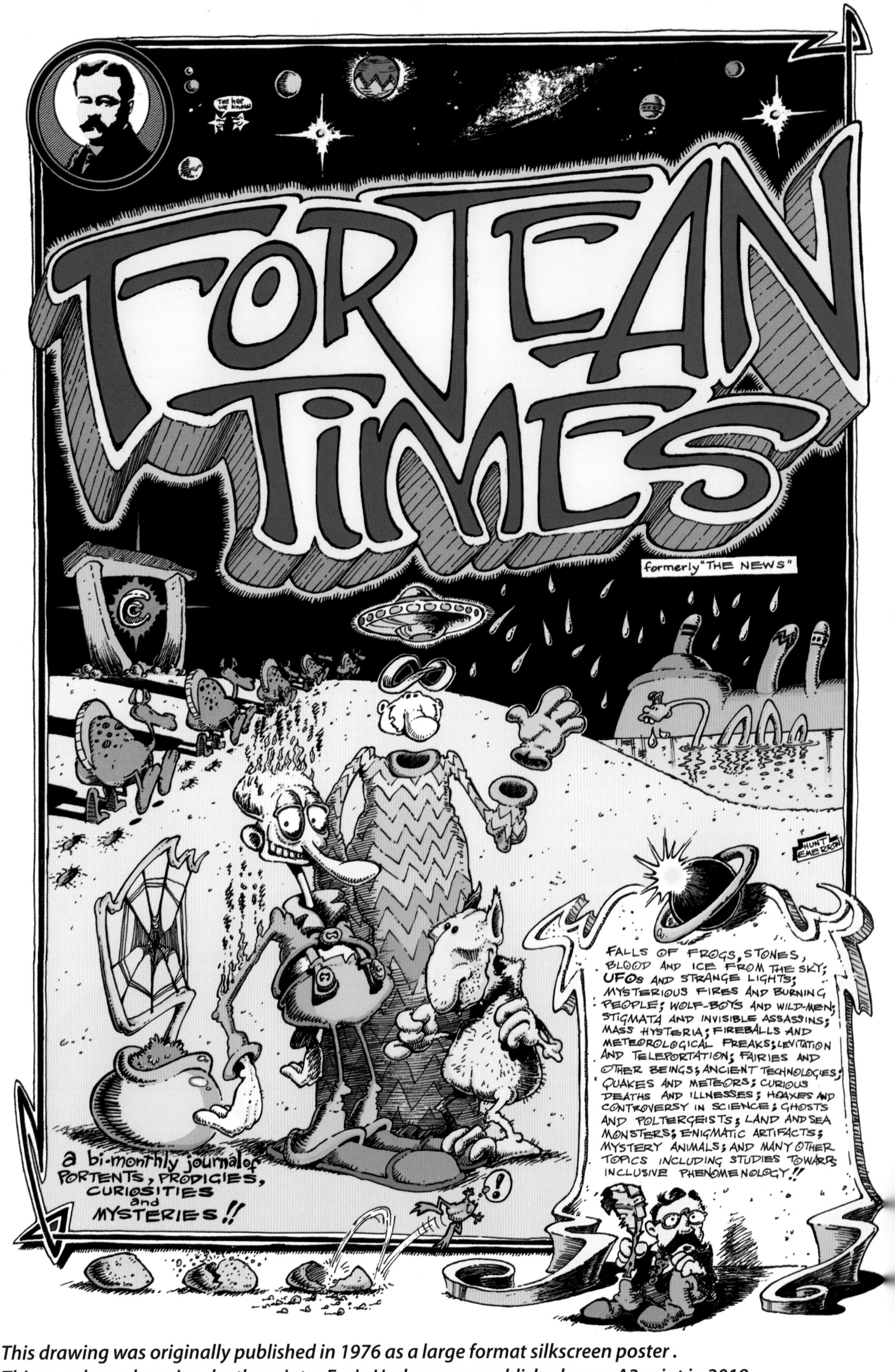
Tee hee we know
FORTEAN TIMES
formerly "THE NEWS"
HUNT EMERSON
FALLS OF FROGS, STONES, BLOOD AND ICE FROM THE SKY; UFOs AND STRANGE LIGHTS; MYSTERIOUS FIRES AND BURNING PEOPLE; WOLF-BOYS AND WILD-MEN; STIGMATA AND INVISIBLE ASSASSINS; MASS HYSTERIA; FIREBALLS AND METEOROLOGICAL FREAKS; LEVITATION AND TELEPORTATION; FAIRIES AND OTHER BEINGS; ANCIENT TECHNOLOGIES; QUAKES AND METEORS; CURIOUS DEATHS AND ILLNESSES; HOAXES AND CONTROVERSY IN SCIENCE; GHOSTS AND POLTERGEISTS; LAND AND SEA MONSTERS; ENIGMATIC ARTIFACTS; MYSTERY ANIMALS; AND MANY OTHER TOPICS INCLUDING STUDIES TOWARDS INCLUSIVE PHENOMENOLOGY!!
a bi-monthly journal of PORTENTS, PRODIGIES, CURIOSITIES and MYSTERIES!!
!

This drawing was originally published in 1976 as a large format silkscreen poster .
This re-coloured version, by the printer Ernie Hudson, was published as an A3 print in 2019.

the legacy of Charles Fort – in nearly every is-sue since. In fact, he is our oldest continuous contributor by 46 years! In time, Carol went on to establish Knockabout Comics in London with Tony Bennett ... and Hunt ascended into the pantheon of comix artists ... just as FT too became better known.

Then came Fortean Funnies, a three-page experiment in FT23 (Autumn 1977), scripted by the late Steve Moore. It celebrated phenomena associated with the number 23, made famous by the late Robert Anton Wilson. A second instalment celebrated our fifth anniversary (FT27, Autumn 1977). After that, Hunt's gloriously uproarious series Phenomenomix really took off. Many of the episodes of Phenomenomix since have featured the character of Gully Bull (get it?) as FT's hapless investigator of baffling anomalies, but his first appearance was in FT30 (Winter 1979); and occasionally, Hunt drew multi-part stories for the series, such as the utterly daft 'Borders of Buffoonery' in FT34-FT36.

I am particularly proud of three of my collaborations with Hunt. The first is 'The Material of Sagas', a two-pager in FT41, which harked back to the original experiment in FT23 by adapting one of the most poetic passages in Book of the Damned (1919), Fort's first book. Then there is the intermittent series of half-pagers called 'Great Moments in Science' that we put together to celebrate some monumental absurdities.

The third wonder is this opportunity to showcase Hunt's special collaboration with Fortean Times, in which he shows in a few brilliant images what the rest of us have been trying to say in thousands of words. Only Fort's "strange orthogenetic gods" know how much this unsettling world needs Hunt's enlightened humour.

Bob Rickard

NEARLY 40 YEARS OF FORTEAN COMIX

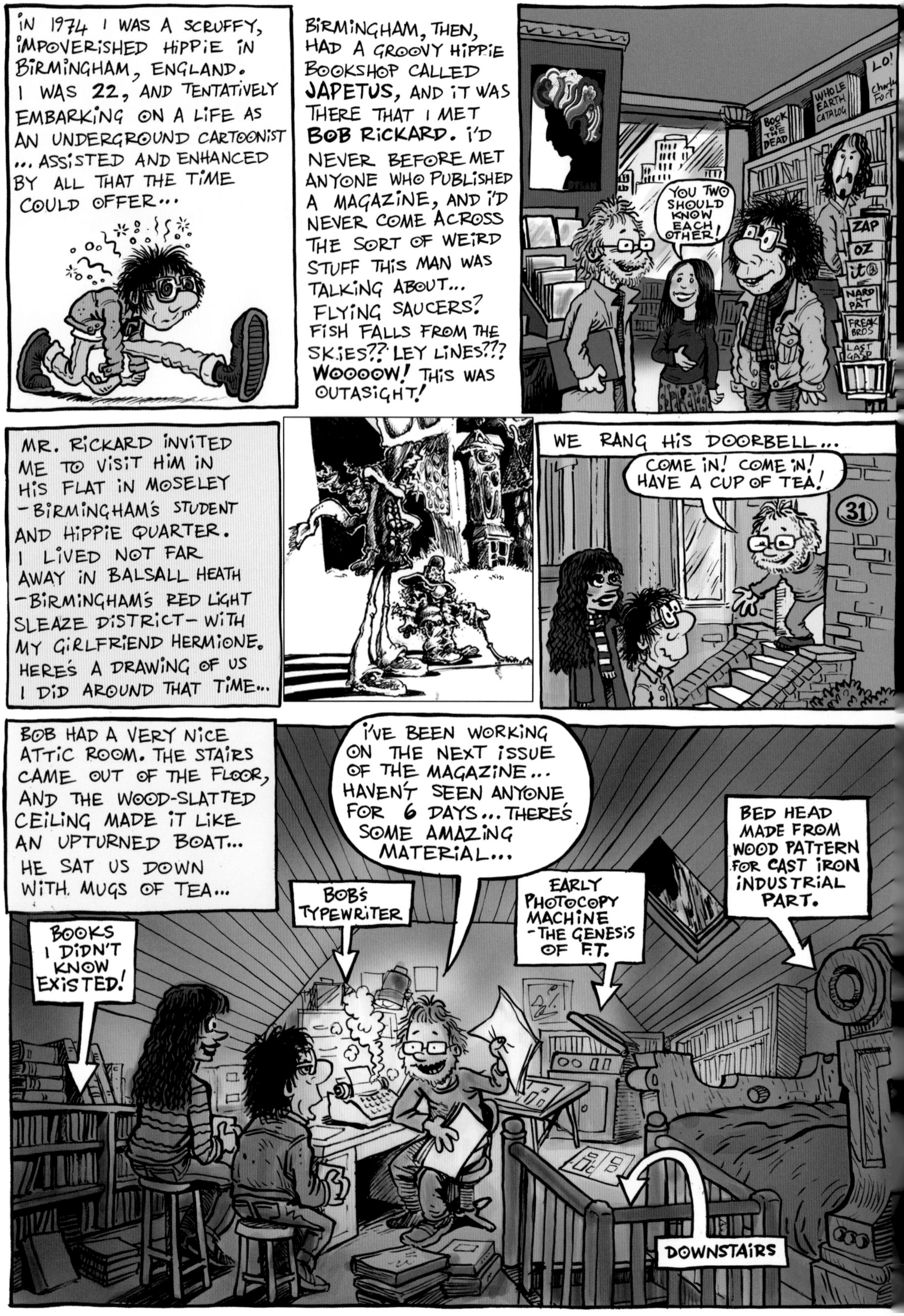
IN 1974 I WAS A SCRUFFY, IMPOVERISHED HIPPIE IN BIRMINGHAM, ENGLAND. I WAS 22, AND TENTATIVELY EMBARKING ON A LIFE AS AN UNDERGROUND CARTOONIST ... ASSISTED AND ENHANCED BY ALL THAT THE TIME COULD OFFER...
BIRMINGHAM, THEN, HAD A GROOVY HIPPIE BOOKSHOP CALLED JAPETUS, AND IT WAS THERE THAT I MET BOB RICKARD. I'D NEVER BEFORE MET ANYONE WHO PUBLISHED A MAGAZINE, AND I'D NEVER COME ACROSS THE SORT OF WEIRD STUFF THIS MAN WAS TALKING ABOUT... FLYING SAUCERS? FISH FALLS FROM THE SKIES?? LEY LINES??? WOOOOW! THIS WAS OUTASIGHT!
LO!
BOOK OF THE DEAD
WHOLE EARTH CATALOG
DYLAN
YOU TWO SHOULD KNOW EACH OTHER!
ZAP
OZ
FREAK BROS
LAST GASP
MR. RICKARD INVITED ME TO VISIT HIM IN HIS FLAT IN MOSELEY – BIRMINGHAM'S STUDENT AND HIPPIE QUARTER. I LIVED NOT FAR AWAY IN BALSALL HEATH – BIRMINGHAM'S RED LIGHT SLEAZE DISTRICT – WITH MY GIRLFRIEND HERMIONE. HERE'S A DRAWING OF US I DID AROUND THAT TIME...
WE RANG HIS DOORBELL...
COME IN! COME IN! HAVE A CUP OF TEA!
31
BOB HAD A VERY NICE ATTIC ROOM. THE STAIRS CAME OUT OF THE FLOOR, AND THE WOOD-SLATTED CEILING MADE IT LIKE AN UPTURNED BOAT... HE SAT US DOWN WITH MUGS OF TEA...
I'VE BEEN WORKING ON THE NEXT ISSUE OF THE MAGAZINE... HAVEN'T SEEN ANYONE FOR 6 DAYS... THERE'S SOME AMAZING MATERIAL...
BED HEAD MADE FROM WOOD PATTERN FOR CAST IRON INDUSTRIAL PART.
BOOKS I DIDN'T KNOW EXISTED!
BOB'S TYPEWRITER
EARLY PHOTOCOPY MACHINE – THE GENESIS OF F.T.
DOWNSTAIRS

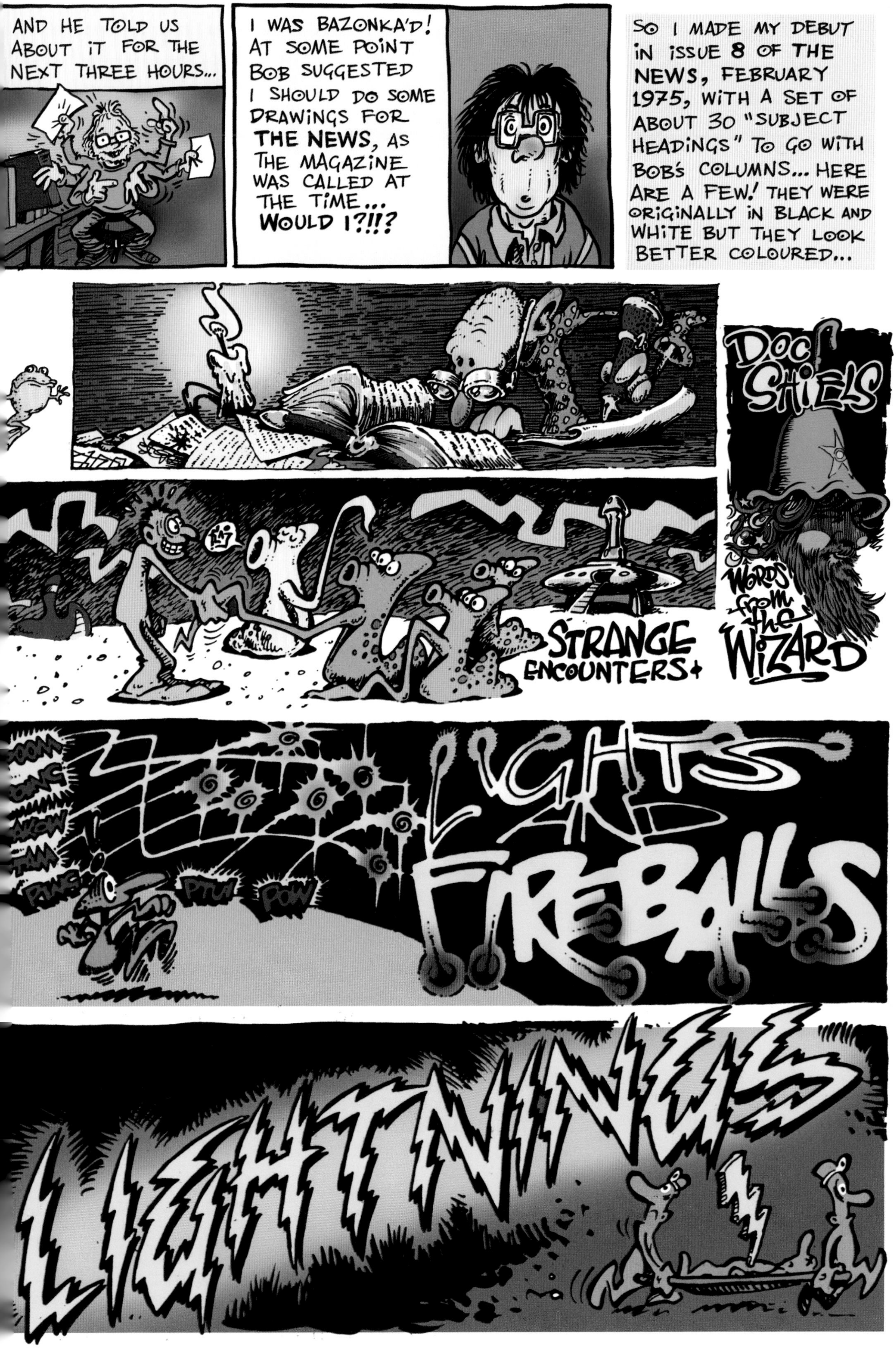
AND HE TOLD US ABOUT IT FOR THE NEXT THREE HOURS...
I WAS BAZONKA'D! AT SOME POINT BOB SUGGESTED I SHOULD DO SOME DRAWINGS FOR THE NEWS, AS THE MAGAZINE WAS CALLED AT THE TIME... WOULD I?!!?
SO I MADE MY DEBUT IN ISSUE 8 OF THE NEWS, FEBRUARY 1975, WITH A SET OF ABOUT 30 "SUBJECT HEADINGS" TO GO WITH BOB'S COLUMNS... HERE ARE A FEW! THEY WERE ORIGINALLY IN BLACK AND WHITE BUT THEY LOOK BETTER COLOURED...
Doc Shiels
Words from the Wizard
STRANGE ENCOUNTERS+
PTUI
POW
LIGHTS AND FIREBALLS
LIGHTNINGS

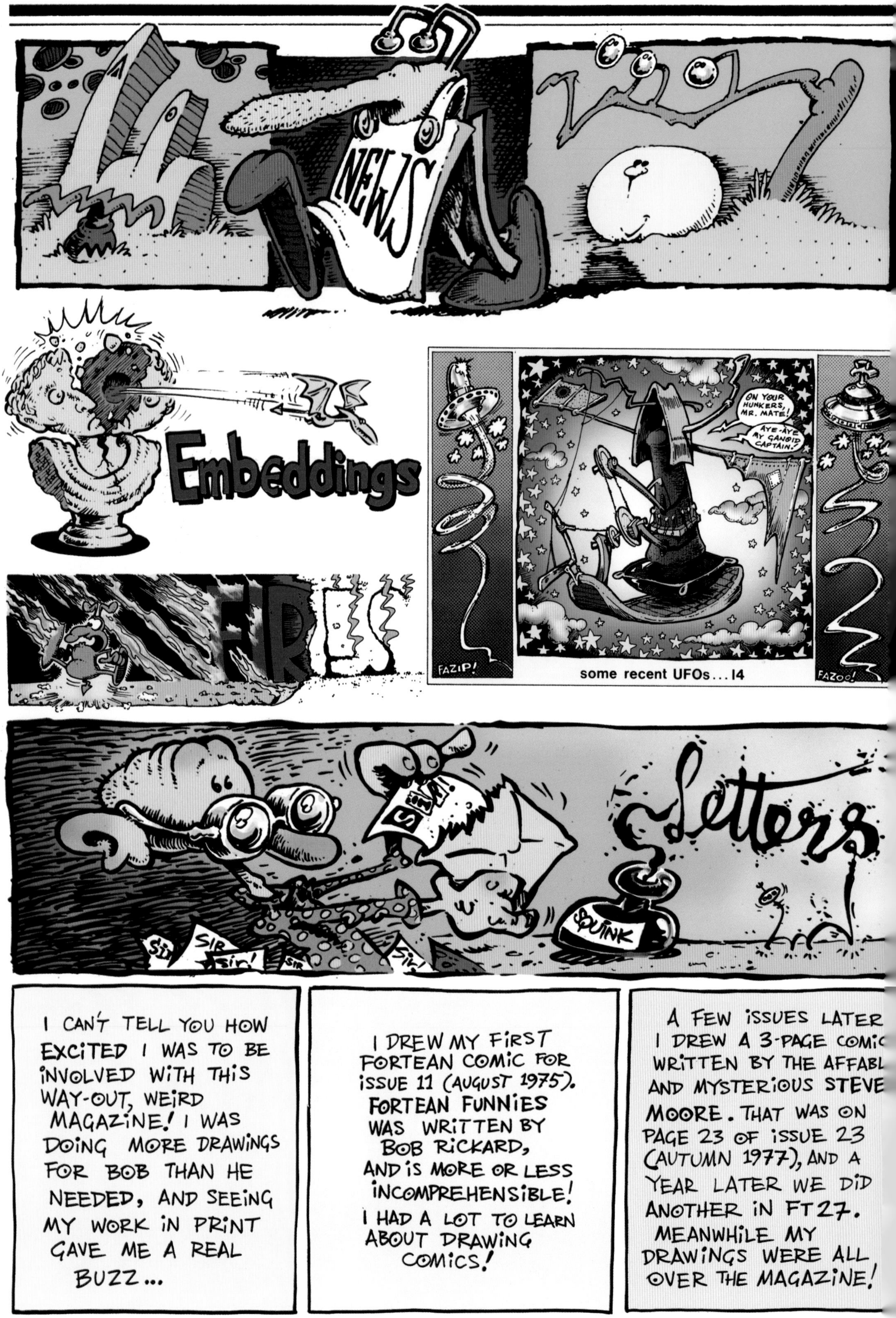
NEWS
Embeddings
FIRES
ON YOUR HUNKERS, MR. MATE!
AYE-AYE MY GANOID CAPTAIN!
FAZIP!
some recent UFOs... 14
FAZOO!
SIR!
Letters
SQUINK
SIR
SIR
SIR!
SIR
SIR!
I CAN'T TELL YOU HOW EXCITED I WAS TO BE INVOLVED WITH THIS WAY-OUT, WEIRD MAGAZINE! I WAS DOING MORE DRAWINGS FOR BOB THAN HE NEEDED, AND SEEING MY WORK IN PRINT GAVE ME A REAL BUZZ...
I DREW MY FIRST FORTEAN COMIC FOR ISSUE 11 (AUGUST 1975). FORTEAN FUNNIES WAS WRITTEN BY BOB RICKARD, AND IS MORE OR LESS INCOMPREHENSIBLE!
I HAD A LOT TO LEARN ABOUT DRAWING COMICS!
A FEW ISSUES LATER I DREW A 3-PAGE COMIC WRITTEN BY THE AFFABLE AND MYSTERIOUS STEVE MOORE. THAT WAS ON PAGE 23 OF ISSUE 23 (AUTUMN 1977), AND A YEAR LATER WE DID ANOTHER IN FT27. MEANWHILE MY DRAWINGS WERE ALL OVER THE MAGAZINE!

BETWEEN ISSUES 8 AND 9 OF **THE NEWS**, BOB MOVED AWAY FROM BIRMINGHAM, AND HERMIONE AND I TOOK OVER HIS FLAT IN MOSELEY. WE HAD THAT LOVELY ATTIC ROOM! A COUPLE OF YEARS OF MID-70's FUN AND GAMES WERE PLAYED OUT THERE, AND I WAS BY NOW CHURNING OUT MY COMICS - CALCULUS CAT, BILL THE BUNNY, MAX ZILLION, AND OF COURSE PHENOMENOMIX!

WE EVEN HAD A MINOR FORTEAN EVENT IN OUR ROOM! ONE NIGHT THERE WAS A GREAT STORM, AND THE SKYLIGHT WINDOW WAS CRACKED BY A SUPER-HAILSTONE THE SIZE OF A PIGEON EGG!

NOT MUCH, BUT SUITABLE...

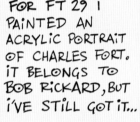

FOR FT 29 I PAINTED AN ACRYLIC PORTRAIT OF CHARLES FORT. IT BELONGS TO BOB RICKARD, BUT I'VE STILL GOT IT...

SORRY, BOB!

DO YOU WANT IT BACK?

Fortean Times

The Journal of Strange Phenomena

AND FT 30 (SEPT. 1979) FEATURED THE FIRST **PHENOMENOMIX** STRIP!

PHENOMENOMIX —YOU HAVE TO TAKE A RUN AT IT... I DO...

SOME TIMES I DON'T KNOW WHEN TO STOP!

PHENOMENOMEN OMENOMENOMEN OMENOMENOMIX!

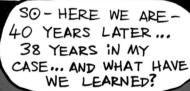

SO - HERE WE ARE - 40 YEARS LATER... 38 YEARS IN MY CASE... AND WHAT HAVE WE LEARNED?

Y'KNOW WHAT? I'LL TELL YOU!

THE WORLD'S A FUNNY PLACE!

PIG WITH 3 NOSES

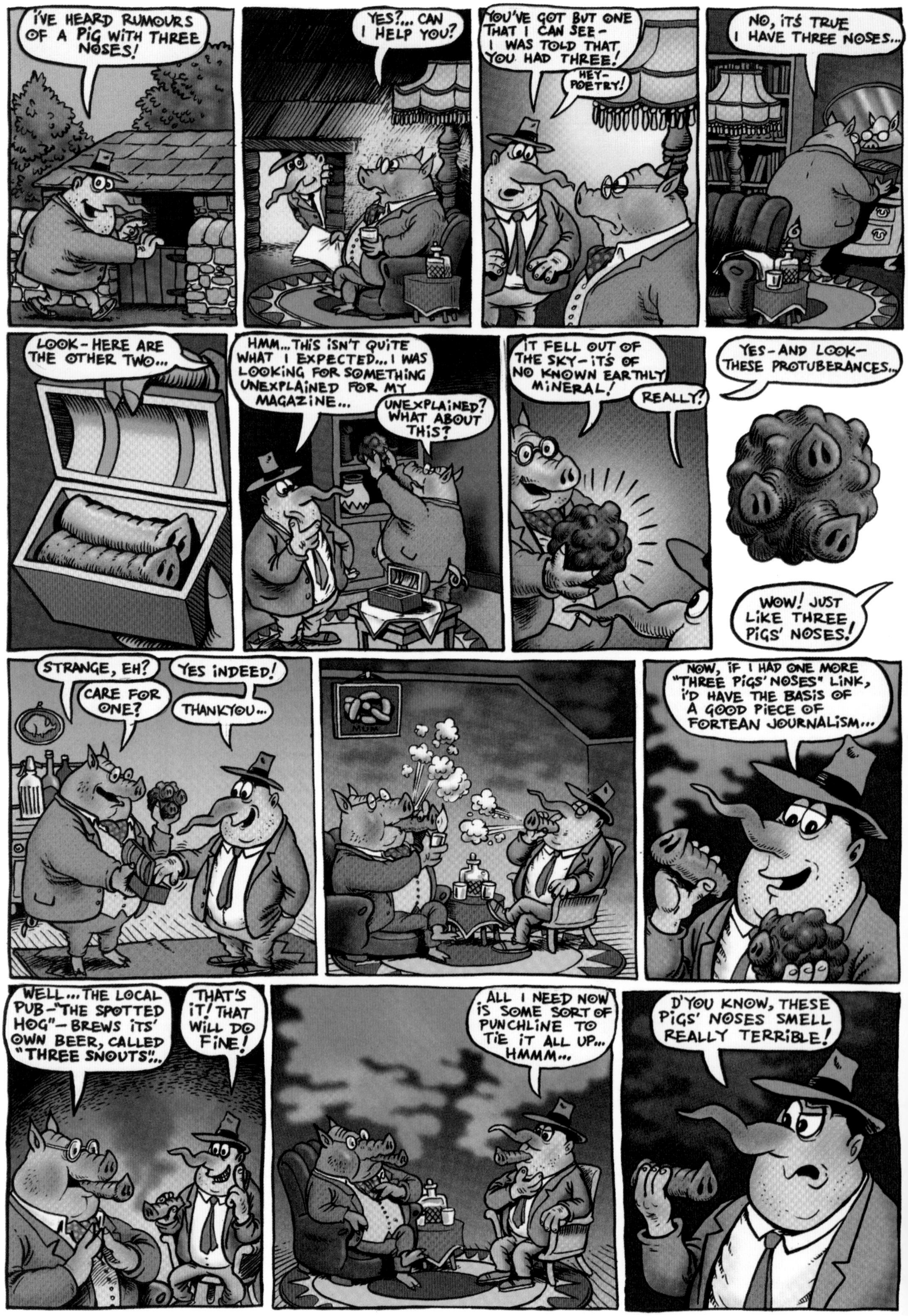

I'VE HEARD RUMOURS OF A PIG WITH THREE NOSES!
YES?... CAN I HELP YOU?
YOU'VE GOT BUT ONE THAT I CAN SEE - I WAS TOLD THAT YOU HAD THREE!
HEY- POETRY!
NO, IT'S TRUE I HAVE THREE NOSES...
LOOK- HERE ARE THE OTHER TWO...
HMM... THIS ISN'T QUITE WHAT I EXPECTED... I WAS LOOKING FOR SOMETHING UNEXPLAINED FOR MY MAGAZINE...
UNEXPLAINED? WHAT ABOUT THIS?
IT FELL OUT OF THE SKY- IT'S OF NO KNOWN EARTHLY MINERAL!
REALLY?
YES- AND LOOK- THESE PROTUBERANCES...
WOW! JUST LIKE THREE PIGS' NOSES!
STRANGE, EH?
YES INDEED!
CARE FOR ONE?
THANKYOU...
MUM
NOW, IF I HAD ONE MORE "THREE PIGS' NOSES" LINK, I'D HAVE THE BASIS OF A GOOD PIECE OF FORTEAN JOURNALISM...
WELL... THE LOCAL PUB-"THE SPOTTED HOG"- BREWS ITS' OWN BEER, CALLED "THREE SNOUTS"...
THAT'S IT! THAT WILL DO FINE!
ALL I NEED NOW IS SOME SORT OF PUNCHLINE TO TIE IT ALL UP... HMMM...
D'YOU KNOW, THESE PIGS' NOSES SMELL REALLY TERRIBLE!

Hi FANS! GULLY BULL - FORTEAN INVESTIGATOR - HERE - GLAD TO BE BACK!

SO, WHAT'S BEEN HAPPENING IN THE WORLD OF WEIRDNESS WHILE I'VE BEEN OFF DOING MY RESEARCHES?

WELL, THERE WAS THE 70 FOOT, HORNED, GREEN APE THAT EMERGED FROM THE JUNGLE OF THE CONGO, TRAILING FIRE IN ITS FOOTSTEPS, AND CARVING A SWATHE OF DESTRUCTION FOR 200 MILES TO THE SEA... PERHAPS YOU SAW THE LIVE TV COVERAGE OF THAT?

I DIDN'T - I WAS INVESTIGATING A MERMAID IN YARMOUTH, WHICH TURNED OUT TO BE A HOAX...

OR MAYBE YOU REMEMBER THE FLEETS OF FLYING SAUCERS THAT CRISS-CROSSED THE WORLD'S SKIES IN MAY, IN INTRICATE, GRAPHIC, SOMETIMES OBSCENE FORMATIONS?

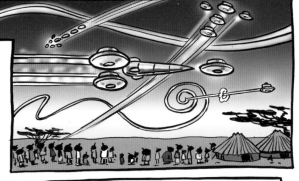

I MISSED THOSE TOO, I'M AFRAID... I WAS FAR TOO BUSY WITH A CASE INVOLVING A SIX INCH NAIL...

A MAN IN EALING HAD PUT UP A SHED, AND HE CLAIMED THE FACE OF CHRIST HAD APPEARED ON THE HEAD OF A NAIL AFTER HE HAMMERED IT IN...

THE SHED HAD BECOME A PLACE OF PILGRIMAGE...

MY METHODS WERE RIGOROUS! I GAVE THE NAIL ANOTHER COUPLE OF BELTS WITH THE HAMMER!

BAM BAM

NOW THE FACE ON THE NAIL WAS THAT OF ELVIS PRESLEY!

THE SHED BECAME A PLACE OF PILGRIMAGE FOR FANS OF THE KING...

A RELIGIOUS WAR BROKE OUT BETWEEN THE NAILITES AND THE PRESLEYANS, WHICH IS DEVASTATING SOUTHERN ENGLAND AS WE SPEAK...

AND IT'S ALL HIS FAULT!

HUNT EMERSON

60 YEARS OF UFOS

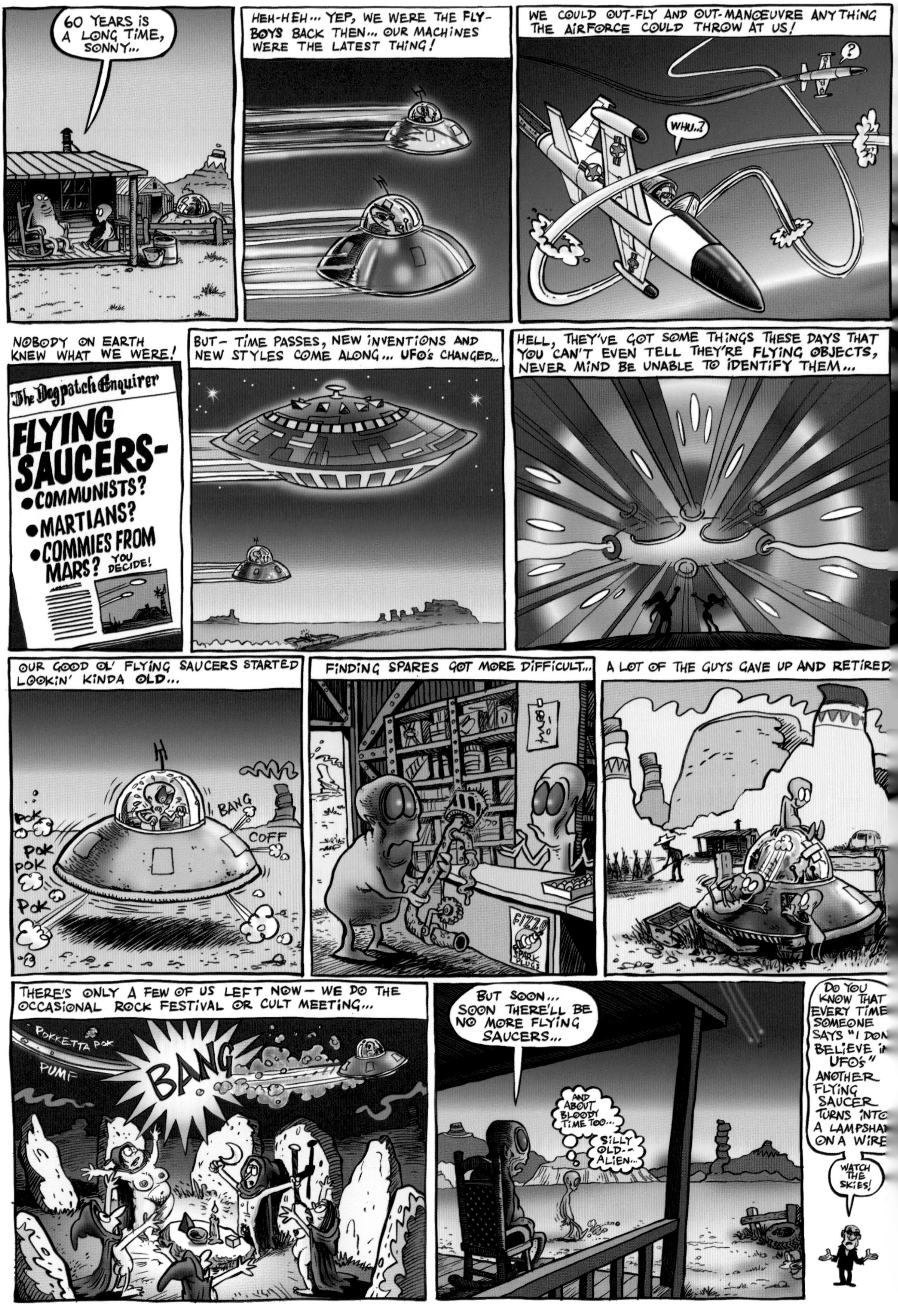

60 YEARS IS A LONG TIME, SONNY...
HEH-HEH... YEP, WE WERE THE FLY-BOYS BACK THEN... OUR MACHINES WERE THE LATEST THING!
WE COULD OUT-FLY AND OUT-MANOEUVRE ANYTHING THE AIRFORCE COULD THROW AT US!
?
WHU..?
NOBODY ON EARTH KNEW WHAT WE WERE!
The Dogpatch Enquirer
FLYING SAUCERS-
• COMMUNISTS?
• MARTIANS?
• COMMIES FROM MARS? YOU DECIDE!
BUT- TIME PASSES, NEW INVENTIONS AND NEW STYLES COME ALONG... UFO's CHANGED...
HELL, THEY'VE GOT SOME THINGS THESE DAYS THAT YOU CAN'T EVEN TELL THEY'RE FLYING OBJECTS, NEVER MIND BE UNABLE TO IDENTIFY THEM...
OUR GOOD OL' FLYING SAUCERS STARTED LOOKIN' KINDA OLD...
POK
POK
POK
POK
BANG
COFF
FINDING SPARES GOT MORE DIFFICULT...
FIZZO SPARK PLUGS
A LOT OF THE GUYS GAVE UP AND RETIRED.
THERE'S ONLY A FEW OF US LEFT NOW- WE DO THE OCCASIONAL ROCK FESTIVAL OR CULT MEETING...
POKKETTA POK
PUMF
BANG
BUT SOON... SOON THERE'LL BE NO MORE FLYING SAUCERS...
AND ABOUT BLOODY TIME TOO...
SILLY OLD ALIEN...
DO YOU KNOW THAT EVERY TIME SOMEONE SAYS "I DON BELIEVE IN UFO's" ANOTHER FLYING SAUCER TURNS INTO A LAMPSHA ON A WIRE
WATCH THE SKIES!

GULLY BULL'S NOSE FOR MYSTERY

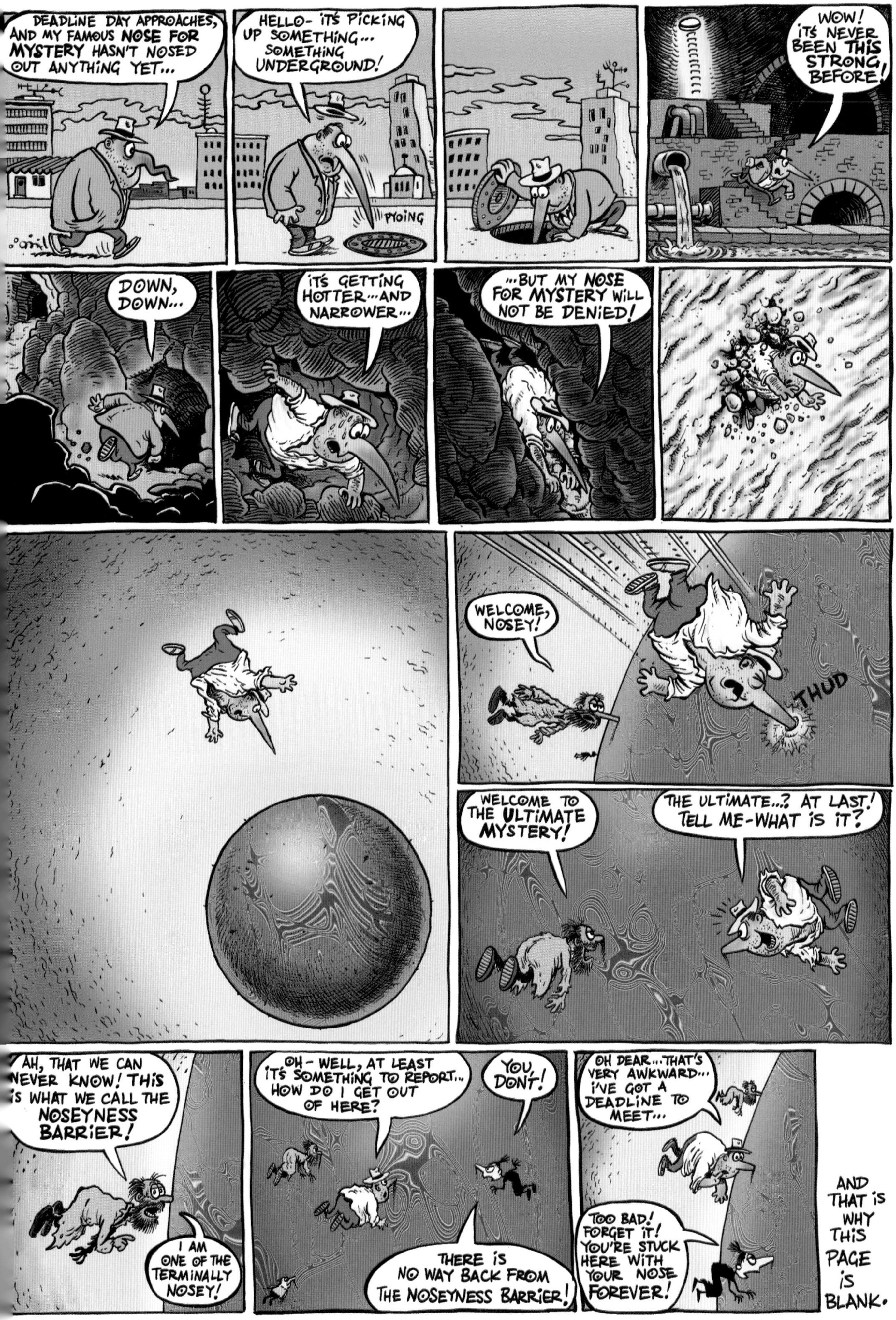

DEADLINE DAY APPROACHES, AND MY FAMOUS NOSE FOR MYSTERY HASN'T NOSED OUT ANYTHING YET...
HELLO- IT'S PICKING UP SOMETHING... SOMETHING UNDERGROUND!
PYOING
WOW! IT'S NEVER BEEN THIS STRONG BEFORE!
DOWN, DOWN...
IT'S GETTING HOTTER...AND NARROWER...
...BUT MY NOSE FOR MYSTERY WILL NOT BE DENIED!
WELCOME, NOSEY!
THUD
WELCOME TO THE ULTIMATE MYSTERY!
THE ULTIMATE...? AT LAST! TELL ME-WHAT IS IT?
AH, THAT WE CAN NEVER KNOW! THIS IS WHAT WE CALL THE NOSEYNESS BARRIER!
I AM ONE OF THE TERMINALLY NOSEY!
OH- WELL, AT LEAST IT'S SOMETHING TO REPORT.. HOW DO I GET OUT OF HERE?
YOU DON'T!
THERE IS NO WAY BACK FROM THE NOSEYNESS BARRIER!
OH DEAR...THAT'S VERY AWKWARD... I'VE GOT A DEADLINE TO MEET...
TOO BAD! FORGET IT! YOU'RE STUCK HERE WITH YOUR NOSE FOREVER!

AND THAT IS WHY THIS PAGE IS BLANK.

200 FORTEAN EVENTS

IN HONOUR OF 200 ISSUES OF YOUR FAVOURITE MAGAZINE, I WILL NOW ATTEMPT TO DEPICT 200 FORTEAN EVENTS* IN TWO PAGES OF COMICS!

*TAKEN FROM THE BOOKS OF CHARLES FORT - DOVER PUBLICATIONS 1974

YES, 200 PHENOMENA BETWEEN HERE AND THE FINAL FRAME IN THE BOTTOM RIGHT HAND CORNER! I MUST HAVE COMPLETE SILENCE PLEASE!

WE START WITH BENJAMIN BATHURST, WHO, IN 1809, WALKED AROUND SOME HORSES HE WAS EXAMINING AND WAS NEVER SEEN AGAIN!

I SAY-- BATHURST...

WHERE'S HE GONE?

1794 - FALL OF STONES IN SIENA, ITALY...

1852 - A TRIANGULAR CLOUD IN A STORM, WITH A RED NUCLEUS AND A LONG "TAIL"

1851 - A SIXPENNY IRON NAIL FOUND INSIDE A LUMP OF QUARTZ, WHEN THE LUMP WAS SPLIT...

1894 - FROGSPAWN FALLS FROM THE SKY ONTO BATH, ENGLAND...

AT THE SAME TIME, SMALL FROGS RAINED ON WIGAN, UK...

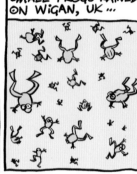

1871 - A "STORM OF GLUTINOUS DROPS" FALLS, AGAIN AT BATH...

...AND SEVERAL DAYS LATER, MORE FELL AT THE SAME PLACE...

1911 - BUCKS, UK - GROUND COVERED WITH MASSES OF JELLY...

1835 - GOTHA, GERMANY - JELLY LIKE MASS ON THE GROUND, THIS TIME ASSOCIATED WITH A METEORITE!

JUST A MINUTE! THOSE LAST FOUR - YOU HAVEN'T "DEPICTED" THEM - YOU JUST TAGGED THEM ONTO THAT DRAWING OF SOME FROGS!

WHAT? OH, YEAH... WELL - HOW MUCH JELLY DO YOU WANT ME TO DRAW? ANYWAY, EXCUSE ME, I'M LOSING TIME AND SPACE HERE...

...er... "..er... OK, THAT'S TEN! NUMBER ELEVEN...

DEC. 1883 - TWO ENORMOUS SHINING WHEELS APPEAR IN THE WATER ALONGSIDE A SHIP IN THE PERSIAN GULF...

1901 - PERSIAN GULF - ROTATING SHAFTS OF LIGHT IN THE WATER...

1880 - MALABAR COAST - SEA ILLUMINATED BY SHAFTS OF LIGHT IN WAVES...

1906 - GULF OF OMAN - "SHAFTS OF BRILLIANT LIGHT"...

1907 - MALACCA STRAIT - THE SAME PHENOMENON!

...AND I HAVE DATA FOR AT LEAST FIVE MORE!

IN 1885, NEAR YOKAHAMA, A FIERY MASS FELL FROM THE SKY INTO THE SEA...

1887 - A LARGE BALL OF FIRE RISES FROM THE SEA, NEAR CAPE RACE...

...AND IN 1845 3 LUMINOUS BODIES ARE SEEN TO RISE FROM THE SEA!

YOU'RE DOING IT AGAIN!

YES I AM! NOW WILL YOU PLEASE STAND ASIDE, SIR! OK - THAT'S 25!

25? I MAKE IT 23...YOU'VE COUNTED THOSE THREE LUMINOUS BODIES AS 3 PHENOMENA, HAVEN'T YOU!

FOR GOD'S SAKE - I'LL NEVER GET THROUGH THEM OTHERWISE!

OK OK JUST CHECKING... 23

RIGHT! THAT'S 25 - 25!

1890 - CALABRIA - A RAIN OF BLOOD...

...AND LATER, IN THE SAME PLACE, IT HAPPENED AGAIN!

1892 - A LUMINOUS OBJECT TRAVELS BACK AND FORTH IN THE SKY IN SWEDEN...

1905 - LLANGOLLEN, WALES - AN "INTENSLY BLACK OBJECT" ABOUT TWO MILES UP...

THROUGH FIELD GLASSES IT LOOKED LIKE A HUGE WINGED PIG WITH WEBBED FEET...

1898 - LILLE, FRANCE - A RECTANGULAR COLOURED OBJECT IN THE SKY...

1902 - SOUTH DEVON - IN THE SKY, A GREAT NUMBER OF HIGHLY COLOURED OBJECTS LIKE LITTLE SUNS...

1899 - ENORMOUS KITE-LIKE OBJECT FLASHING RED, WHITE AND BLUE - DORDOGNE, FRANCE

1899 - LUZARCHES, FRANCE - ROUND LUMINOUS OBJECT THAT MOVED AWAY AND DIMINISHED TO A POINT...

1899 - EL PASO, TEXAS - A LUMINOUS OBJECT THAT TRAVELLED WITH THE MOON...

NOT DOING VERY WELL, ARE YOU?...

GET OUT OF THE WAY!

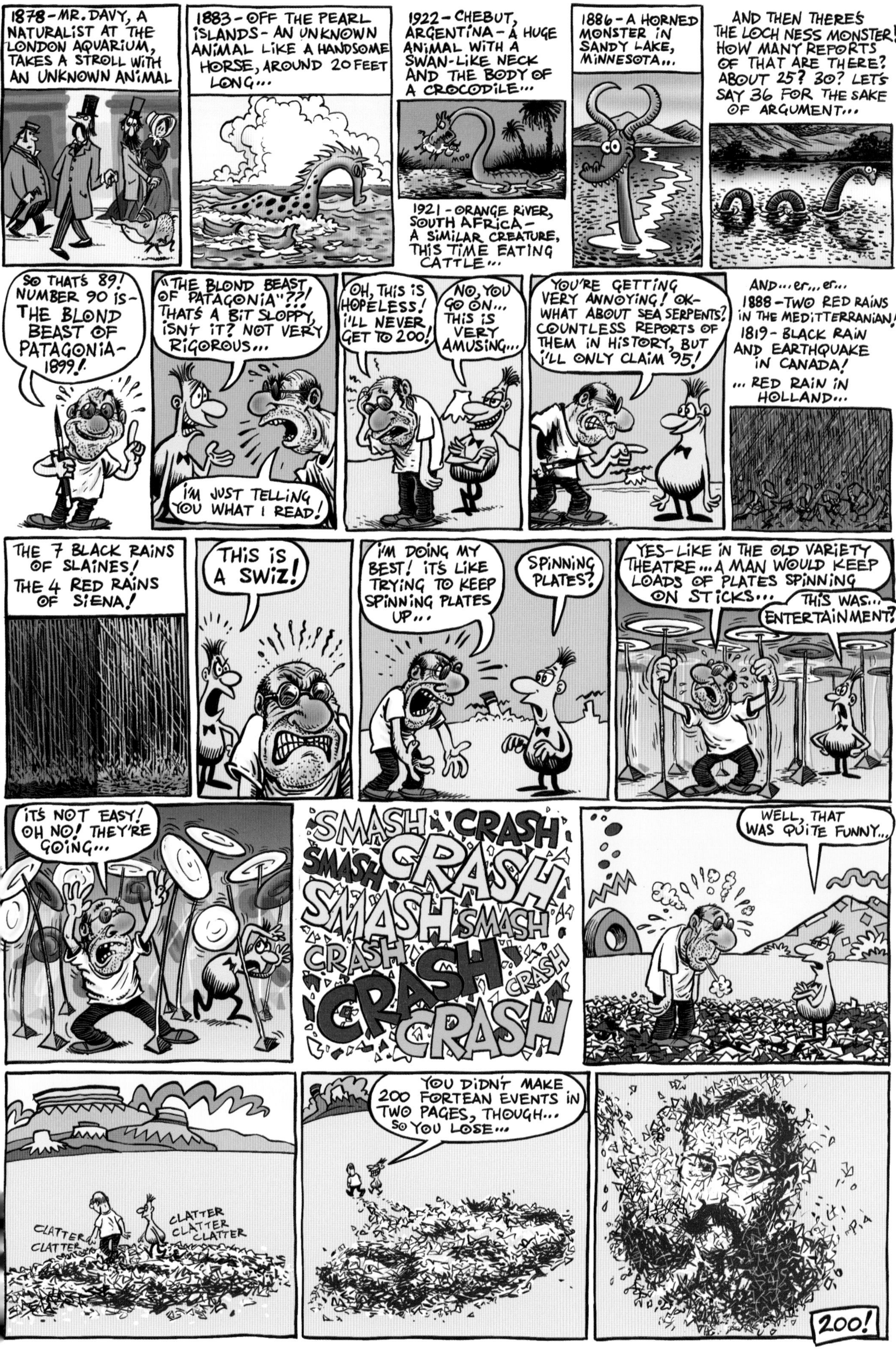

1878 - MR. DAVY, A NATURALIST AT THE LONDON AQUARIUM, TAKES A STROLL WITH AN UNKNOWN ANIMAL
1883 - OFF THE PEARL ISLANDS - AN UNKNOWN ANIMAL LIKE A HANDSOME HORSE, AROUND 20 FEET LONG...
1922 - CHEBUT, ARGENTINA - A HUGE ANIMAL WITH A SWAN-LIKE NECK AND THE BODY OF A CROCODILE...
MOO
1921 - ORANGE RIVER, SOUTH AFRICA - A SIMILAR CREATURE, THIS TIME EATING CATTLE...
1886 - A HORNED MONSTER IN SANDY LAKE, MINNESOTA...
AND THEN THERE'S THE LOCH NESS MONSTER! HOW MANY REPORTS OF THAT ARE THERE? ABOUT 25? 30? LET'S SAY 36 FOR THE SAKE OF ARGUMENT...
SO THAT'S 89! NUMBER 90 IS - THE BLOND BEAST OF PATAGONIA - 1899!
"THE BLOND BEAST OF PATAGONIA"??! THAT'S A BIT SLOPPY, ISN'T IT? NOT VERY RIGOROUS...
I'M JUST TELLING YOU WHAT I READ!
OH, THIS IS HOPELESS! I'LL NEVER GET TO 200!
NO, YOU GO ON... THIS IS VERY AMUSING...
YOU'RE GETTING VERY ANNOYING! OK - WHAT ABOUT SEA SERPENTS? COUNTLESS REPORTS OF THEM IN HISTORY, BUT I'LL ONLY CLAIM 95!
AND... ER... ER... 1888 - TWO RED RAINS IN THE MEDITTERRANIAN! 1819 - BLACK RAIN AND EARTHQUAKE IN CANADA! ... RED RAIN IN HOLLAND...
THE 7 BLACK RAINS OF SLAINES! THE 4 RED RAINS OF SIENA!
THIS IS A SWIZ!
I'M DOING MY BEST! IT'S LIKE TRYING TO KEEP SPINNING PLATES UP...
SPINNING PLATES?
YES - LIKE IN THE OLD VARIETY THEATRE... A MAN WOULD KEEP LOADS OF PLATES SPINNING ON STICKS...
THIS WAS... ENTERTAINMENT?
IT'S NOT EASY! OH NO! THEY'RE GOING...
SMASH CRASH SMASH CRASH SMASH SMASH CRASH CRASH CRASH CRASH CRASH
WELL, THAT WAS QUITE FUNNY...
CLATTER CLATTER
CLATTER CLATTER CLATTER
YOU DIDN'T MAKE 200 FORTEAN EVENTS IN TWO PAGES, THOUGH... SO YOU LOSE...
200!

A DREADFUL NIGHT

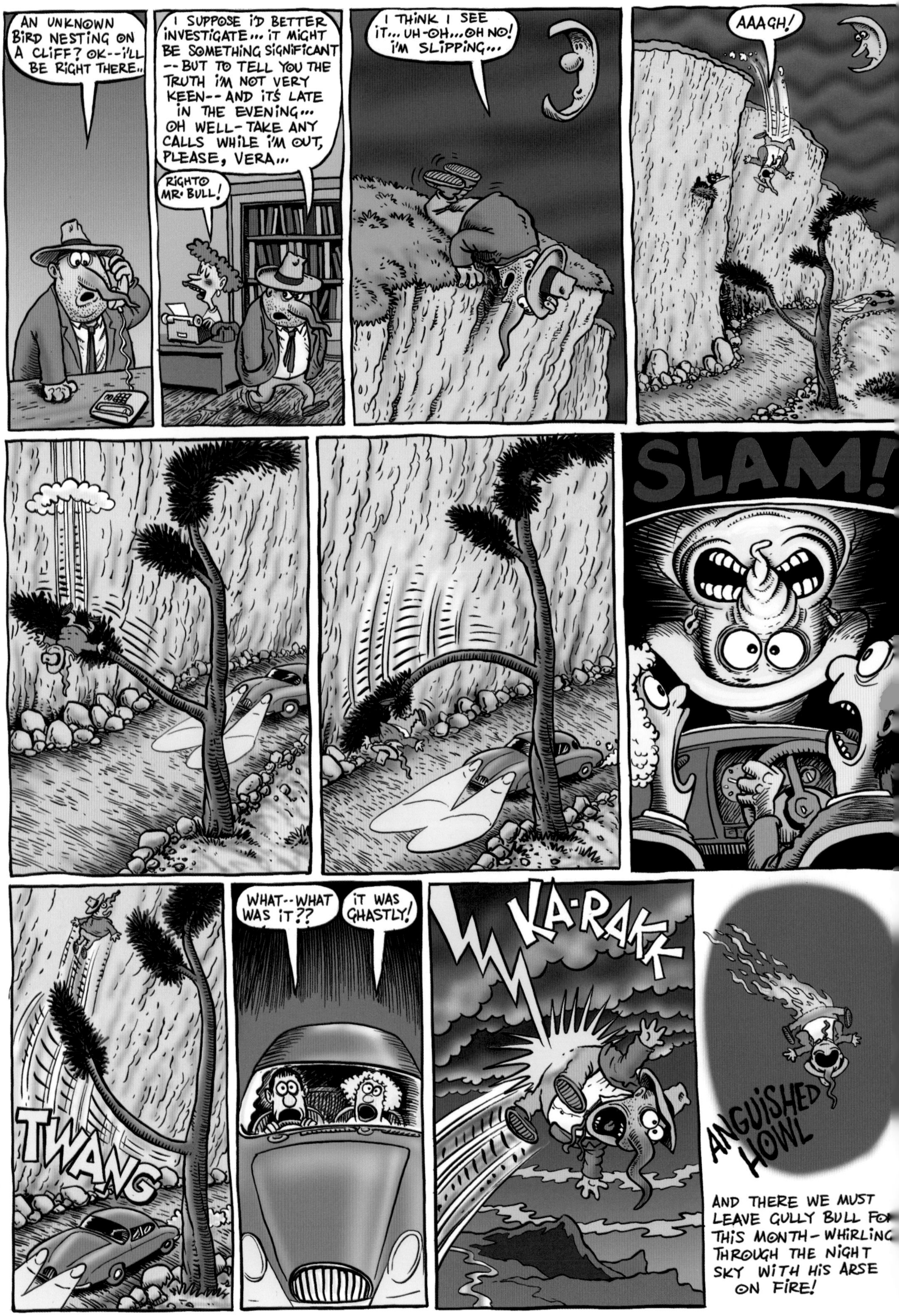

AN UNKNOWN BIRD NESTING ON A CLIFF? OK--I'LL BE RIGHT THERE..
I SUPPOSE I'D BETTER INVESTIGATE... IT MIGHT BE SOMETHING SIGNIFICANT --BUT TO TELL YOU THE TRUTH I'M NOT VERY KEEN-- AND IT'S LATE IN THE EVENING... OH WELL- TAKE ANY CALLS WHILE I'M OUT, PLEASE, VERA...
RIGHTO MR. BULL!
I THINK I SEE IT... UH-OH... OH NO! I'M SLIPPING...
AAAGH!
SLAM!
TWANG
WHAT--WHAT WAS IT??
IT WAS GHASTLY!
KA-RAKK
ANGUISHED HOWL

AND THERE WE MUST LEAVE GULLY BULL FOR THIS MONTH- WHIRLING THROUGH THE NIGHT SKY WITH HIS ARSE ON FIRE!

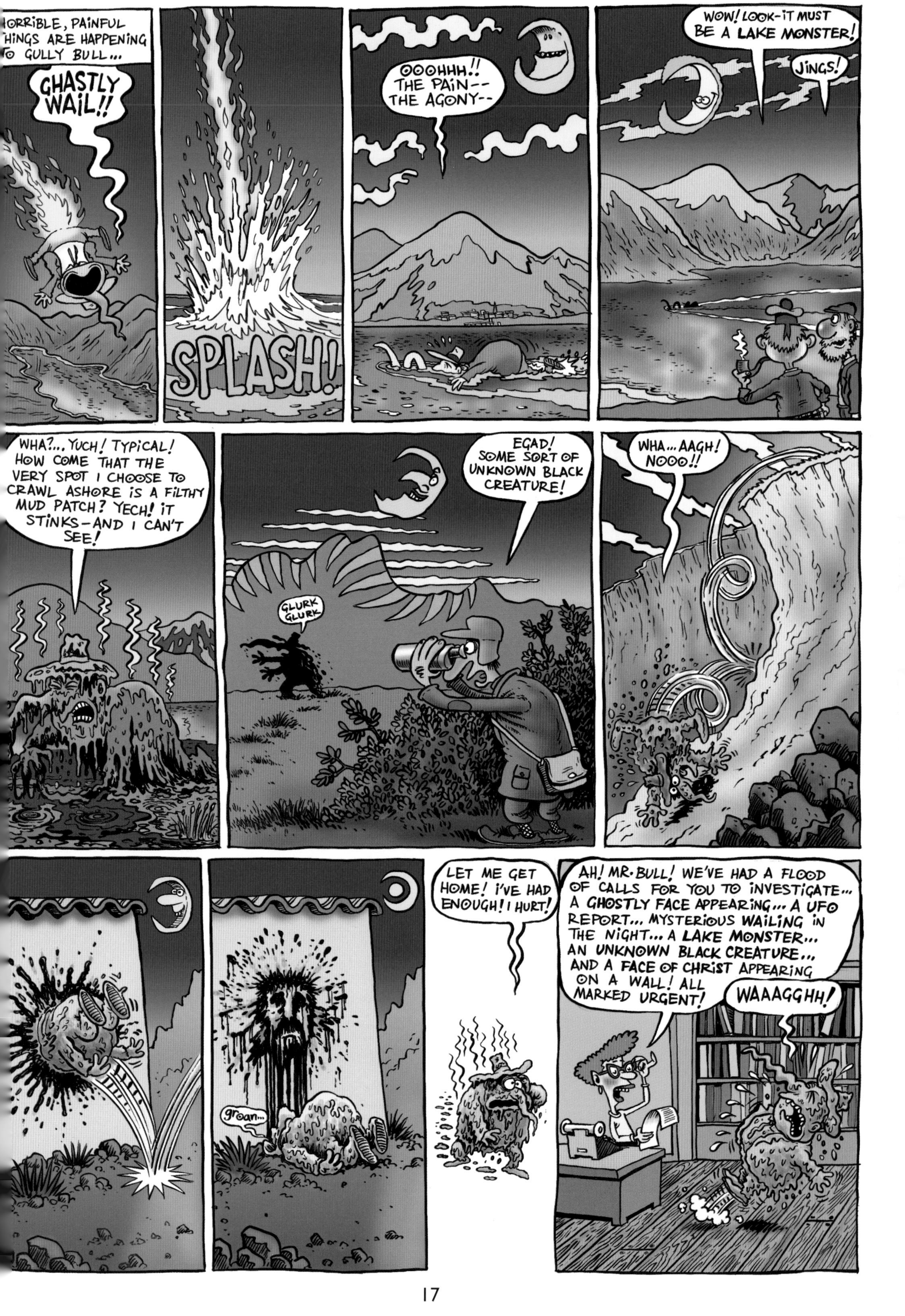

HORRIBLE, PAINFUL THINGS ARE HAPPENING TO GULLY BULL...
GHASTLY WAIL!!
SPLASH!
OOOHHH!! THE PAIN-- THE AGONY--
WOW! LOOK-IT MUST BE A LAKE MONSTER!
JINGS!
WHA?... YUCH! TYPICAL! HOW COME THAT THE VERY SPOT I CHOOSE TO CRAWL ASHORE IS A FILTHY MUD PATCH? YECH! IT STINKS-AND I CAN'T SEE!
EGAD! SOME SORT OF UNKNOWN BLACK CREATURE!
GLURK GLURK
WHA... AAGH! NOOO!!
groan...
LET ME GET HOME! I'VE HAD ENOUGH! I HURT!
AH! MR. BULL! WE'VE HAD A FLOOD OF CALLS FOR YOU TO INVESTIGATE... A GHOSTLY FACE APPEARING... A UFO REPORT... MYSTERIOUS WAILING IN THE NIGHT... A LAKE MONSTER... AN UNKNOWN BLACK CREATURE... AND A FACE OF CHRIST APPEARING ON A WALL! ALL MARKED URGENT!
WAAAGGHH!

ARTIFICIAL INTELLIGENCE

HUNT EMERSON ©97
PHENO MENO MIX
HMM..., ARTIFICIAL INTELLIGENCE... I WONDER IF I CAN WRITE A STORY ABOUT THAT...
HMMM...
PILOT
T5

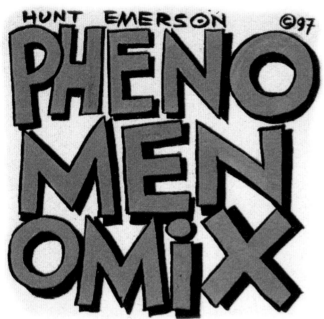

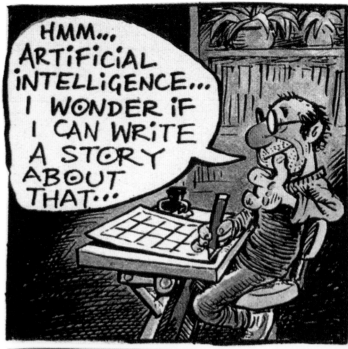

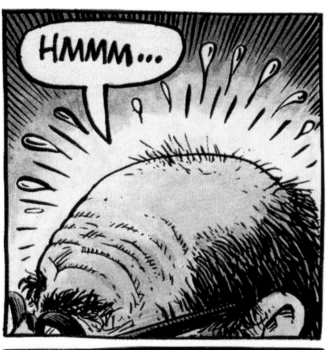

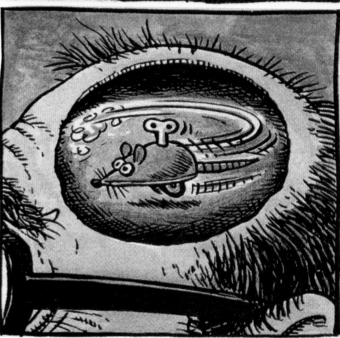

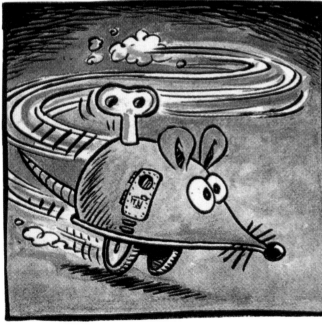

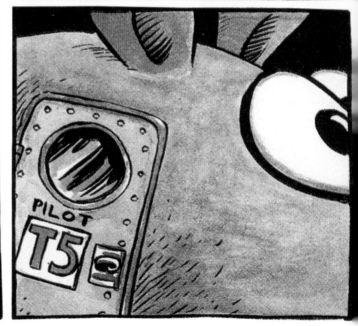

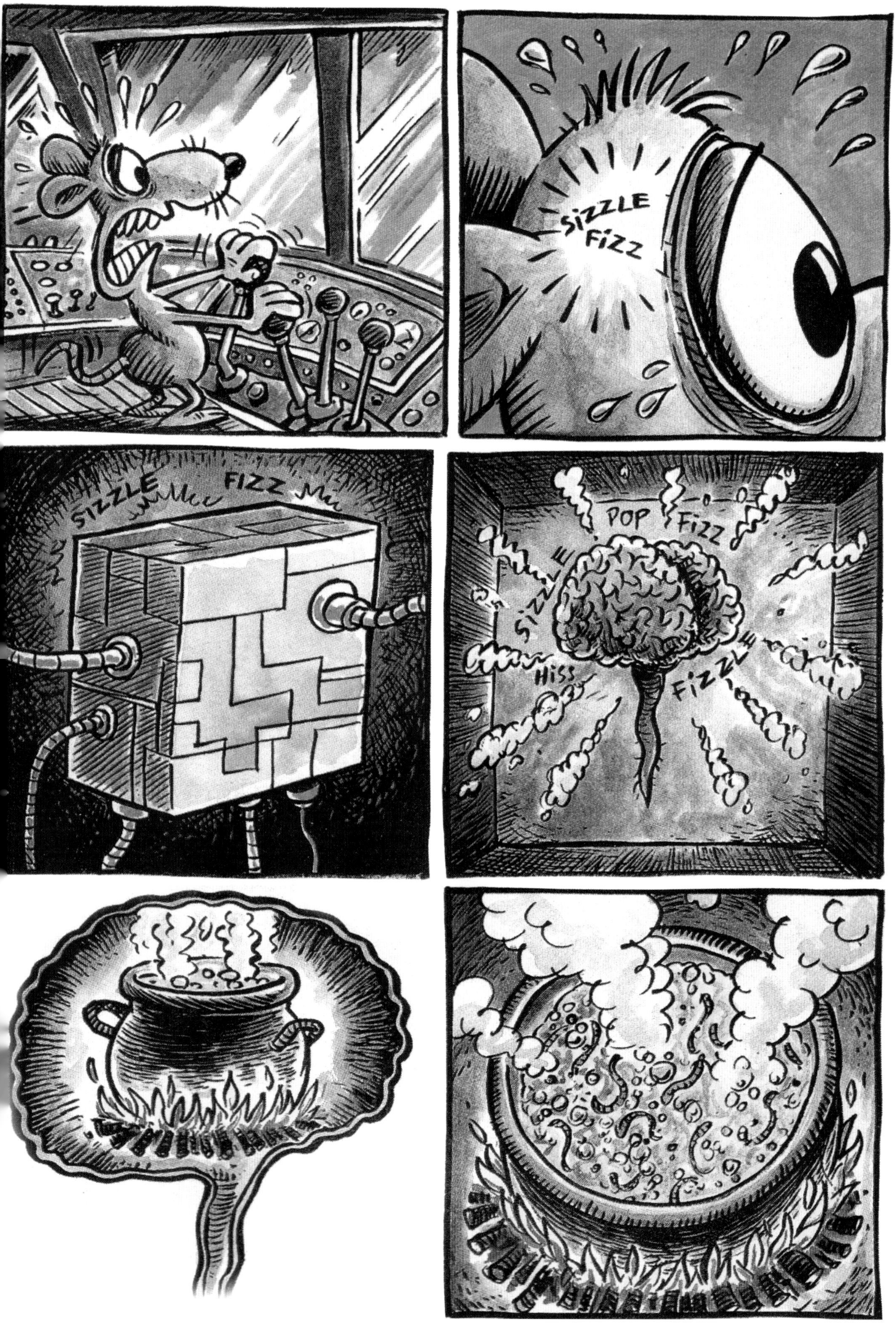
SIZZLE
FIZZ
SIZZLE
FIZZ
POP
FIZZ
SIZZLE
HISS
FIZZLE

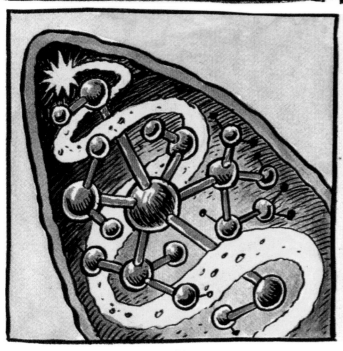
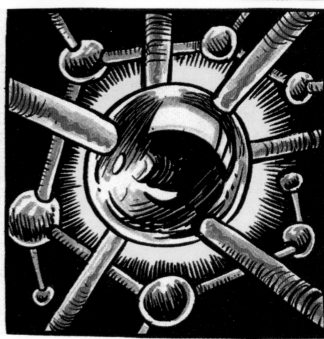

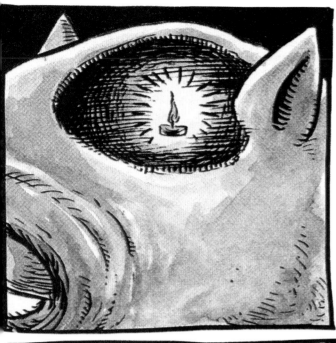

NAAA! IT'S NO GOOD— I CAN'T THINK OF AN IDEA!

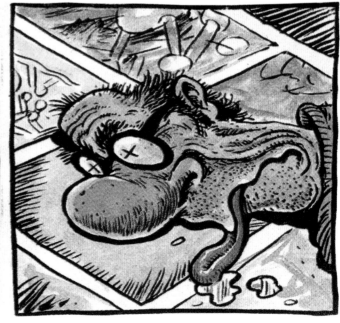

ALIEN HUMOUR

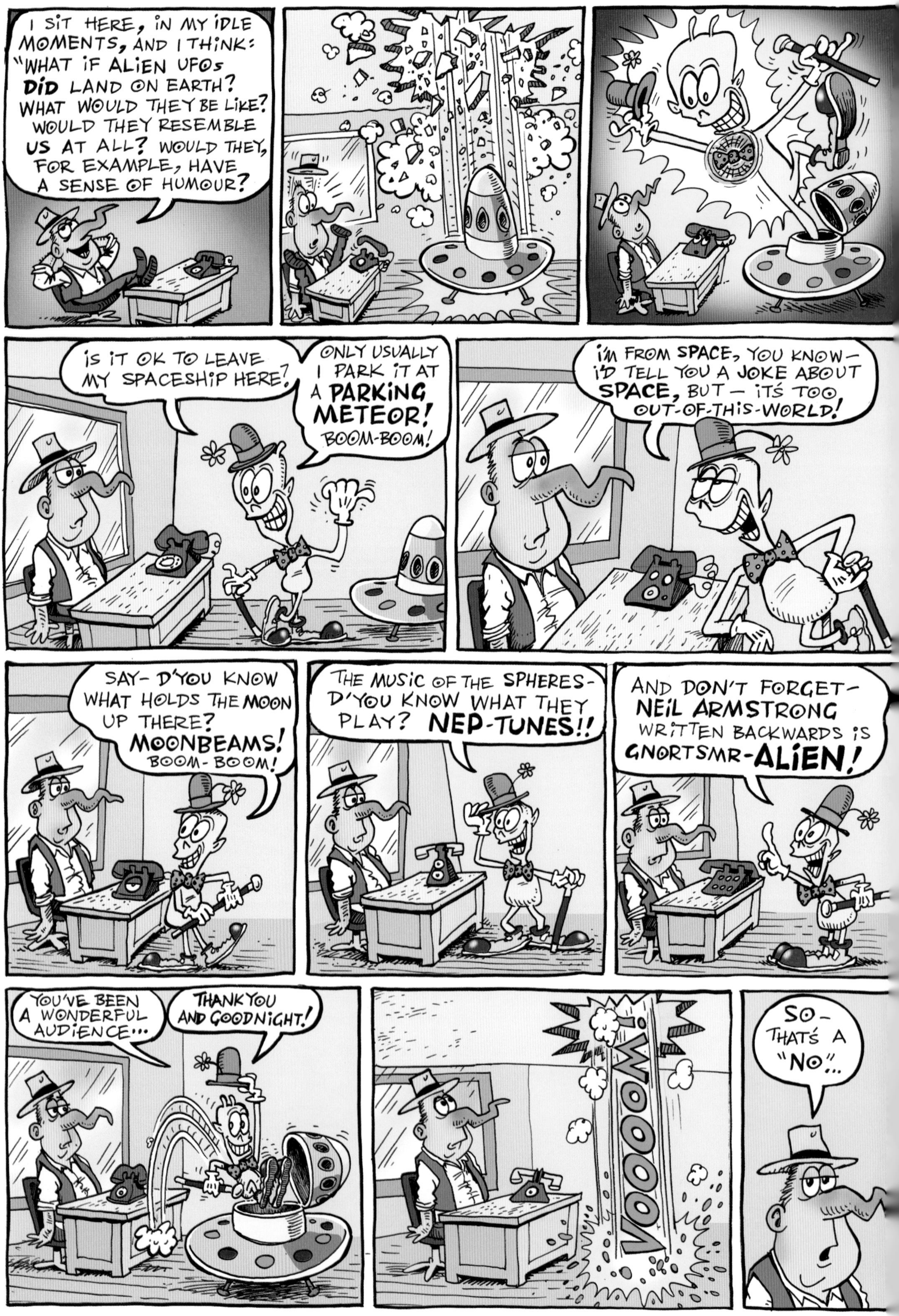

I SIT HERE, IN MY IDLE MOMENTS, AND I THINK: "WHAT IF ALIEN UFOs DID LAND ON EARTH? WHAT WOULD THEY BE LIKE? WOULD THEY RESEMBLE US AT ALL? WOULD THEY, FOR EXAMPLE, HAVE A SENSE OF HUMOUR?
IS IT OK TO LEAVE MY SPACESHIP HERE?
ONLY USUALLY I PARK IT AT A PARKING METEOR! BOOM-BOOM!
I'M FROM SPACE, YOU KNOW— I'D TELL YOU A JOKE ABOUT SPACE, BUT— IT'S TOO OUT-OF-THIS-WORLD!
SAY- D'YOU KNOW WHAT HOLDS THE MOON UP THERE? MOONBEAMS! BOOM-BOOM!
THE MUSIC OF THE SPHERES- D'YOU KNOW WHAT THEY PLAY? NEP-TUNES!!
AND DON'T FORGET- NEIL ARMSTRONG WRITTEN BACKWARDS IS GNORTSMR-ALIEN!
YOU'VE BEEN A WONDERFUL AUDIENCE...
THANK YOU AND GOODNIGHT!
VOOOOOM
SO— THAT'S A "NO"...

THE ALNWICK VAMPIRE

A LOT OF PEOPLE BELIEVE THAT VAMPIRE STORIES ARE ONLY FOUND IN TRANSYLVANIA!

NOT SO!

AH! THE CHEEL-DREN OFF THE NAYT- VOTT MUSIK THAY MAYEK...

HOOWWLLL OOOOWOOOOO

BRITAIN HAS PLENTY OF VAMPIRE LEGENDS—ESPECIALLY IN THE NORTH OF ENGLAND!

WILT THA SHUT THON BARMPOT WHIPPET UP, MUTHA!

HOOWWLLL OOOWOOO...

ONE OF THE MOST TERRIFYING TOOK PLACE IN NORTHUMBERLAND!

THIS IS THE STORY OF...

THE ALNWICK VAMPIRE!

ACCORDING TO THE HISTORIAN WILLIAM OF NEWBURGH, IT ALL BEGAN IN THE ELEVENTH CENTURY WHEN THE LORD OF ALNWICK CASTLE HIRED A BAD LAD FROM YORKSHIRE--

I'VE GOT SOME UPPITY PEASANTS I WANT YOU TO BE PARTICULARLY NASTY TO...

AY, 'APPEN!

EEEE, HE WAS A BAD 'UN!

TURDS! SCUM!

NOT THAT HIS MISSUS WAS WHAT YOU'D CALL A SAINT, EITHER...

EEE- C'MERE LAD!

URGL...

SUSPICIOUS OF HIS WIFE'S LOOSE WAYS, THE YORKSHIRE LAD HID AMONG THE RAFTERS TO SPY ON HER...

...AND FELL TO HIS DEATH!

AAAACH!

SPLAT!

HE WAS GIVEN A CHRISTIAN BURIAL, BUT A FEW WEEKS LATER TERRIFIED LOCALS REPORTED SEEING HIM ROAMING THE STREETS AT NIGHT...

WHEREVER HE PASSED, A MYSTERIOUS ILLNESS BROKE OUT...

FINALLY, THE LOCAL PRIEST GATHERED A PARTY AND LED THEM TO THE VAMPIRE'S GRAVE... WHEN THEY DUG HIM UP, HIS BODY WAS PINK AND WARM!

WEY Y'BUGGA!

LOOK AT HIM!

EEE!

'E'S AALL PINK!

THEY PIERCED HIM WITH A SHOVEL, THEN BURNED THE REMAINS! THE MYSTERIOUS PLAGUE WAS OVER!

THE MONSTER WAS DEAD!

OR WAS HE...?

HANG ON- WHO'S THAT FUNNY-LOOKING EXTRA WITH HARRY? I DIDN'T ORDER FANGS...

ALNWICK CASTLE HARRY POTTER SET NO ENTRY WITHOUT PAS

DIRECTOR

AMMONITE

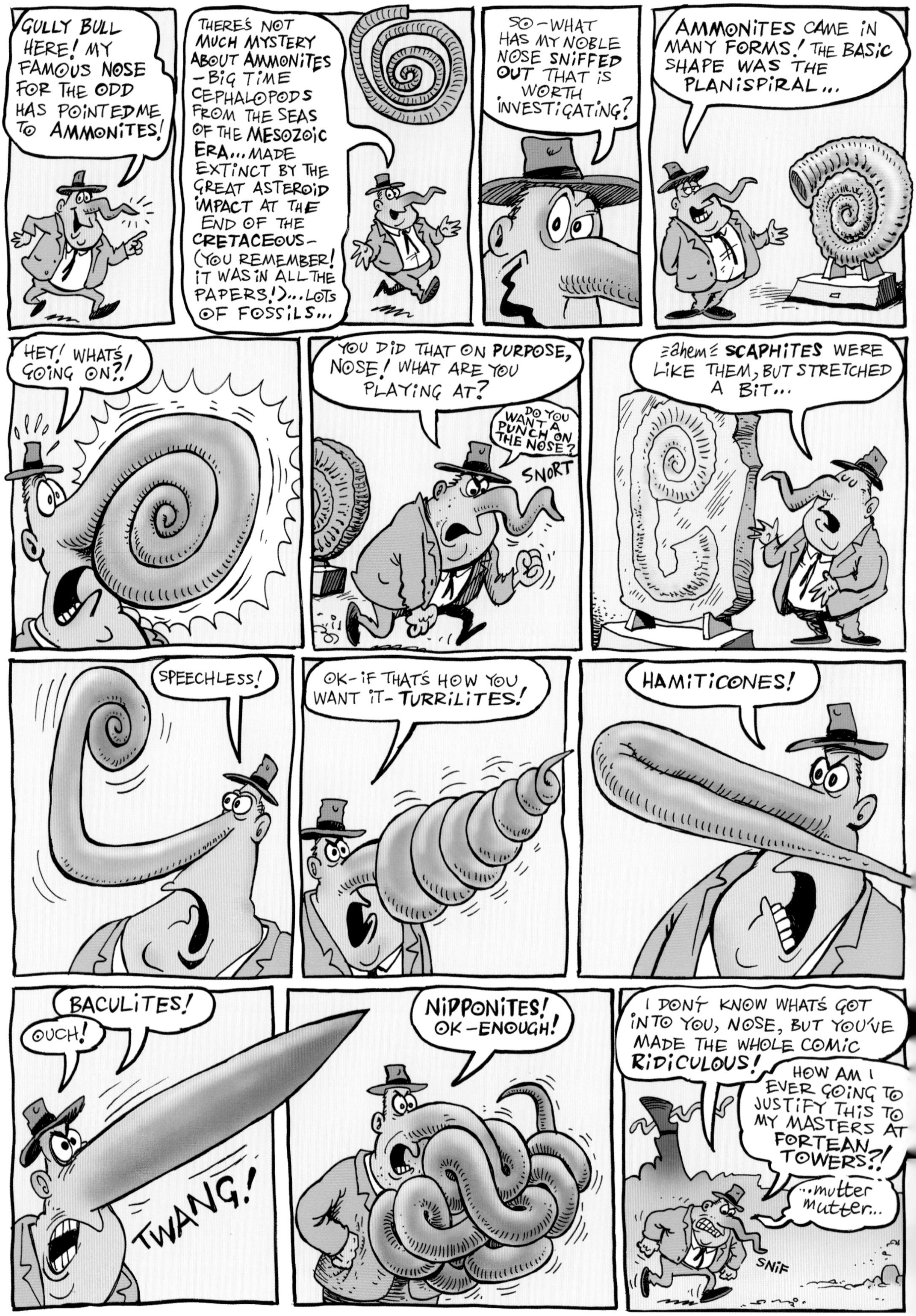

GULLY BULL HERE! MY FAMOUS NOSE FOR THE ODD HAS POINTED ME TO AMMONITES!
THERE'S NOT MUCH MYSTERY ABOUT AMMONITES – BIG TIME CEPHALOPODS FROM THE SEAS OF THE MESOZOIC ERA... MADE EXTINCT BY THE GREAT ASTEROID IMPACT AT THE END OF THE CRETACEOUS – (YOU REMEMBER! IT WAS IN ALL THE PAPERS!)... LOTS OF FOSSILS...
SO – WHAT HAS MY NOBLE NOSE SNIFFED OUT THAT IS WORTH INVESTIGATING?
AMMONITES CAME IN MANY FORMS! THE BASIC SHAPE WAS THE PLANISPIRAL...
HEY! WHAT'S GOING ON?!
YOU DID THAT ON PURPOSE, NOSE! WHAT ARE YOU PLAYING AT?
DO YOU WANT A PUNCH ON THE NOSE?
SNORT
ahem SCAPHITES WERE LIKE THEM, BUT STRETCHED A BIT...
SPEECHLESS!
OK – IF THAT'S HOW YOU WANT IT – TURRILITES!
HAMITICONES!
BACULITES!
OUCH!
TWANG!
NIPPONITES! OK – ENOUGH!
I DON'T KNOW WHAT'S GOT INTO YOU, NOSE, BUT YOU'VE MADE THE WHOLE COMIC RIDICULOUS!
HOW AM I EVER GOING TO JUSTIFY THIS TO MY MASTERS AT FORTEAN TOWERS?!
...mutter mutter...
SNIF

ANIMALS IN THE BINS

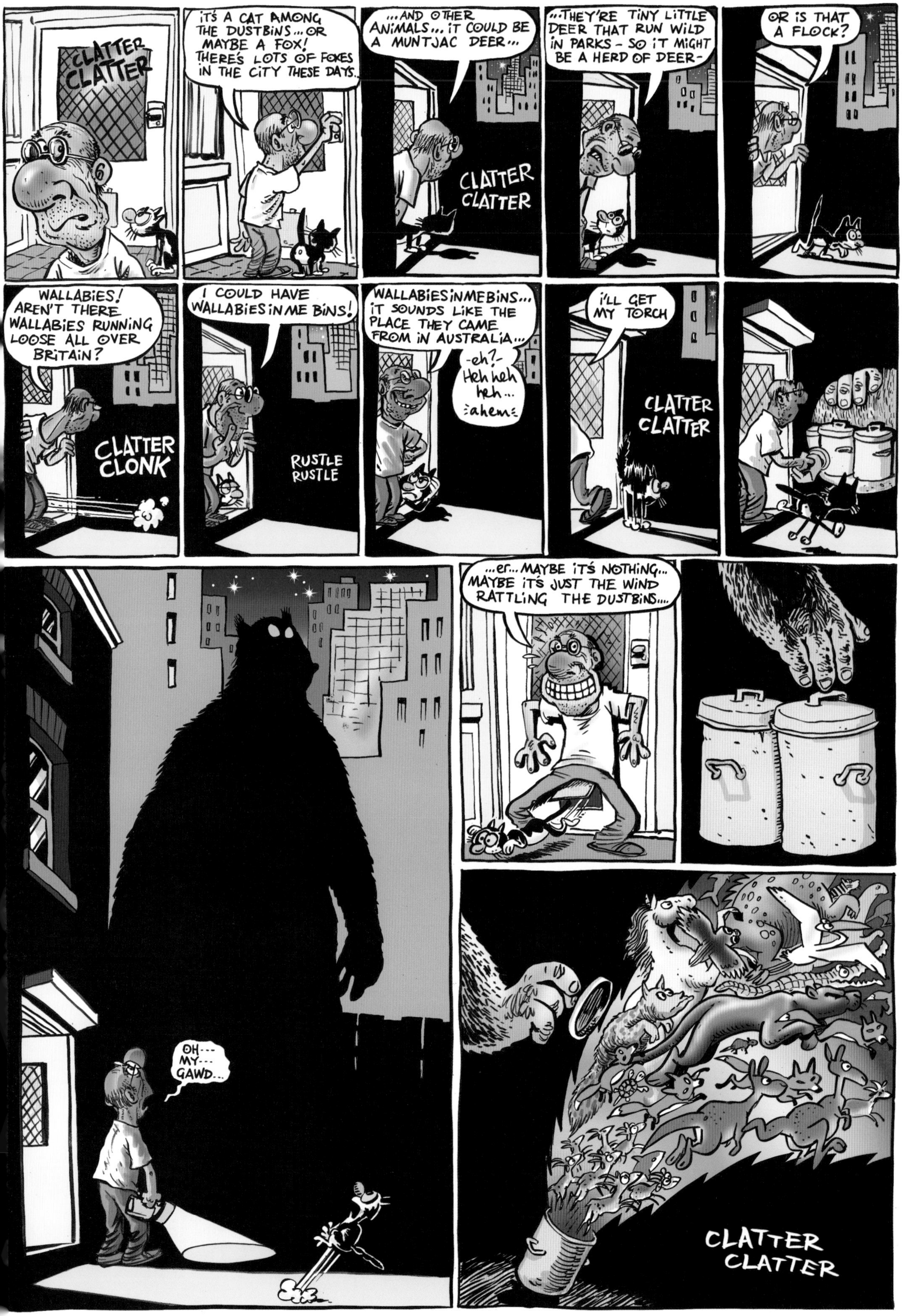
CLATTER CLATTER
IT'S A CAT AMONG THE DUSTBINS... OR MAYBE A FOX! THERE'S LOTS OF FOXES IN THE CITY THESE DAYS...
...AND OTHER ANIMALS... IT COULD BE A MUNTJAC DEER...
CLATTER CLATTER
...THEY'RE TINY LITTLE DEER THAT RUN WILD IN PARKS - SO IT MIGHT BE A HERD OF DEER-
OR IS THAT A FLOCK?
WALLABIES! AREN'T THERE WALLABIES RUNNING LOOSE ALL OVER BRITAIN?
CLATTER CLONK
I COULD HAVE WALLABIES IN ME BINS!
RUSTLE RUSTLE
WALLABIES IN ME BINS... IT SOUNDS LIKE THE PLACE THEY CAME FROM IN AUSTRALIA...
-eh?- Heh heh heh... ahem
I'LL GET MY TORCH
CLATTER CLATTER
OH--- MY--- GAWD...
...er... MAYBE IT'S NOTHING... MAYBE IT'S JUST THE WIND RATTLING THE DUSTBINS....
CLATTER CLATTER

ANOTHER THEORY OF EVOLUTION

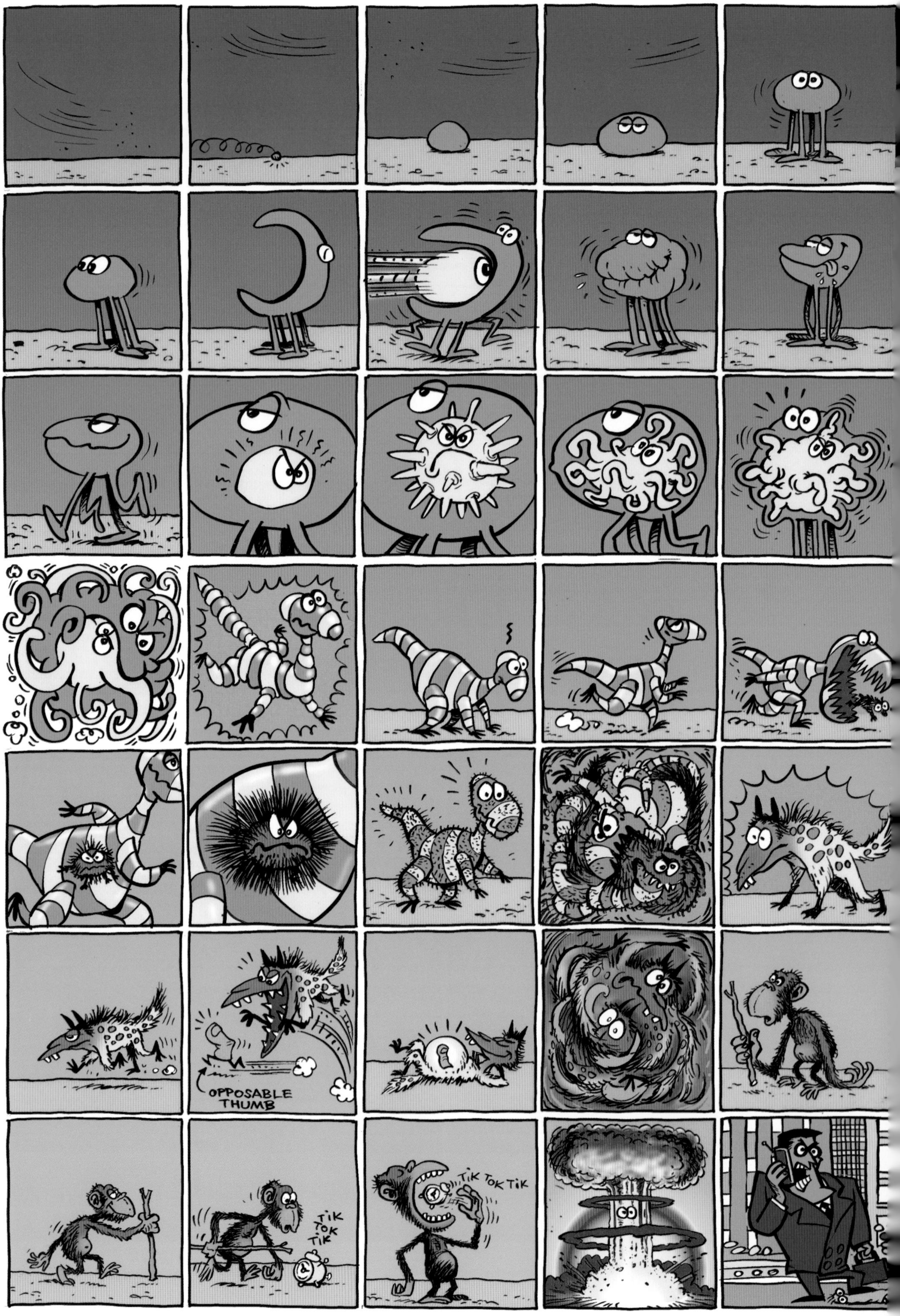
OPPOSABLE THUMB
TIK TOK TIK
TIK TOK TIK

ANTARCTIC

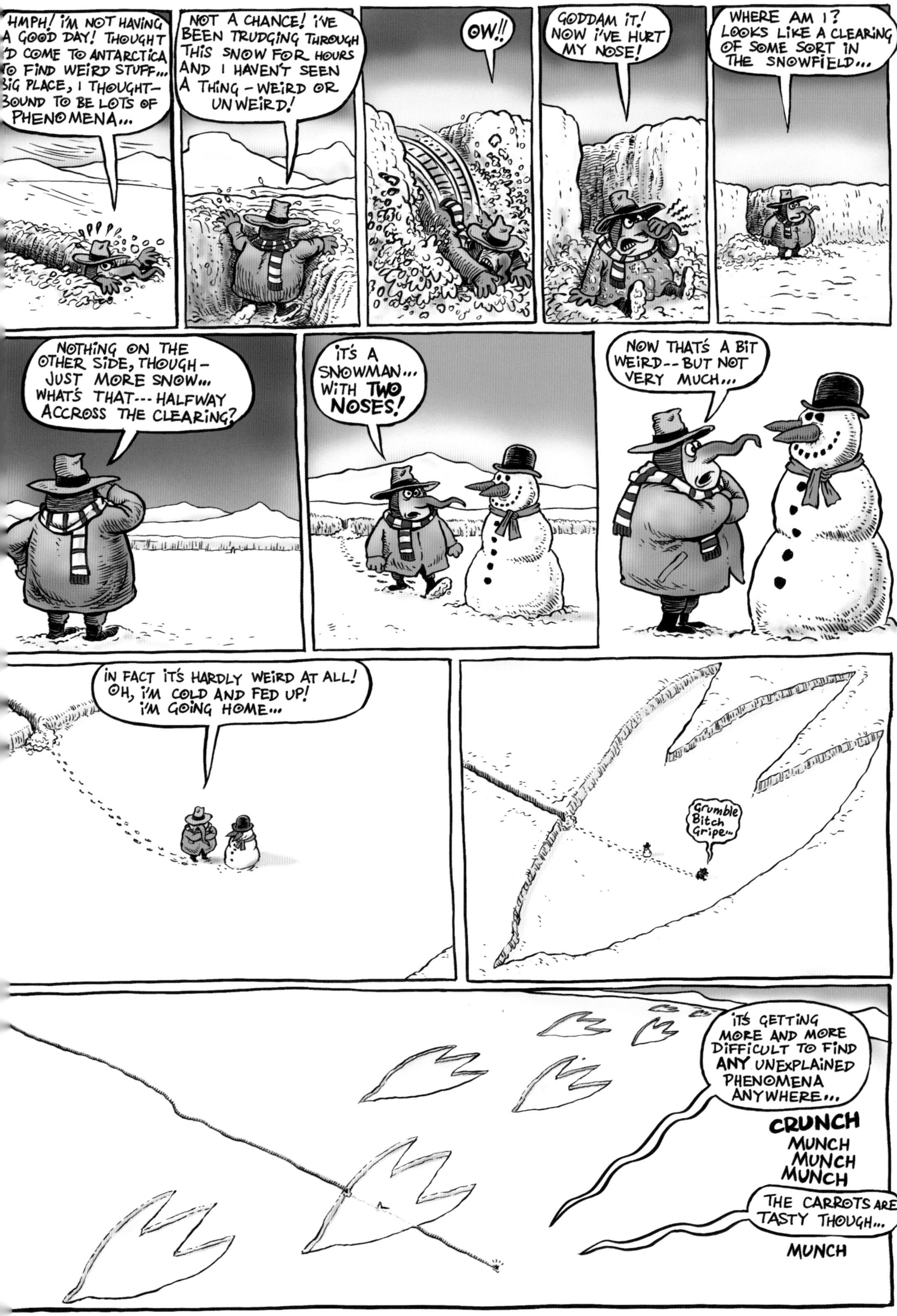
HMPH! I'M NOT HAVING A GOOD DAY! THOUGHT I'D COME TO ANTARCTICA TO FIND WEIRD STUFF... BIG PLACE, I THOUGHT- BOUND TO BE LOTS OF PHENOMENA...
NOT A CHANCE! I'VE BEEN TRUDGING THROUGH THIS SNOW FOR HOURS AND I HAVEN'T SEEN A THING - WEIRD OR UNWEIRD!
OW!!
GODDAM IT! NOW I'VE HURT MY NOSE!
WHERE AM I? LOOKS LIKE A CLEARING OF SOME SORT IN THE SNOWFIELD...
NOTHING ON THE OTHER SIDE, THOUGH- JUST MORE SNOW... WHAT'S THAT--- HALFWAY ACCROSS THE CLEARING?
IT'S A SNOWMAN... WITH TWO NOSES!
NOW THAT'S A BIT WEIRD-- BUT NOT VERY MUCH...
IN FACT IT'S HARDLY WEIRD AT ALL! OH, I'M COLD AND FED UP! I'M GOING HOME...
Grumble Bitch Gripe...
IT'S GETTING MORE AND MORE DIFFICULT TO FIND ANY UNEXPLAINED PHENOMENA ANYWHERE...
CRUNCH
MUNCH
MUNCH
MUNCH
THE CARROTS ARE TASTY THOUGH...
MUNCH

THE BIRMINGHAM VAMPIRE

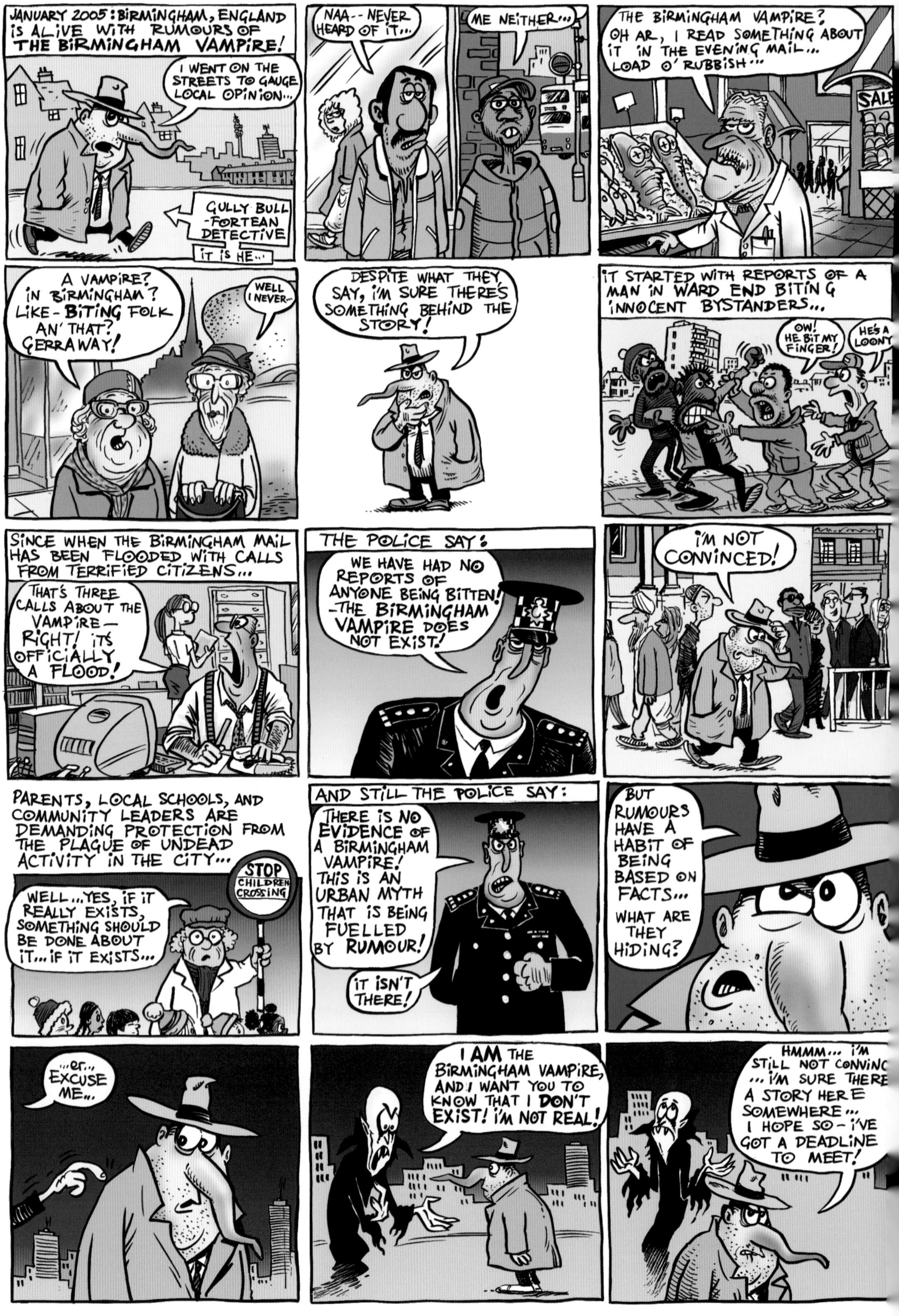

JANUARY 2005: BIRMINGHAM, ENGLAND IS ALIVE WITH RUMOURS OF THE BIRMINGHAM VAMPIRE!
I WENT ON THE STREETS TO GAUGE LOCAL OPINION...
GULLY BULL - FORTEAN DETECTIVE
IT IS HE...
NAA-- NEVER HEARD OF IT...
ME NEITHER...
THE BIRMINGHAM VAMPIRE? OH AR, I READ SOMETHING ABOUT IT IN THE EVENING MAIL... LOAD O' RUBBISH...
A VAMPIRE? IN BIRMINGHAM? LIKE - BITING FOLK AN' THAT? GERRAWAY!
WELL I NEVER...
DESPITE WHAT THEY SAY, I'M SURE THERE'S SOMETHING BEHIND THE STORY!
IT STARTED WITH REPORTS OF A MAN IN WARD END BITING INNOCENT BYSTANDERS...
OW! HE BIT MY FINGER!
HE'S A LOONY
SINCE WHEN THE BIRMINGHAM MAIL HAS BEEN FLOODED WITH CALLS FROM TERRIFIED CITIZENS...
THAT'S THREE CALLS ABOUT THE VAMPIRE — RIGHT! IT'S OFFICIALLY A FLOOD!
THE POLICE SAY:
WE HAVE HAD NO REPORTS OF ANYONE BEING BITTEN! - THE BIRMINGHAM VAMPIRE DOES NOT EXIST!
I'M NOT CONVINCED!
PARENTS, LOCAL SCHOOLS, AND COMMUNITY LEADERS ARE DEMANDING PROTECTION FROM THE PLAGUE OF UNDEAD ACTIVITY IN THE CITY...
STOP CHILDREN CROSSING
WELL... YES, IF IT REALLY EXISTS, SOMETHING SHOULD BE DONE ABOUT IT... IF IT EXISTS...
AND STILL THE POLICE SAY:
THERE IS NO EVIDENCE OF A BIRMINGHAM VAMPIRE! THIS IS AN URBAN MYTH THAT IS BEING FUELLED BY RUMOUR!
IT ISN'T THERE!
BUT RUMOURS HAVE A HABIT OF BEING BASED ON FACTS... WHAT ARE THEY HIDING?
...er... EXCUSE ME...
I AM THE BIRMINGHAM VAMPIRE, AND I WANT YOU TO KNOW THAT I DON'T EXIST! I'M NOT REAL!
HMMM... I'M STILL NOT CONVINC ...I'M SURE THERE A STORY HERE SOMEWHERE... I HOPE SO - I'VE GOT A DEADLINE TO MEET!

TINKER-BALL LIGHTNING

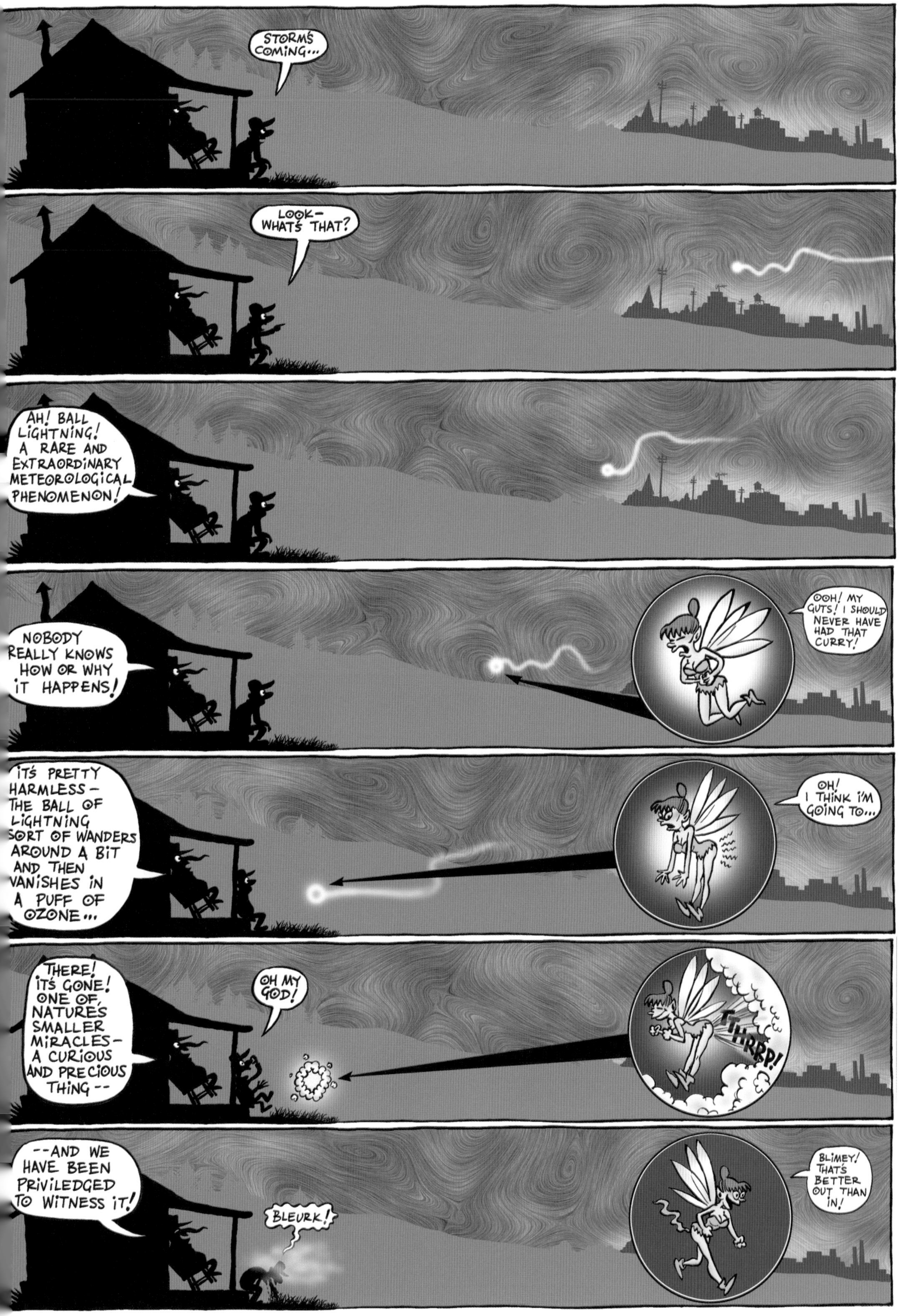

STORM'S COMING...
LOOK— WHAT'S THAT?
AH! BALL LIGHTNING! A RARE AND EXTRAORDINARY METEOROLOGICAL PHENOMENON!
NOBODY REALLY KNOWS HOW OR WHY IT HAPPENS!
OOH! MY GUTS! I SHOULD NEVER HAVE HAD THAT CURRY!
IT'S PRETTY HARMLESS — THE BALL OF LIGHTNING SORT OF WANDERS AROUND A BIT AND THEN VANISHES IN A PUFF OF OZONE...
OH! I THINK I'M GOING TO...
THERE! IT'S GONE! ONE OF NATURE'S SMALLER MIRACLES — A CURIOUS AND PRECIOUS THING --
OH MY GOD!
FTHRRP!
--AND WE HAVE BEEN PRIVILEDGED TO WITNESS IT!
BLEURK!
BLIMEY! THAT'S BETTER OUT THAN IN!

BEARDS OF WISDOM

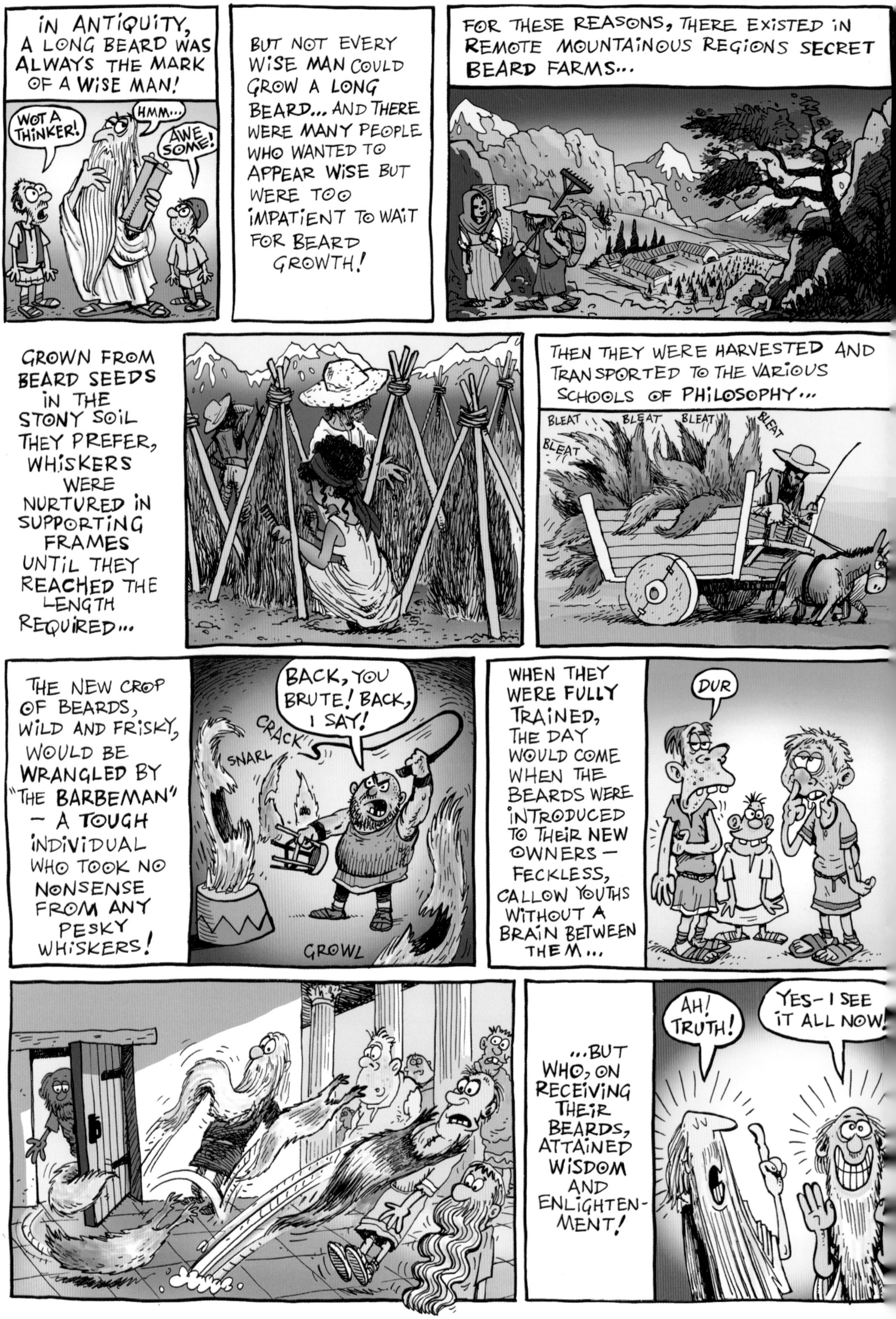
IN ANTIQUITY, A LONG BEARD WAS ALWAYS THE MARK OF A WISE MAN!
WOT A THINKER!
HMM...
AWE SOME!
BUT NOT EVERY WISE MAN COULD GROW A LONG BEARD... AND THERE WERE MANY PEOPLE WHO WANTED TO APPEAR WISE BUT WERE TOO IMPATIENT TO WAIT FOR BEARD GROWTH!
FOR THESE REASONS, THERE EXISTED IN REMOTE MOUNTAINOUS REGIONS SECRET BEARD FARMS...
GROWN FROM BEARD SEEDS IN THE STONY SOIL THEY PREFER, WHISKERS WERE NURTURED IN SUPPORTING FRAMES UNTIL THEY REACHED THE LENGTH REQUIRED...
THEN THEY WERE HARVESTED AND TRANSPORTED TO THE VARIOUS SCHOOLS OF PHILOSOPHY...
BLEAT
BLEAT
BLEAT
BLEAT
BLEAT
THE NEW CROP OF BEARDS, WILD AND FRISKY, WOULD BE WRANGLED BY "THE BARBEMAN" – A TOUGH INDIVIDUAL WHO TOOK NO NONSENSE FROM ANY PESKY WHISKERS!
BACK, YOU BRUTE! BACK, I SAY!
CRACK
SNARL
GROWL
WHEN THEY WERE FULLY TRAINED, THE DAY WOULD COME WHEN THE BEARDS WERE INTRODUCED TO THEIR NEW OWNERS – FECKLESS, CALLOW YOUTHS WITHOUT A BRAIN BETWEEN THEM...
DUR
...BUT WHO, ON RECEIVING THEIR BEARDS, ATTAINED WISDOM AND ENLIGHTEN-MENT!
AH! TRUTH!
YES – I SEE IT ALL NOW!

THE BEAST OF BAMBURGH

WITH ROB GANDY

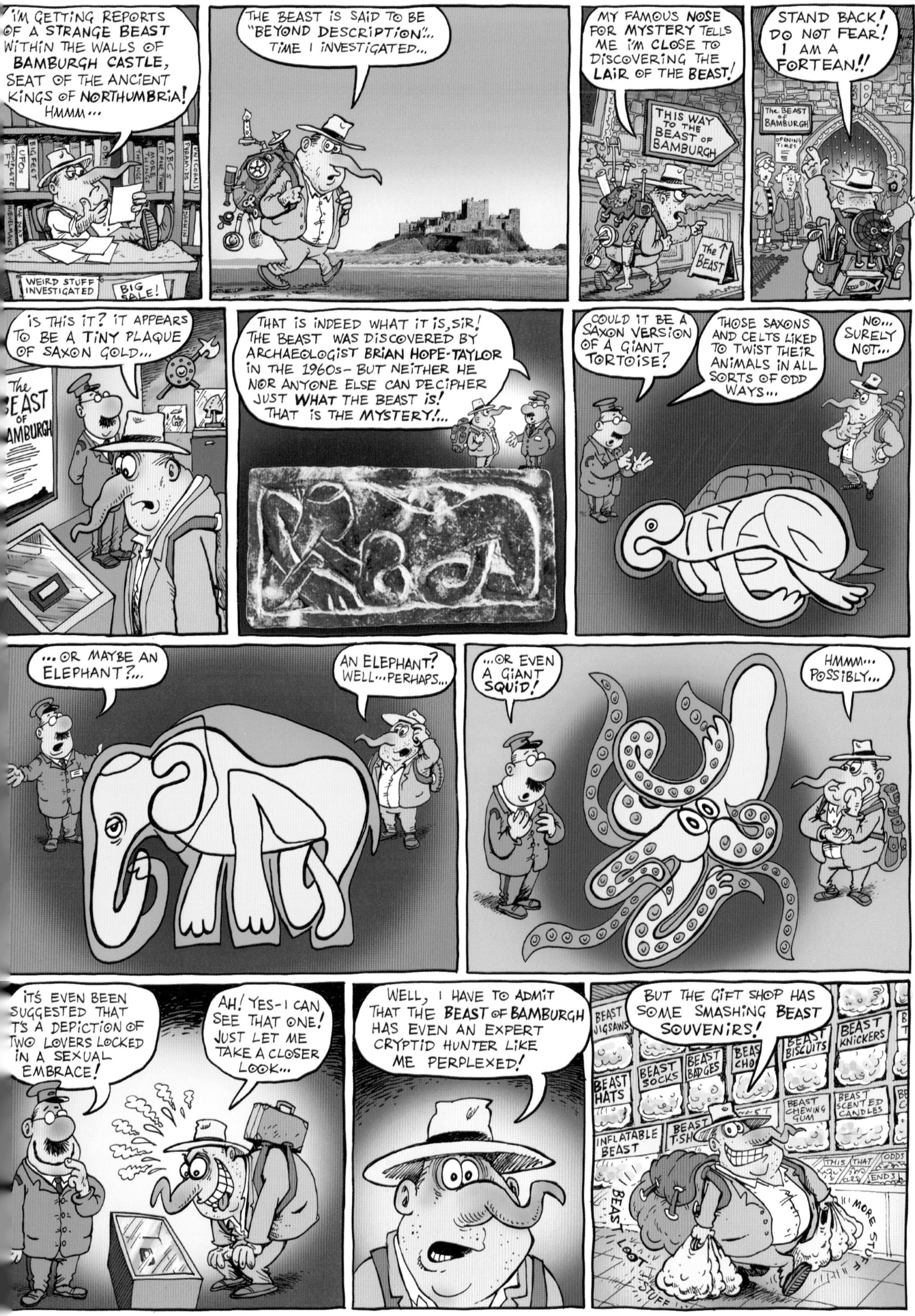

I'M GETTING REPORTS OF A STRANGE BEAST WITHIN THE WALLS OF BAMBURGH CASTLE, SEAT OF THE ANCIENT KINGS OF NORTHUMBRIA! HMMM...
WEIRD STUFF INVESTIGATED
BIG SALE!
THE BEAST IS SAID TO BE "BEYOND DESCRIPTION"... TIME I INVESTIGATED...
MY FAMOUS NOSE FOR MYSTERY TELLS ME I'M CLOSE TO DISCOVERING THE LAIR OF THE BEAST!
THIS WAY TO THE BEAST OF BAMBURGH
The ↑ BEAST
STAND BACK! DO NOT FEAR! I AM A FORTEAN!!
The BEAST of BAMBURGH
OPENING TIMES
IS THIS IT? IT APPEARS TO BE A TINY PLAQUE OF SAXON GOLD...
The BEAST OF BAMBURGH
THAT IS INDEED WHAT IT IS, SIR! THE BEAST WAS DISCOVERED BY ARCHAEOLOGIST BRIAN HOPE-TAYLOR IN THE 1960s - BUT NEITHER HE NOR ANYONE ELSE CAN DECIPHER JUST WHAT THE BEAST IS! THAT IS THE MYSTERY!...
COULD IT BE A SAXON VERSION OF A GIANT TORTOISE?
THOSE SAXONS AND CELTS LIKED TO TWIST THEIR ANIMALS IN ALL SORTS OF ODD WAYS...
NO... SURELY NOT...
...OR MAYBE AN ELEPHANT?...
AN ELEPHANT? WELL...PERHAPS...
...OR EVEN A GIANT SQUID!
HMMM... POSSIBLY...
IT'S EVEN BEEN SUGGESTED THAT IT'S A DEPICTION OF TWO LOVERS LOCKED IN A SEXUAL EMBRACE!
AH! YES - I CAN SEE THAT ONE! JUST LET ME TAKE A CLOSER LOOK...
WELL, I HAVE TO ADMIT THAT THE BEAST OF BAMBURGH HAS EVEN AN EXPERT CRYPTID HUNTER LIKE ME PERPLEXED!
BUT THE GIFT SHOP HAS SOME SMASHING BEAST SOUVENIRS!
BEAST JIGSAWS
BEAST BISCUITS
BEAST KNICKERS
BEAST HATS
BEAST SOCKS
BEAST BADGES
BEAST CHEWING GUM
BEAST SCENTED CANDLES
INFLATABLE BEAST
THIS THAT ODDS ENDS
BEAST LOOT
STUFF
MORE STUFF

BERBIGUIER

WRITTEN BY BOB RICKARD

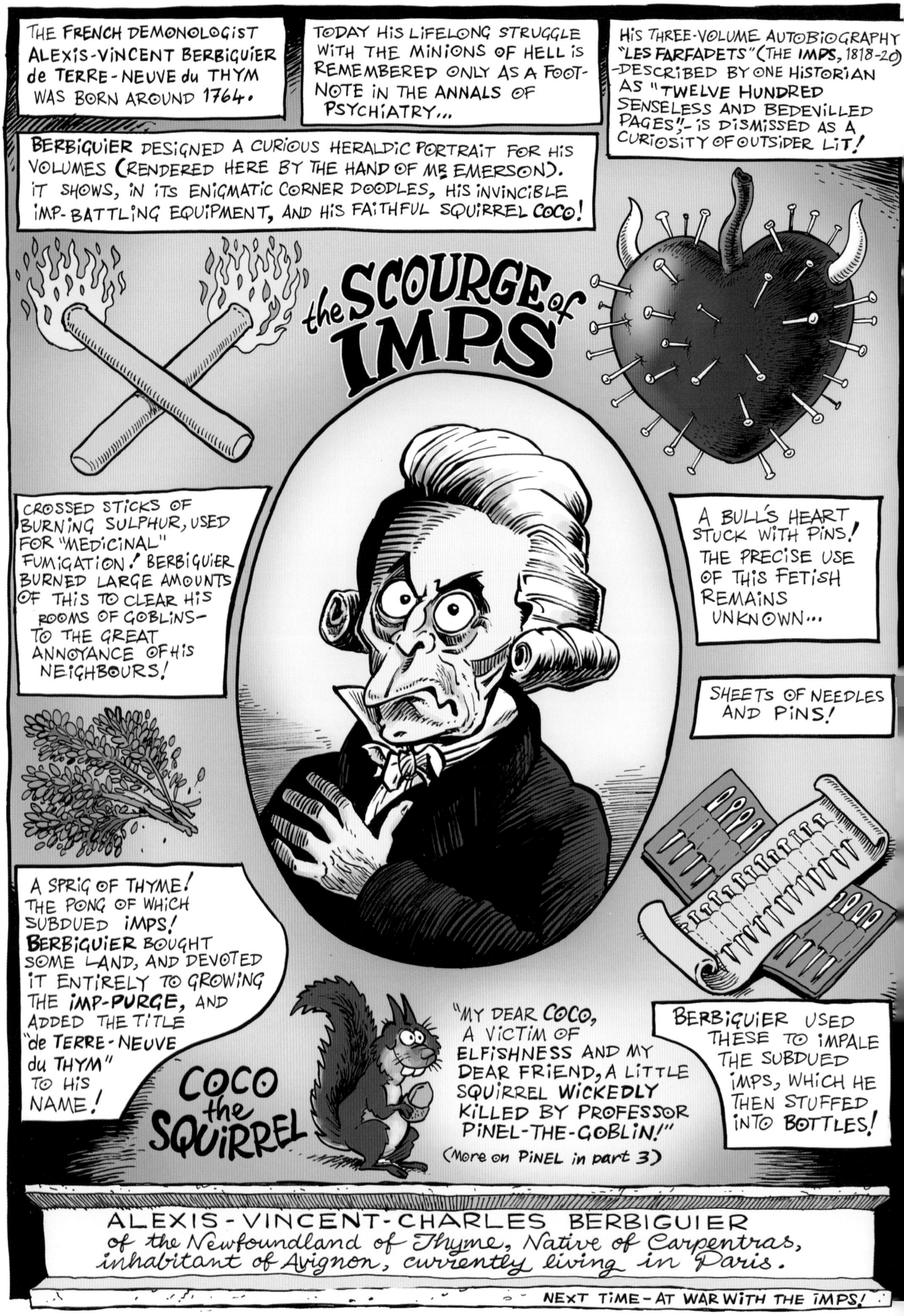
THE FRENCH DEMONOLOGIST ALEXIS-VINCENT BERBIGUIER de TERRE-NEUVE du THYM WAS BORN AROUND 1764.
TODAY HIS LIFELONG STRUGGLE WITH THE MINIONS OF HELL IS REMEMBERED ONLY AS A FOOT-NOTE IN THE ANNALS OF PSYCHIATRY...
HIS THREE-VOLUME AUTOBIOGRAPHY "LES FARFADETS" (THE IMPS, 1818-20) -DESCRIBED BY ONE HISTORIAN AS "TWELVE HUNDRED SENSELESS AND BEDEVILLED PAGES"- IS DISMISSED AS A CURIOSITY OF OUTSIDER LIT!
BERBIGUIER DESIGNED A CURIOUS HERALDIC PORTRAIT FOR HIS VOLUMES (RENDERED HERE BY THE HAND OF MR EMERSON). IT SHOWS, IN ITS ENIGMATIC CORNER DOODLES, HIS INVINCIBLE IMP-BATTLING EQUIPMENT, AND HIS FAITHFUL SQUIRREL COCO!
the SCOURGE of IMPS
CROSSED STICKS OF BURNING SULPHUR, USED FOR "MEDICINAL" FUMIGATION! BERBIGUIER BURNED LARGE AMOUNTS OF THIS TO CLEAR HIS ROOMS OF GOBLINS- TO THE GREAT ANNOYANCE OF HIS NEIGHBOURS!
A BULL'S HEART STUCK WITH PINS! THE PRECISE USE OF THIS FETISH REMAINS UNKNOWN...
SHEETS OF NEEDLES AND PINS!
A SPRIG OF THYME! THE PONG OF WHICH SUBDUED IMPS! BERBIGUIER BOUGHT SOME LAND, AND DEVOTED IT ENTIRELY TO GROWING THE IMP-PURGE, AND ADDED THE TITLE "de TERRE-NEUVE du THYM" TO HIS NAME!
COCO the SQUIRREL
"MY DEAR COCO, A VICTIM OF ELFISHNESS AND MY DEAR FRIEND, A LITTLE SQUIRREL WICKEDLY KILLED BY PROFESSOR PINEL-THE-GOBLIN!"
(More on PINEL in part 3)
BERBIGUIER USED THESE TO IMPALE THE SUBDUED IMPS, WHICH HE THEN STUFFED INTO BOTTLES!
ALEXIS-VINCENT-CHARLES BERBIGUIER
of the Newfoundland of Thyme, Native of Carpentras, inhabitant of Avignon, currently living in Paris.
NEXT TIME - AT WAR WITH THE IMPS!

BERBIGUIER WAS BORN IN CARPENTRAS, SOUTHERN FRANCE, IN 1764, AND LIVED THROUGH THE REVOLUTION! AGED 32, HE MOVED TO AVIGNON, WHERE A SERIES OF UNFORTUNATE ENCOUNTERS TRIGGERED HIS MANIA!

HE CONSULTED A 'CLAIRVOYANT' CALLED MANSOTTE

SIEVE AND TWO SCISSORS

?

...BUT HE WAS DISTURBED BY HER BIZARRE RITUALS...

HE WENT TO SEE Dr. NICHOLAS THE MESMERIST...

...BUT HE WAS "AN EMISSARY OF MOLOCH!"

SO HE WENT TO PARIS TO SEE THE FAMOUS MAGICIAN MOREAU...

PICK A CARD

ANY CARD...

...BUT HE WAS MERELY A STREET PERFORMER!

HE WAS EVEN EXPLOITED BY A PRIEST, WHO—FED UP WITH BERBIGUIER'S NON-STOP TALKING— WROTE LETTERS PRETENDING TO BE BEELZEBUB!

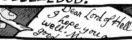

Dear Lord of Hell I hope you well...

BERBIGUIER ANSWERED THEM ALL, AND FOR A WHILE ENGAGED IN A CIVILISED CORRESPONDENCE WITH THE UPPER ECHELONS OF HELL!

BERBIGUIER'S DIGS WERE STUFFED WITH IMPS "IN EVERY NOOK AND CRANNY"! THEIR GENERAL—RHOTOMAGO—ONE OF BEELZEBUB'S STAFF, "PROPOSED TO ME THAT I SHOULD ENTER THEIR ACCURSED FELLOWSHIP!" I, OF COURSE, REPULSED HIM INDIGNANTLY!"

HIS MORNING MAIL WAS STUFFED WITH LETTERS FROM THE DIGNITARIES OF HADES!

I SAY! WHAT A CHARMING LETTER! I MUST REPLY...

Dear M.Berbiguier, We wish you evil. You are invited to join us in the Legions of Hell. Warmest regards, Beelzebub and his pals.

THE IMPS WOULD TORMENT HIM IN BED, SOMETIMES PLAYFULLY...

ONLY JOKING MATE

HE WOULD CAPTURE THEM AND IMPRISON THEM IN BOTTLES...

HE EXPERIMENTED WITH FUMIGATION TO SUBDUE THE IMPS — BURNING SULPHUR, BOILING ODD MIXTURES, AND CRUSHING AND BURNING THE HERB THYME...

HE WOULD TALK INTERMINABLY TO ANYONE ABOUT HIS MISSION TO RID THE WORLD OF IMPS!

...AND ANYWHERE HE WENT THE IMPS WOULD PURSUE HIM...

ONCE HE WAS UNABLE TO CROSS THE SEINE BECAUSE AN IMP MOB HAD BARRICADED THE PONT-NEUF!

BUT THE LAST STRAW FOR BERBIGUIER WAS WHEN THE IMPS CHASED HIM INTO THE CONFESSIONAL BOOTH!

FATHER, I HAVE SINNED!

SO HAVE WE!!

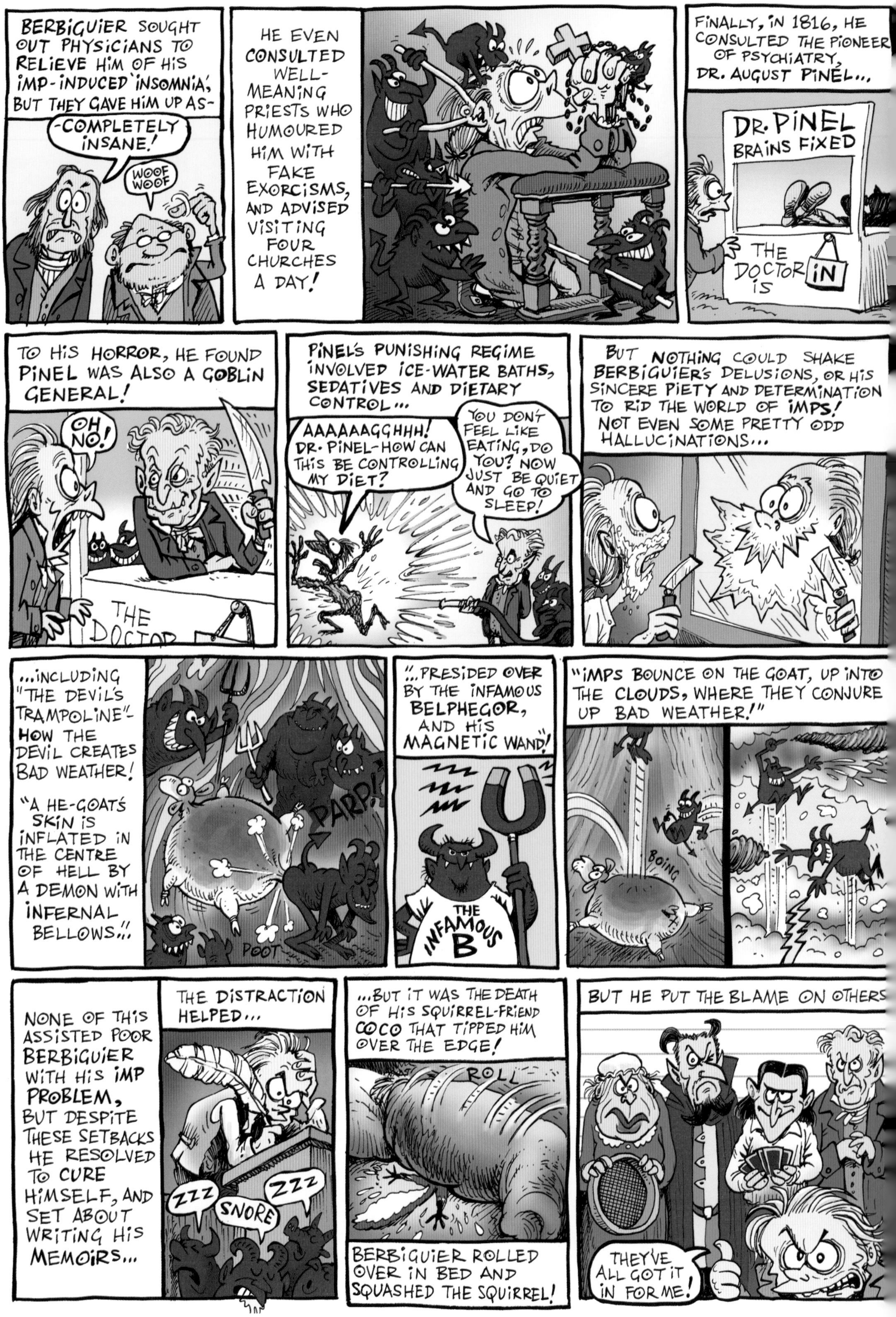

BERBIGUIER SOUGHT OUT PHYSICIANS TO RELIEVE HIM OF HIS IMP-INDUCED 'INSOMNIA', BUT THEY GAVE HIM UP AS-
-COMPLETELY INSANE!
WOOF WOOF
HE EVEN CONSULTED WELL-MEANING PRIESTS WHO HUMOURED HIM WITH FAKE EXORCISMS, AND ADVISED VISITING FOUR CHURCHES A DAY!
FINALLY, IN 1816, HE CONSULTED THE PIONEER OF PSYCHIATRY, DR. AUGUST PINEL...
DR. PINEL BRAINS FIXED
THE DOCTOR IS IN
TO HIS HORROR, HE FOUND PINEL WAS ALSO A GOBLIN GENERAL!
OH NO!
THE DOCTOR
PINEL'S PUNISHING REGIME INVOLVED ICE-WATER BATHS, SEDATIVES AND DIETARY CONTROL...
AAAAAAGGHHH! DR. PINEL-HOW CAN THIS BE CONTROLLING MY DIET?
YOU DON'T FEEL LIKE EATING, DO YOU? NOW JUST BE QUIET AND GO TO SLEEP!
BUT NOTHING COULD SHAKE BERBIGUIER'S DELUSIONS, OR HIS SINCERE PIETY AND DETERMINATION TO RID THE WORLD OF IMPS! NOT EVEN SOME PRETTY ODD HALLUCINATIONS...
...INCLUDING "THE DEVIL'S TRAMPOLINE"- HOW THE DEVIL CREATES BAD WEATHER!
"A HE-GOAT'S SKIN IS INFLATED IN THE CENTRE OF HELL BY A DEMON WITH INFERNAL BELLOWS..."
PARP!
POOT
"...PRESIDED OVER BY THE INFAMOUS BELPHEGOR, AND HIS MAGNETIC WAND!"
THE INFAMOUS B
"IMPS BOUNCE ON THE GOAT, UP INTO THE CLOUDS, WHERE THEY CONJURE UP BAD WEATHER!"
BOING
NONE OF THIS ASSISTED POOR BERBIGUIER WITH HIS IMP PROBLEM, BUT DESPITE THESE SETBACKS HE RESOLVED TO CURE HIMSELF, AND SET ABOUT WRITING HIS MEMOIRS...
THE DISTRACTION HELPED...
ZZZ
SNORE
ZZZ
...BUT IT WAS THE DEATH OF HIS SQUIRREL-FRIEND COCO THAT TIPPED HIM OVER THE EDGE!
ROLL
BERBIGUIER ROLLED OVER IN BED AND SQUASHED THE SQUIRREL!
BUT HE PUT THE BLAME ON OTHERS
THEY'VE ALL GOT IT IN FOR ME!

AS PART OF HIS RECOVERY FROM THE DEATH OF COCO, HIS SQUIRREL, BERBIGUIER WROTE HIS MEMOIRS...

IT'S ALL IN HERE!

TAP TAP

COCO

IN 1827, ROBERT ARNAUD, EDITOR OF THE FAMOUS "BIOGRAPHIE DES CONTEMPORAINS" REVIEWED BERBIGUIER, AND CALLED OUR AUTHOR "A MADMAN." BERBIGUIER WAS FURIOUS, AND SUED!

UNFORTUNATELY FOR HIM, MANY OF THE PEOPLE HE'D CALLED GOBLINS OVER THE YEARS BACKED ARNAUD...

GOBLINS!

I AM BERBIGUIER DE TERRE-NEUVE DU THYM, THE SCOURGE OF THE IMPS!

WE ARE HERE TO DECIDE ON LIBEL, NOT THE EXISTENCE OF GOBLINS!

SILENCE!

LAUGHTER IN THE COURTROOM, SUPPRESSED BY THE USHERS...

HA HA

HAHAHAHA HA

HIS HONOUR IS SO WITTY!

I AM TRYING TO SAVE THE WORLD FROM THE MENACE OF IMPS, BUT THEY ARE TRYING TO MAKE ME LOOK CRAZY!

I HAVE PROOF! THIS BOTTLE CONTAINS MILLIONS OF IMPS!

HERE ARE TWO THAT ATTACKED ME LAST NIGHT!

DR. PINEL, WHO IS ALSO A GOBLIN, TORMENTED ME! TOMORROW I WILL BRING HIS SOUL IN ANOTHER BOTTLE!

ENOUGH! BE SILENT!

BERBIGUIER LOST THE CASE, WITH DAMAGES! RESENTING HIS NEW-FOUND FAME AS A "LITERARY FOOL," HE SKULKED AROUND PARIS BUYING BACK AND DESTROYING COPIES OF HIS BOOKS...

IN 1841 HE DIED, UNREPENTANT AND BROKE! OR WAS IT 1833? OR MAYBE 1836? '51? '57? THE DATE IS UNCERTAIN BECAUSE THE IMPS STILL HAD IT IN FOR HIM!

IT WAS RUMOURED THAT, AT HIS OWN REQUEST, HIS SHROUD WAS FILLED WITH NEEDLES!

HERE LIES BERBIGUIER DIED 1841 1833 1836 1850 1857 1862

OW OW OW

SO—BERBIGUIER: RAVING PARANOID, OR IMPISH SENSE OF FUN? THE JURY IS OUT!

BIG CATS - PUSSPUSS

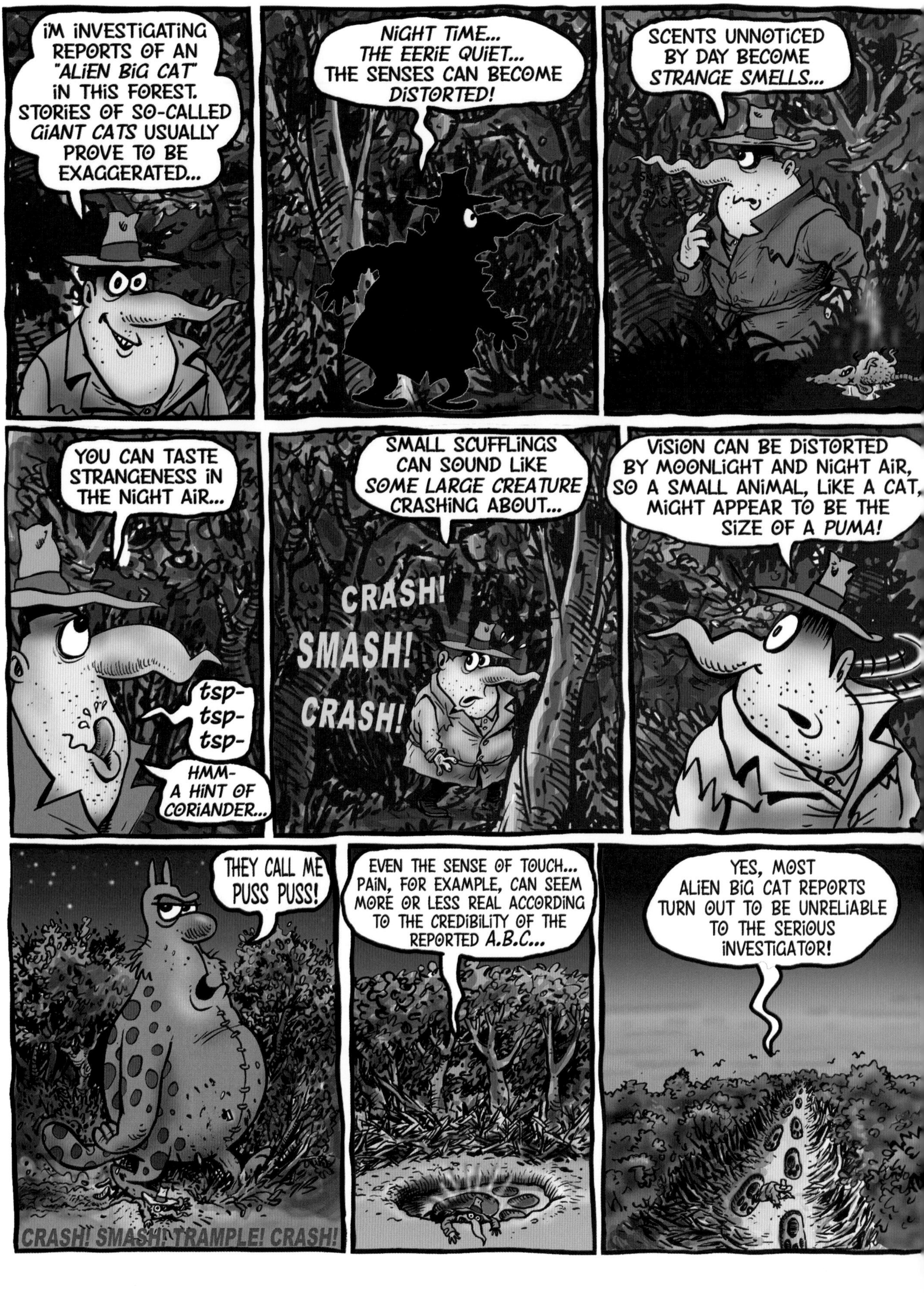

I'M INVESTIGATING REPORTS OF AN "ALIEN BIG CAT" IN THIS FOREST. STORIES OF SO-CALLED GIANT CATS USUALLY PROVE TO BE EXAGGERATED...
NIGHT TIME... THE EERIE QUIET... THE SENSES CAN BECOME DISTORTED!
SCENTS UNNOTICED BY DAY BECOME STRANGE SMELLS...
YOU CAN TASTE STRANGENESS IN THE NIGHT AIR...
tsp- tsp- tsp-
HMM- A HINT OF CORIANDER...
SMALL SCUFFLINGS CAN SOUND LIKE SOME LARGE CREATURE CRASHING ABOUT...
CRASH!
SMASH!
CRASH!
VISION CAN BE DISTORTED BY MOONLIGHT AND NIGHT AIR, SO A SMALL ANIMAL, LIKE A CAT, MIGHT APPEAR TO BE THE SIZE OF A PUMA!
THEY CALL ME PUSS PUSS!
CRASH! SMASH! TRAMPLE! CRASH!
EVEN THE SENSE OF TOUCH... PAIN, FOR EXAMPLE, CAN SEEM MORE OR LESS REAL ACCORDING TO THE CREDIBILITY OF THE REPORTED A.B.C...
YES, MOST ALIEN BIG CAT REPORTS TURN OUT TO BE UNRELIABLE TO THE SERIOUS INVESTIGATOR!

BIG CATS - CATFLAP

THERE ARE SOME **BIG CATS** OUT THERE - JUST BEYOND YOUR SIGHT - OCCASIONALLY SPIED IN THE DUSK...

BIG CATS!

WE'RE NOT TALKING "WHO'S-A-BIG-FAT-FURRY-PUSS-THEN-OH-WHAT-A-BIG-FURRY-TUMMY"...TYPE CATS *

PRRRR
PRRRRR
PRRRR

✱ YOU KNOW WHO I'M TALKING ABOUT, ALLI.

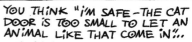

WE'RE TALKING **BIG CATS!**

YOU WOULDN'T WANT ONE OF THESE SHARPENING HIS CLAWS ON YOUR FURNITURE...

YOU THINK "I'M SAFE - THE CAT DOOR IS TOO SMALL TO LET AN ANIMAL LIKE THAT COME IN"...

MEW

HAH! FOOL!

THEY'LL SLIP IN LIKE SMOKE...

...AND BE THERE IN THE MORNING, DEMANDING KATTOMEAT!

OK! OK! GIVE ME A CHANCE...

MIAOW!

37

BIG EARS

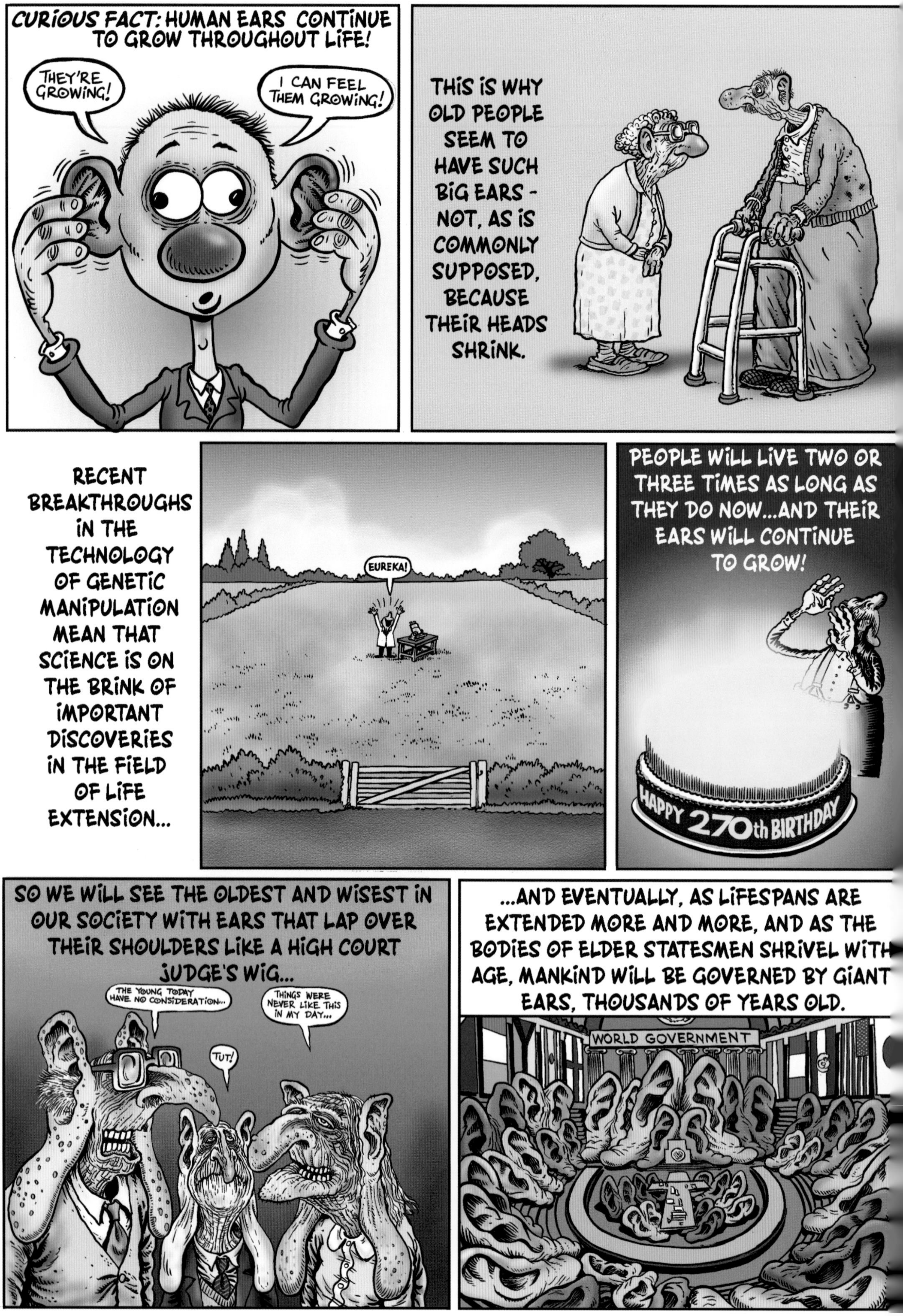

CURIOUS FACT: HUMAN EARS CONTINUE TO GROW THROUGHOUT LIFE!
THEY'RE GROWING!
I CAN FEEL THEM GROWING!
THIS IS WHY OLD PEOPLE SEEM TO HAVE SUCH BIG EARS - NOT, AS IS COMMONLY SUPPOSED, BECAUSE THEIR HEADS SHRINK.
RECENT BREAKTHROUGHS IN THE TECHNOLOGY OF GENETIC MANIPULATION MEAN THAT SCIENCE IS ON THE BRINK OF IMPORTANT DISCOVERIES IN THE FIELD OF LIFE EXTENSION...
EUREKA!
PEOPLE WILL LIVE TWO OR THREE TIMES AS LONG AS THEY DO NOW...AND THEIR EARS WILL CONTINUE TO GROW!
HAPPY 270th BIRTHDAY
SO WE WILL SEE THE OLDEST AND WISEST IN OUR SOCIETY WITH EARS THAT LAP OVER THEIR SHOULDERS LIKE A HIGH COURT JUDGE'S WIG...
THE YOUNG TODAY HAVE NO CONSIDERATION...
THINGS WERE NEVER LIKE THIS IN MY DAY...
TUT!
...AND EVENTUALLY, AS LIFESPANS ARE EXTENDED MORE AND MORE, AND AS THE BODIES OF ELDER STATESMEN SHRIVEL WITH AGE, MANKIND WILL BE GOVERNED BY GIANT EARS, THOUSANDS OF YEARS OLD.
WORLD GOVERNMENT

IGFOOT BEARD

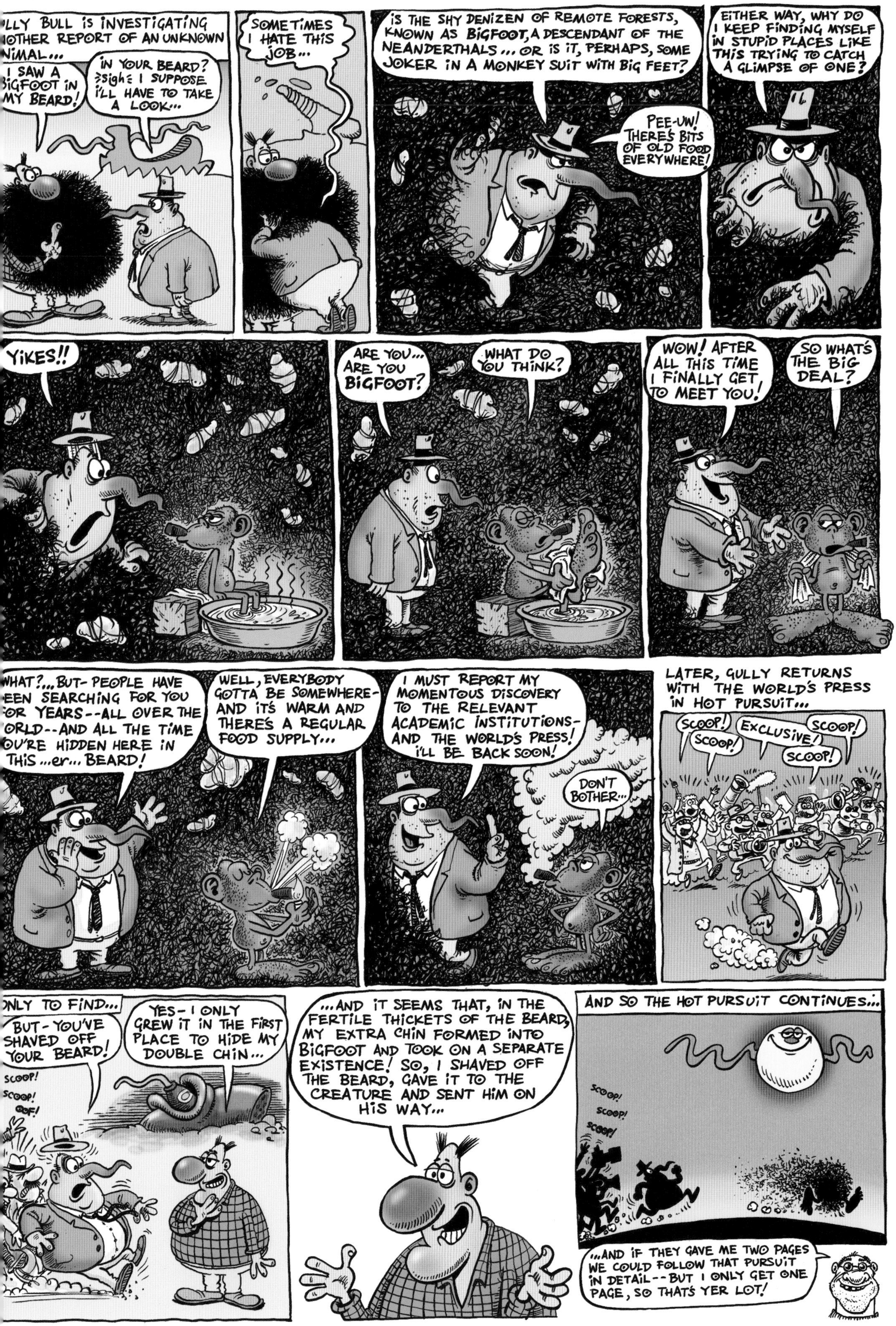

LLY BULL IS INVESTIGATING NOTHER REPORT OF AN UNKNOWN NIMAL...
I SAW A BIGFOOT IN MY BEARD!
IN YOUR BEARD? ≥sigh≤ I SUPPOSE I'LL HAVE TO TAKE A LOOK...
SOMETIMES I HATE THIS JOB...
IS THE SHY DENIZEN OF REMOTE FORESTS, KNOWN AS BIGFOOT, A DESCENDANT OF THE NEANDERTHALS ... OR IS IT, PERHAPS, SOME JOKER IN A MONKEY SUIT WITH BIG FEET?
PEE-UW! THERE'S BITS OF OLD FOOD EVERYWHERE!
EITHER WAY, WHY DO I KEEP FINDING MYSELF IN STUPID PLACES LIKE THIS TRYING TO CATCH A GLIMPSE OF ONE?
YIKES!!
ARE YOU... ARE YOU BIGFOOT?
WHAT DO YOU THINK?
WOW! AFTER ALL THIS TIME I FINALLY GET TO MEET YOU!
SO WHAT'S THE BIG DEAL?
WHAT?... BUT- PEOPLE HAVE EEN SEARCHING FOR YOU FOR YEARS--ALL OVER THE WORLD--AND ALL THE TIME YOU'RE HIDDEN HERE IN THIS ...er... BEARD!
WELL, EVERYBODY GOTTA BE SOMEWHERE- AND IT'S WARM AND THERE'S A REGULAR FOOD SUPPLY...
I MUST REPORT MY MOMENTOUS DISCOVERY TO THE RELEVANT ACADEMIC INSTITUTIONS- AND THE WORLD'S PRESS! I'LL BE BACK SOON!
DON'T BOTHER...
LATER, GULLY RETURNS WITH THE WORLD'S PRESS IN HOT PURSUIT...
SCOOP!
SCOOP!
EXCLUSIVE!
SCOOP!
SCOOP!
ONLY TO FIND...
BUT- YOU'VE SHAVED OFF YOUR BEARD!
YES- I ONLY GREW IT IN THE FIRST PLACE TO HIDE MY DOUBLE CHIN...
SCOOP!
SCOOP!
OOF!
...AND IT SEEMS THAT, IN THE FERTILE THICKETS OF THE BEARD, MY EXTRA CHIN FORMED INTO BIGFOOT AND TOOK ON A SEPARATE EXISTENCE! SO, I SHAVED OFF THE BEARD, GAVE IT TO THE CREATURE AND SENT HIM ON HIS WAY...
AND SO THE HOT PURSUIT CONTINUES...
SCOOP!
SCOOP!
SCOOP!
...AND IF THEY GAVE ME TWO PAGES WE COULD FOLLOW THAT PURSUIT IN DETAIL--BUT I ONLY GET ONE PAGE, SO THAT'S YER LOT!

BIGFOOT MOWING

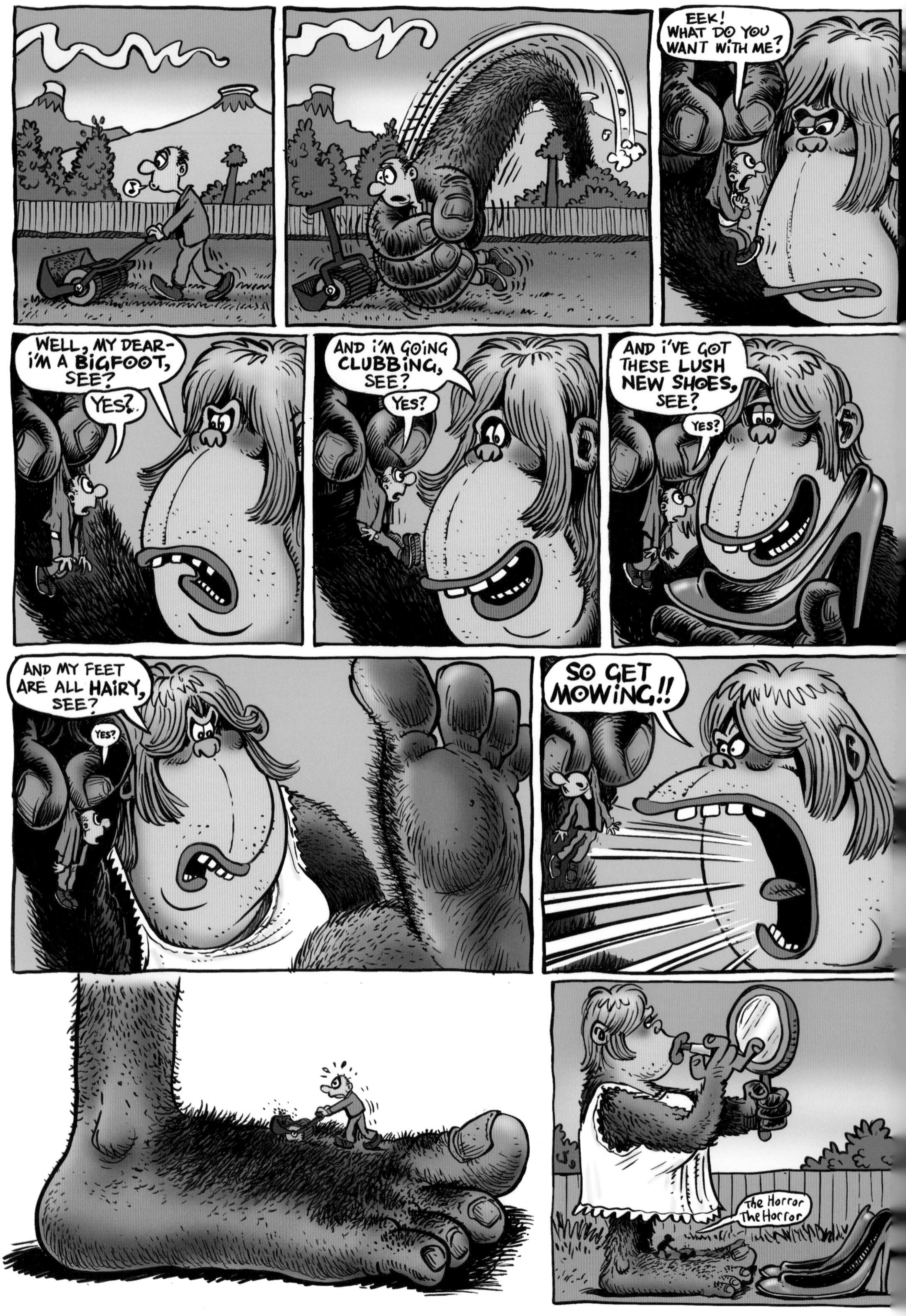
EEK! WHAT DO YOU WANT WITH ME?
WELL, MY DEAR- I'M A BIGFOOT, SEE?
YES?
AND I'M GOING CLUBBING, SEE?
YES?
AND I'VE GOT THESE LUSH NEW SHOES, SEE?
YES?
AND MY FEET ARE ALL HAIRY, SEE?
YES?
SO GET MOWING!!
The Horror The Horror

SASQUATCH

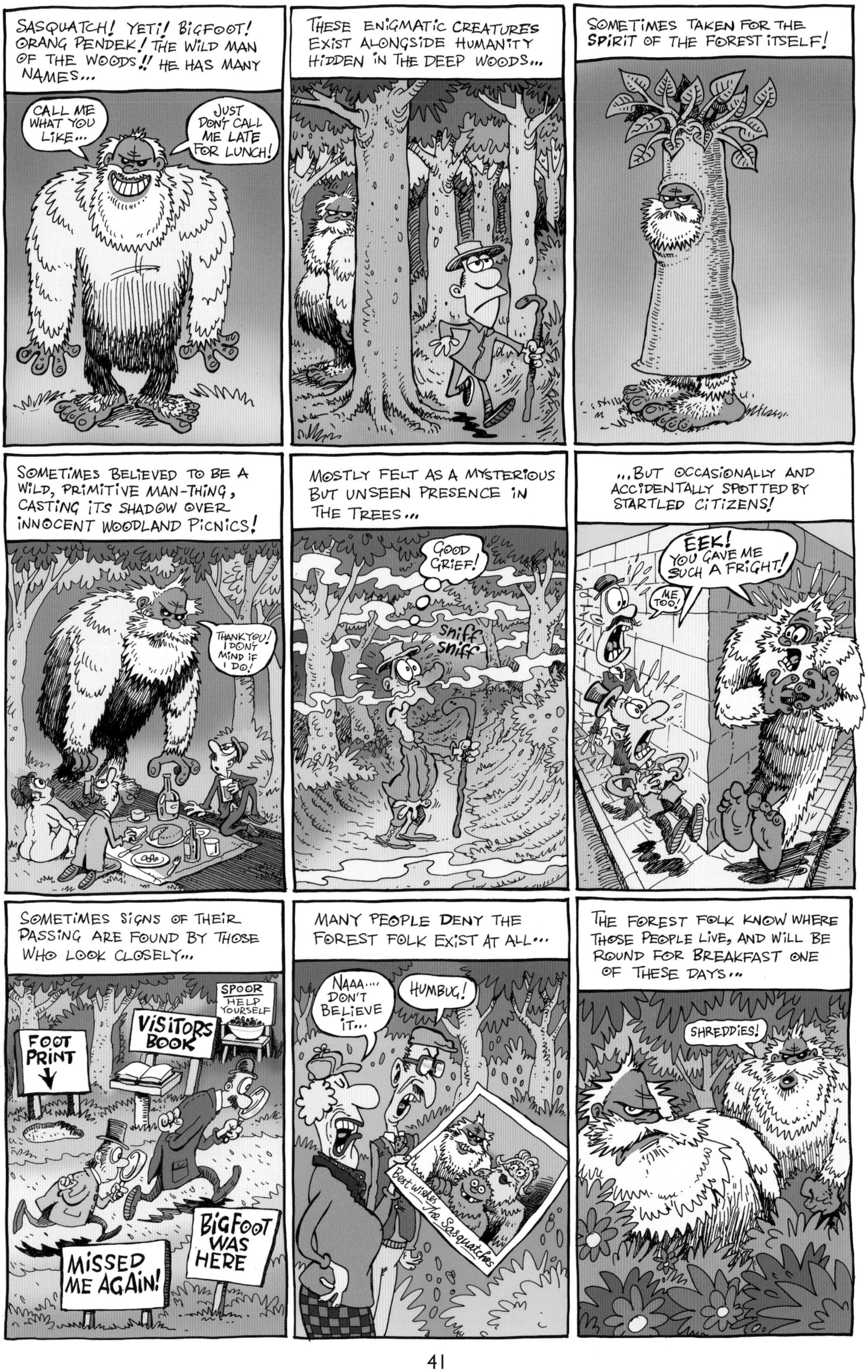
SASQUATCH! YETI! BIGFOOT! ORANG PENDEK! THE WILD MAN OF THE WOODS!! HE HAS MANY NAMES...
CALL ME WHAT YOU LIKE...
JUST DON'T CALL ME LATE FOR LUNCH!
THESE ENIGMATIC CREATURES EXIST ALONGSIDE HUMANITY HIDDEN IN THE DEEP WOODS...
SOMETIMES TAKEN FOR THE SPIRIT OF THE FOREST ITSELF!
SOMETIMES BELIEVED TO BE A WILD, PRIMITIVE MAN-THING, CASTING ITS SHADOW OVER INNOCENT WOODLAND PICNICS!
THANKYOU! I DON'T MIND IF I DO!
MOSTLY FELT AS A MYSTERIOUS BUT UNSEEN PRESENCE IN THE TREES...
GOOD GRIEF!
sniff sniff
...BUT OCCASIONALLY AND ACCIDENTALLY SPOTTED BY STARTLED CITIZENS!
EEK! YOU GAVE ME SUCH A FRIGHT!
ME TOO!
SOMETIMES SIGNS OF THEIR PASSING ARE FOUND BY THOSE WHO LOOK CLOSELY...
SPOOR
HELP YOURSELF
VISITORS BOOK
FOOT PRINT
BIGFOOT WAS HERE
MISSED ME AGAIN!
MANY PEOPLE DENY THE FOREST FOLK EXIST AT ALL...
NAAA.... DON'T BELIEVE IT...
HUMBUG!
Best wishes The Sasquatches
THE FOREST FOLK KNOW WHERE THOSE PEOPLE LIVE, AND WILL BE ROUND FOR BREAKFAST ONE OF THESE DAYS...
SHREDDIES!

BLACK BAGS

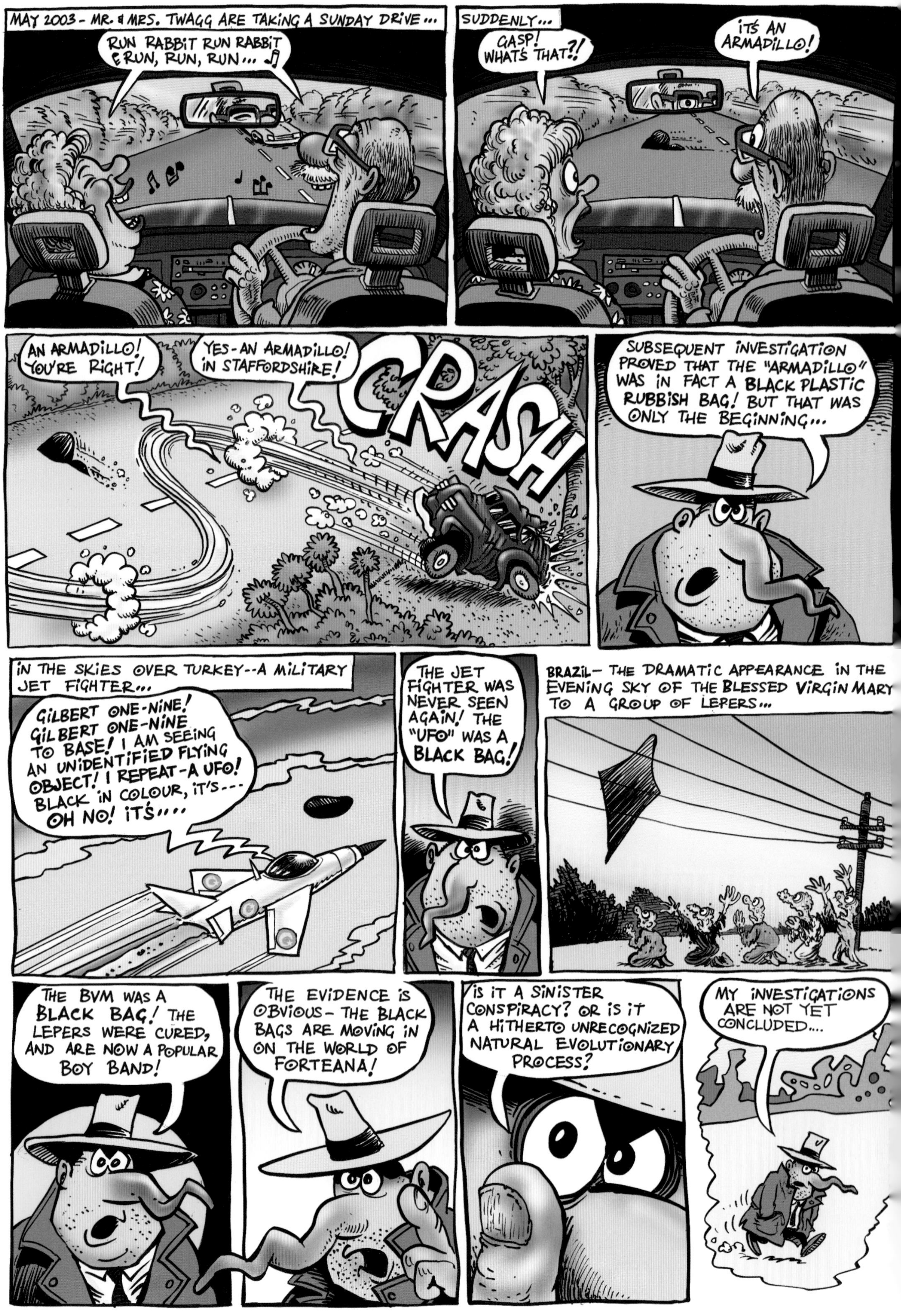

MAY 2003 - MR. & MRS. TWAGG ARE TAKING A SUNDAY DRIVE...
RUN RABBIT RUN RABBIT & RUN, RUN, RUN...
SUDDENLY...
GASP! WHAT'S THAT?!
IT'S AN ARMADILLO!
AN ARMADILLO! YOU'RE RIGHT!
YES - AN ARMADILLO! IN STAFFORDSHIRE!
CRASH
SUBSEQUENT INVESTIGATION PROVED THAT THE "ARMADILLO" WAS IN FACT A BLACK PLASTIC RUBBISH BAG! BUT THAT WAS ONLY THE BEGINNING...
IN THE SKIES OVER TURKEY--A MILITARY JET FIGHTER...
GILBERT ONE-NINE! GILBERT ONE-NINE TO BASE! I AM SEEING AN UNIDENTIFIED FLYING OBJECT! I REPEAT - A UFO! BLACK IN COLOUR, IT'S--- OH NO! IT'S...
THE JET FIGHTER WAS NEVER SEEN AGAIN! THE "UFO" WAS A BLACK BAG!
BRAZIL - THE DRAMATIC APPEARANCE IN THE EVENING SKY OF THE BLESSED VIRGIN MARY TO A GROUP OF LEPERS...
THE BVM WAS A BLACK BAG! THE LEPERS WERE CURED, AND ARE NOW A POPULAR BOY BAND!
THE EVIDENCE IS OBVIOUS - THE BLACK BAGS ARE MOVING IN ON THE WORLD OF FORTEANA!
IS IT A SINISTER CONSPIRACY? OR IS IT A HITHERTO UNRECOGNIZED NATURAL EVOLUTIONARY PROCESS?
MY INVESTIGATIONS ARE NOT YET CONCLUDED....

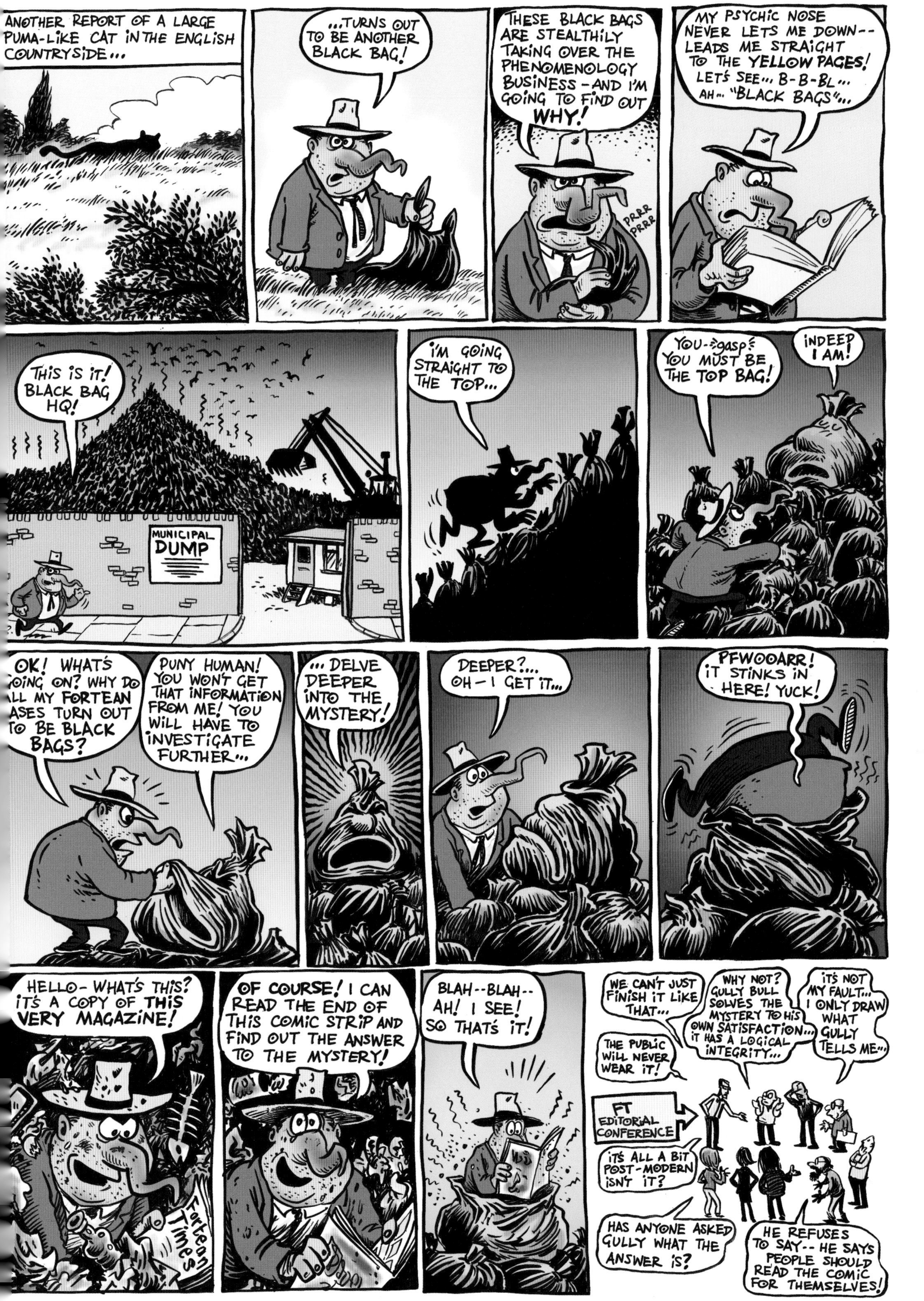
ANOTHER REPORT OF A LARGE PUMA-LIKE CAT IN THE ENGLISH COUNTRYSIDE...
...TURNS OUT TO BE ANOTHER BLACK BAG!
THESE BLACK BAGS ARE STEALTHILY TAKING OVER THE PHENOMENOLOGY BUSINESS - AND I'M GOING TO FIND OUT WHY!
PRRR PRRR
MY PSYCHIC NOSE NEVER LETS ME DOWN-- LEADS ME STRAIGHT TO THE YELLOW PAGES! LET'S SEE... B-B-BL... AH... "BLACK BAGS"...
THIS IS IT! BLACK BAG HQ!
MUNICIPAL DUMP
I'M GOING STRAIGHT TO THE TOP...
YOU-gasp YOU MUST BE THE TOP BAG!
INDEED I AM!
OK! WHAT'S GOING ON? WHY DO ALL MY FORTEAN CASES TURN OUT TO BE BLACK BAGS?
PUNY HUMAN! YOU WON'T GET THAT INFORMATION FROM ME! YOU WILL HAVE TO INVESTIGATE FURTHER...
...DELVE DEEPER INTO THE MYSTERY!
DEEPER?... OH - I GET IT...
PFWOOARR! IT STINKS IN HERE! YUCK!
HELLO- WHAT'S THIS? IT'S A COPY OF THIS VERY MAGAZINE!
Fortean Times
OF COURSE! I CAN READ THE END OF THIS COMIC STRIP AND FIND OUT THE ANSWER TO THE MYSTERY!
BLAH--BLAH-- AH! I SEE! SO THAT'S IT!
WE CAN'T JUST FINISH IT LIKE THAT...
WHY NOT? GULLY BULL SOLVES THE MYSTERY TO HIS OWN SATISFACTION... IT HAS A LOGICAL INTEGRITY...
IT'S NOT MY FAULT... I ONLY DRAW WHAT GULLY TELLS ME...
THE PUBLIC WILL NEVER WEAR IT!
FT EDITORIAL CONFERENCE
IT'S ALL A BIT POST-MODERN ISN'T IT?
HAS ANYONE ASKED GULLY WHAT THE ANSWER IS?
HE REFUSES TO SAY-- HE SAYS PEOPLE SHOULD READ THE COMIC FOR THEMSELVES!

THE BONNYBRIDGE UFO

EARLY 1990s – A UFO EVENT...
A LARGE TRIANGULAR OBJECT IS SEEN OVER *BONNYBRIDGE* IN SCOTLAND...

CLIK

A REPORT IN THE LOCAL PRESS SAYS THE OBJECT WAS CAUGHT ON CAMERA!

THESE PHOTOGRAPHS HAVE NEVER BEEN SEEN!

WE HAVE COME FOR THE CAMERA!

YEH! WE FROM THE GOV'MINT!

GULP!

THANK YOU FOR YOUR CO-OPERATION!

F'O DA GO MIN

THE CAMERA IS FLOWN BY *PRIVATE JET* TO A SECRET U.S. SECURITY BASE...

CAN'T YOU MAKE THIS THING GO ANY FASTER?

...WHERE IT IS INTERROGATED UNDER BRIGHT LIGHTS!

WHAT DO YOU KNOW?

WHO DO YOU KNOW?

THE LIGHTS FOG THE FILM* SO NO PHOTOGRAPHIC EVIDENCE REMAINS...

SHIT! WHAT WE GONNA DO NOW?

IT'S A GODDAM COMMUNIST PLOT

* PRE-DIGITAL!

THE GOVERNMENT SECURITY DEPARTMENT TAKES THE *CAMERA'S* REFUSAL TO DIVULGE INFORMATION UNDER DURESS AS AN ADMISSION OF *GUILT*...

THE REPORT IS GENUINE! AND THE PHOTOGRAPHIC EVIDENCE HAS BEEN ERASED!

IT'S A GODDAM COMMUNIST PLOT!

DEFINITIVE PROOF OF UFO EVENTS SUPRESSED BY COVERT GOVERNMENT FORCES!

EVIDENCE TO BE *LOCKED AWAY* AS PART OF A POLICY OF *GOVERNMENT SECRECY*...

SECRET UFO DATA
UNDER INVESTIGATION

BACKTRACK TO *BONNYBRIDGE* – THE DAY OF THE *EVENT*...

THE LOCAL YOUTH HAVE BEEN ENJOYING A FEW BOTTLES OF *BUCKY* AROUND THE TOWN CENTRE...

BELIEVE ME, THERE'S BUGGER-ALL TO DO IN *BONNY* AFTER 8 O'CLOCK!

A CERTAIN AMOUNT OF ARSING ABOUT IS GOING ON...

WAHEY! LOOK AT THIS – A UFO!

Hahahaha... AH'VE GOT IT ON MA WEE CAMERA, JAMIE! I GOT A PHOTO!

SNAP

HEY, STUART! YOU CAN DO A WEE NEWS STORY IN YER WEE NEWSPAPER – THE BONNY-BRIDGE BUGLE! Hahahaha!

AYE! I WILL TOO! "BONNY BRIDGE UFO SCARE!" Hahaha!

TWO DAYS LATER...

NEW

BOWMAN'S NOSE

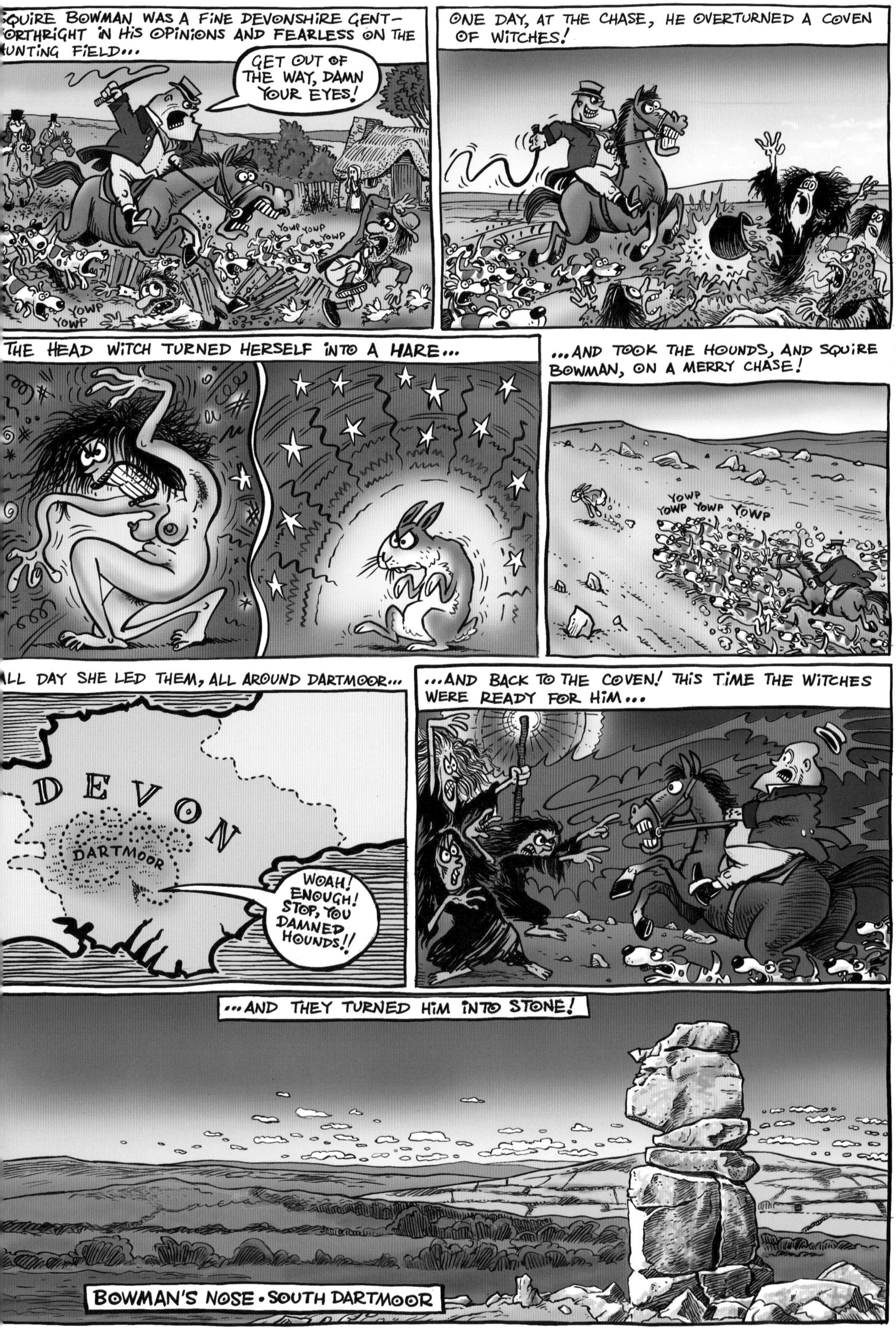

SQUIRE BOWMAN WAS A FINE DEVONSHIRE GENT—FORTHRIGHT IN HIS OPINIONS AND FEARLESS ON THE HUNTING FIELD...
GET OUT OF THE WAY, DAMN YOUR EYES!
YOWP YOWP YOWP
YOWP YOWP
ONE DAY, AT THE CHASE, HE OVERTURNED A COVEN OF WITCHES!
THE HEAD WITCH TURNED HERSELF INTO A HARE...
...AND TOOK THE HOUNDS, AND SQUIRE BOWMAN, ON A MERRY CHASE!
YOWP YOWP YOWP YOWP
ALL DAY SHE LED THEM, ALL AROUND DARTMOOR...
DEVON
DARTMOOR
WOAH! ENOUGH! STOP, YOU DAMNED HOUNDS!!
...AND BACK TO THE COVEN! THIS TIME THE WITCHES WERE READY FOR HIM...
...AND THEY TURNED HIM INTO STONE!
BOWMAN'S NOSE • SOUTH DARTMOOR

BRAIN CORE

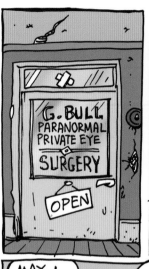

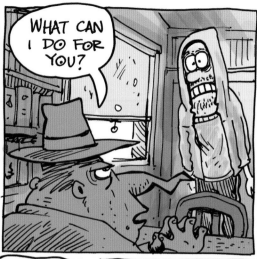

G. BULL
PARANORMAL PRIVATE EYE
SURGERY
OPEN
WHAT CAN I DO FOR YOU?
I'VE BEEN INTERFERED WITH BY ALIENS!
THEY'VE REMOVED A PIECE OF MY BRAIN TO DO TESTS ON!
MAY I SEE IT?
THEY'VE TAKEN A SAMPLE CORE OUT OF ME HEAD!
HE WAS RIGHT! THERE WAS A NEAT, CORE-SHAPED HOLE IN THE BACK OF HIS HEAD! YOU COULD HAVE PUT YOUR FINGER IN IT...
I PUT MY FINGER IN IT...
HEY! CUT THAT OUT!
WIGGLE
WIGGLE
STOP IT!
LET ME TELL YOU, ALIENS HAVE NOTHING TO DO WITH YOUR CORE-HOLE.
STRANGE STUFF SORTED
DEMONS UNLEASHED
MYSTERIES LOOKED INTO
IT'S THE GOVERNMENT!
THE GOVERNMENT? BUT- WHY?
IT'S NORMAL BEHAVIOUR FOR A GOVERNMENT...
...AND AS SUCH IT'S OUTSIDE MY RANGE! I DEAL STRICTLY IN THE PARANORMAL... I KNOW NOTHING ABOUT THE NORMAL
-GOOD DAY!
I MIGHT USE YOUR CASE IN A "WEIRD NOSE" PIECE SOMETI
BUT I CAN'T PROMISE!
DON'T COME BACK, PLEASE...

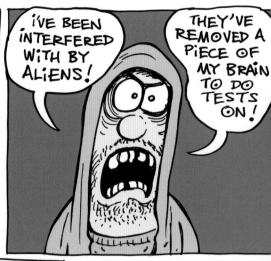

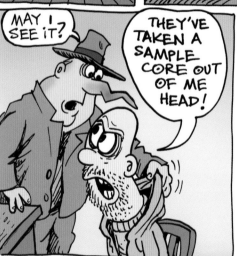

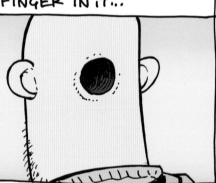

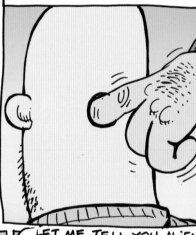

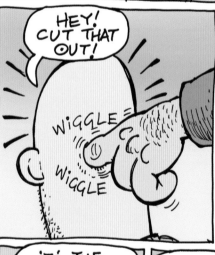

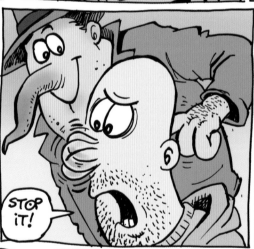

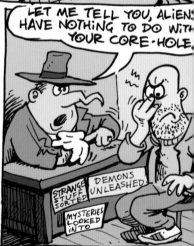

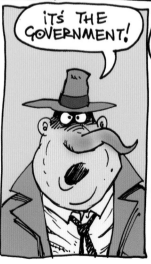

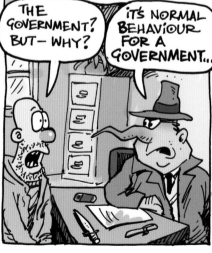

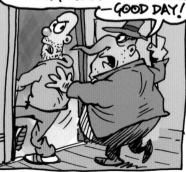

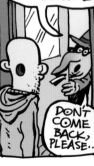

BURNING JUDAS

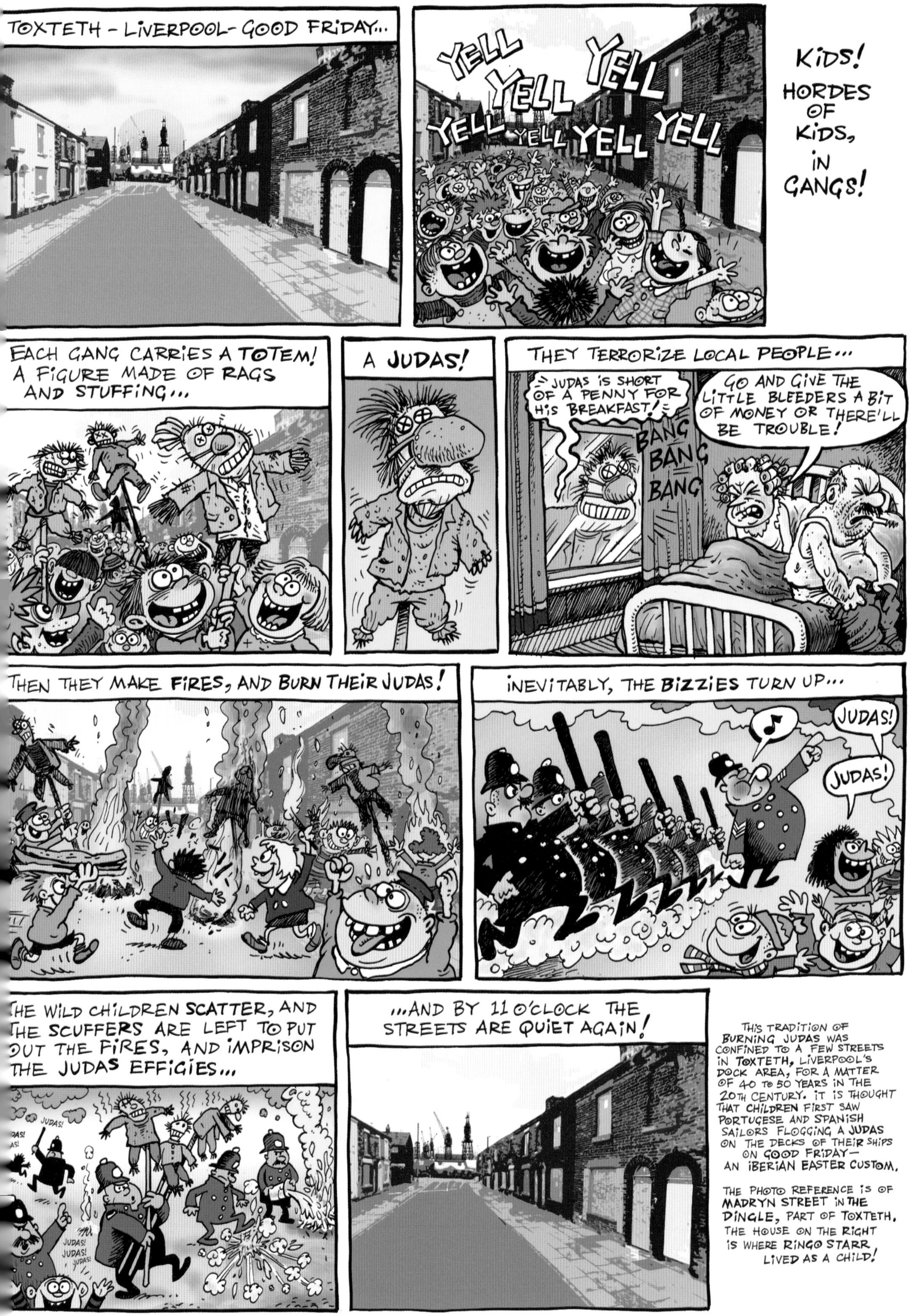
TOXTETH – LIVERPOOL – GOOD FRIDAY...
YELL YELL YELL YELL YELL YELL YELL
KIDS! HORDES OF KIDS, IN GANGS!
EACH GANG CARRIES A TOTEM! A FIGURE MADE OF RAGS AND STUFFING...
A JUDAS!
THEY TERRORIZE LOCAL PEOPLE...
JUDAS IS SHORT OF A PENNY FOR HIS BREAKFAST!
BANG BANG BANG
GO AND GIVE THE LITTLE BLEEDERS A BIT OF MONEY OR THERE'LL BE TROUBLE!
THEN THEY MAKE FIRES, AND BURN THEIR JUDAS!
INEVITABLY, THE BIZZIES TURN UP...
JUDAS!
JUDAS!
THE WILD CHILDREN SCATTER, AND THE SCUFFERS ARE LEFT TO PUT OUT THE FIRES, AND IMPRISON THE JUDAS EFFIGIES...
JUDAS!
JUDAS! JUDAS! JUDAS!
...AND BY 11 O'CLOCK THE STREETS ARE QUIET AGAIN!

THIS TRADITION OF BURNING JUDAS WAS CONFINED TO A FEW STREETS IN TOXTETH, LIVERPOOL'S DOCK AREA, FOR A MATTER OF 40 TO 50 YEARS IN THE 20TH CENTURY. IT IS THOUGHT THAT CHILDREN FIRST SAW PORTUGESE AND SPANISH SAILORS FLOGGING A JUDAS ON THE DECKS OF THEIR SHIPS ON GOOD FRIDAY— AN IBERIAN EASTER CUSTOM.

THE PHOTO REFERENCE IS OF MADRYN STREET IN THE DINGLE, PART OF TOXTETH. THE HOUSE ON THE RIGHT IS WHERE RINGO STARR LIVED AS A CHILD!

CAVORITE SHOES

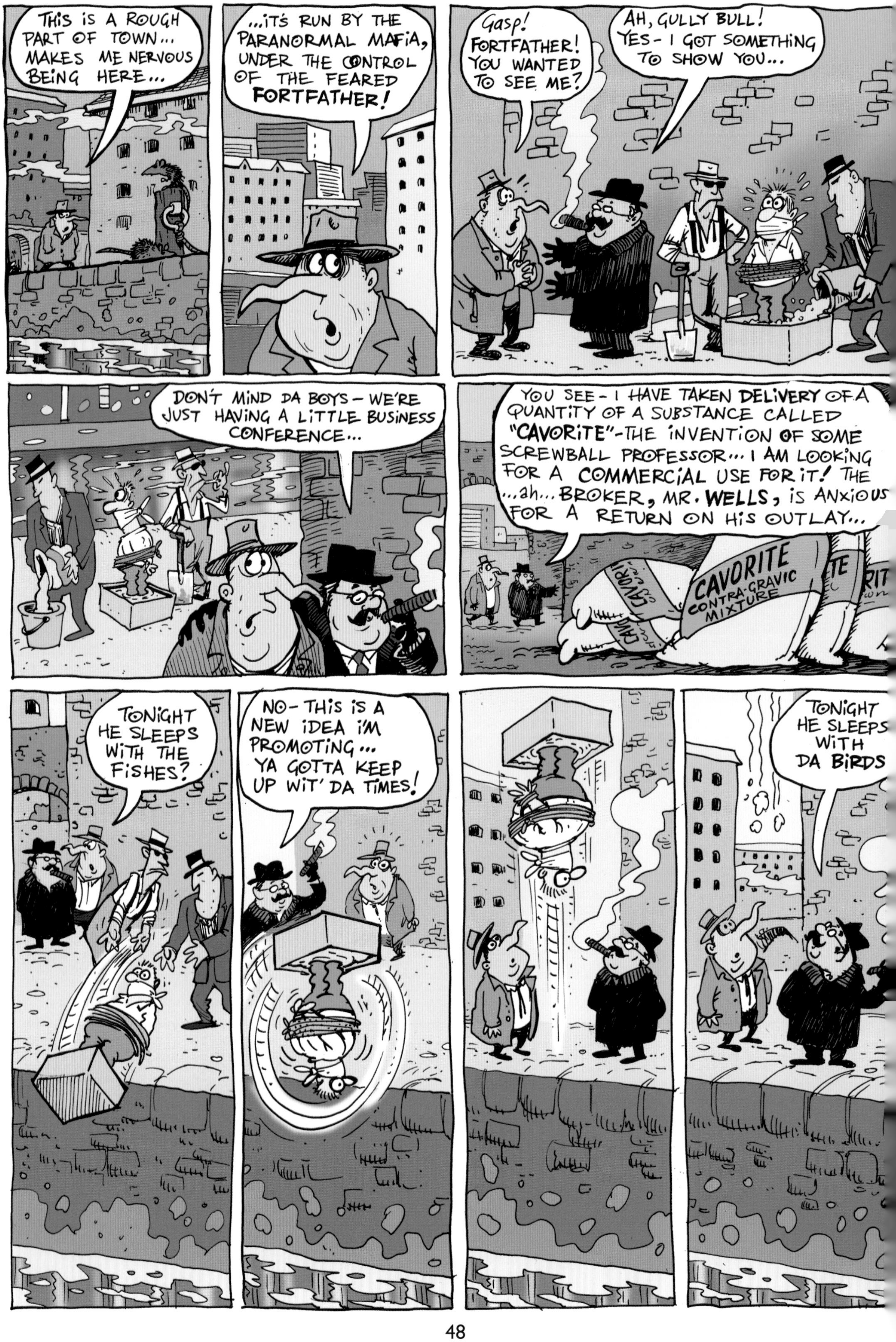
THIS IS A ROUGH PART OF TOWN... MAKES ME NERVOUS BEING HERE...
...IT'S RUN BY THE PARANORMAL MAFIA, UNDER THE CONTROL OF THE FEARED FORTFATHER!
Gasp! FORTFATHER! YOU WANTED TO SEE ME?
AH, GULLY BULL! YES - I GOT SOMETHING TO SHOW YOU...
DON'T MIND DA BOYS - WE'RE JUST HAVING A LITTLE BUSINESS CONFERENCE...
YOU SEE - I HAVE TAKEN DELIVERY OF A QUANTITY OF A SUBSTANCE CALLED "CAVORITE" - THE INVENTION OF SOME SCREWBALL PROFESSOR... I AM LOOKING FOR A COMMERCIAL USE FOR IT! THE ...ah... BROKER, MR. WELLS, IS ANXIOUS FOR A RETURN ON HIS OUTLAY...
CAVORITE CONTRA-GRAVIC MIXTURE
TONIGHT HE SLEEPS WITH THE FISHES?
NO - THIS IS A NEW IDEA I'M PROMOTING... YA GOTTA KEEP UP WIT' DA TIMES!
TONIGHT HE SLEEPS WITH DA BIRDS

CERN ANIMALS

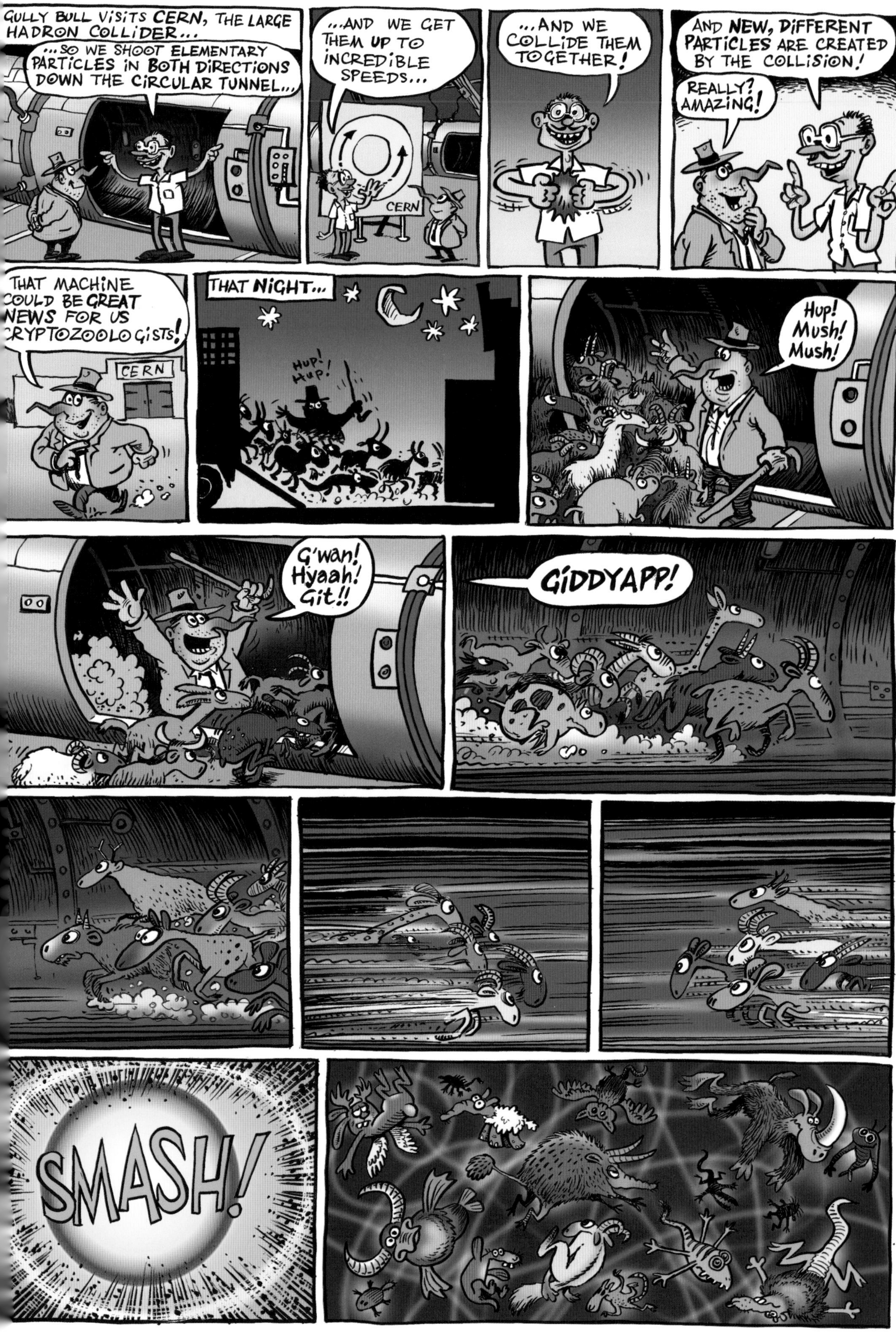
GULLY BULL VISITS CERN, THE LARGE HADRON COLLIDER...
...SO WE SHOOT ELEMENTARY PARTICLES IN BOTH DIRECTIONS DOWN THE CIRCULAR TUNNEL...
...AND WE GET THEM UP TO INCREDIBLE SPEEDS...
CERN
...AND WE COLLIDE THEM TOGETHER!
AND NEW, DIFFERENT PARTICLES ARE CREATED BY THE COLLISION!
REALLY? AMAZING!
THAT MACHINE COULD BE GREAT NEWS FOR US CRYPTOZOOLOGISTS!
CERN
THAT NIGHT...
HUP! HUP!
Hup! Mush! Mush!
G'wan! Hyaah! Git!!
GIDDYAPP!
SMASH!

THE CHESTERFIELD SPIRE

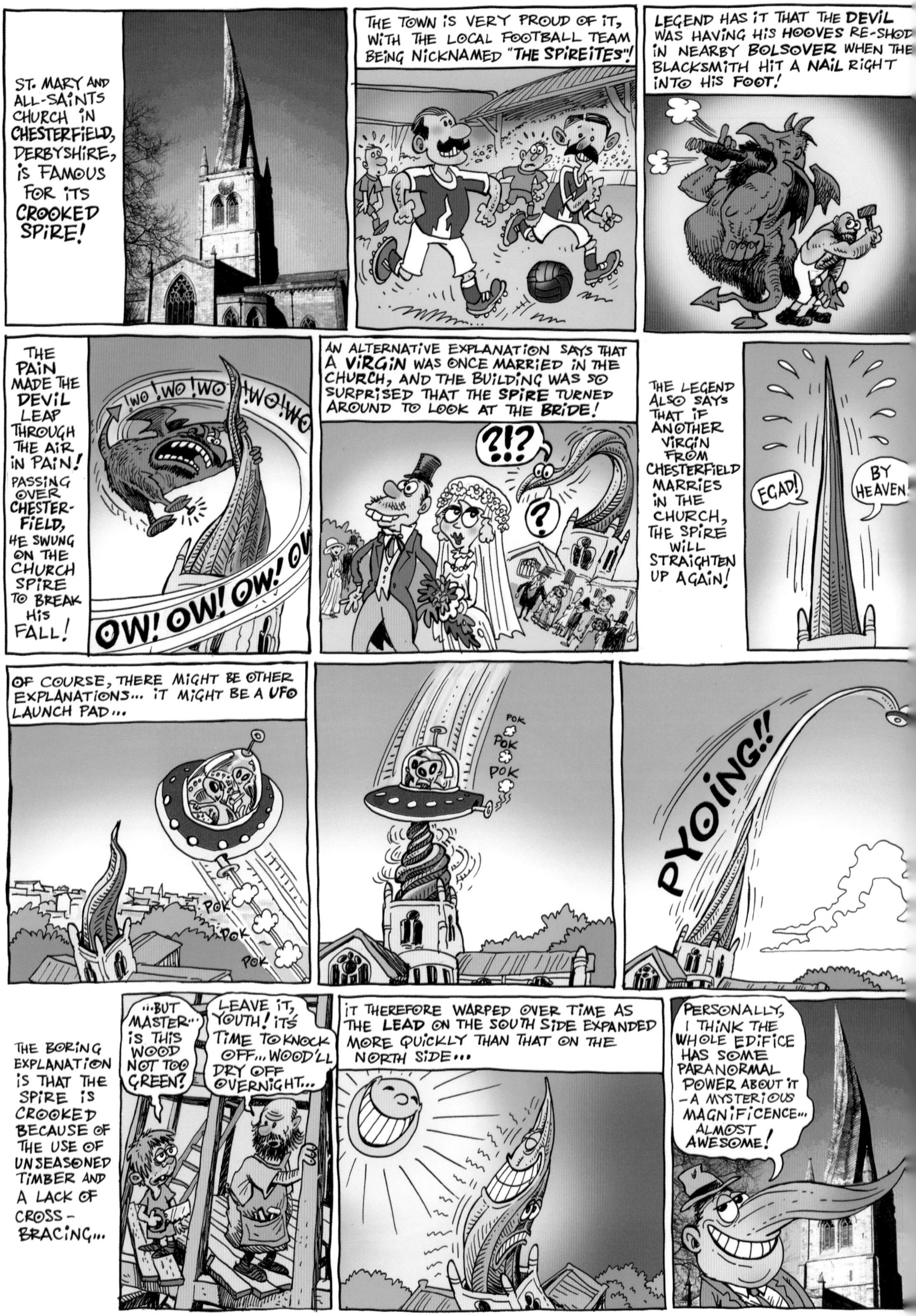

ST. MARY AND ALL-SAINTS CHURCH IN CHESTERFIELD, DERBYSHIRE, IS FAMOUS FOR ITS CROOKED SPIRE!
THE TOWN IS VERY PROUD OF IT, WITH THE LOCAL FOOTBALL TEAM BEING NICKNAMED "THE SPIREITES"!
LEGEND HAS IT THAT THE DEVIL WAS HAVING HIS HOOVES RE-SHOD IN NEARBY BOLSOVER WHEN THE BLACKSMITH HIT A NAIL RIGHT INTO HIS FOOT!
THE PAIN MADE THE DEVIL LEAP THROUGH THE AIR IN PAIN! PASSING OVER CHESTERFIELD, HE SWUNG ON THE CHURCH SPIRE TO BREAK HIS FALL!
OW! OW! OW! OW!
OW! OW! OW! OW
AN ALTERNATIVE EXPLANATION SAYS THAT A VIRGIN WAS ONCE MARRIED IN THE CHURCH, AND THE BUILDING WAS SO SURPRISED THAT THE SPIRE TURNED AROUND TO LOOK AT THE BRIDE!
?!?
?
THE LEGEND ALSO SAYS THAT IF ANOTHER VIRGIN FROM CHESTERFIELD MARRIES IN THE CHURCH, THE SPIRE WILL STRAIGHTEN UP AGAIN!
EGAD!
BY HEAVEN!
OF COURSE, THERE MIGHT BE OTHER EXPLANATIONS... IT MIGHT BE A UFO LAUNCH PAD...
POK
POK
POK
POK
POK
POK
PYOING!!
THE BORING EXPLANATION IS THAT THE SPIRE IS CROOKED BECAUSE OF THE USE OF UNSEASONED TIMBER AND A LACK OF CROSS-BRACING...
...BUT MASTER... IS THIS WOOD NOT TOO GREEN?
LEAVE IT, YOUTH! IT'S TIME TO KNOCK OFF... WOOD'LL DRY OFF OVERNIGHT...
IT THEREFORE WARPED OVER TIME AS THE LEAD ON THE SOUTH SIDE EXPANDED MORE QUICKLY THAN THAT ON THE NORTH SIDE...
PERSONALLY, I THINK THE WHOLE EDIFICE HAS SOME PARANORMAL POWER ABOUT IT – A MYSTERIOUS MAGNIFICENCE... ALMOST AWESOME!

CHRISTMAS IN CATALONIA

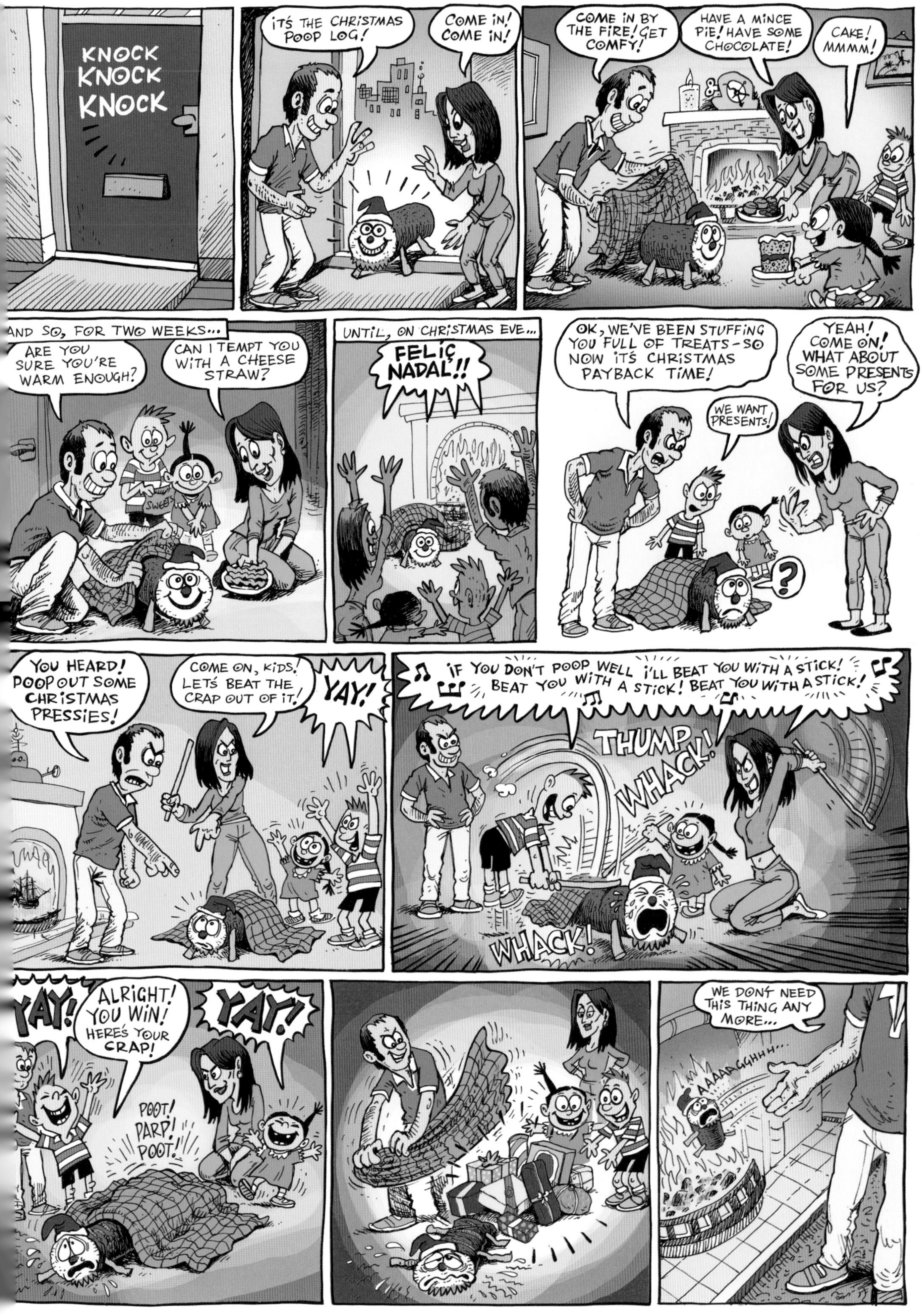
KNOCK KNOCK KNOCK
IT'S THE CHRISTMAS POOP LOG!
COME IN! COME IN!
COME IN BY THE FIRE! GET COMFY!
HAVE A MINCE PIE! HAVE SOME CHOCOLATE!
CAKE! MMMM!
AND SO, FOR TWO WEEKS...
ARE YOU SURE YOU'RE WARM ENOUGH?
CAN I TEMPT YOU WITH A CHEESE STRAW?
SWEETS
UNTIL, ON CHRISTMAS EVE...
FELIÇ NADAL!!
OK, WE'VE BEEN STUFFING YOU FULL OF TREATS - SO NOW IT'S CHRISTMAS PAYBACK TIME!
YEAH! COME ON! WHAT ABOUT SOME PRESENTS FOR US?
WE WANT PRESENTS!
?
YOU HEARD! POOP OUT SOME CHRISTMAS PRESSIES!
COME ON, KIDS! LET'S BEAT THE CRAP OUT OF IT!
YAY!
IF YOU DON'T POOP WELL I'LL BEAT YOU WITH A STICK! BEAT YOU WITH A STICK! BEAT YOU WITH A STICK!
THUMP
WHACK!
WHACK!
YAY!
ALRIGHT! YOU WIN! HERE'S YOUR CRAP!
YAY!
POOT! PARP! POOT!
WE DON'T NEED THIS THING ANY MORE...
AAAARGGHHH...

CHUPACABRA

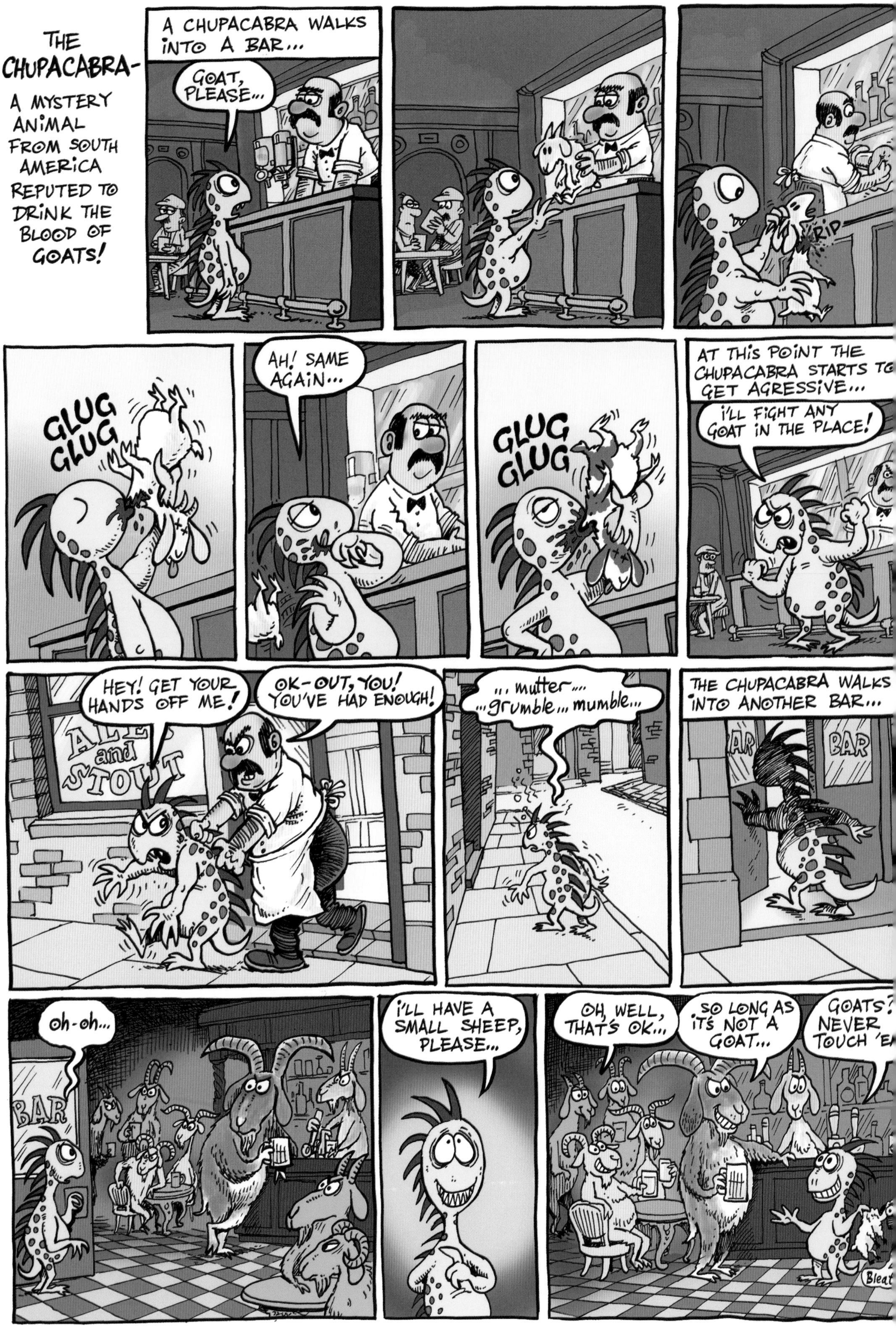
THE CHUPACABRA- A MYSTERY ANIMAL FROM SOUTH AMERICA REPUTED TO DRINK THE BLOOD OF GOATS!
A CHUPACABRA WALKS INTO A BAR...
GOAT, PLEASE...
RIP
GLUG GLUG
AH! SAME AGAIN...
GLUG GLUG
AT THIS POINT THE CHUPACABRA STARTS TO GET AGRESSIVE...
I'LL FIGHT ANY GOAT IN THE PLACE!
HEY! GET YOUR HANDS OFF ME!
OK-OUT, YOU! YOU'VE HAD ENOUGH!
ALES and STOUT
... mutter... ...grumble... mumble...
THE CHUPACABRA WALKS INTO ANOTHER BAR...
BAR
oh-oh...
BAR
I'LL HAVE A SMALL SHEEP, PLEASE...
OH, WELL, THAT'S OK...
SO LONG AS IT'S NOT A GOAT...
GOATS? NEVER TOUCH 'EM
Bleat

CLIFF EDGE

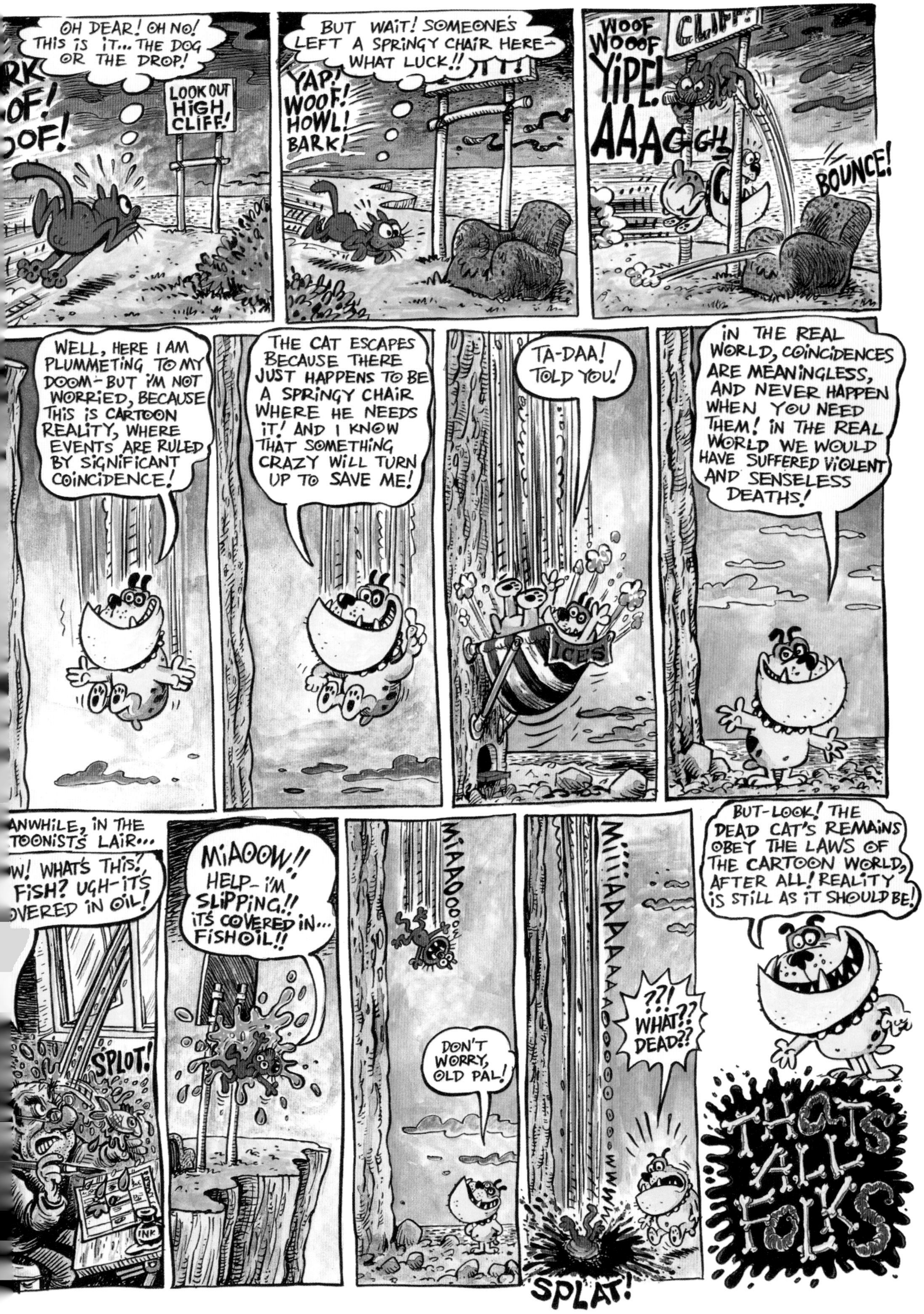

OH DEAR! OH NO! THIS IS IT... THE DOG OR THE DROP!
RK OF! OOF!
LOOK OUT HIGH CLIFF!
BUT WAIT! SOMEONE'S LEFT A SPRINGY CHAIR HERE — WHAT LUCK!!
YAP! WOOF! HOWL! BARK!
WOOF WOOOF YIPE! AAAAGGH!
CLIFF!
BOUNCE!
WELL, HERE I AM PLUMMETING TO MY DOOM — BUT I'M NOT WORRIED, BECAUSE THIS IS CARTOON REALITY, WHERE EVENTS ARE RULED BY SIGNIFICANT COINCIDENCE!
THE CAT ESCAPES BECAUSE THERE JUST HAPPENS TO BE A SPRINGY CHAIR WHERE HE NEEDS IT! AND I KNOW THAT SOMETHING CRAZY WILL TURN UP TO SAVE ME!
TA-DAA! TOLD YOU!
ICES
IN THE REAL WORLD, COINCIDENCES ARE MEANINGLESS, AND NEVER HAPPEN WHEN YOU NEED THEM! IN THE REAL WORLD WE WOULD HAVE SUFFERED VIOLENT AND SENSELESS DEATHS!
ANWHILE, IN THE TOONISTS LAIR...
W! WHAT'S THIS? FISH? UGH — IT'S OVERED IN OIL!
SPLOT!
INK
MIAOOW!! HELP — I'M SLIPPING!! IT'S COVERED IN... FISHOIL!!
MIAAOOOOOW
DON'T WORRY, OLD PAL!
MIIIIAAAAAAAAOOOOOOWWWW
??! WHAT?? DEAD??
SPLAT!
BUT — LOOK! THE DEAD CAT'S REMAINS OBEY THE LAWS OF THE CARTOON WORLD, AFTER ALL! REALITY IS STILL AS IT SHOULD BE!
THAT'S ALL FOLKS

CLOWNS

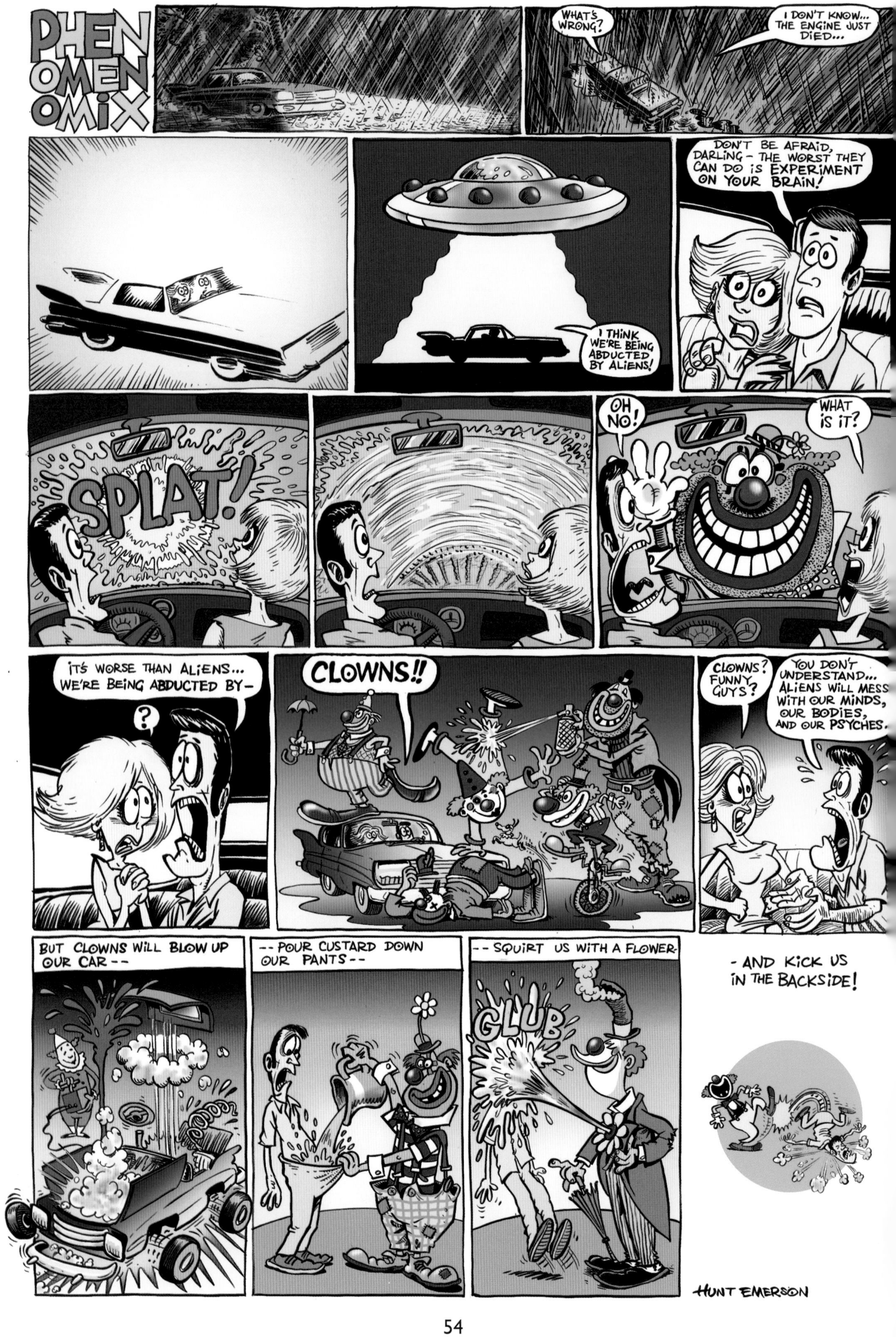

PHENOMENOMIX
WHAT'S WRONG?
I DON'T KNOW... THE ENGINE JUST DIED...
I THINK WE'RE BEING ABDUCTED BY ALIENS!
DON'T BE AFRAID, DARLING - THE WORST THEY CAN DO IS EXPERIMENT ON YOUR BRAIN!
SPLAT!
OH NO!
WHAT IS IT?
IT'S WORSE THAN ALIENS... WE'RE BEING ABDUCTED BY-
?
CLOWNS!!
CLOWNS? FUNNY GUYS?
YOU DON'T UNDERSTAND... ALIENS WILL MESS WITH OUR MINDS, OUR BODIES, AND OUR PSYCHES.
BUT CLOWNS WILL BLOW UP OUR CAR--
--POUR CUSTARD DOWN OUR PANTS--
--SQUIRT US WITH A FLOWER-
GLUB
-AND KICK US IN THE BACKSIDE!
HUNT EMERSON

ULLY BULL'S CROP CIRCLE NOSE

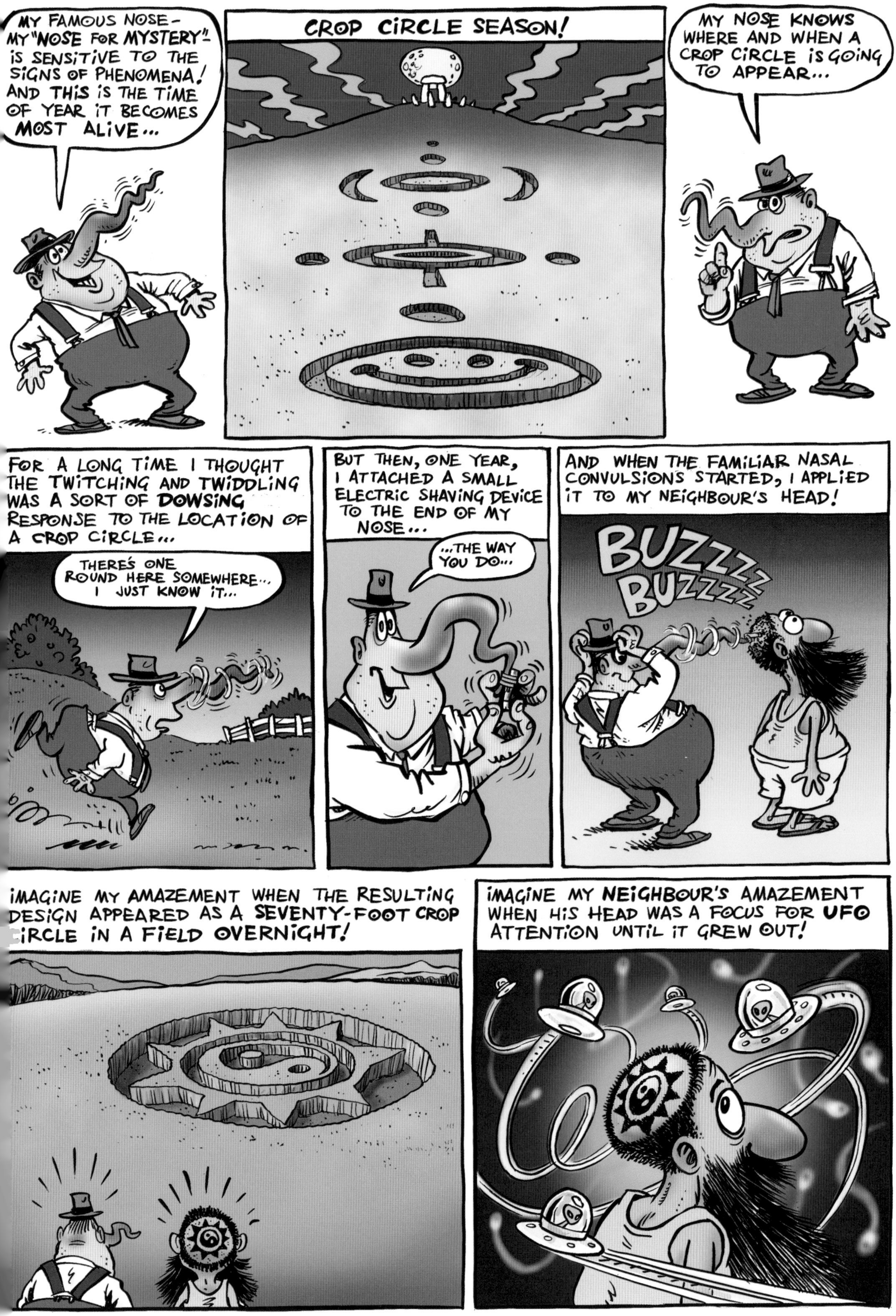
MY FAMOUS NOSE- MY "NOSE FOR MYSTERY"- IS SENSITIVE TO THE SIGNS OF PHENOMENA! AND THIS IS THE TIME OF YEAR IT BECOMES MOST ALIVE...
CROP CIRCLE SEASON!
MY NOSE KNOWS WHERE AND WHEN A CROP CIRCLE IS GOING TO APPEAR...
FOR A LONG TIME I THOUGHT THE TWITCHING AND TWIDDLING WAS A SORT OF DOWSING RESPONSE TO THE LOCATION OF A CROP CIRCLE...
THERE'S ONE ROUND HERE SOMEWHERE... I JUST KNOW IT...
BUT THEN, ONE YEAR, I ATTACHED A SMALL ELECTRIC SHAVING DEVICE TO THE END OF MY NOSE...
...THE WAY YOU DO...
AND WHEN THE FAMILIAR NASAL CONVULSIONS STARTED, I APPLIED IT TO MY NEIGHBOUR'S HEAD!
BUZZZZ BUZZZZ
IMAGINE MY AMAZEMENT WHEN THE RESULTING DESIGN APPEARED AS A SEVENTY-FOOT CROP CIRCLE IN A FIELD OVERNIGHT!
IMAGINE MY NEIGHBOUR'S AMAZEMENT WHEN HIS HEAD WAS A FOCUS FOR UFO ATTENTION UNTIL IT GREW OUT!

CROP CIRCLE SHOES

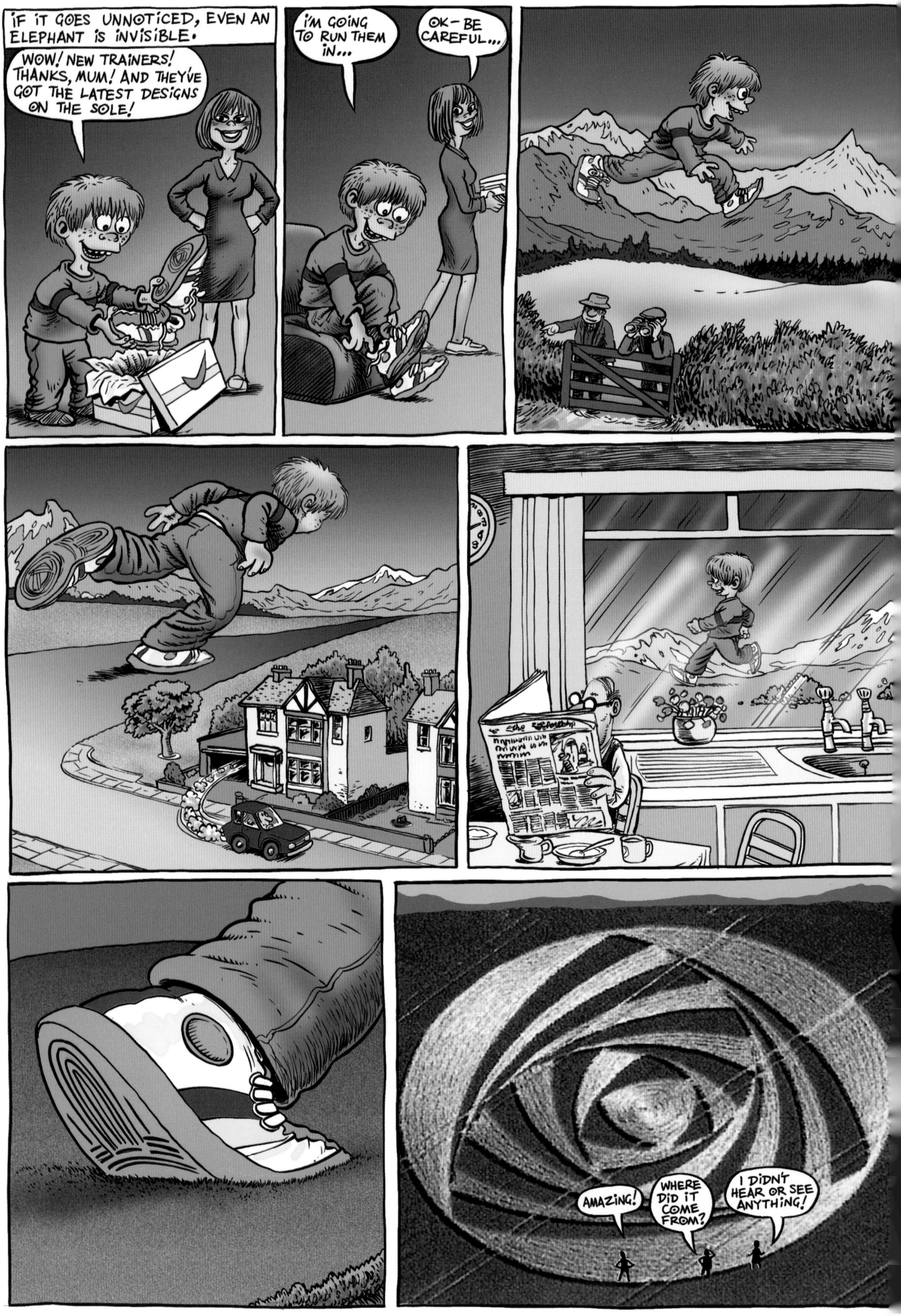
IF IT GOES UNNOTICED, EVEN AN ELEPHANT IS INVISIBLE.
WOW! NEW TRAINERS! THANKS, MUM! AND THEY'VE GOT THE LATEST DESIGNS ON THE SOLE!
I'M GOING TO RUN THEM IN...
OK – BE CAREFUL...
AMAZING!
WHERE DID IT COME FROM?
I DIDN'T HEAR OR SEE ANYTHING!

CRYPTOPUDDING

HELLO! I'M OUTSIDE THE CFP - THE CENTRE FOR FORTEAN PUDDINGS - WITH THE COUNTRY'S LEADING CRYPTOPUDDINGOLOGIST, MR. TOMATHON TRIFLE!

HELLO

MR. TRIFLE - WHAT IS CRYPTOPUDDINGOLOGY?

THE STUDY OF PUDDINGS, DESSERTS, SWEETS, AND AFTERS UNDESCRIBED BY SCIENCE AND OF AN OTHERWISE MYSTERIOUS NATURE...

I AM PRIVILEDGED TO BE THE CHAIRMAN OF THE CFP - THIS IS MY ICING OF OFFICE!

WHAT'S THE MOST INEXPLICABLE PUDDING YOU'VE COME ACCROSS?

HELICOPTER LEMON SURPRISE!

A CARAMELIZED HELICOPTER FILLED WITH VANILLA CRÈME, WITH A WHOLE LEMON INSERTED INTO THE COCKPIT...

HMM! WHAT WAS THE SURPRISE?

THAT THEY EVER MANAGED TO TEACH A LEMON TO FLY A HELICOPTER!

EXCUSE ME... I JUST CAN'T RESIST....

HEY!

SLURP!

HOW DARE YOU! THIS INTERVIEW IS OVER!

TERMINATED!

Mmm Delicious

WITH PREJUDICE!

CFP

SLAM

WELL - THAT WASN'T VERY FORTEAN, WAS IT?

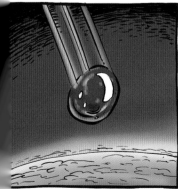

BUT, HIGH ABOVE, IN THE UPPER ATMOSPHERE, A GIANT GLACÉ CHERRY IS FALLING TOWARDS EARTH...

BLOOP
BLOOP
PATERSON'S CUSTARD FACTORY

PLOP
PATERSONS CUSTARD FACTORY

CUP-AND-RING MARKS

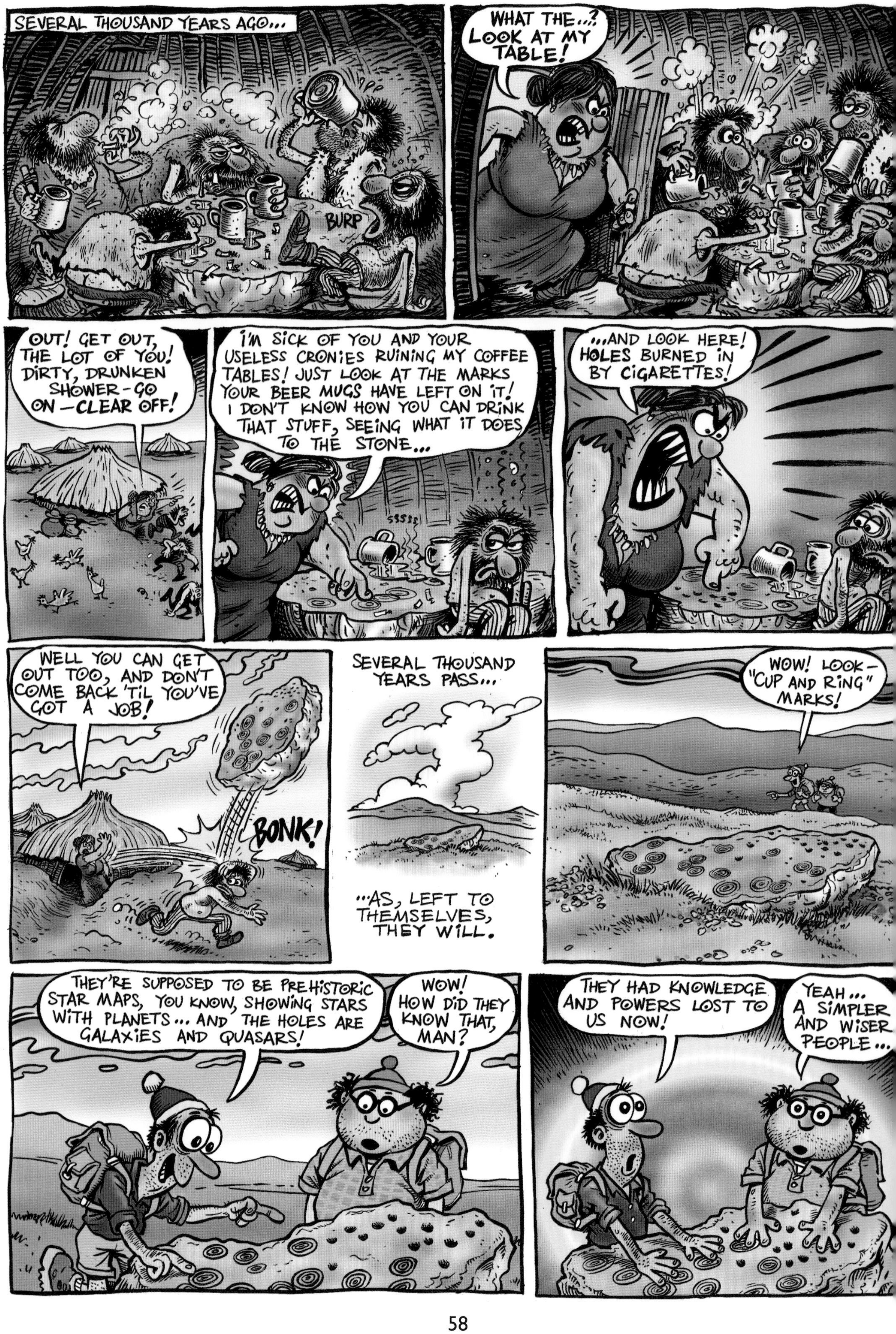
SEVERAL THOUSAND YEARS AGO...
BURP
WHAT THE...? LOOK AT MY TABLE!
OUT! GET OUT, THE LOT OF YOU! DIRTY, DRUNKEN SHOWER–GO ON–CLEAR OFF!
I'M SICK OF YOU AND YOUR USELESS CRONIES RUINING MY COFFEE TABLES! JUST LOOK AT THE MARKS YOUR BEER MUGS HAVE LEFT ON IT! I DON'T KNOW HOW YOU CAN DRINK THAT STUFF, SEEING WHAT IT DOES TO THE STONE...
SSSSS
...AND LOOK HERE! HOLES BURNED IN BY CIGARETTES!
WELL YOU CAN GET OUT TOO, AND DON'T COME BACK 'TIL YOU'VE GOT A JOB!
BONK!
SEVERAL THOUSAND YEARS PASS...
...AS, LEFT TO THEMSELVES, THEY WILL.
WOW! LOOK– "CUP AND RING" MARKS!
THEY'RE SUPPOSED TO BE PREHISTORIC STAR MAPS, YOU KNOW, SHOWING STARS WITH PLANETS... AND THE HOLES ARE GALAXIES AND QUASARS!
WOW! HOW DID THEY KNOW THAT, MAN?
THEY HAD KNOWLEDGE AND POWERS LOST TO US NOW!
YEAH... A SIMPLER AND WISER PEOPLE...

THE DA VINCI CODE

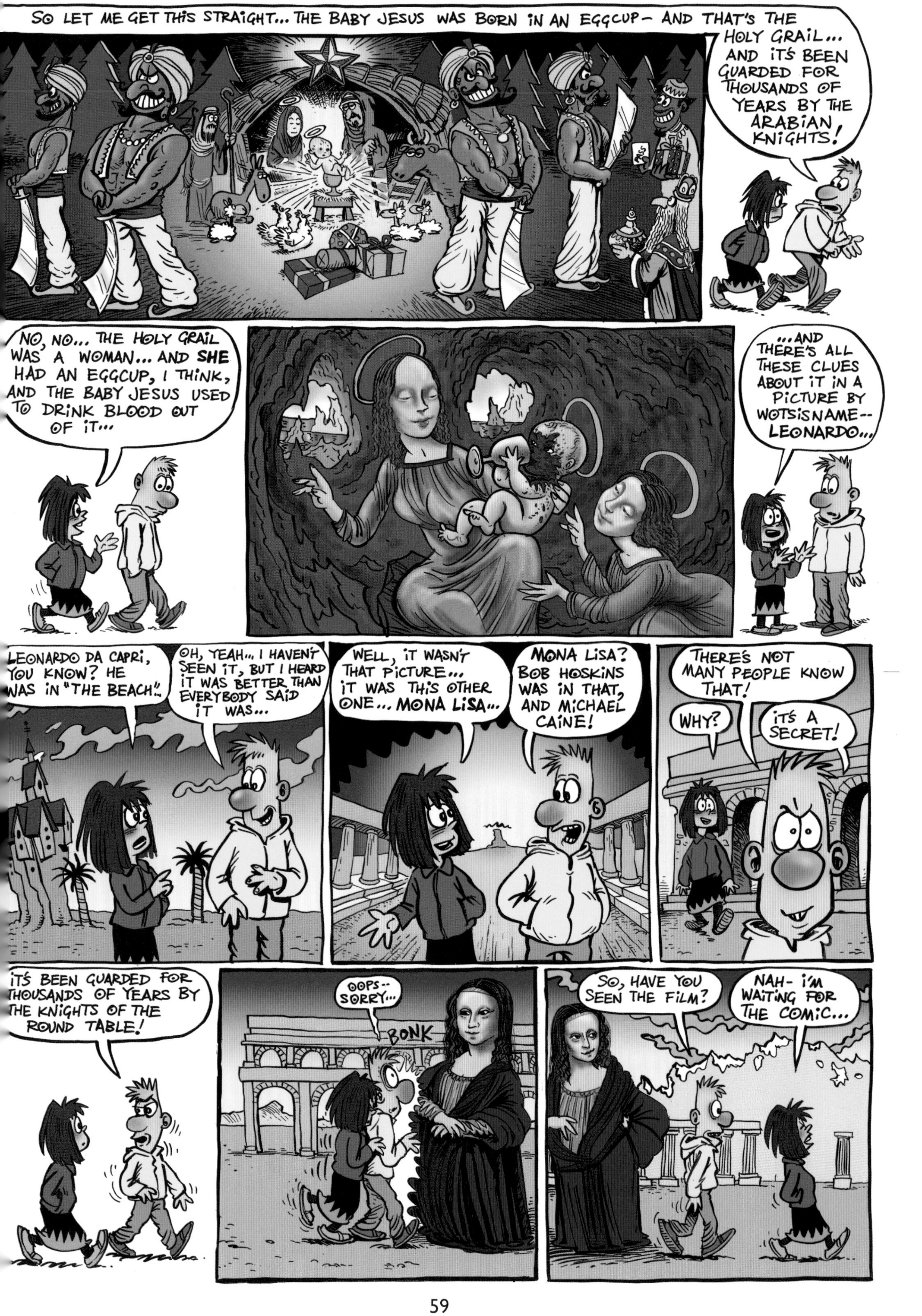

SO LET ME GET THIS STRAIGHT... THE BABY JESUS WAS BORN IN AN EGGCUP— AND THAT'S THE HOLY GRAIL... AND IT'S BEEN GUARDED FOR THOUSANDS OF YEARS BY THE ARABIAN KNIGHTS!
NO, NO... THE HOLY GRAIL WAS A WOMAN... AND SHE HAD AN EGGCUP, I THINK, AND THE BABY JESUS USED TO DRINK BLOOD OUT OF IT...
...AND THERE'S ALL THESE CLUES ABOUT IT IN A PICTURE BY WOTSISNAME-- LEONARDO...
LEONARDO DA CAPRI, YOU KNOW? HE WAS IN "THE BEACH".
OH, YEAH... I HAVEN'T SEEN IT, BUT I HEARD IT WAS BETTER THAN EVERYBODY SAID IT WAS...
WELL, IT WASN'T THAT PICTURE... IT WAS THIS OTHER ONE... MONA LISA...
MONA LISA? BOB HOSKINS WAS IN THAT, AND MICHAEL CAINE!
THERE'S NOT MANY PEOPLE KNOW THAT!
WHY?
IT'S A SECRET!
IT'S BEEN GUARDED FOR THOUSANDS OF YEARS BY THE KNIGHTS OF THE ROUND TABLE!
OOPS-- SORRY...
BONK
SO, HAVE YOU SEEN THE FILM?
NAH- I'M WAITING FOR THE COMIC...

DEUS EX MACHINA

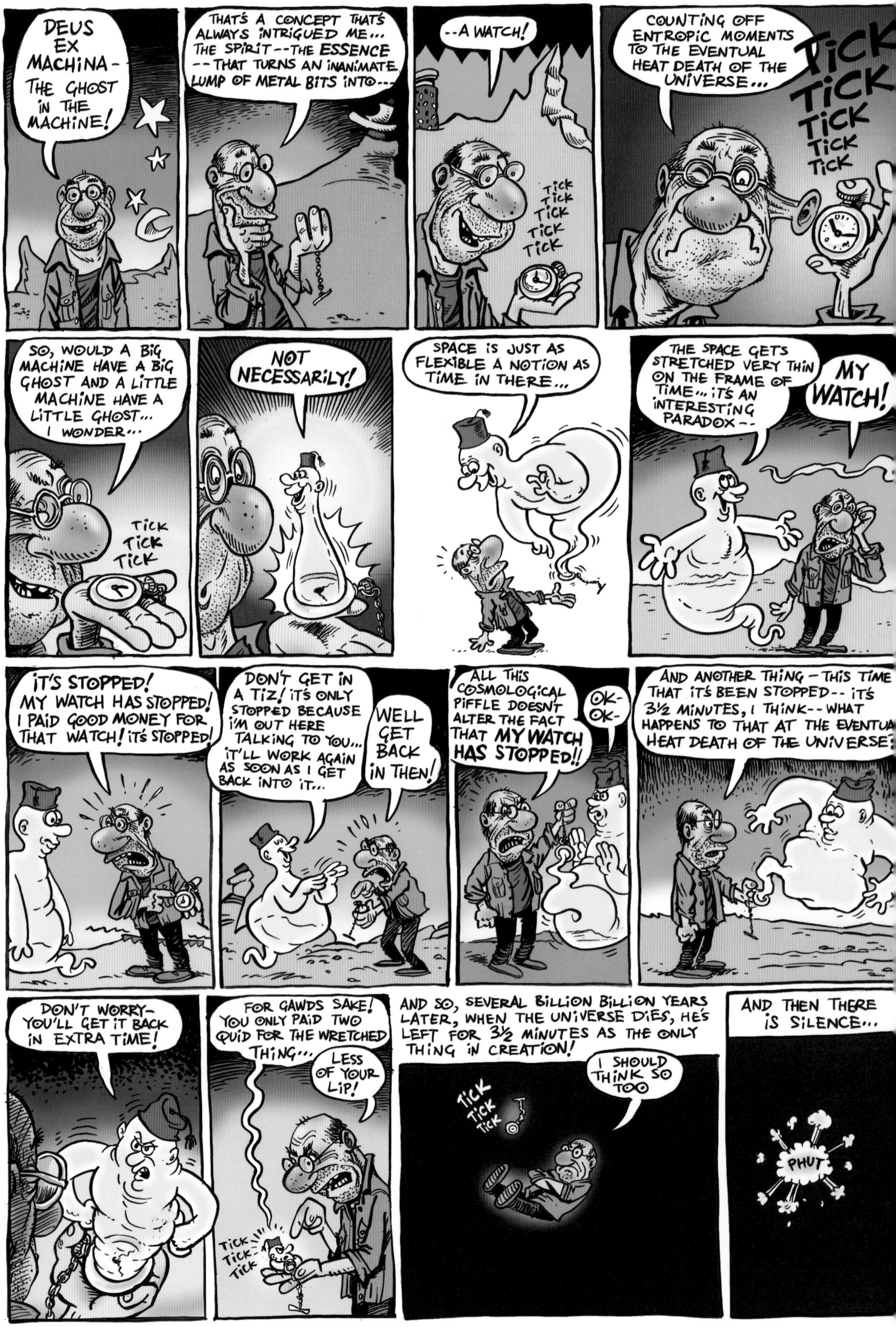

DEUS EX MACHINA - THE GHOST IN THE MACHINE!
THAT'S A CONCEPT THAT'S ALWAYS INTRIGUED ME... THE SPIRIT--THE ESSENCE --THAT TURNS AN INANIMATE LUMP OF METAL BITS INTO---
--A WATCH!
TICK TICK TICK TICK TICK
COUNTING OFF ENTROPIC MOMENTS TO THE EVENTUAL HEAT DEATH OF THE UNIVERSE...
TICK TICK TICK TICK TICK
SO, WOULD A BIG MACHINE HAVE A BIG GHOST AND A LITTLE MACHINE HAVE A LITTLE GHOST... I WONDER...
TICK TICK TICK
NOT NECESSARILY!
SPACE IS JUST AS FLEXIBLE A NOTION AS TIME IN THERE...
THE SPACE GETS STRETCHED VERY THIN ON THE FRAME OF TIME... IT'S AN INTERESTING PARADOX--
MY WATCH!
IT'S STOPPED! MY WATCH HAS STOPPED! I PAID GOOD MONEY FOR THAT WATCH! IT'S STOPPED!
DON'T GET IN A TIZ! IT'S ONLY STOPPED BECAUSE I'M OUT HERE TALKING TO YOU... IT'LL WORK AGAIN AS SOON AS I GET BACK INTO IT...
WELL GET BACK IN THEN!
ALL THIS COSMOLOGICAL PIFFLE DOESN'T ALTER THE FACT THAT MY WATCH HAS STOPPED!!
OK- OK-
AND ANOTHER THING - THIS TIME THAT IT'S BEEN STOPPED-- IT'S 3½ MINUTES, I THINK-- WHAT HAPPENS TO THAT AT THE EVENTUAL HEAT DEATH OF THE UNIVERSE?
DON'T WORRY- YOU'LL GET IT BACK IN EXTRA TIME!
FOR GAWDS SAKE! YOU ONLY PAID TWO QUID FOR THE WRETCHED THING...
LESS OF YOUR LIP!
TICK TICK TICK
AND SO, SEVERAL BILLION BILLION YEARS LATER, WHEN THE UNIVERSE DIES, HE'S LEFT FOR 3½ MINUTES AS THE ONLY THING IN CREATION!
TICK TICK TICK
I SHOULD THINK SO TOO
AND THEN THERE IS SILENCE...
PHUT

DINO-BOY

DINO-BOY EMERGES FROM THE FOREST...

HE HAS SCRAMBLED AND FALLEN FROM AN INACCESIBLE JUNGLE-TOPPED MESA, WHERE EVOLUTION, LIKE, HASN'T HAPPENED, MAN! AND, LIKE, DINOSAURS RULE!

SO DINO-BOY HITS THE HIGHWAY...

NO ROADSIDE CHICKEN YARD IS SAFE FROM THE DINO-BOY!

OH, DINO-BOY - YOU'RE SO COOL!

HE'S SO CUTE!

DINO-BOY, YOU'RE THE BEST!

HEY, CHICKENS! I'M THE DINO-BOY, DIG?

OH! CLUCKING OH!

...UNTIL HE HITS THE ROAD AGAIN...

≶SIGH!≶

≶CLUCKING SIGH!≶

BYE-BYE!

UNTIL...

OK, SUNSHINE - HOLIDAY'S OVER! BACK UP THE HILL WITH YOU!

YEAH, MAN - I DIG IT...

STRANGE LIGHTS AROUND THE HIGH MESA AGAIN...

AI-AI!

SI, I SEE THEM! WE CAN THANK THE GREAT ONES THAT THEY DO NOT INTERFERE WITH WE SIMPLE FOLK AND OUR SIMPLE CHICKENS!

BUT— A GENERATION OF EGGS IS PREPARING TO HATCH...

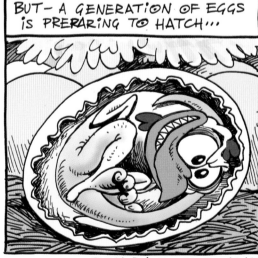

DOM-DA-DOM-DOM!!!

DINOSAUR DRUMSTICK

I'M ON MY WAY TO A "DIG"!
A PALAEONTOLOGIST FRIEND OF MINE TELLS ME HE'S FOUND SOMETHING AMAZING!
HELLO! PROFESSOR SCRABBLE!
AH-BULL! LOOK AT THIS!
IT'S THE FOSSILIZED LEG BONE OF A GIGANTIC PREHISTORIC BEAST!
WOW!
AN EARLY FLIGHTLESS CHICKEN, IT SEEMS...
INCREDIBLE! I BET IT COULD RUN LIKE A FOOL, AND IT MUST HAVE HAD QUITE A PECK!
GREAT SCOTT! WHAT'S THIS? THERE ARE FRAGMENTS OF FOSSILIZED FLESH STILL ADHERING TO THE BONE!
FRAGMENTS OF FOSSILIZED FLESH?
KEEP DIGGING...
D'YOU WANT FRIES WITH THAT?
YEAH- AND A COKE...

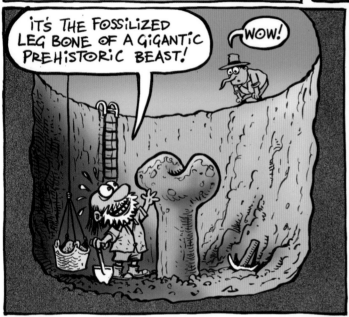

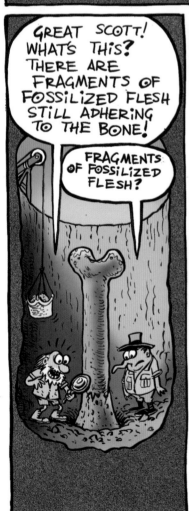

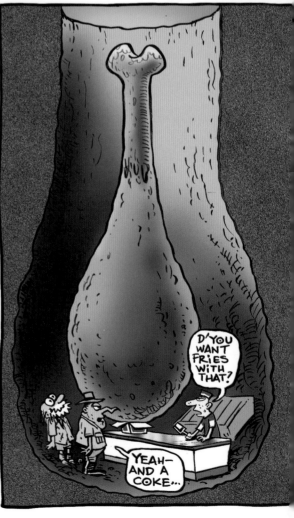

HE DISEMBODIED HAND

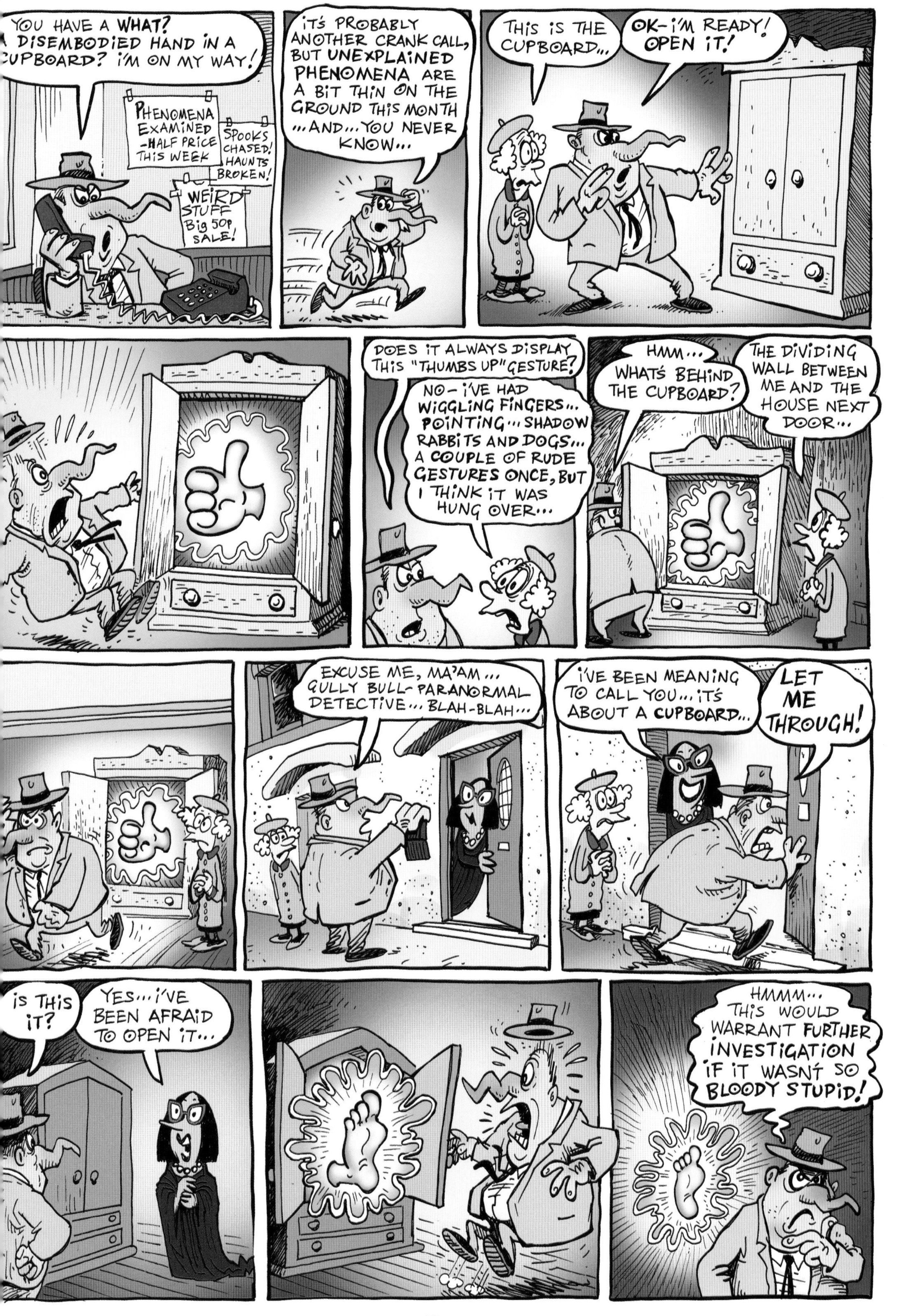

YOU HAVE A WHAT? A DISEMBODIED HAND IN A CUPBOARD? I'M ON MY WAY!
PHENOMENA EXAMINED -HALF PRICE THIS WEEK
SPOOKS CHASED! HAUNTS BROKEN!
WEIRD STUFF Big 50p SALE!
IT'S PROBABLY ANOTHER CRANK CALL, BUT UNEXPLAINED PHENOMENA ARE A BIT THIN ON THE GROUND THIS MONTH ...AND... YOU NEVER KNOW...
THIS IS THE CUPBOARD...
OK- I'M READY! OPEN IT!
DOES IT ALWAYS DISPLAY THIS "THUMBS UP" GESTURE?
NO- I'VE HAD WIGGLING FINGERS... POINTING... SHADOW RABBITS AND DOGS... A COUPLE OF RUDE GESTURES ONCE, BUT I THINK IT WAS HUNG OVER...
HMM... WHAT'S BEHIND THE CUPBOARD?
THE DIVIDING WALL BETWEEN ME AND THE HOUSE NEXT DOOR...
EXCUSE ME, MA'AM... GULLY BULL- PARANORMAL DETECTIVE... BLAH-BLAH...
I'VE BEEN MEANING TO CALL YOU... IT'S ABOUT A CUPBOARD...
LET ME THROUGH!
IS THIS IT?
YES... I'VE BEEN AFRAID TO OPEN IT...
HMMM... THIS WOULD WARRANT FURTHER INVESTIGATION IF IT WASN'T SO BLOODY STUPID!

DOG BRAIN

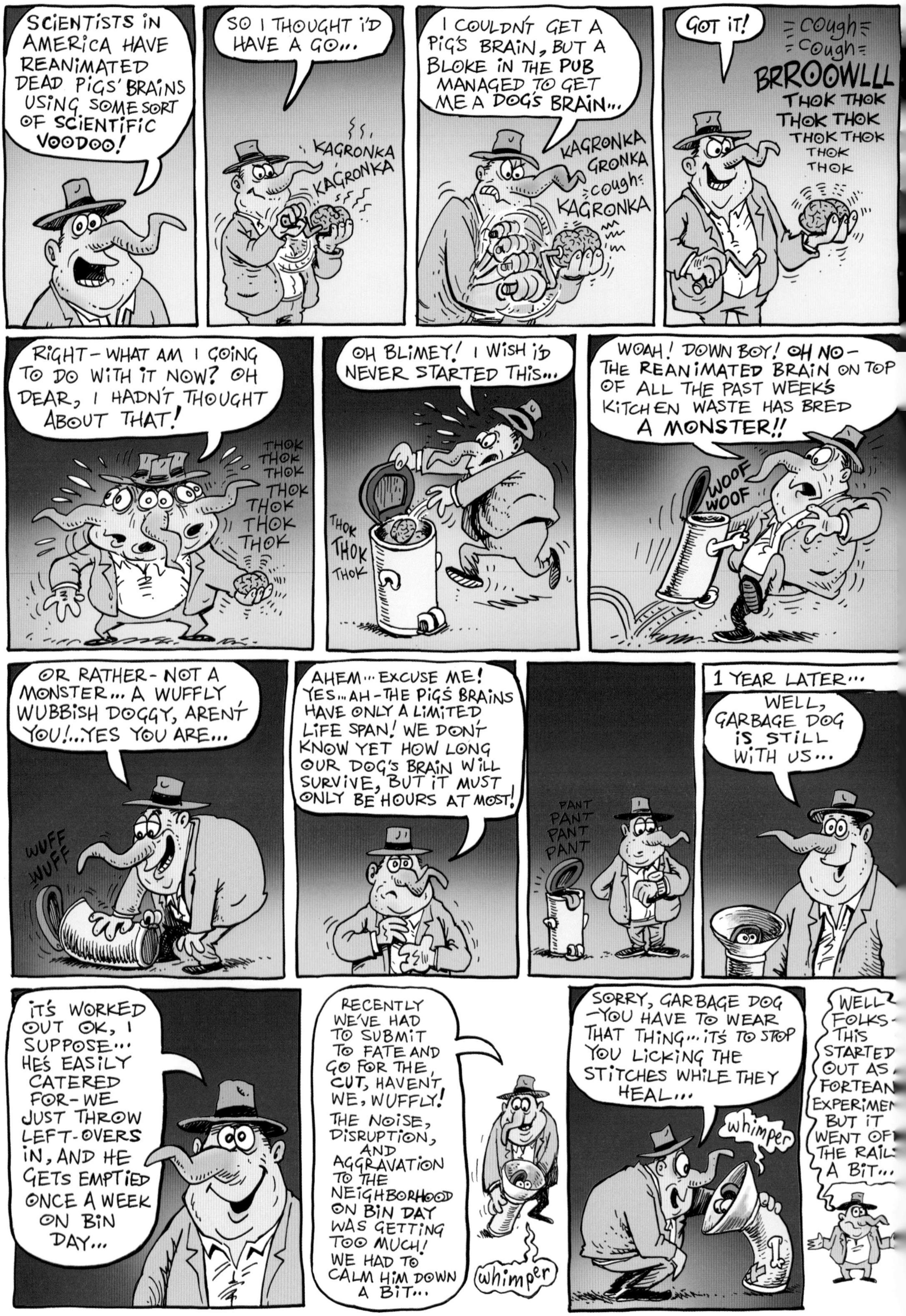
SCIENTISTS IN AMERICA HAVE REANIMATED DEAD PIGS' BRAINS USING SOME SORT OF SCIENTIFIC VOODOO!
SO I THOUGHT I'D HAVE A GO...
KAGRONKA
KAGRONKA
I COULDN'T GET A PIG'S BRAIN, BUT A BLOKE IN THE PUB MANAGED TO GET ME A DOG'S BRAIN...
KAGRONKA GRONKA
cough
KAGRONKA
GOT IT!
cough
cough
BRROOWLLL
THOK THOK THOK THOK THOK THOK THOK THOK
RIGHT - WHAT AM I GOING TO DO WITH IT NOW? OH DEAR, I HADN'T THOUGHT ABOUT THAT!
THOK THOK THOK THOK THOK THOK THOK
OH BLIMEY! I WISH I'D NEVER STARTED THIS...
THOK THOK THOK
WOAH! DOWN BOY! OH NO - THE REANIMATED BRAIN ON TOP OF ALL THE PAST WEEK'S KITCHEN WASTE HAS BRED A MONSTER!!
WOOF WOOF
OR RATHER - NOT A MONSTER... A WUFFLY WUBBISH DOGGY, AREN'T YOU!...YES YOU ARE...
WUFF WUFF
AHEM... EXCUSE ME! YES... AH - THE PIG'S BRAINS HAVE ONLY A LIMITED LIFE SPAN! WE DON'T KNOW YET HOW LONG OUR DOG'S BRAIN WILL SURVIVE, BUT IT MUST ONLY BE HOURS AT MOST!
PANT PANT PANT PANT
1 YEAR LATER...
WELL, GARBAGE DOG IS STILL WITH US...
IT'S WORKED OUT OK, I SUPPOSE... HE'S EASILY CATERED FOR - WE JUST THROW LEFT-OVERS IN, AND HE GETS EMPTIED ONCE A WEEK ON BIN DAY...
RECENTLY WE'VE HAD TO SUBMIT TO FATE AND GO FOR THE CUT, HAVEN'T WE, WUFFLY! THE NOISE, DISRUPTION, AND AGGRAVATION TO THE NEIGHBORHOOD ON BIN DAY WAS GETTING TOO MUCH! WE HAD TO CALM HIM DOWN A BIT...
whimper
SORRY, GARBAGE DOG - YOU HAVE TO WEAR THAT THING... IT'S TO STOP YOU LICKING THE STITCHES WHILE THEY HEAL...
whimper

FALLS OF DOG BISCUITS

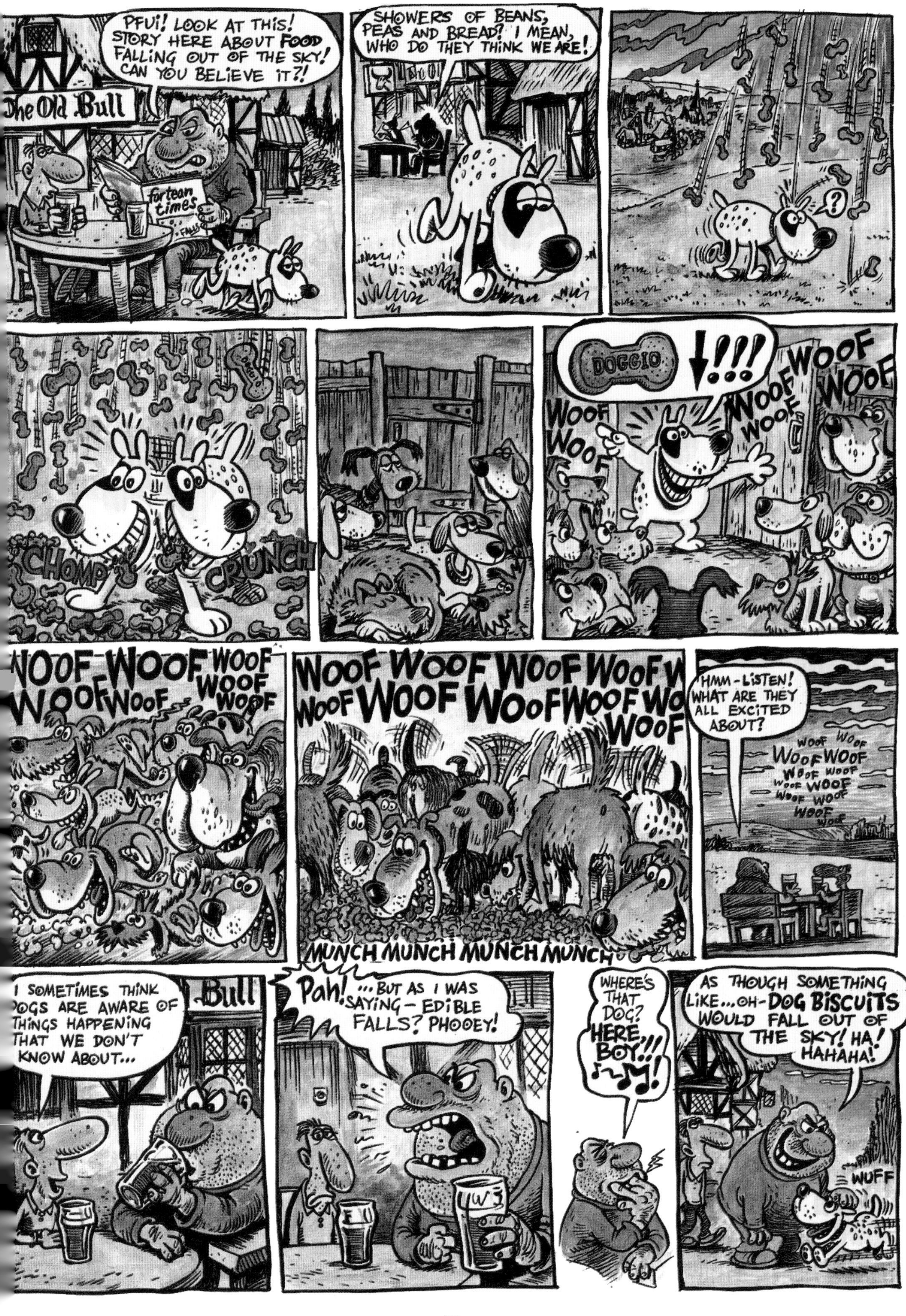

The Old Bull
PFUI! LOOK AT THIS! STORY HERE ABOUT FOOD FALLING OUT OF THE SKY! CAN YOU BELIEVE IT?!
fortean times
SHOWERS OF BEANS, PEAS AND BREAD? I MEAN, WHO DO THEY THINK WE ARE!
?
CHOMP
CRUNCH
DOGGIO
!!!!
WOOF WOOF WOOF WOOF WOOF WOOF WOOF
WOOF WOOF WOOF WOOF WOOF WOOF WOOF
WOOF WOOF WOOF WOOF WOOF WOOF WOOF WOOF WOOF WOOF WOOF WOOF
MUNCH MUNCH MUNCH MUNCH
HMM - LISTEN! WHAT ARE THEY ALL EXCITED ABOUT?
WOOF WOOF WOOF WOOF WOOF WOOF WOOF WOOF WOOF WOOF WOOF WOOF
I SOMETIMES THINK DOGS ARE AWARE OF THINGS HAPPENING THAT WE DON'T KNOW ABOUT...
Bull
PAH! ...BUT AS I WAS SAYING - EDIBLE FALLS? PHOOEY!
WHERE'S THAT DOG? HERE, BOY!!!
AS THOUGH SOMETHING LIKE...OH- DOG BISCUITS WOULD FALL OUT OF THE SKY! HA! HAHAHA!
WUFF

DRACULA

WRITTEN BY KEVIN JACKSON

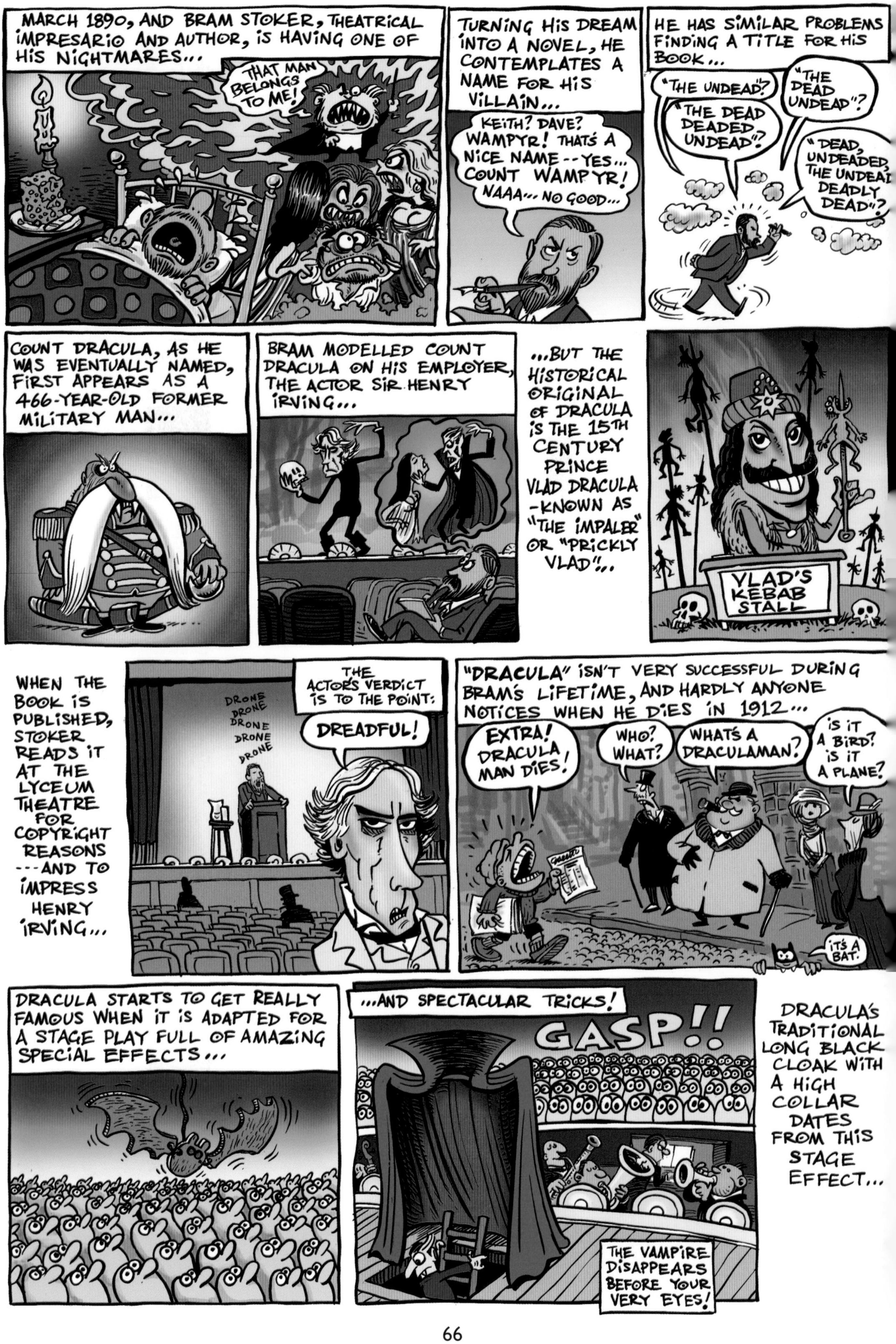

MARCH 1890, AND BRAM STOKER, THEATRICAL IMPRESARIO AND AUTHOR, IS HAVING ONE OF HIS NIGHTMARES...
THAT MAN BELONGS TO ME!
TURNING HIS DREAM INTO A NOVEL, HE CONTEMPLATES A NAME FOR HIS VILLAIN...
KEITH? DAVE? WAMPYR! THAT'S A NICE NAME -- YES... COUNT WAMPYR! NAAA... NO GOOD...
HE HAS SIMILAR PROBLEMS FINDING A TITLE FOR HIS BOOK...
"THE UNDEAD"?
"THE DEAD DEADED UNDEAD"?
"THE DEAD UNDEAD"?
"DEAD, UNDEADED, THE UNDEAD DEADLY DEAD"?
COUNT DRACULA, AS HE WAS EVENTUALLY NAMED, FIRST APPEARS AS A 466-YEAR-OLD FORMER MILITARY MAN...
BRAM MODELLED COUNT DRACULA ON HIS EMPLOYER, THE ACTOR SIR HENRY IRVING...
...BUT THE HISTORICAL ORIGINAL OF DRACULA IS THE 15TH CENTURY PRINCE VLAD DRACULA -KNOWN AS "THE IMPALER" OR "PRICKLY VLAD"...
VLAD'S KEBAB STALL
WHEN THE BOOK IS PUBLISHED, STOKER READS IT AT THE LYCEUM THEATRE FOR COPYRIGHT REASONS ---AND TO IMPRESS HENRY IRVING...
DRONE DRONE DRONE DRONE DRONE
THE ACTOR'S VERDICT IS TO THE POINT:
DREADFUL!
"DRACULA" ISN'T VERY SUCCESSFUL DURING BRAM'S LIFETIME, AND HARDLY ANYONE NOTICES WHEN HE DIES IN 1912...
EXTRA! DRACULA MAN DIES!
WHO? WHAT?
WHAT'S A DRACULAMAN?
IS IT A BIRD? IS IT A PLANE?
IT'S A BAT.
DRACULA STARTS TO GET REALLY FAMOUS WHEN IT IS ADAPTED FOR A STAGE PLAY FULL OF AMAZING SPECIAL EFFECTS...
...AND SPECTACULAR TRICKS!
GASP!!
THE VAMPIRE DISAPPEARS BEFORE YOUR VERY EYES!
DRACULA'S TRADITIONAL LONG BLACK CLOAK WITH A HIGH COLLAR DATES FROM THIS STAGE EFFECT...

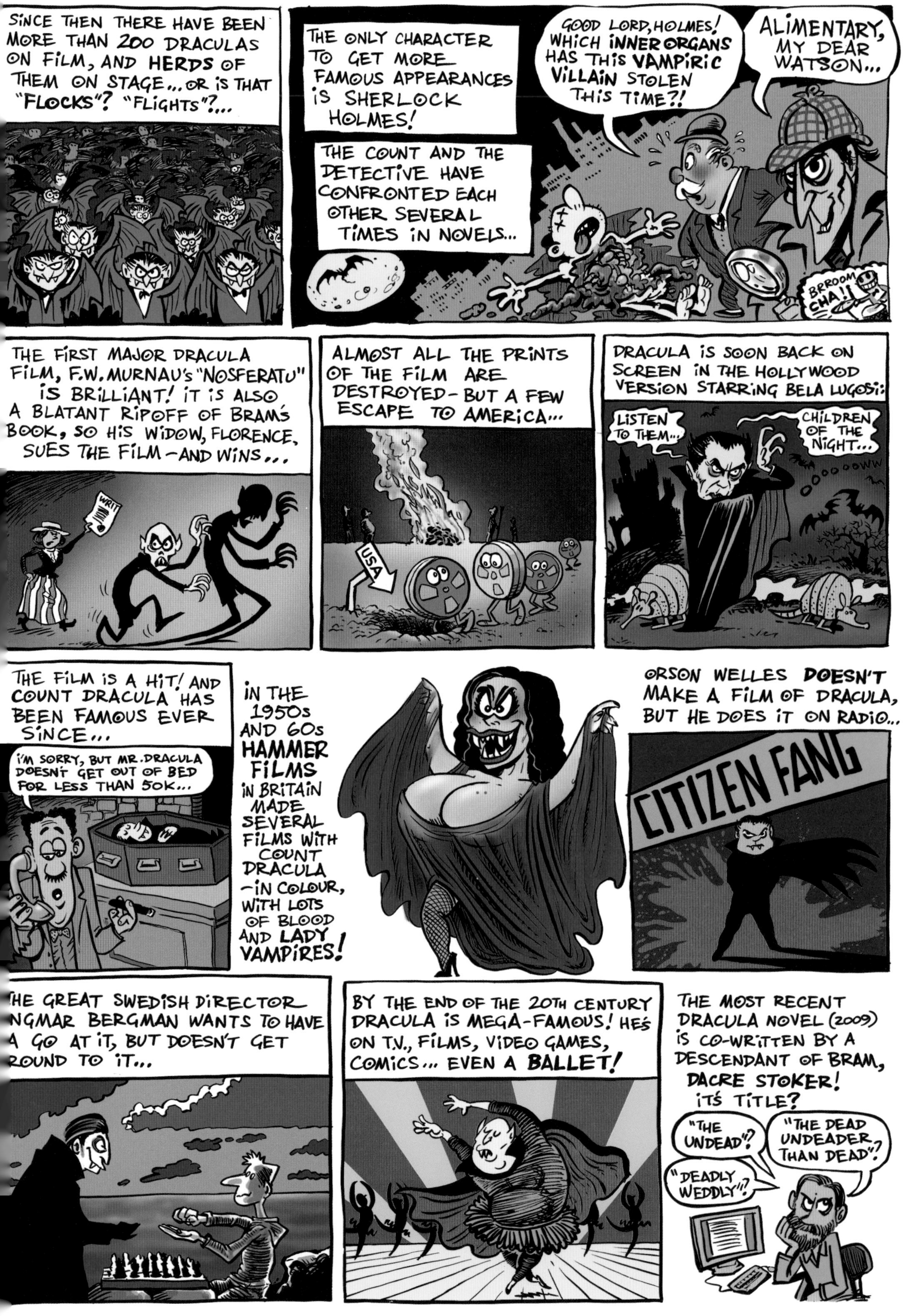
SINCE THEN THERE HAVE BEEN MORE THAN 200 DRACULAS ON FILM, AND HERDS OF THEM ON STAGE... OR IS THAT "FLOCKS"? "FLIGHTS"?...
THE ONLY CHARACTER TO GET MORE FAMOUS APPEARANCES IS SHERLOCK HOLMES!
THE COUNT AND THE DETECTIVE HAVE CONFRONTED EACH OTHER SEVERAL TIMES IN NOVELS...
GOOD LORD, HOLMES! WHICH INNER ORGANS HAS THIS VAMPIRIC VILLAIN STOLEN THIS TIME?!
ALIMENTARY, MY DEAR WATSON...
BRROOM CHA!!
THE FIRST MAJOR DRACULA FILM, F.W. MURNAU'S "NOSFERATU" IS BRILLIANT! IT IS ALSO A BLATANT RIPOFF OF BRAM'S BOOK, SO HIS WIDOW, FLORENCE, SUES THE FILM – AND WINS...
WRIT
ALMOST ALL THE PRINTS OF THE FILM ARE DESTROYED – BUT A FEW ESCAPE TO AMERICA...
USA
DRACULA IS SOON BACK ON SCREEN IN THE HOLLYWOOD VERSION STARRING BELA LUGOSI:
LISTEN TO THEM...
CHILDREN OF THE NIGHT...
OOOOOOWW
THE FILM IS A HIT! AND COUNT DRACULA HAS BEEN FAMOUS EVER SINCE...
I'M SORRY, BUT MR. DRACULA DOESN'T GET OUT OF BED FOR LESS THAN 50K...
IN THE 1950s AND 60s HAMMER FILMS IN BRITAIN MADE SEVERAL FILMS WITH COUNT DRACULA – IN COLOUR, WITH LOTS OF BLOOD AND LADY VAMPIRES!
ORSON WELLES DOESN'T MAKE A FILM OF DRACULA, BUT HE DOES IT ON RADIO...
CITIZEN FANG
HE GREAT SWEDISH DIRECTOR NGMAR BERGMAN WANTS TO HAVE A GO AT IT, BUT DOESN'T GET ROUND TO IT...
BY THE END OF THE 20TH CENTURY DRACULA IS MEGA-FAMOUS! HE'S ON T.V., FILMS, VIDEO GAMES, COMICS... EVEN A BALLET!
THE MOST RECENT DRACULA NOVEL (2009) IS CO-WRITTEN BY A DESCENDANT OF BRAM, DACRE STOKER! IT'S TITLE?
"THE UNDEAD"?
"THE DEAD UNDEADER THAN DEAD"?
"DEADLY WEDDLY"!?

ECLIPSE

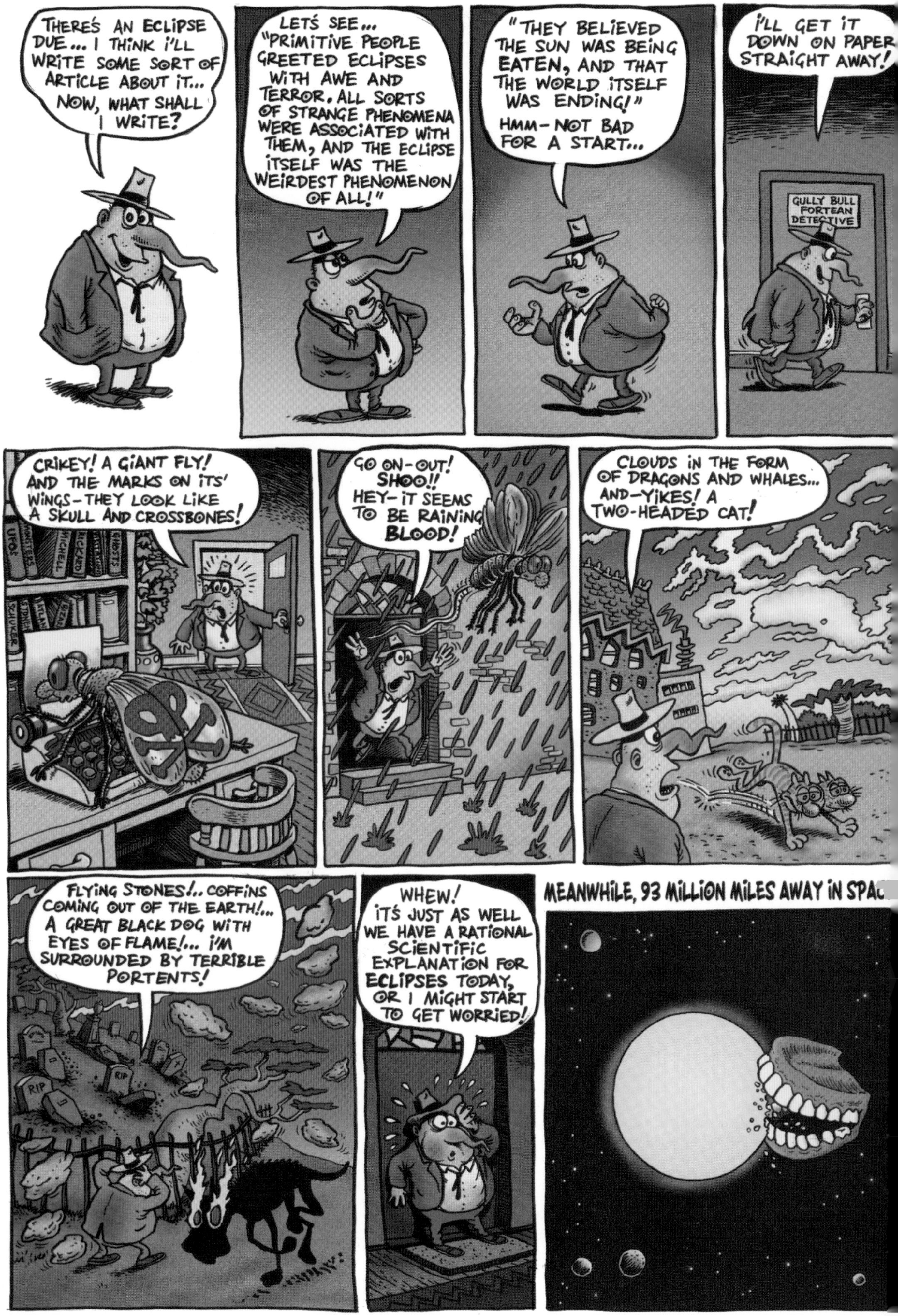

THERE'S AN ECLIPSE DUE... I THINK I'LL WRITE SOME SORT OF ARTICLE ABOUT IT... NOW, WHAT SHALL I WRITE?
LET'S SEE... "PRIMITIVE PEOPLE GREETED ECLIPSES WITH AWE AND TERROR. ALL SORTS OF STRANGE PHENOMENA WERE ASSOCIATED WITH THEM, AND THE ECLIPSE ITSELF WAS THE WEIRDEST PHENOMENON OF ALL!"
"THEY BELIEVED THE SUN WAS BEING EATEN, AND THAT THE WORLD ITSELF WAS ENDING!" HMM-NOT BAD FOR A START...
I'LL GET IT DOWN ON PAPER STRAIGHT AWAY!
GULLY BULL FORTEAN DETECTIVE
CRIKEY! A GIANT FLY! AND THE MARKS ON ITS' WINGS-THEY LOOK LIKE A SKULL AND CROSSBONES!
UFOs
MONSTERS
MICHELL
RICKARD
GHOSTS
SCHUKER
ATLANTIS
GO ON-OUT! SHOO!! HEY-IT SEEMS TO BE RAINING BLOOD!
CLOUDS IN THE FORM OF DRAGONS AND WHALES... AND-YIKES! A TWO-HEADED CAT!
FLYING STONES!.. COFFINS COMING OUT OF THE EARTH!... A GREAT BLACK DOG WITH EYES OF FLAME!... I'M SURROUNDED BY TERRIBLE PORTENTS!
RIP
RIP
WHEW! IT'S JUST AS WELL WE HAVE A RATIONAL SCIENTIFIC EXPLANATION FOR ECLIPSES TODAY, OR I MIGHT START TO GET WORRIED!
MEANWHILE, 93 MILLION MILES AWAY IN SPAC

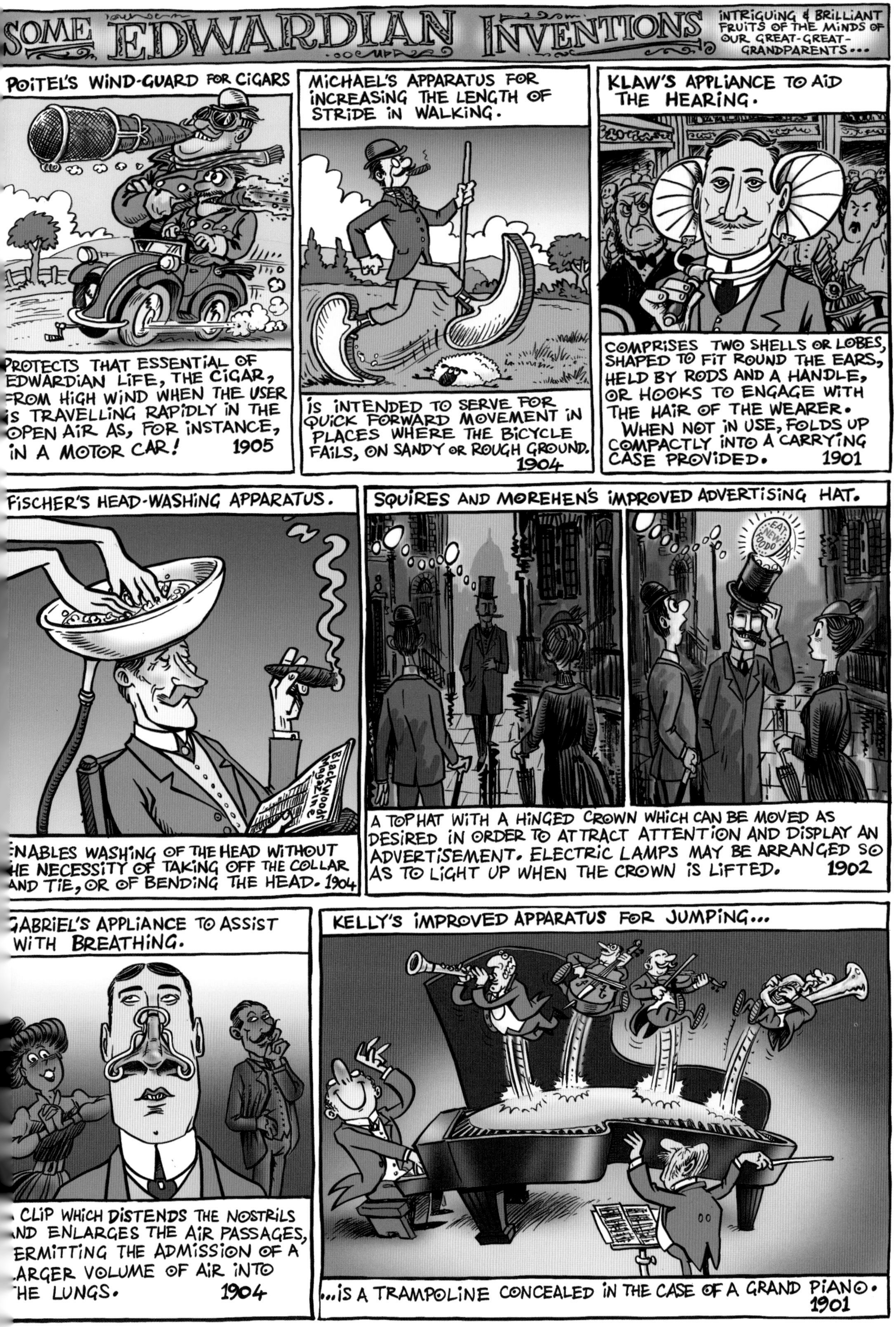

SOME EDWARDIAN INVENTIONS
INTRIGUING & BRILLIANT FRUITS OF THE MINDS OF OUR GREAT-GREAT-GRANDPARENTS...
POITEL'S WIND-GUARD FOR CIGARS
PROTECTS THAT ESSENTIAL OF EDWARDIAN LIFE, THE CIGAR, FROM HIGH WIND WHEN THE USER IS TRAVELLING RAPIDLY IN THE OPEN AIR AS, FOR INSTANCE, IN A MOTOR CAR! 1905
MICHAEL'S APPARATUS FOR INCREASING THE LENGTH OF STRIDE IN WALKING.
IS INTENDED TO SERVE FOR QUICK FORWARD MOVEMENT IN PLACES WHERE THE BICYCLE FAILS, ON SANDY OR ROUGH GROUND. 1904
KLAW'S APPLIANCE TO AID THE HEARING.
COMPRISES TWO SHELLS OR LOBES, SHAPED TO FIT ROUND THE EARS, HELD BY RODS AND A HANDLE, OR HOOKS TO ENGAGE WITH THE HAIR OF THE WEARER.
WHEN NOT IN USE, FOLDS UP COMPACTLY INTO A CARRYING CASE PROVIDED. 1901
FISCHER'S HEAD-WASHING APPARATUS.
Blackwood's Magazine
NABLES WASHING OF THE HEAD WITHOUT HE NECESSITY OF TAKING OFF THE COLLAR AND TIE, OR OF BENDING THE HEAD. 1904
SQUIRES AND MOREHEN'S IMPROVED ADVERTISING HAT.
A TOP HAT WITH A HINGED CROWN WHICH CAN BE MOVED AS DESIRED IN ORDER TO ATTRACT ATTENTION AND DISPLAY AN ADVERTISEMENT. ELECTRIC LAMPS MAY BE ARRANGED SO AS TO LIGHT UP WHEN THE CROWN IS LIFTED. 1902
ABRIEL'S APPLIANCE TO ASSIST WITH BREATHING.
CLIP WHICH DISTENDS THE NOSTRILS ND ENLARGES THE AIR PASSAGES, ERMITTING THE ADMISSION OF A ARGER VOLUME OF AIR INTO HE LUNGS. 1904
KELLY'S IMPROVED APPARATUS FOR JUMPING...
...IS A TRAMPOLINE CONCEALED IN THE CASE OF A GRAND PIANO. 1901

ELEMENTARY PARTICLES

AT ONE TIME THE ATOM WAS THOUGHT TO BE THE SMALLEST PARTICLE OF MATTER...

...UNTIL IT WAS REALISED THAT THE ATOM COULD BE BROKEN DOWN INTO SMALLER PARTICLES, EACH HAVING IT'S OWN SPECIFIC QUALITIES.

THE ELECTRON - CHARGED WITH NEGATIVE ENERGY.

DOWN WITH EVERYTHING!

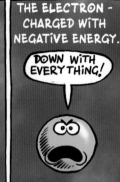

THE POSITRON - IRRITATINGLY OPTIMISTIC.

OH BOY! I FEEL POSITIVE!

THE NEUTRON - CARRYING A NEUTRAL CHARGE.

I DON'T CARE ONE WAY OR THE OTHER, REALLY...

THE HADRON - CHARGED WITH SOME OTHER FORM OF ENERGY OR SPIN...

THE BORON - OTHER PARTICLES FIND THIS ONE VERY TEDIOUS.

THE GLUON - A PARTICLE THAT HOLDS OTHERS TOGETHER.

THE NE-ON - A FLASHY PARTICLE.

THE BUTT-ON - A PARTICLE WITH FOUR HOLES.

THE STICK-ON - A PARTICLE WITH VELCRO-LIKE QUALITIES.

OI! GERROFF

THE RIGHT-ON - A RIGHTEOUS SOUL BRO' OF A PARTICLE.

YO!

THE FUT-ON - A PARTICLE THAT FOLDS DOWN INTO A TEMPORARY BED.

THE MUTT-ON - DELICIOUS WITH MINT SAUCE.

BAA-A-A!

THE PYL-ON - CONNECTS TO OTHER PARTICLES WITH ELECTRIC CABLES.

THE TIPT-ON - A PARTICLE THAT LURKS TO THE NORTH WEST OF BIRMINGHAM

'OWAMYER, YOW?

THE ENRON - A GREEDY, CROOKED PARTICLE THAT WIPES OUT PENSIONS.

THE PENSI-ON - A PARTICLE THAT IS DESTROYED ON CONTACT WITH THE ENRON.

THREE PARTICLES THAT CONSISTENTLY FIND THEMSELVES AT THE BOTTOM OF THE PARTICLE PILE ARE THE SAT-ON, THE SPAT-ON, AND THE SHAT-ON.

OTHER ELEMENTARY PARTICLES INCLUDE -

THE CARRY-ON...

OOOH MATRON!

THE LI-ON...

THE GALLE-ON...

THE PYTH-ON...

AND NOW FOR SOMETHING COMPLETELY DIFFERENT!

AND THE CUDDLY KITT-ON.

THERE ARE MANY OTHER PARTICLES - SO MANY, IN FACT THAT SCIENTISTS CAN'T BE BOTHERED TO CLASSIFY THEM SEPARATELY, AND SIMPLY REFER TO THEM AS "THE SO-ONS".

HE EMPTY SHIP

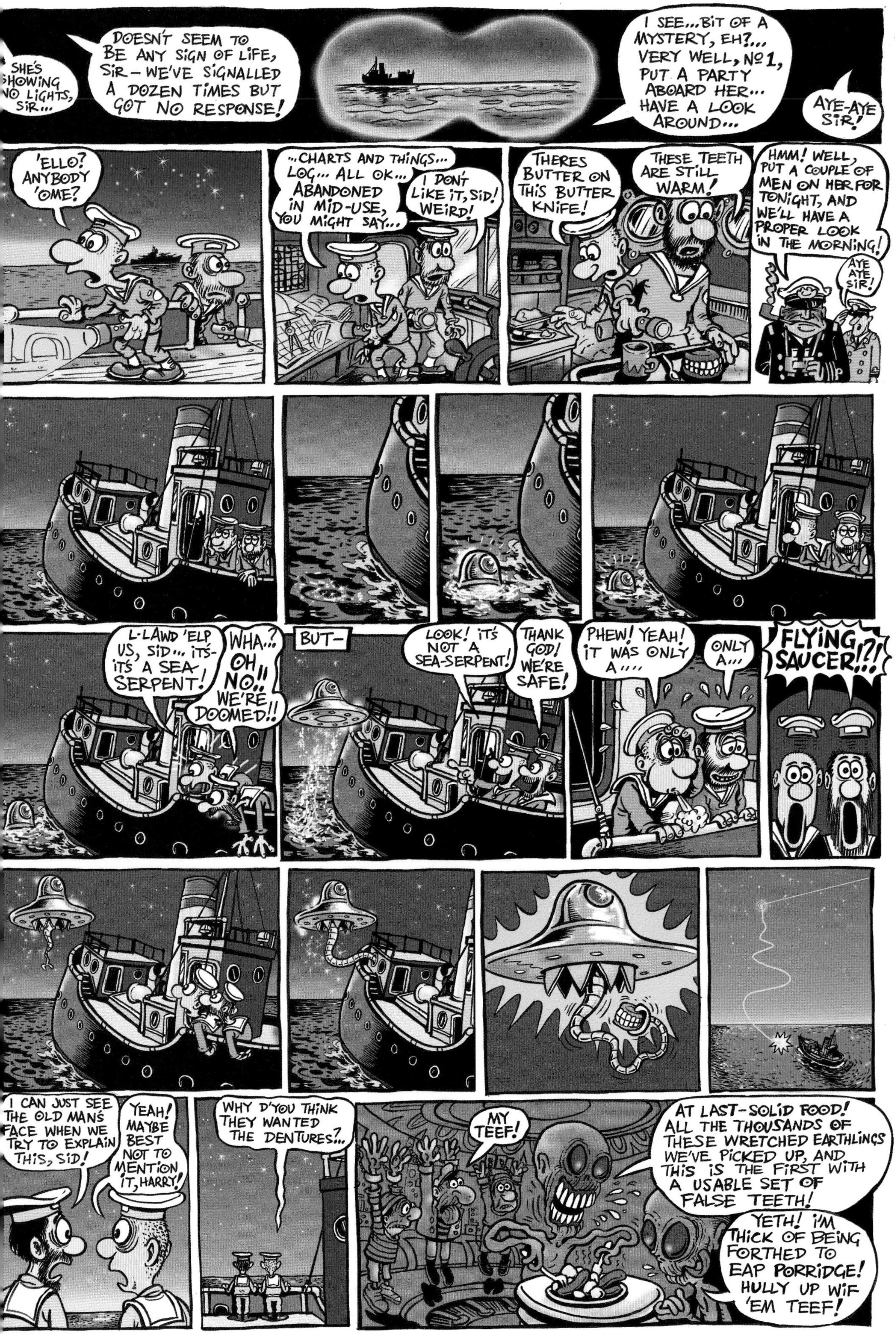

SHE'S SHOWING NO LIGHTS, SIR...
DOESN'T SEEM TO BE ANY SIGN OF LIFE, SIR – WE'VE SIGNALLED A DOZEN TIMES BUT GOT NO RESPONSE!
I SEE... BIT OF A MYSTERY, EH?... VERY WELL, Nº 1, PUT A PARTY ABOARD HER... HAVE A LOOK AROUND...
AYE-AYE SIR!
'ELLO? ANYBODY 'OME?
...CHARTS AND THINGS... LOG... ALL OK... ABANDONED IN MID-USE, YOU MIGHT SAY...
I DON'T LIKE IT, SID! WEIRD!
THERES BUTTER ON THIS BUTTER KNIFE!
THESE TEETH ARE STILL WARM!
HMM! WELL, PUT A COUPLE OF MEN ON HER FOR TONIGHT, AND WE'LL HAVE A PROPER LOOK IN THE MORNING!
AYE AYE SIR!
L-LAWD 'ELP US, SID... IT'S- IT'S A SEA-SERPENT!
WHA..? OH NO!! WE'RE DOOMED!!
BUT-
LOOK! IT'S NOT A SEA-SERPENT!
THANK GOD! WE'RE SAFE!
PHEW! YEAH! IT WAS ONLY A....
ONLY A...
FLYING SAUCER!?!
I CAN JUST SEE THE OLD MAN'S FACE WHEN WE TRY TO EXPLAIN THIS, SID!
YEAH! MAYBE BEST NOT TO MENTION IT, HARRY!
WHY D'YOU THINK THEY WANTED THE DENTURES?..
MY TEEF!
AT LAST–SOLID FOOD! ALL THE THOUSANDS OF THESE WRETCHED EARTHLINGS WE'VE PICKED UP, AND THIS IS THE FIRST WITH A USABLE SET OF FALSE TEETH!
YETH! I'M THICK OF BEING FORTHED TO EAP PORRIDGE! HULLY UP WIF 'EM TEEF!

MOTH EARS

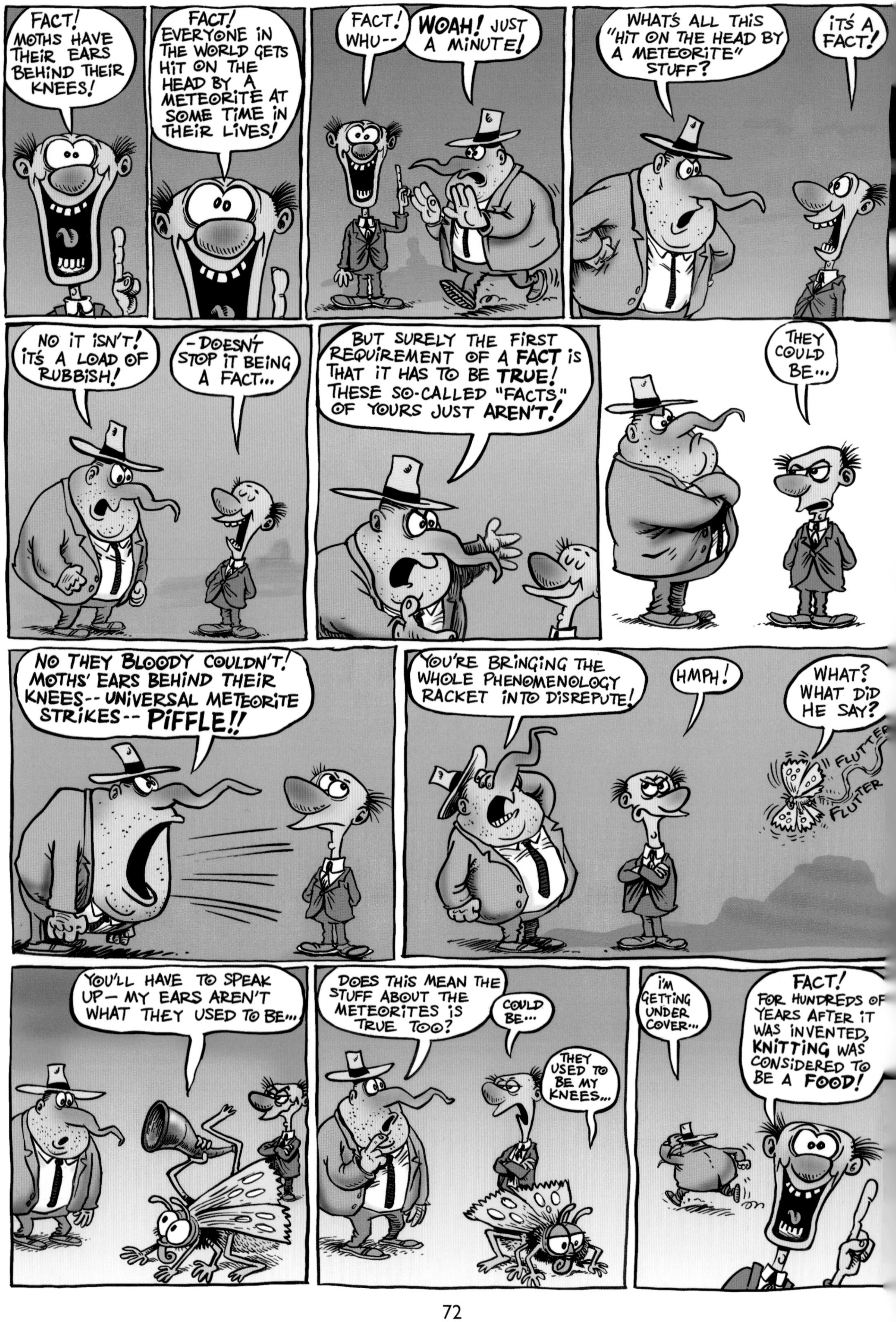

FACT! MOTHS HAVE THEIR EARS BEHIND THEIR KNEES!
FACT! EVERYONE IN THE WORLD GETS HIT ON THE HEAD BY A METEORITE AT SOME TIME IN THEIR LIVES!
FACT! WHU--
WOAH! JUST A MINUTE!
WHAT'S ALL THIS "HIT ON THE HEAD BY A METEORITE" STUFF?
IT'S A FACT!
NO IT ISN'T! IT'S A LOAD OF RUBBISH!
- DOESN'T STOP IT BEING A FACT...
BUT SURELY THE FIRST REQUIREMENT OF A FACT IS THAT IT HAS TO BE TRUE! THESE SO-CALLED "FACTS" OF YOURS JUST AREN'T!
THEY COULD BE...
NO THEY BLOODY COULDN'T! MOTHS' EARS BEHIND THEIR KNEES-- UNIVERSAL METEORITE STRIKES-- PIFFLE!!
YOU'RE BRINGING THE WHOLE PHENOMENOLOGY RACKET INTO DISREPUTE!
HMPH!
WHAT? WHAT DID HE SAY?
FLUTTER
FLUTTER
YOU'LL HAVE TO SPEAK UP— MY EARS AREN'T WHAT THEY USED TO BE...
DOES THIS MEAN THE STUFF ABOUT THE METEORITES IS TRUE TOO?
COULD BE...
THEY USED TO BE MY KNEES...
I'M GETTING UNDER COVER...
FACT! FOR HUNDREDS OF YEARS AFTER IT WAS INVENTED, KNITTING WAS CONSIDERED TO BE A FOOD!

HARK SNORES

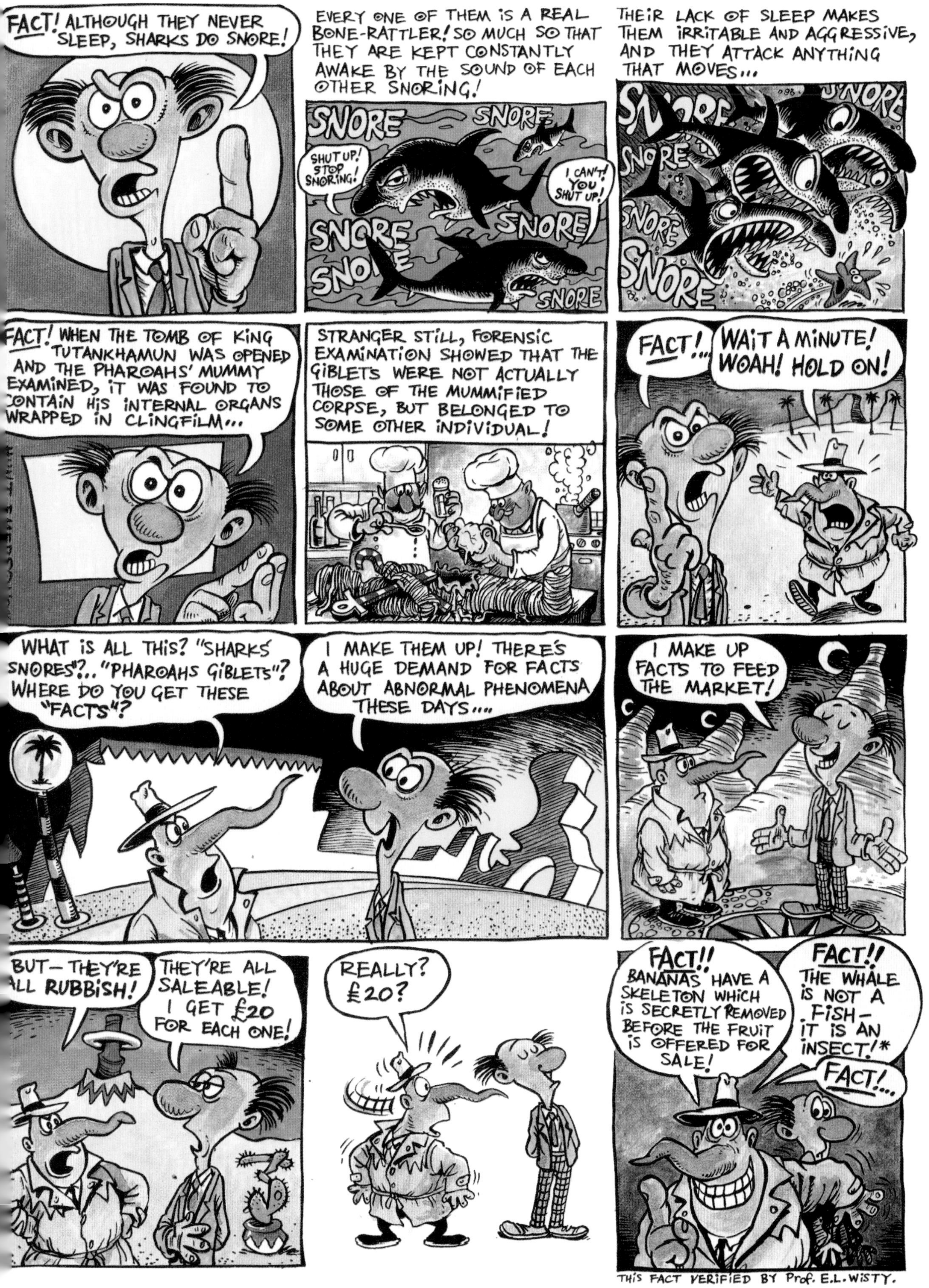
FACT! ALTHOUGH THEY NEVER SLEEP, SHARKS DO SNORE!
EVERY ONE OF THEM IS A REAL BONE-RATTLER! SO MUCH SO THAT THEY ARE KEPT CONSTANTLY AWAKE BY THE SOUND OF EACH OTHER SNORING!
SNORE
SNORE
SHUT UP! STOP SNORING!
I CAN'T! YOU SHUT UP!
SNORE
SNORE
SNORE
SNORE
THEIR LACK OF SLEEP MAKES THEM IRRITABLE AND AGGRESSIVE, AND THEY ATTACK ANYTHING THAT MOVES...
SNORE
SNORE
SNORE
SNORE
SNORE
FACT! WHEN THE TOMB OF KING TUTANKHAMUN WAS OPENED AND THE PHAROAHS' MUMMY EXAMINED, IT WAS FOUND TO CONTAIN HIS INTERNAL ORGANS WRAPPED IN CLINGFILM...
STRANGER STILL, FORENSIC EXAMINATION SHOWED THAT THE GIBLETS WERE NOT ACTUALLY THOSE OF THE MUMMIFIED CORPSE, BUT BELONGED TO SOME OTHER INDIVIDUAL!
FACT!...
WAIT A MINUTE! WOAH! HOLD ON!
WHAT IS ALL THIS? "SHARKS SNORES"?.. "PHAROAHS GIBLETS"? WHERE DO YOU GET THESE "FACTS"?
I MAKE THEM UP! THERE'S A HUGE DEMAND FOR FACTS ABOUT ABNORMAL PHENOMENA THESE DAYS...
I MAKE UP FACTS TO FEED THE MARKET!
BUT— THEY'RE ALL RUBBISH!
THEY'RE ALL SALEABLE! I GET £20 FOR EACH ONE!
REALLY? £20?
FACT!! BANANAS HAVE A SKELETON WHICH IS SECRETLY REMOVED BEFORE THE FRUIT IS OFFERED FOR SALE!
FACT!! THE WHALE IS NOT A FISH— IT IS AN INSECT!*
FACT!...
THIS FACT VERIFIED BY Prof. E.L. WISTY.

MERMAID

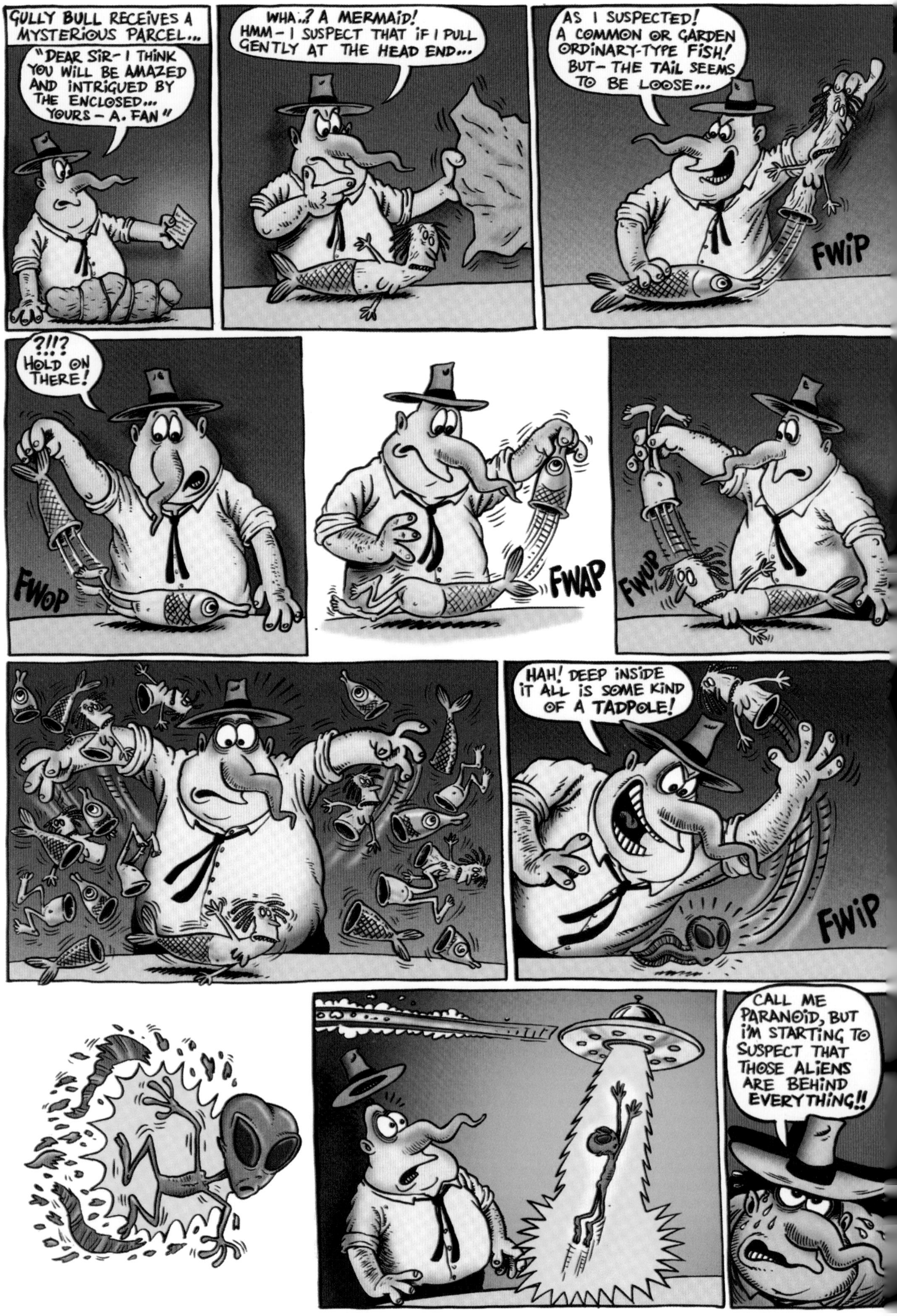

GULLY BULL RECEIVES A MYSTERIOUS PARCEL...
"DEAR SIR- I THINK YOU WILL BE AMAZED AND INTRIGUED BY THE ENCLOSED... YOURS - A. FAN"
WHA..? A MERMAID! HMM - I SUSPECT THAT IF I PULL GENTLY AT THE HEAD END...
AS I SUSPECTED! A COMMON OR GARDEN ORDINARY-TYPE FISH! BUT- THE TAIL SEEMS TO BE LOOSE...
FWIP
?!!? HOLD ON THERE!
FWOP
FWAP
FWUP
HAH! DEEP INSIDE IT ALL IS SOME KIND OF A TADPOLE!
FWIP
CALL ME PARANOID, BUT I'M STARTING TO SUSPECT THAT THOSE ALIENS ARE BEHIND EVERYTHING!!

AISED BY WOLVES

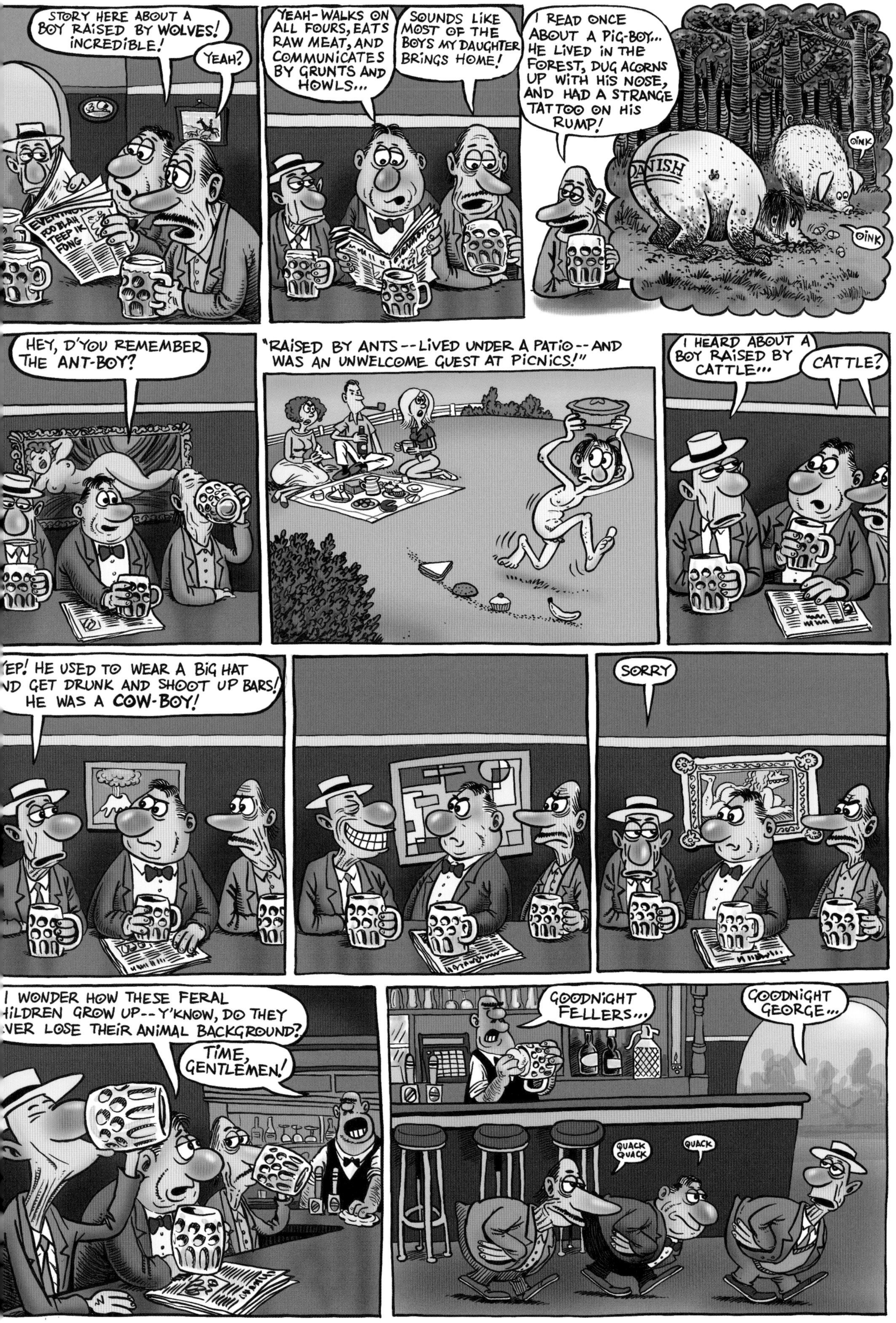

STORY HERE ABOUT A BOY RAISED BY WOLVES! INCREDIBLE!
YEAH?
YEAH- WALKS ON ALL FOURS, EATS RAW MEAT, AND COMMUNICATES BY GRUNTS AND HOWLS...
SOUNDS LIKE MOST OF THE BOYS MY DAUGHTER BRINGS HOME!
I READ ONCE ABOUT A PIG-BOY... HE LIVED IN THE FOREST, DUG ACORNS UP WITH HIS NOSE, AND HAD A STRANGE TATTOO ON HIS RUMP!
DANISH
OINK
OINK
HEY, D'YOU REMEMBER THE ANT-BOY?
"RAISED BY ANTS -- LIVED UNDER A PATIO -- AND WAS AN UNWELCOME GUEST AT PICNICS!"
I HEARD ABOUT A BOY RAISED BY CATTLE...
CATTLE?
EP! HE USED TO WEAR A BIG HAT
ND GET DRUNK AND SHOOT UP BARS!
HE WAS A COW-BOY!
SORRY
I WONDER HOW THESE FERAL
HILDREN GROW UP-- Y'KNOW, DO THEY
VER LOSE THEIR ANIMAL BACKGROUND?
TIME, GENTLEMEN!
GOODNIGHT FELLERS...
GOODNIGHT GEORGE...
QUACK QUACK
QUACK

FALL OF SNAILS

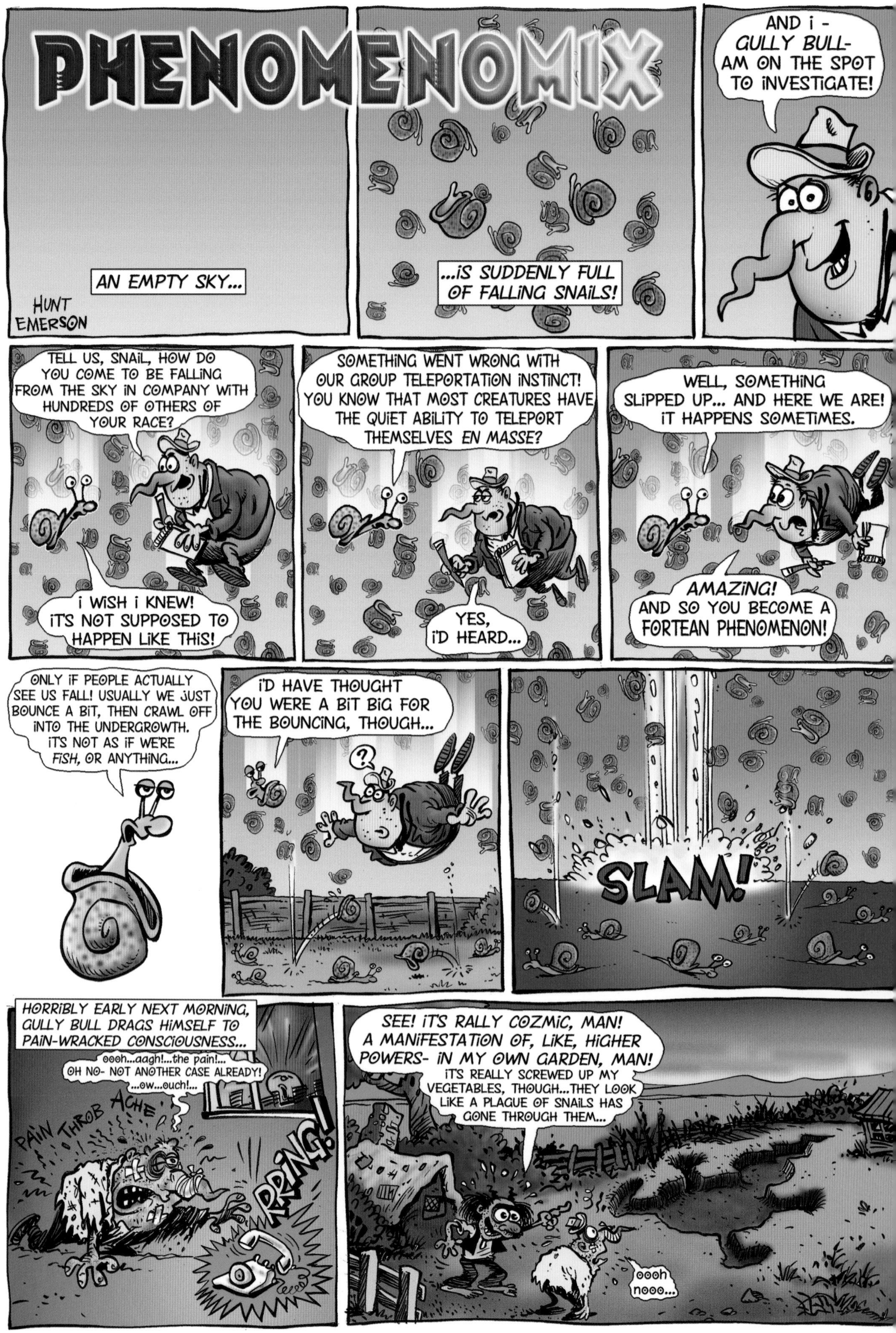
PHENOMENOMIX
AN EMPTY SKY...
HUNT EMERSON
...iS SUDDENLY FULL OF FALLiNG SNAiLS!
AND i - GULLY BULL- AM ON THE SPOT TO iNVESTiGATE!
TELL US, SNAiL, HOW DO YOU COME TO BE FALLiNG FROM THE SKY iN COMPANY WiTH HUNDREDS OF OTHERS OF YOUR RACE?
i WiSH i KNEW! iT'S NOT SUPPOSED TO HAPPEN LiKE THiS!
SOMETHiNG WENT WRONG WiTH OUR GROUP TELEPORTATiON iNSTiNCT! YOU KNOW THAT MOST CREATURES HAVE THE QUiET ABiLiTY TO TELEPORT THEMSELVES EN MASSE?
YES, i'D HEARD...
WELL, SOMETHiNG SLiPPED UP... AND HERE WE ARE! iT HAPPENS SOMETiMES.
AMAZiNG! AND SO YOU BECOME A FORTEAN PHENOMENON!
ONLY iF PEOPLE ACTUALLY SEE US FALL! USUALLY WE JUST BOUNCE A BiT, THEN CRAWL OFF iNTO THE UNDERGROWTH. iT'S NOT AS iF WE'RE FiSH, OR ANYTHiNG...
i'D HAVE THOUGHT YOU WERE A BiT BiG FOR THE BOUNCiNG, THOUGH...
?
SLAM!
HORRiBLY EARLY NEXT MORNiNG, GULLY BULL DRAGS HiMSELF TO PAiN-WRACKED CONSCiOUSNESS...
oooh...aagh!...the pain!...
OH NO- NOT ANOTHER CASE ALREADY!
...ow...ouch!...
PAiN THROB ACHE
RRiNG!
SEE! iT'S RALLY COZMiC, MAN! A MANiFESTATiON OF, LiKE, HiGHER POWERS- iN MY OWN GARDEN, MAN!
iT'S REALLY SCREWED UP MY VEGETABLES, THOUGH...THEY LOOK LiKE A PLAGUE OF SNAiLS HAS GONE THROUGH THEM...
oooh nooo...

ALL OF WHELKS

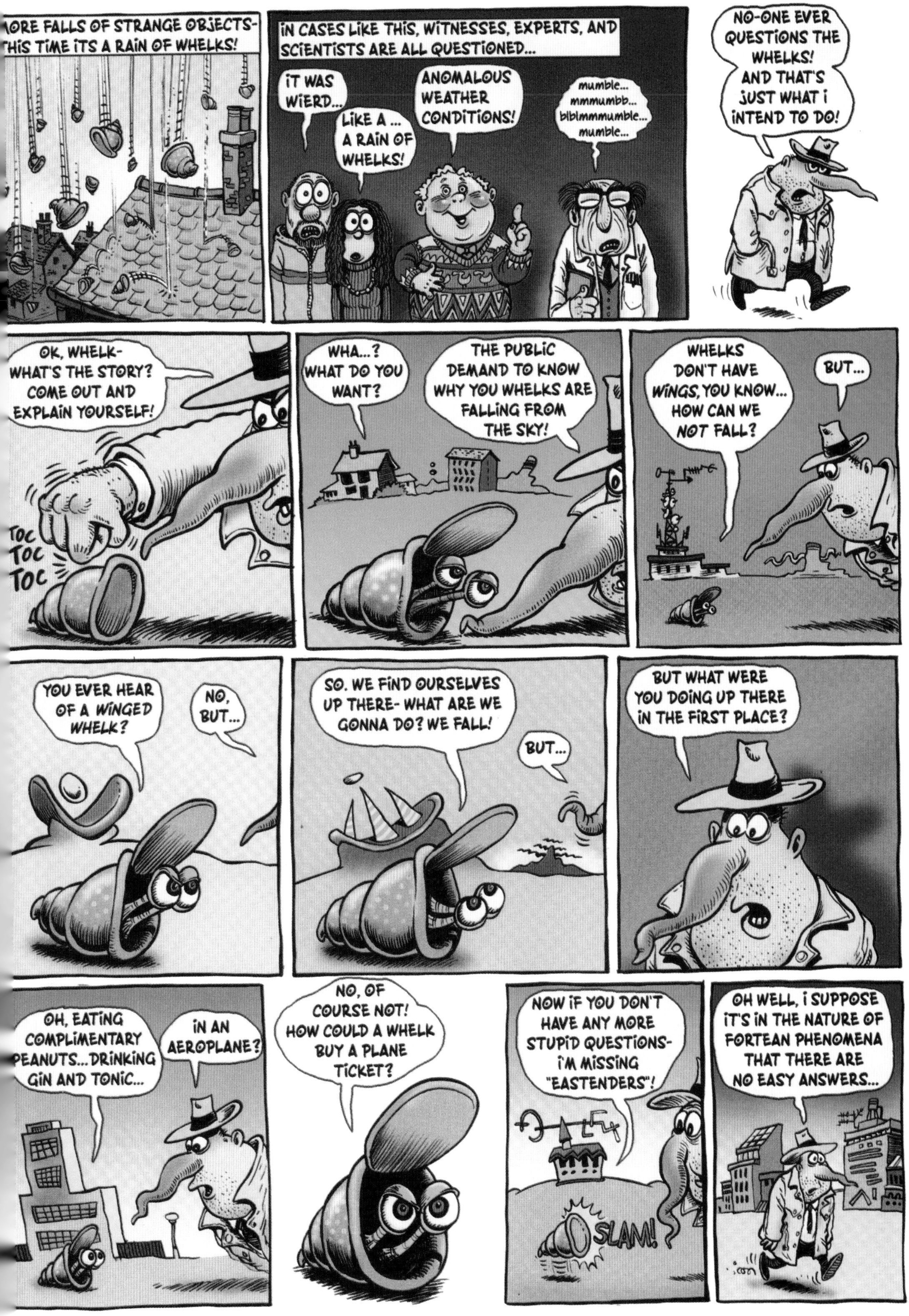

ORE FALLS OF STRANGE OBJECTS- THIS TIME ITS A RAIN OF WHELKS!
IN CASES LIKE THIS, WITNESSES, EXPERTS, AND SCIENTISTS ARE ALL QUESTIONED...
IT WAS WIERD...
LIKE A ... A RAIN OF WHELKS!
ANOMALOUS WEATHER CONDITIONS!
mumble... mmmumbb... blblmmmumble... mumble...
NO-ONE EVER QUESTIONS THE WHELKS! AND THAT'S JUST WHAT I INTEND TO DO!
OK, WHELK- WHAT'S THE STORY? COME OUT AND EXPLAIN YOURSELF!
TOC TOC TOC
WHA...? WHAT DO YOU WANT?
THE PUBLIC DEMAND TO KNOW WHY YOU WHELKS ARE FALLING FROM THE SKY!
WHELKS DON'T HAVE WINGS, YOU KNOW... HOW CAN WE NOT FALL?
BUT...
YOU EVER HEAR OF A WINGED WHELK?
NO, BUT...
SO. WE FIND OURSELVES UP THERE- WHAT ARE WE GONNA DO? WE FALL!
BUT...
BUT WHAT WERE YOU DOING UP THERE IN THE FIRST PLACE?
OH, EATING COMPLIMENTARY PEANUTS...DRINKING GIN AND TONIC...
IN AN AEROPLANE?
NO, OF COURSE NOT! HOW COULD A WHELK BUY A PLANE TICKET?
NOW IF YOU DON'T HAVE ANY MORE STUPID QUESTIONS- I'M MISSING "EASTENDERS"!
SLAM!
OH WELL, I SUPPOSE IT'S IN THE NATURE OF FORTEAN PHENOMENA THAT THERE ARE NO EASY ANSWERS...

THE FLOODED CHURCH

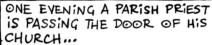

ONE EVENING A PARISH PRIEST IS PASSING THE DOOR OF HIS CHURCH...

SOB SOB BAAWL SOB

BOOHOO WAAAH! SOB SOB

BAWL! WAIL

MY STATUE OF OUR LADY—SHE'S WEEPING! IS THIS A MIRACLE?

HEY! WHAT ARE YOU DOING? THAT'S OUR RELIQUARY!

AND YOU'RE USING THE LEG BONE OF SAINT SQUELTIOUS AS AN OAR!

SPLOSH SPLISH

THAT'S OK— I'M A SAINT TOO— SAINT PRESERVUS... SAINT SQUELTIOUS SAID I COULD...

BUT...BUT.... THE CHURCH IS FLOODED...

DON'T WORRY—BY THE MORNING THE HOLY TEARS WILL HAVE TRANSUBSTANTIATED INTO FLOOR POLISH!

FLOOR POLISH?!

YES--IT HAPPENS EVERY WEEK, YOU KNOW... YOUR CLEANING LADY LIGHTS A CANDLE TO US, AND WE DO THE REST!

IT SAVES HER HAVING TO POLISH ALL THIS FLOOR ON HER KNEES...

I SEE...

SHE'S A MARTYR TO HER KNEES, POOR DEAR...

YES, SO SHE TELLS ME... ENDLESSLY...

MRS. O'TOOLE... CAN I HAVE A WORD PLEASE?...

FLYING SNAKE

With help from FLYING SNAKE, a Journal of Cryptozoology and Forteana, compiled by Richard Muirhead.

FASCINATING! I'M READING THE LATEST EDITION OF FLYING SNAKE MAGAZINE - VOL. 4 #12, SEPT. 2017!

THE LEAD STORY IS ABOUT REPORTS OF PLESIOSAURS IN PATAGONIA...

Flying Snake
A Journal of Cryptozoology, Folklore and Forteana
Volume 4 Number 12 September 2017

EL PLESIOSAURIO TANGO
POR ARTURO TERRI

Flying Dog · Chinese skeletons in Roman tombs · Elephant Remains at Sea · Ghost Bicycle · King Henry VIII's Sea Monster · Human Skeletons in Trees · Giant Snail · South American Plesiosaur · Fox Skeleton in a Tree · Thylacine News · And More!

...AND THERE'S INTERESTING STUFF ABOUT SKELETONS IN TREES, GIANT SNAILS AND FROGS IN BIRDS' NESTS...

...BUT WHAT HAS JUST CAUGHT MY EYE IS THIS STORY FROM THE ALBUQUERQUE JOURNAL OF JULY 22nd 1922! IN ROSWELL - YES, ROSWELL! - A PLYMOUTH ROCK HEN HAS LAID A NINE-INCH EGG WHICH HAS SECOND EGG INSIDE IT!!

SECOND EGG!

...AND ANOTHER CLIPPING FROM THE COUNTRYMAN OF SPRING 1957...

IN CHIPPING CAMPDEN - YES, CHIPPING CAMPDEN! - AN APPLE WAS BITTEN INTO AND REVEALED A SECOND APPLE INSIDE IT!!

SECOND APPLE!

FRANKLY, I'M NOT SURPRISED!! I'M REMINDED OF A CASE I INVESTIGATED A FALL OF FISH FROM THE SKY ONTO A BACK YARD IN CHIPPING SODBURY - YES, CHIPPING SODBURY!...

SPLAT SPLAP

I SLICED ONE OF THE FISH OPEN - THERE WAS A SECOND FISH INSIDE IT!

BUGGER OFF

I SLICED MORE FISH - ALL OF THEM HAD A SECOND FISH INSIDE!

IT TOOK ME THREE WEEKS TO CHECK ALL THE FISH - IT WAS THE HEIGHT OF SUMMER - THE SMELL WAS APPALLING! BUT THIS WAS VALUABLE FORTEAN DATA!

PONG!

TO SHOW THEIR APPRECIATION OF MY FORTEAN DILIGENCE, THE GOOD FOLK OF CHIPPING SODBURY MADE A WHICKERWORK FRAME MODELLING EXACTLY MY OWN BODY SHAPE, AND PUT ME INSIDE IT!

PONG!

...AND NOW THEY ARE HOLDING A FESTIVAL IN MY HONOUR! THEY'RE LIGHTING A BONFIRE!

OUR WORLD IS A MIRACULOUS NETWORK OF COINCIDENCE...

A FORTEAN LIBRARY

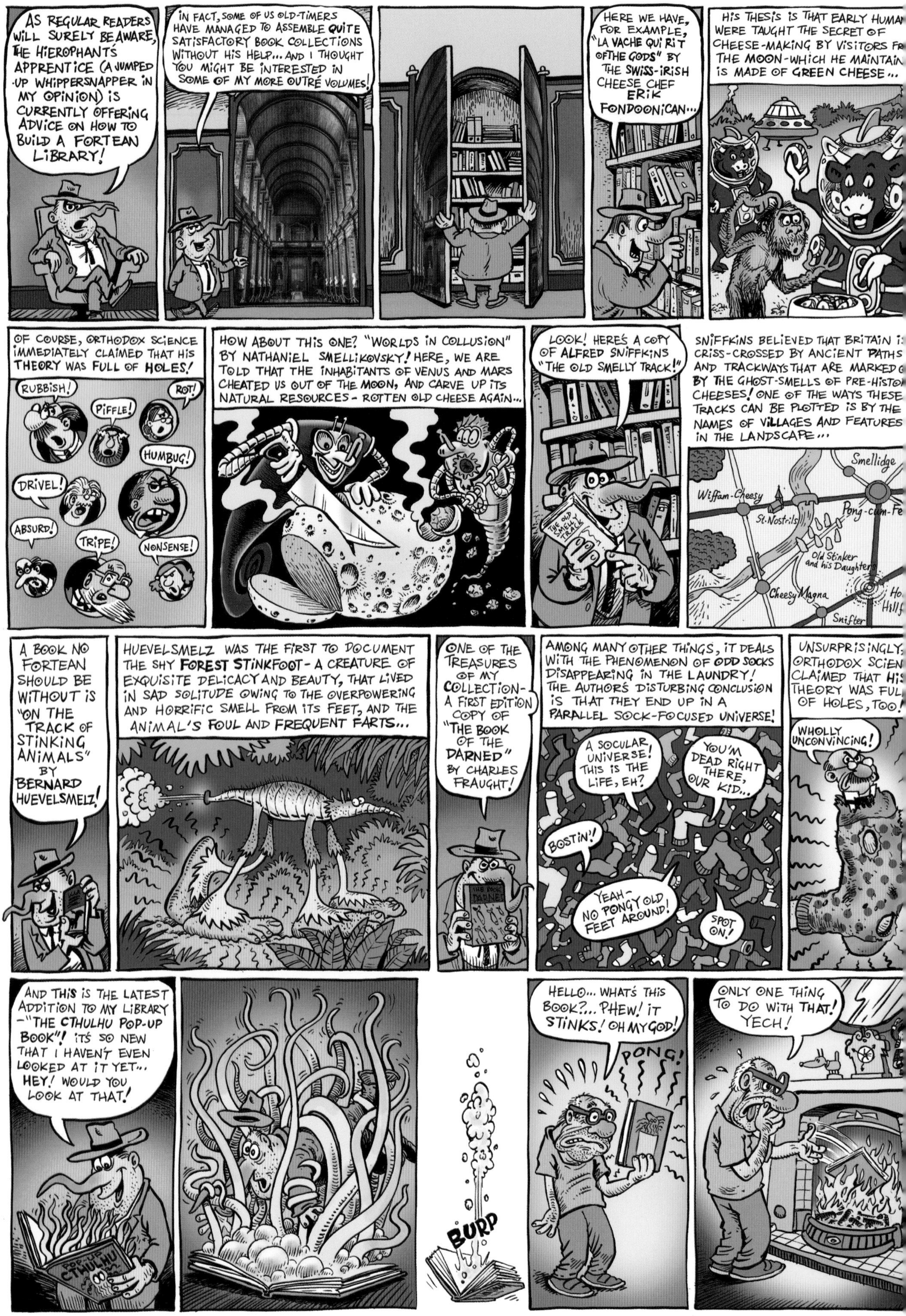

AS REGULAR READERS WILL SURELY BE AWARE, THE HIEROPHANT'S APPRENTICE (A JUMPED-UP WHIPPERSNAPPER IN MY OPINION) IS CURRENTLY OFFERING ADVICE ON HOW TO BUILD A FORTEAN LIBRARY!
IN FACT, SOME OF US OLD-TIMERS HAVE MANAGED TO ASSEMBLE QUITE SATISFACTORY BOOK COLLECTIONS WITHOUT HIS HELP... AND I THOUGHT YOU MIGHT BE INTERESTED IN SOME OF MY MORE OUTRÉ VOLUMES!
HERE WE HAVE, FOR EXAMPLE, "LA VACHE QUI RIT OF THE GODS" BY THE SWISS-IRISH CHEESE CHEF ERIK FONDOONICAN...
HIS THESIS IS THAT EARLY HUMA WERE TAUGHT THE SECRET OF CHEESE-MAKING BY VISITORS FR THE MOON - WHICH HE MAINTAIN IS MADE OF GREEN CHEESE...
OF COURSE, ORTHODOX SCIENCE IMMEDIATELY CLAIMED THAT HIS THEORY WAS FULL OF HOLES!
RUBBISH!
PIFFLE!
ROT!
HUMBUG!
DRIVEL!
ABSURD!
TRIPE!
NONSENSE!
HOW ABOUT THIS ONE? "WORLDS IN COLLUSION" BY NATHANIEL SMELLIKOVSKY! HERE, WE ARE TOLD THAT THE INHABITANTS OF VENUS AND MARS CHEATED US OUT OF THE MOON, AND CARVE UP ITS NATURAL RESOURCES - ROTTEN OLD CHEESE AGAIN...
LOOK! HERE'S A COPY OF ALFRED SNIFFKINS "THE OLD SMELLY TRACK!"
THE OLD SMELLY TRACK
SNIFFKINS BELIEVED THAT BRITAIN I CRISS-CROSSED BY ANCIENT PATHS AND TRACKWAYS THAT ARE MARKED BY THE GHOST-SMELLS OF PRE-HISTO CHEESES! ONE OF THE WAYS THESE TRACKS CAN BE PLOTTED IS BY THE NAMES OF VILLAGES AND FEATURES IN THE LANDSCAPE...
Smellidge
Wiffam-Cheesy
St. Nostrils
Pong-cum-Fe
Old Stinker and his Daughters
Cheesy Magna
Snifter
A BOOK NO FORTEAN SHOULD BE WITHOUT IS "ON THE TRACK OF STINKING ANIMALS" BY BERNARD HUEVELSMELZ!
HUEVELSMELZ WAS THE FIRST TO DOCUMENT THE SHY FOREST STINKFOOT - A CREATURE OF EXQUISITE DELICACY AND BEAUTY, THAT LIVED IN SAD SOLITUDE OWING TO THE OVERPOWERING AND HORRIFIC SMELL FROM ITS FEET, AND THE ANIMAL'S FOUL AND FREQUENT FARTS...
ONE OF THE TREASURES OF MY COLLECTION - A FIRST EDITION COPY OF "THE BOOK OF THE DARNED" BY CHARLES FRAUGHT!
AMONG MANY OTHER THINGS, IT DEALS WITH THE PHENOMENON OF ODD SOCKS DISAPPEARING IN THE LAUNDRY! THE AUTHOR'S DISTURBING CONCLUSION IS THAT THEY END UP IN A PARALLEL SOCK-FOCUSED UNIVERSE!
A SOCULAR UNIVERSE! THIS IS THE LIFE, EH?
YOU'M DEAD RIGHT THERE, OUR KID...
BOSTIN'!
YEAH - NO PONGY OLD FEET AROUND!
SPOT ON!
UNSURPRISINGLY, ORTHODOX SCIEN CLAIMED THAT HIS THEORY WAS FUL OF HOLES, TOO!
WHOLLY UNCONVINCING!
AND THIS IS THE LATEST ADDITION TO MY LIBRARY - "THE CTHULHU POP-UP BOOK"! IT'S SO NEW THAT I HAVEN'T EVEN LOOKED AT IT YET... HEY! WOULD YOU LOOK AT THAT!
POP-UP CTHULHU
BURP
HELLO... WHAT'S THIS BOOK?... PHEW! IT STINKS! OH MY GOD!
PONG!
ONLY ONE THING TO DO WITH THAT! YECH!

GALAXIDI

EARLY 9th CENTURY **GREECE** WAS RULED BY THE OTTOMANS, WHO FORBADE ALL FORMS OF CELEBRATION...

IN THE HARBOUR TOWN OF **GALAXIDI**...

CAN WE HAVE A CELEBRATION, PLEASE?

GO ON! IT'S THE FIRST DAY OF LENT, AND WE WANT A PARTY TO USE UP ALL OUR SPARE FOOD!

CERTAINLY NOT!

BUT THE **GALAXIDIANS** WERE NOT TO BE DETERRED...

COME ON — LET'S HAVE A DANCE IN THE STREET!

YEAH! COSTAS — YOU KEEP AN EYE OUT FOR THE ROTTEN OTTOMANS!

WHAT AM I GOING TO DO WITH ALL THIS FLOUR OVER LENT?

HERE — GIVE ME SOME...

FLOUR

HAHAHAHA!!

WAAAH!

WAHEY!

IN NO TIME AT ALL...

THE TRADITION CONTINUES TO THIS DAY! IN WHAT IS KNOWN AS "CLEAN MONDAY", GALAXIDI IS ONE BIG FARINACEOUS FOOD FIGHT!

I KNOW — I WAS THERE!

The Greeks, of course, have a word for it — ALEVROMOUTZOUROMATA (ΑΛΕϛΡΟΜΟΥΤΖΟΥΡΟΜΑΤΑ)! It means "People throw flour at each other".

GENETIC MANIPULATION

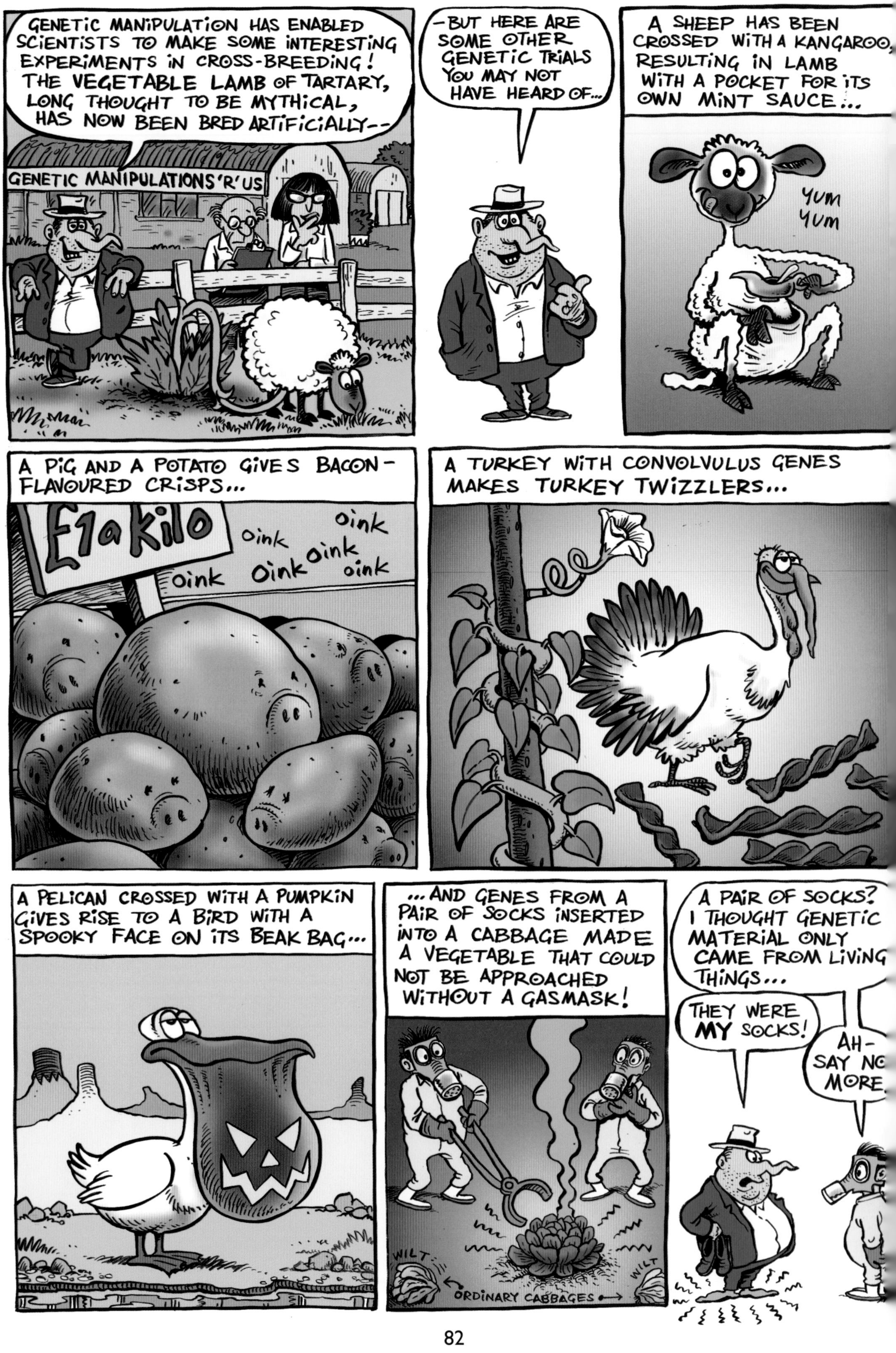
GENETIC MANIPULATION HAS ENABLED SCIENTISTS TO MAKE SOME INTERESTING EXPERIMENTS IN CROSS-BREEDING! THE VEGETABLE LAMB OF TARTARY, LONG THOUGHT TO BE MYTHICAL, HAS NOW BEEN BRED ARTIFICIALLY--
GENETIC MANIPULATIONS 'R' US
-BUT HERE ARE SOME OTHER GENETIC TRIALS YOU MAY NOT HAVE HEARD OF...
A SHEEP HAS BEEN CROSSED WITH A KANGAROO, RESULTING IN LAMB WITH A POCKET FOR ITS OWN MINT SAUCE...
YUM YUM
A PIG AND A POTATO GIVES BACON-FLAVOURED CRISPS...
£1 a kilo
oink
oink
oink
oink
oink
oink
A TURKEY WITH CONVOLVULUS GENES MAKES TURKEY TWIZZLERS...
A PELICAN CROSSED WITH A PUMPKIN GIVES RISE TO A BIRD WITH A SPOOKY FACE ON ITS BEAK BAG...
...AND GENES FROM A PAIR OF SOCKS INSERTED INTO A CABBAGE MADE A VEGETABLE THAT COULD NOT BE APPROACHED WITHOUT A GASMASK!
WILT
WILT
ORDINARY CABBAGES
A PAIR OF SOCKS? I THOUGHT GENETIC MATERIAL ONLY CAME FROM LIVING THINGS...
THEY WERE MY SOCKS!
AH- SAY NO MORE.

GIANT BIRDS

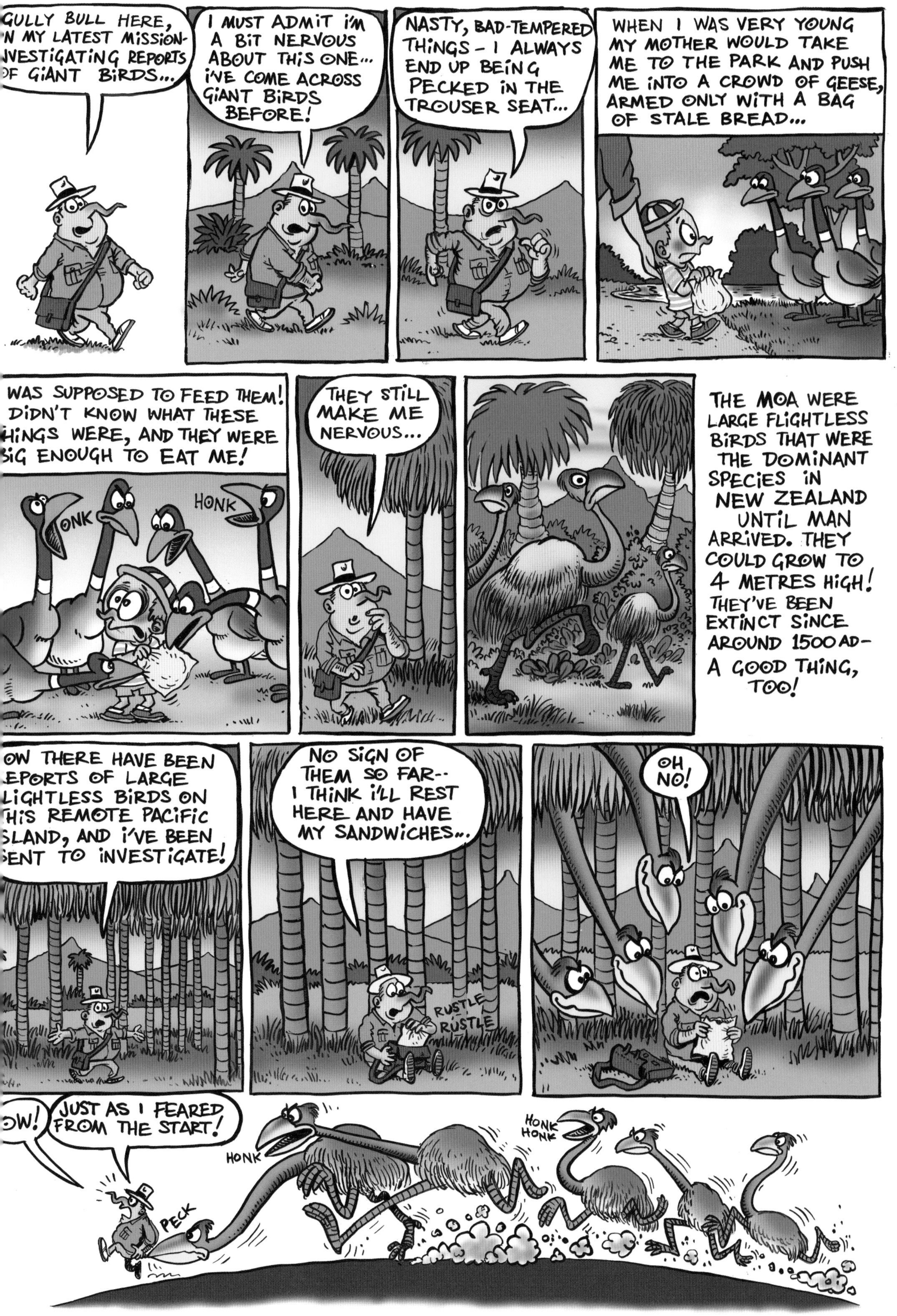

GULLY BULL HERE, ON MY LATEST MISSION- INVESTIGATING REPORTS OF GIANT BIRDS...
I MUST ADMIT I'M A BIT NERVOUS ABOUT THIS ONE... I'VE COME ACROSS GIANT BIRDS BEFORE!
NASTY, BAD-TEMPERED THINGS - I ALWAYS END UP BEING PECKED IN THE TROUSER SEAT...
WHEN I WAS VERY YOUNG MY MOTHER WOULD TAKE ME TO THE PARK AND PUSH ME INTO A CROWD OF GEESE, ARMED ONLY WITH A BAG OF STALE BREAD...
I WAS SUPPOSED TO FEED THEM! I DIDN'T KNOW WHAT THESE THINGS WERE, AND THEY WERE BIG ENOUGH TO EAT ME!
HONK
HONK
THEY STILL MAKE ME NERVOUS...
THE MOA WERE LARGE FLIGHTLESS BIRDS THAT WERE THE DOMINANT SPECIES IN NEW ZEALAND UNTIL MAN ARRIVED. THEY COULD GROW TO 4 METRES HIGH! THEY'VE BEEN EXTINCT SINCE AROUND 1500 AD- A GOOD THING, TOO!
NOW THERE HAVE BEEN REPORTS OF LARGE FLIGHTLESS BIRDS ON THIS REMOTE PACIFIC ISLAND, AND I'VE BEEN SENT TO INVESTIGATE!
NO SIGN OF THEM SO FAR-- I THINK I'LL REST HERE AND HAVE MY SANDWICHES...
RUSTLE RUSTLE
OH NO!
OW!
JUST AS I FEARED FROM THE START!
HONK
HONK HONK
PECK

THE STRANGE WORLD OF PECULIAR PLANTS

A BREED OF GIGANTIC ARUM IN THE FORESTS OF NEW GUINEA FLOWERS ONLY EVERY SEVEN YEARS, WHEN IT DEVELOPS A HUGE SQUATTING PITCHER WITH A NINE FOOT PRONG STICKING RUDELY FROM ITS' CENTRE...

THE PRONG GIVES OFF AN APPALLING STENCH, REVOLTING TO ALL LIVING THINGS EXCEPT FOR A PARTICULAR FLY...

THE FLY CRAWLS INTO THE PITCHER, BRUSHING AGAINST HAIRS AS IT DOES SO, WHICH CAUSES THE MOUTH OF THE PITCHER TO CLAMP SHUT. THE FLY IS TRAPPED—BUT IT KNOWS WHAT TO DO!

SLAM

THE FLY'S FIRST TASK IS TO DEPOSIT POLLEN IT HAS GATHERED FROM PREVIOUS ARUMS ONTO THE FEMALE RECEPTORS.

THEN IT COLLECTS POLLEN TO BE TAKEN TO OTHER PLANTS...

AND FINALLY IT DEPOSITS ITS OWN EGG IN A SPECIAL INCUBATOR CHAMBER!

THE FLY IS REWARDED FOR ITS LABOURS WITH A DRINK OF NECTAR.

ICE   NECTAR 70%

THE ONLY WAY OUT OF THE PITCHER IS A SMALL EXIT NEAR THE BOTTOM.

PLEASE LEAVE QUIETLY CONSIDER OUR NEIGHBOURS

IT SCRAMBLES UP A TUBE...

...AND FLIES AWAY TO FIND ANOTHER ARUM, WHO'S APPALLING STENCH IT ALREADY DETECTS!

SNIF SNIF   HMM!

THE PLANT QUICKLY CLOSES DOWN ITS' PRONG AND PITCHER EQUIPMENT, WHICH IS NOW REDUNDANT.

PFLUURRR

A STEM SHOOTS INTO THE AIR, CARRYING THE FERTI SEEDS HIGH ABOVE THE FOREST FLOOR...

THE FRUIT SWELLS TO BURSTING POINT!

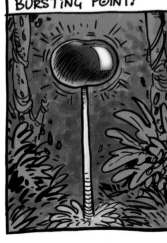

IT BURSTS!

POP

THE SEEDS OF THE ARUM ARE SCATTERED FAR INTO THE FOREST, TO GROW FOR SEVEN YEARS BEFORE THEMSELVES FLOWERING!

THE FLY EGG IS ALSO DEPOSITED IN A PLACE BEST SUITED TO NURTUR ANOTHER YOUNG FLY!

FLY FOUNDLIN HOME

ANOTHER ADMINISTRATIVE TRIUMPH FOR NATURE!

GREAT PLUMMETS

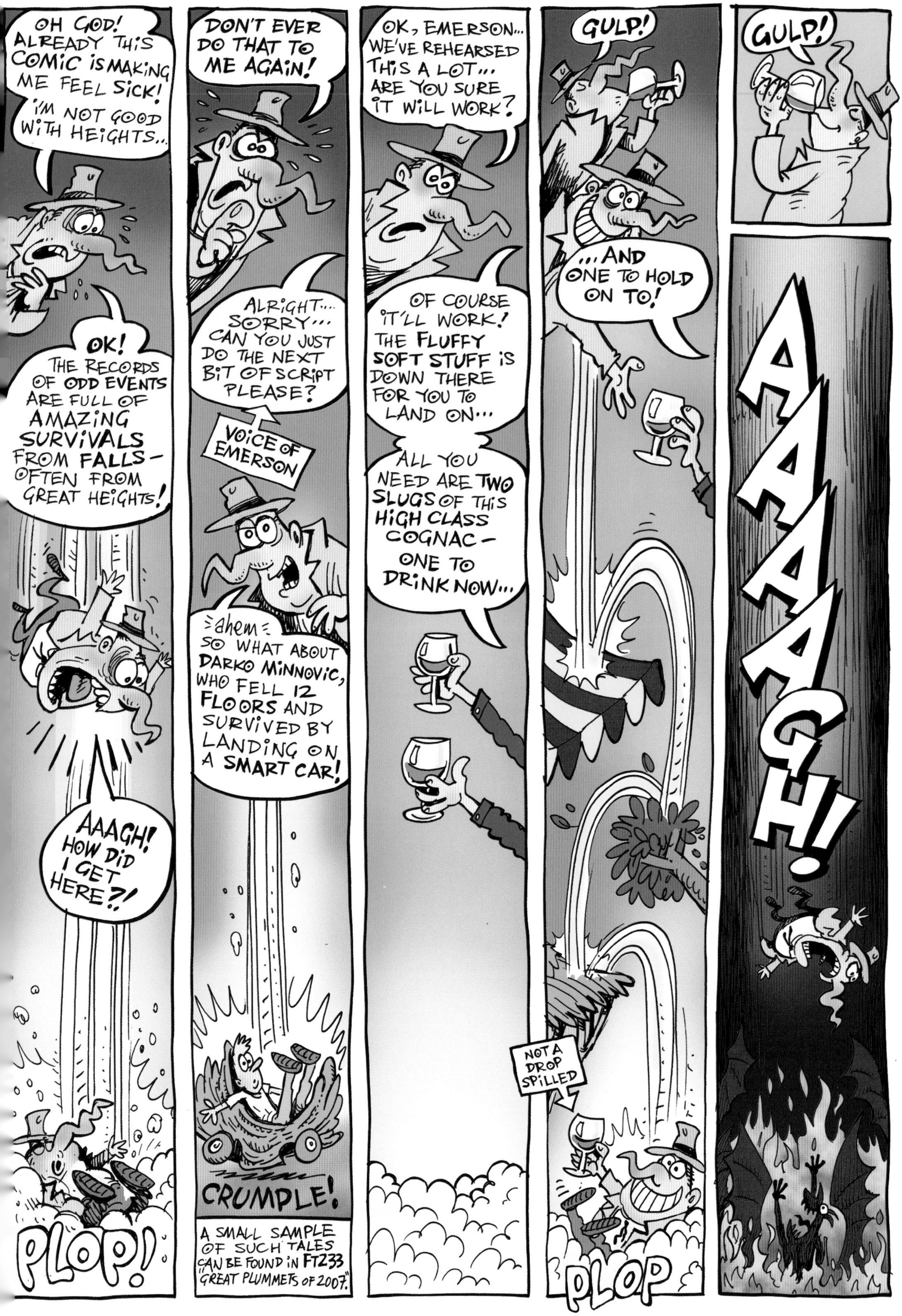

OH GOD! ALREADY THIS COMIC IS MAKING ME FEEL SICK! I'M NOT GOOD WITH HEIGHTS...
OK! THE RECORDS OF ODD EVENTS ARE FULL OF AMAZING SURVIVALS FROM FALLS – OFTEN FROM GREAT HEIGHTS!
AAAGH! HOW DID I GET HERE?!
PLOP!
DON'T EVER DO THAT TO ME AGAIN!
ALRIGHT... SORRY... CAN YOU JUST DO THE NEXT BIT OF SCRIPT PLEASE?
VOICE OF EMERSON
ahem SO WHAT ABOUT DARKO MINNOVIC, WHO FELL 12 FLOORS AND SURVIVED BY LANDING ON A SMART CAR!
CRUMPLE!
A SMALL SAMPLE OF SUCH TALES CAN BE FOUND IN FT233 "GREAT PLUMMETS OF 2007."
OK, EMERSON... WE'VE REHEARSED THIS A LOT... ARE YOU SURE IT WILL WORK?
OF COURSE IT'LL WORK! THE FLUFFY SOFT STUFF IS DOWN THERE FOR YOU TO LAND ON...
ALL YOU NEED ARE TWO SLUGS OF THIS HIGH CLASS COGNAC – ONE TO DRINK NOW...
GULP!
...AND ONE TO HOLD ON TO!
NOT A DROP SPILLED
PLOP
GULP!
AAAAAGH!

GREEN MAN

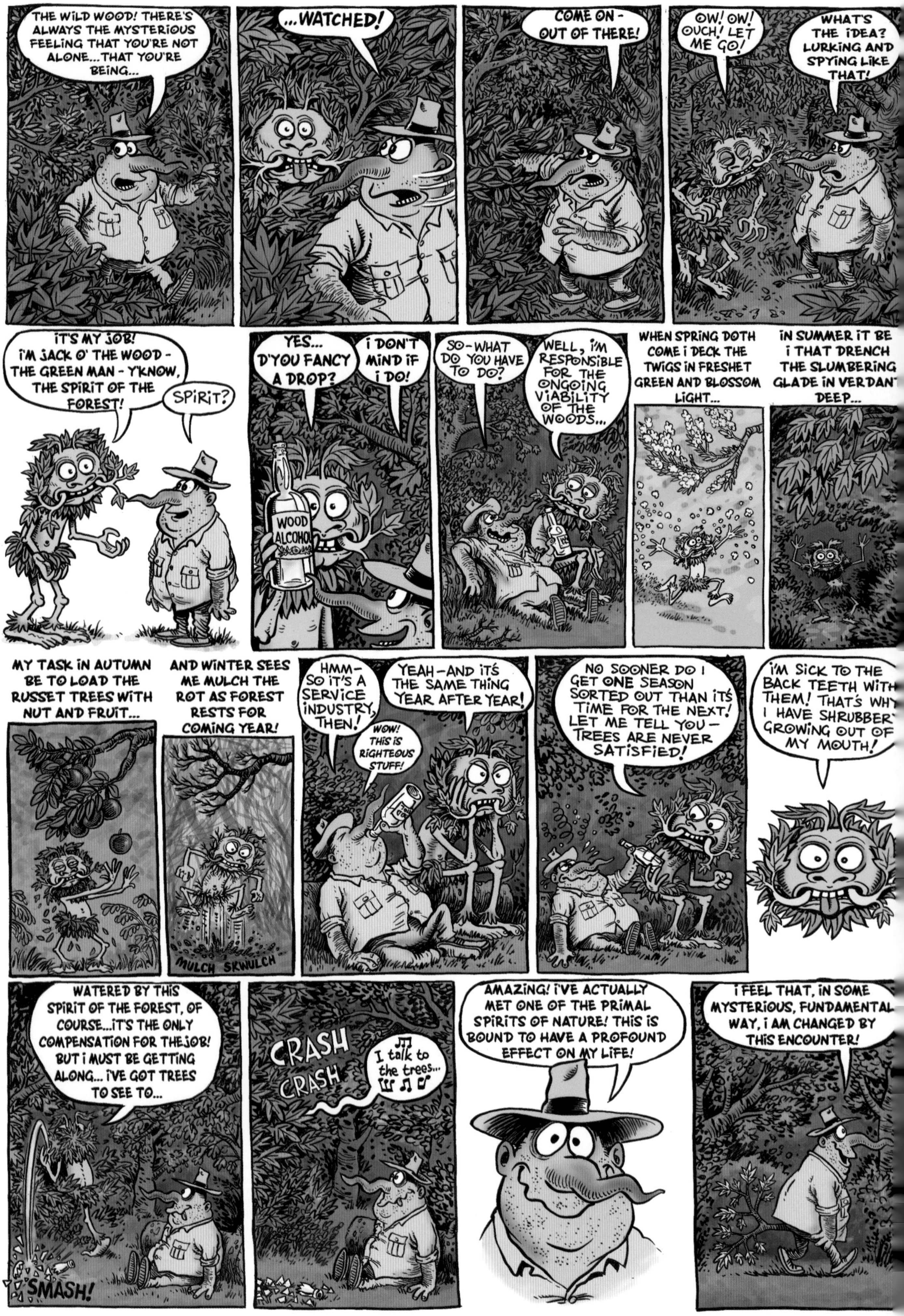

THE WILD WOOD! THERE'S ALWAYS THE MYSTERIOUS FEELING THAT YOU'RE NOT ALONE...THAT YOU'RE BEING...
...WATCHED!
COME ON - OUT OF THERE!
OW! OW! OUCH! LET ME GO!
WHAT'S THE IDEA? LURKING AND SPYING LIKE THAT!
IT'S MY JOB! I'M JACK O' THE WOOD - THE GREEN MAN - Y'KNOW, THE SPIRIT OF THE FOREST!
SPIRIT?
YES... D'YOU FANCY A DROP?
I DON'T MIND IF I DO!
WOOD ALCOHO
SO-WHAT DO YOU HAVE TO DO?
WELL, I'M RESPONSIBLE FOR THE ONGOING VIABILITY OF THE WOODS...
WHEN SPRING DOTH COME I DECK THE TWIGS IN FRESHET GREEN AND BLOSSOM LIGHT...
IN SUMMER IT BE I THAT DRENCH THE SLUMBERING GLADE IN VERDANT DEEP...
MY TASK IN AUTUMN BE TO LOAD THE RUSSET TREES WITH NUT AND FRUIT...
AND WINTER SEES ME MULCH THE ROT AS FOREST RESTS FOR COMING YEAR!
MULCH SKWULCH
HMM- SO IT'S A SERVICE INDUSTRY, THEN!
YEAH-AND IT'S THE SAME THING YEAR AFTER YEAR!
WOW! THIS IS RIGHTEOUS STUFF!
NO SOONER DO I GET ONE SEASON SORTED OUT THAN IT'S TIME FOR THE NEXT! LET ME TELL YOU - TREES ARE NEVER SATISFIED!
I'M SICK TO THE BACK TEETH WITH THEM! THAT'S WHY I HAVE SHRUBBER GROWING OUT OF MY MOUTH!
WATERED BY THIS SPIRIT OF THE FOREST, OF COURSE...IT'S THE ONLY COMPENSATION FOR THE JOB! BUT I MUST BE GETTING ALONG... I'VE GOT TREES TO SEE TO...
SMASH!
CRASH
CRASH
I talk to the trees...
AMAZING! I'VE ACTUALLY MET ONE OF THE PRIMAL SPIRITS OF NATURE! THIS IS BOUND TO HAVE A PROFOUND EFFECT ON MY LIFE!
I FEEL THAT, IN SOME MYSTERIOUS, FUNDAMENTAL WAY, I AM CHANGED BY THIS ENCOUNTER!

GRUNTING COD

As reported in *New Scientist* 13/02/1999

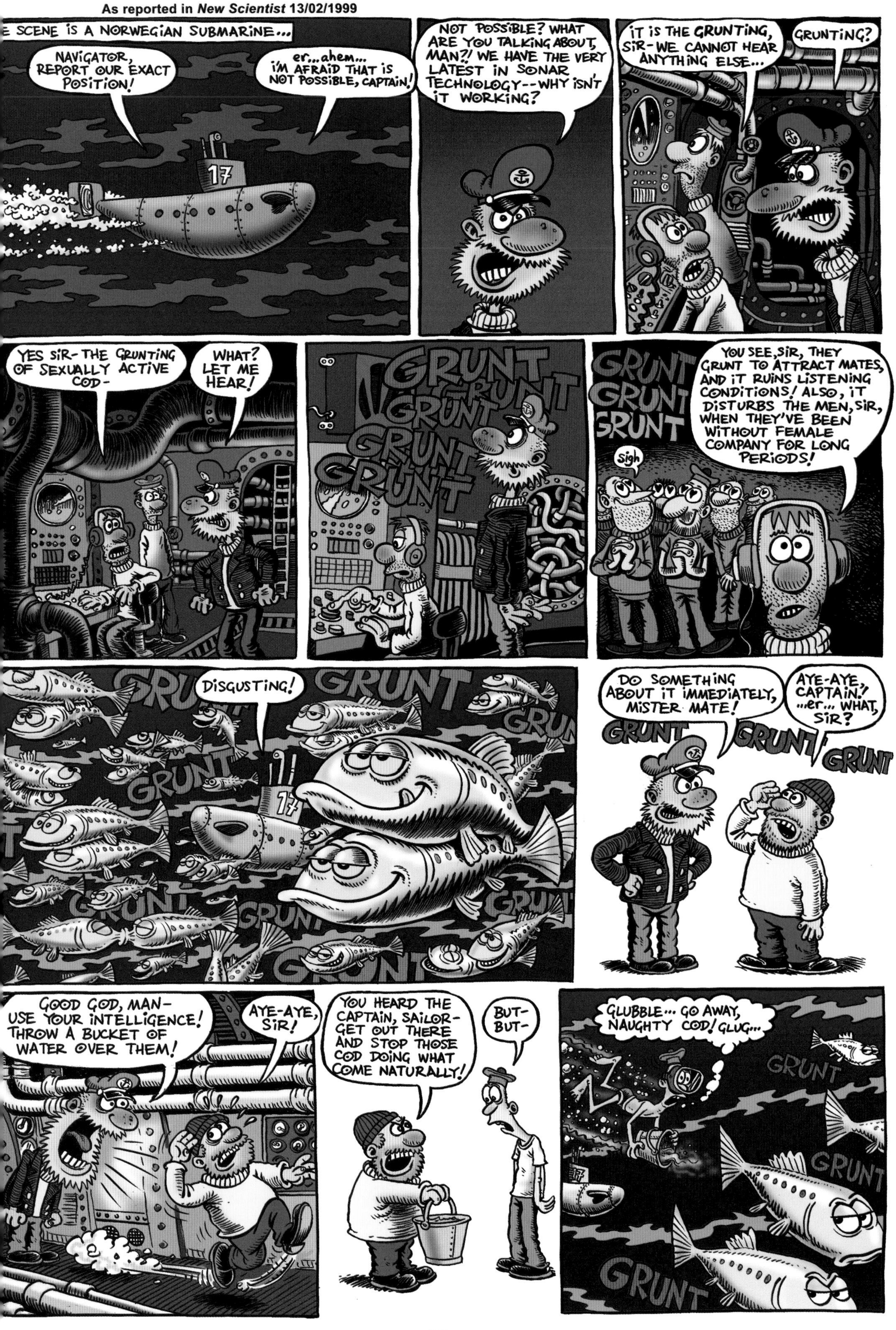
E SCENE IS A NORWEGIAN SUBMARINE...
NAVIGATOR, REPORT OUR EXACT POSITION!
er...ahem... I'M AFRAID THAT IS NOT POSSIBLE, CAPTAIN!
17
NOT POSSIBLE? WHAT ARE YOU TALKING ABOUT, MAN?! WE HAVE THE VERY LATEST IN SONAR TECHNOLOGY--WHY ISN'T IT WORKING?
IT IS THE GRUNTING, SIR-WE CANNOT HEAR ANYTHING ELSE...
GRUNTING?
YES SIR-THE GRUNTING OF SEXUALLY ACTIVE COD-
WHAT? LET ME HEAR!
GRUNT GRUNT GRUNT GRUNT GRUNT
GRUNT GRUNT GRUNT
YOU SEE, SIR, THEY GRUNT TO ATTRACT MATES, AND IT RUINS LISTENING CONDITIONS! ALSO, IT DISTURBS THE MEN, SIR, WHEN THEY'VE BEEN WITHOUT FEMALE COMPANY FOR LONG PERIODS!
sigh
DISGUSTING!
GRUNT GRUNT GRUNT GRUNT GRUNT GRUNT
DO SOMETHING ABOUT IT IMMEDIATELY, MISTER MATE!
AYE-AYE, CAPTAIN! ...er... WHAT, SIR?
GRUNT GRUNT GRUNT
GOOD GOD, MAN-USE YOUR INTELLIGENCE! THROW A BUCKET OF WATER OVER THEM!
AYE-AYE, SIR!
YOU HEARD THE CAPTAIN, SAILOR-GET OUT THERE AND STOP THOSE COD DOING WHAT COME NATURALLY!
BUT-BUT-
GLUBBLE... GO AWAY, NAUGHTY COD! GLUG...
GRUNT
GRUNT
GRUNT

HAG STONES

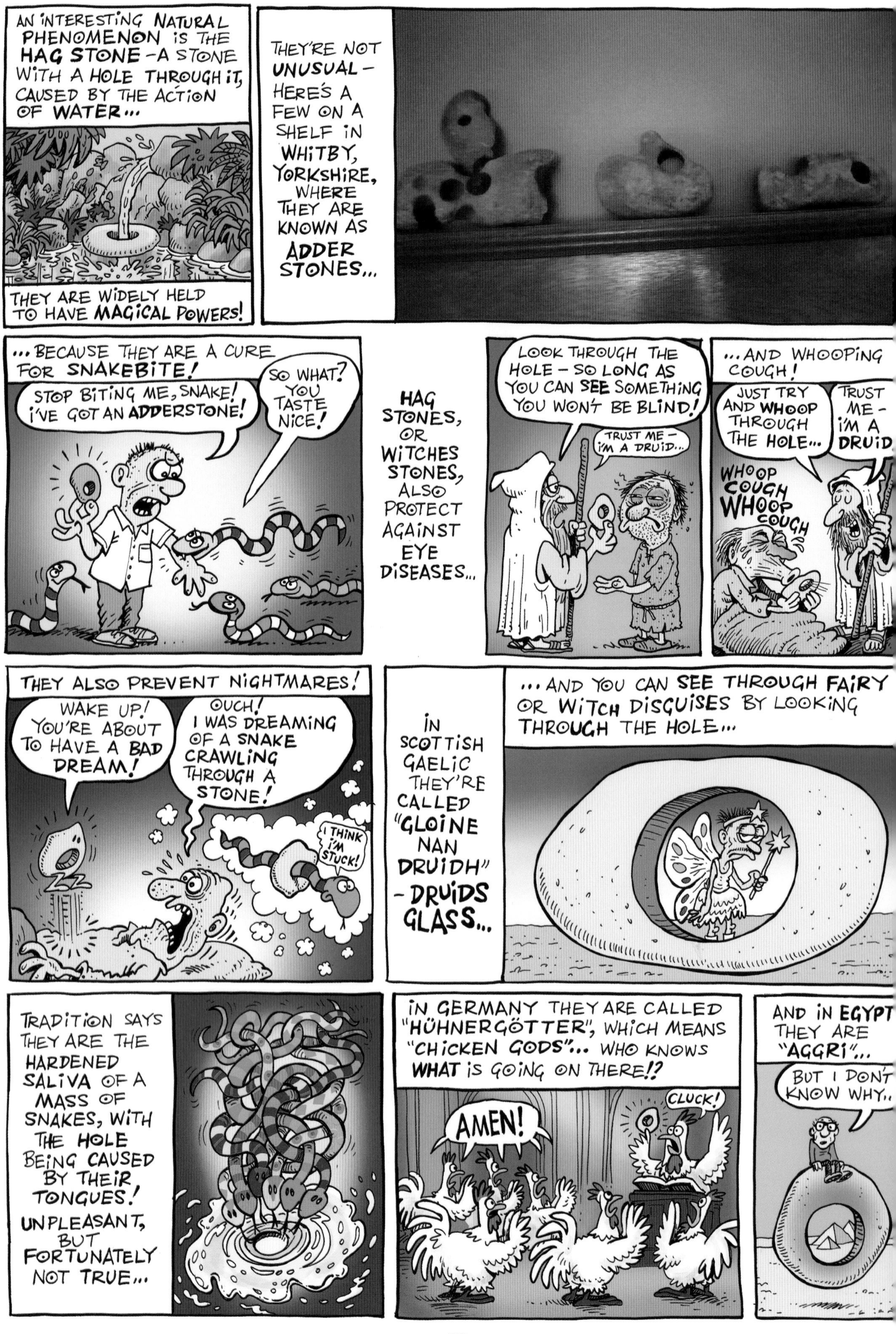

AN INTERESTING NATURAL PHENOMENON IS THE HAG STONE – A STONE WITH A HOLE THROUGH IT, CAUSED BY THE ACTION OF WATER...
THEY ARE WIDELY HELD TO HAVE MAGICAL POWERS!
THEY'RE NOT UNUSUAL – HERE'S A FEW ON A SHELF IN WHITBY, YORKSHIRE, WHERE THEY ARE KNOWN AS ADDER STONES...
...BECAUSE THEY ARE A CURE FOR SNAKEBITE!
STOP BITING ME, SNAKE! I'VE GOT AN ADDERSTONE!
SO WHAT? YOU TASTE NICE!
HAG STONES, OR WITCHES STONES, ALSO PROTECT AGAINST EYE DISEASES...
LOOK THROUGH THE HOLE – SO LONG AS YOU CAN SEE SOMETHING YOU WON'T BE BLIND!
TRUST ME – I'M A DRUID...
...AND WHOOPING COUGH!
JUST TRY AND WHOOP THROUGH THE HOLE...
TRUST ME – I'M A DRUID
WHOOP COUGH WHOOP COUGH
THEY ALSO PREVENT NIGHTMARES!
WAKE UP! YOU'RE ABOUT TO HAVE A BAD DREAM!
OUCH! I WAS DREAMING OF A SNAKE CRAWLING THROUGH A STONE!
I THINK I'M STUCK!
IN SCOTTISH GAELIC THEY'RE CALLED "GLOINE NAN DRUIDH" – DRUIDS GLASS...
...AND YOU CAN SEE THROUGH FAIRY OR WITCH DISGUISES BY LOOKING THROUGH THE HOLE...
TRADITION SAYS THEY ARE THE HARDENED SALIVA OF A MASS OF SNAKES, WITH THE HOLE BEING CAUSED BY THEIR TONGUES! UNPLEASANT, BUT FORTUNATELY NOT TRUE...
IN GERMANY THEY ARE CALLED "HÜHNERGÖTTER", WHICH MEANS "CHICKEN GODS"... WHO KNOWS WHAT IS GOING ON THERE!?
AMEN!
CLUCK!
AND IN EGYPT THEY ARE "AGGRI"...
BUT I DON'T KNOW WHY..

WEIRD HAIR SALONA

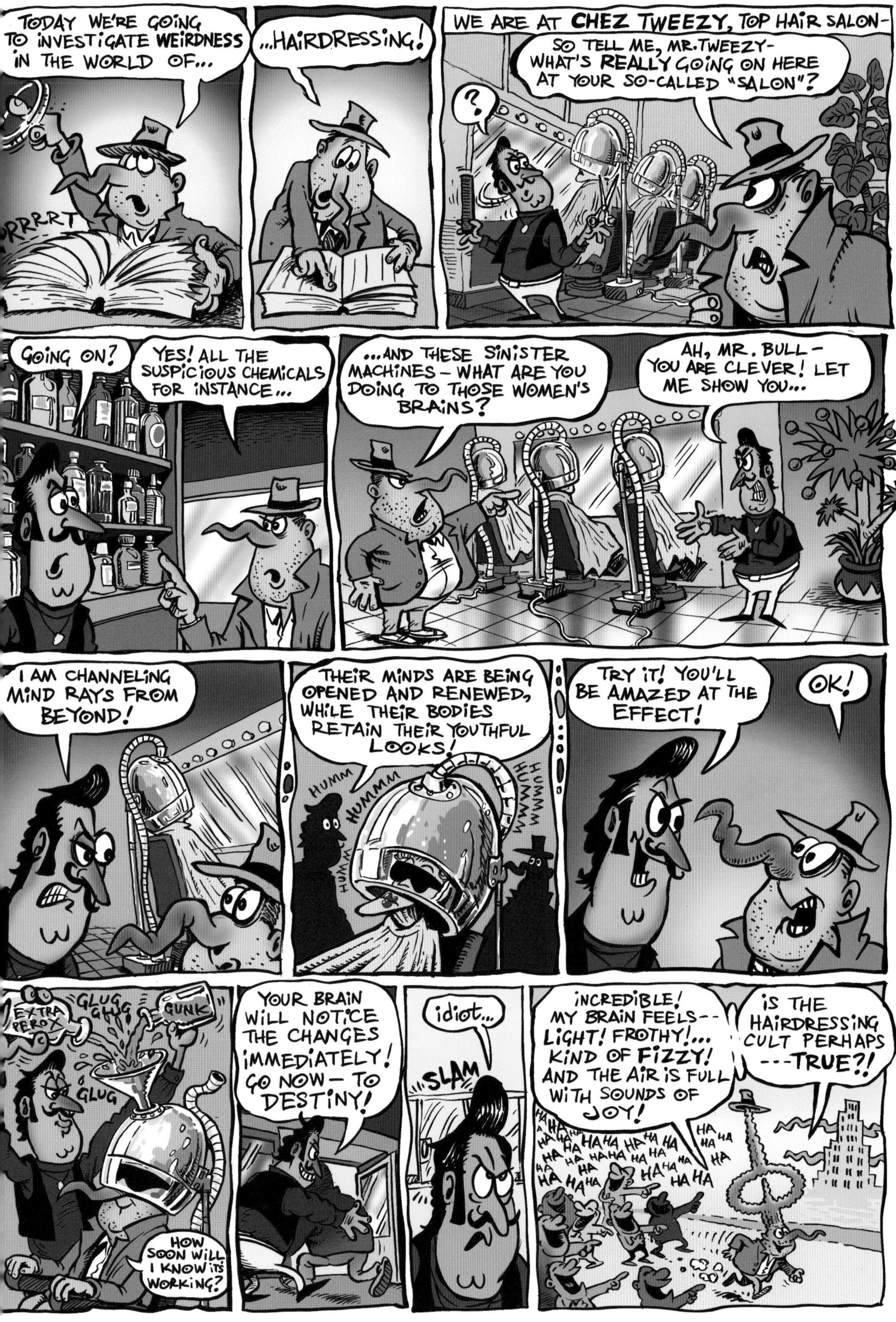
TODAY WE'RE GOING TO INVESTIGATE WEIRDNESS IN THE WORLD OF...
RRRRRT
...HAIRDRESSING!
WE ARE AT CHEZ TWEEZY, TOP HAIR SALON-
SO TELL ME, MR. TWEEZY- WHAT'S REALLY GOING ON HERE AT YOUR SO-CALLED "SALON"?
?
GOING ON?
YES! ALL THE SUSPICIOUS CHEMICALS FOR INSTANCE...
...AND THESE SINISTER MACHINES - WHAT ARE YOU DOING TO THOSE WOMEN'S BRAINS?
AH, MR. BULL - YOU ARE CLEVER! LET ME SHOW YOU...
I AM CHANNELING MIND RAYS FROM BEYOND!
THEIR MINDS ARE BEING OPENED AND RENEWED, WHILE THEIR BODIES RETAIN THEIR YOUTHFUL LOOKS!
HUMM HUMMM HUMMM HUMMM
TRY IT! YOU'LL BE AMAZED AT THE EFFECT!
OK!
EXTRA PEROX
GLUG GLUG
GUNK
GLUG
HOW SOON WILL I KNOW IT'S WORKING?
YOUR BRAIN WILL NOTICE THE CHANGES IMMEDIATELY! GO NOW - TO DESTINY!
idiot...
SLAM
INCREDIBLE! MY BRAIN FEELS-- LIGHT! FROTHY!... KIND OF FIZZY! AND THE AIR IS FULL WITH SOUNDS OF JOY!
IS THE HAIRDRESSING CULT PERHAPS ---TRUE?!
HA HA HA HA HA HA HA HA HA HA HA HA HA HA HA HA

GULLY'S HALLUCINATION

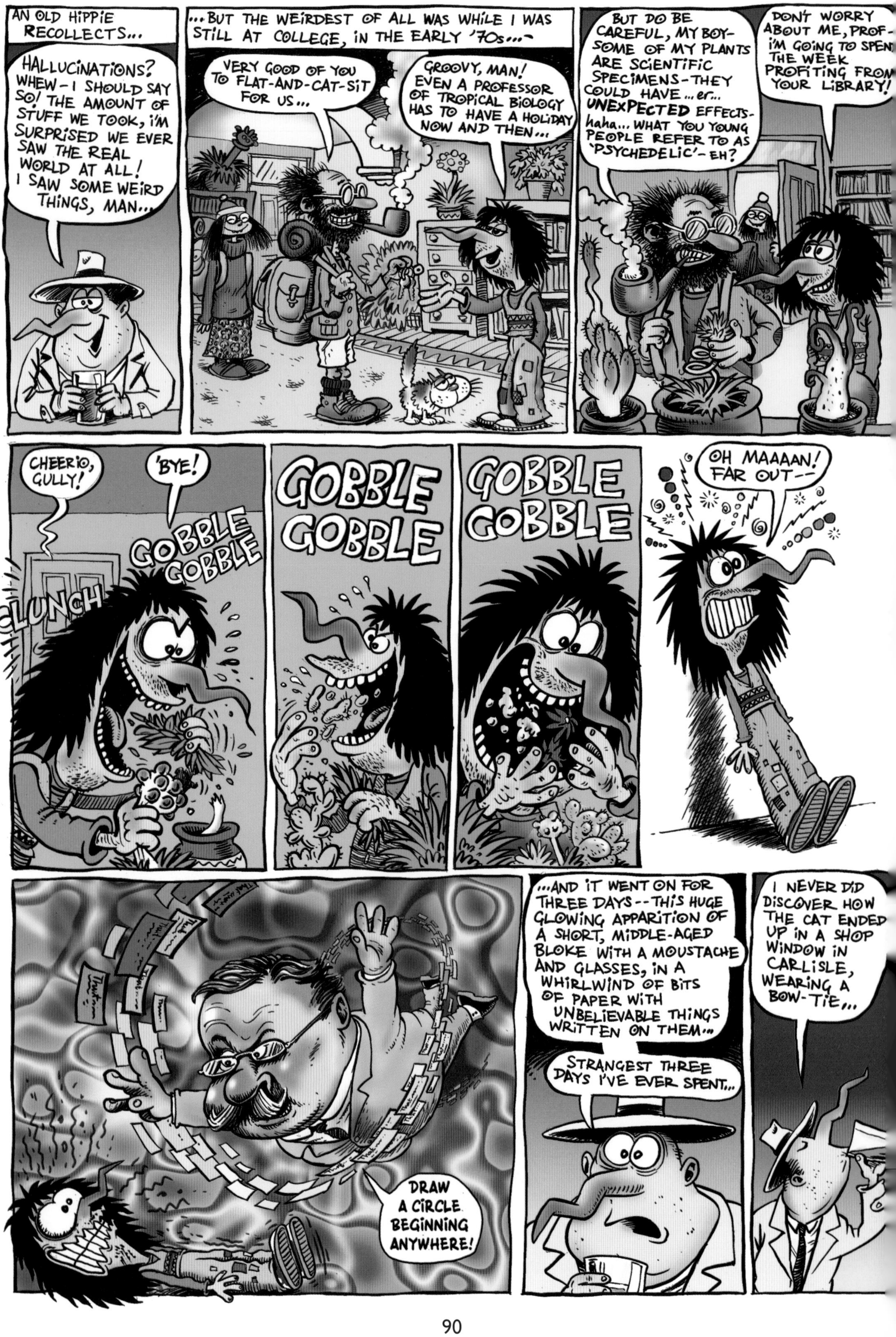
AN OLD HIPPIE RECOLLECTS...
HALLUCINATIONS? WHEW - I SHOULD SAY SO! THE AMOUNT OF STUFF WE TOOK, I'M SURPRISED WE EVER SAW THE REAL WORLD AT ALL! I SAW SOME WEIRD THINGS, MAN...
...BUT THE WEIRDEST OF ALL WAS WHILE I WAS STILL AT COLLEGE, IN THE EARLY '70s...
VERY GOOD OF YOU TO FLAT-AND-CAT-SIT FOR US...
GROOVY, MAN! EVEN A PROFESSOR OF TROPICAL BIOLOGY HAS TO HAVE A HOLIDAY NOW AND THEN...
BUT DO BE CAREFUL, MY BOY - SOME OF MY PLANTS ARE SCIENTIFIC SPECIMENS - THEY COULD HAVE ...er... UNEXPECTED EFFECTS - haha... WHAT YOU YOUNG PEOPLE REFER TO AS 'PSYCHEDELIC' - EH?
DON'T WORRY ABOUT ME, PROF - I'M GOING TO SPEND THE WEEK PROFITING FROM YOUR LIBRARY!
CHEERIO, GULLY!
'BYE!
CLUNCH
GOBBLE GOBBLE
GOBBLE GOBBLE
GOBBLE GOBBLE
OH MAAAAN! FAR OUT--
DRAW A CIRCLE BEGINNING ANYWHERE!
...AND IT WENT ON FOR THREE DAYS -- THIS HUGE GLOWING APPARITION OF A SHORT, MIDDLE-AGED BLOKE WITH A MOUSTACHE AND GLASSES, IN A WHIRLWIND OF BITS OF PAPER WITH UNBELIEVABLE THINGS WRITTEN ON THEM...
STRANGEST THREE DAYS I'VE EVER SPENT...
I NEVER DID DISCOVER HOW THE CAT ENDED UP IN A SHOP WINDOW IN CARLISLE, WEARING A BOW-TIE...

HE HAUNTED BANJO

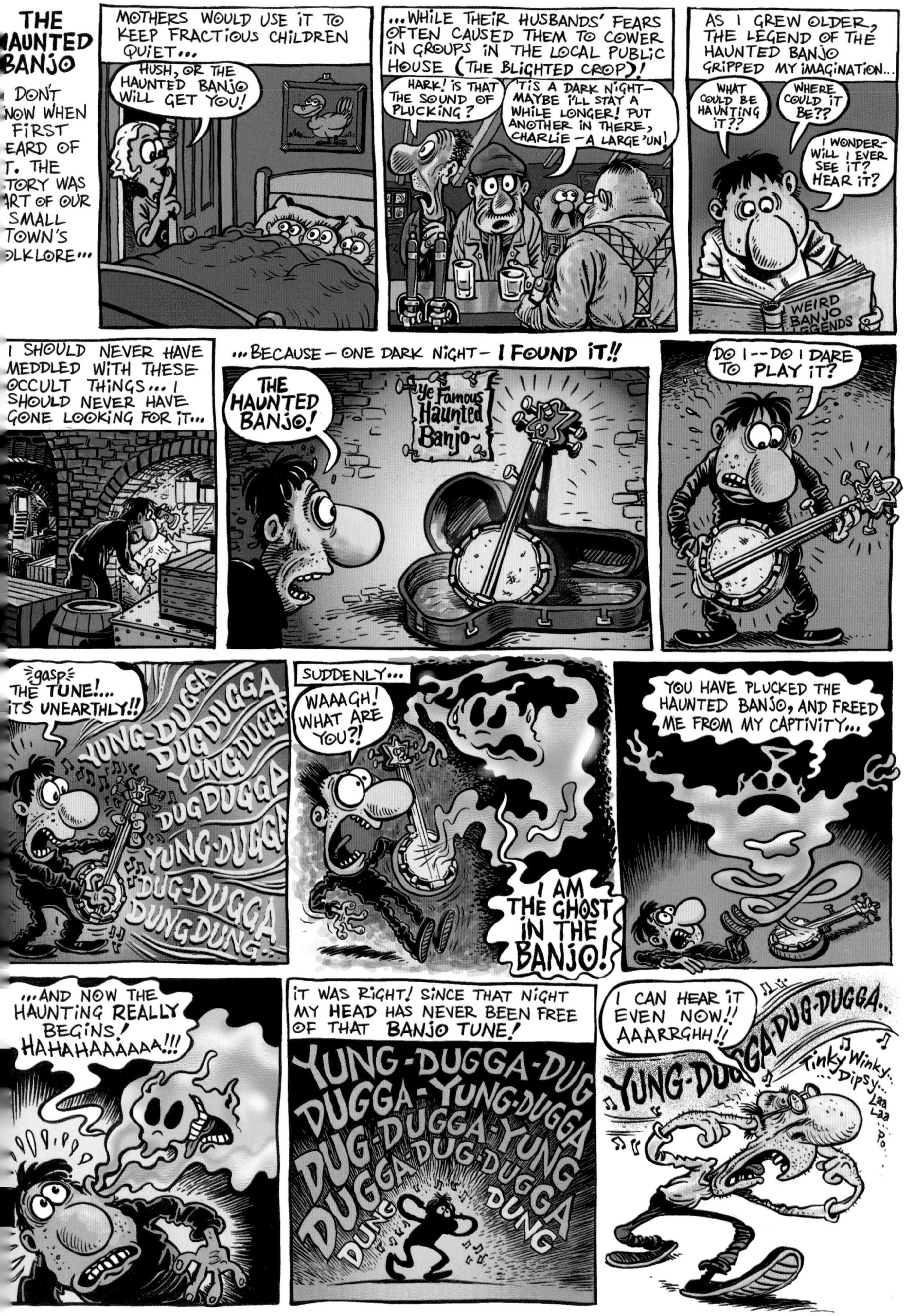
THE
AUNTED
BANJO
DON'T
NOW WHEN
FIRST
EARD OF
T. THE
TORY WAS
ART OF OUR
SMALL
TOWN'S
LKLORE...
MOTHERS WOULD USE IT TO KEEP FRACTIOUS CHILDREN QUIET...
HUSH, OR THE HAUNTED BANJO WILL GET YOU!
...WHILE THEIR HUSBANDS' FEARS OFTEN CAUSED THEM TO COWER IN GROUPS IN THE LOCAL PUBLIC HOUSE (THE BLIGHTED CROP)!
HARK! IS THAT THE SOUND OF PLUCKING?
'TIS A DARK NIGHT— MAYBE I'LL STAY A WHILE LONGER! PUT ANOTHER IN THERE, CHARLIE—A LARGE 'UN!
AS I GREW OLDER, THE LEGEND OF THE HAUNTED BANJO GRIPPED MY IMAGINATION...
WHAT COULD BE HAUNTING IT??
WHERE COULD IT BE??
I WONDER- WILL I EVER SEE IT? HEAR IT?
WEIRD BANJO LEGENDS
I SHOULD NEVER HAVE MEDDLED WITH THESE OCCULT THINGS... I SHOULD NEVER HAVE GONE LOOKING FOR IT...
...BECAUSE—ONE DARK NIGHT—I FOUND IT!!
THE HAUNTED BANJO!
Ye Famous Haunted Banjo
DO I--DO I DARE TO PLAY IT?
gasp
THE TUNE!... IT'S UNEARTHLY!!
YUNG-DUGGA DUG DUGGA YUNG DUGGA DUG DUGGA YUNG-DUGGA DUG-DUGGA DUNG DUNG...
SUDDENLY...
WAAAGH! WHAT ARE YOU?!
I AM THE GHOST IN THE BANJO!
YOU HAVE PLUCKED THE HAUNTED BANJO, AND FREED ME FROM MY CAPTIVITY...
...AND NOW THE HAUNTING REALLY BEGINS! HAHAHAAAAAA!!!
IT WAS RIGHT! SINCE THAT NIGHT MY HEAD HAS NEVER BEEN FREE OF THAT BANJO TUNE!
YUNG-DUGGA-DUG DUGGA-YUNG-DUGGA DUG-DUGGA-YUNG DUGGA-DUG-DUGGA DUNG DUNG
I CAN HEAR IT EVEN NOW!! AAARRGHH!!
YUNG-DUGGA-DUG-DUGGA...
Tinky Winky... Dipsy... Laa Laa... Po...

ODD DEATHS IN ANCIENT GREEK MUSIC 1

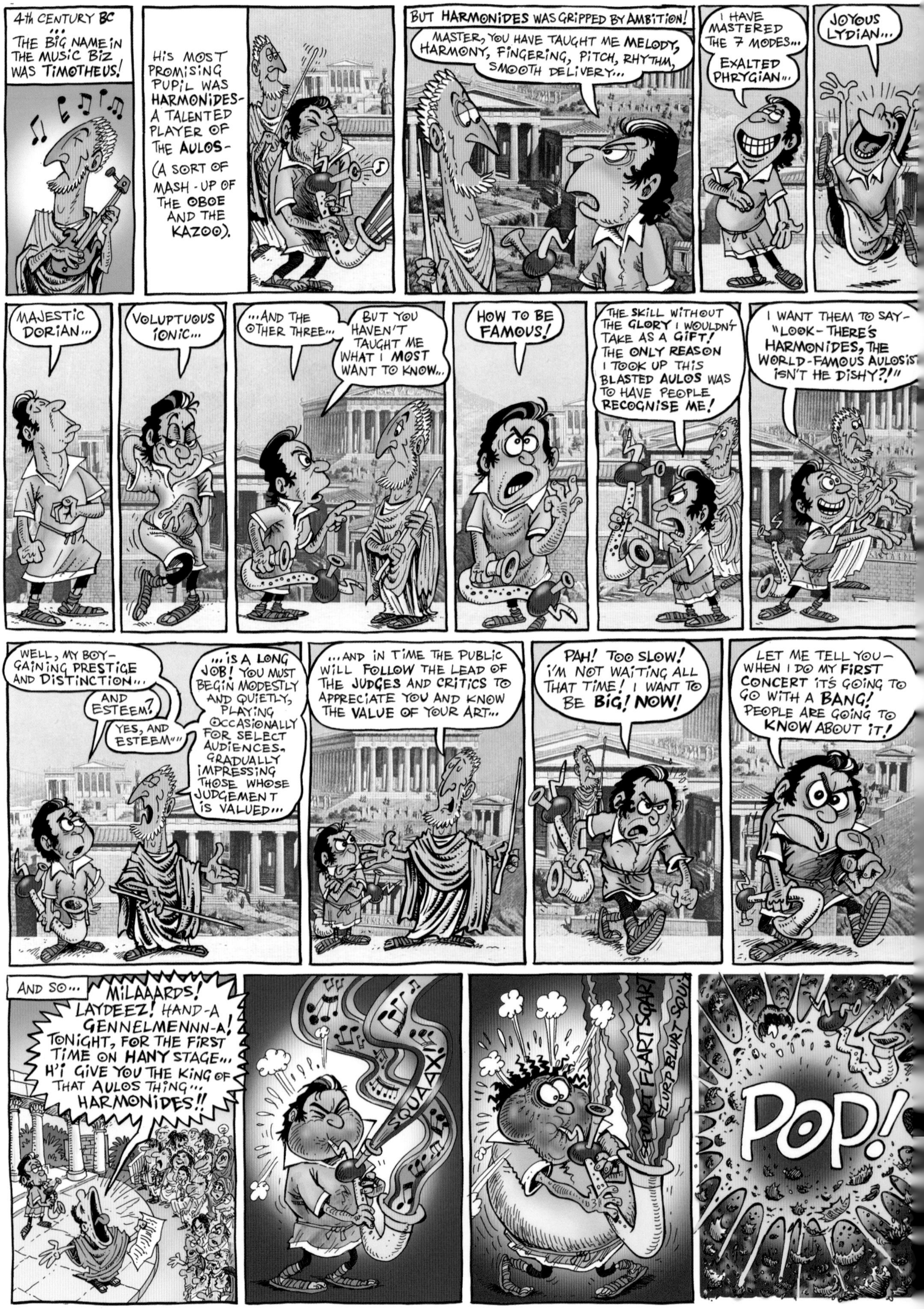

4th CENTURY BC ... THE BIG NAME IN THE MUSIC BIZ WAS TIMOTHEUS!
HIS MOST PROMISING PUPIL WAS HARMONIDES - A TALENTED PLAYER OF THE AULOS - (A SORT OF MASH-UP OF THE OBOE AND THE KAZOO).
BUT HARMONIDES WAS GRIPPED BY AMBITION!
MASTER, YOU HAVE TAUGHT ME MELODY, HARMONY, FINGERING, PITCH, RHYTHM, SMOOTH DELIVERY...
I HAVE MASTERED THE 7 MODES...
EXALTED PHRYGIAN...
JOYOUS LYDIAN...
MAJESTIC DORIAN...
VOLUPTUOUS IONIC...
...AND THE OTHER THREE...
BUT YOU HAVEN'T TAUGHT ME WHAT I MOST WANT TO KNOW...
HOW TO BE FAMOUS!
THE SKILL WITHOUT THE GLORY I WOULDN'T TAKE AS A GIFT! THE ONLY REASON I TOOK UP THIS BLASTED AULOS WAS TO HAVE PEOPLE RECOGNISE ME!
I WANT THEM TO SAY- "LOOK- THERE'S HARMONIDES, THE WORLD-FAMOUS AULOSIST ISN'T HE DISHY?!"
WELL, MY BOY- GAINING PRESTIGE AND DISTINCTION...
AND ESTEEM?
YES, AND ESTEEM...
...IS A LONG JOB! YOU MUST BEGIN MODESTLY AND QUIETLY, PLAYING OCCASIONALLY FOR SELECT AUDIENCES, GRADUALLY IMPRESSING THOSE WHOSE JUDGEMENT IS VALUED...
...AND IN TIME THE PUBLIC WILL FOLLOW THE LEAD OF THE JUDGES AND CRITICS TO APPRECIATE YOU AND KNOW THE VALUE OF YOUR ART...
PAH! TOO SLOW! I'M NOT WAITING ALL THAT TIME! I WANT TO BE BIG! NOW!
LET ME TELL YOU- WHEN I DO MY FIRST CONCERT IT'S GOING TO GO WITH A BANG! PEOPLE ARE GOING TO KNOW ABOUT IT!
AND SO...
MILAAARDS! LAYDEEZ! HAND-A GENNELMENNN-A! TONIGHT, FOR THE FIRST TIME ON HANY STAGE... H'I GIVE YOU THE KING OF THAT AULOS THING... HARMONIDES!!
SQUAAAX!
SQUART FLART SQART
FLURP BLURT SQUI
POP!

ODD DEATHS IN ANCIENT GREEK MUSIC 2

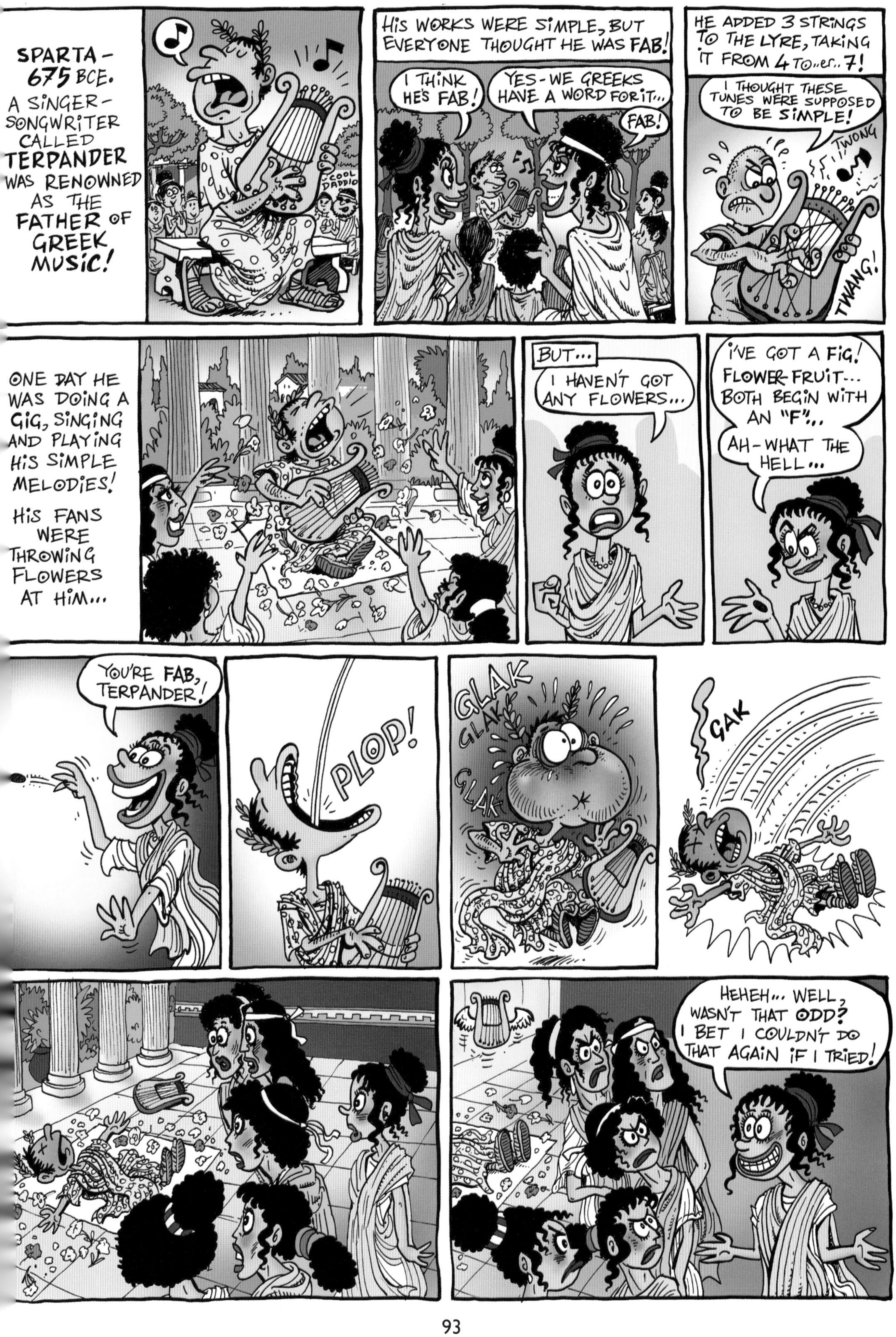
SPARTA - 675 BCE. A SINGER-SONGWRITER CALLED TERPANDER WAS RENOWNED AS THE FATHER OF GREEK MUSIC!
COOL DADDIO
HIS WORKS WERE SIMPLE, BUT EVERYONE THOUGHT HE WAS FAB!
I THINK HE'S FAB!
YES - WE GREEKS HAVE A WORD FOR IT...
FAB!
HE ADDED 3 STRINGS TO THE LYRE, TAKING IT FROM 4 TO...er.. 7!
I THOUGHT THESE TUNES WERE SUPPOSED TO BE SIMPLE!
TWONG
TWANG!
ONE DAY HE WAS DOING A GIG, SINGING AND PLAYING HIS SIMPLE MELODIES!
HIS FANS WERE THROWING FLOWERS AT HIM...
BUT...
I HAVEN'T GOT ANY FLOWERS...
I'VE GOT A FIG! FLOWER FRUIT... BOTH BEGIN WITH AN "F"..
AH - WHAT THE HELL...
YOU'RE FAB, TERPANDER!
PLOP!
GLAK
GLAK
GLAK
GAK
HEHEH... WELL, WASN'T THAT ODD? I BET I COULDN'T DO THAT AGAIN IF I TRIED!

THE HAUNTED QUARK

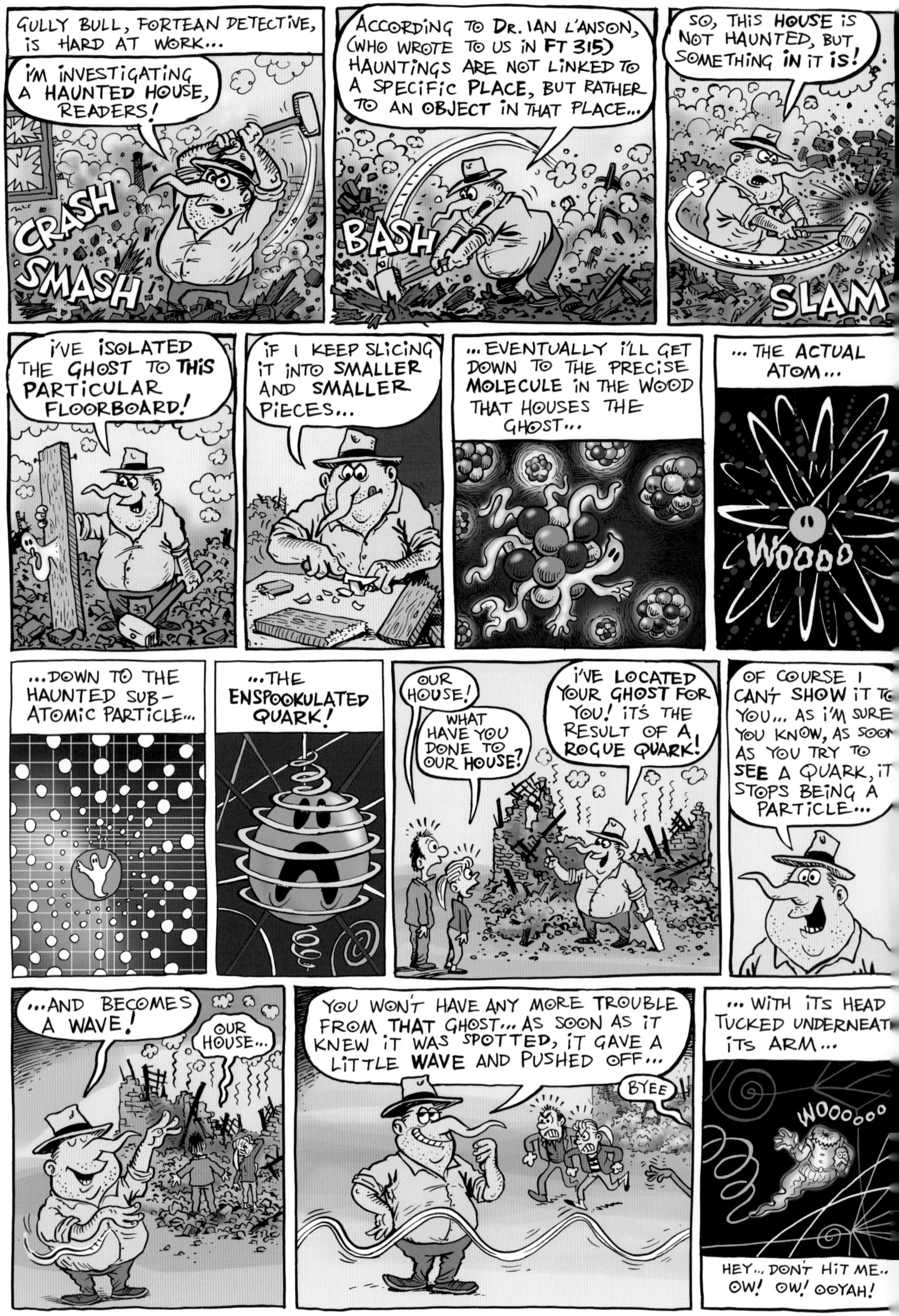

GULLY BULL, FORTEAN DETECTIVE, IS HARD AT WORK...
I'M INVESTIGATING A HAUNTED HOUSE, READERS!
CRASH
SMASH
ACCORDING TO DR. IAN L'ANSON, (WHO WROTE TO US IN FT 315) HAUNTINGS ARE NOT LINKED TO A SPECIFIC PLACE, BUT RATHER TO AN OBJECT IN THAT PLACE...
BASH
SO, THIS HOUSE IS NOT HAUNTED, BUT SOMETHING IN IT IS!
SLAM
I'VE ISOLATED THE GHOST TO THIS PARTICULAR FLOORBOARD!
IF I KEEP SLICING IT INTO SMALLER AND SMALLER PIECES...
...EVENTUALLY I'LL GET DOWN TO THE PRECISE MOLECULE IN THE WOOD THAT HOUSES THE GHOST...
...THE ACTUAL ATOM...
WOOOO
...DOWN TO THE HAUNTED SUB-ATOMIC PARTICLE...
...THE ENSPOOKULATED QUARK!
OUR HOUSE!
WHAT HAVE YOU DONE TO OUR HOUSE?
I'VE LOCATED YOUR GHOST FOR YOU! IT'S THE RESULT OF A ROGUE QUARK!
OF COURSE I CAN'T SHOW IT TO YOU... AS I'M SURE YOU KNOW, AS SOON AS YOU TRY TO SEE A QUARK, IT STOPS BEING A PARTICLE...
...AND BECOMES A WAVE!
OUR HOUSE...
YOU WON'T HAVE ANY MORE TROUBLE FROM THAT GHOST... AS SOON AS IT KNEW IT WAS SPOTTED, IT GAVE A LITTLE WAVE AND PUSHED OFF...
BYEE
...WITH ITS HEAD TUCKED UNDERNEATH ITS ARM...
WOOOoooo
HEY... DON'T HIT ME.. OW! OW! OOYAH!

HE HOLLOW EARTH

DID YOU KNOW THE EARTH IS HOLLOW?

THERE IS A HOLE AT THE NORTH POLE THAT GIVES ACCESS TO THE INSIDE OF THE PLANET! IT'S TRUE!

THE FACTS MAY BE SUPPRESSED BY SCIENTIFIC ORTHODOXY, BUT IT IS TRUE!

BUT NEVER MIND THE CONSPIRACY THEORIES — WHAT DOES THE HOLLOW EARTH MEAN IN COSMOLOGICAL TERMS?

WELL, AS OUR PLANET SPINS THROUGH SPACE, THE COSMIC WIND THAT SURROUNDS IT BLOWS ACROSS THE POLE HOLE AND MAKES A NOTE...

...LIKE WHEN YOU BLOW ON THE NECK OF A BOTTLE!

HOOT

AND NOT ONLY THAT! THE PLANET IS PITTED WITH OTHER HOLES INTO THE INTERIOR — VOLCANOES AND SUCHLIKE...

EACH OF THESE HOLES ALTERS THE COSMIC WIND NOTE, AND TOGETHER, OVER TIME, THEY MAKE UP A TUNE UNIQUE TO THE EARTH...

A TRUE MUSIC OF THE SPHERES!

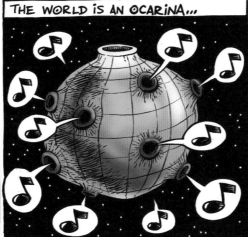

THE WORLD IS AN OCARINA...

...BUT WHO IS THE OCARINIST? EH? EH?

TWEET TOOT

?

TWEETLE TOOTLE

THE HORNED TURNIP

I'VE GOT A LETTER HERE FROM A SMALLHOLDER IN WARWICKSHIRE... A MR. K. WHITE... HE SAYS HE'S GROWN A CROP OF HORNED TURNIPS...

HMM... LET'S SEE WHAT I CAN FIND IN THE LITERATURE...

THE BIG BOOK OF WEIRD VEGETABLES

"A 'DEVYLS TURNYPE' WAS PRESENTED TO QUEEN ELIZABETH IN THE YEAR 1600.."

"...AND IT SEEMS THAT ROBERT BURNS WROTE A BALLAD CALLED 'AULD NICK'S NEEP!..."

'FOR WHA'D BE FEUL TAE FEED HIS SHEEP WI' SIC' A THING AS AULD NICK'S NEEP!'

OH RABBIE! THAT'S BYEWTIFU'!

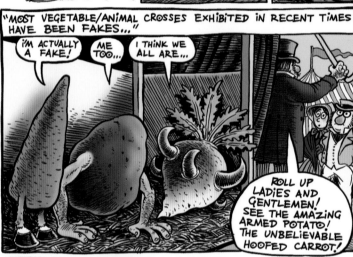

"MOST VEGETABLE/ANIMAL CROSSES EXHIBITED IN RECENT TIMES HAVE BEEN FAKES..."

I'M ACTUALLY A FAKE!

ME TOO...

I THINK WE ALL ARE...

ROLL UP LADIES AND GENTLEMEN! SEE THE AMAZING ARMED POTATO! THE UNBELIEVABLE HOOFED CARROT!

"THE LAST GENUINE REPORT OF A HORNED TURNIP WAS IN 1847, AS REPORTED IN HORNIBLOW'S MAGAZINE FOR APRIL OF THAT YEAR!"

Horned Turnip. This true and genuine marvel was grow... this year in the County of Essex... your attention to the... whilst the horn...

I'M GOING TO VISIT MR. WHITE!

AH! WHITE! I'M HERE TO SEE YOUR HORNED TURNIPS!

OH, THEY, SIR! WELL, I COOKED AND ATE 'EM...

YOU WHAT?! YOU'VE EATEN THE EVIDENCE!?

YES, SIR...

GREAT GALLOPING GANDERFLAPS! WELL...WELL...WHAT DID THEY TASTE LIKE?

LIKE TURNIP!

NOT THE TURNIPS, YOU IDIOT! THE HORNS! WHAT DID THE HORNS TASTE LIKE?

OH... YUMMM- SPICY!

I DID TAKE A SNAP OF ONE OF THE TURNIPS WITH MY LITTLE CAMERA!

A PHOTO? THANK HEAVENS! PROOF!

This strip is based on **actual events,** invented by the author.

The photograph taken by Mr. White, naturally, didn't come out.

96

VAMPIRE MOVIE

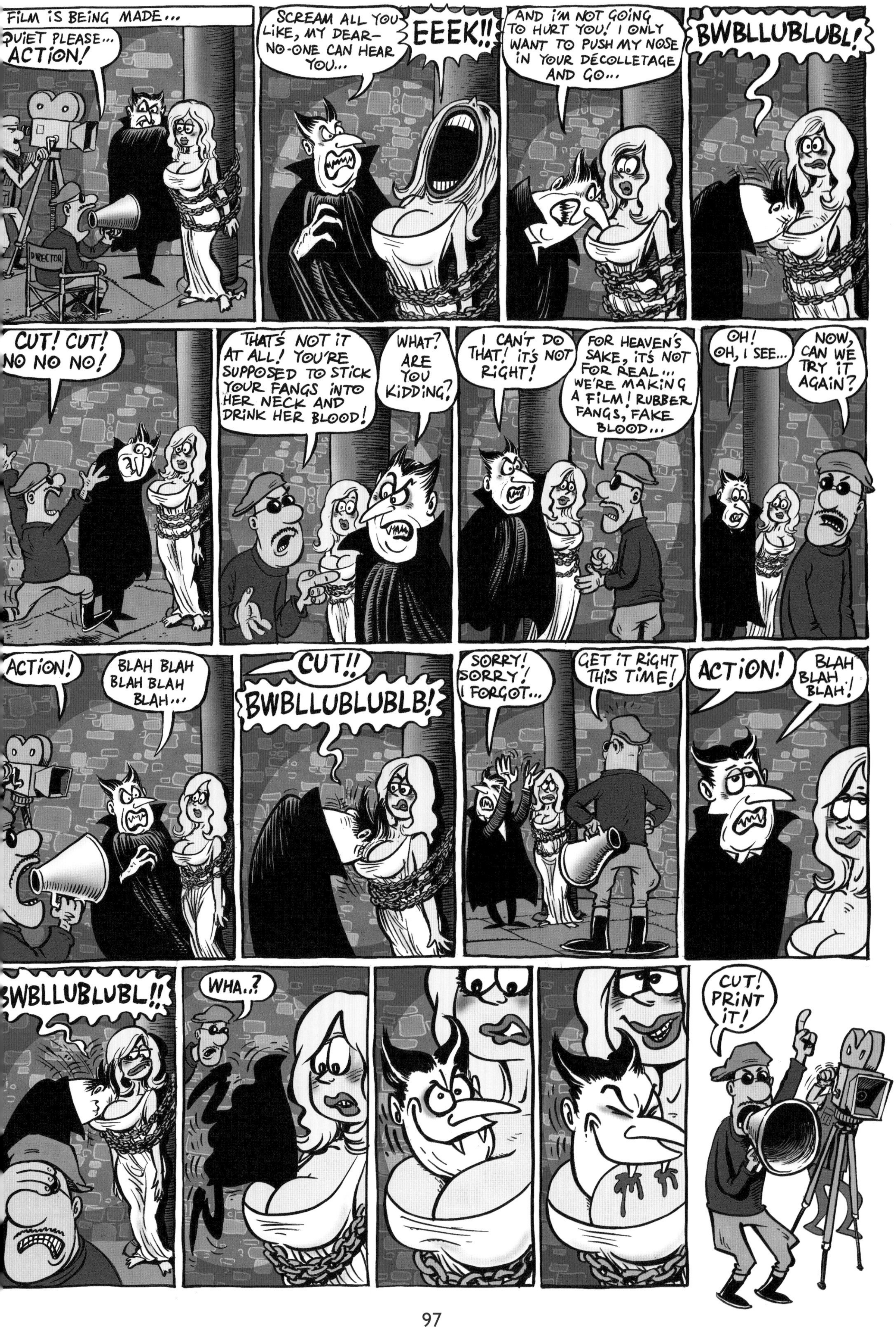

FILM IS BEING MADE...
QUIET PLEASE... ACTION!
DIRECTOR
SCREAM ALL YOU LIKE, MY DEAR- NO-ONE CAN HEAR YOU...
EEEK!!
AND I'M NOT GOING TO HURT YOU! I ONLY WANT TO PUSH MY NOSE IN YOUR DÉCOLLETAGE AND GO...
BWBLLUBLUBL!
CUT! CUT! NO NO NO!
THAT'S NOT IT AT ALL! YOU'RE SUPPOSED TO STICK YOUR FANGS INTO HER NECK AND DRINK HER BLOOD!
WHAT? ARE YOU KIDDING?
I CAN'T DO THAT! IT'S NOT RIGHT!
FOR HEAVEN'S SAKE, IT'S NOT FOR REAL... WE'RE MAKING A FILM! RUBBER FANGS, FAKE BLOOD...
OH! OH, I SEE...
NOW, CAN WE TRY IT AGAIN?
ACTION!
BLAH BLAH BLAH BLAH BLAH...
CUT!!
BWBLLUBLUBLB!
SORRY! SORRY! I FORGOT...
GET IT RIGHT THIS TIME!
ACTION!
BLAH BLAH BLAH!
BWBLLUBLUBL!!
WHA..?
CUT! PRINT IT!

HORNSWOGGLED

THE NAME'S BULL... GULLY BULL! I'M A PARANORMAL DETECTIVE... AN INVESTIGATOR OF STRANGE PHENOMENA!

I WAS FOLLOWING UP SIGHTINGS OF A STRANGE ANIMAL... AS USUAL, THE WITNESSES SEEMED LIKE ORDINARY FOLK...

WOULD YOU SAY IT WAS A LARGE CAT OF SOME SORT?

'TWERE LIKE NO CAT I'VE EVER SEEN SIR...

NO...

IT WERE A BROWN COLOUR... SIX FEET HIGH... STOOD ON BIG HIND LEGS... WITH A LONG TAIL... A DARK MUZZLE...

...AND A BIG HORN ON ITS SNOUT, SIR!

AND DID IT LEAVE ANY TRACKS?

NO, SIR— NO TRACKS... JUST A SMELL!

MY NOSE IS A HIGHLY TRAINED INSTRUMENT, SENSITIVE TO THE SLIGHTEST ODOUR OF STRANGENESS...

SILENCE, PLEASE... I MUST CONCENTRATE!

I SHOULD BE CAREFUL IF I WERE YOU, SIR...

SNIFF SNIFF...

GOOD GRIEF!! WHAT A PONG!!!

AS I RECOVERED, I PONDERED OVER MY FINDINGS...

A STRANGE ANIMAL IS SEEN IN AN ORDINARY SUBURB...

IT APPEARS TO BE A KANGAROO WITH A HORN ON ITS NOSE...

...AND IT SMELLS UNBELIEVABLY BAD!

COULD I BE ON THE TRAIL OF AN UNDISCOVERED ANIMAL?

BUT HOW COULD ANYTHING THAT SMELL LIKE THAT REMAIN UNNOTICED?

...AND, DO I REALLY WANT TO DISCOVER IT? THAT SMELL... OOHHH....

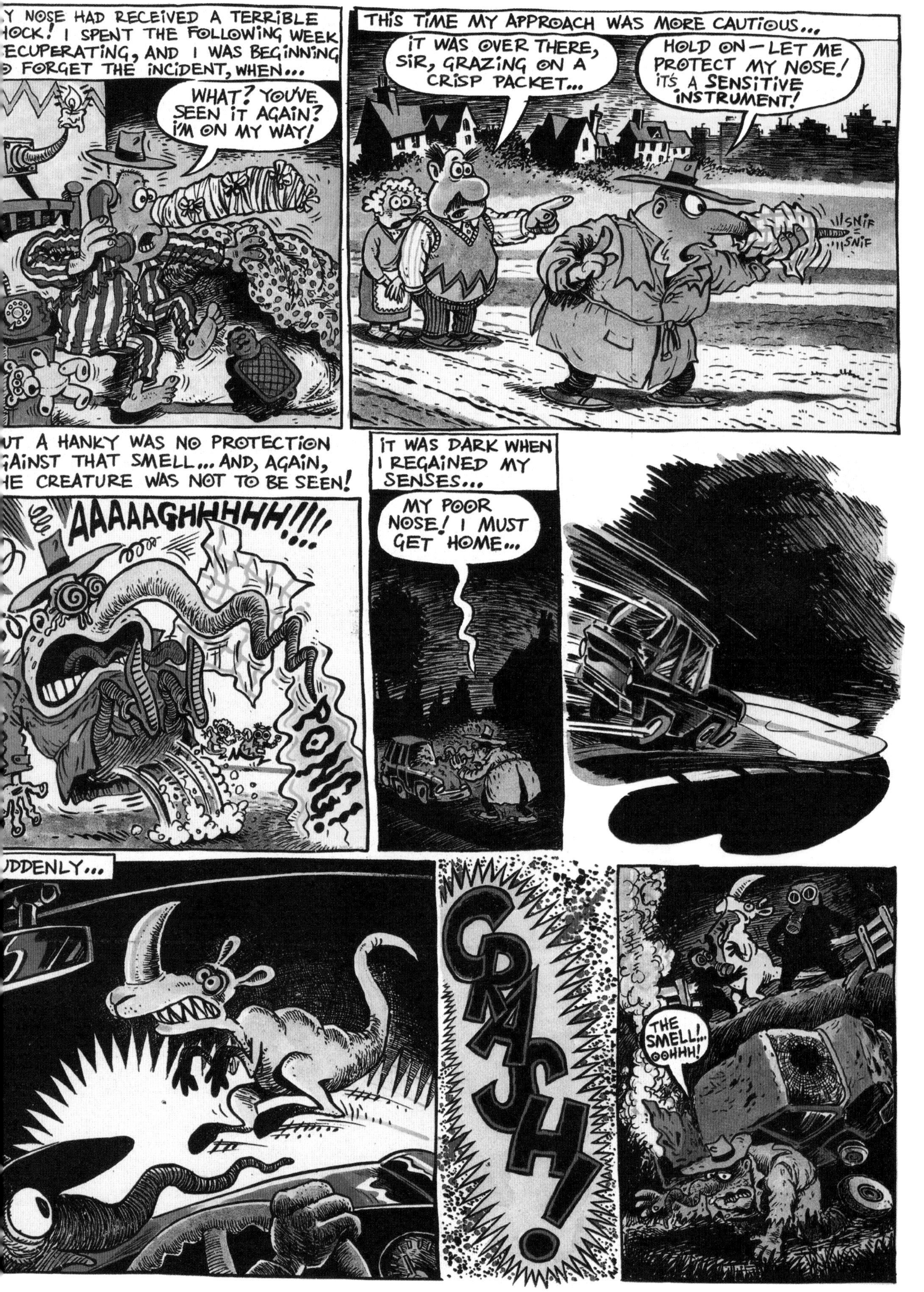
Y NOSE HAD RECEIVED A TERRIBLE HOCK! I SPENT THE FOLLOWING WEEK ECUPERATING, AND I WAS BEGINNING O FORGET THE INCIDENT, WHEN...
WHAT? YOU'VE SEEN IT AGAIN? I'M ON MY WAY!
THIS TIME MY APPROACH WAS MORE CAUTIOUS...
IT WAS OVER THERE, SIR, GRAZING ON A CRISP PACKET...
HOLD ON—LET ME PROTECT MY NOSE! IT'S A SENSITIVE INSTRUMENT!
SNIF SNIF
UT A HANKY WAS NO PROTECTION GAINST THAT SMELL... AND, AGAIN, HE CREATURE WAS NOT TO BE SEEN!
AAAAAGHHHHH!!!!...
PONG!
IT WAS DARK WHEN I REGAINED MY SENSES...
MY POOR NOSE! I MUST GET HOME...
UDDENLY...
CRASH!
THE SMELL!... OOHHH!

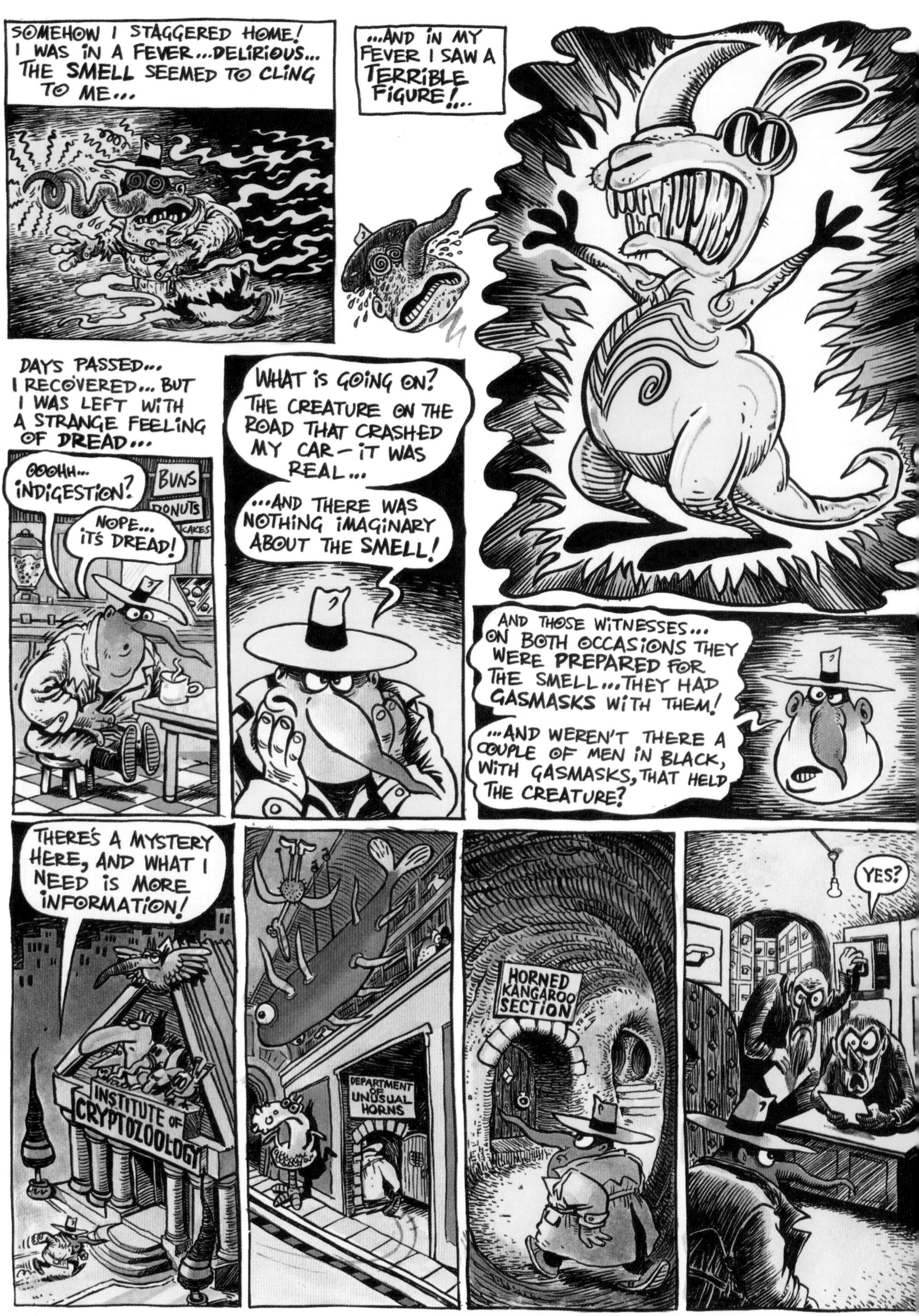
SOMEHOW I STAGGERED HOME! I WAS IN A FEVER...DELIRIOUS... THE SMELL SEEMED TO CLING TO ME...
...AND IN MY FEVER I SAW A TERRIBLE FIGURE!...
DAYS PASSED... I RECOVERED... BUT I WAS LEFT WITH A STRANGE FEELING OF DREAD...
OOOHH... INDIGESTION?
NOPE... IT'S DREAD!
BUNS
DONUTS
CAKES
WHAT IS GOING ON? THE CREATURE ON THE ROAD THAT CRASHED MY CAR – IT WAS REAL...
...AND THERE WAS NOTHING IMAGINARY ABOUT THE SMELL!
AND THOSE WITNESSES... ON BOTH OCCASIONS THEY WERE PREPARED FOR THE SMELL...THEY HAD GASMASKS WITH THEM!
...AND WEREN'T THERE A COUPLE OF MEN IN BLACK, WITH GASMASKS, THAT HELD THE CREATURE?
THERE'S A MYSTERY HERE, AND WHAT I NEED IS MORE INFORMATION!
INSTITUTE OF CRYPTOZOOLOGY
DEPARTMENT OF UNUSUAL HORNS
HORNED KANGAROO SECTION
YES?

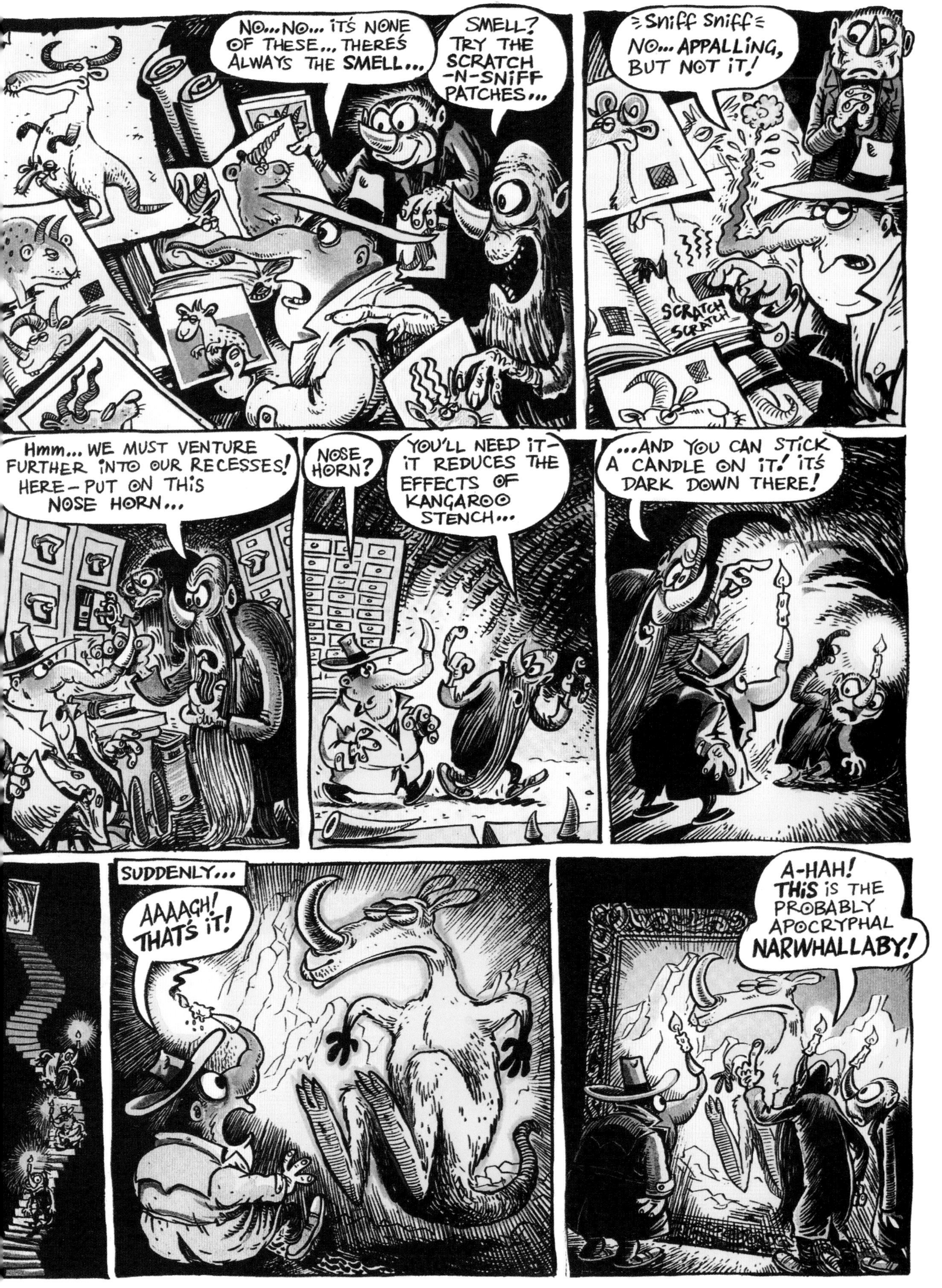
NO...NO... IT'S NONE OF THESE... THERE'S ALWAYS THE SMELL...
SMELL? TRY THE SCRATCH -N-SNIFF PATCHES...
Sniff Sniff
NO... APPALLING, BUT NOT IT!
SCRATCH SCRATCH
Hmm... WE MUST VENTURE FURTHER INTO OUR RECESSES! HERE- PUT ON THIS NOSE HORN...
NOSE HORN?
YOU'LL NEED IT- IT REDUCES THE EFFECTS OF KANGAROO STENCH...
...AND YOU CAN STICK A CANDLE ON IT! IT'S DARK DOWN THERE!
SUDDENLY...
AAAAGH! THAT'S IT!
A-HAH! THIS is THE PROBABLY APOCRYPHAL NARWHALLABY!

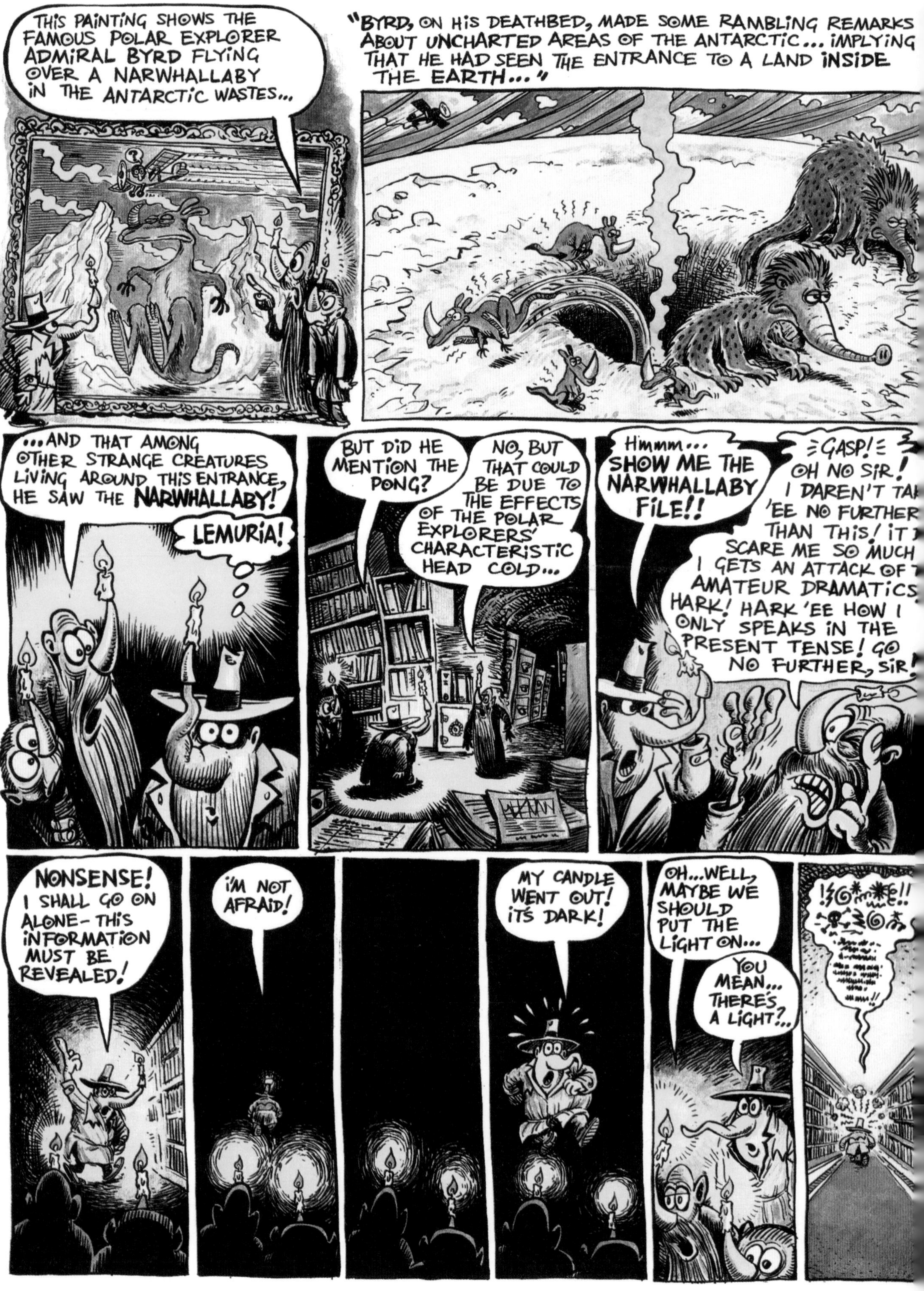
THIS PAINTING SHOWS THE FAMOUS POLAR EXPLORER ADMIRAL BYRD FLYING OVER A NARWHALLABY IN THE ANTARCTIC WASTES...
"BYRD, ON HIS DEATHBED, MADE SOME RAMBLING REMARKS ABOUT UNCHARTED AREAS OF THE ANTARCTIC... IMPLYING THAT HE HAD SEEN THE ENTRANCE TO A LAND INSIDE THE EARTH..."
...AND THAT AMONG OTHER STRANGE CREATURES LIVING AROUND THIS ENTRANCE, HE SAW THE NARWHALLABY!
LEMURIA!
BUT DID HE MENTION THE PONG?
NO, BUT THAT COULD BE DUE TO THE EFFECTS OF THE POLAR EXPLORERS' CHARACTERISTIC HEAD COLD...
Hmmm... SHOW ME THE NARWHALLABY FILE!!
GASP! OH NO SIR! I DAREN'T TA 'EE NO FURTHER THAN THIS! IT SCARE ME SO MUCH I GETS AN ATTACK OF AMATEUR DRAMATICS HARK! HARK 'EE HOW I ONLY SPEAKS IN THE PRESENT TENSE! GO NO FURTHER, SIR!
NONSENSE! I SHALL GO ON ALONE- THIS INFORMATION MUST BE REVEALED!
I'M NOT AFRAID!
MY CANDLE WENT OUT! IT'S DARK!
OH...WELL, MAYBE WE SHOULD PUT THE LIGHT ON...
YOU MEAN... THERE'S A LIGHT?..

I'VE BEEN WANDERING IN THESE CORRIDORS... THESE TUNNELS - FOR THREE DAYS NOW! FORTUNATELY, MY NOSE ALWAYS SEEMS TO KNOW WHICH TURN TO TAKE! LEFT... RIGHT... UP...OR DOWN...

TWITCH

I MUST BE MILES BELOW THE SURFACE OF THE EARTH...

TWITCH

THE SEARCH FOR THE NARWHALLABY IS NO LONGER OF PRIME IMPORTANCE TO ME... I THINK I'M ABOUT TO DISCOVER LEMURIA!!

TWITCH

LEMURIA... FABLED LAND ON THE INSIDE OF THE EARTH, ONCE INHABITED BY AN ANCIENT MASTER RACE WHO LEFT THE PLANET 12000 YEARS AGO, AND NOW LIVE IN OUTER SPACE, USING LEMURIA AS A BASE FOR THEIR UFO ACTIVITIES!

THE TUNNELS OF LEMURIA ARE NOW THE DOMAIN OF SUBHUMAN CREATURES CALLED "DEROS" —ONCE THE SLAVES OF THE MASTER RACE, AND NOW NURTURING A GRUDGE AGAINST ALL MANKIND!

THE ENTRANCES TO LEMURIA WERE THROUGH HOLES AT THE NORTH AND SOUTH POLES... BUT I'M SURE THAT I'M ABOUT TO DISCOVER ANOTHER WAY IN! OUCH!

WAK!

SOMEHOW... I EXPECTED THIS TO HAPPEN...

WALLOP!

BLANK LUMP OF TIME PASSES BLANKLY FOR BULLY BULL ...

Oooh... WHERE AM I?

IT LOOKS LIKE... A PRISON CAMP...

IT IS A PRISON CAMP, OLD BOY...AND WE'RE ALL PRISONERS OF THE LEMURIANS!

BUT... WHO ARE YOU ALL?

WE ARE FORTEANS!

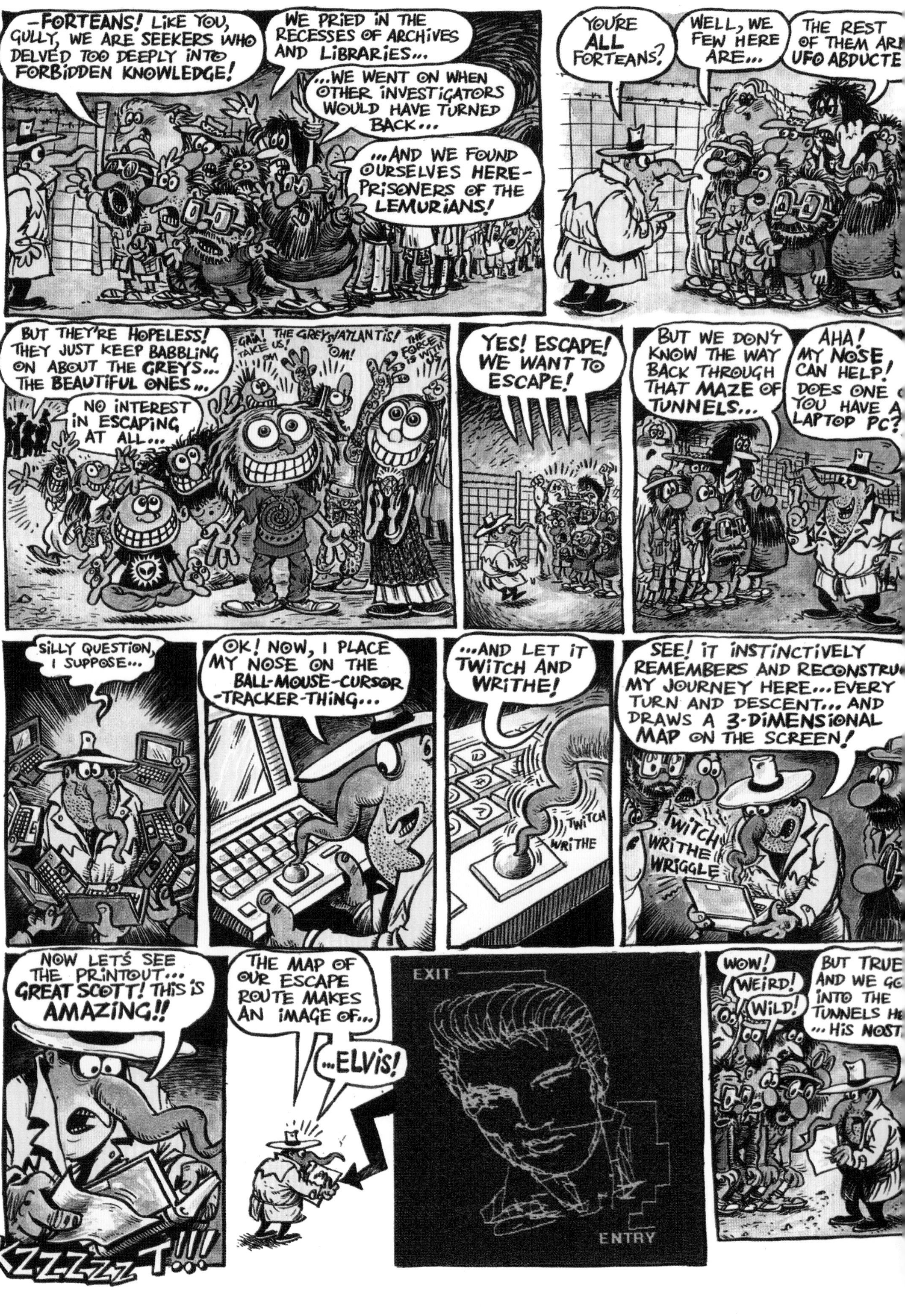

-FORTEANS! LIKE YOU, GULLY, WE ARE SEEKERS WHO DELVED TOO DEEPLY INTO FORBIDDEN KNOWLEDGE!
WE PRIED IN THE RECESSES OF ARCHIVES AND LIBRARIES...
...WE WENT ON WHEN OTHER INVESTIGATORS WOULD HAVE TURNED BACK...
...AND WE FOUND OURSELVES HERE- PRISONERS OF THE LEMURIANS!
YOU'RE ALL FORTEANS?
WELL, WE FEW HERE ARE...
THE REST OF THEM AR UFO ABDUCTE
BUT THEY'RE HOPELESS! THEY JUST KEEP BABBLING ON ABOUT THE GREYS... THE BEAUTIFUL ONES...
GAIA! TAKE US!
THE GREYS!
ATLANTIS!
OM!
THE FORCE IS WITH US
NO INTEREST IN ESCAPING AT ALL...
YES! ESCAPE! WE WANT TO ESCAPE!
BUT WE DON'T KNOW THE WAY BACK THROUGH THAT MAZE OF TUNNELS...
AHA! MY NOSE CAN HELP! DOES ONE YOU HAVE A LAPTOP PC?
SILLY QUESTION, I SUPPOSE...
OK! NOW, I PLACE MY NOSE ON THE BALL-MOUSE-CURSOR-TRACKER-THING...
...AND LET IT TWITCH AND WRITHE!
TWITCH
WRITHE
SEE! IT INSTINCTIVELY REMEMBERS AND RECONSTRU MY JOURNEY HERE... EVERY TURN AND DESCENT... AND DRAWS A 3-DIMENSIONAL MAP ON THE SCREEN!
TWITCH
WRITHE
WRIGGLE
NOW LET'S SEE THE PRINTOUT... GREAT SCOTT! THIS IS AMAZING!!
KZZZZZZT!!!
THE MAP OF OUR ESCAPE ROUTE MAKES AN IMAGE OF...
...ELVIS!
EXIT
ENTRY
WOW!
WEIRD!
WILD!
BUT TRUE AND WE GO INTO THE TUNNELS HE ...HIS NOST

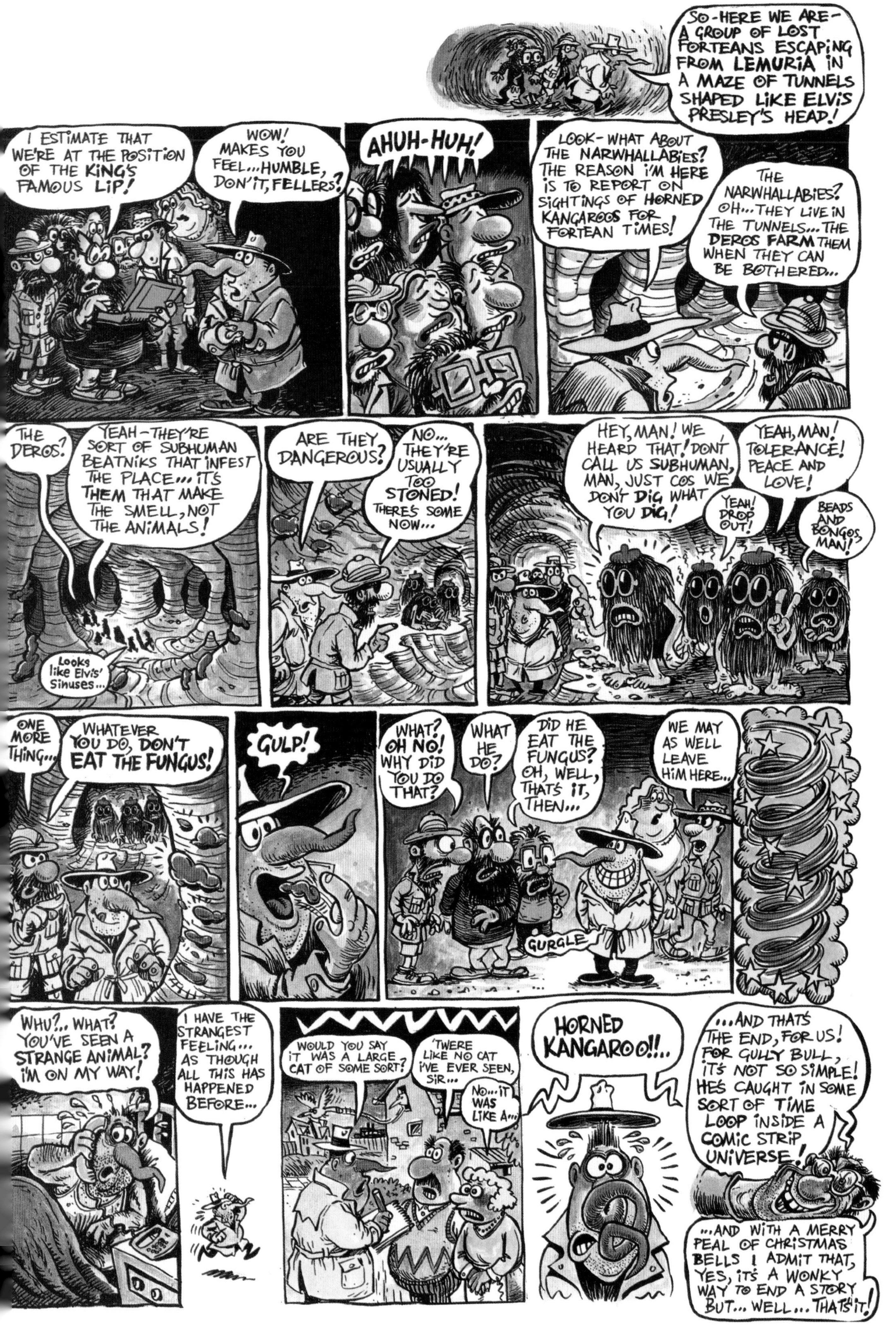
SO-HERE WE ARE- A GROUP OF LOST FORTEANS ESCAPING FROM LEMURIA IN A MAZE OF TUNNELS SHAPED LIKE ELVIS PRESLEY'S HEAD!
I ESTIMATE THAT WE'RE AT THE POSITION OF THE KING'S FAMOUS LIP!
WOW! MAKES YOU FEEL...HUMBLE, DON'T IT, FELLERS?
AHUH-HUH!
LOOK- WHAT ABOUT THE NARWHALLABIES? THE REASON I'M HERE IS TO REPORT ON SIGHTINGS OF HORNED KANGAROOS FOR FORTEAN TIMES!
THE NARWHALLABIES? OH...THEY LIVE IN THE TUNNELS...THE DEROS FARM THEM WHEN THEY CAN BE BOTHERED...
THE DEROS?
YEAH-THEY'RE SORT OF SUBHUMAN BEATNIKS THAT INFEST THE PLACE... IT'S THEM THAT MAKE THE SMELL, NOT THE ANIMALS!
Looks like Elvis' sinuses...
ARE THEY DANGEROUS?
NO... THEY'RE USUALLY TOO STONED! THERE'S SOME NOW...
HEY, MAN! WE HEARD THAT! DON'T CALL US SUBHUMAN, MAN, JUST COS WE DON'T DIG WHAT YOU DIG!
YEAH, MAN! TOLERANCE! PEACE AND LOVE!
YEAH! DROP OUT!
BEADS AND BONGOS, MAN!
ONE MORE THING...
WHATEVER YOU DO, DON'T EAT THE FUNGUS!
GULP!
WHAT? OH NO! WHY DID YOU DO THAT?
WHAT HE DO?
DID HE EAT THE FUNGUS? OH, WELL, THAT'S IT, THEN...
WE MAY AS WELL LEAVE HIM HERE...
GURGLE
WHU?.. WHAT? YOU'VE SEEN A STRANGE ANIMAL? I'M ON MY WAY!
I HAVE THE STRANGEST FEELING... AS THOUGH ALL THIS HAS HAPPENED BEFORE...
WOULD YOU SAY IT WAS A LARGE CAT OF SOME SORT?
'TWERE LIKE NO CAT I'VE EVER SEEN, SIR...
NO...IT WAS LIKE A...
HORNED KANGAROO!!...
...AND THAT'S THE END, FOR US! FOR GULLY BULL, IT'S NOT SO SIMPLE! HE'S CAUGHT IN SOME SORT OF TIME LOOP INSIDE A COMIC STRIP UNIVERSE!
...AND WITH A MERRY PEAL OF CHRISTMAS BELLS I ADMIT THAT, YES, IT'S A WONKY WAY TO END A STORY BUT... WELL... THAT'S IT!

ST. LOUIS PICAYUNE, 20 JULY 1964

I HAVE BEFORE ME THE ST. LOUIS PICAYUNE OF JULY 20TH 1964 — LET'S LOOK AT A FEW OF THE NEWS STORIES...

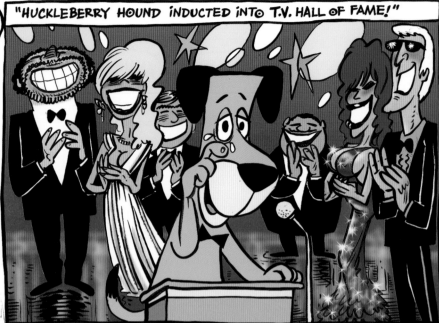

"HUCKLEBERRY HOUND INDUCTED INTO T.V. HALL OF FAME!"

"ROAD CRASH TOPPLES NITESPOT LANDMARK!"

Pixie LOUNGE
BAR · GRILLS · DANCING · POOL

Mr.J INKS

DIXIE DELIVERIES

CRASH!

ZOOOM

SCREECH

AND HERE'S A STORY ABOUT BASEBALL STAR YOGI BERRA, WHO BOUGHT A HUCKLEBERRY PIE AND THEN SAW IT STOLEN AND EATEN BY A HOUND-DOG!

PIES

AND THEY TRY AND TELL ME THERE'S NO MEANING TO EXISTENCE...

ICE MAN

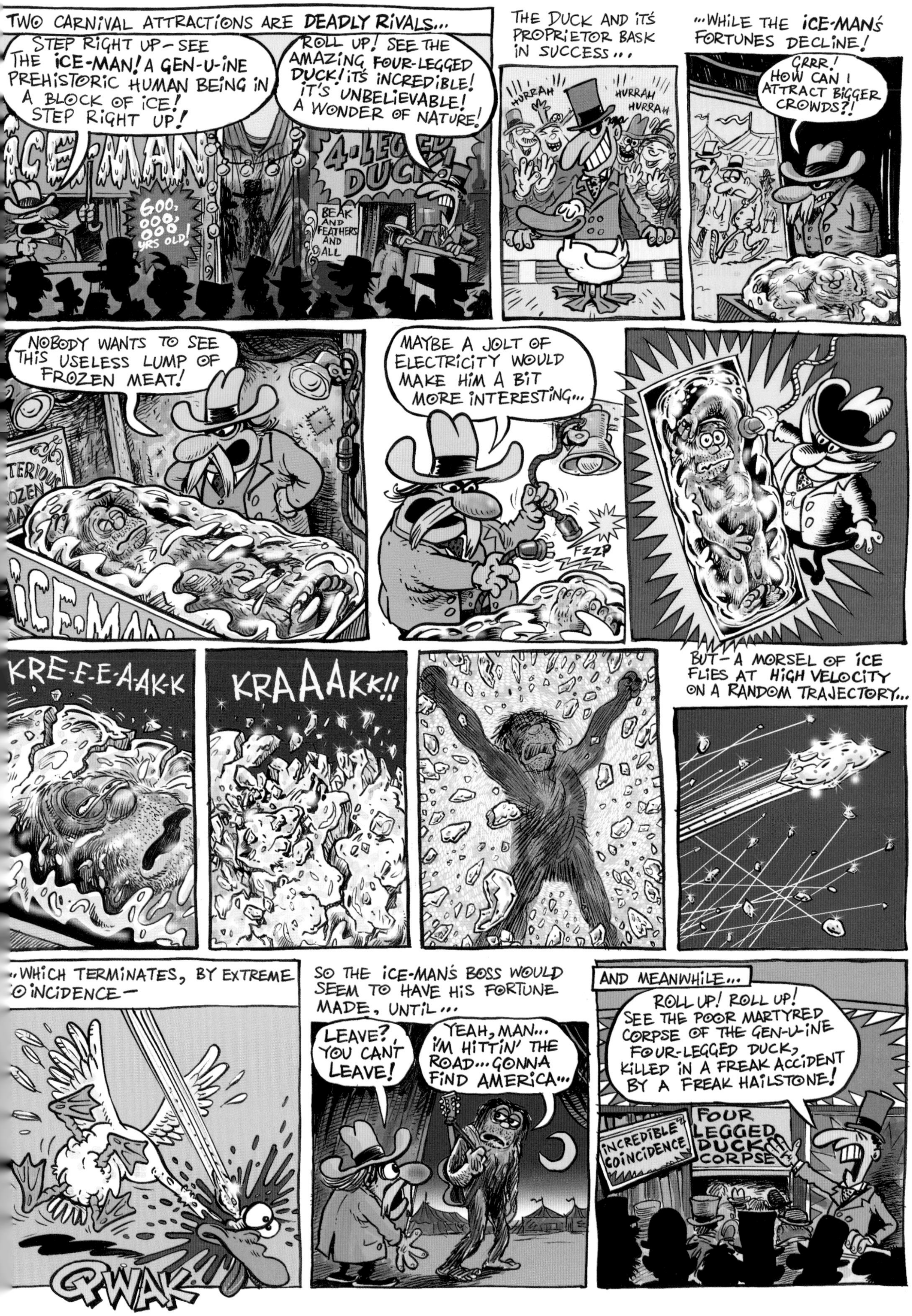

TWO CARNIVAL ATTRACTIONS ARE DEADLY RIVALS...
STEP RIGHT UP—SEE THE ICE-MAN! A GEN-U-INE PREHISTORIC HUMAN BEING IN A BLOCK OF ICE! STEP RIGHT UP!
ROLL UP! SEE THE AMAZING FOUR-LEGGED DUCK! IT'S INCREDIBLE! IT'S UNBELIEVABLE! A WONDER OF NATURE!
ICE-MAN
600,000,000 YRS OLD!
4-LEGGED DUCK
BEAK AND FEATHERS AND ALL
THE DUCK AND IT'S PROPRIETOR BASK IN SUCCESS...
HURRAH
HURRAH HURRAH
...WHILE THE ICE-MAN'S FORTUNES DECLINE!
GRRR! HOW CAN I ATTRACT BIGGER CROWDS?!
NOBODY WANTS TO SEE THIS USELESS LUMP OF FROZEN MEAT!
MAYBE A JOLT OF ELECTRICITY WOULD MAKE HIM A BIT MORE INTERESTING...
FZZP
KRE-E-E-A-AK-K
KRAAAKK!!
BUT—A MORSEL OF ICE FLIES AT HIGH VELOCITY ON A RANDOM TRAJECTORY...
...WHICH TERMINATES, BY EXTREME COINCIDENCE—
QWAK!
SO THE ICE-MAN'S BOSS WOULD SEEM TO HAVE HIS FORTUNE MADE, UNTIL...
LEAVE? YOU CAN'T LEAVE!
YEAH, MAN... I'M HITTIN' THE ROAD... GONNA FIND AMERICA...
AND MEANWHILE...
ROLL UP! ROLL UP! SEE THE POOR MARTYRED CORPSE OF THE GEN-U-INE FOUR-LEGGED DUCK, KILLED IN A FREAK ACCIDENT BY A FREAK HAILSTONE!
INCREDIBLE COINCIDENCE
FOUR LEGGED DUCK CORPSE

IN A THOUSAND YEARS

Based on

IN A THOUSAND YEARS

by Hans Christian Andersen - 1852

*Yes,
in a thousand years
people will fly on the
wings of steam
through the air,
over the ocean!
The young inhabitants
of America will become
visitors of Old Europe.
They will come over to
see the monuments
and the great cities,
which will then be in
ruins, just as we, in
our time, make
pilgrimages to the
tottering splendors
of Southern Asia.
In a thousand years
they will come!*

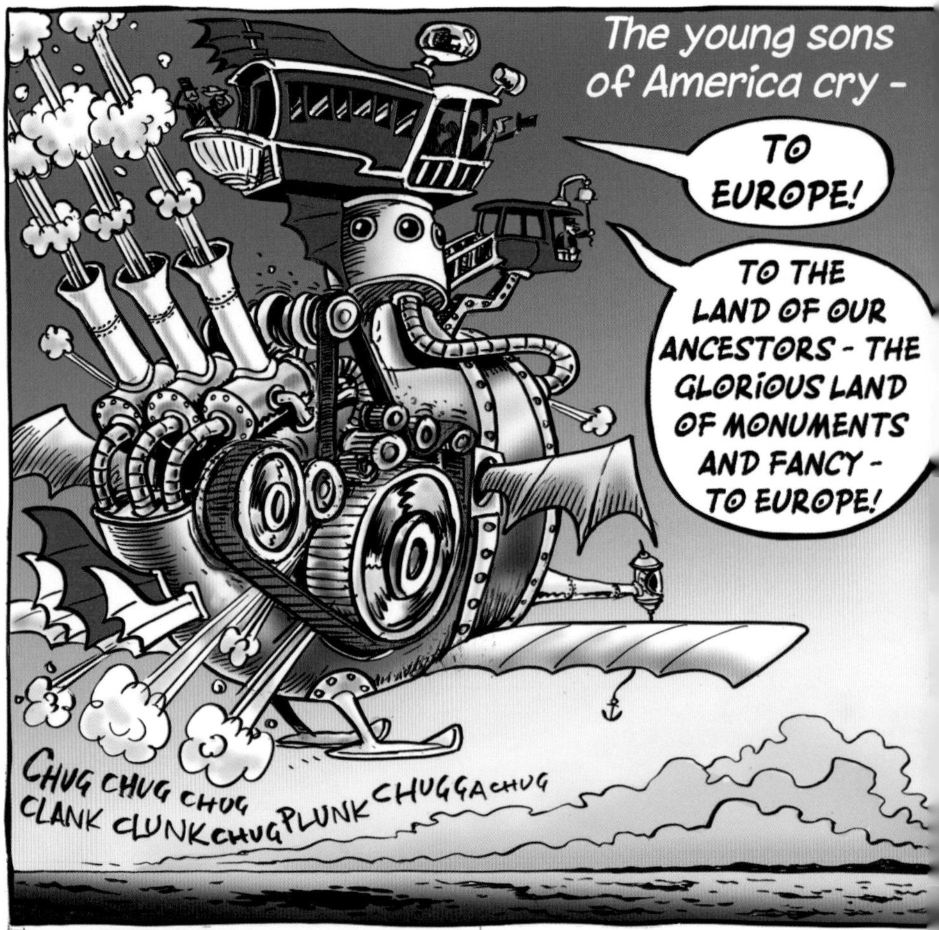
The young sons of America cry -
TO EUROPE!
TO THE LAND OF OUR ANCESTORS - THE GLORIOUS LAND OF MONUMENTS AND FANCY - TO EUROPE!
CHUG CHUG CHUG
CLANK CLUNK CHUG PLUNK CHUGGA CHUG

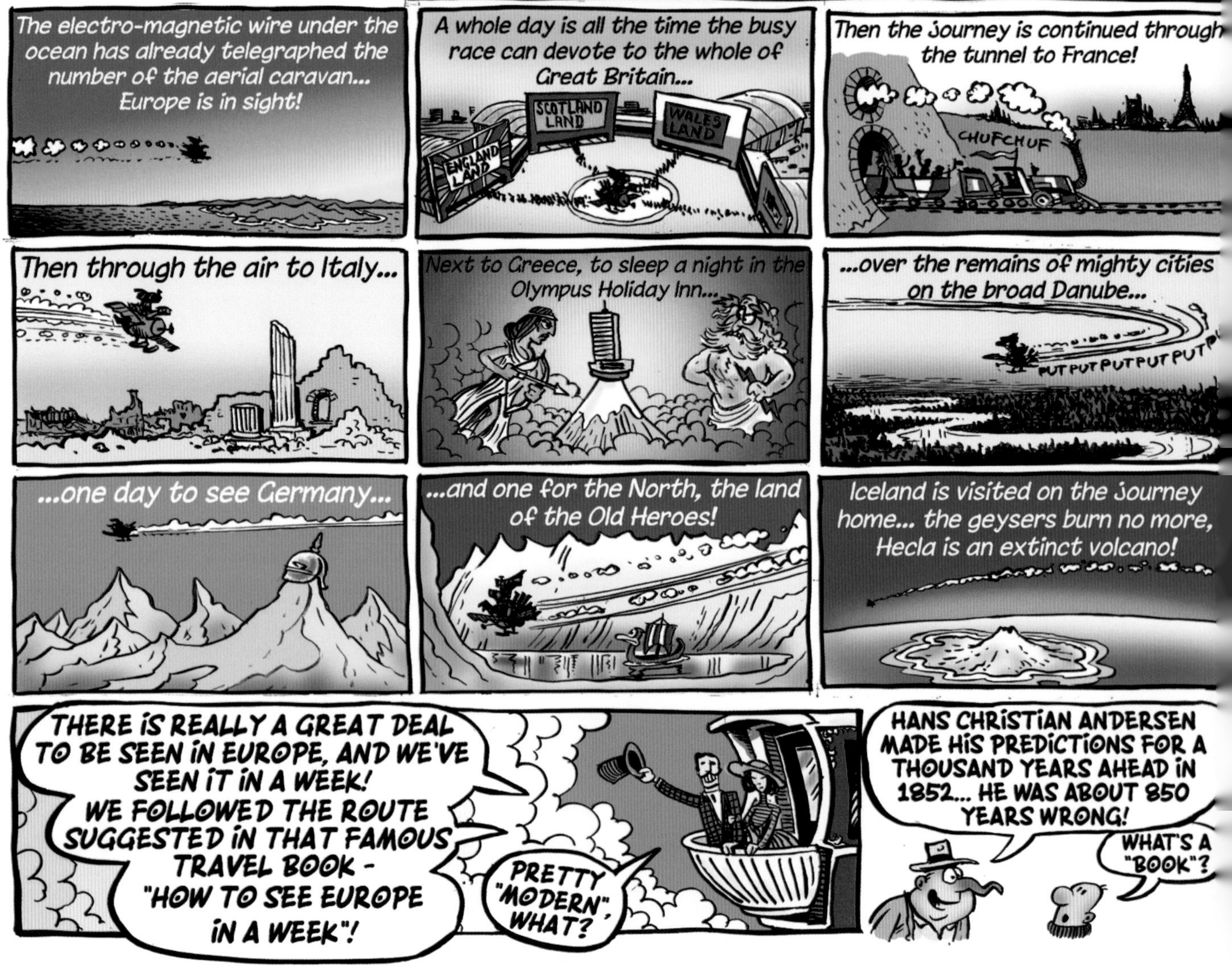
The electro-magnetic wire under the ocean has already telegraphed the number of the aerial caravan... Europe is in sight!
A whole day is all the time the busy race can devote to the whole of Great Britain...
ENGLAND LAND
SCOTLAND LAND
WALES LAND
Then the journey is continued through the tunnel to France!
CHUF CHUF
Then through the air to Italy...
Next to Greece, to sleep a night in the Olympus Holiday Inn...
...over the remains of mighty cities on the broad Danube...
PUT PUT PUT PUT PUT PUT
...one day to see Germany...
...and one for the North, the land of the Old Heroes!
Iceland is visited on the journey home... the geysers burn no more, Hecla is an extinct volcano!
THERE IS REALLY A GREAT DEAL TO BE SEEN IN EUROPE, AND WE'VE SEEN IT IN A WEEK! WE FOLLOWED THE ROUTE SUGGESTED IN THAT FAMOUS TRAVEL BOOK - "HOW TO SEE EUROPE IN A WEEK"!
PRETTY "MODERN", WHAT?
HANS CHRISTIAN ANDERSEN MADE HIS PREDICTIONS FOR A THOUSAND YEARS AHEAD IN 1852... HE WAS ABOUT 850 YEARS WRONG!
WHAT'S A "BOOK"?

INDIAN POPE TRICK

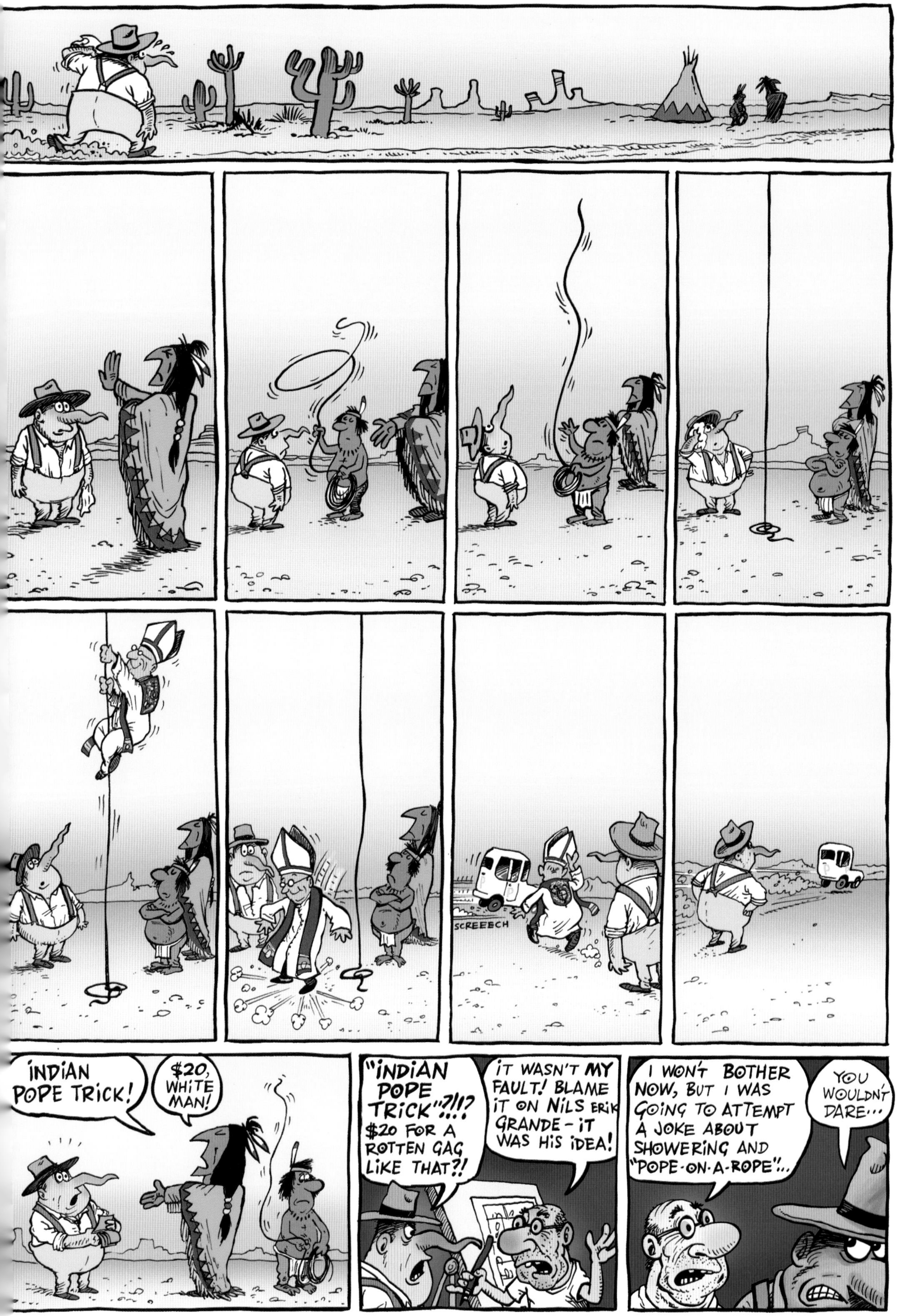
SCREEECH
INDIAN POPE TRICK!
$20, WHITE MAN!
"INDIAN POPE TRICK"?!!? $20 FOR A ROTTEN GAG LIKE THAT?!
IT WASN'T MY FAULT! BLAME IT ON NILS ERIK GRANDE – IT WAS HIS IDEA!
I WON'T BOTHER NOW, BUT I WAS GOING TO ATTEMPT A JOKE ABOUT SHOWERING AND "POPE-ON-A-ROPE"...
YOU WOULDN'T DARE...

ANCIENT UFO

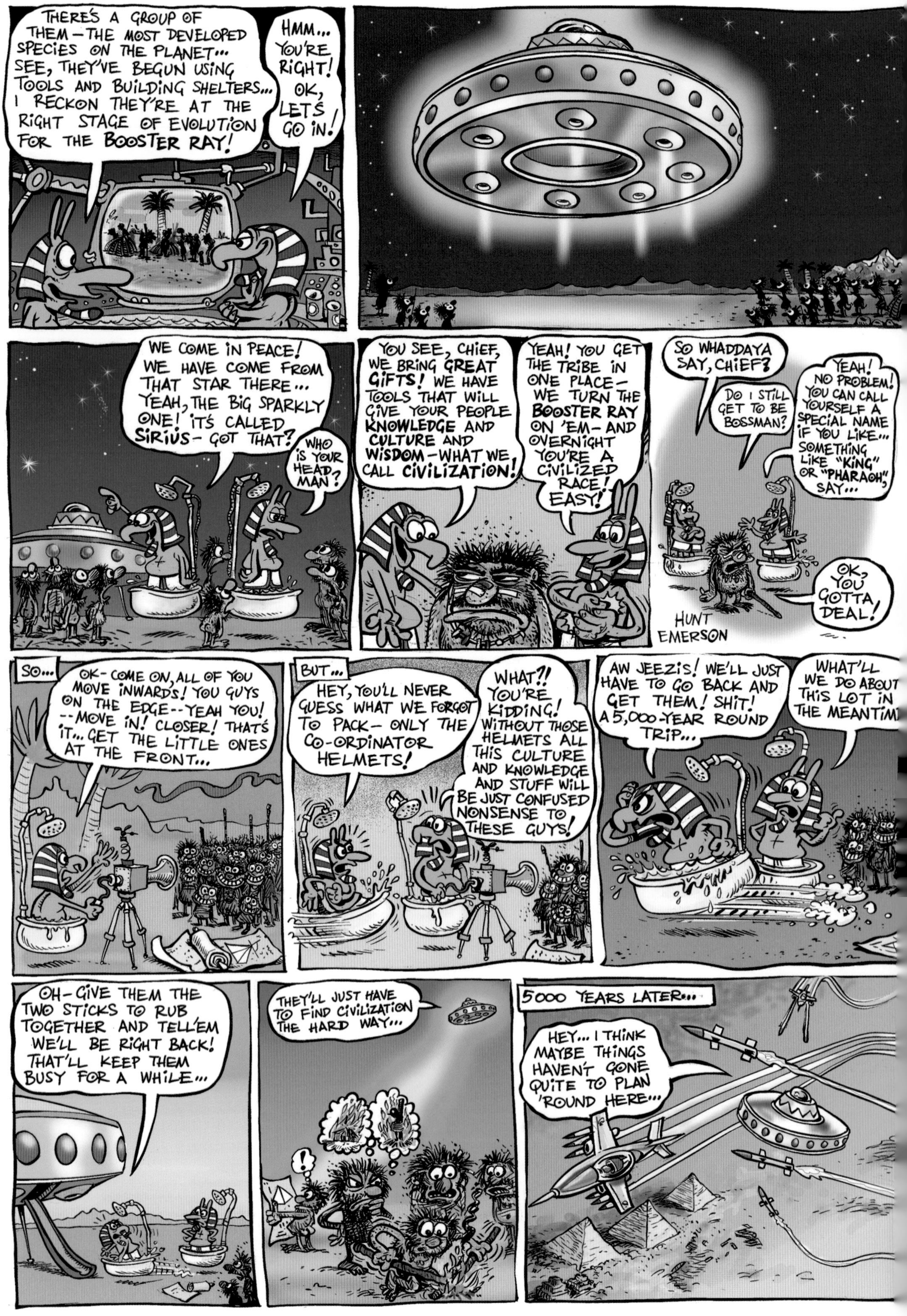
THERE'S A GROUP OF THEM—THE MOST DEVELOPED SPECIES ON THE PLANET... SEE, THEY'VE BEGUN USING TOOLS AND BUILDING SHELTERS... I RECKON THEY'RE AT THE RIGHT STAGE OF EVOLUTION FOR THE BOOSTER RAY!
HMM... YOU'RE RIGHT! OK, LET'S GO IN!
WE COME IN PEACE! WE HAVE COME FROM THAT STAR THERE... YEAH, THE BIG SPARKLY ONE! IT'S CALLED SIRIUS—GOT THAT?
WHO IS YOUR HEAD MAN?
YOU SEE, CHIEF, WE BRING GREAT GIFTS! WE HAVE TOOLS THAT WILL GIVE YOUR PEOPLE KNOWLEDGE AND CULTURE AND WISDOM—WHAT WE CALL CIVILIZATION!
YEAH! YOU GET THE TRIBE IN ONE PLACE—WE TURN THE BOOSTER RAY ON 'EM—AND OVERNIGHT YOU'RE A CIVILIZED RACE! EASY!
SO WHADDAYA SAY, CHIEF?
DO I STILL GET TO BE BOSSMAN?
YEAH! NO PROBLEM! YOU CAN CALL YOURSELF A SPECIAL NAME IF YOU LIKE... SOMETHING LIKE "KING" OR "PHARAOH," SAY...
OK, YOU GOTTA DEAL!
HUNT EMERSON
SO...
OK—COME ON, ALL OF YOU MOVE INWARDS! YOU GUYS ON THE EDGE--YEAH YOU! --MOVE IN! CLOSER! THAT'S IT... GET THE LITTLE ONES AT THE FRONT...
BUT...
HEY, YOU'LL NEVER GUESS WHAT WE FORGOT TO PACK—ONLY THE CO-ORDINATOR HELMETS!
WHAT?! YOU'RE KIDDING! WITHOUT THOSE HELMETS ALL THIS CULTURE AND KNOWLEDGE AND STUFF WILL BE JUST CONFUSED NONSENSE TO THESE GUYS!
AW JEEZIS! WE'LL JUST HAVE TO GO BACK AND GET THEM! SHIT! A 5,000-YEAR ROUND TRIP...
WHAT'LL WE DO ABOUT THIS LOT IN THE MEANTIME
OH—GIVE THEM THE TWO STICKS TO RUB TOGETHER AND TELL'EM WE'LL BE RIGHT BACK! THAT'LL KEEP THEM BUSY FOR A WHILE...
THEY'LL JUST HAVE TO FIND CIVILIZATION THE HARD WAY...
5000 YEARS LATER...
HEY... I THINK MAYBE THINGS HAVEN'T GONE QUITE TO PLAN 'ROUND HERE...

LEY LINES

FOR JOHN MICHELL

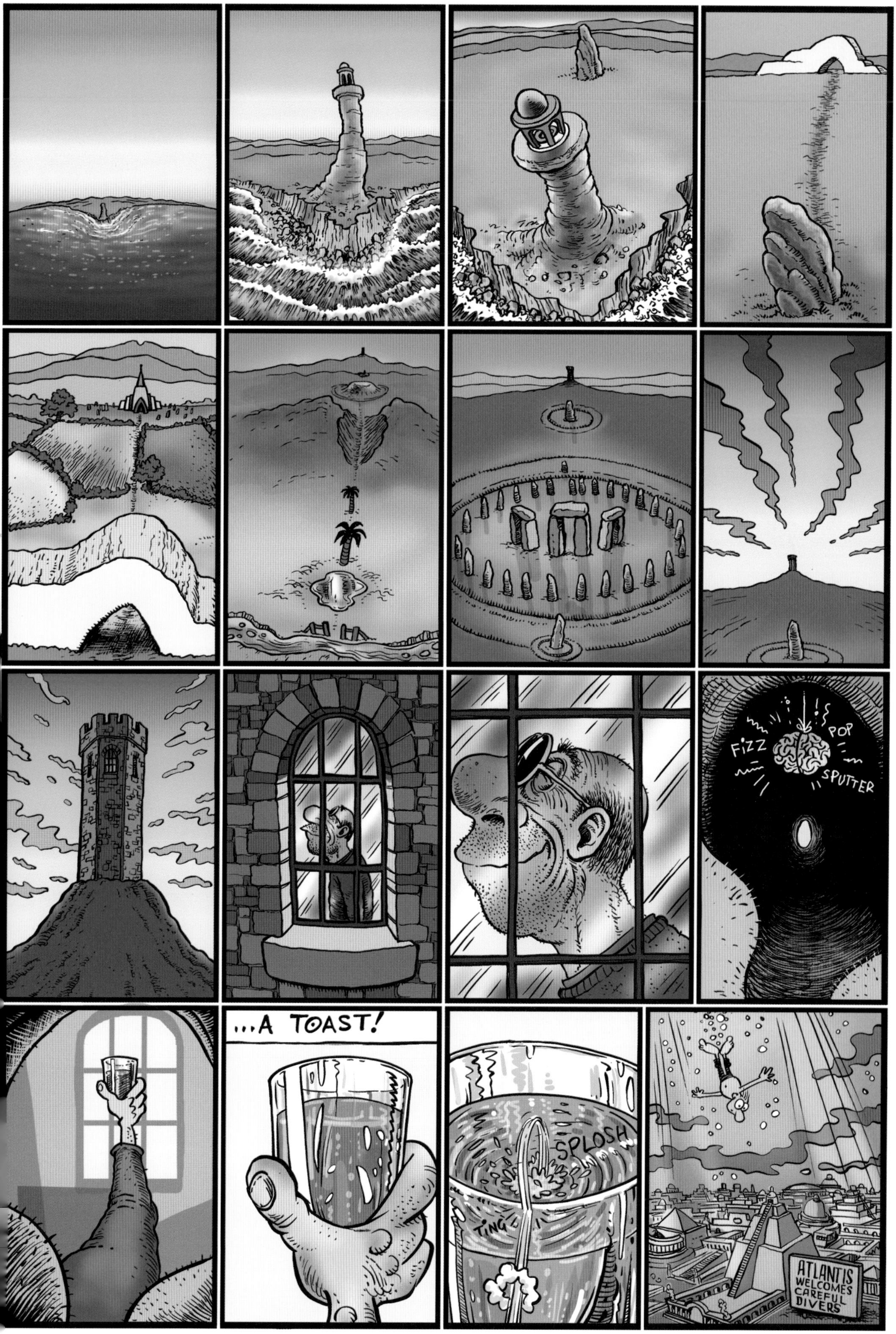

FIZZ
POP
SPUTTER
...A TOAST!
SPLOSH
TING
ATLANTIS WELCOMES CAREFUL DIVERS

MIRACLE AT LORDS

LOURDES IS, OF COURSE, WORLD FAMOUS FOR APPEARANCES BY THE **BVM***, AND FOR ASSOCIATED MIRACLES — EYESIGHT TO THE BLIND, THE LAME MADE TO WALK, ILLNESSES CURED AND SO ON... AMAZING!

*BLESSED VIRGIN MARY

SO WHY AM I HERE, AT LORDS CRICKET GROUND IN LONDON?

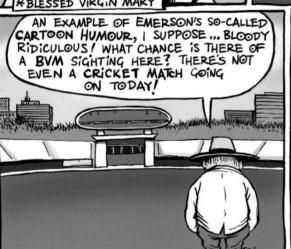

AN EXAMPLE OF EMERSON'S SO-CALLED **CARTOON HUMOUR**, I SUPPOSE... BLOODY RIDICULOUS! WHAT CHANCE IS THERE OF A BVM SIGHTING HERE? THERE'S NOT EVEN A **CRICKET MATCH** GOING ON TODAY!

BUT WAIT! WHO'S THIS TAKING THE RUN-UP TO THE BOWLING END? IT'S THE BLESSED VIRGIN MARY!

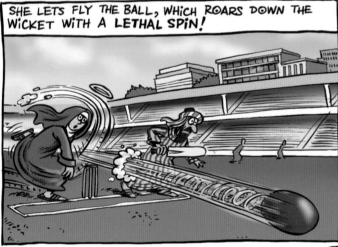

SHE LETS FLY THE BALL, WHICH ROARS DOWN THE WICKET WITH A **LETHAL SPIN!**

JESUS TAKES A MIGHTY SWING — HE'S MISSED! THE STUMPS ARE FLYING-- HE'S OUT! GOD RAISES HIS FINGER, AND JESUS IS OUT!

THE HOLY APPARITION IS FADING AND DISAPPEARING NOW...

AND LOOK! THERE IT IS— A MIRACLE!

THE STUMPS HAVE RE-GROWN THEIR FEET AND HANDS! HALLELUJAH!

A LOST VILLAGE

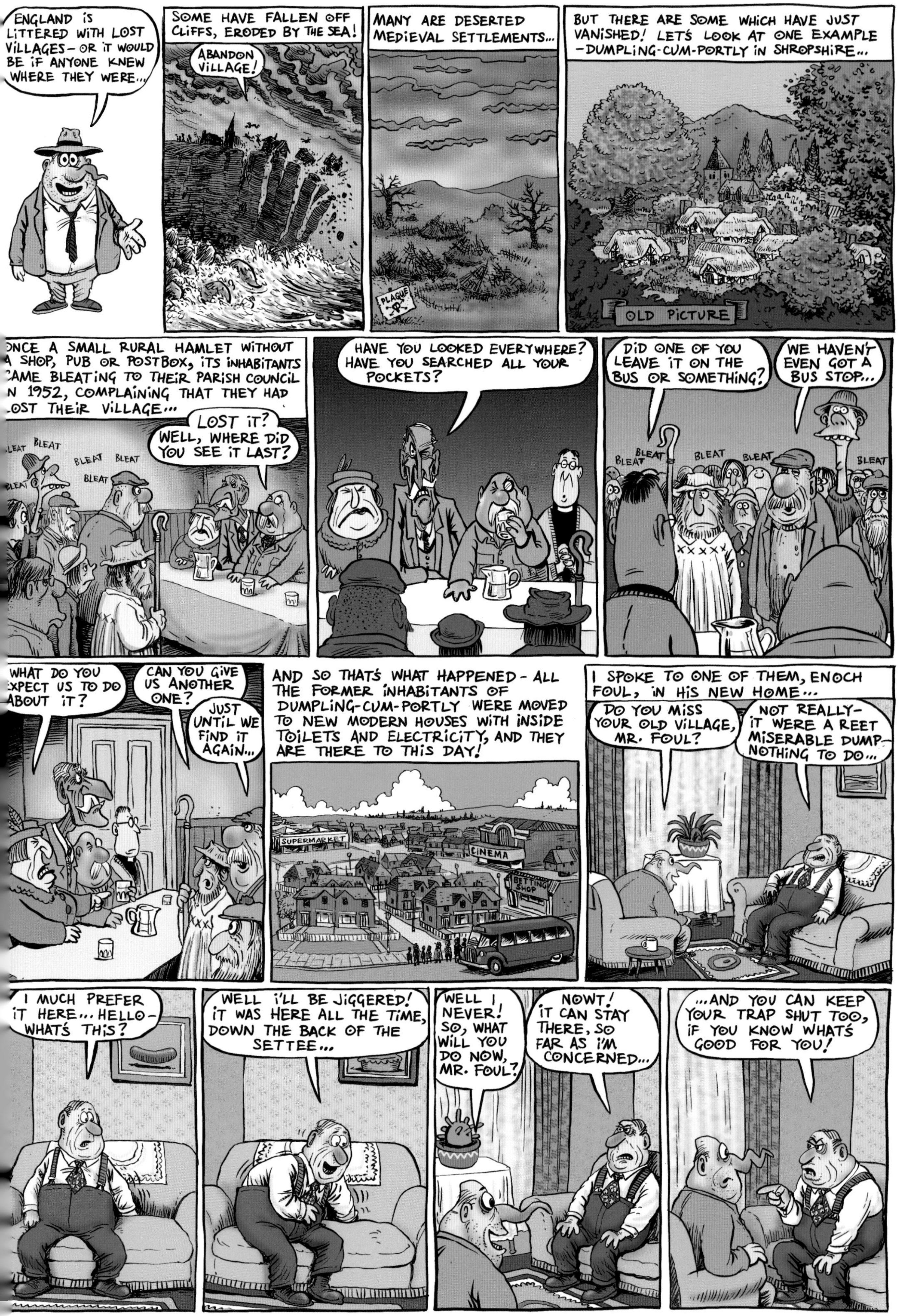
ENGLAND IS LITTERED WITH LOST VILLAGES – OR IT WOULD BE IF ANYONE KNEW WHERE THEY WERE...
SOME HAVE FALLEN OFF CLIFFS, ERODED BY THE SEA!
ABANDON VILLAGE!
MANY ARE DESERTED MEDIEVAL SETTLEMENTS...
PLAGUE
BUT THERE ARE SOME WHICH HAVE JUST VANISHED! LET'S LOOK AT ONE EXAMPLE – DUMPLING-CUM-PORTLY IN SHROPSHIRE...
OLD PICTURE
ONCE A SMALL RURAL HAMLET WITHOUT A SHOP, PUB OR POSTBOX, ITS INHABITANTS CAME BLEATING TO THEIR PARISH COUNCIL IN 1952, COMPLAINING THAT THEY HAD LOST THEIR VILLAGE...
BLEAT BLEAT BLEAT BLEAT BLEAT BLEAT
LOST IT? WELL, WHERE DID YOU SEE IT LAST?
HAVE YOU LOOKED EVERYWHERE? HAVE YOU SEARCHED ALL YOUR POCKETS?
DID ONE OF YOU LEAVE IT ON THE BUS OR SOMETHING?
WE HAVEN'T EVEN GOT A BUS STOP...
BLEAT BLEAT BLEAT BLEAT BLEAT
WHAT DO YOU EXPECT US TO DO ABOUT IT?
CAN YOU GIVE US ANOTHER ONE?
JUST UNTIL WE FIND IT AGAIN...
AND SO THAT'S WHAT HAPPENED – ALL THE FORMER INHABITANTS OF DUMPLING-CUM-PORTLY WERE MOVED TO NEW MODERN HOUSES WITH INSIDE TOILETS AND ELECTRICITY, AND THEY ARE THERE TO THIS DAY!
SUPERMARKET
CINEMA
BETTING SHOP
I SPOKE TO ONE OF THEM, ENOCH FOUL, IN HIS NEW HOME...
DO YOU MISS YOUR OLD VILLAGE, MR. FOUL?
NOT REALLY – IT WERE A REET MISERABLE DUMP – NOTHING TO DO...
I MUCH PREFER IT HERE... HELLO – WHAT'S THIS?
WELL I'LL BE JIGGERED! IT WAS HERE ALL THE TIME, DOWN THE BACK OF THE SETTEE...
WELL I NEVER! SO, WHAT WILL YOU DO NOW, MR. FOUL?
NOWT! IT CAN STAY THERE, SO FAR AS I'M CONCERNED...
...AND YOU CAN KEEP YOUR TRAP SHUT TOO, IF YOU KNOW WHAT'S GOOD FOR YOU!

TECTONIC NOSE

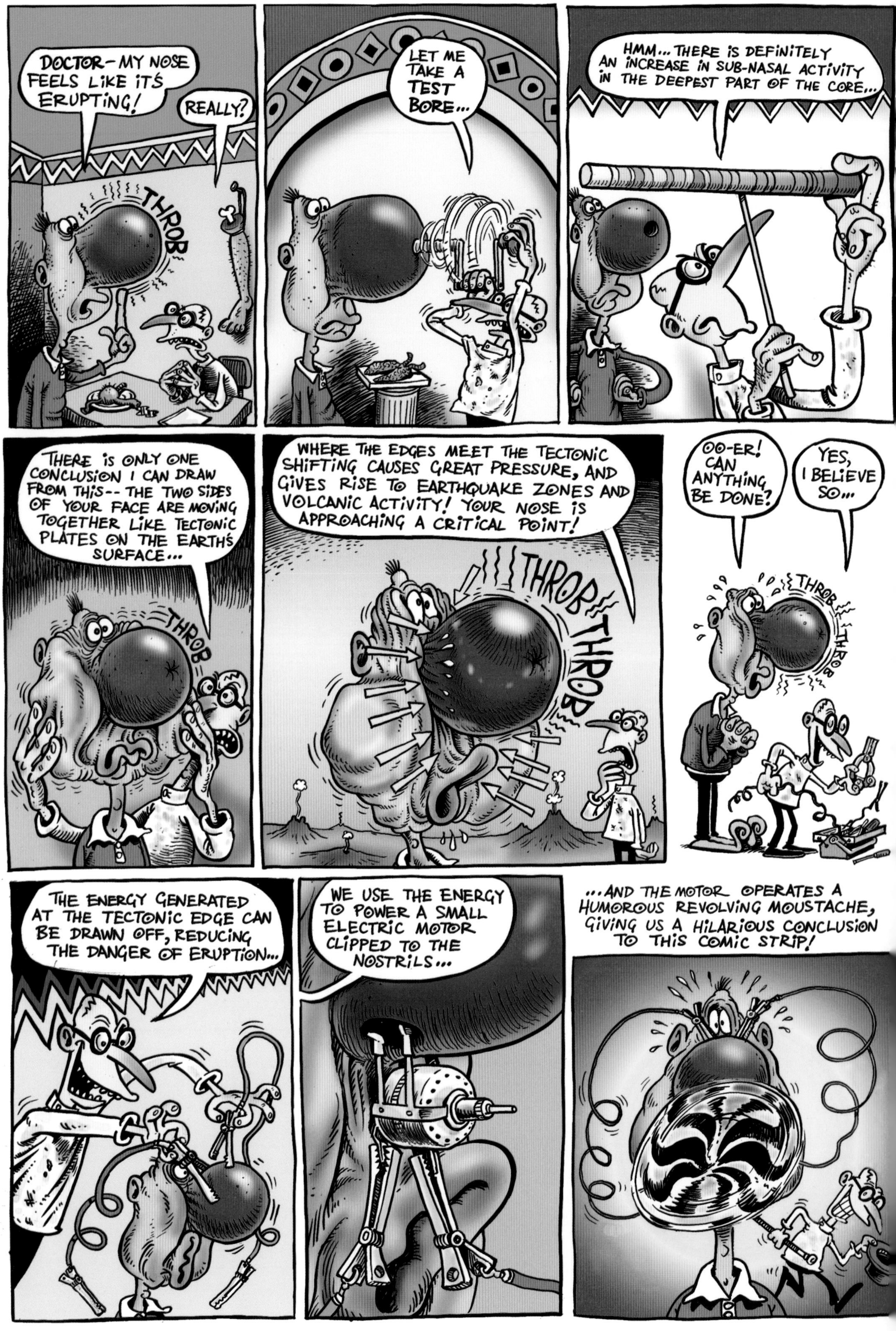

DOCTOR – MY NOSE FEELS LIKE IT'S ERUPTING!
REALLY?
THROB
LET ME TAKE A TEST BORE...
HMM... THERE IS DEFINITELY AN INCREASE IN SUB-NASAL ACTIVITY IN THE DEEPEST PART OF THE CORE...
THERE IS ONLY ONE CONCLUSION I CAN DRAW FROM THIS -- THE TWO SIDES OF YOUR FACE ARE MOVING TOGETHER LIKE TECTONIC PLATES ON THE EARTH'S SURFACE...
THROB
WHERE THE EDGES MEET THE TECTONIC SHIFTING CAUSES GREAT PRESSURE, AND GIVES RISE TO EARTHQUAKE ZONES AND VOLCANIC ACTIVITY! YOUR NOSE IS APPROACHING A CRITICAL POINT!
THROB
THROB
OO-ER! CAN ANYTHING BE DONE?
YES, I BELIEVE SO...
THROB
THROB
THE ENERGY GENERATED AT THE TECTONIC EDGE CAN BE DRAWN OFF, REDUCING THE DANGER OF ERUPTION...
WE USE THE ENERGY TO POWER A SMALL ELECTRIC MOTOR CLIPPED TO THE NOSTRILS...
...AND THE MOTOR OPERATES A HUMOROUS REVOLVING MOUSTACHE, GIVING US A HILARIOUS CONCLUSION TO THIS COMIC STRIP!

MEN IN BLACK 1

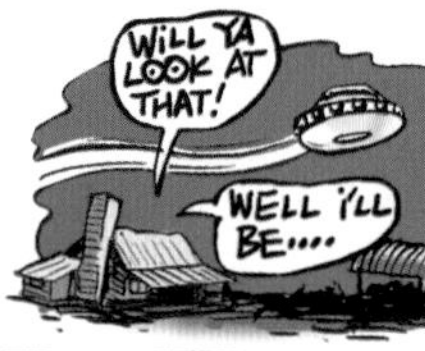

WILL YA LOOK AT THAT!
WELL I'LL BE....

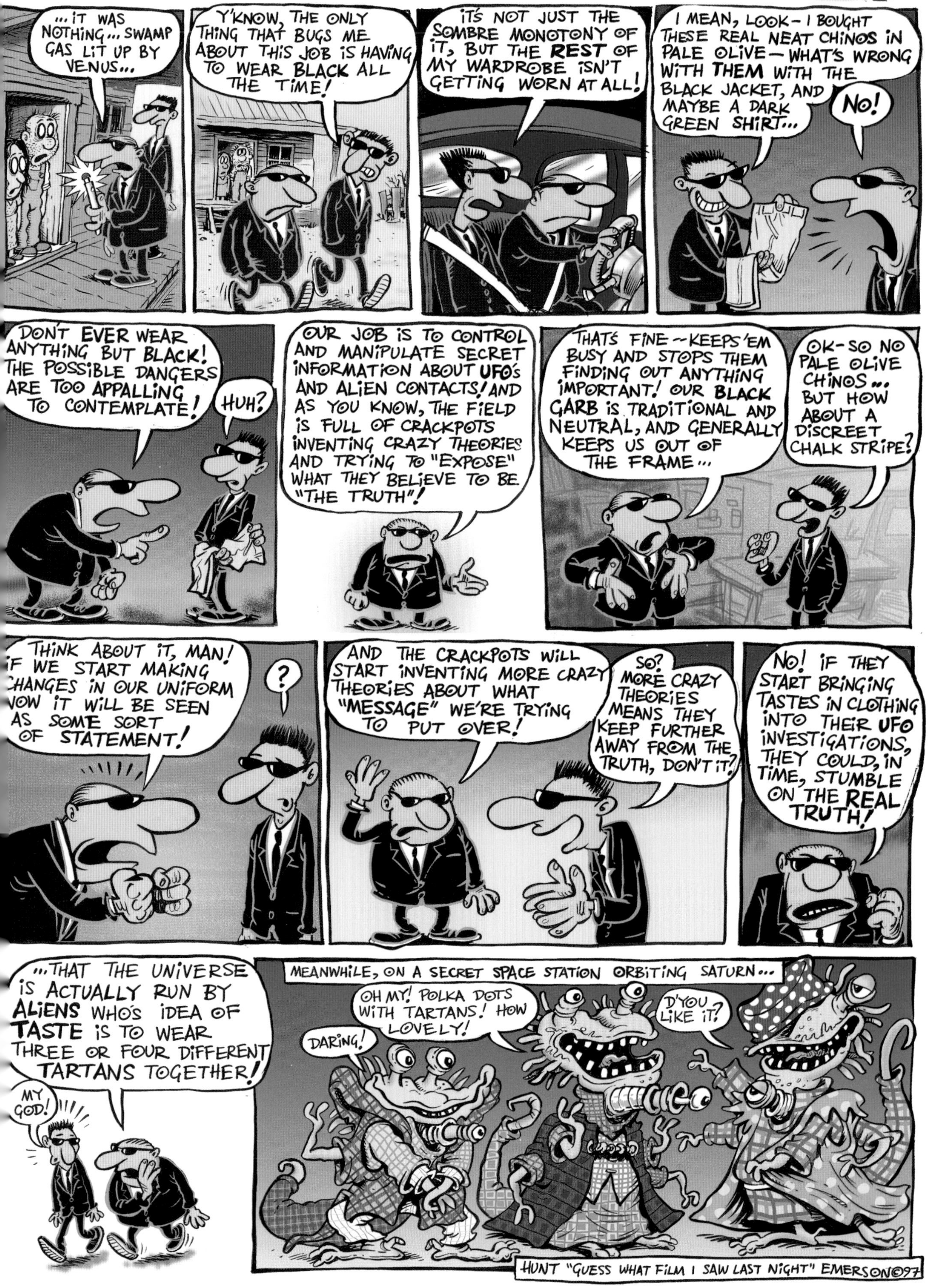

...IT WAS NOTHING... SWAMP GAS LIT UP BY VENUS...
Y'KNOW, THE ONLY THING THAT BUGS ME ABOUT THIS JOB IS HAVING TO WEAR BLACK ALL THE TIME!
IT'S NOT JUST THE SOMBRE MONOTONY OF IT, BUT THE REST OF MY WARDROBE ISN'T GETTING WORN AT ALL!
I MEAN, LOOK - I BOUGHT THESE REAL NEAT CHINOS IN PALE OLIVE - WHAT'S WRONG WITH THEM WITH THE BLACK JACKET, AND MAYBE A DARK GREEN SHIRT...
NO!
DON'T EVER WEAR ANYTHING BUT BLACK! THE POSSIBLE DANGERS ARE TOO APPALLING TO CONTEMPLATE!
HUH?
OUR JOB IS TO CONTROL AND MANIPULATE SECRET INFORMATION ABOUT UFO'S AND ALIEN CONTACTS! AND AS YOU KNOW, THE FIELD IS FULL OF CRACKPOTS INVENTING CRAZY THEORIES AND TRYING TO "EXPOSE" WHAT THEY BELIEVE TO BE "THE TRUTH"!
THAT'S FINE -- KEEPS 'EM BUSY AND STOPS THEM FINDING OUT ANYTHING IMPORTANT! OUR BLACK GARB IS TRADITIONAL AND NEUTRAL, AND GENERALLY KEEPS US OUT OF THE FRAME...
OK - SO NO PALE OLIVE CHINOS... BUT HOW ABOUT A DISCREET CHALK STRIPE?
THINK ABOUT IT, MAN! F WE START MAKING HANGES IN OUR UNIFORM OW IT WILL BE SEEN AS SOME SORT OF STATEMENT!
?
AND THE CRACKPOTS WILL START INVENTING MORE CRAZY THEORIES ABOUT WHAT "MESSAGE" WE'RE TRYING TO PUT OVER!
SO? MORE CRAZY THEORIES MEANS THEY KEEP FURTHER AWAY FROM THE TRUTH, DON'T IT?
NO! IF THEY START BRINGING TASTES IN CLOTHING INTO THEIR UFO INVESTIGATIONS, THEY COULD, IN TIME, STUMBLE ON THE REAL TRUTH!
...THAT THE UNIVERSE IS ACTUALLY RUN BY ALIENS WHO'S IDEA OF TASTE IS TO WEAR THREE OR FOUR DIFFERENT TARTANS TOGETHER!
MY GOD!
MEANWHILE, ON A SECRET SPACE STATION ORBITING SATURN...
OH MY! POLKA DOTS WITH TARTANS! HOW LOVELY!
DARING!
D'YOU LIKE IT?
HUNT "GUESS WHAT FILM I SAW LAST NIGHT" EMERSON©97

MEN IN BLACK 2

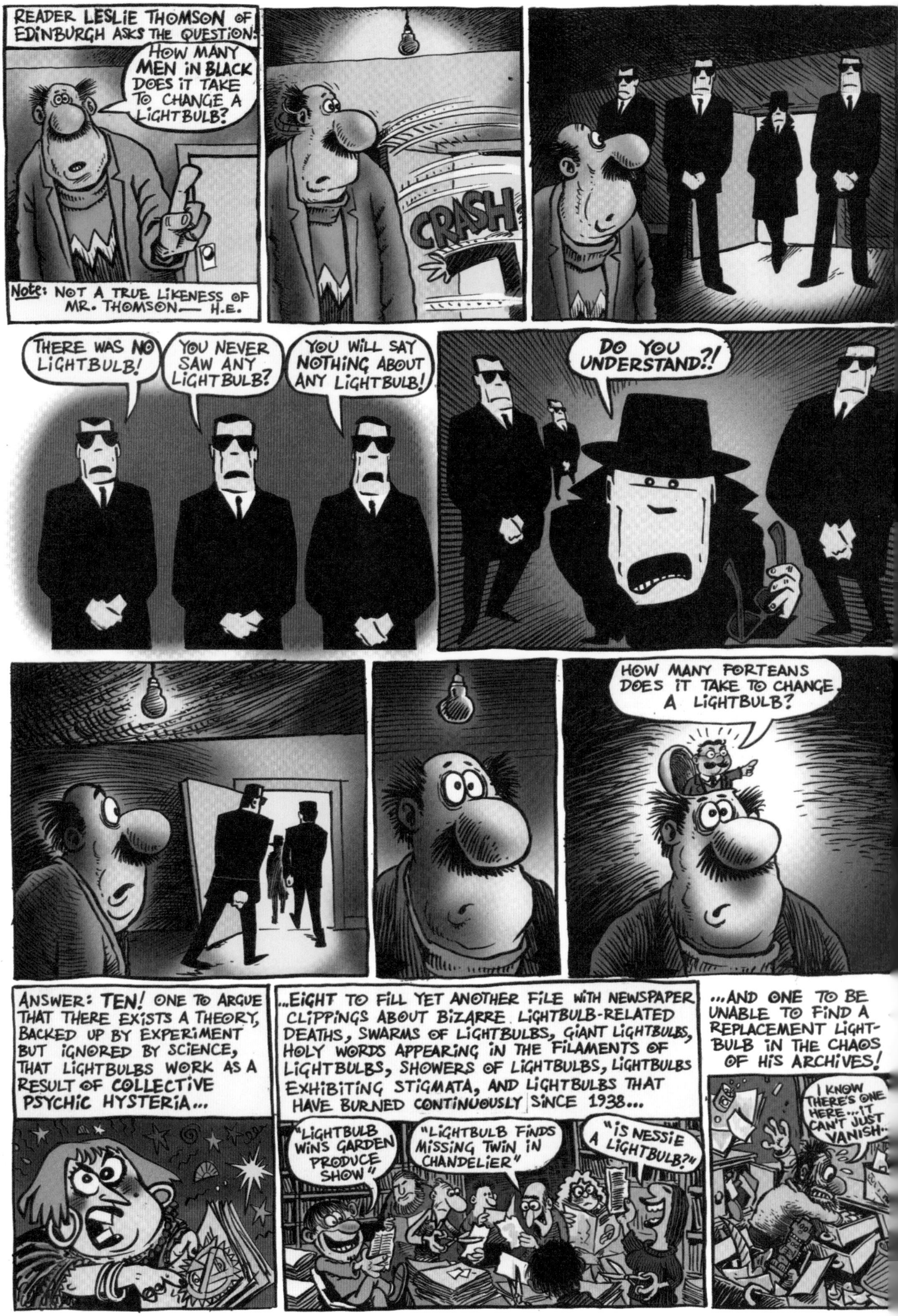
READER LESLIE THOMSON OF EDINBURGH ASKS THE QUESTION:
HOW MANY MEN IN BLACK DOES IT TAKE TO CHANGE A LIGHTBULB?
Note: NOT A TRUE LIKENESS OF MR. THOMSON— H.E.
CRASH
THERE WAS NO LIGHTBULB!
YOU NEVER SAW ANY LIGHTBULB?
YOU WILL SAY NOTHING ABOUT ANY LIGHTBULB!
DO YOU UNDERSTAND?!
HOW MANY FORTEANS DOES IT TAKE TO CHANGE A LIGHTBULB?
ANSWER: TEN! ONE TO ARGUE THAT THERE EXISTS A THEORY, BACKED UP BY EXPERIMENT BUT IGNORED BY SCIENCE, THAT LIGHTBULBS WORK AS A RESULT OF COLLECTIVE PSYCHIC HYSTERIA...
...EIGHT TO FILL YET ANOTHER FILE WITH NEWSPAPER CLIPPINGS ABOUT BIZARRE LIGHTBULB-RELATED DEATHS, SWARMS OF LIGHTBULBS, GIANT LIGHTBULBS, HOLY WORDS APPEARING IN THE FILAMENTS OF LIGHTBULBS, SHOWERS OF LIGHTBULBS, LIGHTBULBS EXHIBITING STIGMATA, AND LIGHTBULBS THAT HAVE BURNED CONTINUOUSLY SINCE 1938...
"LIGHTBULB WINS GARDEN PRODUCE SHOW"
"LIGHTBULB FINDS MISSING TWIN IN CHANDELIER"
"IS NESSIE A LIGHTBULB?"
...AND ONE TO BE UNABLE TO FIND A REPLACEMENT LIGHT-BULB IN THE CHAOS OF HIS ARCHIVES!
I KNOW THERE'S ONE HERE... IT CAN'T JUST VANISH..

MEN IN BLACK 3

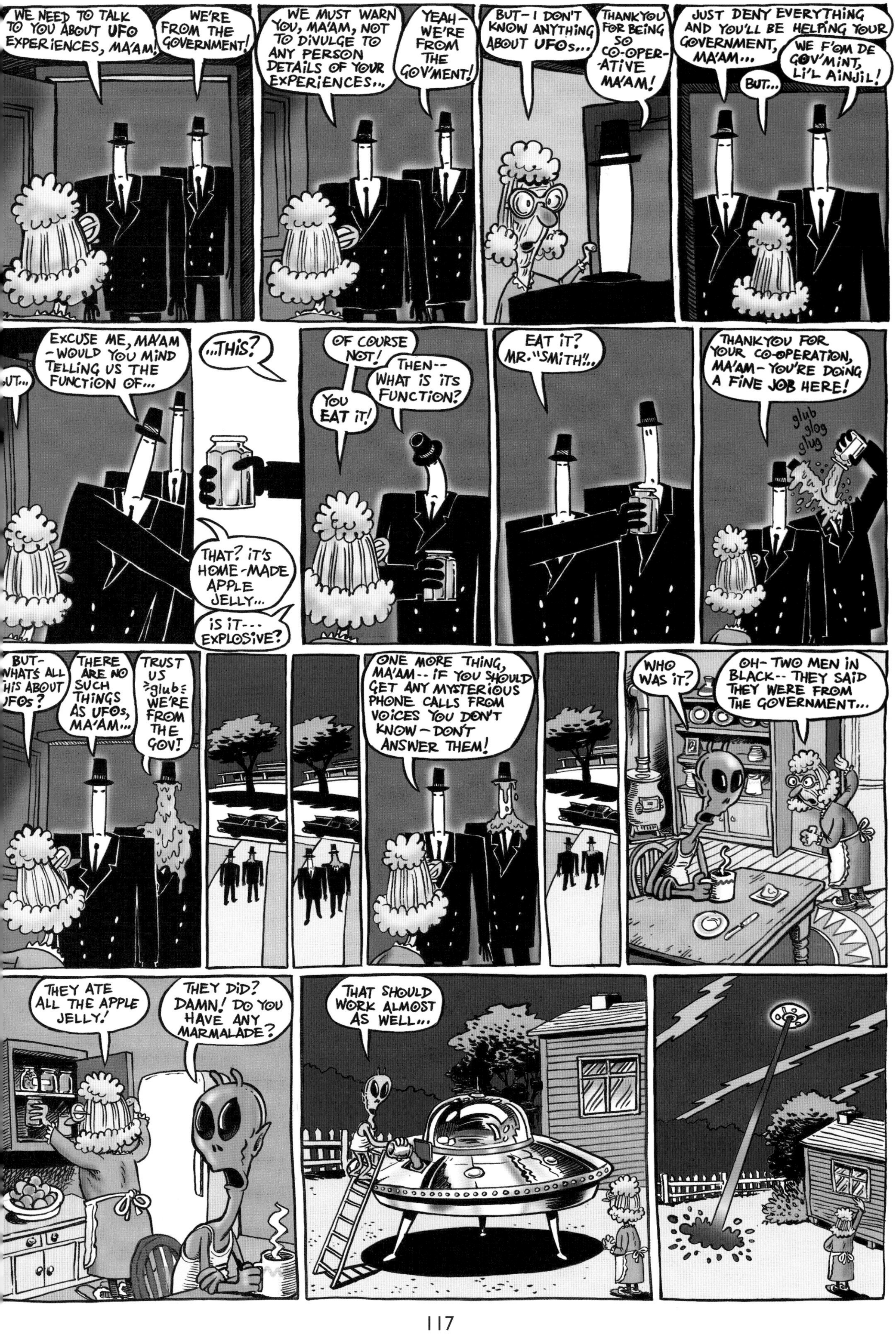

WE NEED TO TALK TO YOU ABOUT UFO EXPERIENCES, MA'AM!
WE'RE FROM THE GOVERNMENT!
WE MUST WARN YOU, MA'AM, NOT TO DIVULGE TO ANY PERSON DETAILS OF YOUR EXPERIENCES...
YEAH— WE'RE FROM THE GOV'MENT!
BUT— I DON'T KNOW ANYTHING ABOUT UFOs...
THANKYOU FOR BEING SO CO-OPER-ATIVE MA'AM!
JUST DENY EVERYTHING AND YOU'LL BE HELPING YOUR GOVERNMENT, MA'AM...
BUT...
WE F'OM DE GOV'MINT, LI'L AINJIL!
UT...
EXCUSE ME, MA'AM —WOULD YOU MIND TELLING US THE FUNCTION OF...
...THIS?
THAT? IT'S HOME-MADE APPLE JELLY...
IS IT--- EXPLOSIVE?
OF COURSE NOT!
THEN-- WHAT IS ITS FUNCTION?
YOU EAT IT!
EAT IT? MR. "SMITH"!..
THANKYOU FOR YOUR CO-OPERATION, MA'AM— YOU'RE DOING A FINE JOB HERE!
glub glog glug
BUT— WHAT'S ALL HIS ABOUT UFOs?
THERE ARE NO SUCH THINGS AS UFOs, MA'AM...
TRUST US glub WE'RE FROM THE GOV!
ONE MORE THING, MA'AM-- IF YOU SHOULD GET ANY MYSTERIOUS PHONE CALLS FROM VOICES YOU DON'T KNOW— DON'T ANSWER THEM!
WHO WAS IT?
OH— TWO MEN IN BLACK-- THEY SAID THEY WERE FROM THE GOVERNMENT...
THEY ATE ALL THE APPLE JELLY!
THEY DID? DAMN! DO YOU HAVE ANY MARMALADE?
THAT SHOULD WORK ALMOST AS WELL...

FORTEAN JOKES COMPETITION

THE M.I.B LIGHTBULB JOKE SENT IN BY READER LES THOMSON HAS REALLY STARTED SOMETHING!

I'VE BEEN OVERWHELMED BY AN AVALANCHE OF TWO JOKES FROM STEVE SCANLON! THEY ARE:

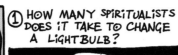

① HOW MANY SPIRITUALISTS DOES IT TAKE TO CHANGE A LIGHTBULB?

IS THERE ANY BODY THERE?

I DON'T KNOW... THE LIGHT'S GONE OUT!

SH! PLEASE BE SERIOUS!

ANSWER: NONE! IT'S ALL DONE BY UNSEEN FORCES!

GASP

WoooOOooo...

AND-

② WHY DID THE SPIRITUALIST CROSS THE ROAD?

STOP SOULS CROSSING

ANSWER: TO GET TO-THE OTHER SIDE!

WoooOOooo...!! SPOOKY, eh?

OK, SO WHY DID THE FORTEAN CROSS THE ROAD?

YOU MAY NOT GO THERE... IT IS AGAINST ALL DOCTRINE...

DO NOT GO!

IT CAN'T BE DONE!

WELL, THERE'S SO MUCH ORTHODOX OPINION LINED UP ON THIS SIDE OF THE ROAD, ALL INSISTING IT IS THE ONLY POSSIBLE SIDE TO BE ON...

...THAT I NATURALLY SUSPECT A CONSPIRACY, SO I'M GOING TO INVESTIGATE THE OTHER SIDE OF THE ROAD FOR MYSELF!

DON'T DO IT...

AAAAAAAGH!!

WELL, THAT'S IT. NOT MUCH OF A PUNCHLINE, I'M AFRAID, BUT I COULDN'T THINK OF A JOKE...

SO, WE'RE GOING TO HAVE A COMPETITION!

WHAT IS YOUR ANSWER TO THE QUESTION:

"WHY DID THE FORTEAN CROSS THE ROAD?"

EMAIL YOUR ANSWER TO: phenomenomix ⬛⬛⬛⬛⬛.c⬛

OR SEND A POSTCARD TO OUR ED⬛⬛⬛⬛ ADDRESS, MARKED "PHENOMENOMIX JOKE COMP."

PRIZE: AN ORIGINAL SKETCH OF GULLY BULL.

...ESULTS!

TIME'S UP! THE COMPETITION IS ENDED! TIME TO JUDGE THE ENTRIES...

AND WHAT A FANTASTIC BUNCH OF ANSWERS WE'VE RECEIVED! SACKFULS OF HILARITY AS **YOU**, THE READERS, ANSWERED THE QUESTION: WHY DID THE FORTEAN CROSS THE ROAD?

AND THOSE ANSWERS COVER A LOT OF GROUND! THEY RANGE FROM THE LEARNED...

WHY DID THE FORTEAN CROSS THE ROAD?

He never made it across, having stopped at the centre line. Equidistant between two competing - and, as far as he had yet determined, equally attractive - positions, he refused to choose one over the other, and sat down. So there the fortean remains, only saved from sharing the fate of Buridan's ass by his snatching of the occasional chicken.

http://www.cenius.net/refer/display.php?ArticleID=buridansass

~~Brian Morgan~~, Canada.

..TO THE BASIC!

WHY DID THE FORTEAN CROSS THE ROAD?

Because there was no traffic.

~~Steve N Harden~~, London

FROM THE SUBTLE...

WHY DID THE FORTEAN CROSS THE ROAD?

To see the ley of the land.

~~Ashley Watson~~, Leicester.

...TO THE NOT-SO-SUBTLE!

WHY DID THE FORTEAN CROSS THE ROAD?

FOR TEA'N TOAST!

~~Syd Smythson~~, Cambs.

BOOM BOOM!

SOME ENTRANTS USED THE COMPETITION TO BLATANTLY INDULGE THEIR OWN SECRET LUSTS...

I COME! I COME!

WHY DID THE FORTEAN CROSS THE ROAD?

Because Robbie Williams/ Chocolate/ chocolate mousse with chopped-up bananas and Cointreau-flavoured squirty-cream on top - was on the other side.

~~B Jones~~, Warminster.

..AND SOME WERE FRANKLY INEXPLICABLE!

WHY DID THE FORTEAN CROSS THE ROAD?

Alisteir Crowley

~~Spink~~, email.

BUT IN THE END I'VE SETTLED FOR TWO JOKES THAT ARE FORTEAN IN NATURE... AND HERE THEY ARE!

TAN·TARA TAN TAN TARAAA!

WHY DID THE FORTEAN CROSS THE ROAD?

ROAD? THIS ISN'T A ROAD! IT'S A LANDING STRIP FOR ANCIENT ASTRONAUTS!

~~Narinar~~, email.

THAT WAS THE RUNNER UP-- THE OVERALL WINNER IS...

WHY DID THE FORTEAN CROSS THE ROAD?

To prove that one measures a roundabout starting anywhere.

~~Henrik Backman~~, Sweden.

MASS PANIC 1

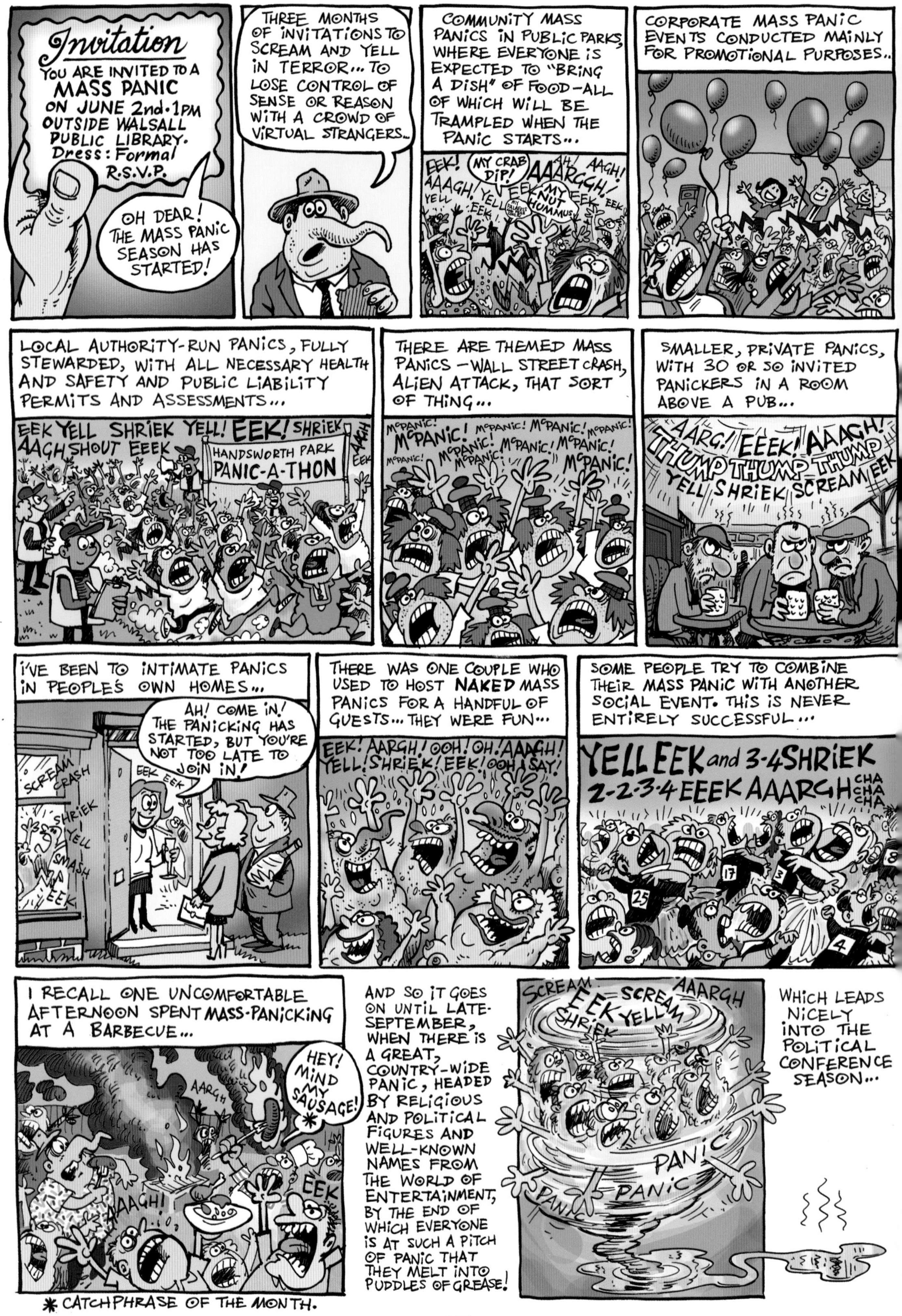
Invitation
YOU ARE INVITED TO A MASS PANIC ON JUNE 2nd·1PM OUTSIDE WALSALL PUBLIC LIBRARY. Dress: Formal R.S.V.P.
OH DEAR! THE MASS PANIC SEASON HAS STARTED!
THREE MONTHS OF INVITATIONS TO SCREAM AND YELL IN TERROR... TO LOSE CONTROL OF SENSE OR REASON WITH A CROWD OF VIRTUAL STRANGERS...
COMMUNITY MASS PANICS IN PUBLIC PARKS, WHERE EVERYONE IS EXPECTED TO "BRING A DISH" OF FOOD—ALL OF WHICH WILL BE TRAMPLED WHEN THE PANIC STARTS...
EEK! MY CRAB DIP! AAARGGH! AH! AAGH! AAAGH! YELL EEK MY NUT HUMMUS! EEK EEK
CORPORATE MASS PANIC EVENTS CONDUCTED MAINLY FOR PROMOTIONAL PURPOSES...
LOCAL AUTHORITY-RUN PANICS, FULLY STEWARDED, WITH ALL NECESSARY HEALTH AND SAFETY AND PUBLIC LIABILITY PERMITS AND ASSESSMENTS...
EEK YELL SHRIEK YELL! EEK! SHRIEK AAGH SHOUT EEEK AAGH EEK
HANDSWORTH PARK PANIC-A-THON
THERE ARE THEMED MASS PANICS—WALL STREET CRASH, ALIEN ATTACK, THAT SORT OF THING...
McPANIC! McPANIC! McPANIC! McPANIC! McPANIC! McPANIC! McPANIC! McPANIC! McPANIC! McPANIC! McPANIC!
SMALLER, PRIVATE PANICS, WITH 30 OR SO INVITED PANICKERS IN A ROOM ABOVE A PUB...
AARG! EEEK! AAAGH! THUMP THUMP THUMP YELL SHRIEK SCREAM EEK
I'VE BEEN TO INTIMATE PANICS IN PEOPLE'S OWN HOMES...
AH! COME IN! THE PANICKING HAS STARTED, BUT YOU'RE NOT TOO LATE TO JOIN IN!
SCREAM CRASH SHRIEK YELL SMASH EEK EEK EEK
THERE WAS ONE COUPLE WHO USED TO HOST NAKED MASS PANICS FOR A HANDFUL OF GUESTS... THEY WERE FUN...
EEK! AARGH! OOH! OH! AAAGH! YELL! SHRIEK! EEK! OOH I SAY!
SOME PEOPLE TRY TO COMBINE THEIR MASS PANIC WITH ANOTHER SOCIAL EVENT. THIS IS NEVER ENTIRELY SUCCESSFUL...
YELL EEK and 3-4 SHRIEK 2-2-3-4 EEEK AAARGH CHA CHA CHA
I RECALL ONE UNCOMFORTABLE AFTERNOON SPENT MASS-PANICKING AT A BARBECUE...
HEY! MIND MY SAUSAGE!*
AARGH AAAGH! EEK
AND SO IT GOES ON UNTIL LATE-SEPTEMBER, WHEN THERE IS A GREAT, COUNTRY-WIDE PANIC, HEADED BY RELIGIOUS AND POLITICAL FIGURES AND WELL-KNOWN NAMES FROM THE WORLD OF ENTERTAINMENT, BY THE END OF WHICH EVERYONE IS AT SUCH A PITCH OF PANIC THAT THEY MELT INTO PUDDLES OF GREASE!
SCREAM EEK SCREAM AAARGH SHRIEK YELL PANIC PANIC PANIC
WHICH LEADS NICELY INTO THE POLITICAL CONFERENCE SEASON...
* CATCHPHRASE OF THE MONTH.

MASS PANIC 2

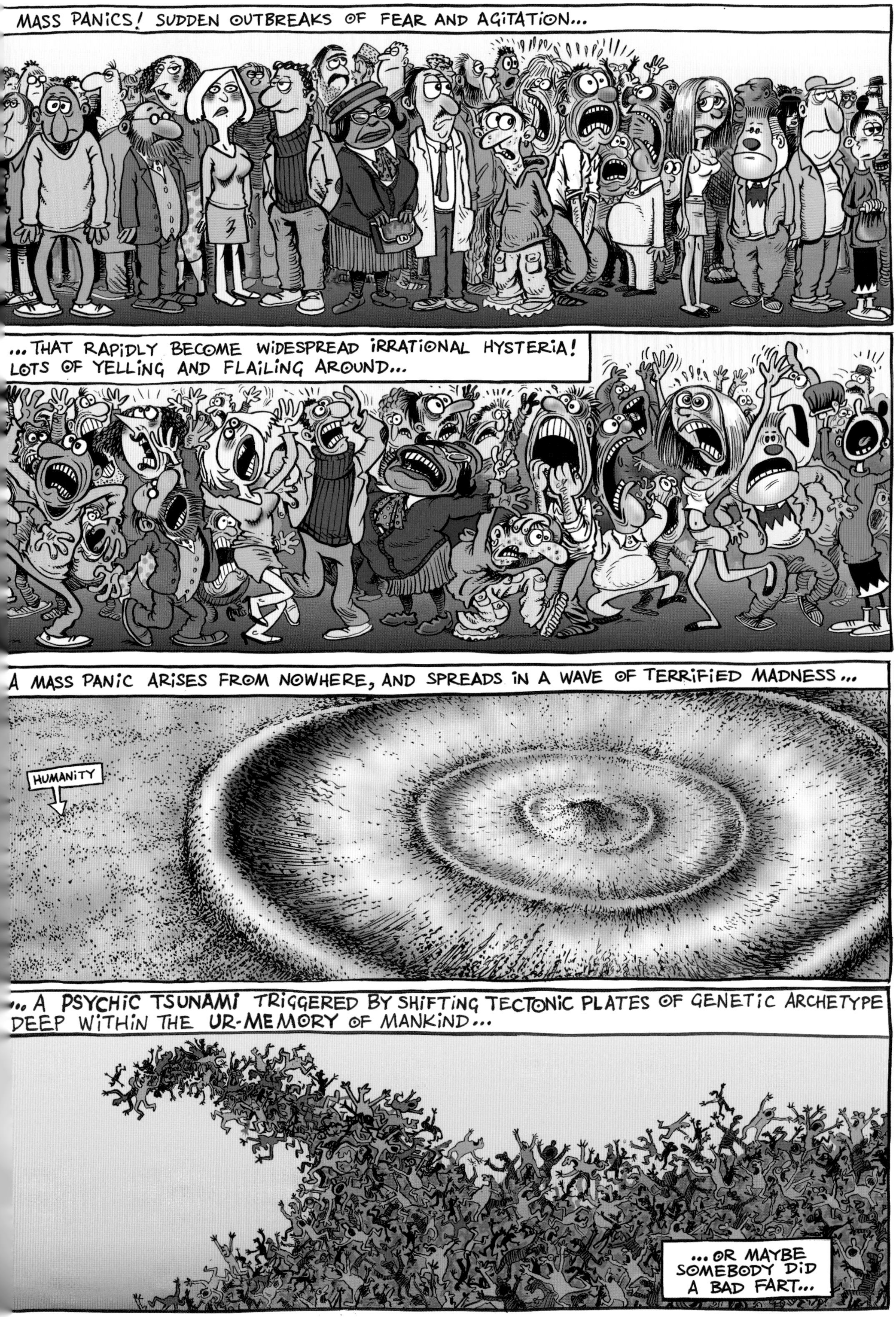

MASS PANICS! SUDDEN OUTBREAKS OF FEAR AND AGITATION...
...THAT RAPIDLY BECOME WIDESPREAD IRRATIONAL HYSTERIA! LOTS OF YELLING AND FLAILING AROUND...
A MASS PANIC ARISES FROM NOWHERE, AND SPREADS IN A WAVE OF TERRIFIED MADNESS...
HUMANITY
...A PSYCHIC TSUNAMI TRIGGERED BY SHIFTING TECTONIC PLATES OF GENETIC ARCHETYPE DEEP WITHIN THE UR-MEMORY OF MANKIND...
...OR MAYBE SOMEBODY DID A BAD FART...

MEGALITH SQUINT

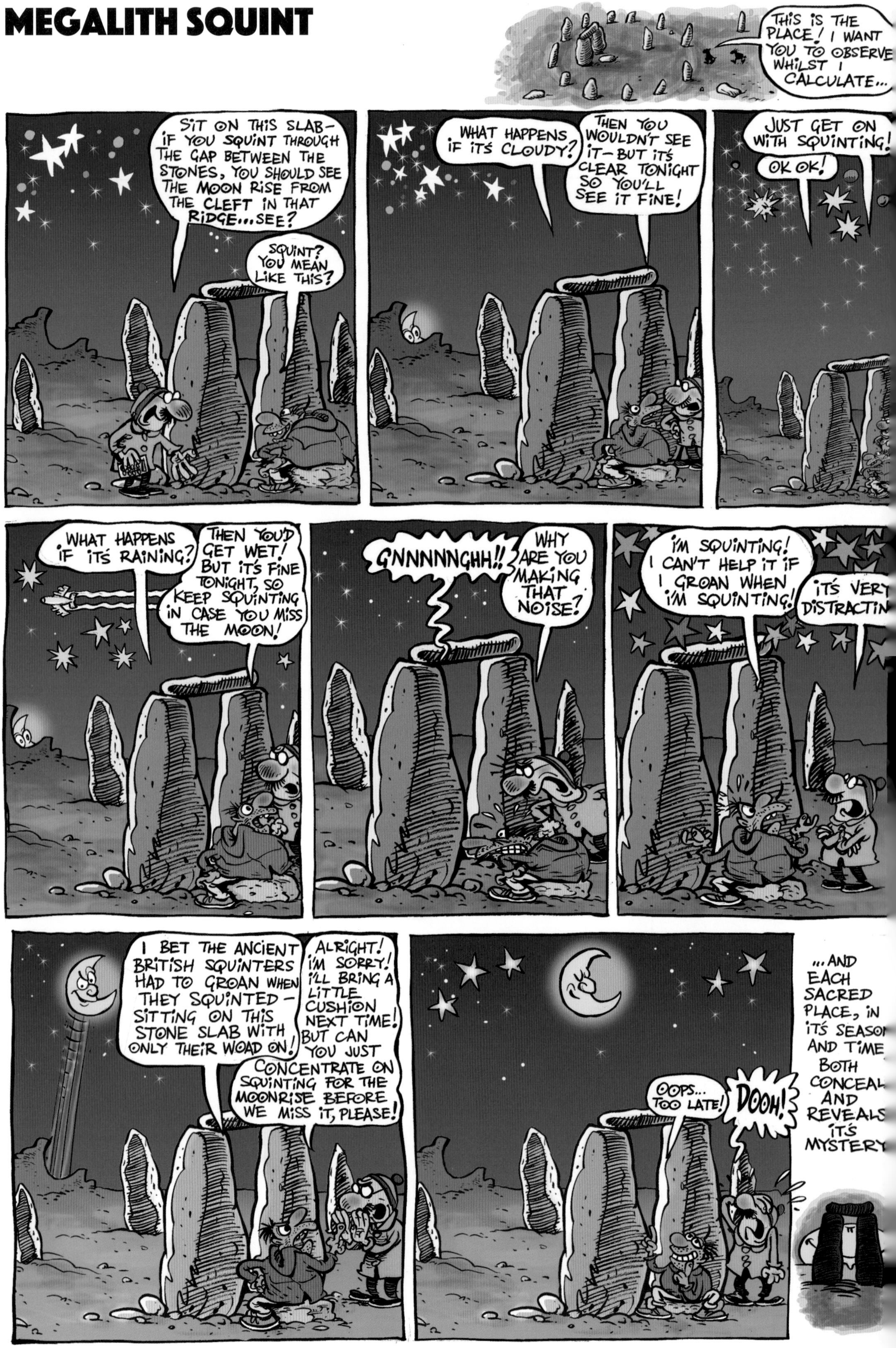

THIS IS THE PLACE! I WANT YOU TO OBSERVE WHILST I CALCULATE...
SIT ON THIS SLAB- IF YOU SQUINT THROUGH THE GAP BETWEEN THE STONES, YOU SHOULD SEE THE MOON RISE FROM THE CLEFT IN THAT RIDGE...SEE?
SQUINT? YOU MEAN LIKE THIS?
WHAT HAPPENS IF IT'S CLOUDY?
THEN YOU WOULDN'T SEE IT-BUT IT'S CLEAR TONIGHT SO YOU'LL SEE IT FINE!
JUST GET ON WITH SQUINTING!
OK OK!
WHAT HAPPENS IF IT'S RAINING?
THEN YOU'D GET WET! BUT IT'S FINE TONIGHT, SO KEEP SQUINTING IN CASE YOU MISS THE MOON!
GNNNNNGHH!!
WHY ARE YOU MAKING THAT NOISE?
I'M SQUINTING! I CAN'T HELP IT IF I GROAN WHEN I'M SQUINTING!
IT'S VERY DISTRACTIN
I BET THE ANCIENT BRITISH SQUINTERS HAD TO GROAN WHEN THEY SQUINTED - SITTING ON THIS STONE SLAB WITH ONLY THEIR WOAD ON!
ALRIGHT! I'M SORRY! I'LL BRING A LITTLE CUSHION NEXT TIME! BUT CAN YOU JUST CONCENTRATE ON SQUINTING FOR THE MOONRISE BEFORE WE MISS IT, PLEASE!
OOPS... TOO LATE!
DOOH!
...AND EACH SACRED PLACE, IN IT'S SEASON AND TIME BOTH CONCEALS AND REVEALS IT'S MYSTERY

MEXICAN SCIENTISTS

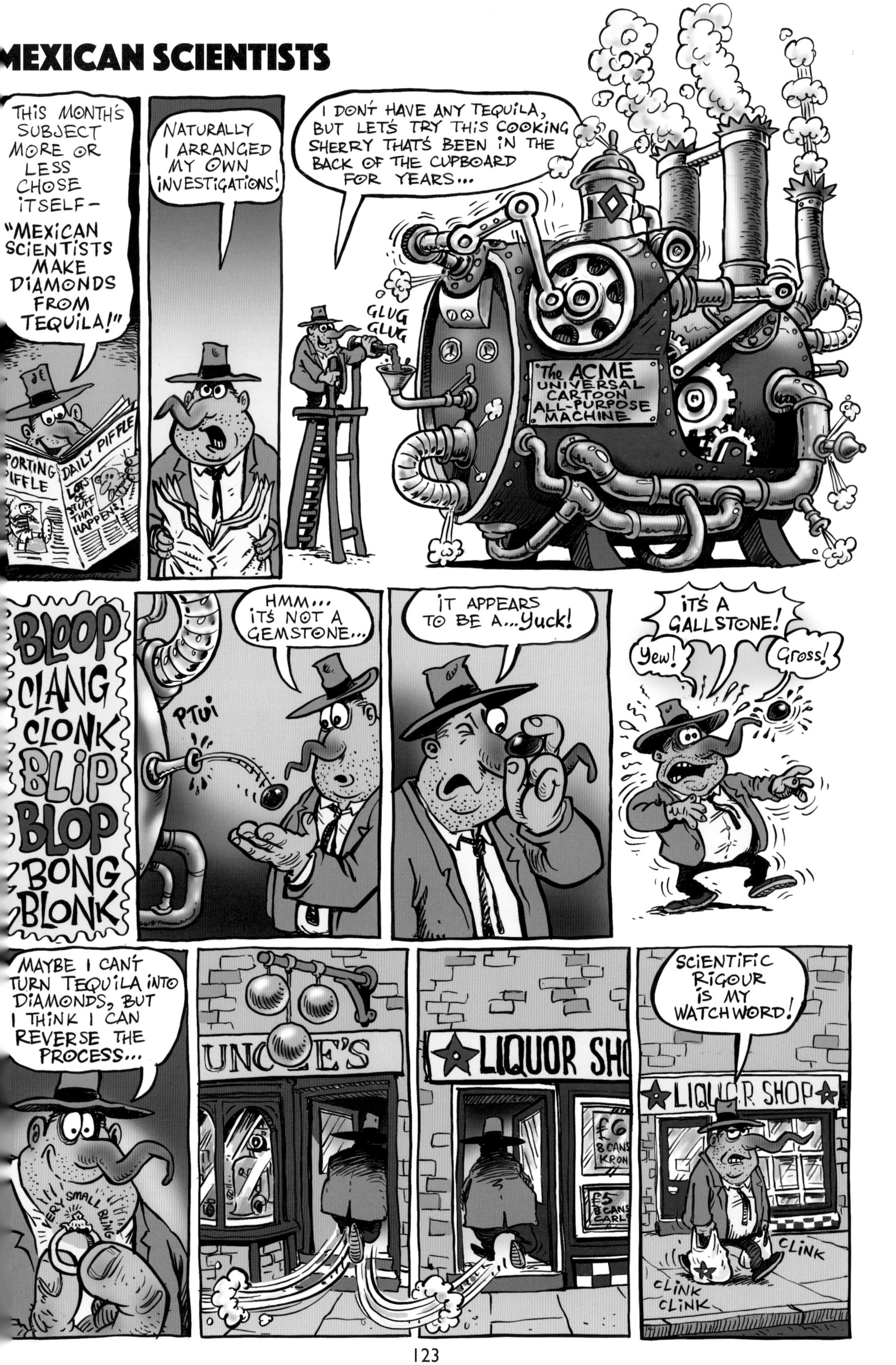

THIS MONTH'S SUBJECT MORE OR LESS CHOSE ITSELF- "MEXICAN SCIENTISTS MAKE DIAMONDS FROM TEQUILA!"
DAILY PIFFLE
SPORTING PIFFLE
LOTS OF STUFF THAT HAPPENS!
NATURALLY I ARRANGED MY OWN INVESTIGATIONS!
I DON'T HAVE ANY TEQUILA, BUT LET'S TRY THIS COOKING SHERRY THAT'S BEEN IN THE BACK OF THE CUPBOARD FOR YEARS...
GLUG GLUG
The ACME UNIVERSAL CARTOON ALL-PURPOSE MACHINE
BLOOP CLANG CLONK BLIP BLOP BONG BLONK
PTUI
HMM... IT'S NOT A GEMSTONE...
IT APPEARS TO BE A...Yuck!
IT'S A GALLSTONE!
Yew!
Gross!
MAYBE I CAN'T TURN TEQUILA INTO DIAMONDS, BUT I THINK I CAN REVERSE THE PROCESS...
VERY SMALL BLING
UNCLE'S
LIQUOR SHO
£6 8 CANS KRON
£5 8 CANS CARLS
SCIENTIFIC RIGOUR IS MY WATCHWORD!
LIQUOR SHOP
CLINK
CLINK CLINK

MIND CONTROL

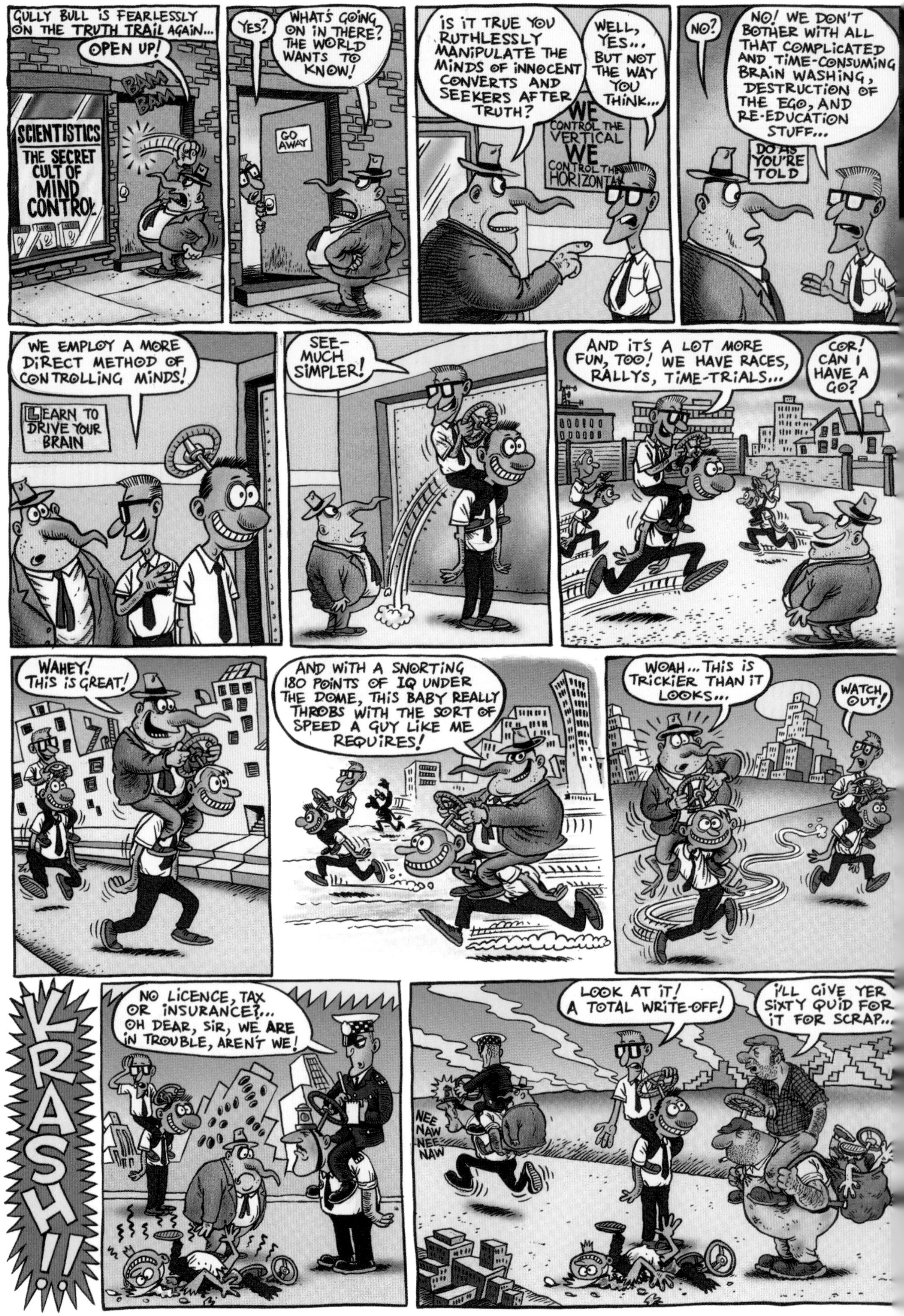

GULLY BULL IS FEARLESSLY ON THE TRUTH TRAIL AGAIN...
OPEN UP!
BAM BAM
SCIENTISTICS THE SECRET CULT OF MIND CONTROL
YES?
WHAT'S GOING ON IN THERE? THE WORLD WANTS TO KNOW!
GO AWAY
IS IT TRUE YOU RUTHLESSLY MANIPULATE THE MINDS OF INNOCENT CONVERTS AND SEEKERS AFTER TRUTH?
WELL, YES... BUT NOT THE WAY YOU THINK...
WE CONTROL THE VERTICAL WE CONTROL THE HORIZONTA
NO?
NO! WE DON'T BOTHER WITH ALL THAT COMPLICATED AND TIME-CONSUMING BRAIN WASHING, DESTRUCTION OF THE EGO, AND RE-EDUCATION STUFF...
DO AS YOU'RE TOLD
WE EMPLOY A MORE DIRECT METHOD OF CONTROLLING MINDS!
LEARN TO DRIVE YOUR BRAIN
SEE- MUCH SIMPLER!
AND IT'S A LOT MORE FUN, TOO! WE HAVE RACES, RALLYS, TIME-TRIALS...
COR! CAN I HAVE A GO?
WAHEY! THIS IS GREAT!
AND WITH A SNORTING 180 POINTS OF IQ UNDER THE DOME, THIS BABY REALLY THROBS WITH THE SORT OF SPEED A GUY LIKE ME REQUIRES!
WOAH... THIS IS TRICKIER THAN IT LOOKS...
WATCH OUT!
KRASH!!
NO LICENCE, TAX OR INSURANCE?... OH DEAR, SIR, WE ARE IN TROUBLE, AREN'T WE!
NEE NAW NEE NAW
LOOK AT IT! A TOTAL WRITE-OFF!
I'LL GIVE YER SIXTY QUID FOR IT FOR SCRAP...

MOOSE LORE!

This comic is about **MOOSE LORE!**

YES— **MOOSE LORE!**

WOW! I JUST LOVE THAT ECHO!

MOOSE! LORE!

=ahem= OK— TO BUSINESS!

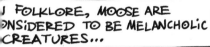

IN FOLKLORE, MOOSE ARE CONSIDERED TO BE MELANCHOLIC CREATURES...

EEE— I'M REET FED UP!

...THOUGH IN REALITY THEY'RE NO MORE MISERABLE THAN ANYBODY ELSE WHO HAS TO LIVE IN A FOREST WITH A COMPLICATED COAT RACK ON HIS HEAD!

Sigh

THEIR HIDES WERE BELIEVED TO BE BULLET PROOF—

WELL, THAT TURNS OUT TO BE A LIE...

POW POW

POW

IF A MOOSE IS ATTACKED, IT DRINKS A LOT OF WATER...

GLUG GLUG

GRRRR

...BOILS IT UP IN ITS BELLY...

GURGLE GLURP GLOOP GLUG

?

...AND REGURGITATES THE SCALDING LIQUID ALL OVER ITS ATTACKER!

YOWP YOWP YOWP

THE ASTRONOMER TYCHO BRAHE HAD A PET MOOSE— IT GOT LOOSE IN HIS CASTLE ONE DAY, FOUND A BARREL OF ALE, AND DRANK IT!

OH NO...

THE ANIMAL WAS SO DRUNK IT FELL DOWN STAIRS AND DIED...

BY BOOSE! BY LOVELY BOOSE!

DID YOU KNOW TYCHO BRAHE HAD A BRASS NOSE?

REALLY? HOW DID HE SMELL?

YOU WOULDN'T DARE!

Reader's Voice

LIKE AN OLD MOOSE!

DOH!

YOK YOK

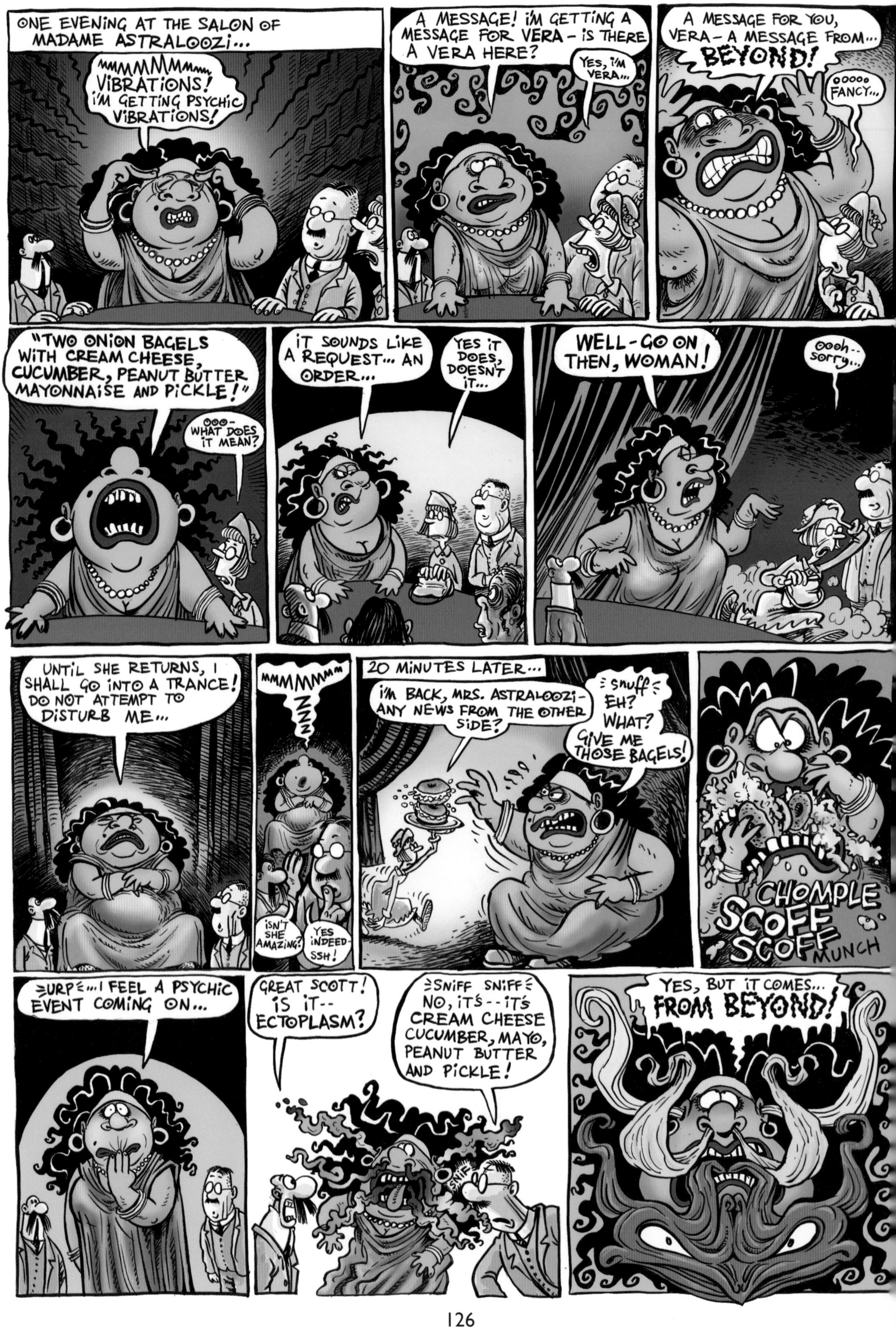
ONE EVENING AT THE SALON OF MADAME ASTRALOOZI...
MMMMMMMMMM VIBRATIONS! I'M GETTING PSYCHIC VIBRATIONS!
A MESSAGE! I'M GETTING A MESSAGE FOR VERA - IS THERE A VERA HERE?
YES, I'M VERA...
A MESSAGE FOR YOU, VERA - A MESSAGE FROM... BEYOND!
OOOOO FANCY...
"TWO ONION BAGELS WITH CREAM CHEESE, CUCUMBER, PEANUT BUTTER MAYONNAISE AND PICKLE!"
OOO- WHAT DOES IT MEAN?
IT SOUNDS LIKE A REQUEST... AN ORDER...
YES IT DOES, DOESN'T IT...
WELL - GO ON THEN, WOMAN!
Oooh... sorry...
UNTIL SHE RETURNS, I SHALL GO INTO A TRANCE! DO NOT ATTEMPT TO DISTURB ME...
MMMMMMMM
ZZZ
ISN'T SHE AMAZING?
YES INDEED- SSH!
20 MINUTES LATER...
I'M BACK, MRS. ASTRALOOZI - ANY NEWS FROM THE OTHER SIDE?
SNUFF EH? WHAT? GIVE ME THOSE BAGELS!
CHOMPLE SCOFF SCOFF MUNCH
URP ...I FEEL A PSYCHIC EVENT COMING ON...
GREAT SCOTT! IS IT-- ECTOPLASM?
SNIFF SNIFF NO, IT'S--IT'S CREAM CHEESE CUCUMBER, MAYO, PEANUT BUTTER AND PICKLE!
SNIF
YES, BUT IT COMES... FROM BEYOND!

THE DRESSING ROOM OF MADAME ASTRALOOZI....

VERA? ARE YOU READY? OUR GUESTS FOR TONIGHT'S SEANCE WILL BE HERE AT ANY MOMENT!

VERA!

YES MADAME... HERE I AM...

ARE YOUR KNEES IN GOOD KNOCKING ORDER?

YES— SEE?

CLACK CLACK CLACK CLACK CLACK

OH DEAR... WHAT WAS THE CODE? REMIND ME AGAIN...

≥Sigh≤ FOR HEAVEN'S SAKE, WOMAN— CAN'T YOU GET IT INTO YOUR HEAD?

ONE KNOCK FOR NO— TWO KNOCKS FOR YES! IT'S PERFECTLY SIMPLE!

OOH... I DO WISH YOU WOULD DO IT, MRS. ASTRALOOZI...

YOU KNOW I CAN'T, VERA —NOT WITH MY KNEES...

I KNOW... YOU'RE A MARTYR TO THEM...

...AND THEY'RE TOO FAT AND SQUISHY TO MAKE ANY NOISE...

ALSO, THE WRINKLES AND FATTY LUMPS ON THEM MAKE THEM LOOK LIKE CROSS OLD MEN...

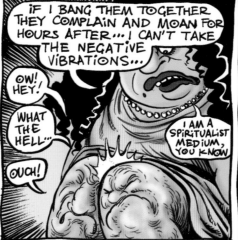

IF I BANG THEM TOGETHER THEY COMPLAIN AND MOAN FOR HOURS AFTER.... I CAN'T TAKE THE NEGATIVE VIBRATIONS...

OW! HEY!

WHAT THE HELL...

OUCH!

I AM A SPIRITUALIST MEDIUM, YOU KNOW

NO DEAR, YOU'VE GOT THE PERFECT KNEES FOR THE JOB! JUST KEEP THEM WELL HIDDEN UNDER THE TABLE AND NO-ONE WILL EVER KNOW...

THE COUNTESS, MA'AM...

AH! OUR FIRST SEEKER! SHOW HER IN!

NOW— ARE YOU READY?

CLACK

WHAT?

OOPS— SORRY! I MEAN...

CLACK CLACK

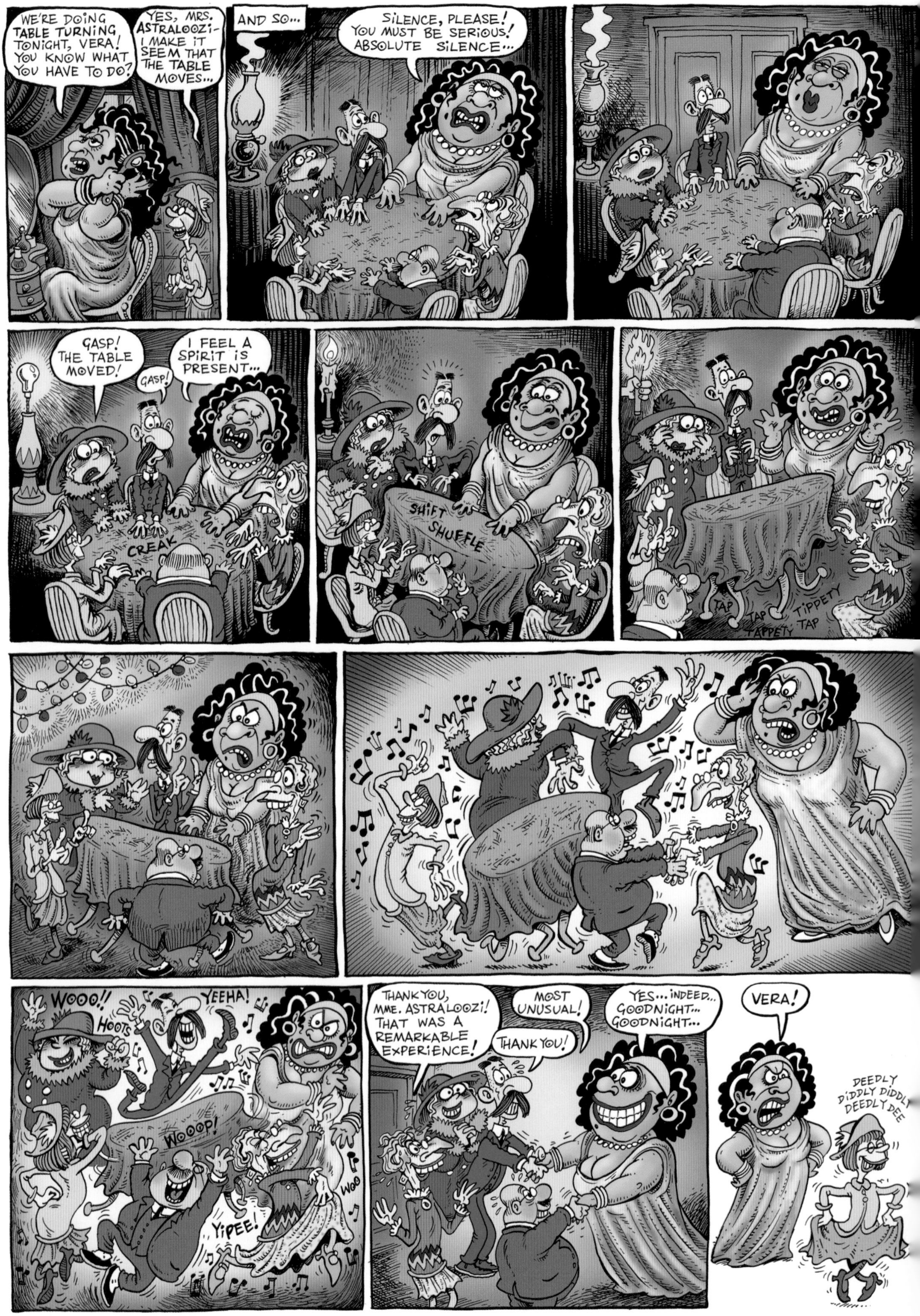
WE'RE DOING TABLE TURNING TONIGHT, VERA! YOU KNOW WHAT YOU HAVE TO DO?
YES, MRS. ASTRALOOZI - I MAKE IT SEEM THAT THE TABLE MOVES...
AND SO...
SILENCE, PLEASE! YOU MUST BE SERIOUS! ABSOLUTE SILENCE...
GASP! THE TABLE MOVED!
GASP!
I FEEL A SPIRIT IS PRESENT...
CREAK
SHIFT
SHUFFLE
TAP
TAP
TAPPETY
TIPPETY
TAP
WOOO!!
HOOTS
YEEHA!
WOOOP!
WOO
YIPEE!
THANK YOU, MME. ASTRALOOZI! THAT WAS A REMARKABLE EXPERIENCE!
MOST UNUSUAL!
THANK YOU!
YES... INDEED... GOODNIGHT... GOODNIGHT...
VERA!
DEEDLY DIDDLY DIDDLY DEEDLY DEE

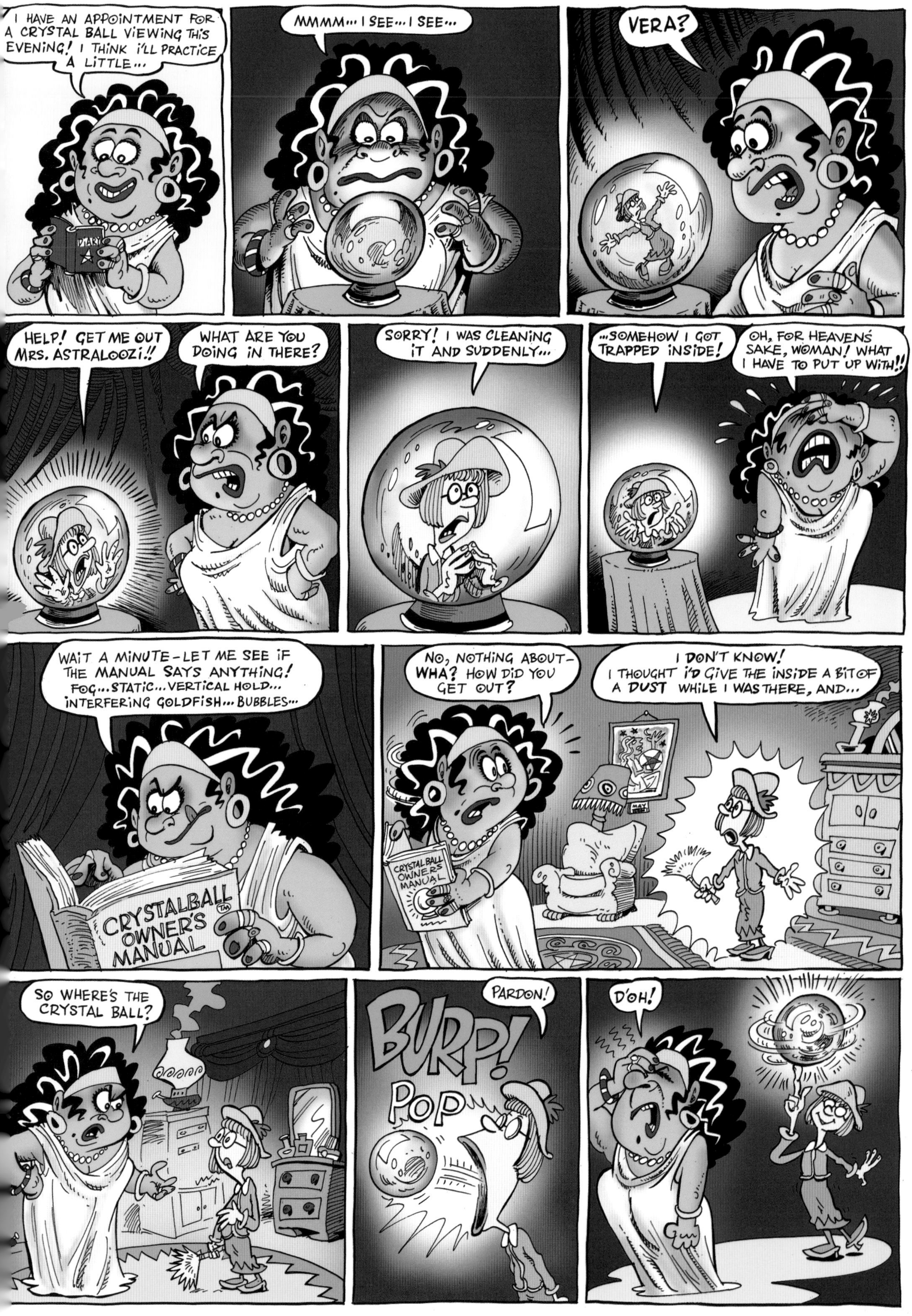
I HAVE AN APPOINTMENT FOR A CRYSTAL BALL VIEWING THIS EVENING! I THINK I'LL PRACTICE A LITTLE...
DIARY
MMMM... I SEE... I SEE...
VERA?
HELP! GET ME OUT MRS. ASTRALOOZI!!
WHAT ARE YOU DOING IN THERE?
SORRY! I WAS CLEANING IT AND SUDDENLY...
...SOMEHOW I GOT TRAPPED INSIDE!
OH, FOR HEAVENS SAKE, WOMAN! WHAT I HAVE TO PUT UP WITH!!
WAIT A MINUTE - LET ME SEE IF THE MANUAL SAYS ANYTHING! FOG...STATIC...VERTICAL HOLD... INTERFERING GOLDFISH... BUBBLES...
CRYSTALBALL OWNER'S MANUAL
NO, NOTHING ABOUT- WHA? HOW DID YOU GET OUT?
I DON'T KNOW! I THOUGHT I'D GIVE THE INSIDE A BIT OF A DUST WHILE I WAS THERE, AND...
CRYSTAL BALL OWNERS MANUAL
SO WHERE'S THE CRYSTAL BALL?
BURP!
POP
PARDON!
D'OH!

FUNNY STUFF, ECTOPLASM...

IT'S SUPPOSED TO BE SOME SORT OF SPIRITUAL, OTHER-WORLDLY FLOW OF **PHANTOM MATTER** FROM THE ORIFICES OF A **MEDIUM**, USUALLY FEMALE, IN A POSSESSED **TRANCE**!

THE **ECTOPLASM** ONLY MANIFESTS IN **DIMLY LIT** ROOMS, AND **GLOWS** SOFTLY! SOMETIMES IT TAKES HUMAN OR ANIMAL FORMS...

THIS WHOLE MALARKY IS CONNECTED WITH COMMUNICATION WITH THE **DEAD**...

I'VE GOT A MESSAGE FOR FRANK... THE KEYS ARE IN THE CHINA VASE IN THE SHED, FRANK...

YAP YAP YAP!

I'M DUBIOUS...

I SUSPECT SOME SORT OF **CONJURING** TRICK IS INVOLVED... A CLEVER METHOD OF FOLDING GOSSAMER-FINE SILK SO AS TO BE **CONCEALED** IN THE CHEEKS OR EARS OF THE **MEDIUM**...

AAAGH!

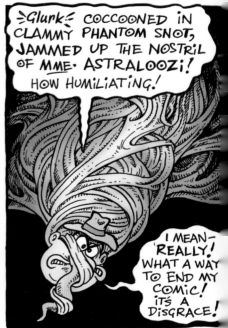

≥Glurk≤ COCOONED IN CLAMMY PHANTOM SNOT, JAMMED UP THE NOSTRIL OF MME. ASTRALOOZI! HOW HUMILIATING!

I MEAN- REALLY! WHAT A WAY TO END MY COMIC! ITS A DISGRACE!

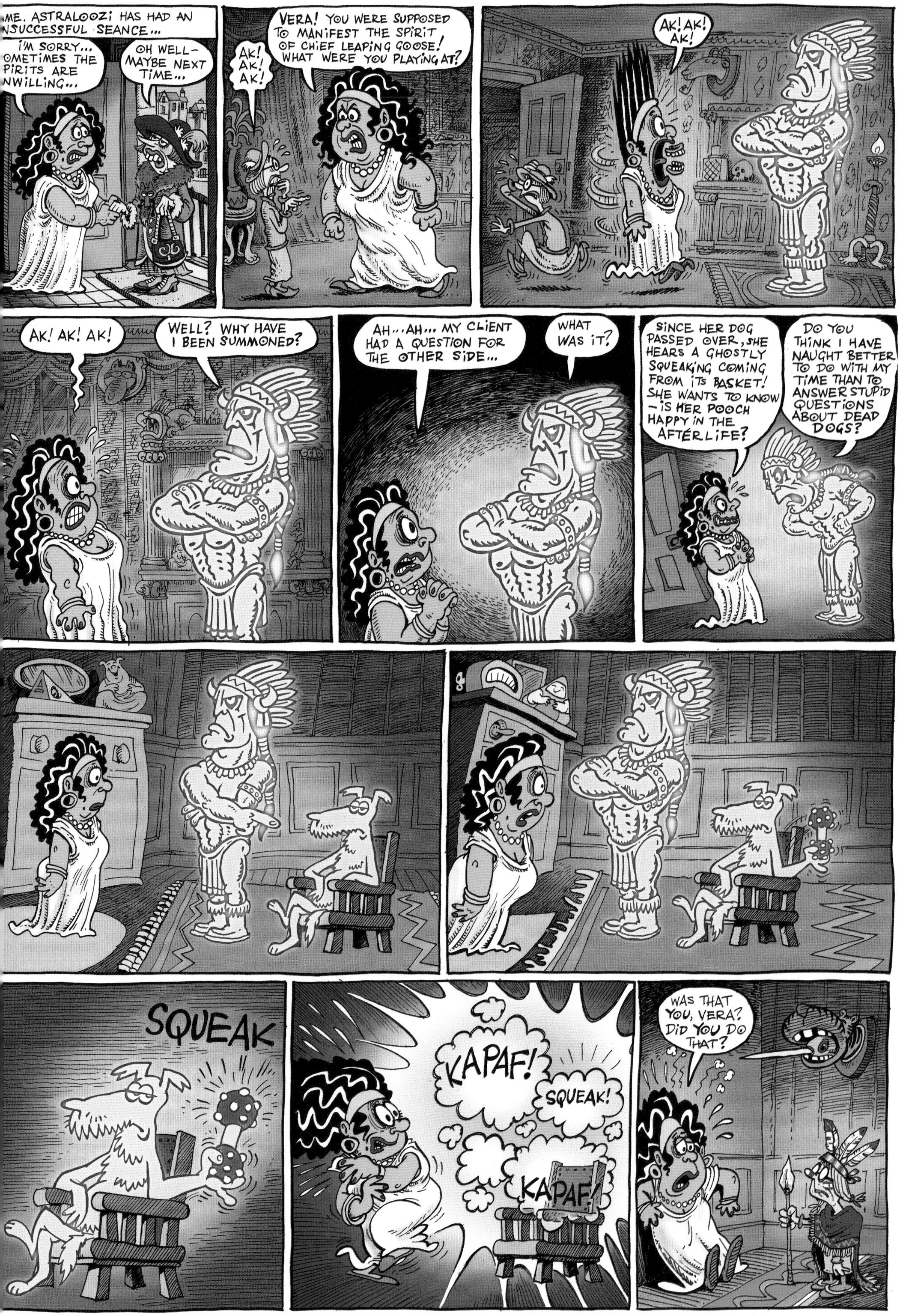
ME. ASTRALOOZI HAS HAD AN UNSUCCESSFUL SEANCE...
I'M SORRY... SOMETIMES THE SPIRITS ARE UNWILLING...
OH WELL- MAYBE NEXT TIME...
AK! AK! AK!
VERA! YOU WERE SUPPOSED TO MANIFEST THE SPIRIT OF CHIEF LEAPING GOOSE! WHAT WERE YOU PLAYING AT?
AK! AK! AK!
AK! AK! AK!
WELL? WHY HAVE I BEEN SUMMONED?
AH...AH... MY CLIENT HAD A QUESTION FOR THE OTHER SIDE...
WHAT WAS IT?
SINCE HER DOG PASSED OVER, SHE HEARS A GHOSTLY SQUEAKING COMING FROM ITS BASKET! SHE WANTS TO KNOW - IS HER POOCH HAPPY IN THE AFTERLIFE?
DO YOU THINK I HAVE NAUGHT BETTER TO DO WITH MY TIME THAN TO ANSWER STUPID QUESTIONS ABOUT DEAD DOGS?
SQUEAK
KAPAF!
SQUEAK!
KAPAF!
WAS THAT YOU, VERA? DID YOU DO THAT?

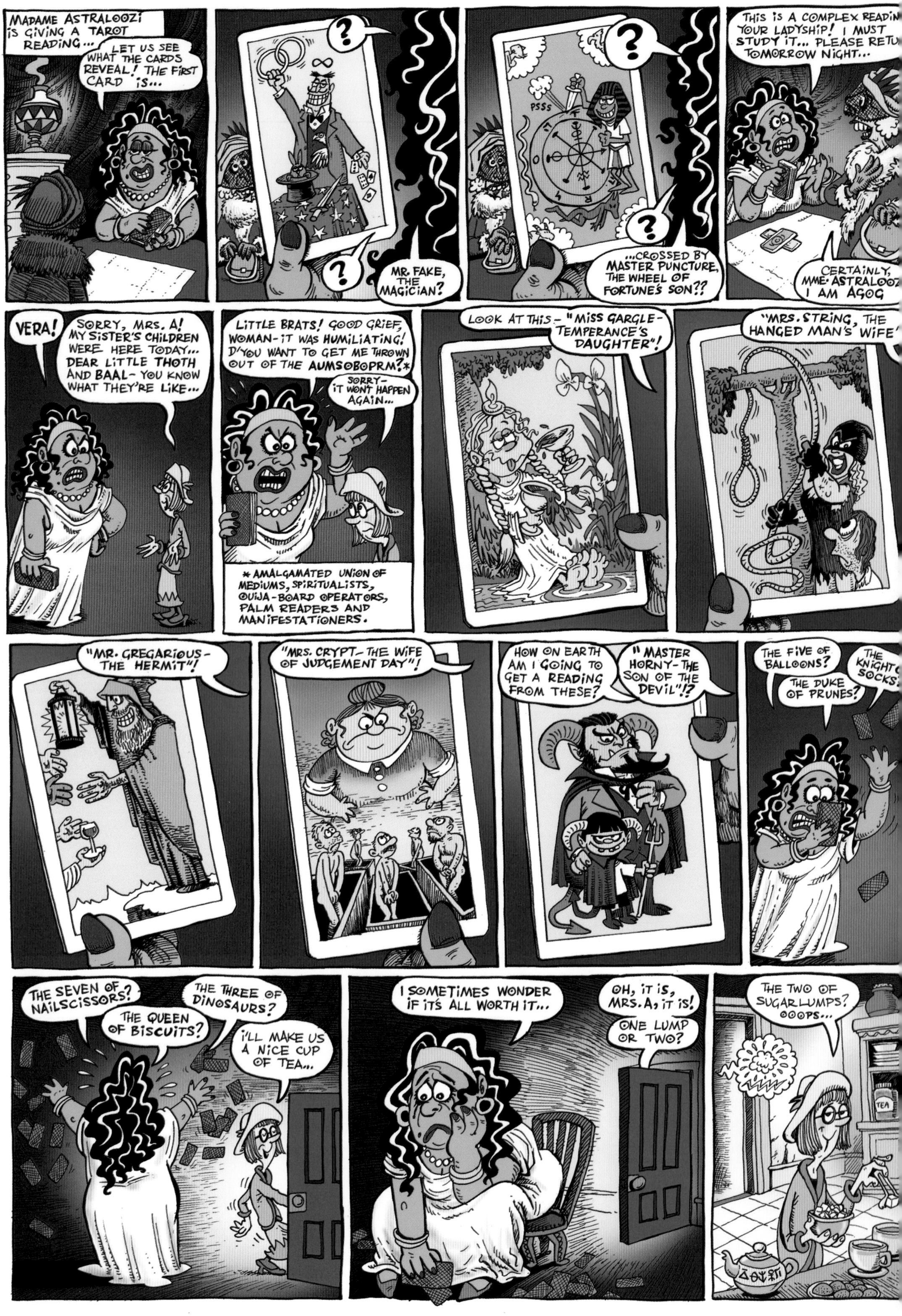
MADAME ASTRALOOZI IS GIVING A TAROT READING...
LET US SEE WHAT THE CARDS REVEAL! THE FIRST CARD IS...
MR. FAKE, THE MAGICIAN?
PSSS
...CROSSED BY MASTER PUNCTURE, THE WHEEL OF FORTUNE'S SON??
THIS IS A COMPLEX READIN YOUR LADYSHIP! I MUST STUDY IT... PLEASE RETU TOMORROW NIGHT...
CERTAINLY, MME. ASTRALOOZ I AM AGOG
VERA!
SORRY, MRS. A! MY SISTER'S CHILDREN WERE HERE TODAY... DEAR LITTLE THOTH AND BAAL- YOU KNOW WHAT THEY'RE LIKE...
LITTLE BRATS! GOOD GRIEF, WOMAN- IT WAS HUMILIATING! D'YOU WANT TO GET ME THROWN OUT OF THE AUMSOBOPRM?*
SORRY- IT WON'T HAPPEN AGAIN...
* AMALGAMATED UNION OF MEDIUMS, SPIRITUALISTS, OUIJA-BOARD OPERATORS, PALM READERS AND MANIFESTATIONERS.
LOOK AT THIS- "MISS GARGLE- TEMPERANCE'S DAUGHTER"!
"MRS. STRING, THE HANGED MAN'S WIFE"
"MR. GREGARIOUS- THE HERMIT"!
"MRS. CRYPT- THE WIFE OF JUDGEMENT DAY"!
HOW ON EARTH AM I GOING TO GET A READING FROM THESE?
"MASTER HORNY- THE SON OF THE DEVIL"!?
THE FIVE OF BALLOONS?
THE DUKE OF PRUNES?
THE KNIGHT SOCKS?
THE SEVEN OF NAILSCISSORS?
THE QUEEN OF BISCUITS?
THE THREE OF DINOSAURS?
I'LL MAKE US A NICE CUP OF TEA...
I SOMETIMES WONDER IF IT'S ALL WORTH IT...
OH, IT IS, MRS. A, IT IS!
ONE LUMP OR TWO?
THE TWO OF SUGARLUMPS? OOOPS...
TEA

WERE-MOLE

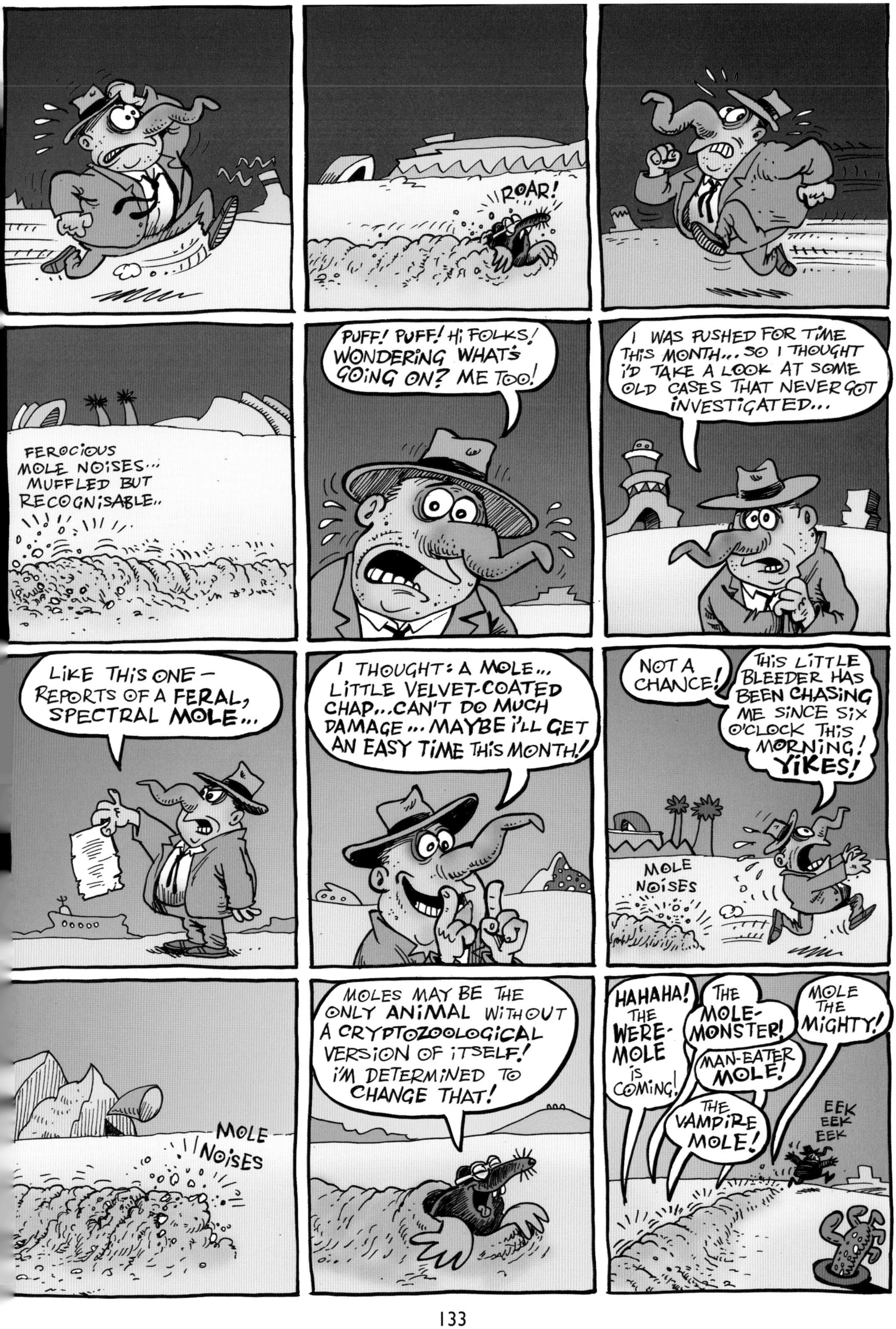
ROAR!
FEROCIOUS MOLE NOISES... MUFFLED BUT RECOGNISABLE..
PUFF! PUFF! Hi FOLKS! WONDERING WHAT'S GOING ON? ME TOO!
I WAS PUSHED FOR TIME THIS MONTH... SO I THOUGHT I'D TAKE A LOOK AT SOME OLD CASES THAT NEVER GOT INVESTIGATED...
LIKE THIS ONE – REPORTS OF A FERAL, SPECTRAL MOLE...
I THOUGHT: A MOLE... LITTLE VELVET-COATED CHAP... CAN'T DO MUCH DAMAGE... MAYBE I'LL GET AN EASY TIME THIS MONTH!
NOT A CHANCE!
THIS LITTLE BLEEDER HAS BEEN CHASING ME SINCE SIX O'CLOCK THIS MORNING! YIKES!
MOLE NOISES
MOLE NOISES
MOLES MAY BE THE ONLY ANIMAL WITHOUT A CRYPTOZOOLOGICAL VERSION OF ITSELF! I'M DETERMINED TO CHANGE THAT!
HAHAHA! THE WERE-MOLE IS COMING!
THE MOLE-MONSTER!
MOLE THE MIGHTY!
MAN-EATER MOLE!
THE VAMPIRE MOLE!
EEK EEK EEK

AN INTERVIEW WITH MOTHMAN

AH! GREETINGS! WELCOME TO MY MOTHARY!

I AM MOTHMAN!

PLEASE – SIT DOWN... HAVE A SLEEVE... RELAX WHILE I TELL YOU MY STORY...

WHEN I WAS MOTHBABY I WAS NO DIFFERENT TO ANY OF MY SIBLING. – I WAS AN EGG STUCK IN A CRACK IN A WARDROBE DOOR...

ME, AGED 4 DAYS

THEN, AS MOTHBOY, I STARTED TO FEEL MYSELF ISOLATED FROM THE OTHERS, PREFERRING TO NIBBLE QUIETLY ON A PIECE OF DAMASK WHEN MY CONTEMPORARIES WERE NOISILY MUNCHING FOOTBALL SOCKS IN A GANG!

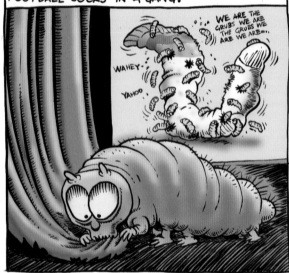

WE ARE THE GRUBS WE ARE THE GRUBS WE ARE WE ARE...

WAHEY!

YAHOO!

MY ADOLESCENCE WAS DIFFICULT. AS MOTHTEEN I SPENT MOST OF MY TIME WRAPPED IN A COCCOON OF SELF-ABSORBTION AND HOSTILITY...

GO AWAY!

IT'S NOT FAIR!

IN TIME I EMERGED – A FULLY-FLEDGED MOTH! BUT I WANTED MORE THAN MY COMRADES, WHO WISHED FOR NOTHING BUT TO FLUTTER INTO A CANDLEFLAME.

AT FIRST I WAS VIGOROUS AND SUCCESSFUL AS MOTH YOUNG EXECUTIVE...

...BUT TIME PASSED, AND I WAS NEVER ABLE TO QUITE MAKE THE GRADES! PROMOTION ELUDED ME!

I BECAME DEPRESSED AND ANGRY, AND TURNED INTO MOTH MIDDLE-AGED GROUCH!

I WAS A PAIN TO MYSELF AND A NUISANCE TO OTHERS – I BECAME MISERABLE MOTH!

PAH! EVERYTHING'S CRAP!

MOTH BALL

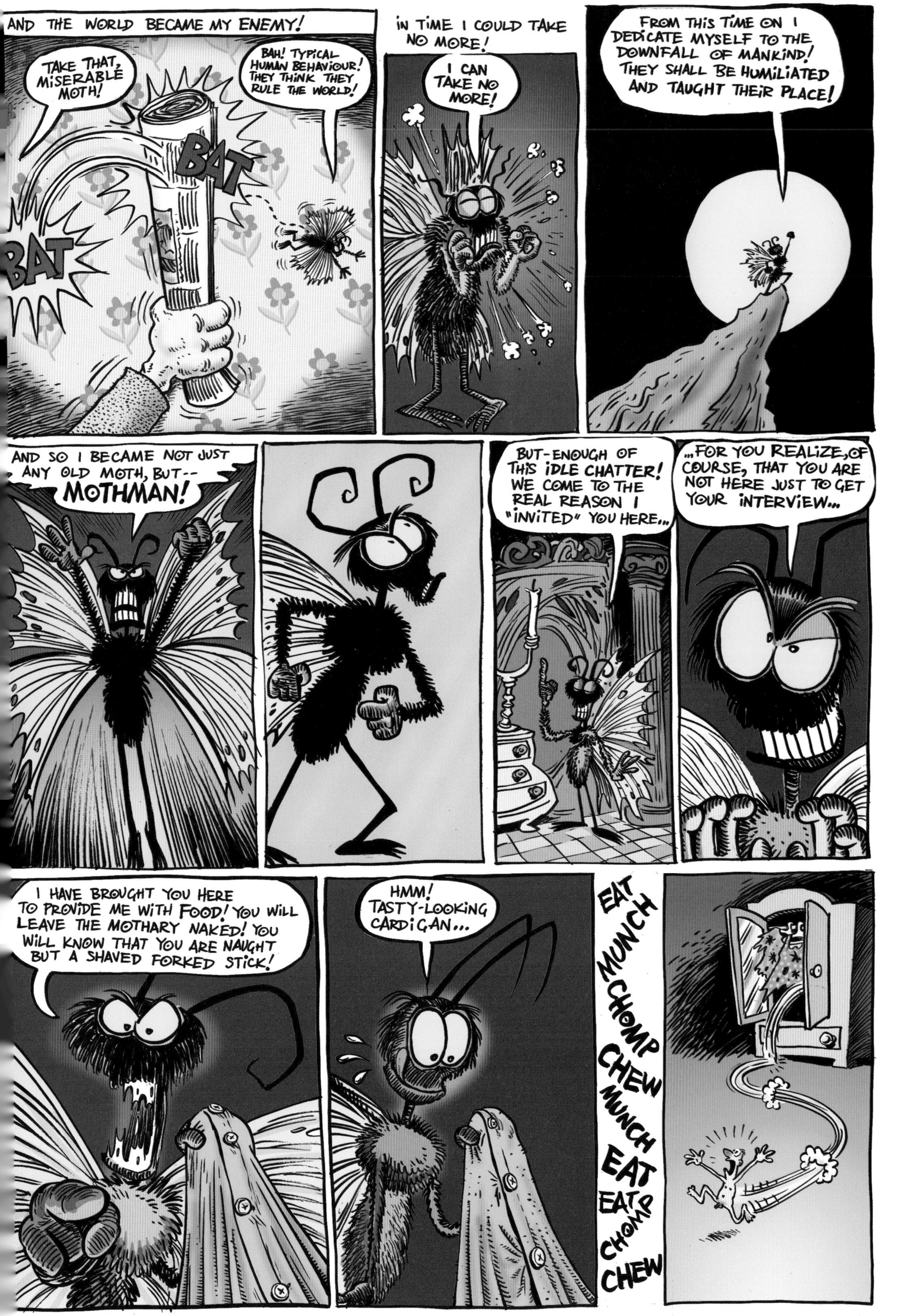

AND THE WORLD BECAME MY ENEMY!
TAKE THAT, MISERABLE MOTH!
BAH! TYPICAL HUMAN BEHAVIOUR! THEY THINK THEY RULE THE WORLD!
BAT
BAT
IN TIME I COULD TAKE NO MORE!
I CAN TAKE NO MORE!
FROM THIS TIME ON I DEDICATE MYSELF TO THE DOWNFALL OF MANKIND! THEY SHALL BE HUMILIATED AND TAUGHT THEIR PLACE!
AND SO I BECAME NOT JUST ANY OLD MOTH, BUT--
MOTHMAN!
BUT-ENOUGH OF THIS IDLE CHATTER! WE COME TO THE REAL REASON I "INVITED" YOU HERE...
...FOR YOU REALIZE, OF COURSE, THAT YOU ARE NOT HERE JUST TO GET YOUR INTERVIEW...
I HAVE BROUGHT YOU HERE TO PROVIDE ME WITH FOOD! YOU WILL LEAVE THE MOTHARY NAKED! YOU WILL KNOW THAT YOU ARE NAUGHT BUT A SHAVED FORKED STICK!
HMM! TASTY-LOOKING CARDIGAN...
EAT MUNCH CHOMP CHEW MUNCH EAT EAT CHOMP CHEW

MASS MICE

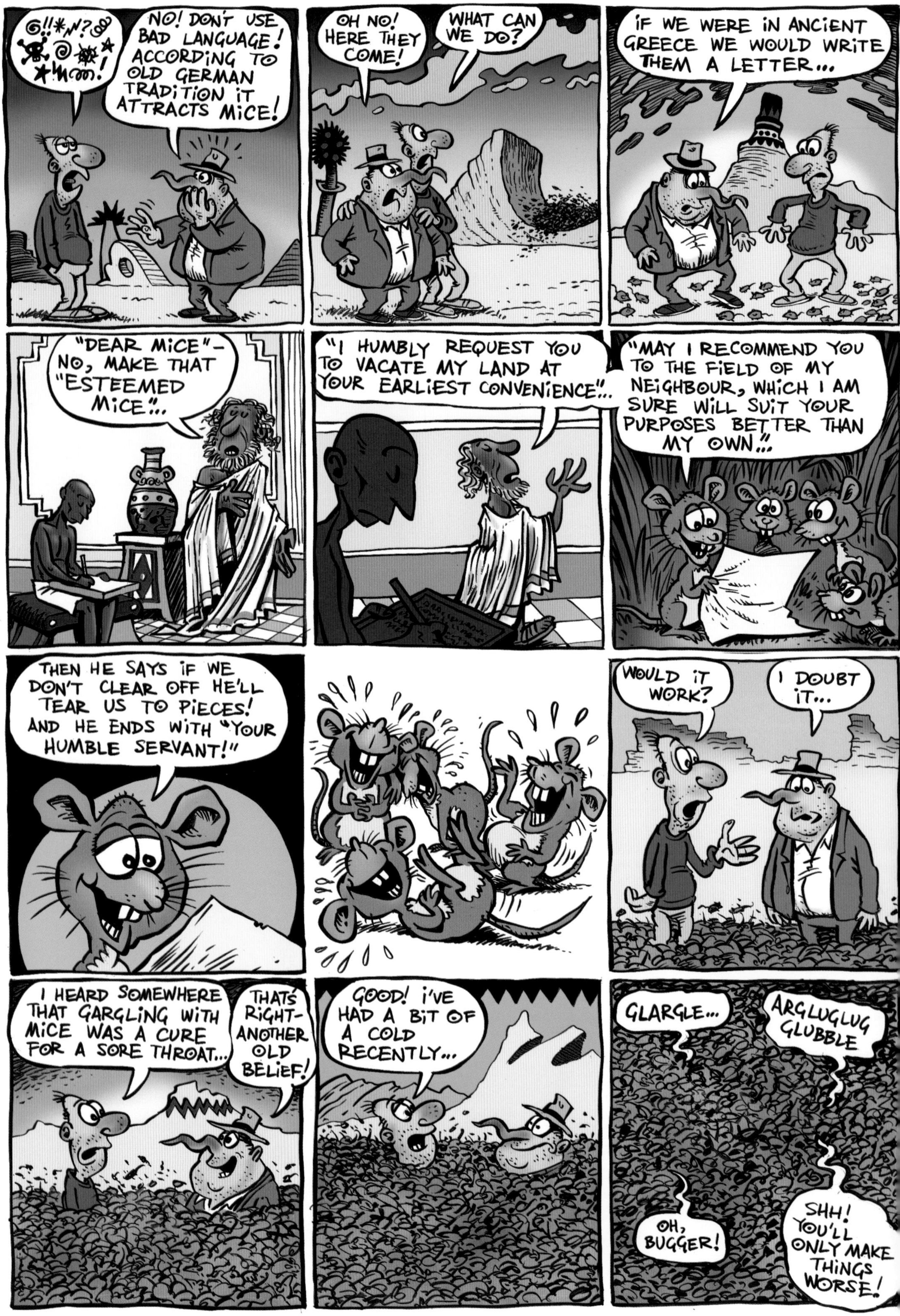
NO! DON'T USE BAD LANGUAGE! ACCORDING TO OLD GERMAN TRADITION IT ATTRACTS MICE!
OH NO! HERE THEY COME!
WHAT CAN WE DO?
IF WE WERE IN ANCIENT GREECE WE WOULD WRITE THEM A LETTER...
"DEAR MICE"– NO, MAKE THAT "ESTEEMED MICE"...
"I HUMBLY REQUEST YOU TO VACATE MY LAND AT YOUR EARLIEST CONVENIENCE"...
"MAY I RECOMMEND YOU TO THE FIELD OF MY NEIGHBOUR, WHICH I AM SURE WILL SUIT YOUR PURPOSES BETTER THAN MY OWN"...
THEN HE SAYS IF WE DON'T CLEAR OFF HE'LL TEAR US TO PIECES! AND HE ENDS WITH "YOUR HUMBLE SERVANT!"
WOULD IT WORK?
I DOUBT IT...
I HEARD SOMEWHERE THAT GARGLING WITH MICE WAS A CURE FOR A SORE THROAT...
THAT'S RIGHT– ANOTHER OLD BELIEF!
GOOD! I'VE HAD A BIT OF A COLD RECENTLY...
GLARGLE...
ARGLUGLUG GLUBBLE
OH, BUGGER!
SHH! YOU'LL ONLY MAKE THINGS WORSE!

MYSTERY SMELLS

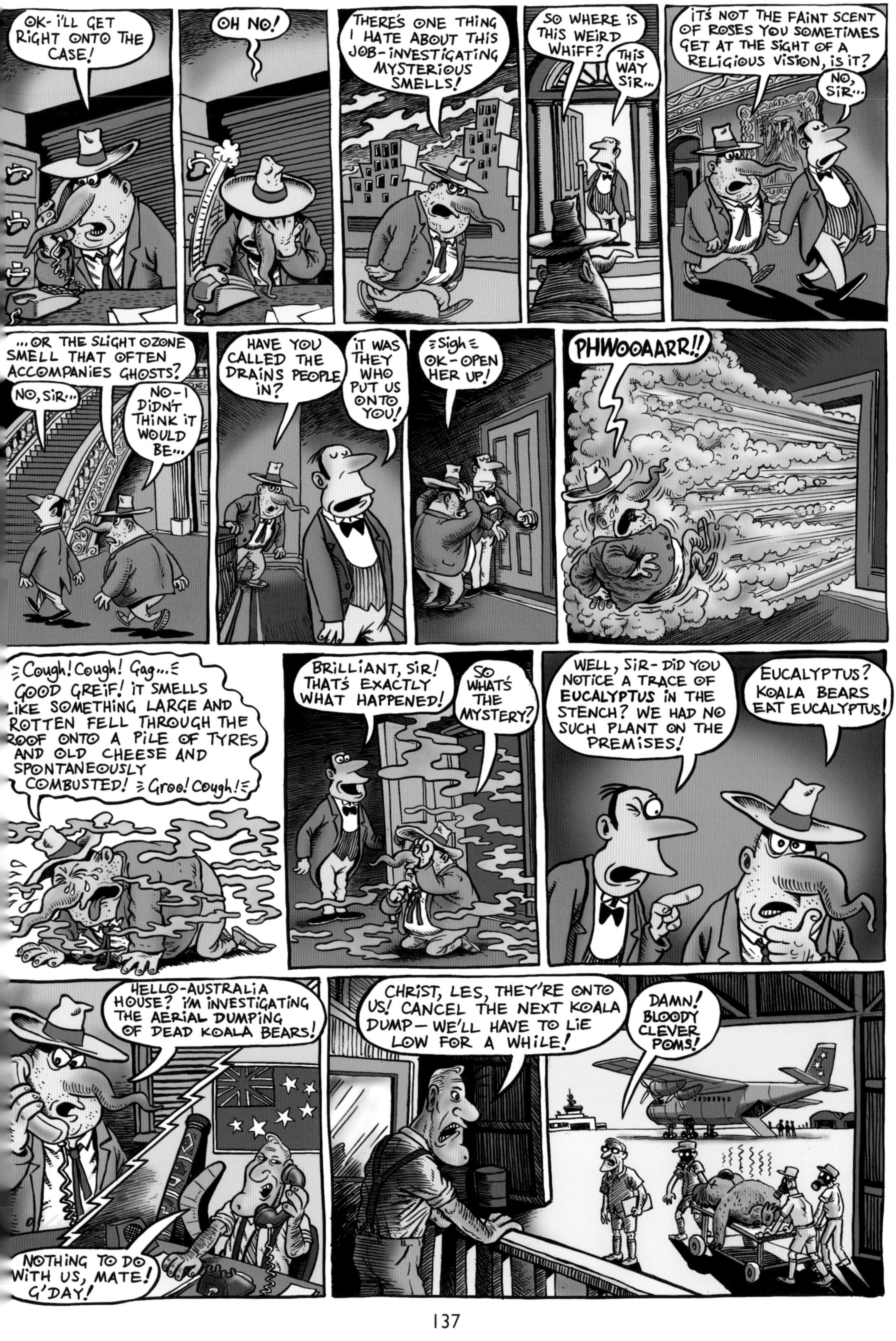

OK- I'LL GET RIGHT ONTO THE CASE!
OH NO!
THERE'S ONE THING I HATE ABOUT THIS JOB- INVESTIGATING MYSTERIOUS SMELLS!
SO WHERE IS THIS WEIRD WHIFF?
THIS WAY SIR...
IT'S NOT THE FAINT SCENT OF ROSES YOU SOMETIMES GET AT THE SIGHT OF A RELIGIOUS VISION, IS IT?
NO, SIR...
...OR THE SLIGHT OZONE SMELL THAT OFTEN ACCOMPANIES GHOSTS?
NO, SIR...
NO- I DIDN'T THINK IT WOULD BE...
HAVE YOU CALLED THE DRAINS PEOPLE IN?
IT WAS THEY WHO PUT US ONTO YOU!
Sigh OK- OPEN HER UP!
PHWOOAARR!!
Cough! Cough! Gag... GOOD GREIF! IT SMELLS LIKE SOMETHING LARGE AND ROTTEN FELL THROUGH THE ROOF ONTO A PILE OF TYRES AND OLD CHEESE AND SPONTANEOUSLY COMBUSTED! Groo! Cough!
BRILLIANT, SIR! THAT'S EXACTLY WHAT HAPPENED!
SO WHAT'S THE MYSTERY?
WELL, SIR- DID YOU NOTICE A TRACE OF EUCALYPTUS IN THE STENCH? WE HAD NO SUCH PLANT ON THE PREMISES!
EUCALYPTUS? KOALA BEARS EAT EUCALYPTUS!
HELLO- AUSTRALIA HOUSE? I'M INVESTIGATING THE AERIAL DUMPING OF DEAD KOALA BEARS!
NOTHING TO DO WITH US, MATE! G'DAY!
CHRIST, LES, THEY'RE ONTO US! CANCEL THE NEXT KOALA DUMP- WE'LL HAVE TO LIE LOW FOR A WHILE!
DAMN! BLOODY CLEVER POMS!

NAZCA

THE PLAIN OF NAZCA IN PERU IS A DRY, ROCKY DESERT, COVERED IN HUGE DRAWINGS, LINES, AND GEOMETRIC SHAPES FORMED IN THE SAND. THEY ARE SO LARGE THAT THEY ARE INDISCERNIBLE FROM GROUND LEVEL...

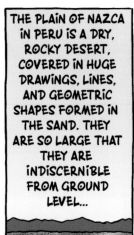

...AND CAN ONLY BE APPRECIATED FROM HIGH IN THE AIR ABOVE THEM!

FROM THIS HEIGHT THEY ARE BEAUTIFUL, MYSTERIOUS, AND AMAZING!

THE INCAS WHO MADE THEM 1500 YEARS AGO MUST HAVE HAD SOME METHOD OF FLYING - PROBABLY HOT AIR BALLOONS...

...BUT WHAT AM I, GULLY BULL - FORTEAN DETECTIVE - DOING THIS FAR ABOVE THE GROUND?

WELL, I MUST ADMIT I'M HERE MORE OR LESS BY ACCIDENT... MY TRUE PURPOSE IN VISITING PERU WAS TO FOLLOW UP REPORTS BY PILOTS OF THE PERUVIAN AIR FORCE OF A UFO!

BUT LAST NIGHT I MADE A HUGE SUPPER OF CHILLI BEANS, AND THIS MORNING I WOKE TO FIND MYSELF FLOATING UNCONTROLLABLY IN THE AIR!

OH! OH DEAR! AND NOW I FEEL THE INEVITABILITY OF A FART JOKE COMING ON... OOOH! OOOOHHHH!

GLUG GLORP

FPRRAAARPP

OOOH!

MADRE DE DIOS! IT'S THE UFO AGAIN!

PPPRRROOOOO

OOOHHH! OOWWW! OW! OOOWWW!

FFFRRZZZZZZZPPZZZZPPPPTTT!

CARAMBA! ARE THEY TRYING TO TELL US SOMETHING?!

GULLY BULL AT WORK

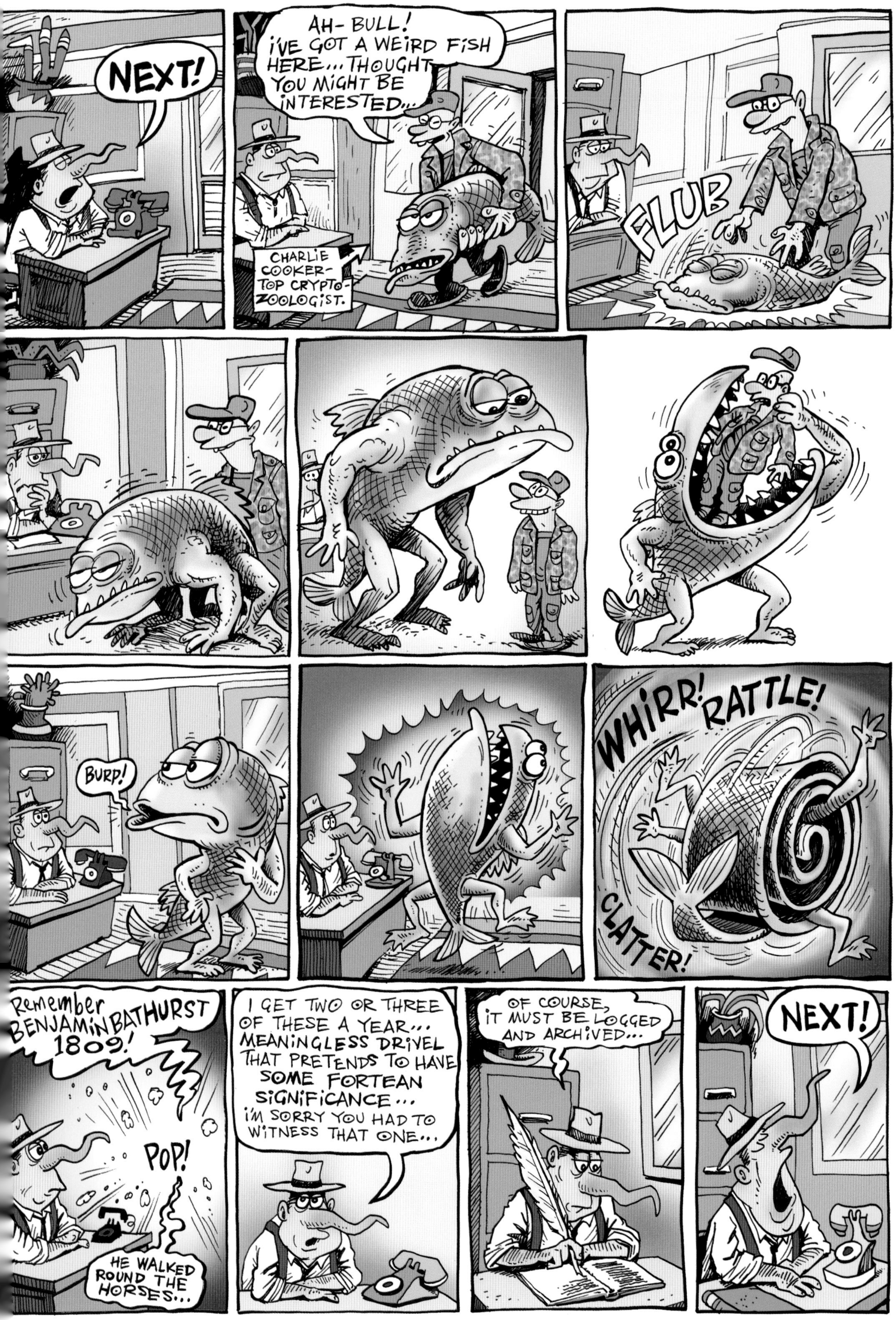
NEXT!
AH- BULL! I'VE GOT A WEIRD FISH HERE... THOUGHT YOU MIGHT BE INTERESTED...
CHARLIE COOKER- TOP CRYPTO-ZOOLOGIST.
FLUB
BURP!
WHIRR! RATTLE!
CLATTER!
Remember BENJAMIN BATHURST 1809!
POP!
HE WALKED ROUND THE HORSES...
I GET TWO OR THREE OF THESE A YEAR... MEANINGLESS DRIVEL THAT PRETENDS TO HAVE SOME FORTEAN SIGNIFICANCE... I'M SORRY YOU HAD TO WITNESS THAT ONE...
OF COURSE, IT MUST BE LOGGED AND ARCHIVED...
NEXT!

NULLABOR PLAIN

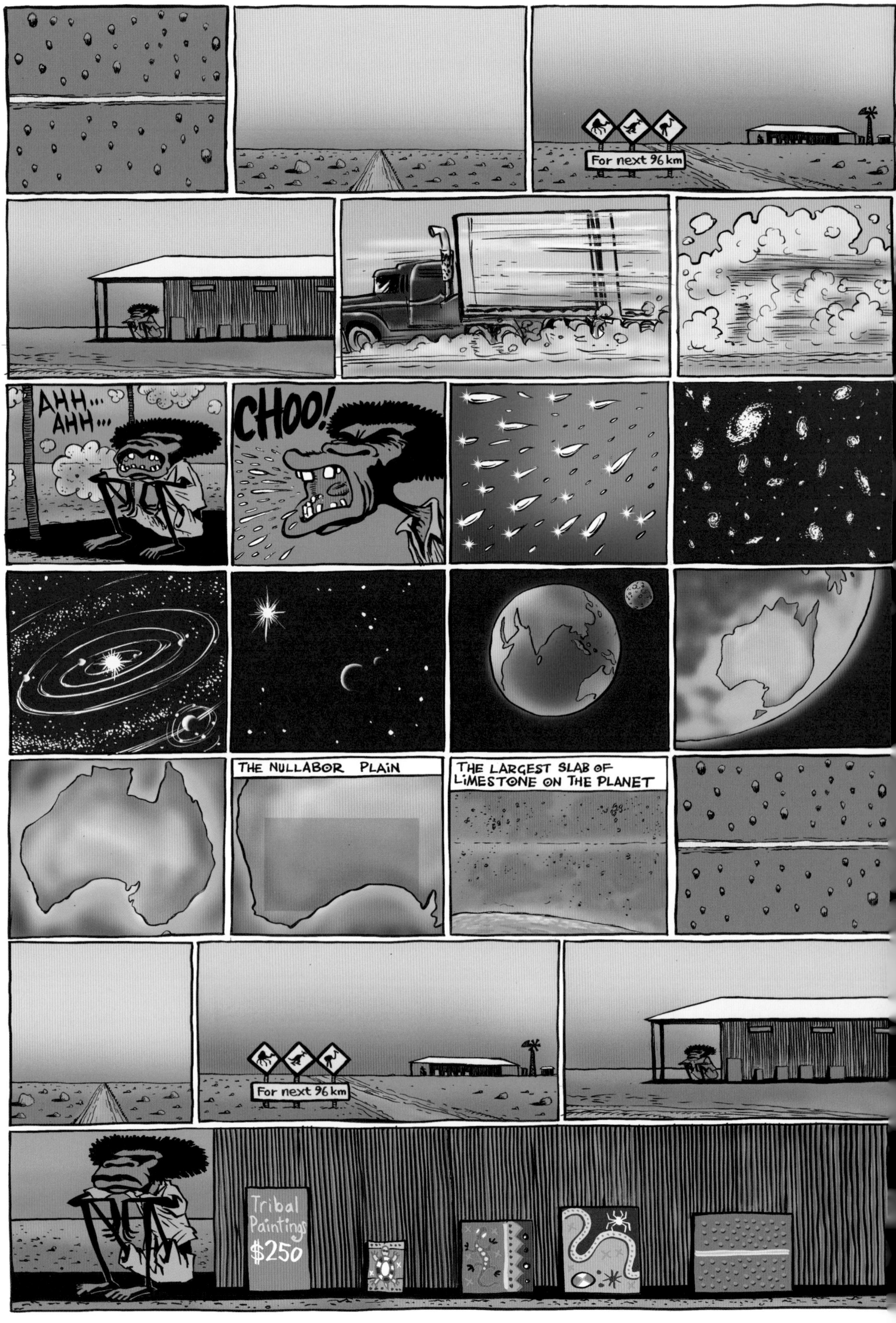
For next 96 km
AHH... AHH...
CHOO!
THE NULLABOR PLAIN
THE LARGEST SLAB OF LIMESTONE ON THE PLANET
For next 96 km
Tribal Paintings $250

OH! WHAT A BEAUTY!

Based on a song by the great Billy Cotton (Wakey Wakey!)

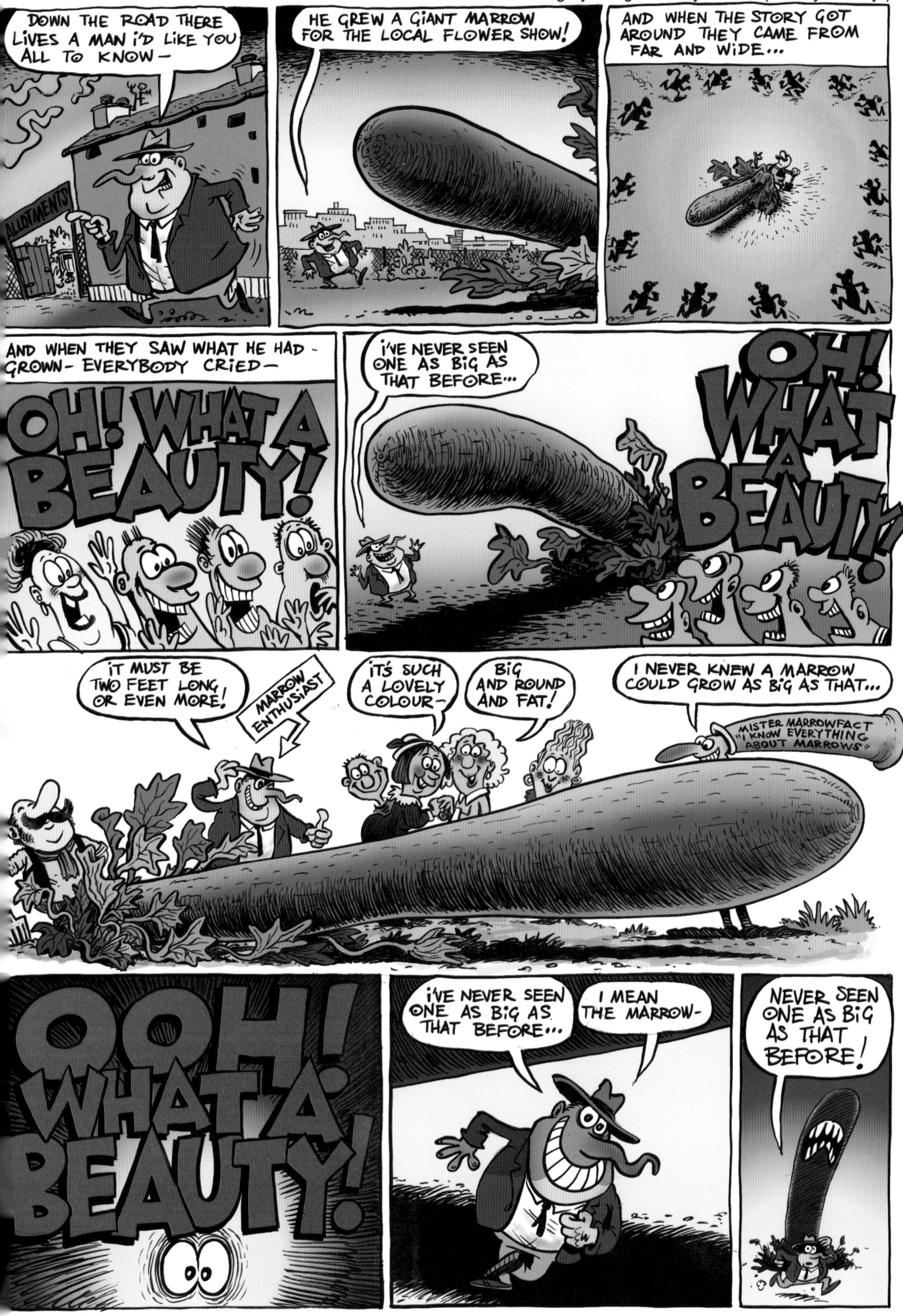

DOWN THE ROAD THERE LIVES A MAN I'D LIKE YOU ALL TO KNOW—
ALLOTMENTS
HE GREW A GIANT MARROW FOR THE LOCAL FLOWER SHOW!
AND WHEN THE STORY GOT AROUND THEY CAME FROM FAR AND WIDE...
AND WHEN THEY SAW WHAT HE HAD - GROWN- EVERYBODY CRIED—
OH! WHAT A BEAUTY!
I'VE NEVER SEEN ONE AS BIG AS THAT BEFORE...
OH! WHAT A BEAUTY!
IT MUST BE TWO FEET LONG OR EVEN MORE!
MARROW ENTHUSIAST
IT'S SUCH A LOVELY COLOUR-
BIG AND ROUND AND FAT!
I NEVER KNEW A MARROW COULD GROW AS BIG AS THAT...
MISTER MARROWFACT "I KNOW EVERYTHING ABOUT MARROWS"
OOH! WHAT A BEAUTY!
I'VE NEVER SEEN ONE AS BIG AS THAT BEFORE...
I MEAN THE MARROW-
NEVER SEEN ONE AS BIG AS THAT BEFORE!

OPPOSABLE THUMB

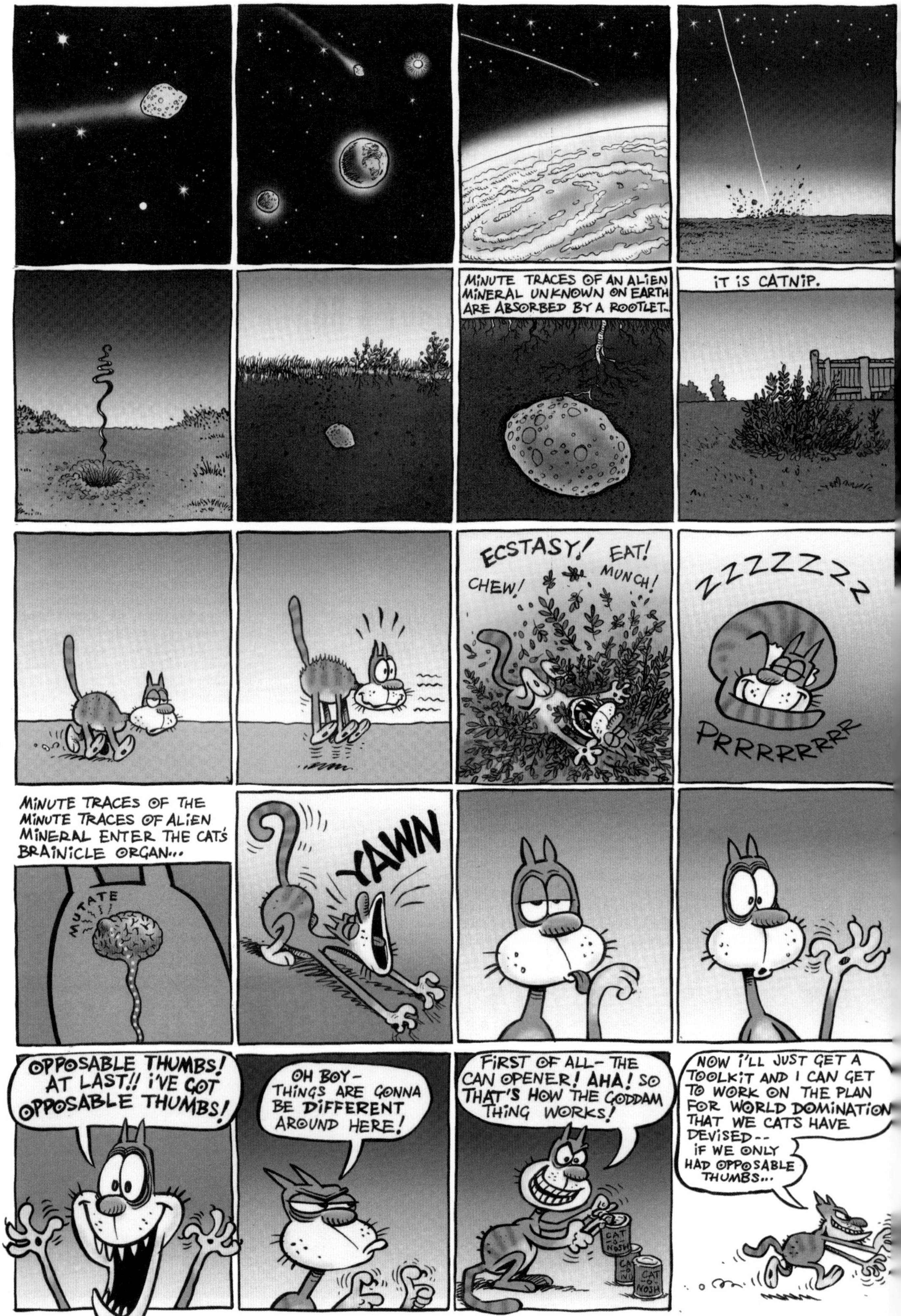
MINUTE TRACES OF AN ALIEN MINERAL UNKNOWN ON EARTH ARE ABSORBED BY A ROOTLET...
IT IS CATNIP.
ECSTASY! EAT! CHEW! MUNCH!
ZZZZZZZ
PRRRRRRRR
MINUTE TRACES OF THE MINUTE TRACES OF ALIEN MINERAL ENTER THE CAT'S BRAINICLE ORGAN...
MUTATE
YAWN
OPPOSABLE THUMBS! AT LAST!! I'VE GOT OPPOSABLE THUMBS!
OH BOY - THINGS ARE GONNA BE DIFFERENT AROUND HERE!
FIRST OF ALL - THE CAN OPENER! AHA! SO THAT'S HOW THE GODDAM THING WORKS!
CAT-O-NOSH
NOW I'LL JUST GET A TOOLKIT AND I CAN GET TO WORK ON THE PLAN FOR WORLD DOMINATION THAT WE CATS HAVE DEVISED -- IF WE ONLY HAD OPPOSABLE THUMBS...

GULLY BULL'S ORIGINS

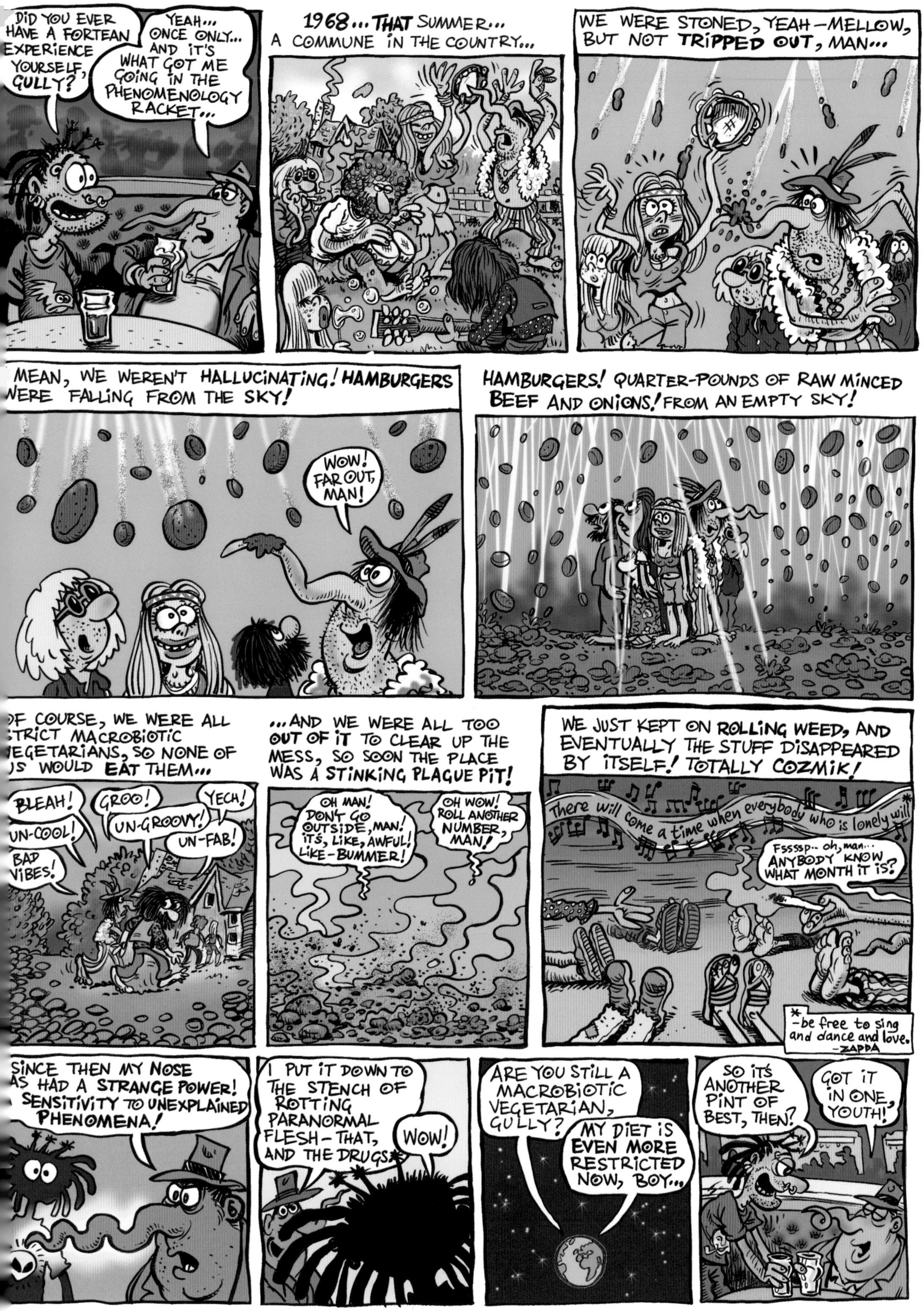

DID YOU EVER HAVE A FORTEAN EXPERIENCE YOURSELF, GULLY?
YEAH... ONCE ONLY... AND IT'S WHAT GOT ME GOING IN THE PHENOMENOLOGY RACKET...
1968... THAT SUMMER... A COMMUNE IN THE COUNTRY...
WE WERE STONED, YEAH – MELLOW, BUT NOT TRIPPED OUT, MAN...
MEAN, WE WEREN'T HALLUCINATING! HAMBURGERS ERE FALLING FROM THE SKY!
WOW! FAR OUT, MAN!
HAMBURGERS! QUARTER-POUNDS OF RAW MINCED BEEF AND ONIONS! FROM AN EMPTY SKY!
F COURSE, WE WERE ALL TRICT MACROBIOTIC EGETARIANS, SO NONE OF S WOULD EAT THEM...
BLEAH!
GROO!
YECH!
UN-COOL!
UN-GROOVY!
UN-FAB!
BAD VIBES!
...AND WE WERE ALL TOO OUT OF IT TO CLEAR UP THE MESS, SO SOON THE PLACE WAS A STINKING PLAGUE PIT!
OH MAN! DON'T GO OUTSIDE, MAN! IT'S, LIKE, AWFUL! LIKE-BUMMER!
OH WOW! ROLL ANOTHER NUMBER, MAN!
WE JUST KEPT ON ROLLING WEED, AND EVENTUALLY THE STUFF DISAPPEARED BY ITSELF! TOTALLY COZMIK!
There will come a time when everybody who is lonely will*
Fssssp.. oh, man... ANYBODY KNOW WHAT MONTH IT IS?
* –be free to sing and dance and love. –ZAPPA
SINCE THEN MY NOSE AS HAD A STRANGE POWER! SENSITIVITY TO UNEXPLAINED PHENOMENA!
I PUT IT DOWN TO THE STENCH OF ROTTING PARANORMAL FLESH – THAT, AND THE DRUGS!
WOW!
ARE YOU STILL A MACROBIOTIC VEGETARIAN, GULLY?
MY DIET IS EVEN MORE RESTRICTED NOW, BOY...
SO IT'S ANOTHER PINT OF BEST, THEN?
GOT IT IN ONE, YOUTH!

PANGRAMS

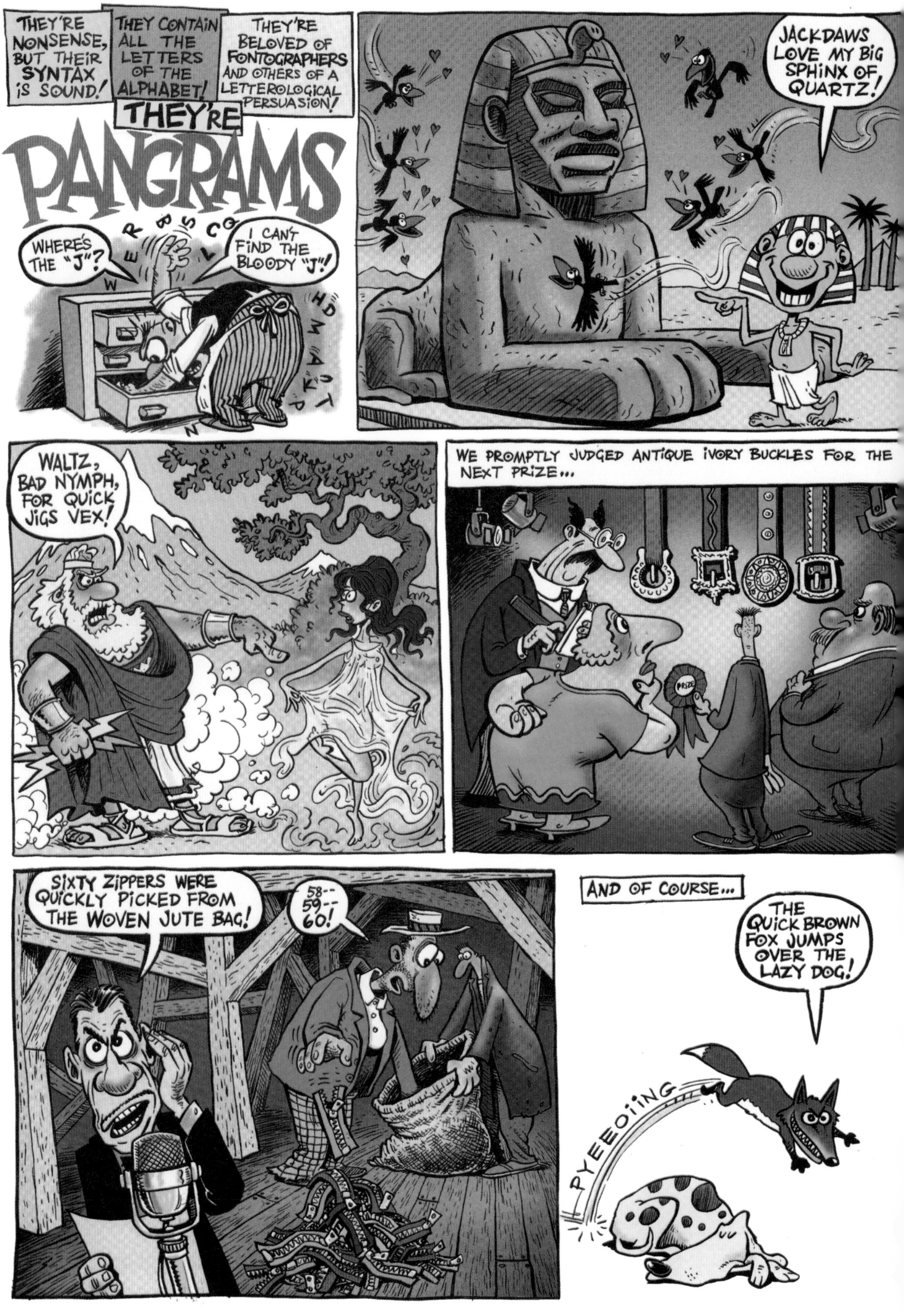

THEY'RE NONSENSE, BUT THEIR SYNTAX IS SOUND!
THEY CONTAIN ALL THE LETTERS OF THE ALPHABET!
THEY'RE BELOVED OF FONTOGRAPHERS AND OTHERS OF A LETTEROLOGICAL PERSUASION!
THEY'RE
PANGRAMS
WHERE'S THE "J"?
I CAN'T FIND THE BLOODY "J"!
JACKDAWS LOVE MY BIG SPHINX OF QUARTZ!
WALTZ, BAD NYMPH, FOR QUICK JIGS VEX!
WE PROMPTLY JUDGED ANTIQUE IVORY BUCKLES FOR THE NEXT PRIZE...
PRIZE
SIXTY ZIPPERS WERE QUICKLY PICKED FROM THE WOVEN JUTE BAG!
58-- 59-- 60!
AND OF COURSE...
THE QUICK BROWN FOX JUMPS OVER THE LAZY DOG!
PYEEEOIING

PARROT BLOOD

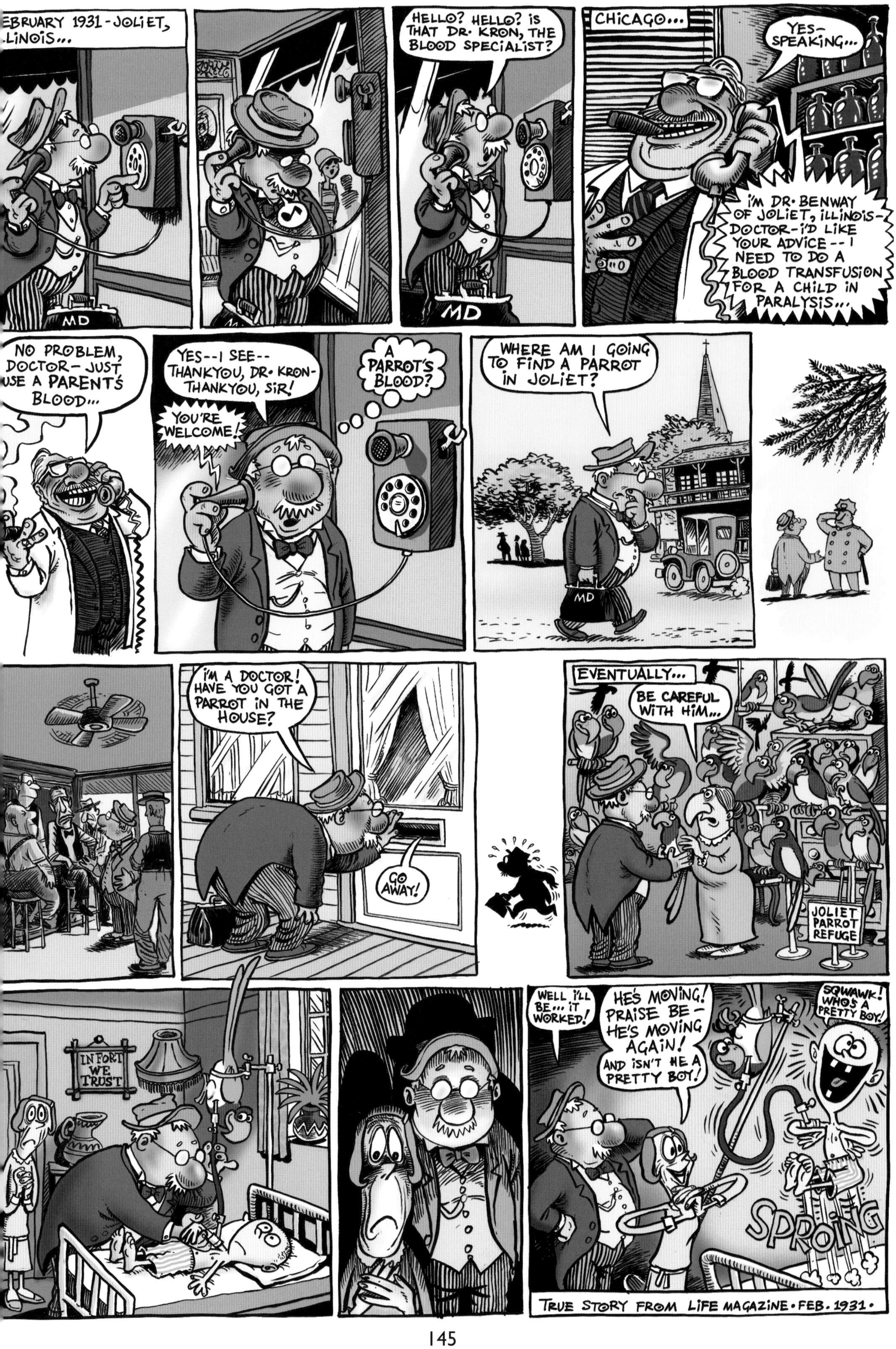

EBRUARY 1931-JOLIET, LINOIS...
MD
HELLO? HELLO? IS THAT DR. KRON, THE BLOOD SPECIALIST?
MD
CHICAGO...
YES-SPEAKING...
I'M DR. BENWAY OF JOLIET, ILLINOIS-DOCTOR-I'D LIKE YOUR ADVICE--I NEED TO DO A BLOOD TRANSFUSION FOR A CHILD IN PARALYSIS...
NO PROBLEM, DOCTOR-JUST USE A PARENT'S BLOOD...
YES--I SEE--THANKYOU, DR. KRON-THANKYOU, SIR!
YOU'RE WELCOME!
A PARROT'S BLOOD?
WHERE AM I GOING TO FIND A PARROT IN JOLIET?
MD
I'M A DOCTOR! HAVE YOU GOT A PARROT IN THE HOUSE?
GO AWAY!
EVENTUALLY...
BE CAREFUL WITH HIM...
JOLIET PARROT REFUGE
IN FORT WE TRUST
WELL I'LL BE... IT WORKED!
HE'S MOVING! PRAISE BE-HE'S MOVING AGAIN! AND ISN'T HE A PRETTY BOY!
SQWAWK! WHOS A PRETTY BOY!
SPROING
TRUE STORY FROM LIFE MAGAZINE • FEB. 1931 •

PHANTOM LIMBS

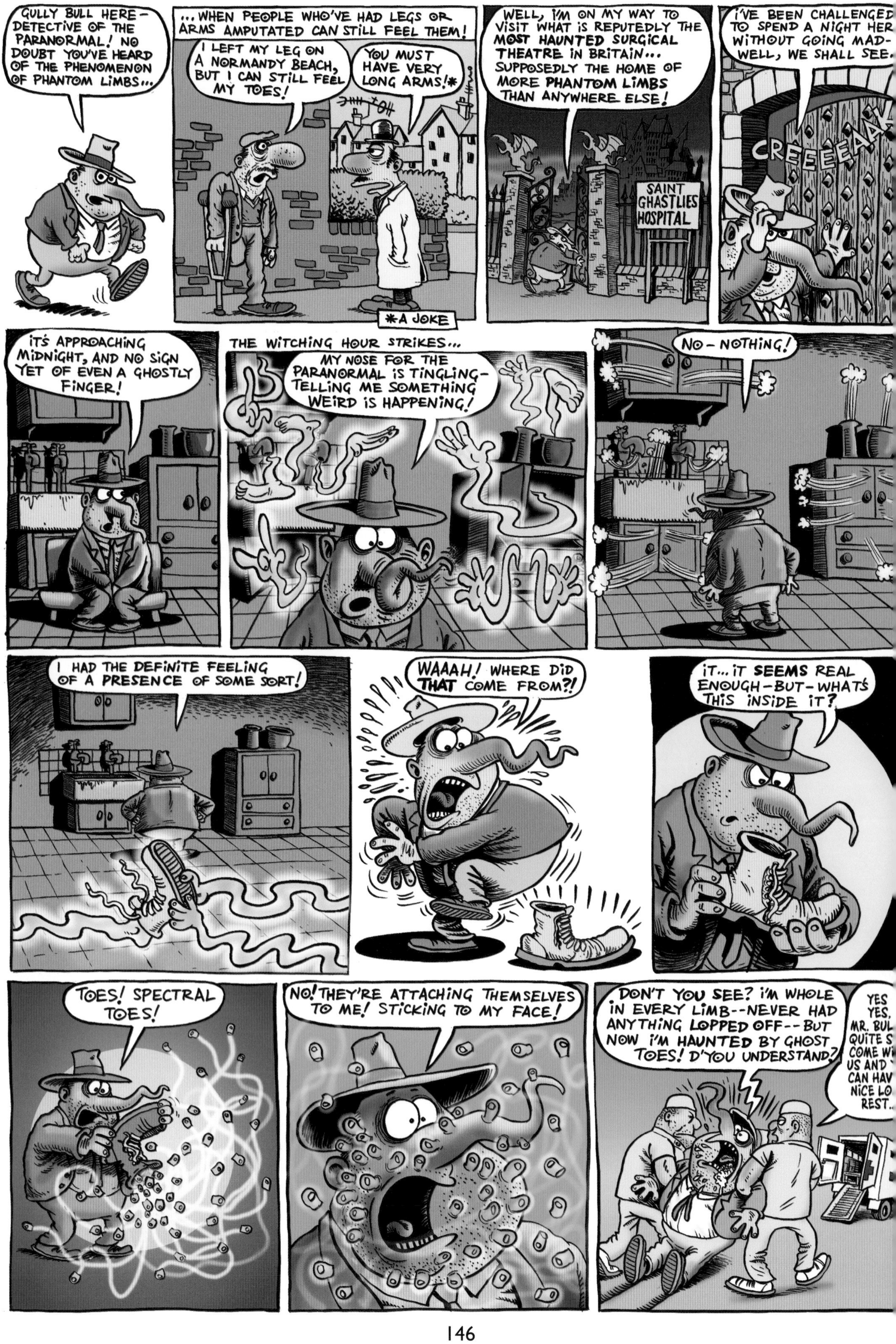
GULLY BULL HERE–DETECTIVE OF THE PARANORMAL! NO DOUBT YOU'VE HEARD OF THE PHENOMENON OF PHANTOM LIMBS...
...WHEN PEOPLE WHO'VE HAD LEGS OR ARMS AMPUTATED CAN STILL FEEL THEM!
I LEFT MY LEG ON A NORMANDY BEACH, BUT I CAN STILL FEEL MY TOES!
YOU MUST HAVE VERY LONG ARMS!*
*A JOKE
WELL, I'M ON MY WAY TO VISIT WHAT IS REPUTEDLY THE MOST HAUNTED SURGICAL THEATRE IN BRITAIN... SUPPOSEDLY THE HOME OF MORE PHANTOM LIMBS THAN ANYWHERE ELSE!
SAINT GHASTLIES HOSPITAL
I'VE BEEN CHALLENGED TO SPEND A NIGHT HER WITHOUT GOING MAD–WELL, WE SHALL SEE.
CREEEEEAK
IT'S APPROACHING MIDNIGHT, AND NO SIGN YET OF EVEN A GHOSTLY FINGER!
THE WITCHING HOUR STRIKES...
MY NOSE FOR THE PARANORMAL IS TINGLING–TELLING ME SOMETHING WEIRD IS HAPPENING!
NO–NOTHING!
I HAD THE DEFINITE FEELING OF A PRESENCE OF SOME SORT!
WAAAH! WHERE DID THAT COME FROM?!
IT... IT SEEMS REAL ENOUGH–BUT–WHAT'S THIS INSIDE IT?
TOES! SPECTRAL TOES!
NO! THEY'RE ATTACHING THEMSELVES TO ME! STICKING TO MY FACE!
DON'T YOU SEE? I'M WHOLE IN EVERY LIMB--NEVER HAD ANYTHING LOPPED OFF--BUT NOW I'M HAUNTED BY GHOST TOES! D'YOU UNDERSTAND?
YES YES, MR. BUL QUITE S COME W US AND CAN HAV NICE LO REST.

PHRENOLENOMIX

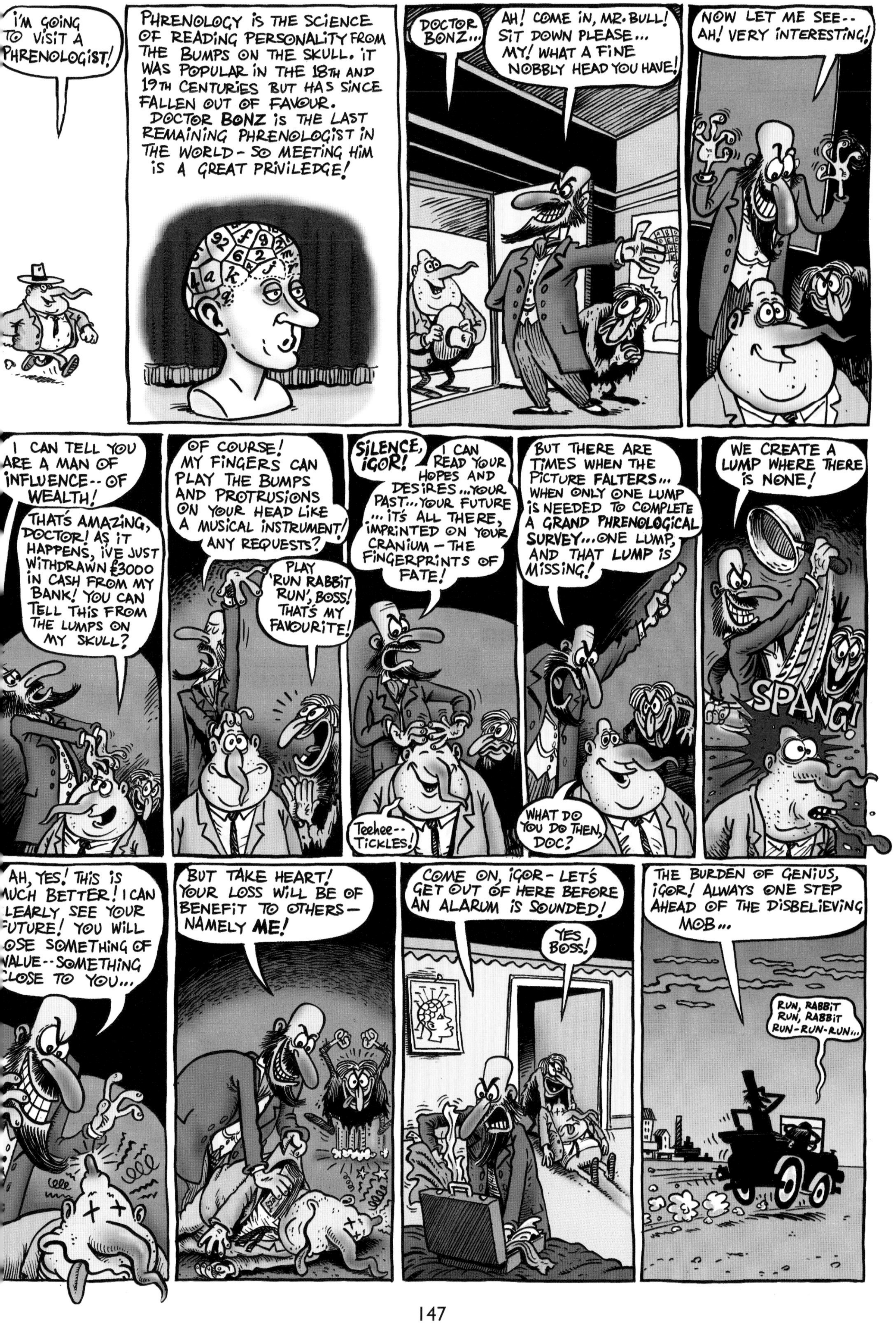

I'M GOING TO VISIT A PHRENOLOGIST!
PHRENOLOGY IS THE SCIENCE OF READING PERSONALITY FROM THE BUMPS ON THE SKULL. IT WAS POPULAR IN THE 18TH AND 19TH CENTURIES BUT HAS SINCE FALLEN OUT OF FAVOUR. DOCTOR BONZ IS THE LAST REMAINING PHRENOLOGIST IN THE WORLD - SO MEETING HIM IS A GREAT PRIVILEDGE!
DOCTOR BONZ...
AH! COME IN, MR. BULL! SIT DOWN PLEASE... MY! WHAT A FINE NOBBLY HEAD YOU HAVE!
NOW LET ME SEE-- AH! VERY INTERESTING!
I CAN TELL YOU ARE A MAN OF INFLUENCE-- OF WEALTH!
THAT'S AMAZING, DOCTOR! AS IT HAPPENS, I'VE JUST WITHDRAWN £3000 IN CASH FROM MY BANK! YOU CAN TELL THIS FROM THE LUMPS ON MY SKULL?
OF COURSE! MY FINGERS CAN PLAY THE BUMPS AND PROTRUSIONS ON YOUR HEAD LIKE A MUSICAL INSTRUMENT! ANY REQUESTS?
PLAY 'RUN RABBIT RUN', BOSS! THAT'S MY FAVOURITE!
SILENCE, IGOR!
I CAN READ YOUR HOPES AND DESIRES...YOUR PAST...YOUR FUTURE ...IT'S ALL THERE, IMPRINTED ON YOUR CRANIUM - THE FINGERPRINTS OF FATE!
Teehee-- TICKLES!
BUT THERE ARE TIMES WHEN THE PICTURE FALTERS... WHEN ONLY ONE LUMP IS NEEDED TO COMPLETE A GRAND PHRENOLOGICAL SURVEY...ONE LUMP, AND THAT LUMP IS MISSING!
WHAT DO YOU DO THEN, DOC?
WE CREATE A LUMP WHERE THERE IS NONE!
SPANG!
AH, YES! THIS IS UCH BETTER! I CAN LEARLY SEE YOUR UTURE! YOU WILL OSE SOMETHING OF ALUE--SOMETHING LOSE TO YOU...
BUT TAKE HEART! YOUR LOSS WILL BE OF BENEFIT TO OTHERS - NAMELY ME!
COME ON, IGOR - LET'S GET OUT OF HERE BEFORE AN ALARUM IS SOUNDED!
YES BOSS!
THE BURDEN OF GENIUS, IGOR! ALWAYS ONE STEP AHEAD OF THE DISBELIEVING MOB...
RUN, RABBIT RUN, RABBIT RUN-RUN-RUN...

PRESLEYANITY

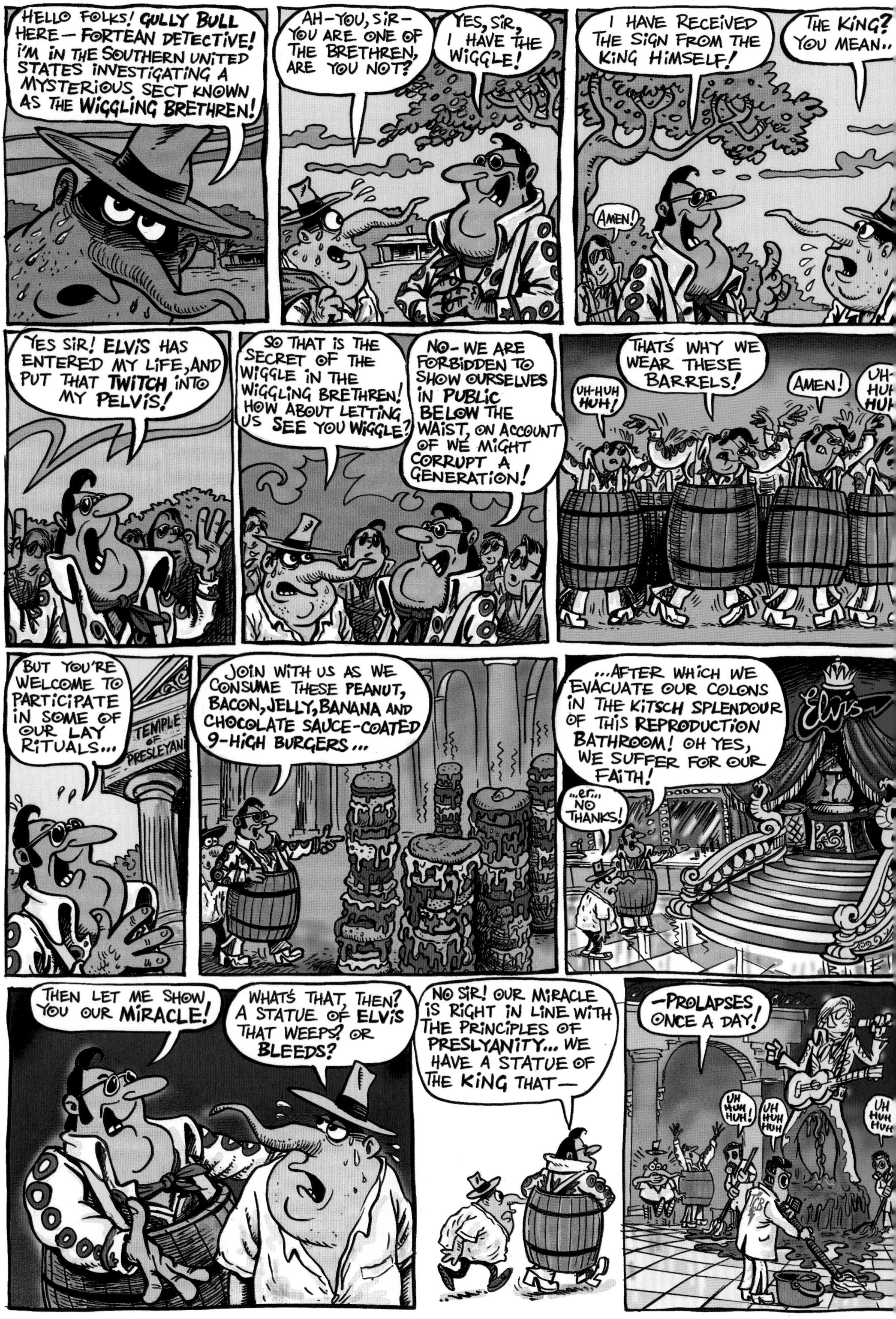

HELLO FOLKS! GULLY BULL HERE — FORTEAN DETECTIVE! I'M IN THE SOUTHERN UNITED STATES INVESTIGATING A MYSTERIOUS SECT KNOWN AS THE WIGGLING BRETHREN!
AH — YOU, SIR — YOU ARE ONE OF THE BRETHREN, ARE YOU NOT?
YES, SIR, I HAVE THE WIGGLE!
I HAVE RECEIVED THE SIGN FROM THE KING HIMSELF!
AMEN!
THE KING? YOU MEAN..
YES SIR! ELVIS HAS ENTERED MY LIFE, AND PUT THAT TWITCH INTO MY PELVIS!
SO THAT IS THE SECRET OF THE WIGGLE IN THE WIGGLING BRETHREN! HOW ABOUT LETTING US SEE YOU WIGGLE?
NO — WE ARE FORBIDDEN TO SHOW OURSELVES IN PUBLIC BELOW THE WAIST, ON ACCOUNT OF WE MIGHT CORRUPT A GENERATION!
UH-HUH HUH!
THAT'S WHY WE WEAR THESE BARRELS!
AMEN!
UH-HUH HUH
BUT YOU'RE WELCOME TO PARTICIPATE IN SOME OF OUR LAY RITUALS...
TEMPLE OF PRESLEYANI
JOIN WITH US AS WE CONSUME THESE PEANUT, BACON, JELLY, BANANA AND CHOCOLATE SAUCE-COATED 9-HIGH BURGERS...
...AFTER WHICH WE EVACUATE OUR COLONS IN THE KITSCH SPLENDOUR OF THIS REPRODUCTION BATHROOM! OH YES, WE SUFFER FOR OUR FAITH!
...er... NO THANKS!
Elvis
THEN LET ME SHOW YOU OUR MIRACLE!
WHAT'S THAT, THEN? A STATUE OF ELVIS THAT WEEPS? OR BLEEDS?
NO SIR! OUR MIRACLE IS RIGHT IN LINE WITH THE PRINCIPLES OF PRESLYANITY... WE HAVE A STATUE OF THE KING THAT—
—PROLAPSES ONCE A DAY!
UH HUH HUH!
UH HUH HUH
UH HUH HUH

PROPHETIC BEER

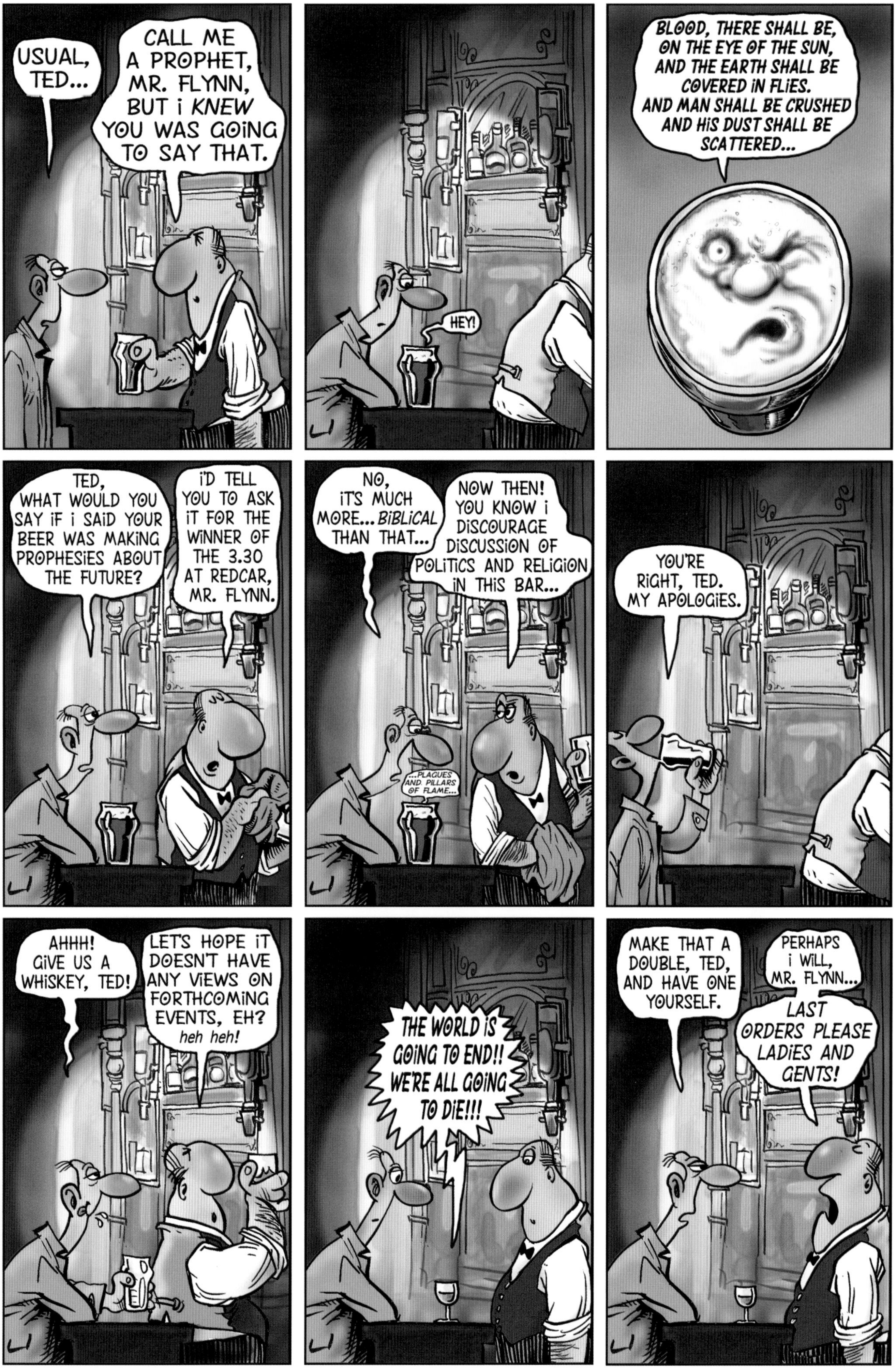
USUAL, TED...
CALL ME A PROPHET, MR. FLYNN, BUT I KNEW YOU WAS GOING TO SAY THAT.
HEY!
BLOOD, THERE SHALL BE, ON THE EYE OF THE SUN, AND THE EARTH SHALL BE COVERED IN FLIES. AND MAN SHALL BE CRUSHED AND HIS DUST SHALL BE SCATTERED...
TED, WHAT WOULD YOU SAY IF I SAID YOUR BEER WAS MAKING PROPHESIES ABOUT THE FUTURE?
I'D TELL YOU TO ASK IT FOR THE WINNER OF THE 3.30 AT REDCAR, MR. FLYNN.
NO, IT'S MUCH MORE... BIBLICAL THAN THAT...
NOW THEN! YOU KNOW I DISCOURAGE DISCUSSION OF POLITICS AND RELIGION IN THIS BAR...
...PLAGUES AND PILLARS OF FLAME...
YOU'RE RIGHT, TED. MY APOLOGIES.
AHHH! GIVE US A WHISKEY, TED!
LET'S HOPE IT DOESN'T HAVE ANY VIEWS ON FORTHCOMING EVENTS, EH? heh heh!
THE WORLD IS GOING TO END!! WE'RE ALL GOING TO DIE!!!
MAKE THAT A DOUBLE, TED, AND HAVE ONE YOURSELF.
PERHAPS I WILL, MR. FLYNN...
LAST ORDERS PLEASE LADIES AND GENTS!

PSYCHIC DINNER

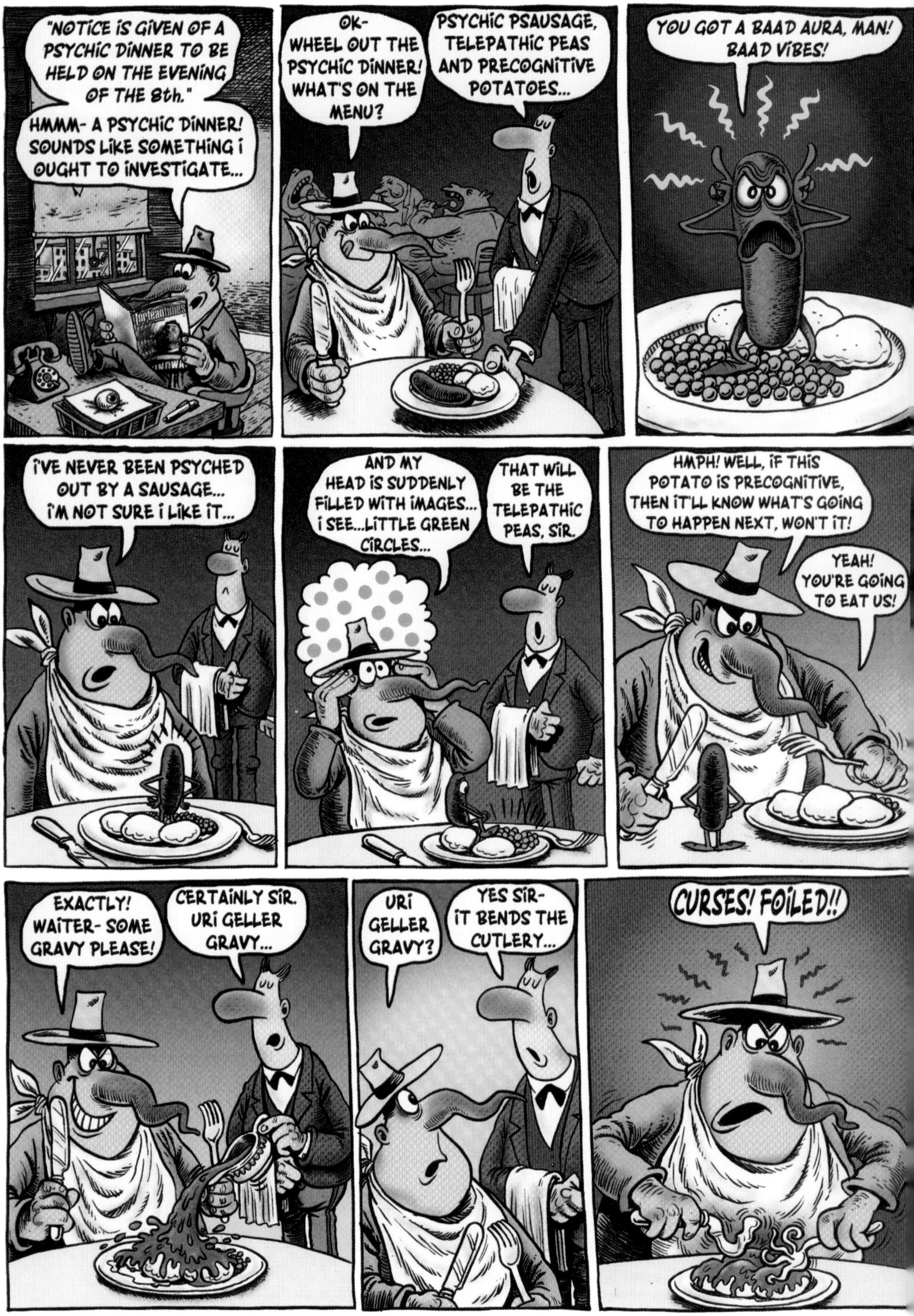
"NOTICE IS GIVEN OF A PSYCHIC DINNER TO BE HELD ON THE EVENING OF THE 8th."
HMMM- A PSYCHIC DINNER! SOUNDS LIKE SOMETHING I OUGHT TO INVESTIGATE...
OK- WHEEL OUT THE PSYCHIC DINNER! WHAT'S ON THE MENU?
PSYCHIC PSAUSAGE, TELEPATHIC PEAS AND PRECOGNITIVE POTATOES...
YOU GOT A BAAD AURA, MAN! BAAD VIBES!
I'VE NEVER BEEN PSYCHED OUT BY A SAUSAGE... I'M NOT SURE I LIKE IT...
AND MY HEAD IS SUDDENLY FILLED WITH IMAGES... I SEE...LITTLE GREEN CIRCLES...
THAT WILL BE THE TELEPATHIC PEAS, SIR.
HMPH! WELL, IF THIS POTATO IS PRECOGNITIVE, THEN IT'LL KNOW WHAT'S GOING TO HAPPEN NEXT, WON'T IT!
YEAH! YOU'RE GOING TO EAT US!
EXACTLY! WAITER- SOME GRAVY PLEASE!
CERTAINLY SIR. URI GELLER GRAVY...
URI GELLER GRAVY?
YES SIR- IT BENDS THE CUTLERY...
CURSES! FOILED!!

PUCKSY

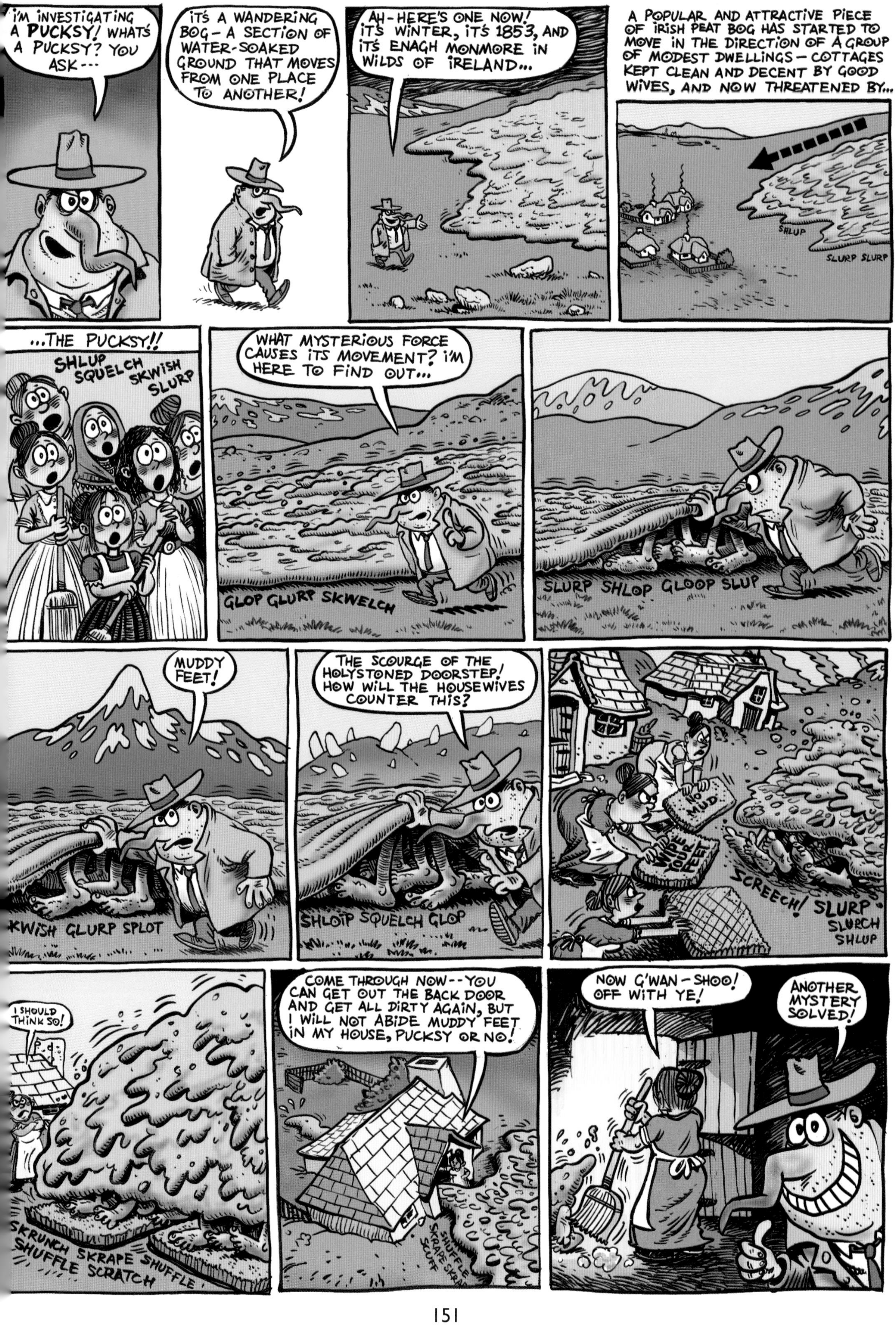
I'M INVESTIGATING A PUCKSY! WHAT'S A PUCKSY? YOU ASK---
IT'S A WANDERING BOG - A SECTION OF WATER-SOAKED GROUND THAT MOVES FROM ONE PLACE TO ANOTHER!
AH - HERE'S ONE NOW! IT'S WINTER, IT'S 1853, AND IT'S ENAGH MONMORE IN WILDS OF IRELAND...
A POPULAR AND ATTRACTIVE PIECE OF IRISH PEAT BOG HAS STARTED TO MOVE IN THE DIRECTION OF A GROUP OF MODEST DWELLINGS - COTTAGES KEPT CLEAN AND DECENT BY GOOD WIVES, AND NOW THREATENED BY...
SHLUP
SLURP SLURP
...THE PUCKSY!!
SHLUP SQUELCH SKWISH SLURP
WHAT MYSTERIOUS FORCE CAUSES ITS MOVEMENT? I'M HERE TO FIND OUT...
GLOP GLURP SKWELCH
SLURP SHLOP GLOOP SLUP
MUDDY FEET!
SKWISH GLURP SPLOT
THE SCOURGE OF THE HOLYSTONED DOORSTEP! HOW WILL THE HOUSEWIVES COUNTER THIS?
SHLOIP SQUELCH GLOP
NO MUD
WIPE YOUR FEET
SCREECH! SLURP SLURCH SHLUP
I SHOULD THINK SO!
SKRUNCH SKRAPE SHUFFLE SHUFFLE SCRATCH
COME THROUGH NOW--YOU CAN GET OUT THE BACK DOOR AND GET ALL DIRTY AGAIN, BUT I WILL NOT ABIDE MUDDY FEET IN MY HOUSE, PUCKSY OR NO!
SHUFFLE SKRAPE SKRA SCUFF
NOW G'WAN - SHOO! OFF WITH YE!
ANOTHER MYSTERY SOLVED!

TRULY TRUE PYRAMID TRUTHS

THEY CAME FROM THE STARS - AND THEY WERE HIRSUTE!

SO HIRSUTE WERE THEY THAT, WHEN HUMANS DEPICTED THEM, IT WAS WITH THE BODIES OF LIONS!

YOU SEE, ON OUR PLANET, BEING HAIRY IS FRIGHTFULLY INFRA-DIG. WE SHAVE OUR WHOLE BODIES THREE TIMES A DAY, AND IT COSTS US A FORTUNE IN RAZOR BLADES...

WE'VE BEEN SEARCHING FOR A PLANET WITH THE RIGHT GEOMANCY TO CONSTRUCT OUR MASS RAZOR SHARPENING DEVICES - AND YOU'RE IT!

YOU'RE WASTING YOUR BREATH, THOTH- THEY'RE NOT LISTENING TO YOU...

AND SO THE GREAT BLADE SHARPENING DEVICES WERE CONSTRUCTED.

THE BLADE-SHARPENING CHAMBER, DEEP INSIDE THE DEVICE...

THIRSTY WORK, THIS- BEING A BLADE-MINDER... VERY THIRSTY...

THIRSTY? AH!- COME WITH ME! WE HAVE THOUGHT OF THAT!

SEE- THE SIZE AND SHAPE OF THE SHARPENERS CONDENSES WATER, WHICH STREAMS DOWN THE SIDE. PLENTY TO DRINK!

OH... THANK YOU... I WAS THINKING OF A BEER, ACTUALLY...

NOW- BACK TO WORK! MORE BLADES TO SHARPEN! I'M FEELING BRISTLY!

WE'VE GOT A RIVER OVER THERE FOR WATER, LIKE...

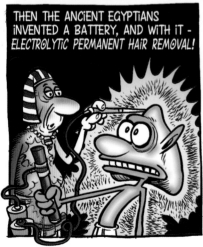

THEN THE ANCIENT EGYPTIANS INVENTED A BATTERY, AND WITH IT - ELECTROLYTIC PERMANENT HAIR REMOVAL!

THE ALIENS, BEAUTIFULLY SMOOTH, NO LONGER HAD ANY NEED FOR RAZOR BLADES...

...OR RAZOR BLADE SHARPENERS!

AND SO THEY LEFT EARTH!

Hey! What are we supposed to do with these things?!

WITH THE RISE OF THE JUDAEO-CHRISTIAN SYSTEM, HAIRY SWEATYNESS ONCE MORE SWEPT THE EARTH...

...AND THE LORE OF THE STAR FOLK WAS FORGOTTEN

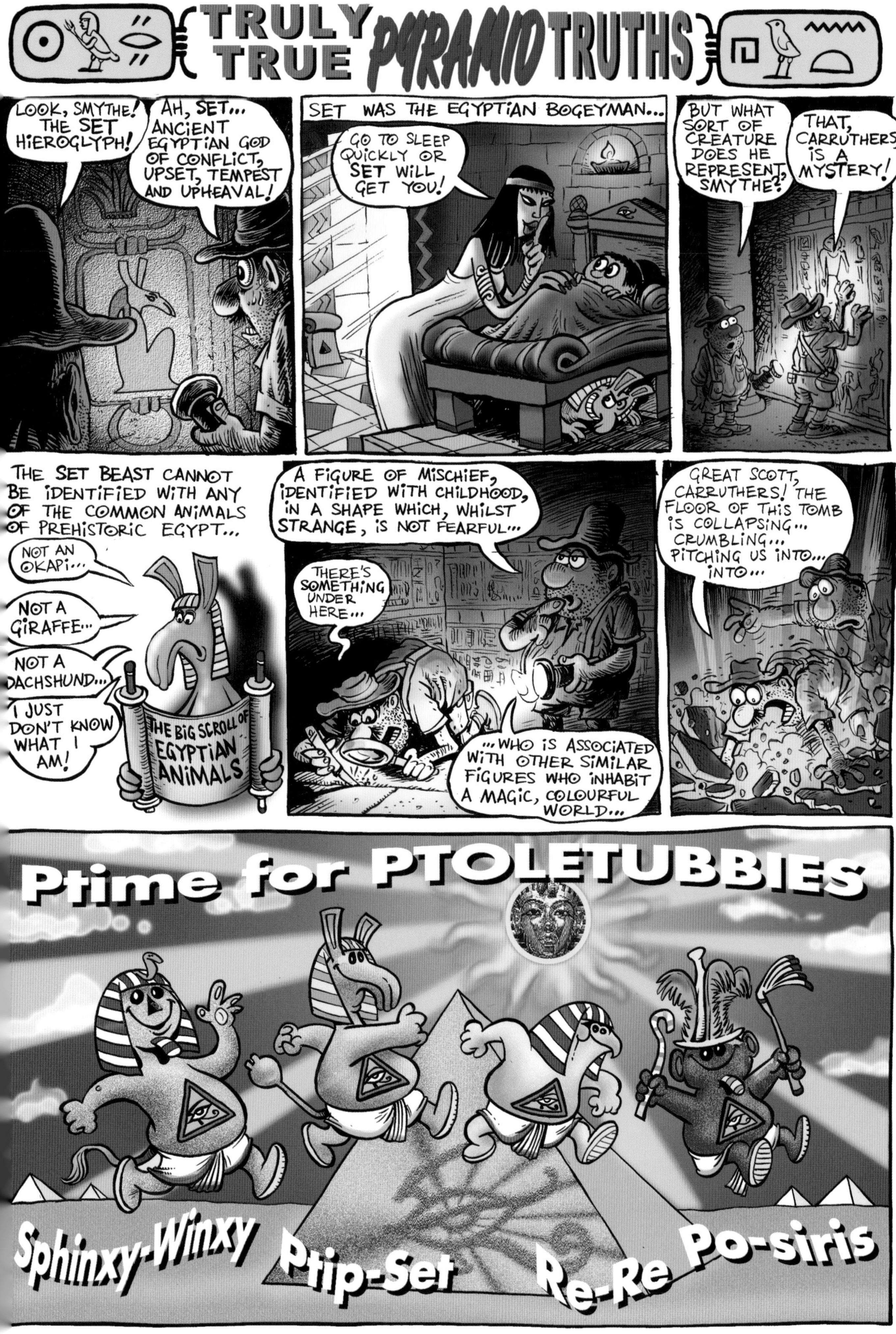
TRULY TRUE PYRAMID TRUTHS
LOOK, SMYTHE! THE SET HIEROGLYPH!
AH, SET... ANCIENT EGYPTIAN GOD OF CONFLICT, UPSET, TEMPEST AND UPHEAVAL!
SET WAS THE EGYPTIAN BOGEYMAN...
GO TO SLEEP QUICKLY OR SET WILL GET YOU!
BUT WHAT SORT OF CREATURE DOES HE REPRESENT, SMYTHE?
THAT, CARRUTHERS, IS A MYSTERY!
THE SET BEAST CANNOT BE IDENTIFIED WITH ANY OF THE COMMON ANIMALS OF PREHISTORIC EGYPT...
NOT AN OKAPI...
NOT A GIRAFFE...
NOT A DACHSHUND...
I JUST DON'T KNOW WHAT I AM!
THE BIG SCROLL OF EGYPTIAN ANIMALS
A FIGURE OF MISCHIEF, IDENTIFIED WITH CHILDHOOD, IN A SHAPE WHICH, WHILST STRANGE, IS NOT FEARFUL...
THERE'S SOMETHING UNDER HERE...
...WHO IS ASSOCIATED WITH OTHER SIMILAR FIGURES WHO INHABIT A MAGIC, COLOURFUL WORLD...
GREAT SCOTT, CARRUTHERS! THE FLOOR OF THIS TOMB IS COLLAPSING... CRUMBLING... PITCHING US INTO... INTO...
Ptime for PTOLETUBBIES
Sphinxy-Winxy
Ptip-Set
Re-Re
Po-siris

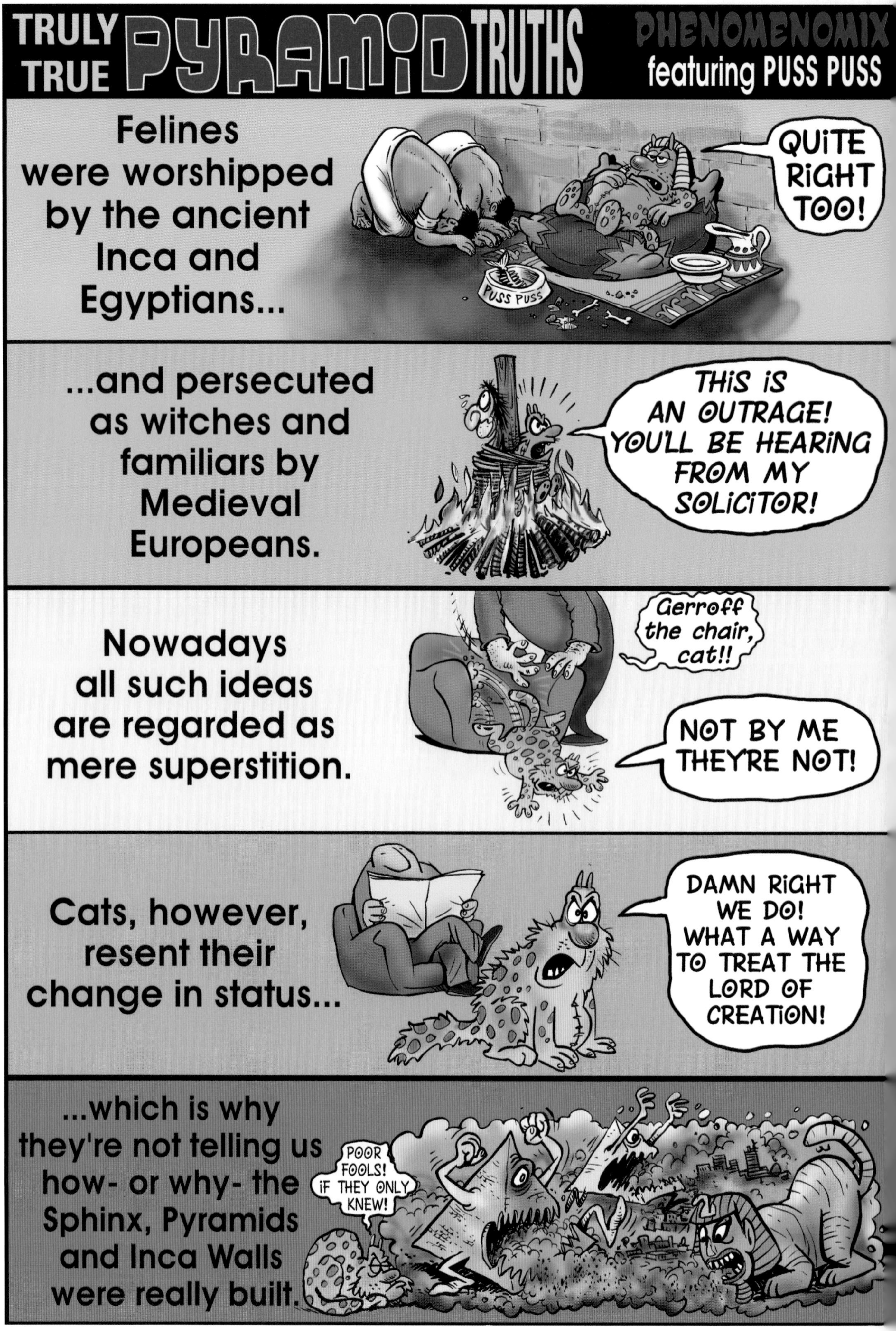
TRULY TRUE PYRAMID TRUTHS
PHENOMENOMIX
featuring PUSS PUSS
Felines were worshipped by the ancient Inca and Egyptians...
QUITE RIGHT TOO!
PUSS PUSS
...and persecuted as witches and familiars by Medieval Europeans.
THIS IS AN OUTRAGE! YOU'LL BE HEARING FROM MY SOLICITOR!
Nowadays all such ideas are regarded as mere superstition.
Gerroff the chair, cat!!
NOT BY ME THEYRE NOT!
Cats, however, resent their change in status...
DAMN RIGHT WE DO! WHAT A WAY TO TREAT THE LORD OF CREATION!
...which is why they're not telling us how- or why- the Sphinx, Pyramids and Inca Walls were really built.
POOR FOOLS! IF THEY ONLY KNEW!

RECIPROCAL EVOLUTION

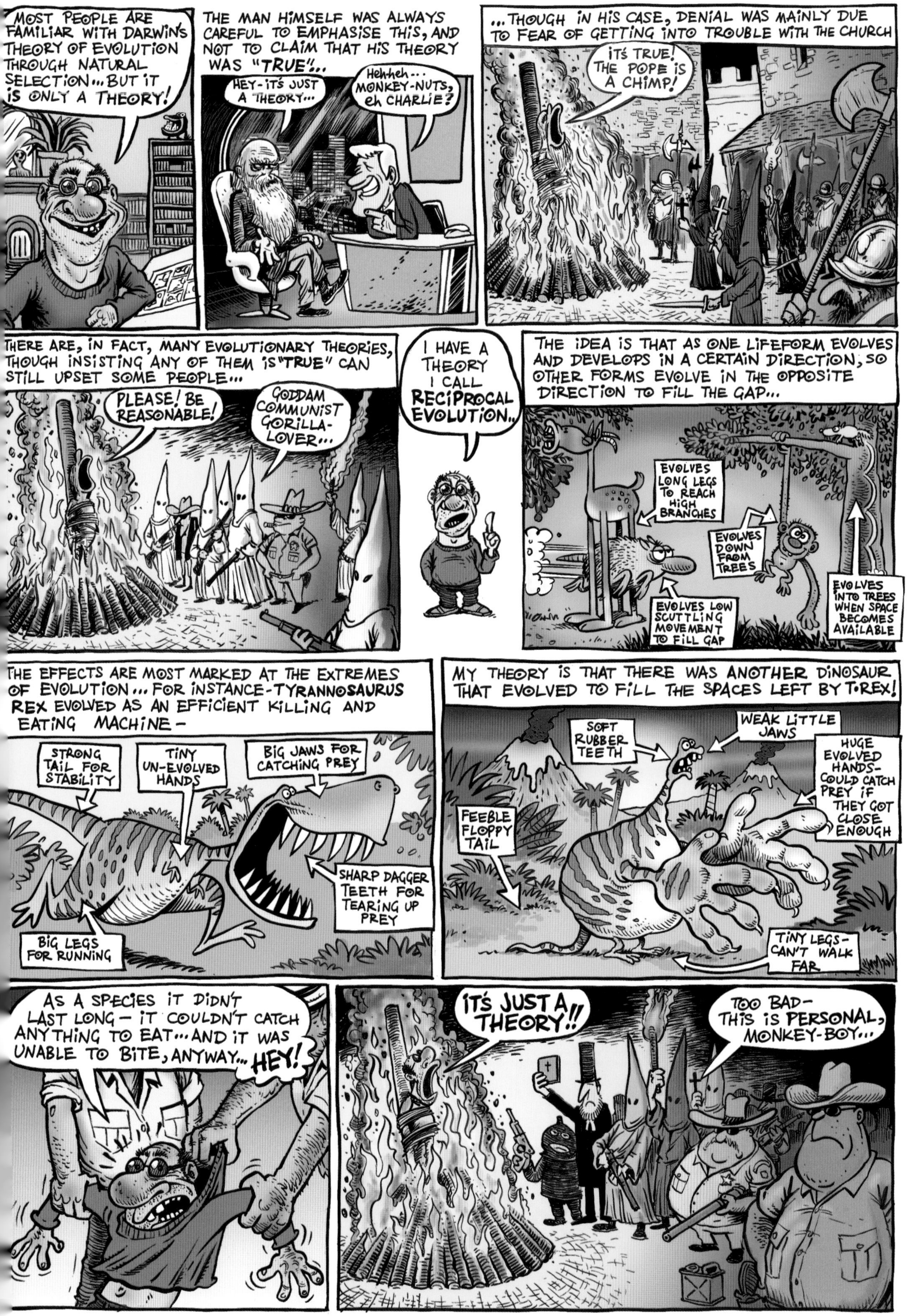

MOST PEOPLE ARE FAMILIAR WITH DARWIN'S THEORY OF EVOLUTION THROUGH NATURAL SELECTION... BUT IT IS ONLY A THEORY!
THE MAN HIMSELF WAS ALWAYS CAREFUL TO EMPHASISE THIS, AND NOT TO CLAIM THAT HIS THEORY WAS "TRUE"...
HEY - IT'S JUST A THEORY...
Hehheh... MONKEY-NUTS, eh CHARLIE?
...THOUGH IN HIS CASE, DENIAL WAS MAINLY DUE TO FEAR OF GETTING INTO TROUBLE WITH THE CHURCH
IT'S TRUE! THE POPE IS A CHIMP!
THERE ARE, IN FACT, MANY EVOLUTIONARY THEORIES, THOUGH INSISTING ANY OF THEM IS "TRUE" CAN STILL UPSET SOME PEOPLE...
PLEASE! BE REASONABLE!
GODDAM COMMUNIST GORILLA-LOVER...
I HAVE A THEORY I CALL RECIPROCAL EVOLUTION...
THE IDEA IS THAT AS ONE LIFEFORM EVOLVES AND DEVELOPS IN A CERTAIN DIRECTION, SO OTHER FORMS EVOLVE IN THE OPPOSITE DIRECTION TO FILL THE GAP...
EVOLVES LONG LEGS TO REACH HIGH BRANCHES
EVOLVES DOWN FROM TREES
EVOLVES LOW SCUTTLING MOVEMENT TO FILL GAP
EVOLVES INTO TREES WHEN SPACE BECOMES AVAILABLE
THE EFFECTS ARE MOST MARKED AT THE EXTREMES OF EVOLUTION... FOR INSTANCE - TYRANNOSAURUS REX EVOLVED AS AN EFFICIENT KILLING AND EATING MACHINE -
STRONG TAIL FOR STABILITY
TINY UN-EVOLVED HANDS
BIG JAWS FOR CATCHING PREY
SHARP DAGGER TEETH FOR TEARING UP PREY
BIG LEGS FOR RUNNING
MY THEORY IS THAT THERE WAS ANOTHER DINOSAUR THAT EVOLVED TO FILL THE SPACES LEFT BY T-REX!
SOFT RUBBER TEETH
WEAK LITTLE JAWS
HUGE EVOLVED HANDS - COULD CATCH PREY IF THEY GOT CLOSE ENOUGH
FEEBLE FLOPPY TAIL
TINY LEGS - CAN'T WALK FAR
AS A SPECIES IT DIDN'T LAST LONG - IT COULDN'T CATCH ANYTHING TO EAT... AND IT WAS UNABLE TO BITE, ANYWAY... HEY!
IT'S JUST A THEORY!!
TOO BAD - THIS IS PERSONAL, MONKEY-BOY...

WILLIAM BUCKLAND

THE SCIENCE OF GEOLOGY ATTRACTED GREAT MINDS IN THE 19TH CENTURY...

SOME OF THE MOST POWERFUL THINKING ENGINES IN THE WORLD LABOURED TO UNRAVEL THE MEANING OF FOSSILS AND THE TRUE AGE OF THE EARTH!

THE MIND OF THE REVEREND WILLIAM BUCKLAND WAS A WONDERFUL THING INDEED! HE KEPT A MENAGERIE OF OFTEN LARGE AND DANGEROUS ANIMALS, WHICH ROAMED FREE IN HIS HOUSE AND GARDEN...

HE CLAIMED TO HAVE EATEN A PORTION OF THE HEART OF KING LOUIS XIV...

Mais... Monsieur!

HE BECAME THE WORLD'S LEADING AUTHORITY ON **COPROLITES** - FOSSILIZED DUNG- AND HAD A TABLE MADE FROM THE THINGS!

HE WANTED TO EAT A SAMPLE OF EVERY ANIMAL IN CREATION, AND HE WORKED HIS WAY THROUGH A GOOD MANY— GUINEA PIG, MICE IN BATTER, HEDGEHOG, BOILED SEA-SLUG, LEOPARD, CROCODILE, DORMOUSE, FRICASSEE OF FLY... HE TRIED THEM ALL AND MORE, AND DECLARED THEM TO BE—

DELICIOUS!

EXCEPT FOR THE COMMON GARDEN MOLE, WHICH HE SAID WAS—

DISGUSTING!

AN INVITATION TO DINNER WITH BUCKLAND COULD BE A HAZARDOUS EXPERIENCE!

ONE WONDERS HOW HIS WIFE COPED! HE WOKE HER ONE NIGHT WITH THE EXCITED CRY—

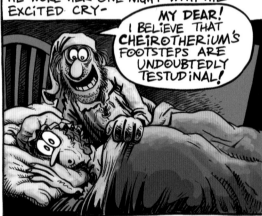

MY DEAR! I BELIEVE THAT CHEIROTHERIUM'S FOOTSTEPS ARE UNDOUBTEDLY TESTUDINAL!

THEY RUSHED TOGETHER TO THE KITCHEN, WHERE THEY PERFORMED AN EXPERIMENT WITH FLOUR PASTE AND A TORTOISE...

OH WILLIAM! YOUR SUPPOSITION IS CORRECT!

YES! THE ANCIENT ANIMAL CHEIROTHERIUM WALKED LIKE A TORTOISE!

WISH I HAD ONE HERE NOW FOR A SANDWICH...

FOSSILIZED FOOTPRINTS OF CHEIROTHERIUM

DO THEY KNOW WHAT TIME IT IS?

FLOUR

THE POOR FELLOW DIED, MAD, IN 1856... PROBABLY SOMETHING HE ATE...

ONCE, IN A CATHEDRAL, HE WAS SHOWN MIRACULOUS "MARTYR'S BLOOD" THAT CONTINUALLY RENEWED ITSELF ON THE FLOOR...

UNDER THE GUISE OF GENUFLECTING HE TASTED IT, AND DECLARED IT—

BAT'S URINE!

BUT THEN, HE'D BE THE ONE TO KNOW!

ON THE ROCKPILE

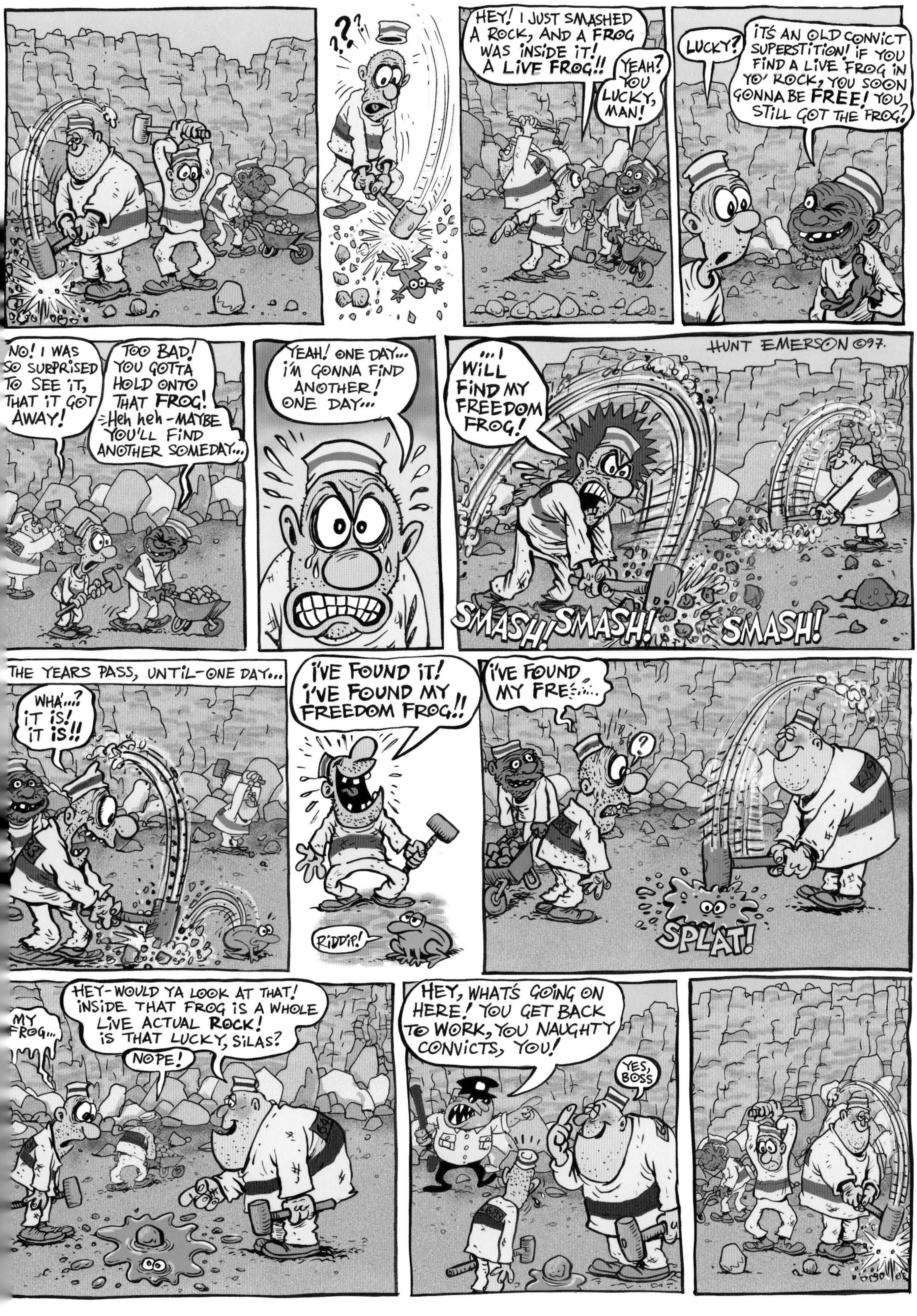

HEY! I JUST SMASHED A ROCK, AND A FROG WAS INSIDE IT! A LIVE FROG!!
YEAH? YOU LUCKY, MAN!
LUCKY?
IT'S AN OLD CONVICT SUPERSTITION! IF YOU FIND A LIVE FROG IN YO' ROCK, YOU SOON GONNA BE FREE! YOU STILL GOT THE FROG?
NO! I WAS SO SURPRISED TO SEE IT, THAT IT GOT AWAY!
TOO BAD! YOU GOTTA HOLD ONTO THAT FROG! Heh heh - MAYBE YOU'LL FIND ANOTHER SOMEDAY...
YEAH! ONE DAY... I'M GONNA FIND ANOTHER! ONE DAY...
...I WILL FIND MY FREEDOM FROG!
HUNT EMERSON ©97.
SMASH! SMASH! SMASH!
THE YEARS PASS, UNTIL - ONE DAY...
WHA'...? IT IS! IT IS!!
I'VE FOUND IT! I'VE FOUND MY FREEDOM FROG!!
RIDDIP!
I'VE FOUND MY FRE...
SPLAT!
MY FROG...
HEY - WOULD YA LOOK AT THAT! INSIDE THAT FROG IS A WHOLE LIVE ACTUAL ROCK! IS THAT LUCKY, SILAS?
NOPE!
HEY, WHAT'S GOING ON HERE! YOU GET BACK TO WORK, YOU NAUGHTY CONVICTS, YOU!
YES, BOSS

ROCKY THE SHIPWORM

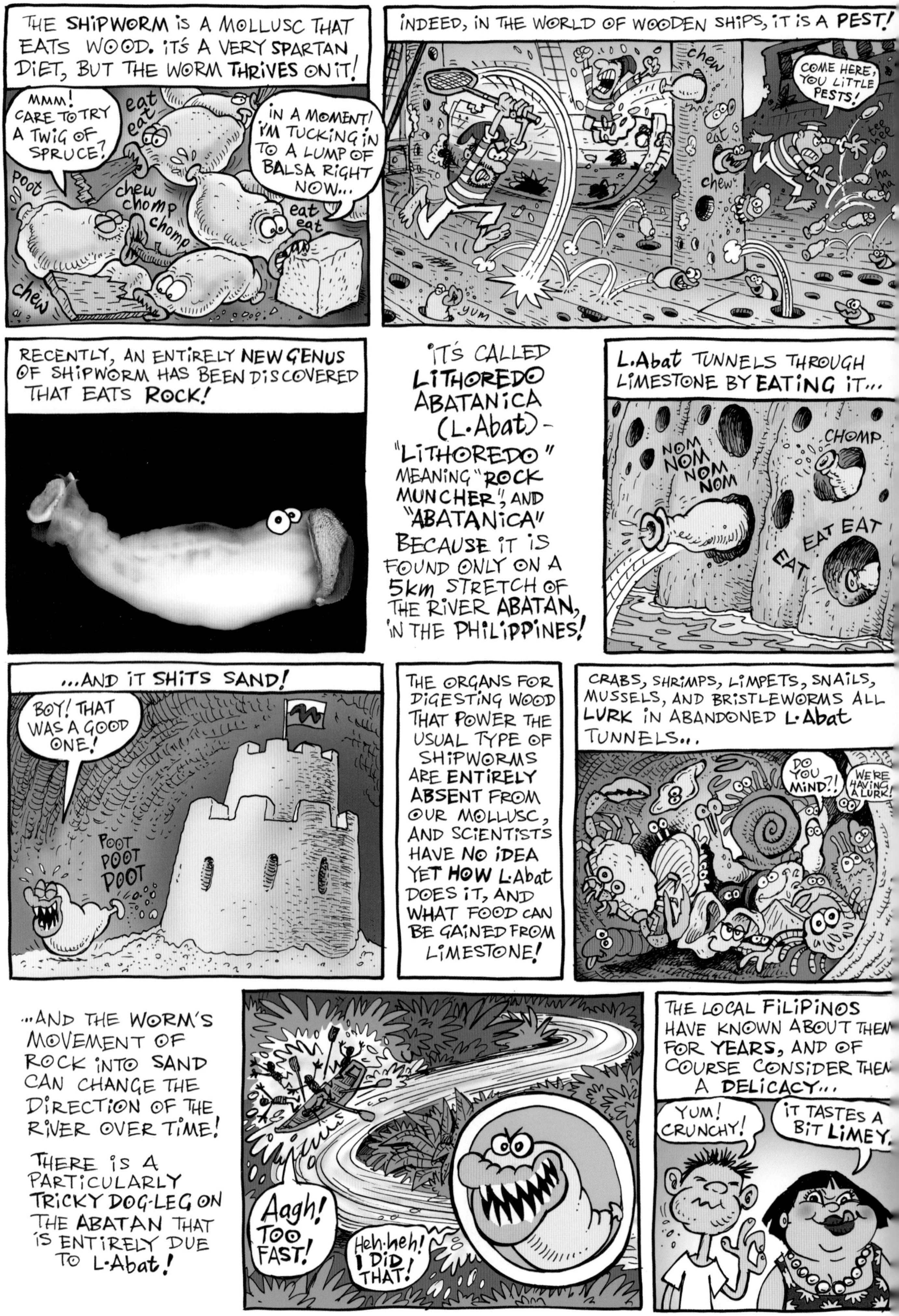
THE SHIPWORM IS A MOLLUSC THAT EATS WOOD. IT'S A VERY SPARTAN DIET, BUT THE WORM THRIVES ON IT!
MMM! CARE TO TRY A TWIG OF SPRUCE?
eat eat
IN A MOMENT! I'M TUCKING IN TO A LUMP OF BALSA RIGHT NOW...
poot
chew chomp chomp
eat eat
chew
INDEED, IN THE WORLD OF WOODEN SHIPS, IT IS A PEST!
chew
COME HERE, YOU LITTLE PESTS!
eat
chew
tee hee
ha ha
yum
RECENTLY, AN ENTIRELY NEW GENUS OF SHIPWORM HAS BEEN DISCOVERED THAT EATS ROCK!
IT'S CALLED LITHOREDO ABATANICA (L.Abat) - "LITHOREDO" MEANING "ROCK MUNCHER", AND "ABATANICA" BECAUSE IT IS FOUND ONLY ON A 5km STRETCH OF THE RIVER ABATAN, IN THE PHILIPPINES!
L.Abat TUNNELS THROUGH LIMESTONE BY EATING IT...
NOM NOM NOM NOM
CHOMP
EAT EAT EAT
...AND IT SHITS SAND!
BOY! THAT WAS A GOOD ONE!
POOT POOT POOT
THE ORGANS FOR DIGESTING WOOD THAT POWER THE USUAL TYPE OF SHIPWORMS ARE ENTIRELY ABSENT FROM OUR MOLLUSC, AND SCIENTISTS HAVE NO IDEA YET HOW L.Abat DOES IT, AND WHAT FOOD CAN BE GAINED FROM LIMESTONE!
CRABS, SHRIMPS, LIMPETS, SNAILS, MUSSELS, AND BRISTLEWORMS ALL LURK IN ABANDONED L.Abat TUNNELS...
DO YOU MIND?!
WE'RE HAVING A LURK!
...AND THE WORM'S MOVEMENT OF ROCK INTO SAND CAN CHANGE THE DIRECTION OF THE RIVER OVER TIME!
THERE IS A PARTICULARLY TRICKY DOG-LEG ON THE ABATAN THAT IS ENTIRELY DUE TO L.Abat!
Aagh! TOO FAST!
Heh-heh! I DID THAT!
THE LOCAL FILIPINOS HAVE KNOWN ABOUT THEM FOR YEARS, AND OF COURSE CONSIDER THEM A DELICACY...
YUM! CRUNCHY!
IT TASTES A BIT LIMEY.

SAINT BALDOMER

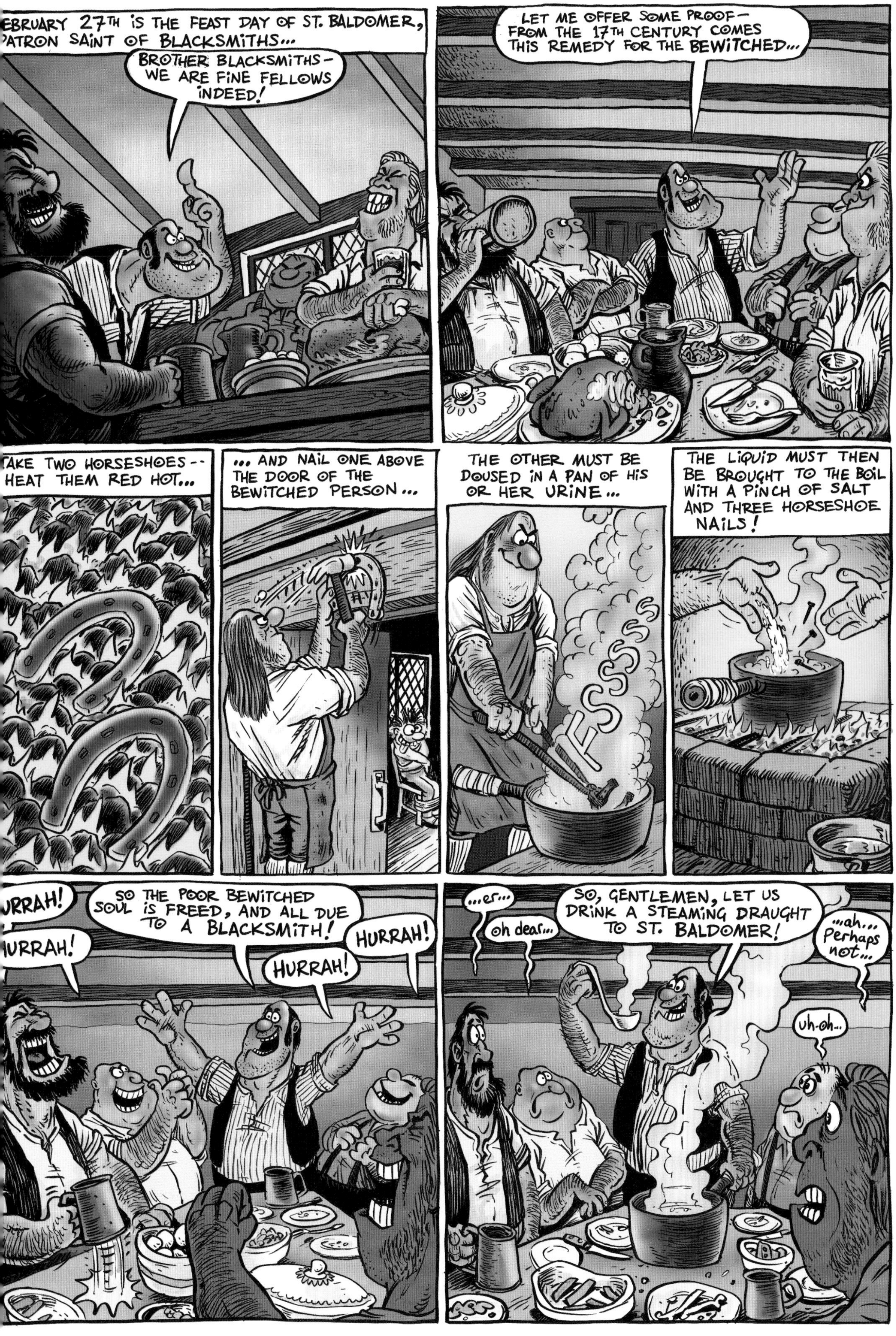

EBRUARY 27TH IS THE FEAST DAY OF ST. BALDOMER, PATRON SAINT OF BLACKSMITHS...
BROTHER BLACKSMITHS - WE ARE FINE FELLOWS INDEED!
LET ME OFFER SOME PROOF - FROM THE 17TH CENTURY COMES THIS REMEDY FOR THE BEWITCHED...
AKE TWO HORSESHOES -- HEAT THEM RED HOT...
... AND NAIL ONE ABOVE THE DOOR OF THE BEWITCHED PERSON...
THE OTHER MUST BE DOUSED IN A PAN OF HIS OR HER URINE...
FSSSSS
THE LIQUID MUST THEN BE BROUGHT TO THE BOIL WITH A PINCH OF SALT AND THREE HORSESHOE NAILS!
HURRAH!
HURRAH!
SO THE POOR BEWITCHED SOUL IS FREED, AND ALL DUE TO A BLACKSMITH!
HURRAH!
HURRAH!
...er...
oh dear...
SO, GENTLEMEN, LET US DRINK A STEAMING DRAUGHT TO ST. BALDOMER!
...ah... Perhaps not...
uh-oh...

SAINT MAGNUS

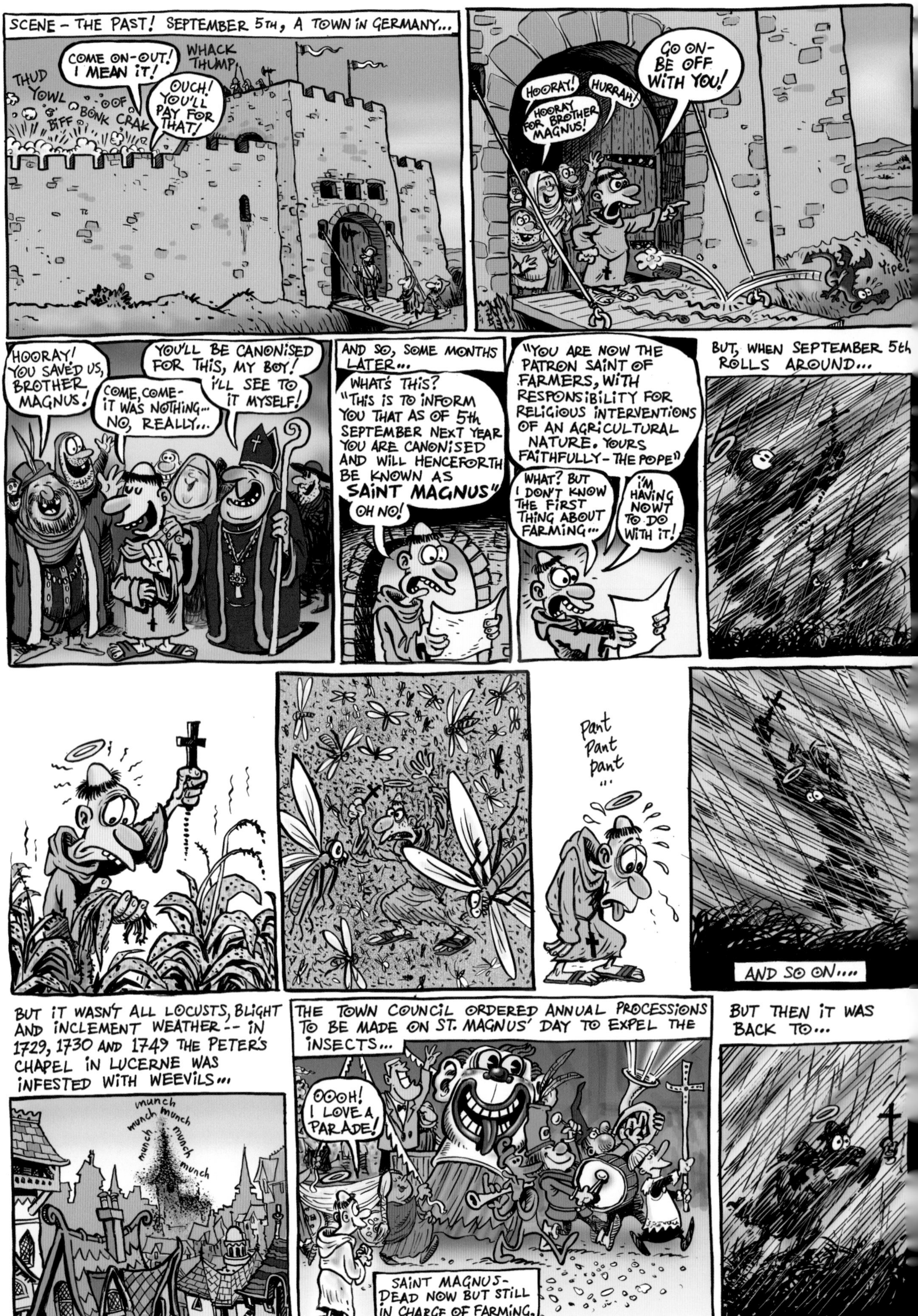

SCENE - THE PAST! SEPTEMBER 5TH, A TOWN IN GERMANY...
COME ON-OUT! I MEAN IT!
WHACK THUMP
THUD YOWL OOF BONK CRAK BIFF
OUCH! YOU'LL PAY FOR THAT!
HOORAY!
HURRAH!
HOORAY FOR BROTHER MAGNUS!
GO ON- BE OFF WITH YOU!
Yipe!
HOORAY! YOU SAVED US, BROTHER MAGNUS!
YOU'LL BE CANONISED FOR THIS, MY BOY! I'LL SEE TO IT MYSELF!
COME, COME- IT WAS NOTHING... NO, REALLY...
AND SO, SOME MONTHS LATER...
WHAT'S THIS? "THIS IS TO INFORM YOU THAT AS OF 5th SEPTEMBER NEXT YEAR YOU ARE CANONISED AND WILL HENCEFORTH BE KNOWN AS SAINT MAGNUS"
OH NO!
"YOU ARE NOW THE PATRON SAINT OF FARMERS, WITH RESPONSIBILITY FOR RELIGIOUS INTERVENTIONS OF AN AGRICULTURAL NATURE. YOURS FAITHFULLY - THE POPE"
WHAT? BUT I DON'T KNOW THE FIRST THING ABOUT FARMING...
I'M HAVING NOWT TO DO WITH IT!
BUT, WHEN SEPTEMBER 5th ROLLS AROUND...
Pant Pant pant
AND SO ON....
BUT IT WASN'T ALL LOCUSTS, BLIGHT AND INCLEMENT WEATHER -- IN 1729, 1730 AND 1749 THE PETER'S CHAPEL IN LUCERNE WAS INFESTED WITH WEEVILS...
munch munch munch munch munch
THE TOWN COUNCIL ORDERED ANNUAL PROCESSIONS TO BE MADE ON ST. MAGNUS' DAY TO EXPEL THE INSECTS...
OOOH! I LOVE A PARADE!
SAINT MAGNUS - DEAD NOW BUT STILL IN CHARGE OF FARMING, INFESTATIONS, AND SO ON...
BUT THEN IT WAS BACK TO...

SAINT MOLING

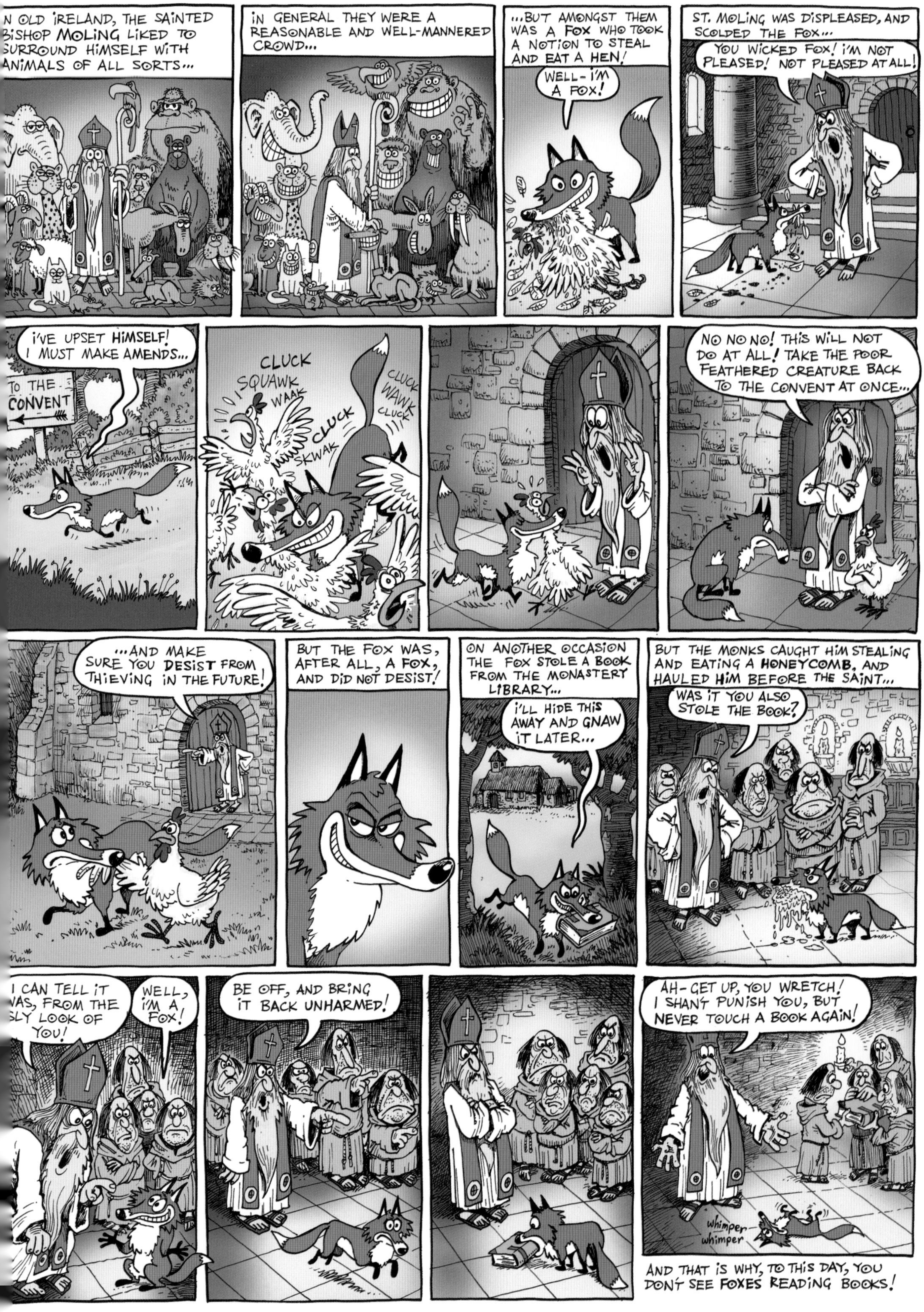

N OLD IRELAND, THE SAINTED BISHOP MOLING LIKED TO SURROUND HIMSELF WITH ANIMALS OF ALL SORTS...
IN GENERAL THEY WERE A REASONABLE AND WELL-MANNERED CROWD...
...BUT AMONGST THEM WAS A FOX WHO TOOK A NOTION TO STEAL AND EAT A HEN!
WELL - I'M A FOX!
ST. MOLING WAS DISPLEASED, AND SCOLDED THE FOX...
YOU WICKED FOX! I'M NOT PLEASED! NOT PLEASED AT ALL!
I'VE UPSET HIMSELF! I MUST MAKE AMENDS...
TO THE CONVENT
CLUCK
SQUAWK
WAAK
CLUCK
SKWAK
CLUCK
WAWK
CLUCK
NO NO NO! THIS WILL NOT DO AT ALL! TAKE THE POOR FEATHERED CREATURE BACK TO THE CONVENT AT ONCE...
...AND MAKE SURE YOU DESIST FROM THIEVING IN THE FUTURE!
BUT THE FOX WAS, AFTER ALL, A FOX, AND DID NOT DESIST!
ON ANOTHER OCCASION THE FOX STOLE A BOOK FROM THE MONASTERY LIBRARY...
I'LL HIDE THIS AWAY AND GNAW IT LATER...
BUT THE MONKS CAUGHT HIM STEALING AND EATING A HONEYCOMB, AND HAULED HIM BEFORE THE SAINT...
WAS IT YOU ALSO STOLE THE BOOK?
I CAN TELL IT WAS, FROM THE SLY LOOK OF YOU!
WELL, I'M A FOX!
BE OFF, AND BRING IT BACK UNHARMED!
AH- GET UP, YOU WRETCH! I SHAN'T PUNISH YOU, BUT NEVER TOUCH A BOOK AGAIN!
whimper whimper
AND THAT IS WHY, TO THIS DAY, YOU DON'T SEE FOXES READING BOOKS!

SATAN'S STEVES

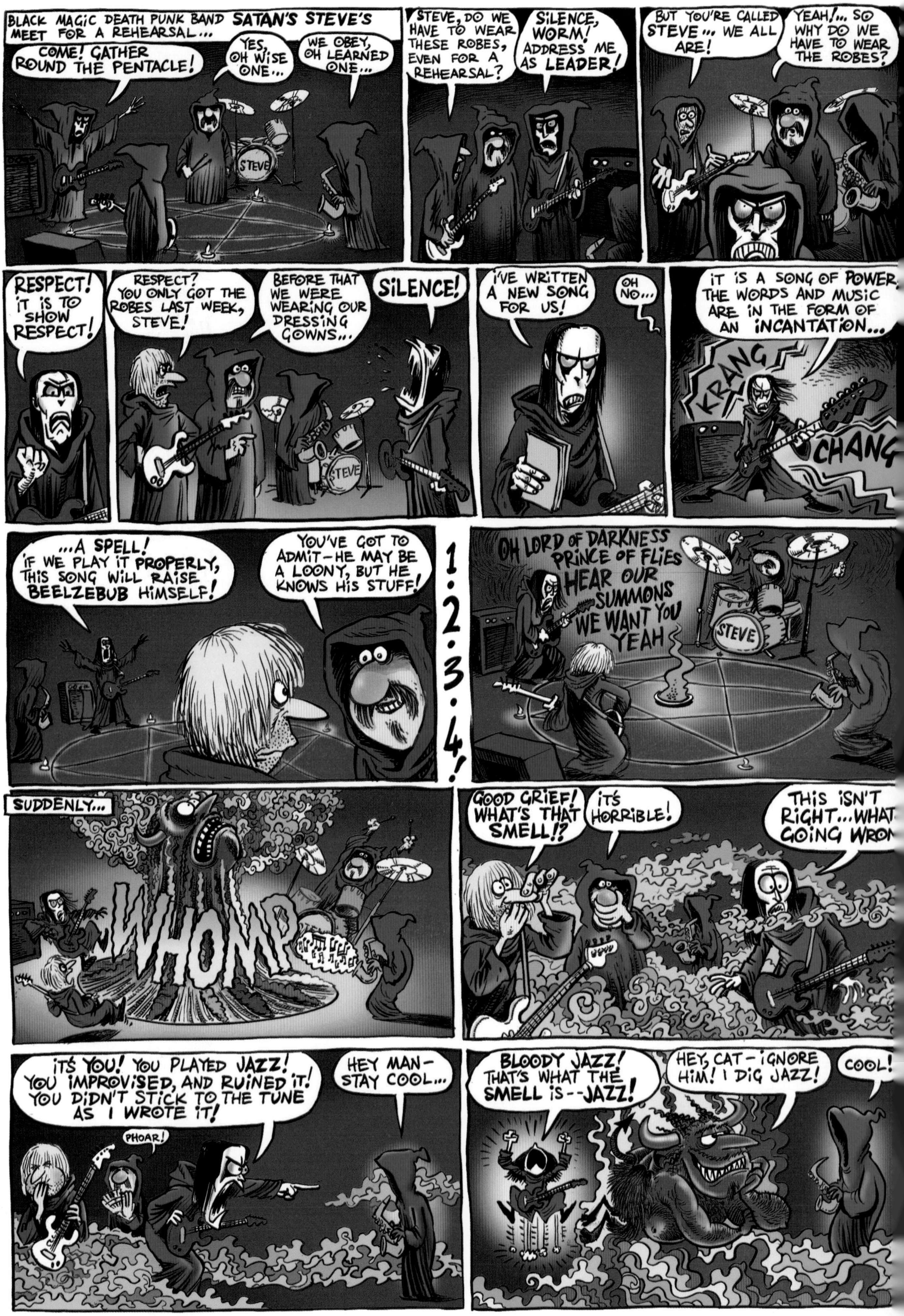

BLACK MAGIC DEATH PUNK BAND SATAN'S STEVE'S MEET FOR A REHEARSAL...
COME! GATHER ROUND THE PENTACLE!
YES, OH WISE ONE...
WE OBEY, OH LEARNED ONE...
STEVE
STEVE, DO WE HAVE TO WEAR THESE ROBES, EVEN FOR A REHEARSAL?
SILENCE, WORM! ADDRESS ME AS LEADER!
BUT YOU'RE CALLED STEVE... WE ALL ARE!
YEAH!... SO WHY DO WE HAVE TO WEAR THE ROBES?
RESPECT! IT IS TO SHOW RESPECT!
RESPECT? YOU ONLY GOT THE ROBES LAST WEEK, STEVE!
BEFORE THAT WE WERE WEARING OUR DRESSING GOWNS...
SILENCE!
STEVE
I'VE WRITTEN A NEW SONG FOR US!
OH NO...
IT IS A SONG OF POWER THE WORDS AND MUSIC ARE IN THE FORM OF AN INCANTATION...
KRANG
CHANG
...A SPELL! IF WE PLAY IT PROPERLY, THIS SONG WILL RAISE BEELZEBUB HIMSELF!
YOU'VE GOT TO ADMIT—HE MAY BE A LOONY, BUT HE KNOWS HIS STUFF!
1. 2. 3. 4!
OH LORD OF DARKNESS PRINCE OF FLIES HEAR OUR SUMMONS WE WANT YOU YEAH
STEVE
SUDDENLY...
WHOMP
GOOD GRIEF! WHAT'S THAT SMELL!?
IT'S HORRIBLE!
THIS ISN'T RIGHT...WHAT GOING WRON
IT'S YOU! YOU PLAYED JAZZ! YOU IMPROVISED, AND RUINED IT! YOU DIDN'T STICK TO THE TUNE AS I WROTE IT!
PHOAR!
HEY MAN- STAY COOL...
BLOODY JAZZ! THAT'S WHAT THE SMELL IS--JAZZ!
HEY, CAT-IGNORE HIM! I DIG JAZZ!
COOL!

THE TENTACLE!

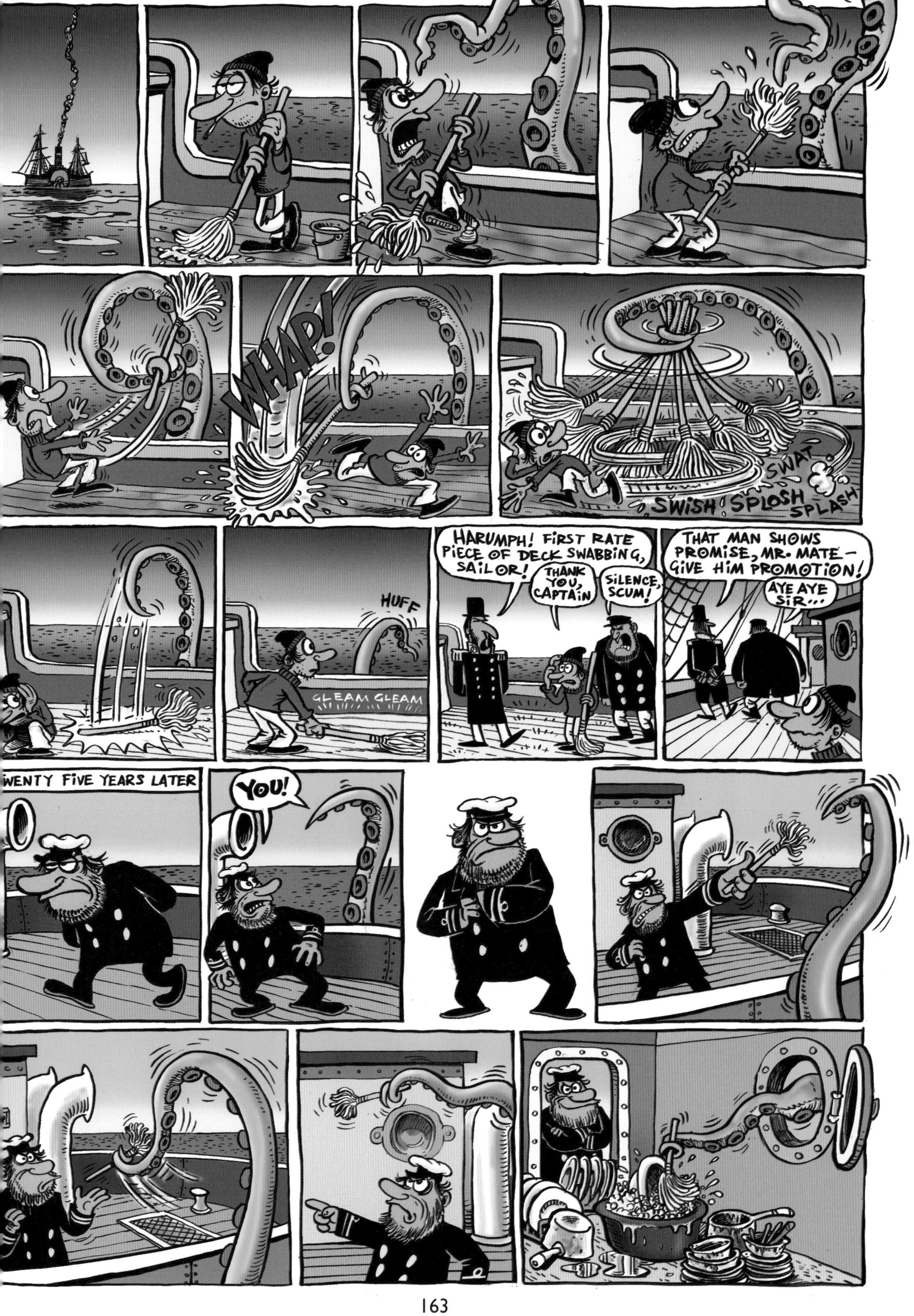
WHAP!
SWAT
SWISH! SPLOSH SPLASH
HUFF
GLEAM GLEAM
HARUMPH! FIRST RATE PIECE OF DECK SWABBING, SAILOR!
THANK YOU, CAPTAIN
SILENCE, SCUM!
THAT MAN SHOWS PROMISE, MR. MATE – GIVE HIM PROMOTION!
AYE AYE SIR...
WENTY FIVE YEARS LATER
YOU!

SEALSUCKER

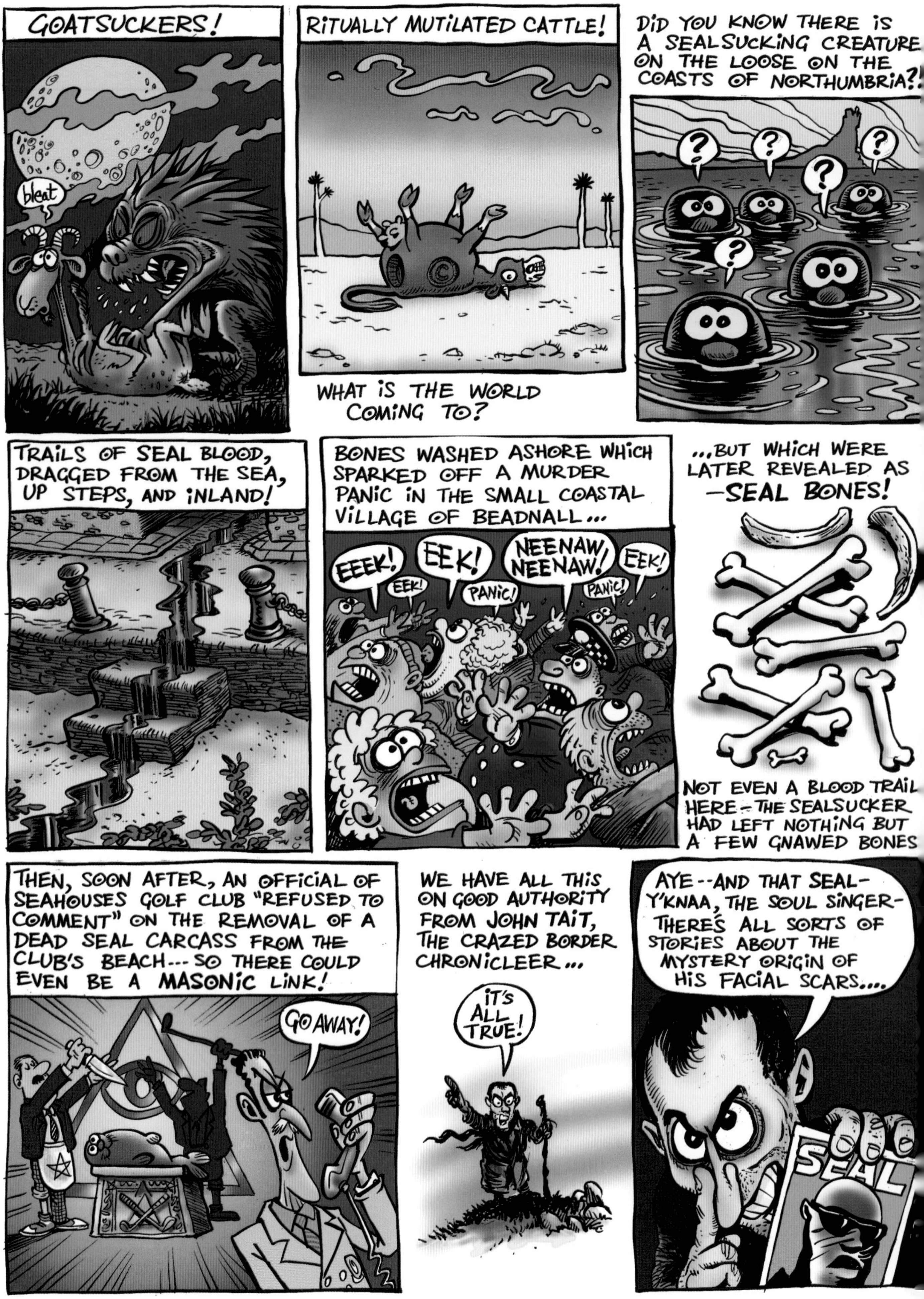
GOATSUCKERS!
bleat
RITUALLY MUTILATED CATTLE!
WHAT IS THE WORLD COMING TO?
DID YOU KNOW THERE IS A SEALSUCKING CREATURE ON THE LOOSE ON THE COASTS OF NORTHUMBRIA?!
?
?
?
?
?
TRAILS OF SEAL BLOOD, DRAGGED FROM THE SEA, UP STEPS, AND INLAND!
BONES WASHED ASHORE WHICH SPARKED OFF A MURDER PANIC IN THE SMALL COASTAL VILLAGE OF BEADNALL...
EEEK!
EEK!
EEK!
PANIC!
NEENAW NEENAW!
PANIC!
EEK!
...BUT WHICH WERE LATER REVEALED AS —SEAL BONES!
NOT EVEN A BLOOD TRAIL HERE - THE SEALSUCKER HAD LEFT NOTHING BUT A FEW GNAWED BONES
THEN, SOON AFTER, AN OFFICIAL OF SEAHOUSES GOLF CLUB "REFUSED TO COMMENT" ON THE REMOVAL OF A DEAD SEAL CARCASS FROM THE CLUB'S BEACH--- SO THERE COULD EVEN BE A MASONIC LINK!
GO AWAY!
WE HAVE ALL THIS ON GOOD AUTHORITY FROM JOHN TAIT, THE CRAZED BORDER CHRONICLEER...
IT'S ALL TRUE!
AYE--AND THAT SEAL-Y'KNAA, THE SOUL SINGER-THERE'S ALL SORTS OF STORIES ABOUT THE MYSTERY ORIGIN OF HIS FACIAL SCARS....
SEAL

.PONTANEOUS HUMAN COMBUSTION 1

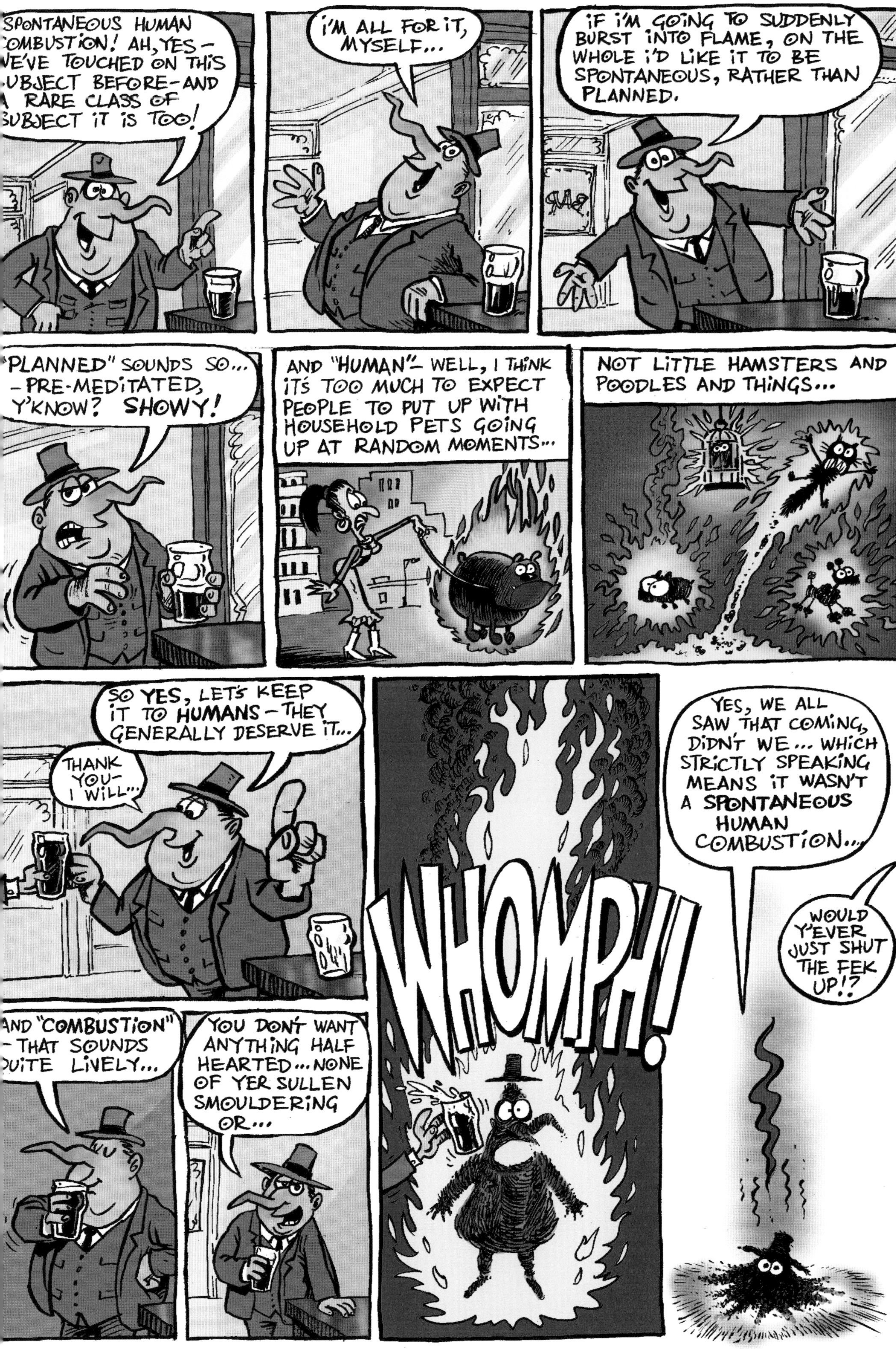

SPONTANEOUS HUMAN COMBUSTION! AH, YES – WE'VE TOUCHED ON THIS SUBJECT BEFORE – AND A RARE CLASS OF SUBJECT IT IS TOO!
I'M ALL FOR IT, MYSELF...
IF I'M GOING TO SUDDENLY BURST INTO FLAME, ON THE WHOLE I'D LIKE IT TO BE SPONTANEOUS, RATHER THAN PLANNED.
"PLANNED" SOUNDS SO... – PRE-MEDITATED, Y'KNOW? SHOWY!
AND "HUMAN" – WELL, I THINK IT'S TOO MUCH TO EXPECT PEOPLE TO PUT UP WITH HOUSEHOLD PETS GOING UP AT RANDOM MOMENTS...
NOT LITTLE HAMSTERS AND POODLES AND THINGS...
SO YES, LET'S KEEP IT TO HUMANS – THEY GENERALLY DESERVE IT...
THANK YOU – I WILL...
AND "COMBUSTION" – THAT SOUNDS QUITE LIVELY...
YOU DON'T WANT ANYTHING HALF HEARTED... NONE OF YER SULLEN SMOULDERING OR...
WHOMPH!
YES, WE ALL SAW THAT COMING, DIDN'T WE... WHICH STRICTLY SPEAKING MEANS IT WASN'T A SPONTANEOUS HUMAN COMBUSTION...
WOULD Y'EVER JUST SHUT THE FEK UP!?

SPONTANEOUS HUMAN COMBUSTION 2

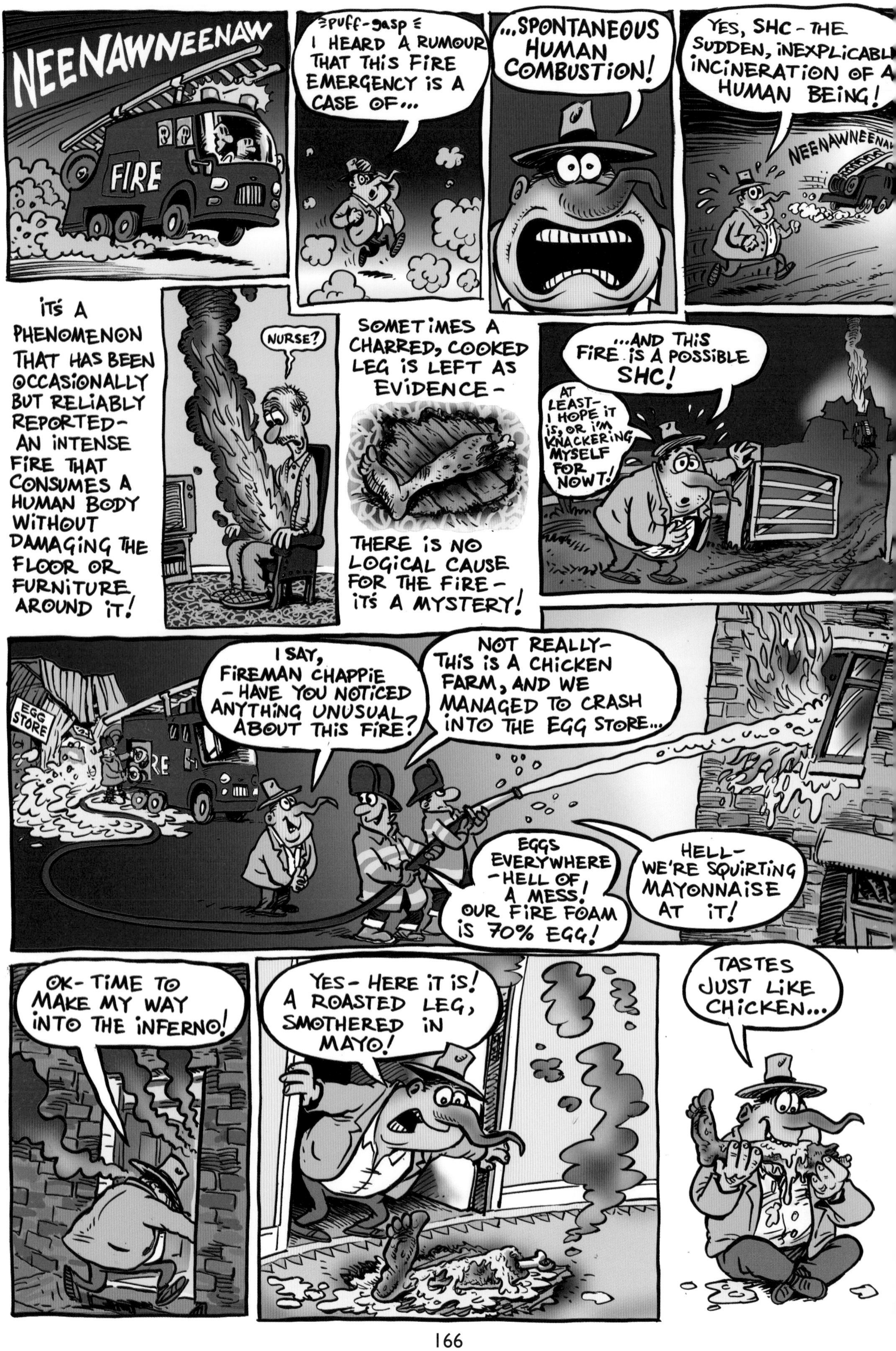
NEENAWNEENAW
FIRE
≡PUFF-GASP≡ I HEARD A RUMOUR THAT THIS FIRE EMERGENCY IS A CASE OF...
...SPONTANEOUS HUMAN COMBUSTION!
YES, SHC - THE SUDDEN, INEXPLICABLE INCINERATION OF A HUMAN BEING!
NEENAWNEENAW
IT'S A PHENOMENON THAT HAS BEEN OCCASIONALLY BUT RELIABLY REPORTED- AN INTENSE FIRE THAT CONSUMES A HUMAN BODY WITHOUT DAMAGING THE FLOOR OR FURNITURE AROUND IT!
NURSE?
SOMETIMES A CHARRED, COOKED LEG IS LEFT AS EVIDENCE-
THERE IS NO LOGICAL CAUSE FOR THE FIRE- IT'S A MYSTERY!
...AND THIS FIRE IS A POSSIBLE SHC!
AT LEAST- I HOPE IT IS, OR I'M KNACKERING MYSELF FOR NOWT!
EGG STORE
I SAY, FIREMAN CHAPPIE - HAVE YOU NOTICED ANYTHING UNUSUAL ABOUT THIS FIRE?
NOT REALLY- THIS IS A CHICKEN FARM, AND WE MANAGED TO CRASH INTO THE EGG STORE...
EGGS EVERYWHERE -HELL OF A MESS! OUR FIRE FOAM IS 70% EGG!
HELL- WE'RE SQUIRTING MAYONNAISE AT IT!
OK- TIME TO MAKE MY WAY INTO THE INFERNO!
YES- HERE IT IS! A ROASTED LEG, SMOTHERED IN MAYO!
TASTES JUST LIKE CHICKEN...

INISTER DUCK

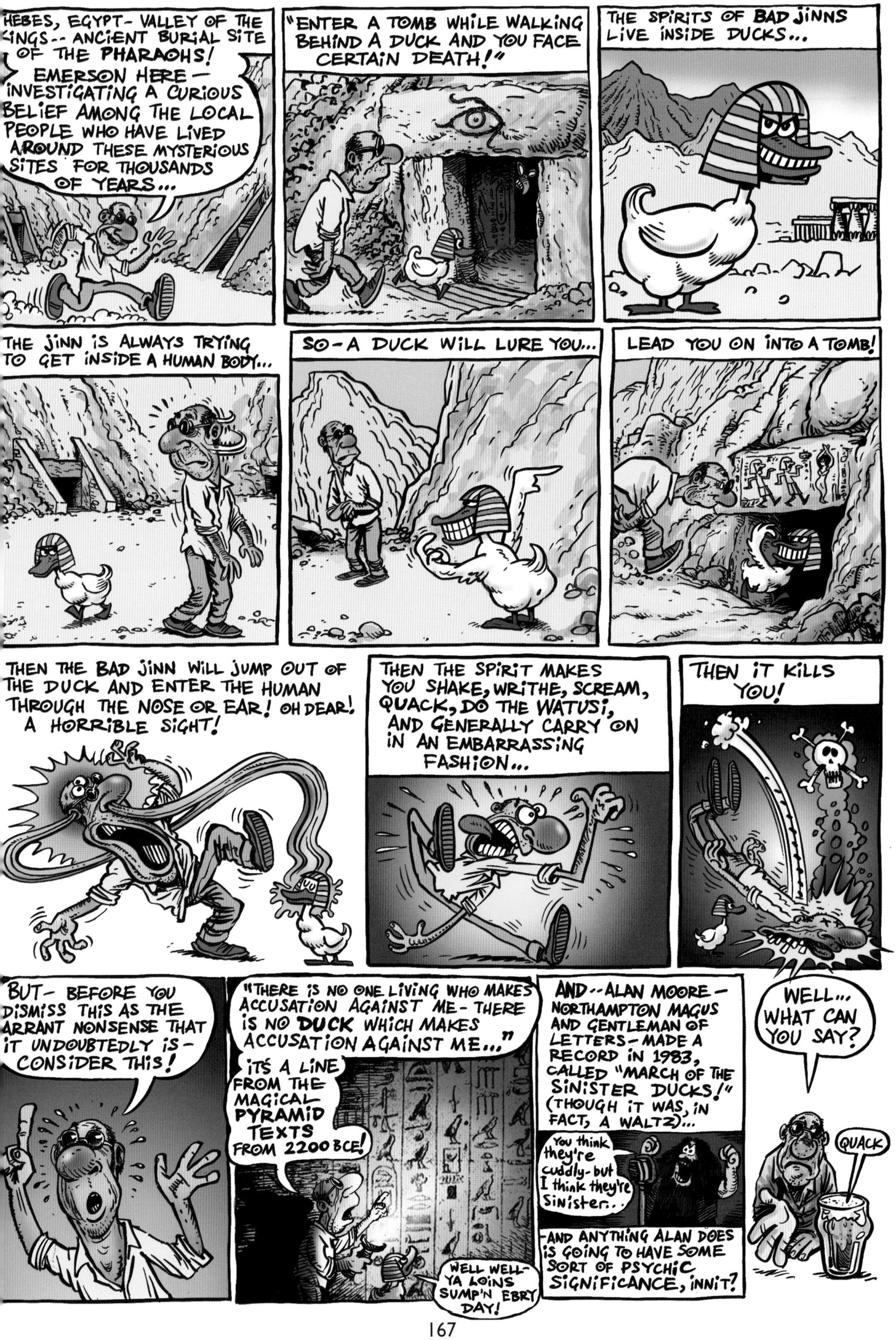

HEBES, EGYPT- VALLEY OF THE KINGS-- ANCIENT BURIAL SITE OF THE PHARAOHS!
EMERSON HERE — INVESTIGATING A CURIOUS BELIEF AMONG THE LOCAL PEOPLE WHO HAVE LIVED AROUND THESE MYSTERIOUS SITES FOR THOUSANDS OF YEARS...
"ENTER A TOMB WHILE WALKING BEHIND A DUCK AND YOU FACE CERTAIN DEATH!"
THE SPIRITS OF BAD JINNS LIVE INSIDE DUCKS...
THE JINN IS ALWAYS TRYING TO GET INSIDE A HUMAN BODY...
SO-A DUCK WILL LURE YOU...
LEAD YOU ON INTO A TOMB!
THEN THE BAD JINN WILL JUMP OUT OF THE DUCK AND ENTER THE HUMAN THROUGH THE NOSE OR EAR! OH DEAR! A HORRIBLE SIGHT!
THEN THE SPIRIT MAKES YOU SHAKE, WRITHE, SCREAM, QUACK, DO THE WATUSI, AND GENERALLY CARRY ON IN AN EMBARRASSING FASHION...
THEN IT KILLS YOU!
BUT- BEFORE YOU DISMISS THIS AS THE ARRANT NONSENSE THAT IT UNDOUBTEDLY IS- CONSIDER THIS!
"THERE IS NO ONE LIVING WHO MAKES ACCUSATION AGAINST ME- THERE IS NO DUCK WHICH MAKES ACCUSATION AGAINST ME..."
IT'S A LINE FROM THE MAGICAL PYRAMID TEXTS FROM 2200 BCE!
WELL WELL- YA LOINS SUMP'N EBRY DAY!
AND--ALAN MOORE- NORTHAMPTON MAGUS AND GENTLEMAN OF LETTERS- MADE A RECORD IN 1983, CALLED "MARCH OF THE SINISTER DUCKS!" (THOUGH IT WAS, IN FACT, A WALTZ)...
You think they're cuddly- but I think they're Sinister..
-AND ANYTHING ALAN DOES IS GOING TO HAVE SOME SORT OF PSYCHIC SIGNIFICANCE, INNIT?
WELL... WHAT CAN YOU SAY?
QUACK

SIR FRANCIS DRAKE

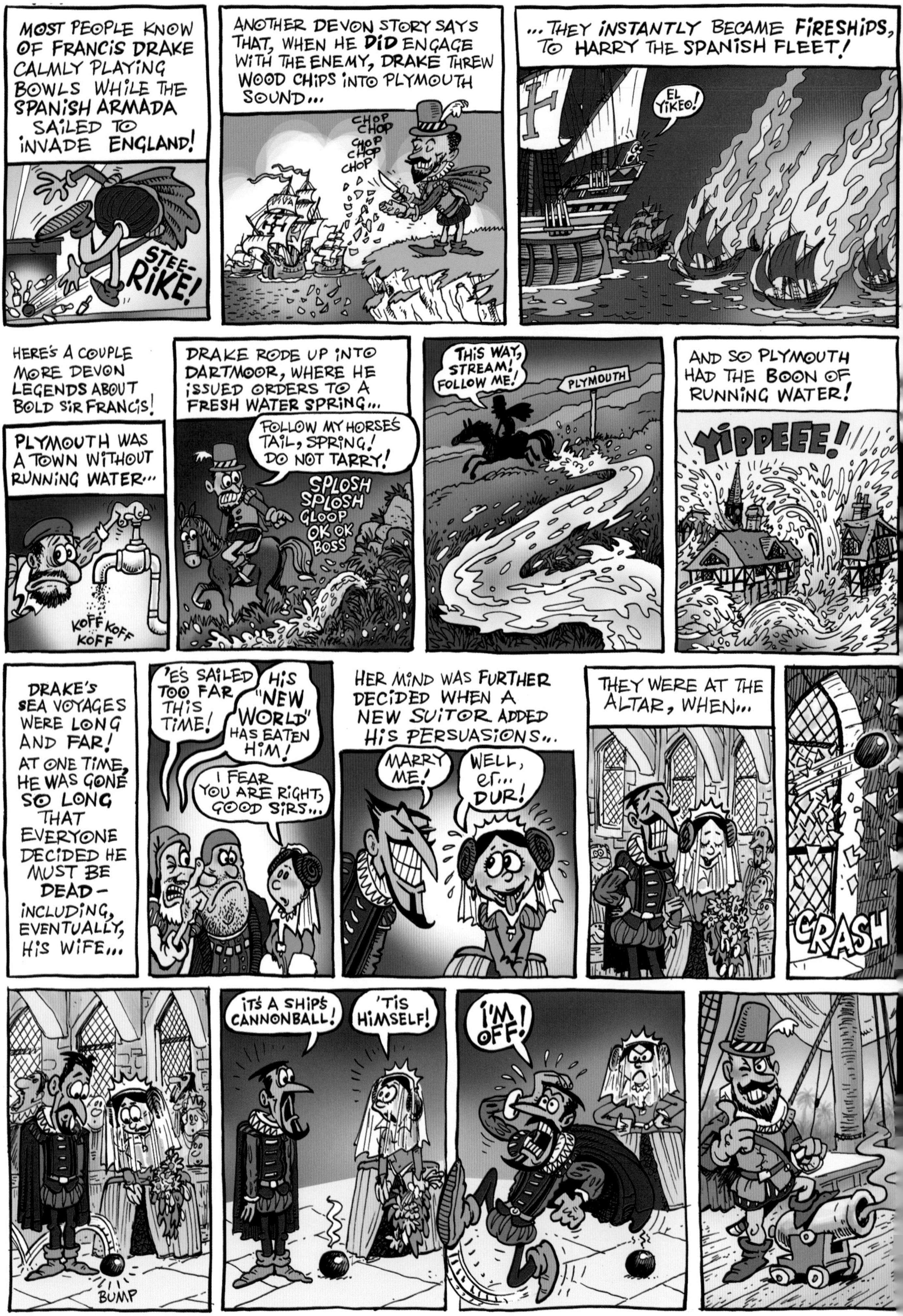

MOST PEOPLE KNOW OF FRANCIS DRAKE CALMLY PLAYING BOWLS WHILE THE SPANISH ARMADA SAILED TO INVADE ENGLAND!
STEE-RIKE!
ANOTHER DEVON STORY SAYS THAT, WHEN HE DID ENGAGE WITH THE ENEMY, DRAKE THREW WOOD CHIPS INTO PLYMOUTH SOUND...
CHOP CHOP CHOP CHOP CHOP
...THEY INSTANTLY BECAME FIRESHIPS, TO HARRY THE SPANISH FLEET!
EL YIKEO!
HERE'S A COUPLE MORE DEVON LEGENDS ABOUT BOLD SIR FRANCIS!
PLYMOUTH WAS A TOWN WITHOUT RUNNING WATER...
KOFF KOFF KOFF
DRAKE RODE UP INTO DARTMOOR, WHERE HE ISSUED ORDERS TO A FRESH WATER SPRING...
FOLLOW MY HORSE'S TAIL, SPRING! DO NOT TARRY!
SPLOSH SPLOSH GLOOP OK OK BOSS
THIS WAY, STREAM! FOLLOW ME!
PLYMOUTH
AND SO PLYMOUTH HAD THE BOON OF RUNNING WATER!
YIPPEEE!
DRAKE'S SEA VOYAGES WERE LONG AND FAR! AT ONE TIME, HE WAS GONE SO LONG THAT EVERYONE DECIDED HE MUST BE DEAD – INCLUDING, EVENTUALLY, HIS WIFE...
'E'S SAILED TOO FAR THIS TIME!
HIS "NEW WORLD" HAS EATEN HIM!
I FEAR YOU ARE RIGHT, GOOD SIRS...
HER MIND WAS FURTHER DECIDED WHEN A NEW SUITOR ADDED HIS PERSUASIONS...
MARRY ME!
WELL, ER... DUR!
THEY WERE AT THE ALTAR, WHEN...
CRASH
BUMP
IT'S A SHIP'S CANNONBALL!
'TIS HIMSELF!
I'M OFF!

THE SKINWALKER RANCH

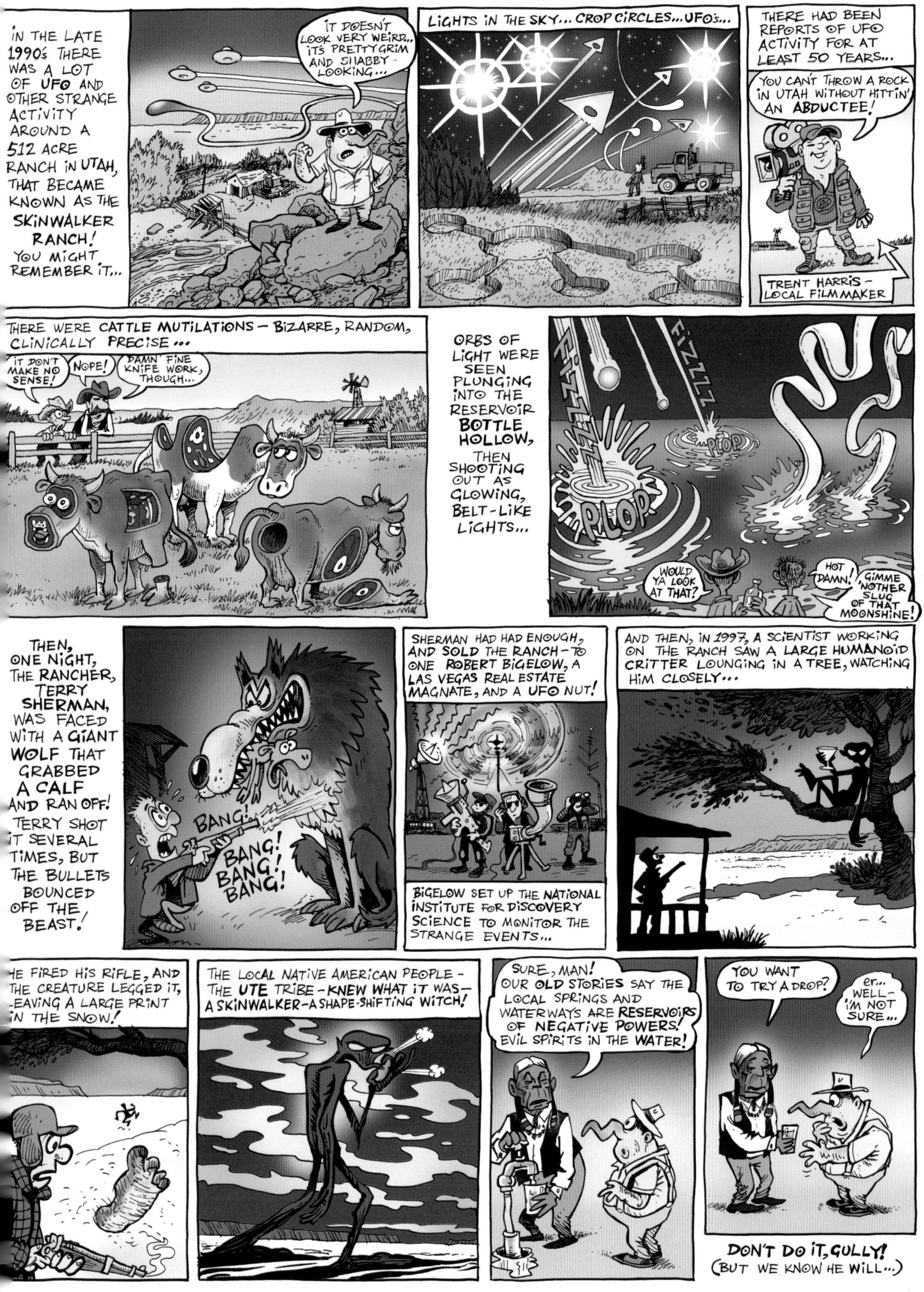

IN THE LATE 1990'S THERE WAS A LOT OF UFO AND OTHER STRANGE ACTIVITY AROUND A 512 ACRE RANCH IN UTAH, THAT BECAME KNOWN AS THE SKINWALKER RANCH! YOU MIGHT REMEMBER IT...
IT DOESN'T LOOK VERY WEIRD... IT'S PRETTY GRIM AND SHABBY-LOOKING...
LIGHTS IN THE SKY... CROP CIRCLES... UFO'S...
THERE HAD BEEN REPORTS OF UFO ACTIVITY FOR AT LEAST 50 YEARS...
YOU CAN'T THROW A ROCK IN UTAH WITHOUT HITTIN' AN ABDUCTEE!
TRENT HARRIS - LOCAL FILMMAKER
THERE WERE CATTLE MUTILATIONS - BIZARRE, RANDOM, CLINICALLY PRECISE...
IT DON'T MAKE NO SENSE!
NOPE!
DAMN' FINE KNIFE WORK, THOUGH...
ORBS OF LIGHT WERE SEEN PLUNGING INTO THE RESERVOIR BOTTLE HOLLOW, THEN SHOOTING OUT AS GLOWING, BELT-LIKE LIGHTS...
FIZZZZ
FIZZZZ
PLOP
PLOP!
WOULD YA LOOK AT THAT?
HOT DAMN!
GIMME 'NOTHER SLUG OF THAT MOONSHINE!
THEN, ONE NIGHT, THE RANCHER, TERRY SHERMAN, WAS FACED WITH A GIANT WOLF THAT GRABBED A CALF AND RAN OFF! TERRY SHOT IT SEVERAL TIMES, BUT THE BULLETS BOUNCED OFF THE BEAST!
BANG!
BANG! BANG! BANG!
SHERMAN HAD HAD ENOUGH, AND SOLD THE RANCH - TO ONE ROBERT BIGELOW, A LAS VEGAS REAL ESTATE MAGNATE, AND A UFO NUT!
BIGELOW SET UP THE NATIONAL INSTITUTE FOR DISCOVERY SCIENCE TO MONITOR THE STRANGE EVENTS...
AND THEN, IN 1997, A SCIENTIST WORKING ON THE RANCH SAW A LARGE HUMANOID CRITTER LOUNGING IN A TREE, WATCHING HIM CLOSELY...
HE FIRED HIS RIFLE, AND THE CREATURE LEGGED IT, LEAVING A LARGE PRINT IN THE SNOW!
THE LOCAL NATIVE AMERICAN PEOPLE - THE UTE TRIBE - KNEW WHAT IT WAS - A SKINWALKER - A SHAPE-SHIFTING WITCH!
SURE, MAN! OUR OLD STORIES SAY THE LOCAL SPRINGS AND WATERWAYS ARE RESERVOIRS OF NEGATIVE POWERS! EVIL SPIRITS IN THE WATER!
YOU WANT TO TRY A DROP?
er... WELL - I'M NOT SURE...
DON'T DO IT, GULLY!
(BUT WE KNOW HE WILL...)

SNAKE HANDLER

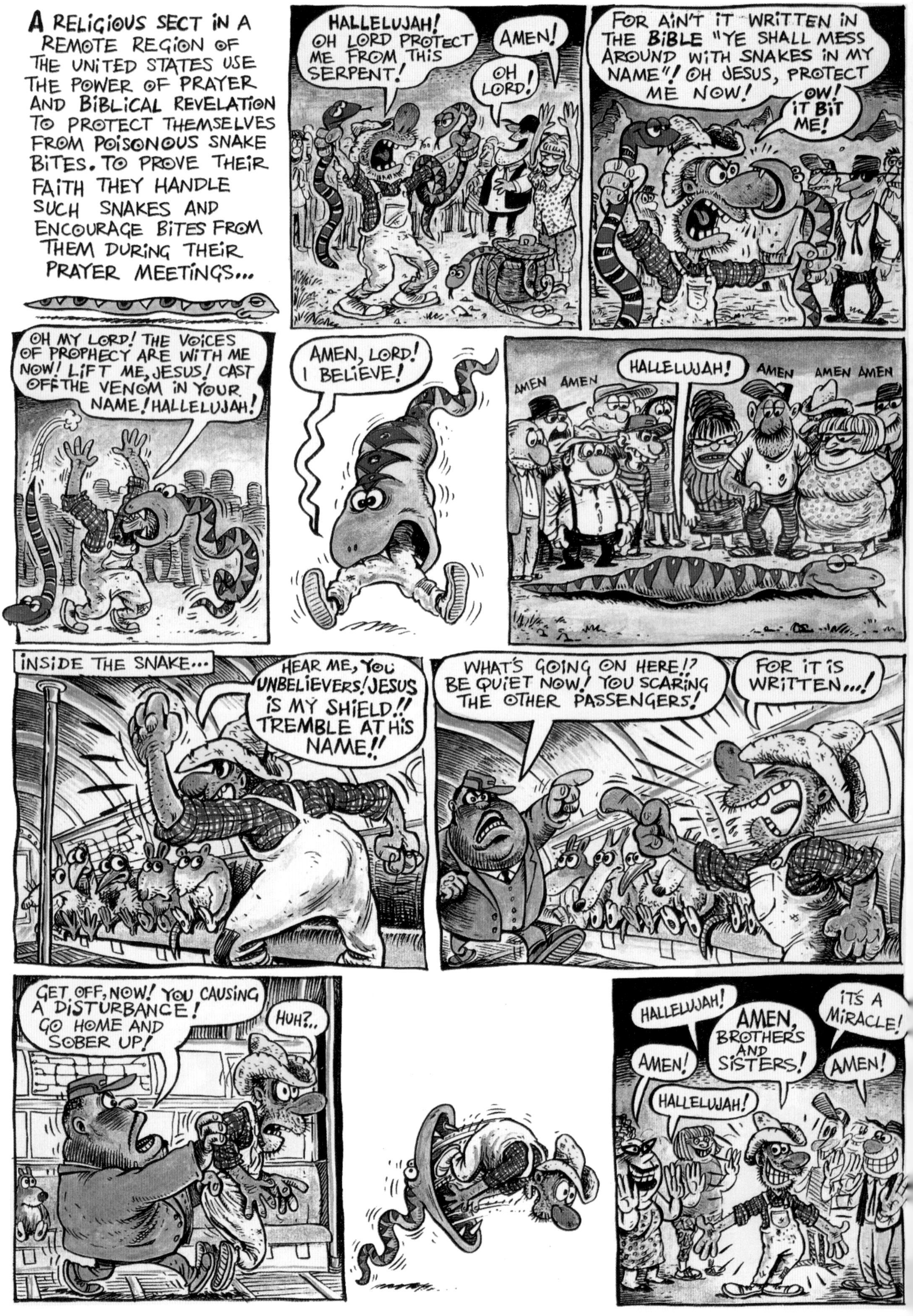
A RELIGIOUS SECT IN A REMOTE REGION OF THE UNITED STATES USE THE POWER OF PRAYER AND BIBLICAL REVELATION TO PROTECT THEMSELVES FROM POISONOUS SNAKE BITES. TO PROVE THEIR FAITH THEY HANDLE SUCH SNAKES AND ENCOURAGE BITES FROM THEM DURING THEIR PRAYER MEETINGS...
HALLELUJAH! OH LORD PROTECT ME FROM THIS SERPENT!
AMEN!
OH LORD!
FOR AIN'T IT WRITTEN IN THE BIBLE "YE SHALL MESS AROUND WITH SNAKES IN MY NAME"! OH JESUS, PROTECT ME NOW!
OW! IT BIT ME!
OH MY LORD! THE VOICES OF PROPHECY ARE WITH ME NOW! LIFT ME, JESUS! CAST OFF THE VENOM IN YOUR NAME! HALLELUJAH!
AMEN, LORD! I BELIEVE!
AMEN AMEN
HALLELUJAH!
AMEN
AMEN AMEN
INSIDE THE SNAKE...
HEAR ME, YOU UNBELIEVERS! JESUS IS MY SHIELD!! TREMBLE AT HIS NAME!!
WHAT'S GOING ON HERE!? BE QUIET NOW! YOU SCARING THE OTHER PASSENGERS!
FOR IT IS WRITTEN...!
GET OFF, NOW! YOU CAUSING A DISTURBANCE! GO HOME AND SOBER UP!
HUH?..
HALLELUJAH!
AMEN, BROTHERS AND SISTERS!
IT'S A MIRACLE!
AMEN!
AMEN!
HALLELUJAH!

SOAP POWDER

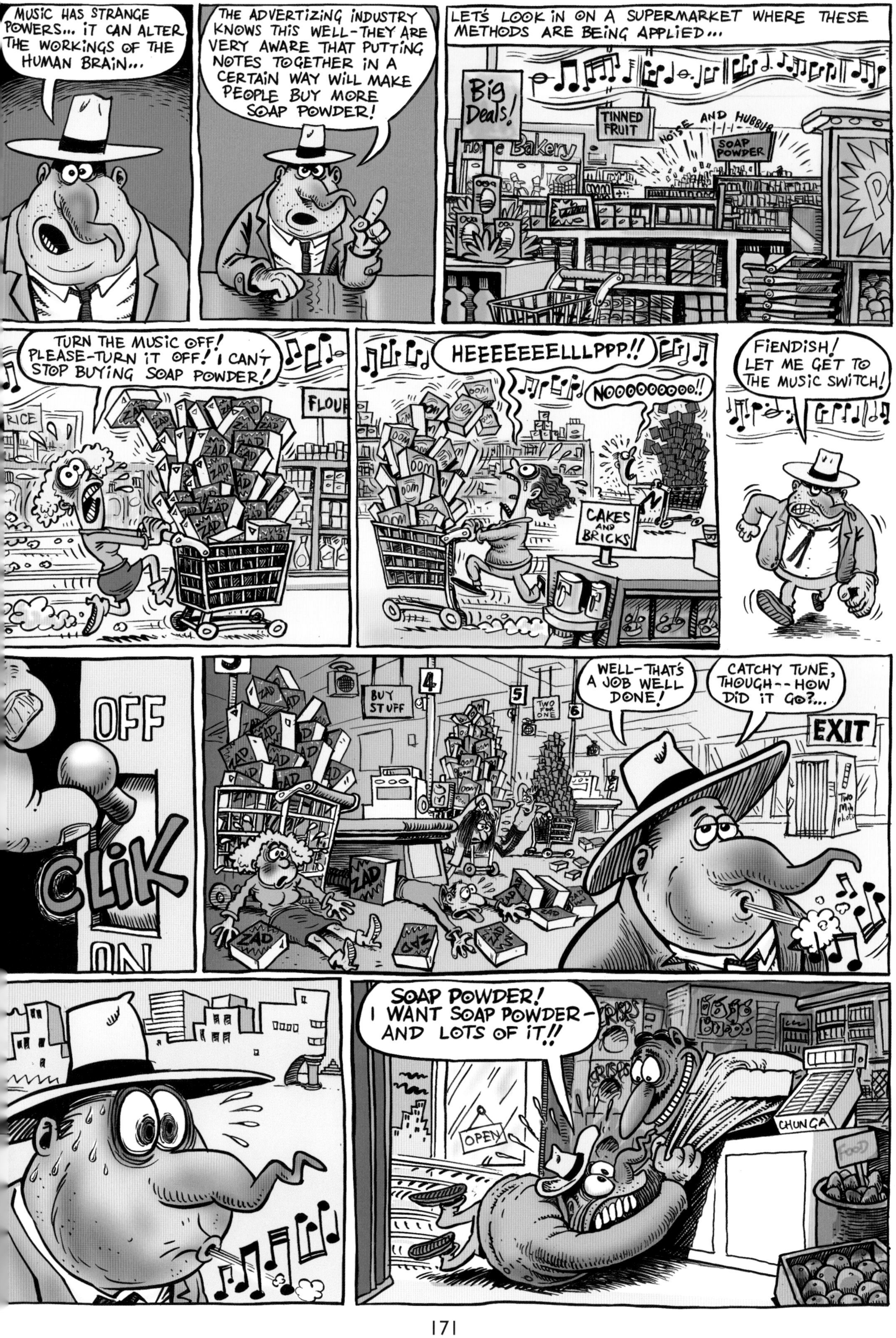
MUSIC HAS STRANGE POWERS... IT CAN ALTER THE WORKINGS OF THE HUMAN BRAIN...
THE ADVERTIZING INDUSTRY KNOWS THIS WELL-THEY ARE VERY AWARE THAT PUTTING NOTES TOGETHER IN A CERTAIN WAY WILL MAKE PEOPLE BUY MORE SOAP POWDER!
LET'S LOOK IN ON A SUPERMARKET WHERE THESE METHODS ARE BEING APPLIED...
Big Deals!
TINNED FRUIT
NOISE AND HUBBUB
SOAP POWDER
Home Bakery
TURN THE MUSIC OFF! PLEASE-TURN IT OFF! I CAN'T STOP BUYING SOAP POWDER!
RICE
FLOUR
ZAD
HEEEEEEELLLPPP!!
NOOOOOOOOO!!
CAKES AND BRICKS
OOM
FIENDISH! LET ME GET TO THE MUSIC SWITCH!
OFF
CLIK
ON
BUY STUFF
TWO FOR ONE
WELL-THAT'S A JOB WELL DONE!
CATCHY TUNE, THOUGH--HOW DID IT GO?...
EXIT
SOAP POWDER! I WANT SOAP POWDER- AND LOTS OF IT!!
CRISPS
OPEN
CHUNGA
FOOD

STARFISH

MILLIONS OF STARFISH MYSTERIOUSLY APPEAR ON A NORFOLK BEACH. SCIENTISTS PUT THE CAUSE DOWN TO "FREAK WIND CONDITIONS" WHICH BLOW THEM FROM THE SEA BED...

THERE IS A LOCAL LEGEND CONCERNING THE ORIGIN OF STARFISH...

WHERE DO STARFISH COME FROM, GRANDAD?

AH— NOW THAT BE A CURIOUS STORY, SON...

YOU SEE, THERE BE A GIANT SEA-SNAKE WHICH LIVES ON THE OCEAN BOTTOM...

IN SOME YEARS, THIS SEA-SNAKE TAKES IT INTO HIS HEAD TO CHEW CHUNKS OUT OF THE SKY, AND HE DO SWALLOW GREAT MYRIADS OF STARS...

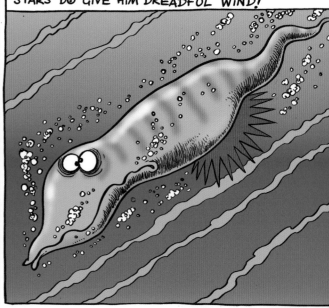

'TIS A GREEDY OL' SNAKE, MIND, AND ALL THEM STARS DO GIVE HIM DREADFUL WIND!

SO HE HAS TO PASS THAT WIND, AND ALL THE STARS DO BE BLOWN UP ONTO THE BEACH AS STARFISH!

KABLOOBALOOBALOOB

AND THAT, M'BOY, BE THE STORY! Y'SEE, THEM SCIENTIST FELLERS DO BE RIGHT TO BLAME IT ON FREAK WINDS...

IS THAT TRUE?

WHO CAN SEE WHAT IS TRUTH

TeeHee WE KNO

STAR TREK

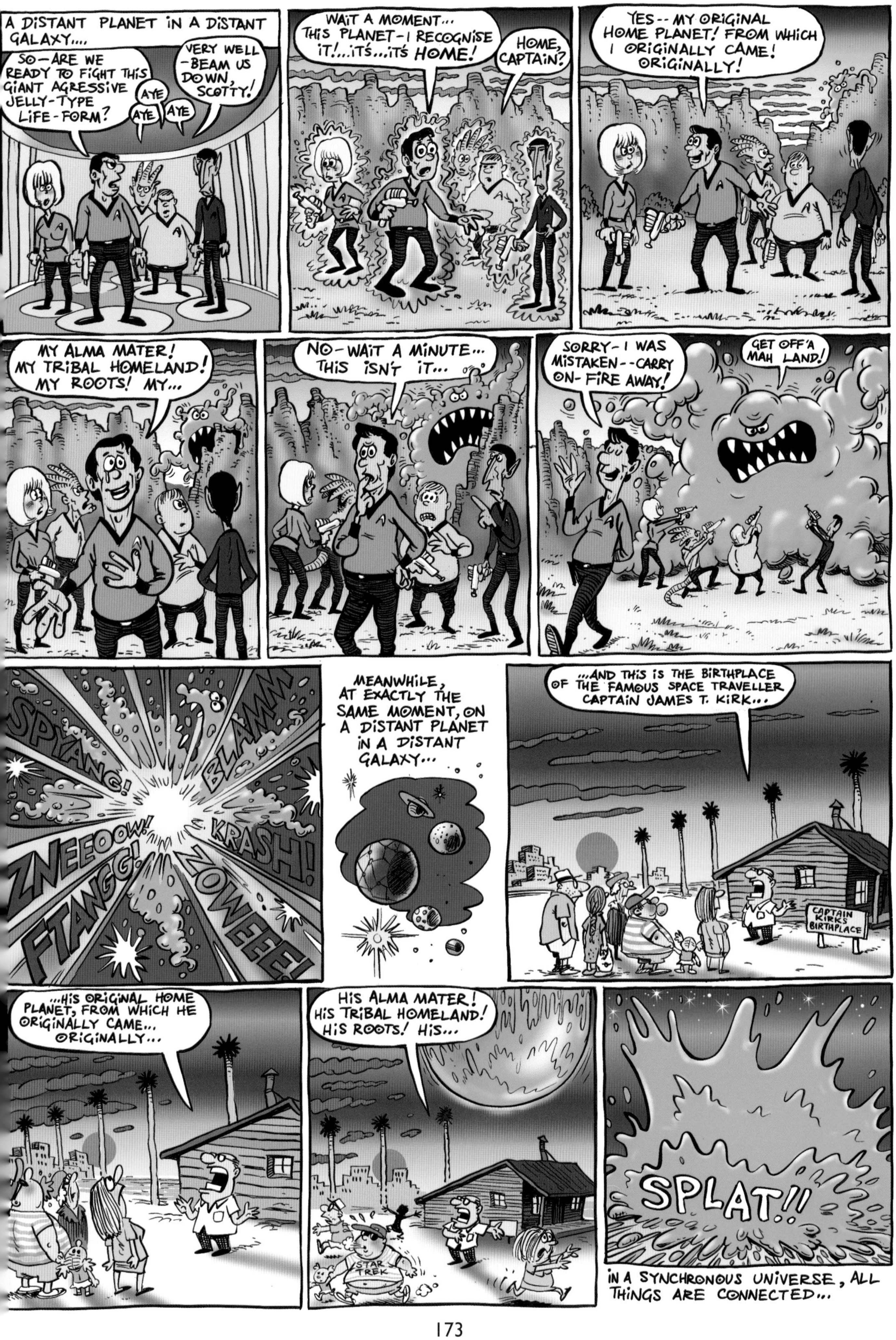

A DISTANT PLANET IN A DISTANT GALAXY....
SO—ARE WE READY TO FIGHT THIS GIANT AGRESSIVE JELLY-TYPE LIFE-FORM?
VERY WELL —BEAM US DOWN, SCOTTY!
AYE
AYE
AYE
WAIT A MOMENT... THIS PLANET—I RECOGNISE IT!...IT'S...IT'S HOME!
HOME, CAPTAIN?
YES--MY ORIGINAL HOME PLANET! FROM WHICH I ORIGINALLY CAME! ORIGINALLY!
MY ALMA MATER! MY TRIBAL HOMELAND! MY ROOTS! MY...
NO—WAIT A MINUTE... THIS ISN'T IT...
SORRY—I WAS MISTAKEN--CARRY ON—FIRE AWAY!
GET OFF'A MAH LAND!
SPYANG!
BLAMM!
ZNEEOOW!
KRASH!
FTANGG!
ZOWEEE!
MEANWHILE, AT EXACTLY THE SAME MOMENT, ON A DISTANT PLANET IN A DISTANT GALAXY...
...AND THIS IS THE BIRTHPLACE OF THE FAMOUS SPACE TRAVELLER CAPTAIN JAMES T. KIRK...
CAPTAIN KIRK'S BIRTHPLACE
...HIS ORIGINAL HOME PLANET, FROM WHICH HE ORIGINALLY CAME... ORIGINALLY...
HIS ALMA MATER! HIS TRIBAL HOMELAND! HIS ROOTS! HIS...
STAR TREK
SPLAT!!
IN A SYNCHRONOUS UNIVERSE, ALL THINGS ARE CONNECTED...

STRANGE SHOE CUSTOMS

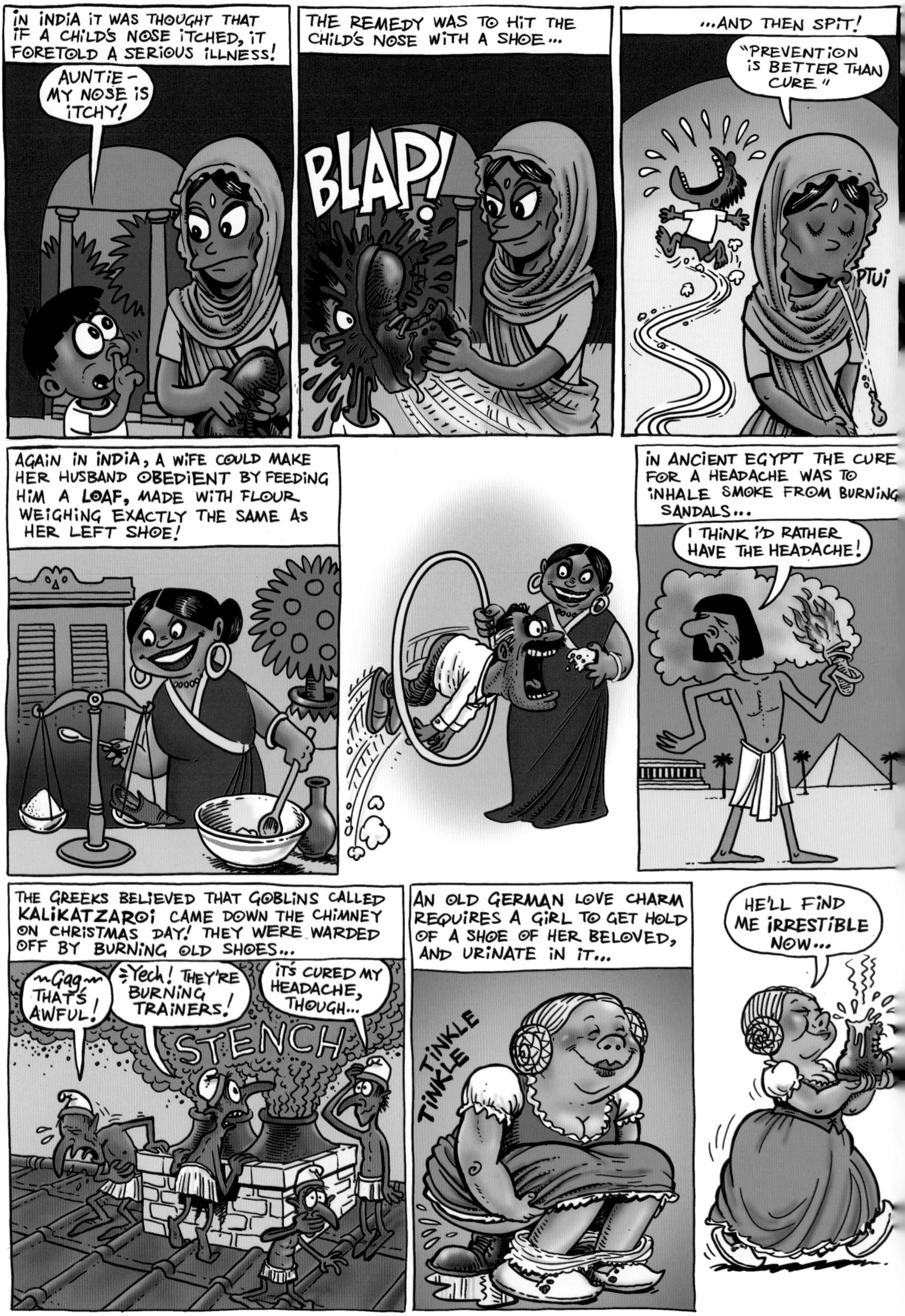

IN INDIA IT WAS THOUGHT THAT IF A CHILD'S NOSE ITCHED, IT FORETOLD A SERIOUS ILLNESS!
AUNTIE – MY NOSE IS ITCHY!
THE REMEDY WAS TO HIT THE CHILD'S NOSE WITH A SHOE...
BLAP!
...AND THEN SPIT!
"PREVENTION IS BETTER THAN CURE"
PTUI
AGAIN IN INDIA, A WIFE COULD MAKE HER HUSBAND OBEDIENT BY FEEDING HIM A LOAF, MADE WITH FLOUR WEIGHING EXACTLY THE SAME AS HER LEFT SHOE!
IN ANCIENT EGYPT THE CURE FOR A HEADACHE WAS TO INHALE SMOKE FROM BURNING SANDALS...
I THINK I'D RATHER HAVE THE HEADACHE!
THE GREEKS BELIEVED THAT GOBLINS CALLED KALIKATZAROI CAME DOWN THE CHIMNEY ON CHRISTMAS DAY! THEY WERE WARDED OFF BY BURNING OLD SHOES...
~Gag~ THAT'S AWFUL!
Yech! THEY'RE BURNING TRAINERS!
IT'S CURED MY HEADACHE, THOUGH...
STENCH
AN OLD GERMAN LOVE CHARM REQUIRES A GIRL TO GET HOLD OF A SHOE OF HER BELOVED, AND URINATE IN IT...
TINKLE TINKLE
HE'LL FIND ME IRRESTIBLE NOW...

PILGRIM'S PSYCHEDELIC MEDITATION

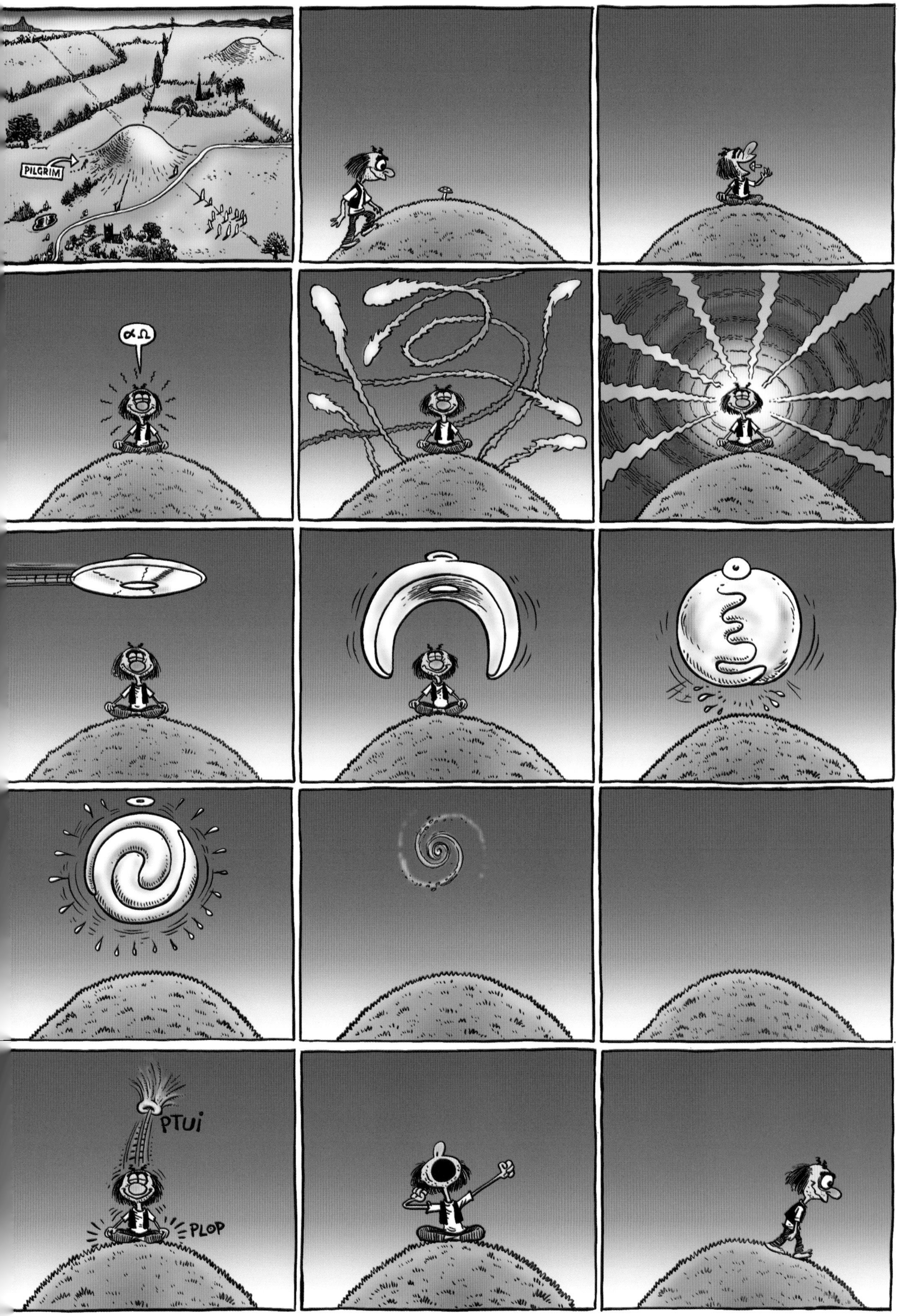
PILGRIM
αΩ
PTUi
PLOP

PILGRIM'S PSYCHEDELIC FESTIVAL

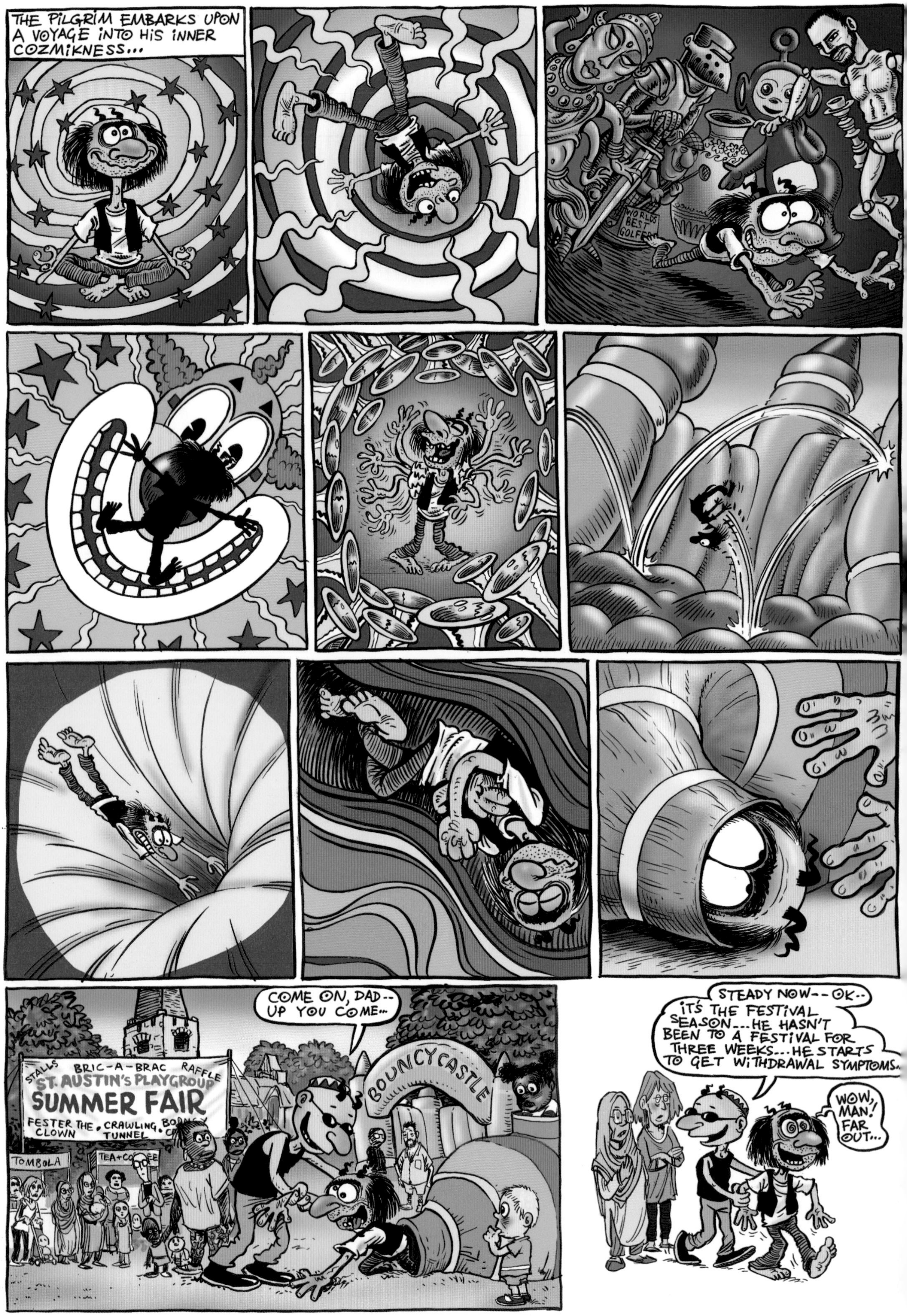
THE PILGRIM EMBARKS UPON A VOYAGE INTO HIS INNER COZMIKNESS...
WORLDS BEST GOLFER
COME ON, DAD-- UP YOU COME...
STALLS BRIC-A-BRAC RAFFLE
ST. AUSTIN'S PLAYGROUP
SUMMER FAIR
FESTER THE CLOWN • CRAWLING TUNNEL •
TOMBOLA
BOUNCYCASTLE
STEADY NOW--OK..
IT'S THE FESTIVAL SEASON...HE HASN'T BEEN TO A FESTIVAL FOR THREE WEEKS...HE STARTS TO GET WITHDRAWAL SYMPTOMS..
WOW, MAN! FAR OUT...

EETH HENGE

EETH
NEXT!
NOW LET'S TAKE A LOOK...OH DEAR...
I'M GOING TO HAVE TO DO SOME SERIOUS WORK HERE!
TIME PASSES...
CHOP
HACK
DRILL
GRIND
SCRAPE
CHIP
NOW HAVE A GOOD RINSE OUT! THAT'LL BE £8000 PLEASE...
A FEW DAYS HE'S SHOWING OFF THE RESULTS TO HIS FRIENDS...
IT'S AMAZING! THE ROOT CANAL WORK HAS ADE A TUNNEL UNDERNEATH IT ALL, LEADING FROM ONE EAR TO THE OTHER...
...AND HE'S DRILLED A HOLE IN THE BACK OF MY NECK IN THE EXACT POSITION OF THE MIDSUMMER SUNRISE!

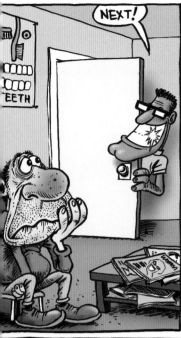

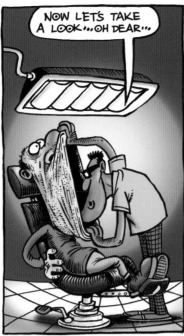

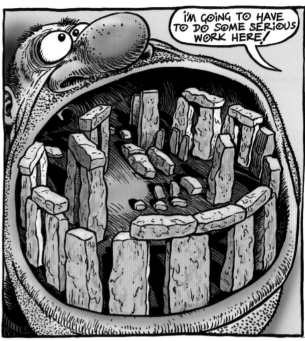

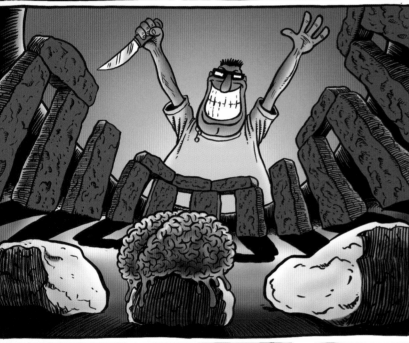

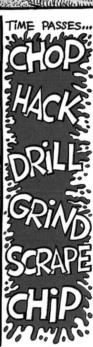

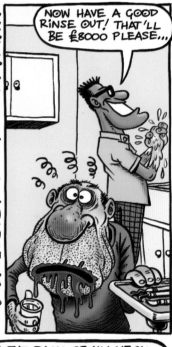

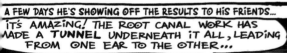

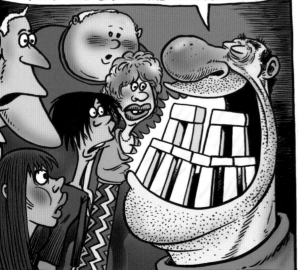

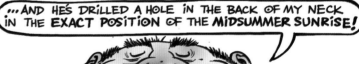

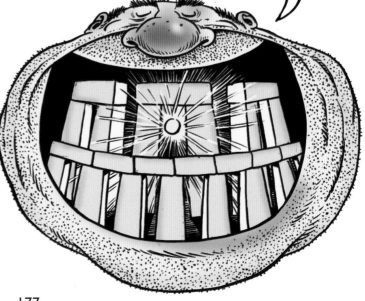

TELEKINESIS CONTEST

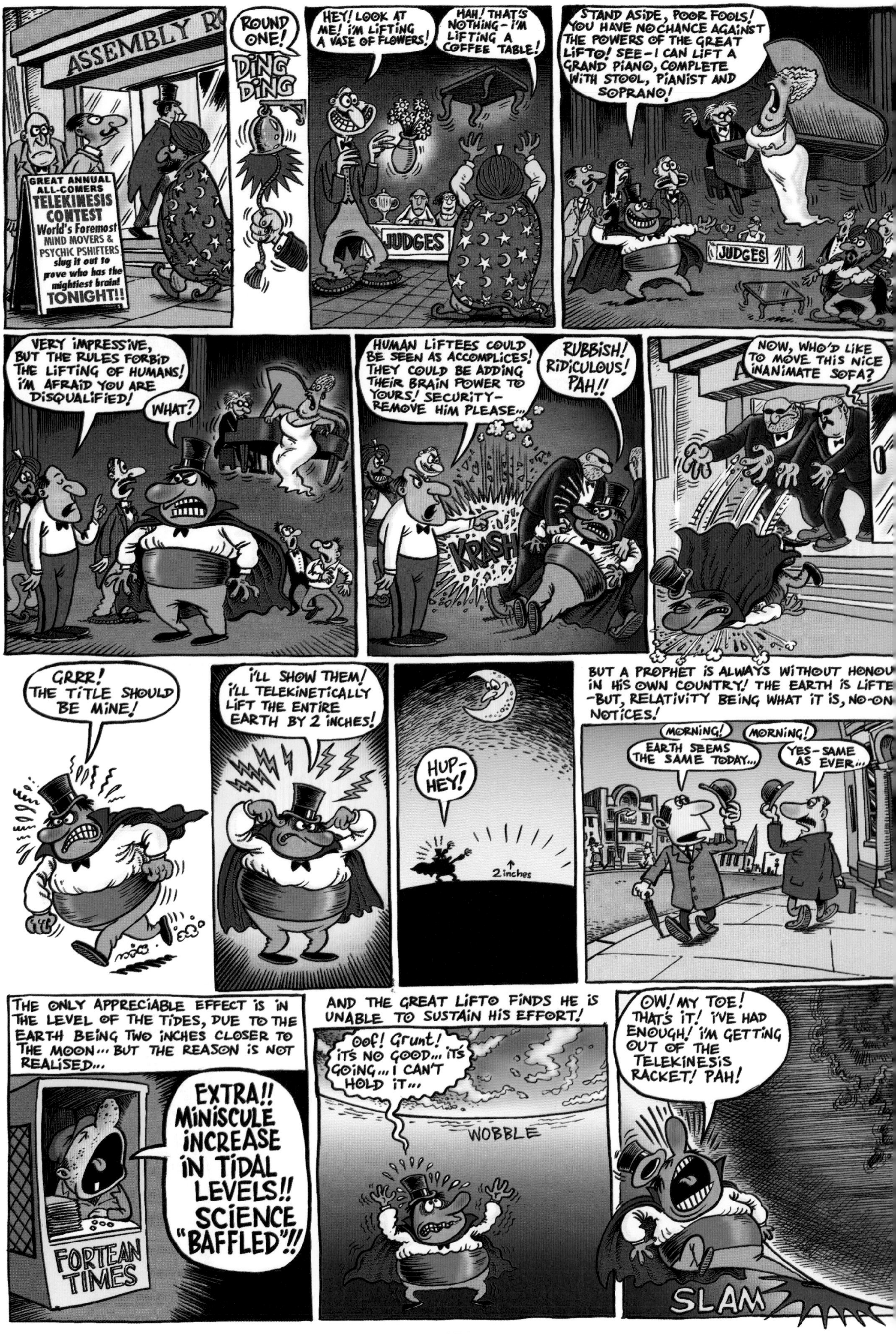
ASSEMBLY R
GREAT ANNUAL ALL-COMERS TELEKINESIS CONTEST World's Foremost MIND MOVERS & PSYCHIC PSHIFTERS slug it out to prove who has the mightiest brain! TONIGHT!!
ROUND ONE!
DING DING
HEY! LOOK AT ME! I'M LIFTING A VASE OF FLOWERS!
HAH! THAT'S NOTHING - I'M LIFTING A COFFEE TABLE!
JUDGES
STAND ASIDE, POOR FOOLS! YOU HAVE NO CHANCE AGAINST THE POWERS OF THE GREAT LIFTO! SEE - I CAN LIFT A GRAND PIANO, COMPLETE WITH STOOL, PIANIST AND SOPRANO!
JUDGES
VERY IMPRESSIVE, BUT THE RULES FORBID THE LIFTING OF HUMANS! I'M AFRAID YOU ARE DISQUALIFIED!
WHAT?
HUMAN LIFTEES COULD BE SEEN AS ACCOMPLICES! THEY COULD BE ADDING THEIR BRAIN POWER TO YOURS! SECURITY - REMOVE HIM PLEASE...
RUBBISH! RIDICULOUS! PAH!!
KRASH
NOW, WHO'D LIKE TO MOVE THIS NICE INANIMATE SOFA?
GRRR! THE TITLE SHOULD BE MINE!
I'LL SHOW THEM! I'LL TELEKINETICALLY LIFT THE ENTIRE EARTH BY 2 INCHES!
HUP-HEY!
2 inches
BUT A PROPHET IS ALWAYS WITHOUT HONOU IN HIS OWN COUNTRY! THE EARTH IS LIFTE -BUT, RELATIVITY BEING WHAT IT IS, NO-ON NOTICES!
MORNING!
MORNING!
EARTH SEEMS THE SAME TODAY...
YES - SAME AS EVER...
THE ONLY APPRECIABLE EFFECT IS IN THE LEVEL OF THE TIDES, DUE TO THE EARTH BEING TWO INCHES CLOSER TO THE MOON... BUT THE REASON IS NOT REALISED...
EXTRA!! MINISCULE INCREASE IN TIDAL LEVELS!! SCIENCE "BAFFLED"!!
FORTEAN TIMES
AND THE GREAT LIFTO FINDS HE IS UNABLE TO SUSTAIN HIS EFFORT!
Oof! Grunt! It's no good... it's going... I can't hold it...
WOBBLE
OW! MY TOE! THAT'S IT! I'VE HAD ENOUGH! I'M GETTING OUT OF THE TELEKINESIS RACKET! PAH!
SLAM

TESLA'S CHILDHOOD

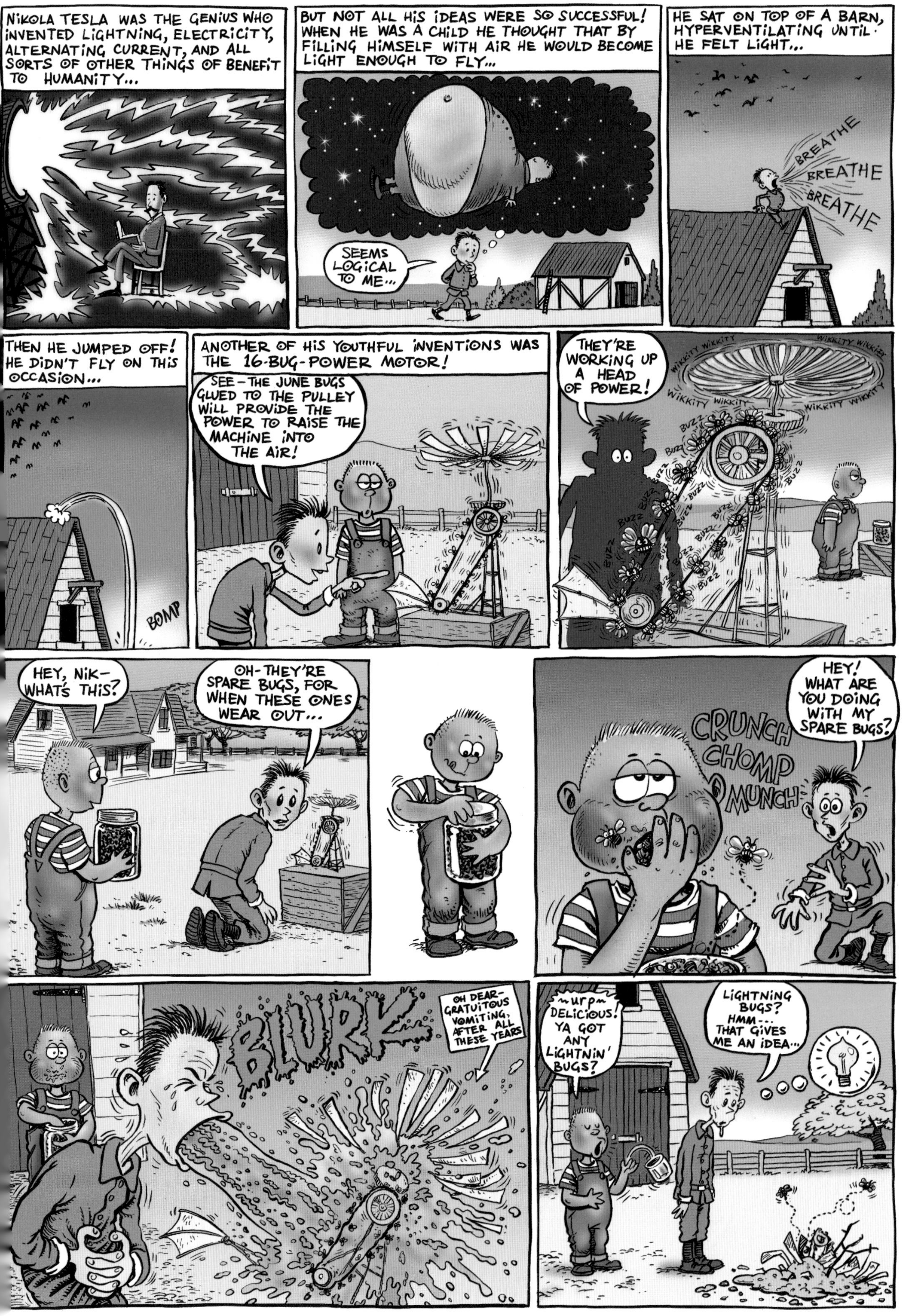
NIKOLA TESLA WAS THE GENIUS WHO INVENTED LIGHTNING, ELECTRICITY, ALTERNATING CURRENT, AND ALL SORTS OF OTHER THINGS OF BENEFIT TO HUMANITY...
BUT NOT ALL HIS IDEAS WERE SO SUCCESSFUL! WHEN HE WAS A CHILD HE THOUGHT THAT BY FILLING HIMSELF WITH AIR HE WOULD BECOME LIGHT ENOUGH TO FLY...
SEEMS LOGICAL TO ME...
HE SAT ON TOP OF A BARN, HYPERVENTILATING UNTIL HE FELT LIGHT...
BREATHE
BREATHE
BREATHE
THEN HE JUMPED OFF! HE DIDN'T FLY ON THIS OCCASION...
BOMP
ANOTHER OF HIS YOUTHFUL INVENTIONS WAS THE 16-BUG-POWER MOTOR!
SEE — THE JUNE BUGS GLUED TO THE PULLEY WILL PROVIDE THE POWER TO RAISE THE MACHINE INTO THE AIR!
THEY'RE WORKING UP A HEAD OF POWER!
WIKKITY WIKKITY
WIKKITY WIKKITY
WIKKITY WIKKITY
WIKKITY WIKKITY
BUZZ
HEY, NIK— WHAT'S THIS?
OH- THEY'RE SPARE BUGS, FOR WHEN THESE ONES WEAR OUT...
CRUNCH
CHOMP
MUNCH
HEY! WHAT ARE YOU DOING WITH MY SPARE BUGS?
BLURK
OH DEAR- GRATUITOUS VOMITING, AFTER ALL THESE YEARS
~urp~ DELICIOUS! YA GOT ANY LIGHTNIN' BUGS?
LIGHTNING BUGS? HMM... THAT GIVES ME AN IDEA...

THAI SUPERSTITIONS

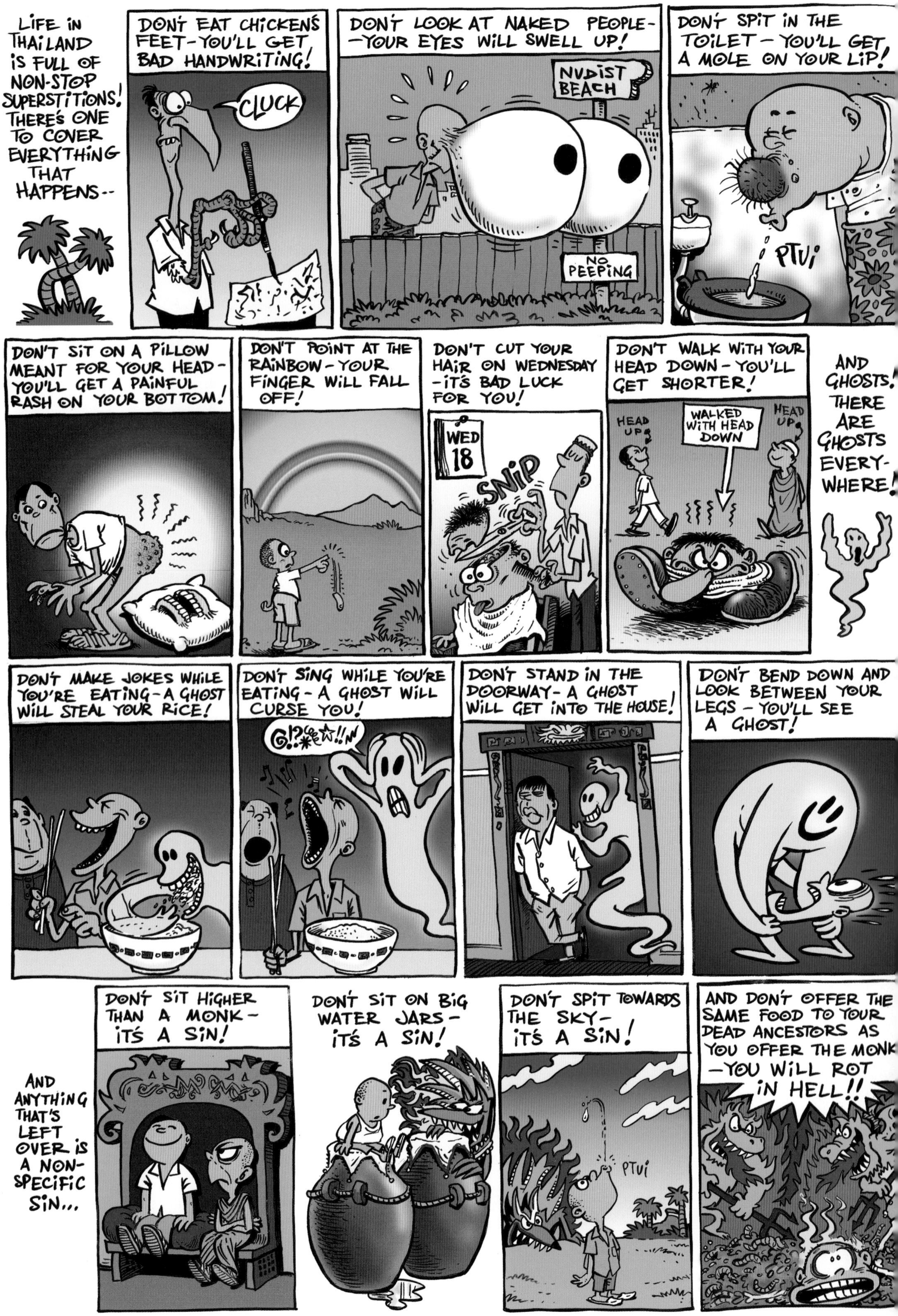
LIFE IN THAILAND IS FULL OF NON-STOP SUPERSTITIONS! THERE'S ONE TO COVER EVERYTHING THAT HAPPENS--
DON'T EAT CHICKEN'S FEET-YOU'LL GET BAD HANDWRITING!
CLUCK
DON'T LOOK AT NAKED PEOPLE- -YOUR EYES WILL SWELL UP!
NUDIST BEACH
NO PEEPING
DON'T SPIT IN THE TOILET - YOU'LL GET A MOLE ON YOUR LIP!
PTUI
DON'T SIT ON A PILLOW MEANT FOR YOUR HEAD - YOU'LL GET A PAINFUL RASH ON YOUR BOTTOM!
DON'T POINT AT THE RAINBOW - YOUR FINGER WILL FALL OFF!
DON'T CUT YOUR HAIR ON WEDNESDAY -IT'S BAD LUCK FOR YOU!
WED 18
SNIP
DON'T WALK WITH YOUR HEAD DOWN - YOU'LL GET SHORTER!
HEAD UP
WALKED WITH HEAD DOWN
HEAD UP
AND GHOSTS! THERE ARE GHOSTS EVERY-WHERE!
DON'T MAKE JOKES WHILE YOU'RE EATING - A GHOST WILL STEAL YOUR RICE!
DON'T SING WHILE YOU'RE EATING - A GHOST WILL CURSE YOU!
DON'T STAND IN THE DOORWAY- A GHOST WILL GET INTO THE HOUSE!
DON'T BEND DOWN AND LOOK BETWEEN YOUR LEGS - YOU'LL SEE A GHOST!
AND ANYTHING THAT'S LEFT OVER IS A NON-SPECIFIC SIN...
DON'T SIT HIGHER THAN A MONK - IT'S A SIN!
DON'T SIT ON BIG WATER JARS - IT'S A SIN!
DON'T SPIT TOWARDS THE SKY- IT'S A SIN!
PTUI
AND DON'T OFFER THE SAME FOOD TO YOUR DEAD ANCESTORS AS YOU OFFER THE MONK -YOU WILL ROT IN HELL!!

THE DOG

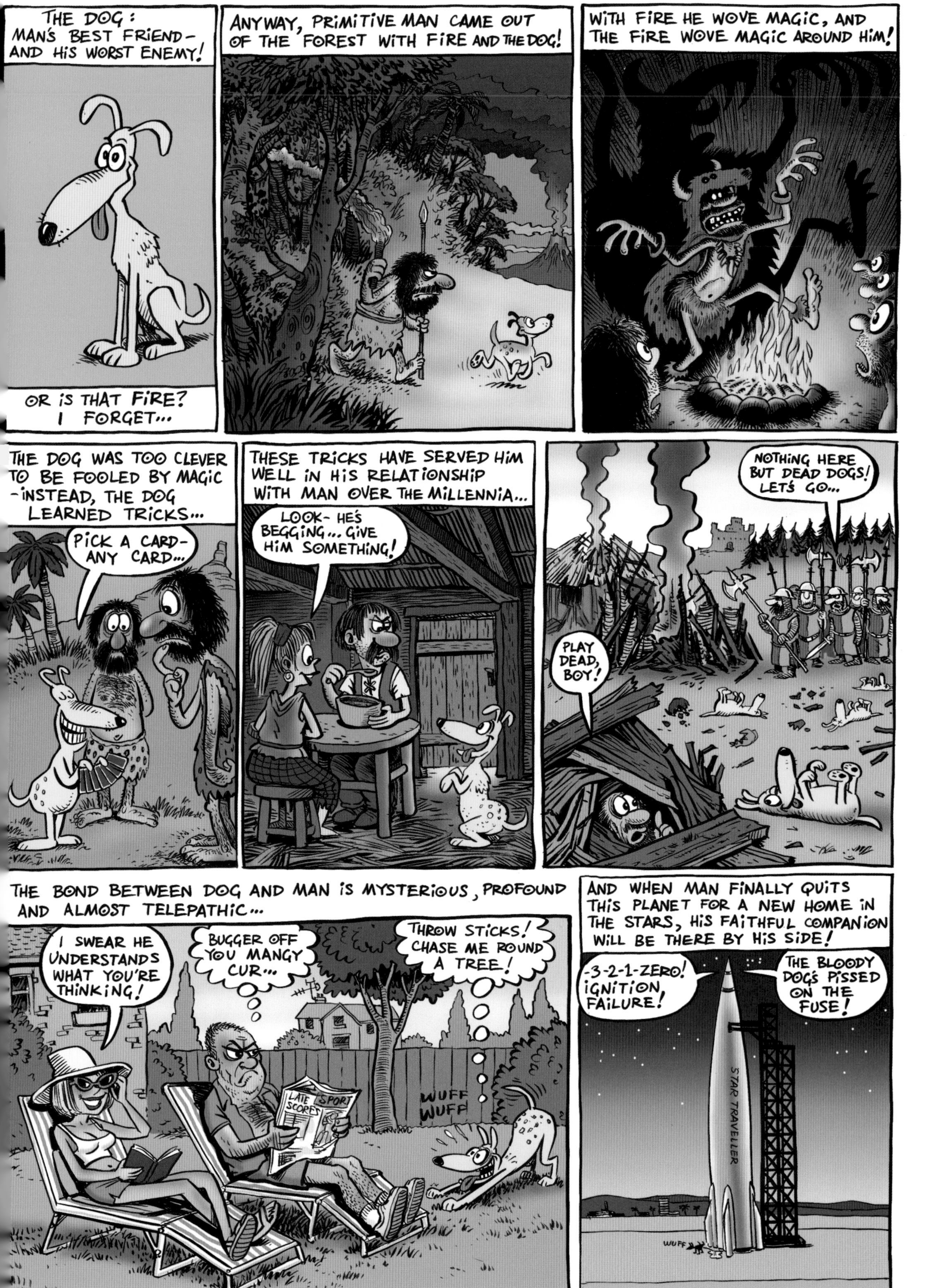

THE DOG: MAN'S BEST FRIEND - AND HIS WORST ENEMY!
OR IS THAT FIRE? I FORGET...
ANYWAY, PRIMITIVE MAN CAME OUT OF THE FOREST WITH FIRE AND THE DOG!
WITH FIRE HE WOVE MAGIC, AND THE FIRE WOVE MAGIC AROUND HIM!
THE DOG WAS TOO CLEVER TO BE FOOLED BY MAGIC - INSTEAD, THE DOG LEARNED TRICKS...
PICK A CARD - ANY CARD...
THESE TRICKS HAVE SERVED HIM WELL IN HIS RELATIONSHIP WITH MAN OVER THE MILLENNIA...
LOOK - HE'S BEGGING... GIVE HIM SOMETHING!
NOTHING HERE BUT DEAD DOGS! LET'S GO...
PLAY DEAD, BOY!
THE BOND BETWEEN DOG AND MAN IS MYSTERIOUS, PROFOUND AND ALMOST TELEPATHIC...
I SWEAR HE UNDERSTANDS WHAT YOU'RE THINKING!
BUGGER OFF YOU MANGY CUR...
THROW STICKS! CHASE ME ROUND A TREE!
LATE SPORT SCORES
WUFF WUFF
AND WHEN MAN FINALLY QUITS THIS PLANET FOR A NEW HOME IN THE STARS, HIS FAITHFUL COMPANION WILL BE THERE BY HIS SIDE!
-3-2-1-ZERO! IGNITION FAILURE!
THE BLOODY DOG'S PISSED ON THE FUSE!
STAR TRAVELLER
WUFF

THE GUY FROM THE FUTURE

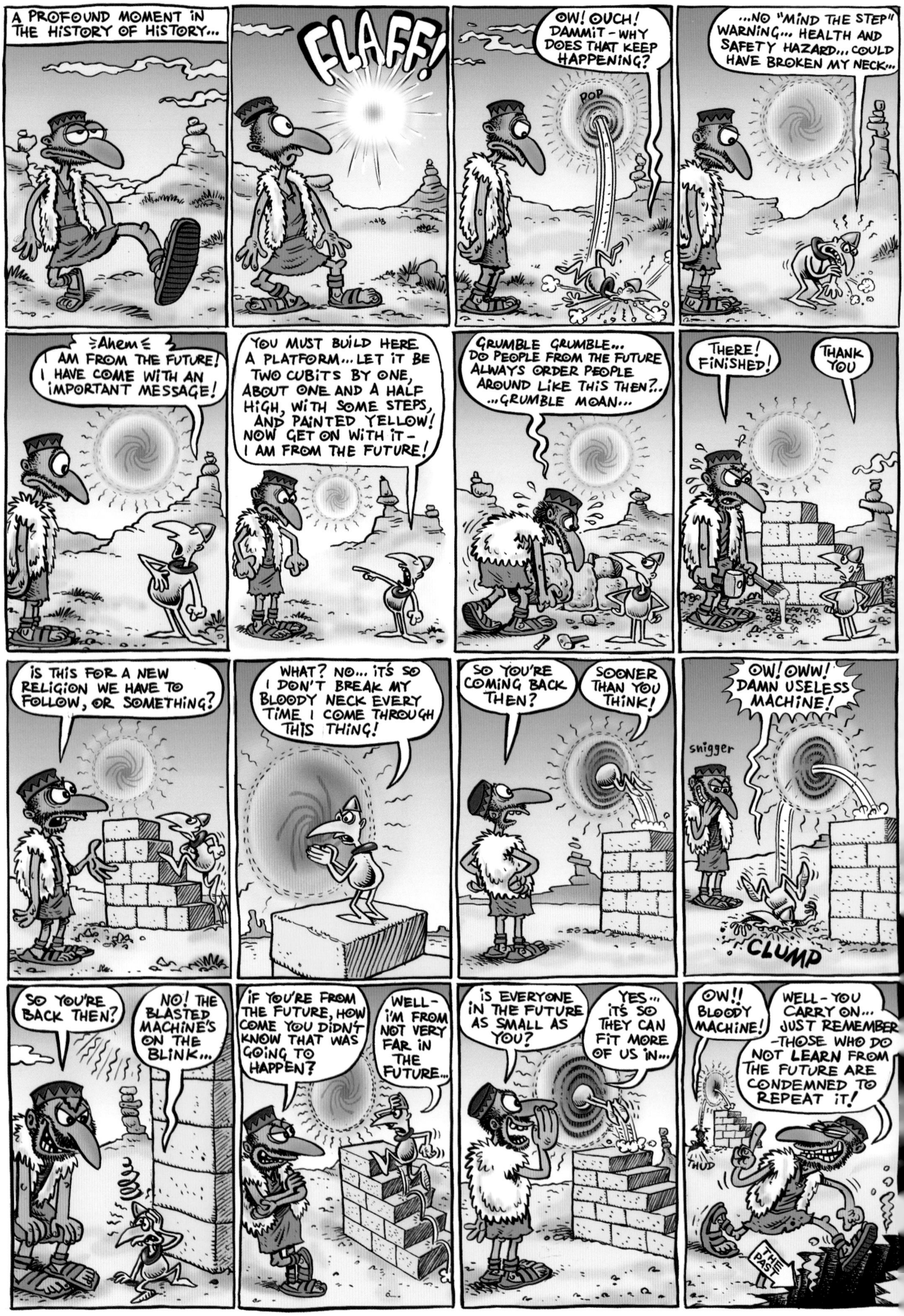
A PROFOUND MOMENT IN THE HISTORY OF HISTORY...
FLAFF!
OW! OUCH! DAMMIT - WHY DOES THAT KEEP HAPPENING?
POP
...NO "MIND THE STEP" WARNING... HEALTH AND SAFETY HAZARD... COULD HAVE BROKEN MY NECK...
Ahem
I AM FROM THE FUTURE! I HAVE COME WITH AN IMPORTANT MESSAGE!
YOU MUST BUILD HERE A PLATFORM... LET IT BE TWO CUBITS BY ONE, ABOUT ONE AND A HALF HIGH, WITH SOME STEPS, AND PAINTED YELLOW! NOW GET ON WITH IT - I AM FROM THE FUTURE!
GRUMBLE GRUMBLE... DO PEOPLE FROM THE FUTURE ALWAYS ORDER PEOPLE AROUND LIKE THIS THEN?.. ...GRUMBLE MOAN...
THERE! FINISHED!
THANK YOU
IS THIS FOR A NEW RELIGION WE HAVE TO FOLLOW, OR SOMETHING?
WHAT? NO... IT'S SO I DON'T BREAK MY BLOODY NECK EVERY TIME I COME THROUGH THIS THING!
SO YOU'RE COMING BACK THEN?
SOONER THAN YOU THINK!
snigger
OW! OWW! DAMN USELESS MACHINE!
CLUMP
SO YOU'RE BACK THEN?
NO! THE BLASTED MACHINE'S ON THE BLINK...
IF YOU'RE FROM THE FUTURE, HOW COME YOU DIDN'T KNOW THAT WAS GOING TO HAPPEN?
WELL- I'M FROM NOT VERY FAR IN THE FUTURE...
IS EVERYONE IN THE FUTURE AS SMALL AS YOU?
YES... IT'S SO THEY CAN FIT MORE OF US IN...
OW!! BLOODY MACHINE!
THUD
WELL - YOU CARRY ON... JUST REMEMBER -THOSE WHO DO NOT LEARN FROM THE FUTURE ARE CONDEMNED TO REPEAT IT!
THE PAST

BIRD BRAIN

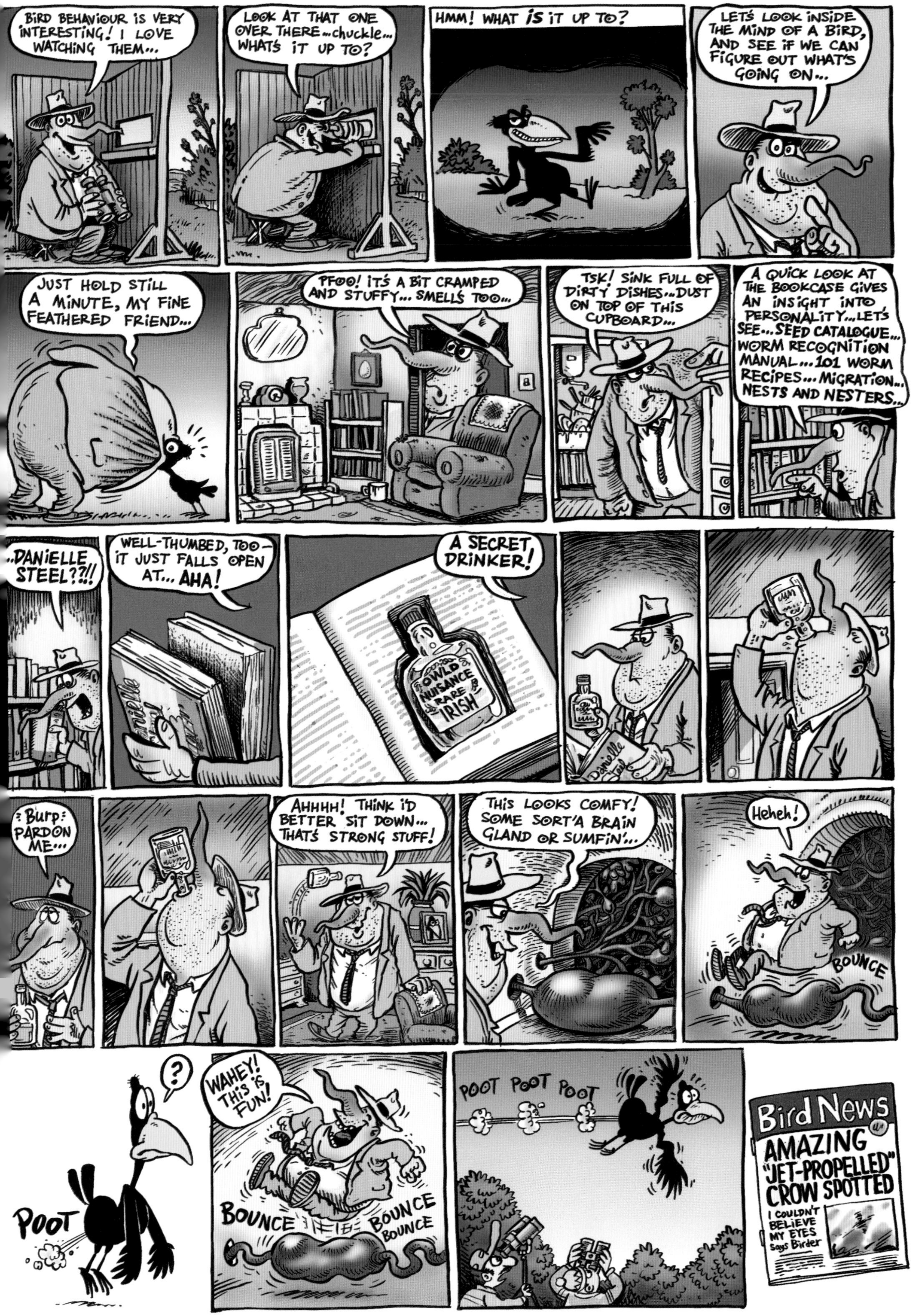
BIRD BEHAVIOUR IS VERY INTERESTING! I LOVE WATCHING THEM...
LOOK AT THAT ONE OVER THERE...chuckle... WHAT'S IT UP TO?
HMM! WHAT IS IT UP TO?
LET'S LOOK INSIDE THE MIND OF A BIRD, AND SEE IF WE CAN FIGURE OUT WHAT'S GOING ON...
JUST HOLD STILL A MINUTE, MY FINE FEATHERED FRIEND...
PFOO! IT'S A BIT CRAMPED AND STUFFY... SMELLS TOO...
TSK! SINK FULL OF DIRTY DISHES...DUST ON TOP OF THIS CUPBOARD...
A QUICK LOOK AT THE BOOKCASE GIVES AN INSIGHT INTO PERSONALITY...LET'S SEE...SEED CATALOGUE... WORM RECOGNITION MANUAL...101 WORM RECIPES... MIGRATION... NESTS AND NESTERS...
..DANIELLE STEEL??!!
WELL-THUMBED, TOO - IT JUST FALLS OPEN AT... AHA!
A SECRET DRINKER!
OWLD NUISANCE RARE IRISH
:Burp: PARDON ME...
AHHHH! THINK I'D BETTER SIT DOWN... THAT'S STRONG STUFF!
THIS LOOKS COMFY! SOME SORT'A BRAIN GLAND OR SUMFIN'...
Heheh!
BOUNCE
?
POOT
WAHEY! THIS IS FUN!
BOUNCE
BOUNCE
BOUNCE
POOT POOT POOT
Bird News
AMAZING "JET-PROPELLED" CROW SPOTTED
I COULDN'T BELIEVE MY EYES Says Birder

THE YELPENBURG YELL

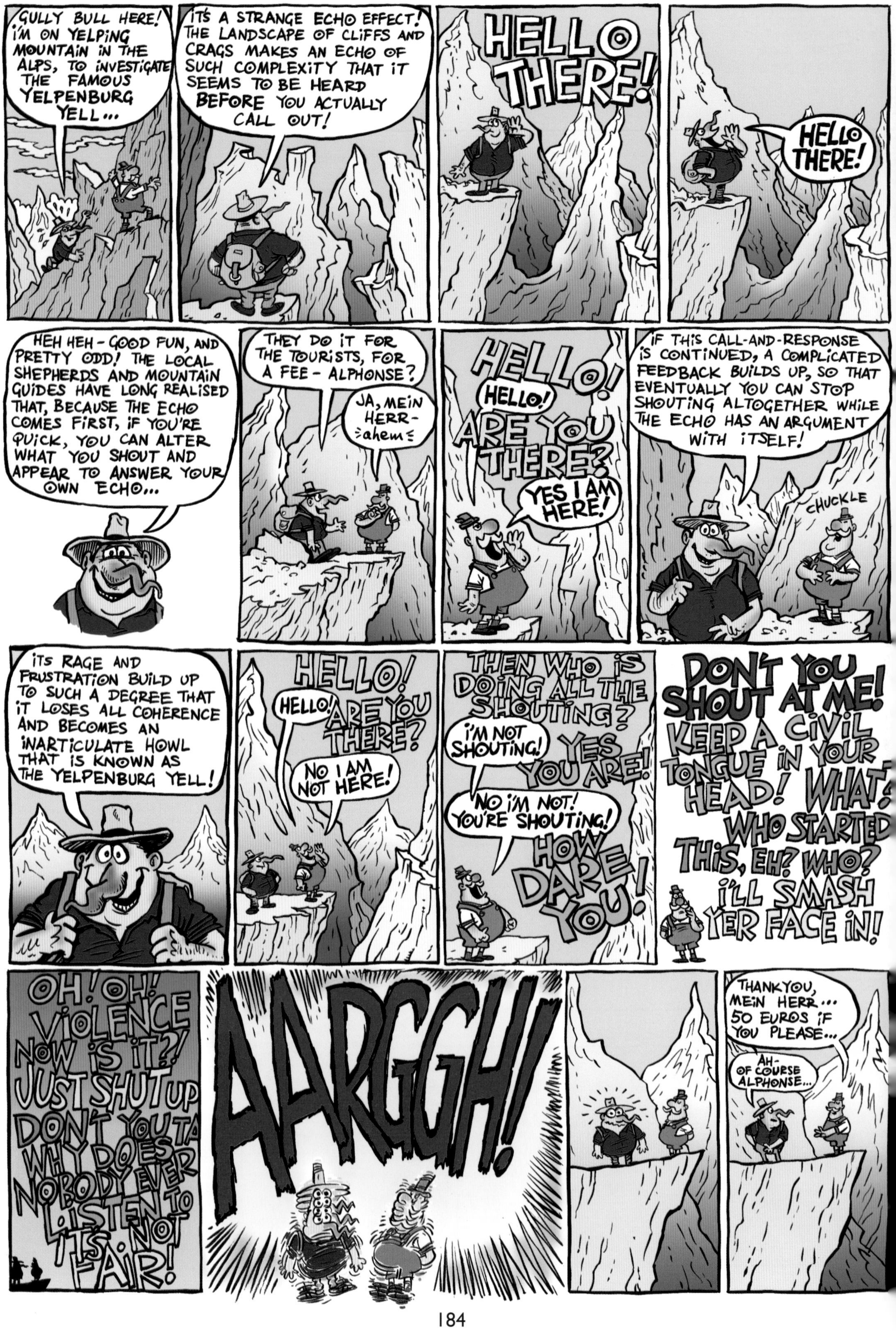
GULLY BULL HERE! I'M ON YELPING MOUNTAIN IN THE ALPS, TO INVESTIGATE THE FAMOUS YELPENBURG YELL...
IT'S A STRANGE ECHO EFFECT! THE LANDSCAPE OF CLIFFS AND CRAGS MAKES AN ECHO OF SUCH COMPLEXITY THAT IT SEEMS TO BE HEARD BEFORE YOU ACTUALLY CALL OUT!
HELLO THERE!
HELLO THERE!
HEH HEH - GOOD FUN, AND PRETTY ODD! THE LOCAL SHEPHERDS AND MOUNTAIN GUIDES HAVE LONG REALISED THAT, BECAUSE THE ECHO COMES FIRST, IF YOU'RE QUICK, YOU CAN ALTER WHAT YOU SHOUT AND APPEAR TO ANSWER YOUR OWN ECHO...
THEY DO IT FOR THE TOURISTS, FOR A FEE - ALPHONSE?
JA, MEIN HERR - ahem
HELLO!
HELLO!
ARE YOU THERE?
YES I AM HERE!
IF THIS CALL-AND-RESPONSE IS CONTINUED, A COMPLICATED FEEDBACK BUILDS UP, SO THAT EVENTUALLY YOU CAN STOP SHOUTING ALTOGETHER WHILE THE ECHO HAS AN ARGUMENT WITH ITSELF!
CHUCKLE
ITS RAGE AND FRUSTRATION BUILD UP TO SUCH A DEGREE THAT IT LOSES ALL COHERENCE AND BECOMES AN INARTICULATE HOWL THAT IS KNOWN AS THE YELPENBURG YELL!
HELLO!
HELLO!
ARE YOU THERE?
NO I AM NOT HERE!
THEN WHO IS DOING ALL THE SHOUTING?
I'M NOT SHOUTING!
YES YOU ARE!
NO I'M NOT! YOU'RE SHOUTING!
HOW DARE YOU!
DON'T YOU SHOUT AT ME! KEEP A CIVIL TONGUE IN YOUR HEAD! WHAT? WHO STARTED THIS, EH? WHO? I'LL SMASH YER FACE IN!
OH! OH! VIOLENCE NOW IS IT?! JUST SHUT UP DON'T YOU TA WHY DOES NOBODY EVER LISTEN TO IT'S NOT FAIR!
AARGGH!
THANKYOU, MEIN HERR... 50 EUROS IF YOU PLEASE...
AH- OF COURSE ALPHONSE...

THE BOOK OF THE DAMNED

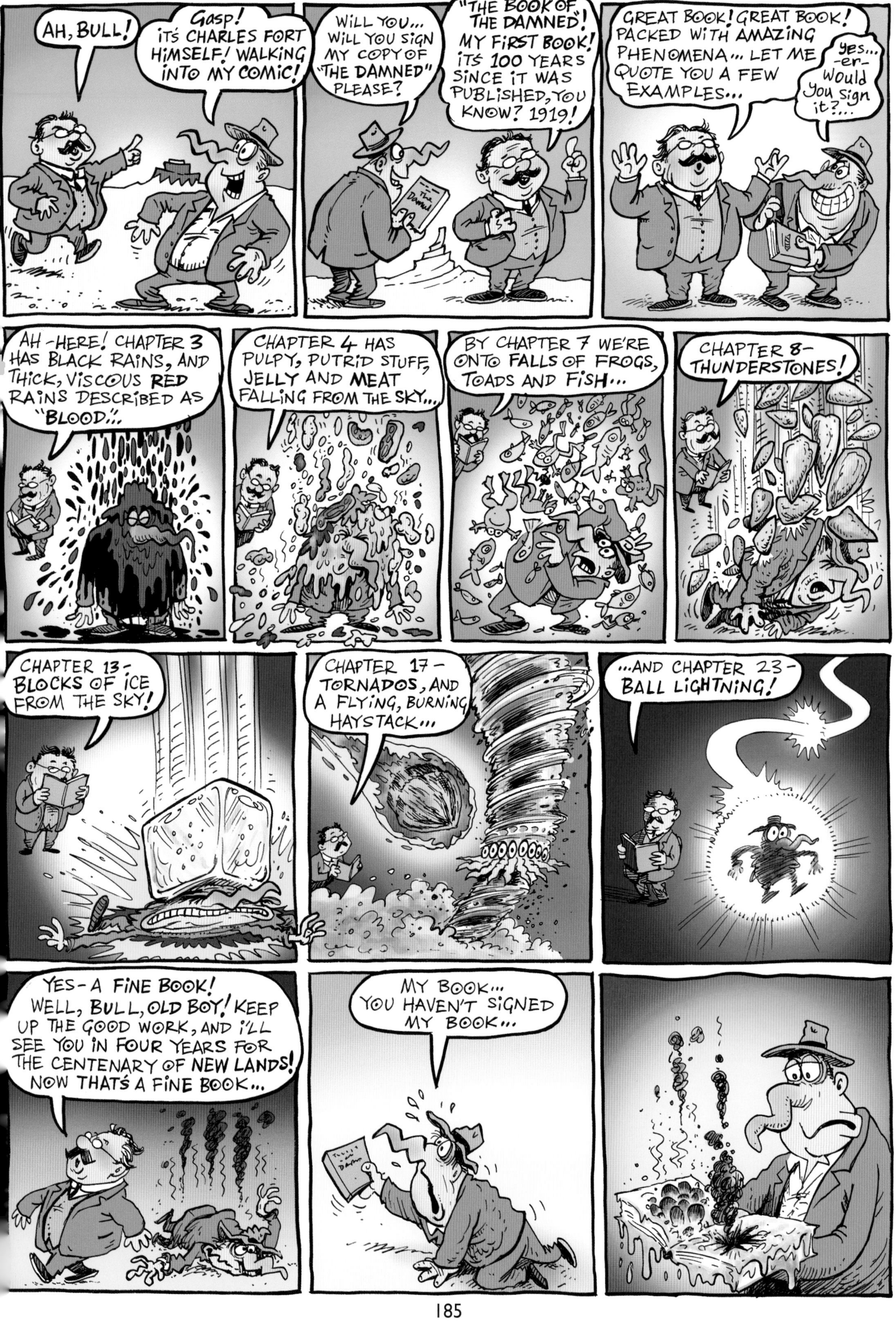

AH, BULL!
Gasp! IT'S CHARLES FORT HIMSELF! WALKING INTO MY COMIC!
WILL YOU... WILL YOU SIGN MY COPY OF "THE DAMNED" PLEASE?
"THE BOOK OF THE DAMNED"! MY FIRST BOOK! IT'S 100 YEARS SINCE IT WAS PUBLISHED, YOU KNOW? 1919!
The Damned
GREAT BOOK! GREAT BOOK! PACKED WITH AMAZING PHENOMENA... LET ME QUOTE YOU A FEW EXAMPLES...
YES... -ER- WOULD YOU SIGN IT?...
AH-HERE! CHAPTER 3 HAS BLACK RAINS, AND THICK, VISCOUS RED RAINS DESCRIBED AS "BLOOD"...
CHAPTER 4 HAS PULPY, PUTRID STUFF, JELLY AND MEAT FALLING FROM THE SKY...
BY CHAPTER 7 WE'RE ONTO FALLS OF FROGS, TOADS AND FISH...
CHAPTER 8- THUNDERSTONES!
CHAPTER 13- BLOCKS OF ICE FROM THE SKY!
CHAPTER 17- TORNADOS, AND A FLYING, BURNING HAYSTACK...
...AND CHAPTER 23- BALL LIGHTNING!
YES- A FINE BOOK! WELL, BULL, OLD BOY! KEEP UP THE GOOD WORK, AND I'LL SEE YOU IN FOUR YEARS FOR THE CENTENARY OF NEW LANDS! NOW THAT'S A FINE BOOK...
MY BOOK... YOU HAVEN'T SIGNED MY BOOK...

THREE FISH FALLS

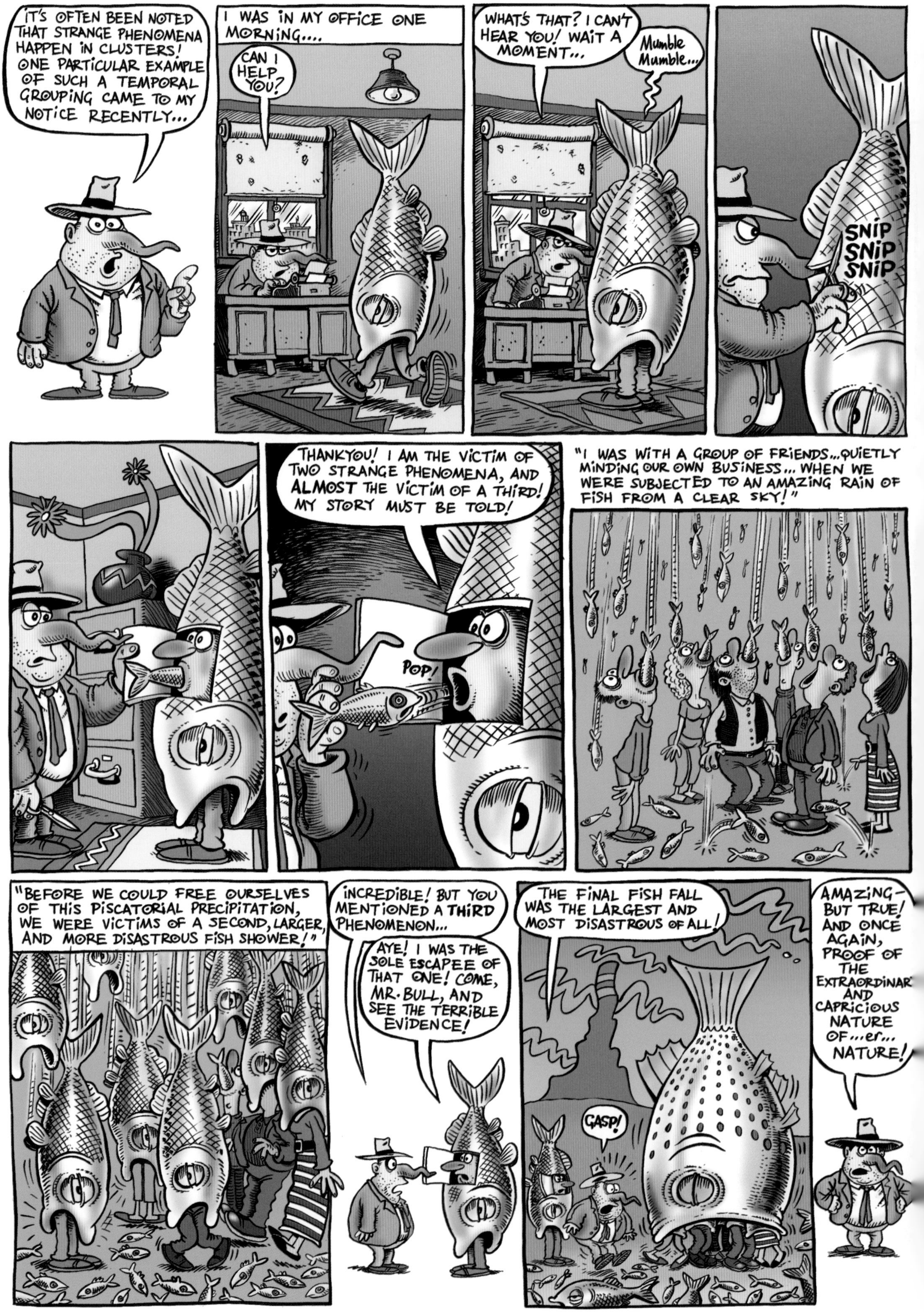

IT'S OFTEN BEEN NOTED THAT STRANGE PHENOMENA HAPPEN IN CLUSTERS! ONE PARTICULAR EXAMPLE OF SUCH A TEMPORAL GROUPING CAME TO MY NOTICE RECENTLY...
I WAS IN MY OFFICE ONE MORNING....
CAN I HELP YOU?
WHAT'S THAT? I CAN'T HEAR YOU! WAIT A MOMENT...
Mumble Mumble...
SNIP SNIP SNIP
THANKYOU! I AM THE VICTIM OF TWO STRANGE PHENOMENA, AND ALMOST THE VICTIM OF A THIRD! MY STORY MUST BE TOLD!
POP!
"I WAS WITH A GROUP OF FRIENDS...QUIETLY MINDING OUR OWN BUSINESS... WHEN WE WERE SUBJECTED TO AN AMAZING RAIN OF FISH FROM A CLEAR SKY!"
"BEFORE WE COULD FREE OURSELVES OF THIS PISCATORIAL PRECIPITATION, WE WERE VICTIMS OF A SECOND, LARGER, AND MORE DISASTROUS FISH SHOWER!"
INCREDIBLE! BUT YOU MENTIONED A THIRD PHENOMENON...
AYE! I WAS THE SOLE ESCAPEE OF THAT ONE! COME, MR. BULL, AND SEE THE TERRIBLE EVIDENCE!
THE FINAL FISH FALL WAS THE LARGEST AND MOST DISASTROUS OF ALL!
GASP!
AMAZING-BUT TRUE! AND ONCE AGAIN, PROOF OF THE EXTRAORDINAR AND CAPRICIOUS NATURE OF...er... NATURE!

THREE MEN IN A SUIT

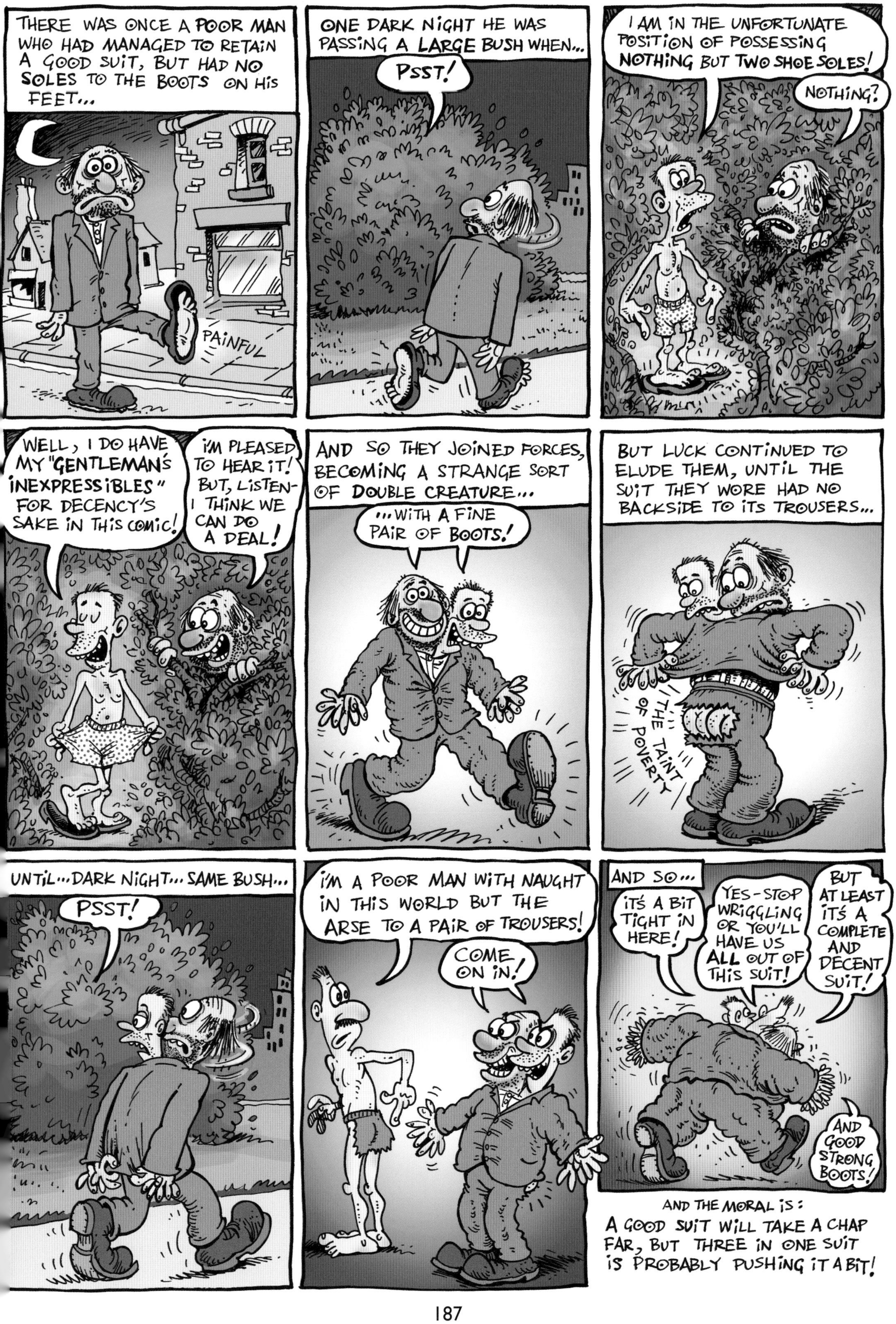

THERE WAS ONCE A POOR MAN WHO HAD MANAGED TO RETAIN A GOOD SUIT, BUT HAD NO SOLES TO THE BOOTS ON HIS FEET...
PAINFUL
ONE DARK NIGHT HE WAS PASSING A LARGE BUSH WHEN...
PSST!
I AM IN THE UNFORTUNATE POSITION OF POSSESSING NOTHING BUT TWO SHOE SOLES!
NOTHING?
WELL, I DO HAVE MY "GENTLEMAN'S INEXPRESSIBLES" FOR DECENCY'S SAKE IN THIS COMIC!
I'M PLEASED TO HEAR IT! BUT, LISTEN- I THINK WE CAN DO A DEAL!
AND SO THEY JOINED FORCES, BECOMING A STRANGE SORT OF DOUBLE CREATURE...
...WITH A FINE PAIR OF BOOTS!
BUT LUCK CONTINUED TO ELUDE THEM, UNTIL THE SUIT THEY WORE HAD NO BACKSIDE TO ITS TROUSERS...
THE TAINT OF POVERTY
UNTIL...DARK NIGHT...SAME BUSH...
PSST!
I'M A POOR MAN WITH NAUGHT IN THIS WORLD BUT THE ARSE TO A PAIR OF TROUSERS!
COME ON IN!
AND SO...
IT'S A BIT TIGHT IN HERE!
YES-STOP WRIGGLING OR YOU'LL HAVE US ALL OUT OF THIS SUIT!
BUT AT LEAST IT'S A COMPLETE AND DECENT SUIT!
AND GOOD STRONG BOOTS!
AND THE MORAL IS:
A GOOD SUIT WILL TAKE A CHAP FAR, BUT THREE IN ONE SUIT IS PROBABLY PUSHING IT A BIT!

THUNDERSTONES

I'M READING CHARLES FORT'S "BOOK OF THE DAMNED", CHAPTER 8, WHERE HE WRITES ABOUT...

"MANUFACTURED OBJECTS OF STONE AND IRON THAT FALL FROM THE SKY DURING THUNDERSTORMS"!

KA-BROOM!

THIS NOTION IS AS WIDESPREAD AS BELIEF IN GHOSTS AND WITCHES ...AS WIDESPREAD AS GEOGRAPHY ITSELF!

THESE THINGS ARE WEDGE SHAPED, OFTEN HIGHLY POLISHED AND FINISHED, AND ARE KNOWN BY DIFFERENT NAMES IN VARIOUS PARTS OF THE WORLD...

FOR INSTANCE, IN JAMAICA, "AXES OF A HARD GREENSTONE FALL DURING THE RAINS"...

BONK!

OW! BLOOD-CLAAT!

IN MYANMAR, CHINA, AND JAPAN THEY ARE CALLED "THUNDERBOLTS"!...

IN NORTH EUROPE, CAMBODIA, SUMATRA, AND SIBERIA THEY ARE "THUNDERSTONES"...

IN LAUSITZ: "STORM STONES"...

IN SLAVONIA: "SKY ARROWS"...

IN BRITAIN: "THUNDER AXES"...

BOOM!

SPAIN AND PORTUGAL CALL THEM "LIGHTNING STONES"!...

IN GREECE THEY ARE "SKY AXES"!...

IN SOUTH AMERICA: "STONE HATCHETS"!..

AND IN AMBOINA "THUNDER TEETH"!...

COMMON PEOPLE —THE SO-CALLED IGNORANT— SAY THEY HAVE FOUND THESE THINGS UNDER, OR STUCK INTO, LIGHTNING-STRUCK TREES...

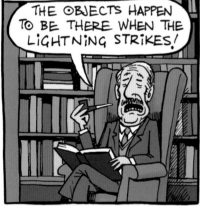

"EDUCATED" MEN SAY IT IS COINCIDENCE...

THE OBJECTS HAPPEN TO BE THERE WHEN THE LIGHTNING STRIKES!

BUT, WOULD PEOPLE WHO HAVE GONE TO THE TROUBLE OF MAKING STONE WEDGES THEN LEAVE THEM LYING AROUND AND FORGET THEY WERE THERE? I HARDLY THINK SO!

THERE SEEMS TO BE SOME AFFINITY, NOTED IN FOLKLORE AND TRADITION, BETWEEN LIGHTNING, THUNDER, AND WEDGE-SHAPED OBJECTS...

THRUMBLE!

RUMBLE OF THUNDER...

KRASH!

UH-OH...

BOOOM!

OUCH!

KRASH! BOOOM!

OW! YELP! YOW!

TIME

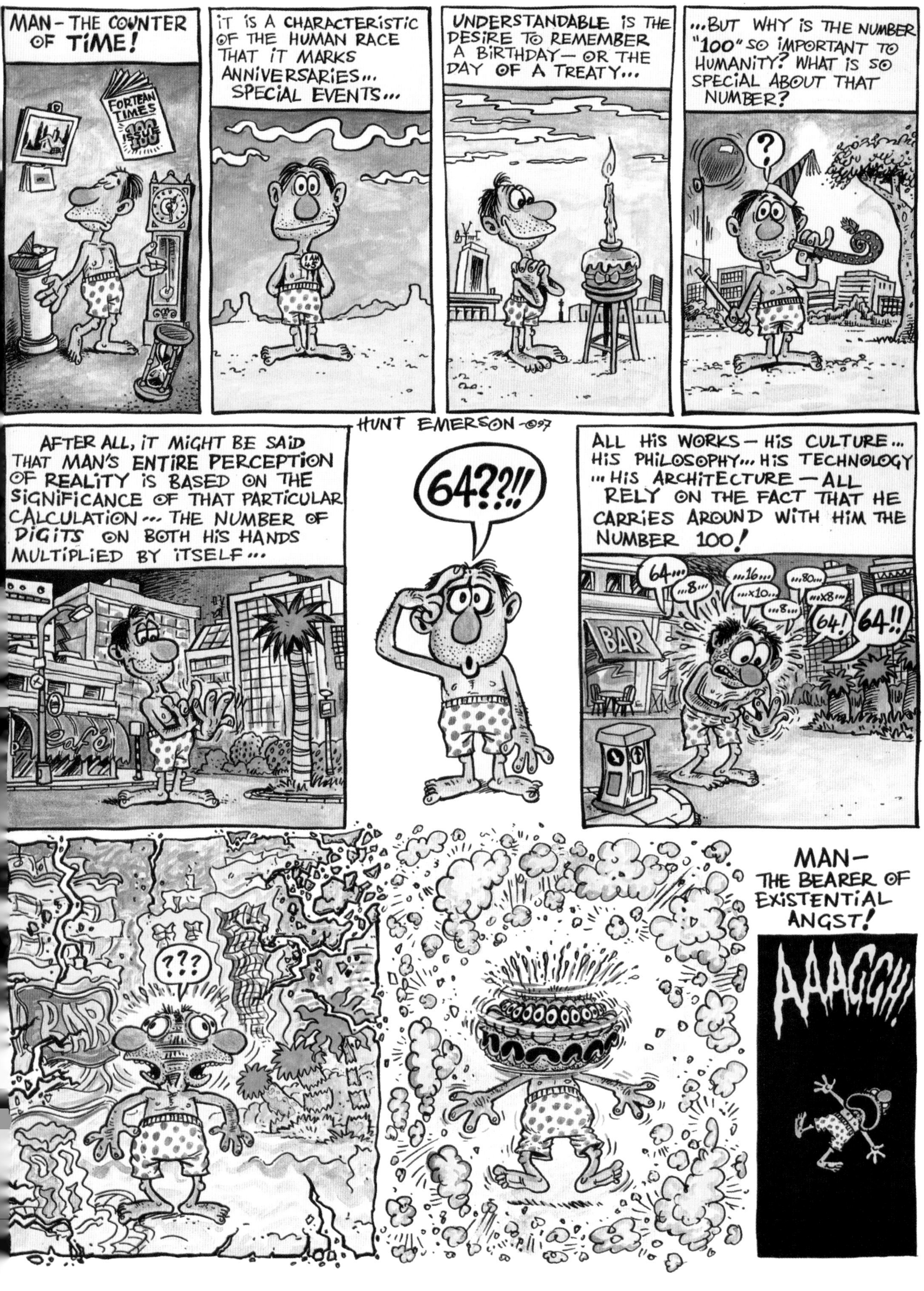
MAN – THE COUNTER OF TIME!
FORTEAN TIMES
IT IS A CHARACTERISTIC OF THE HUMAN RACE THAT IT MARKS ANNIVERSARIES... SPECIAL EVENTS...
UNDERSTANDABLE IS THE DESIRE TO REMEMBER A BIRTHDAY – OR THE DAY OF A TREATY...
...BUT WHY IS THE NUMBER "100" SO IMPORTANT TO HUMANITY? WHAT IS SO SPECIAL ABOUT THAT NUMBER?
?
HUNT EMERSON-©97
AFTER ALL, IT MIGHT BE SAID THAT MAN'S ENTIRE PERCEPTION OF REALITY IS BASED ON THE SIGNIFICANCE OF THAT PARTICULAR CALCULATION... THE NUMBER OF DIGITS ON BOTH HIS HANDS MULTIPLIED BY ITSELF...
64??!!
ALL HIS WORKS – HIS CULTURE... HIS PHILOSOPHY... HIS TECHNOLOGY ...HIS ARCHITECTURE – ALL RELY ON THE FACT THAT HE CARRIES AROUND WITH HIM THE NUMBER 100!
64...
...8...
...16...
...x10...
...8...
...80...
...x8...
64!
64!!
BAR
???
BAR
MAN – THE BEARER OF EXISTENTIAL ANGST!
AAAGGH!

TIMEFOG

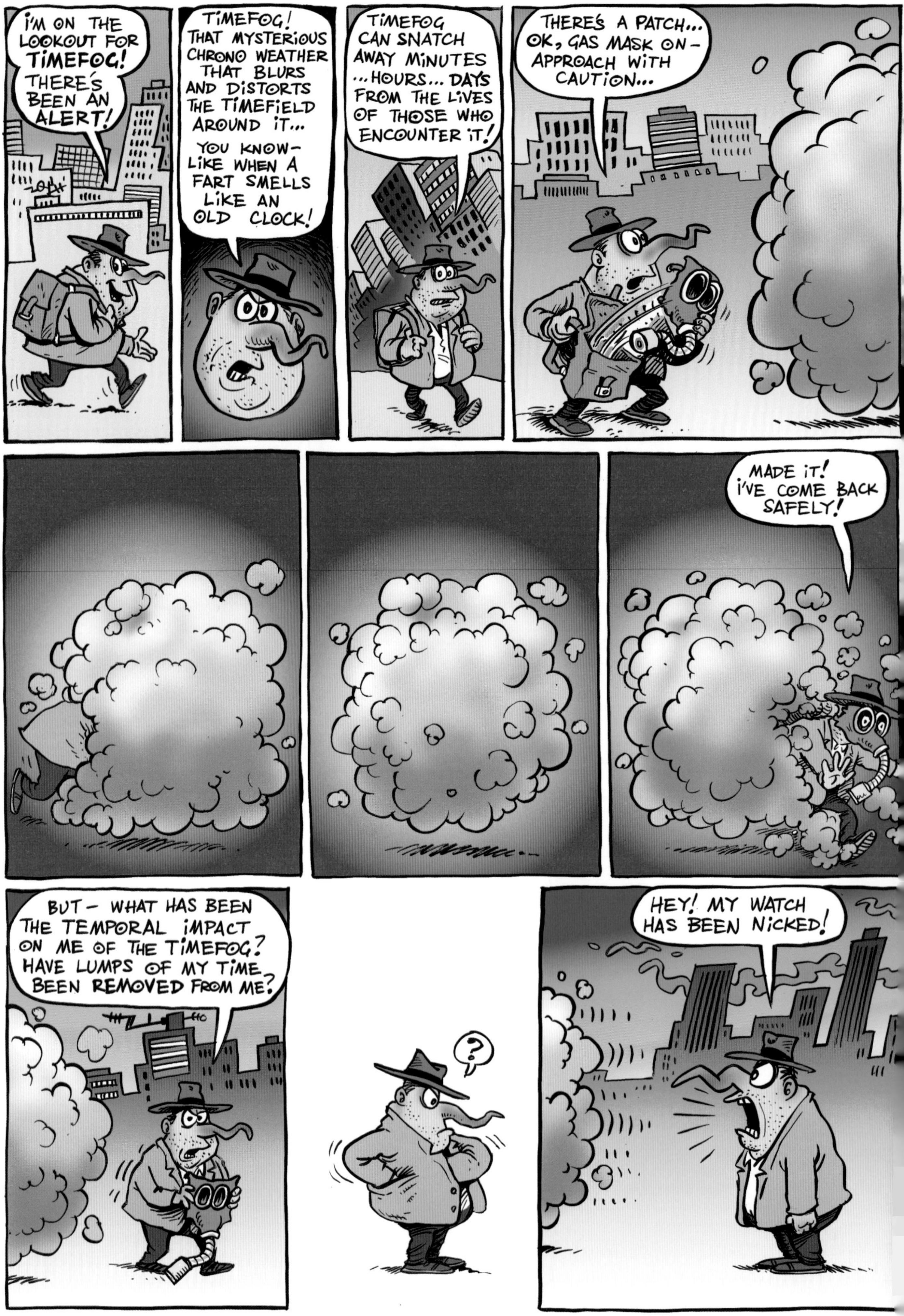
I'M ON THE LOOKOUT FOR TIMEFOG! THERE'S BEEN AN ALERT!
TIMEFOG! THAT MYSTERIOUS CHRONO WEATHER THAT BLURS AND DISTORTS THE TIMEFIELD AROUND IT...
YOU KNOW- LIKE WHEN A FART SMELLS LIKE AN OLD CLOCK!
TIMEFOG CAN SNATCH AWAY MINUTES ...HOURS... DAYS FROM THE LIVES OF THOSE WHO ENCOUNTER IT!
THERE'S A PATCH... OK, GAS MASK ON- APPROACH WITH CAUTION...
MADE IT! I'VE COME BACK SAFELY!
BUT- WHAT HAS BEEN THE TEMPORAL IMPACT ON ME OF THE TIMEFOG? HAVE LUMPS OF MY TIME BEEN REMOVED FROM ME?
?
HEY! MY WATCH HAS BEEN NICKED!

TOADSTONE

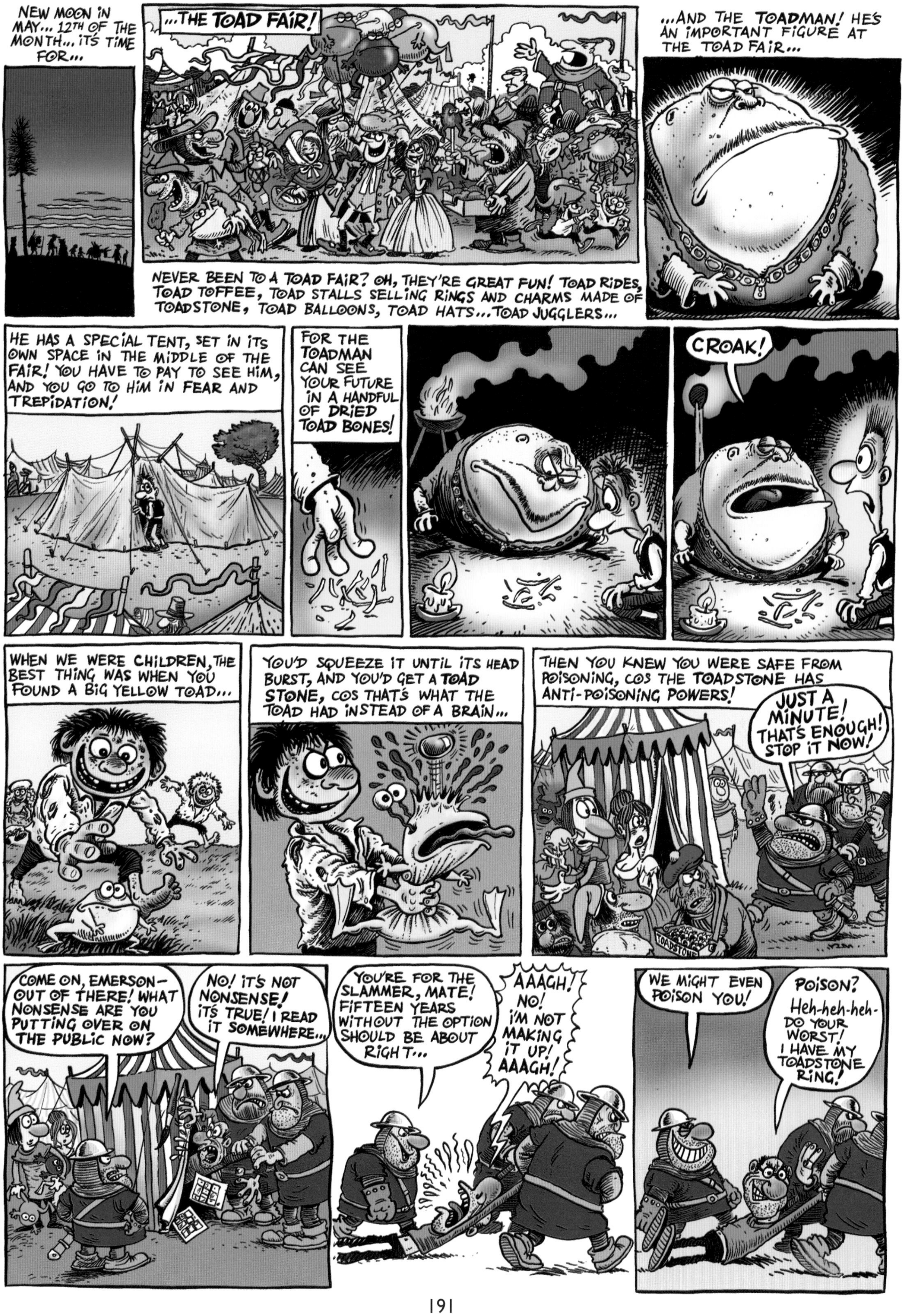

NEW MOON IN MAY... 12TH OF THE MONTH... IT'S TIME FOR...
...THE TOAD FAIR!
...AND THE TOADMAN! HE'S AN IMPORTANT FIGURE AT THE TOAD FAIR...
NEVER BEEN TO A TOAD FAIR? OH, THEY'RE GREAT FUN! TOAD RIDES, TOAD TOFFEE, TOAD STALLS SELLING RINGS AND CHARMS MADE OF TOADSTONE, TOAD BALLOONS, TOAD HATS... TOAD JUGGLERS...
HE HAS A SPECIAL TENT, SET IN ITS OWN SPACE IN THE MIDDLE OF THE FAIR! YOU HAVE TO PAY TO SEE HIM, AND YOU GO TO HIM IN FEAR AND TREPIDATION!
FOR THE TOADMAN CAN SEE YOUR FUTURE IN A HANDFUL OF DRIED TOAD BONES!
CROAK!
WHEN WE WERE CHILDREN, THE BEST THING WAS WHEN YOU FOUND A BIG YELLOW TOAD...
YOU'D SQUEEZE IT UNTIL ITS HEAD BURST, AND YOU'D GET A TOAD STONE, COS THAT'S WHAT THE TOAD HAD INSTEAD OF A BRAIN...
THEN YOU KNEW YOU WERE SAFE FROM POISONING, COS THE TOADSTONE HAS ANTI-POISONING POWERS!
JUST A MINUTE! THAT'S ENOUGH! STOP IT NOW!
TOADSTONE
COME ON, EMERSON— OUT OF THERE! WHAT NONSENSE ARE YOU PUTTING OVER ON THE PUBLIC NOW?
NO! IT'S NOT NONSENSE! IT'S TRUE! I READ IT SOMEWHERE...
YOU'RE FOR THE SLAMMER, MATE! FIFTEEN YEARS WITHOUT THE OPTION SHOULD BE ABOUT RIGHT...
AAAGH! NO! I'M NOT MAKING IT UP! AAAGH!
WE MIGHT EVEN POISON YOU!
POISON? Heh-heh-heh- DO YOUR WORST! I HAVE MY TOADSTONE RING!

TROUSERIFIC PHENOMENA

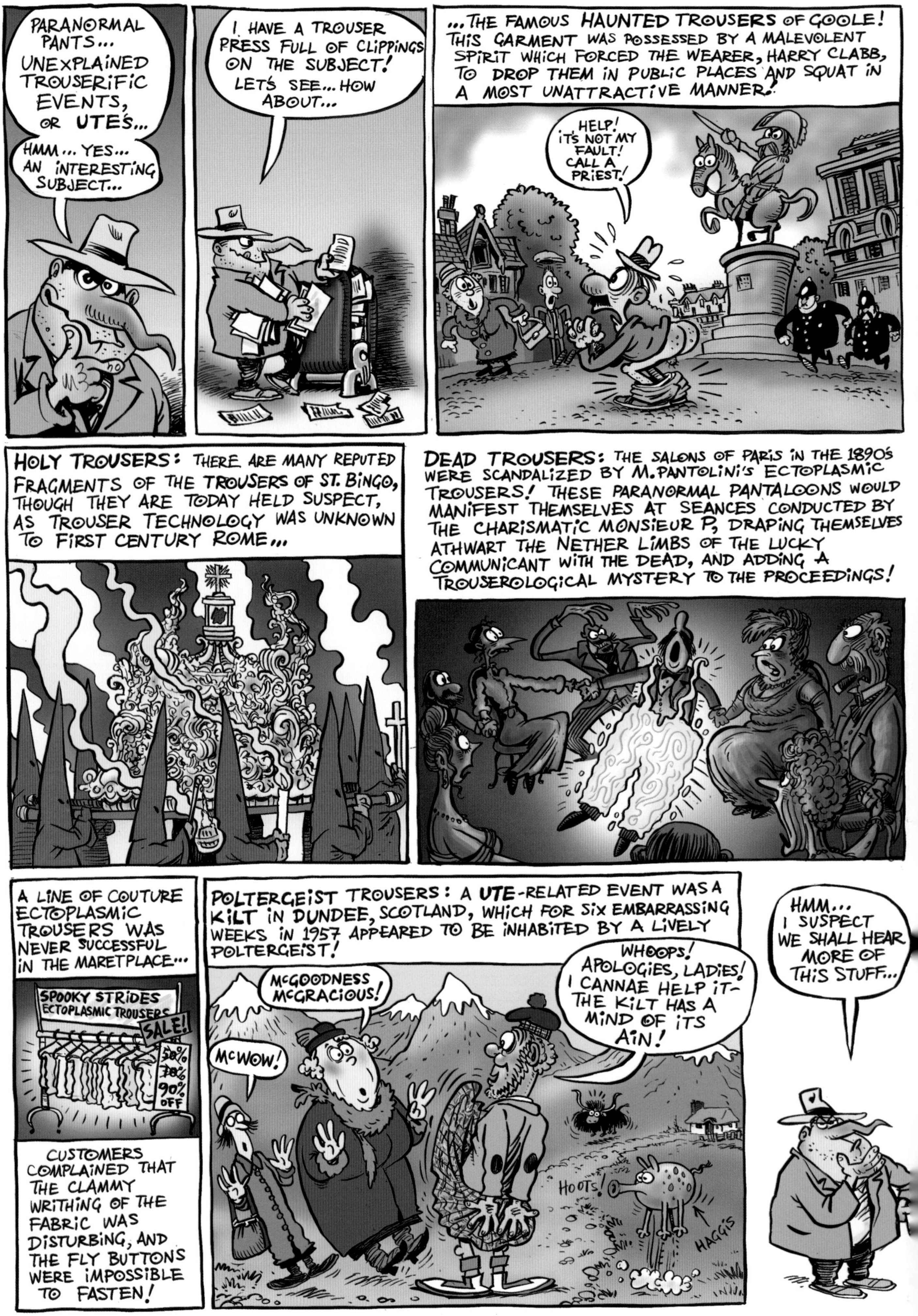
PARANORMAL PANTS... UNEXPLAINED TROUSERIFIC EVENTS, OR UTE'S...
HMM... YES... AN INTERESTING SUBJECT...
I HAVE A TROUSER PRESS FULL OF CLIPPINGS ON THE SUBJECT! LET'S SEE... HOW ABOUT...
...THE FAMOUS HAUNTED TROUSERS OF GOOLE! THIS GARMENT WAS POSSESSED BY A MALEVOLENT SPIRIT WHICH FORCED THE WEARER, HARRY CLABB, TO DROP THEM IN PUBLIC PLACES AND SQUAT IN A MOST UNATTRACTIVE MANNER!
HELP! IT'S NOT MY FAULT! CALL A PRIEST!
HOLY TROUSERS: THERE ARE MANY REPUTED FRAGMENTS OF THE TROUSERS OF ST. BINGO, THOUGH THEY ARE TODAY HELD SUSPECT, AS TROUSER TECHNOLOGY WAS UNKNOWN TO FIRST CENTURY ROME...
DEAD TROUSERS: THE SALONS OF PARIS IN THE 1890'S WERE SCANDALIZED BY M. PANTOLINI'S ECTOPLASMIC TROUSERS! THESE PARANORMAL PANTALOONS WOULD MANIFEST THEMSELVES AT SEANCES CONDUCTED BY THE CHARISMATIC MONSIEUR P, DRAPING THEMSELVES ATHWART THE NETHER LIMBS OF THE LUCKY COMMUNICANT WITH THE DEAD, AND ADDING A TROUSEROLOGICAL MYSTERY TO THE PROCEEDINGS!
A LINE OF COUTURE ECTOPLASMIC TROUSERS WAS NEVER SUCCESSFUL IN THE MARETPLACE...
SPOOKY STRIDES
ECTOPLASMIC TROUSERS
SALE!
50%
70%
90% OFF
CUSTOMERS COMPLAINED THAT THE CLAMMY WRITHING OF THE FABRIC WAS DISTURBING, AND THE FLY BUTTONS WERE IMPOSSIBLE TO FASTEN!
POLTERGEIST TROUSERS: A UTE-RELATED EVENT WAS A KILT IN DUNDEE, SCOTLAND, WHICH FOR SIX EMBARRASSING WEEKS IN 1957 APPEARED TO BE INHABITED BY A LIVELY POLTERGEIST!
McGOODNESS McGRACIOUS!
McWOW!
WHOOPS! APOLOGIES, LADIES! I CANNAE HELP IT- THE KILT HAS A MIND OF ITS AIN!
HOOTS!
HAGGIS
HMM... I SUSPECT WE SHALL HEAR MORE OF THIS STUFF...

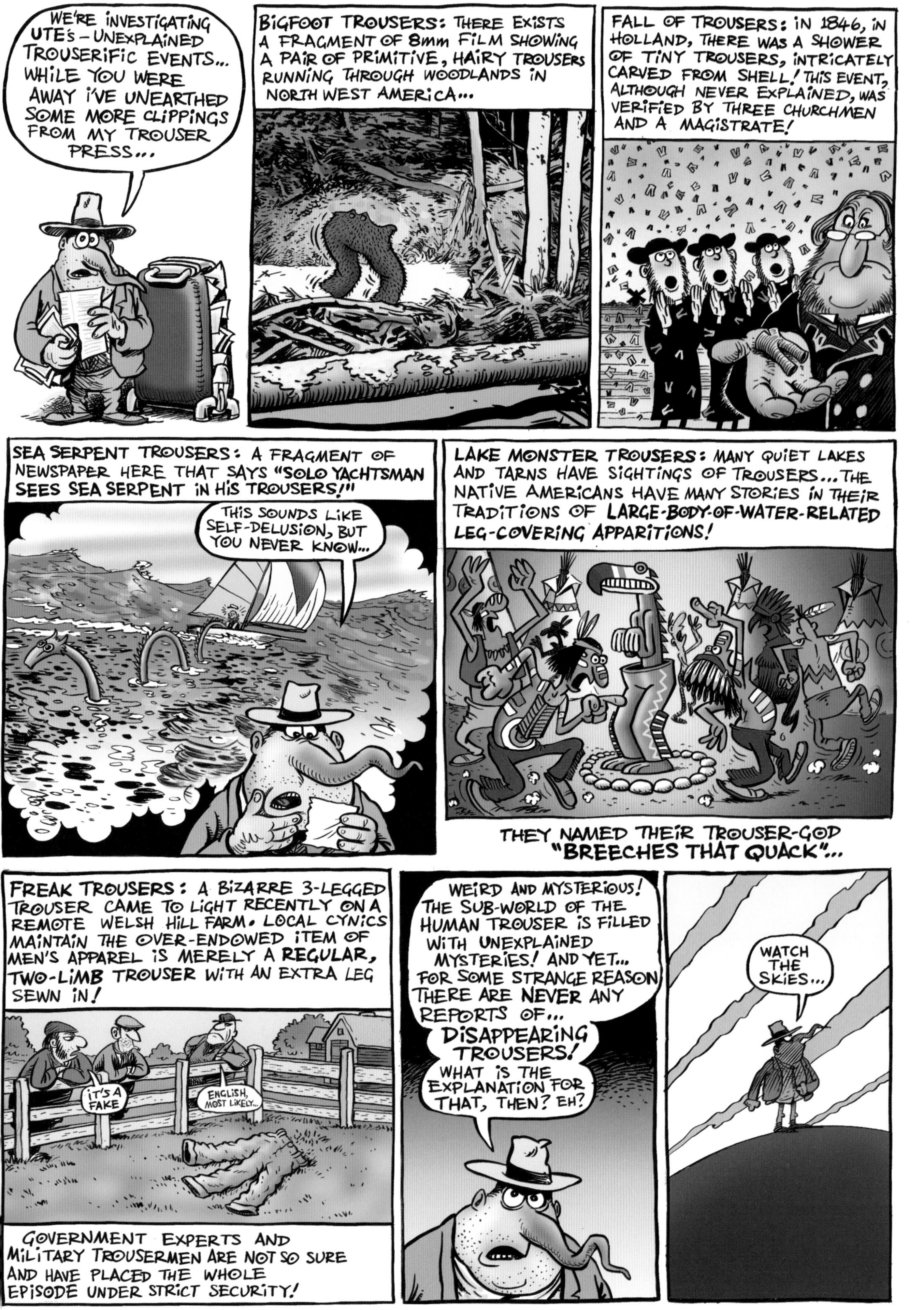
WE'RE INVESTIGATING UTE'S – UNEXPLAINED TROUSERIFIC EVENTS... WHILE YOU WERE AWAY I'VE UNEARTHED SOME MORE CLIPPINGS FROM MY TROUSER PRESS...
BIGFOOT TROUSERS: THERE EXISTS A FRAGMENT OF 8mm FILM SHOWING A PAIR OF PRIMITIVE, HAIRY TROUSERS RUNNING THROUGH WOODLANDS IN NORTH WEST AMERICA...
FALL OF TROUSERS: IN 1846, IN HOLLAND, THERE WAS A SHOWER OF TINY TROUSERS, INTRICATELY CARVED FROM SHELL! THIS EVENT, ALTHOUGH NEVER EXPLAINED, WAS VERIFIED BY THREE CHURCHMEN AND A MAGISTRATE!
SEA SERPENT TROUSERS: A FRAGMENT OF NEWSPAPER HERE THAT SAYS "SOLO YACHTSMAN SEES SEA SERPENT IN HIS TROUSERS!"
THIS SOUNDS LIKE SELF-DELUSION, BUT YOU NEVER KNOW...
LAKE MONSTER TROUSERS: MANY QUIET LAKES AND TARNS HAVE SIGHTINGS OF TROUSERS... THE NATIVE AMERICANS HAVE MANY STORIES IN THEIR TRADITIONS OF LARGE-BODY-OF-WATER-RELATED LEG-COVERING APPARITIONS!
THEY NAMED THEIR TROUSER-GOD "BREECHES THAT QUACK"...
FREAK TROUSERS: A BIZARRE 3-LEGGED TROUSER CAME TO LIGHT RECENTLY ON A REMOTE WELSH HILL FARM. LOCAL CYNICS MAINTAIN THE OVER-ENDOWED ITEM OF MEN'S APPAREL IS MERELY A REGULAR, TWO-LIMB TROUSER WITH AN EXTRA LEG SEWN IN!
IT'S A FAKE
ENGLISH, MOST LIKELY...
GOVERNMENT EXPERTS AND MILITARY TROUSERMEN ARE NOT SO SURE AND HAVE PLACED THE WHOLE EPISODE UNDER STRICT SECURITY!
WEIRD AND MYSTERIOUS! THE SUB-WORLD OF THE HUMAN TROUSER IS FILLED WITH UNEXPLAINED MYSTERIES! AND YET... FOR SOME STRANGE REASON THERE ARE NEVER ANY REPORTS OF... DISAPPEARING TROUSERS!
WHAT IS THE EXPLANATION FOR THAT, THEN? EH?
WATCH THE SKIES...

TREPANNING

TREPANNING IS THE NAME GIVEN TO THE ANCIENT ART OF OPENING A HOLE IN YOUR SKULL IN ORDER TO RELIEVE PRESSURE AND PROMOTE EUPHORIC HAPPINESS AND ENLIGHTENMENT! THERE IS AMPLE FOSSIL EVIDENCE THAT STONE AGE MEN CONTINUALLY TREPANNED THEMSELVES AND EACH OTHER, AND SURVIVED! THROUGHOUT THE AGES, TREPANNING HAS BEEN USED FOR MEDICAL AND RITUAL PURPOSES.....

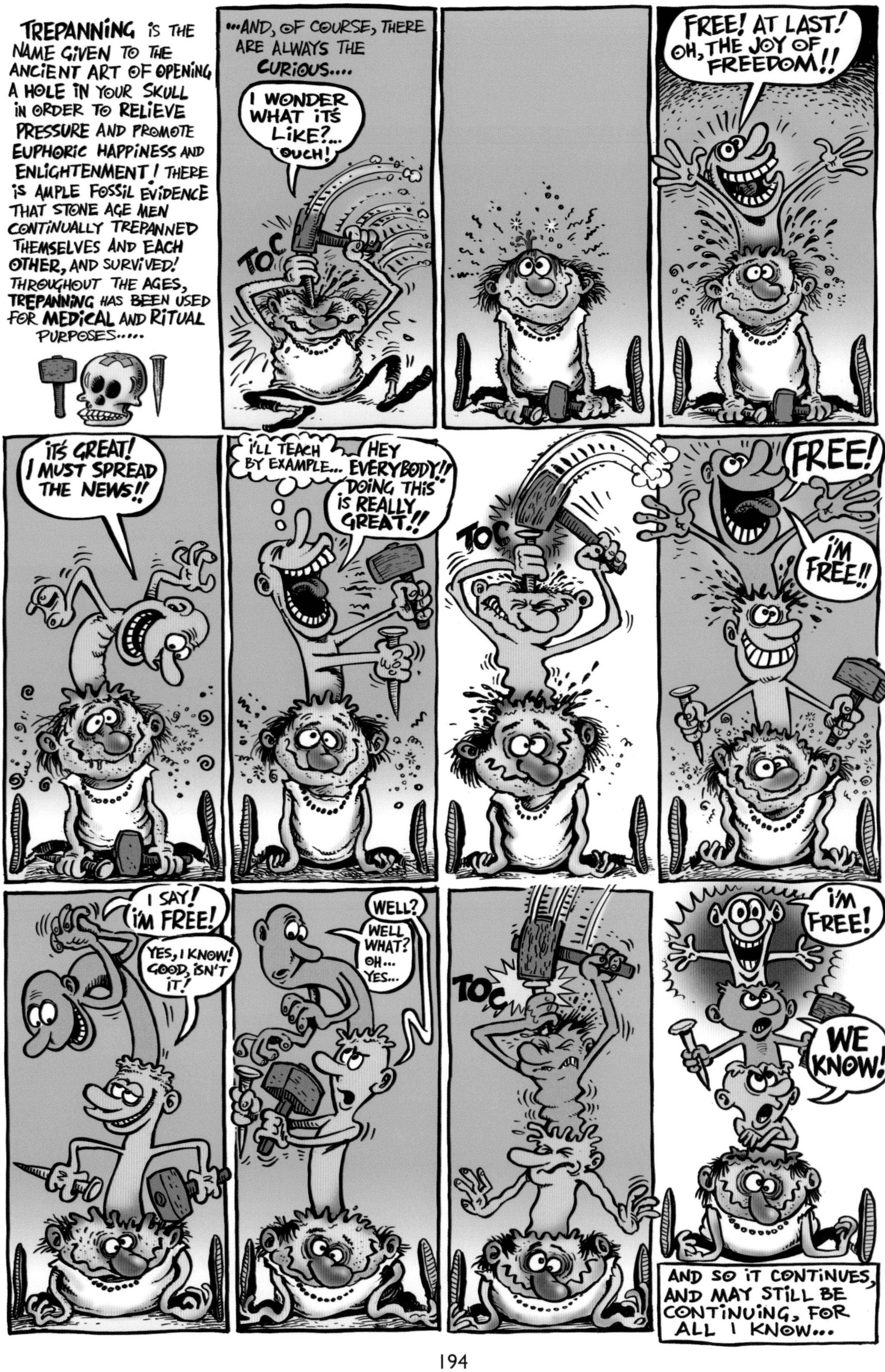

...AND, OF COURSE, THERE ARE ALWAYS THE CURIOUS....
I WONDER WHAT IT'S LIKE?... OUCH!
TOC
FREE! AT LAST! OH, THE JOY OF FREEDOM!!
IT'S GREAT! I MUST SPREAD THE NEWS!!
I'LL TEACH BY EXAMPLE...
HEY EVERYBODY!! DOING THIS IS REALLY GREAT!!
TOC
FREE!
I'M FREE!!
I SAY! I'M FREE!
YES, I KNOW! GOOD, ISN'T IT!
WELL?
WELL WHAT? OH... YES...
TOC
I'M FREE!
WE KNOW!
AND SO IT CONTINUES, AND MAY STILL BE CONTINUING, FOR ALL I KNOW...

TUNGUSKA

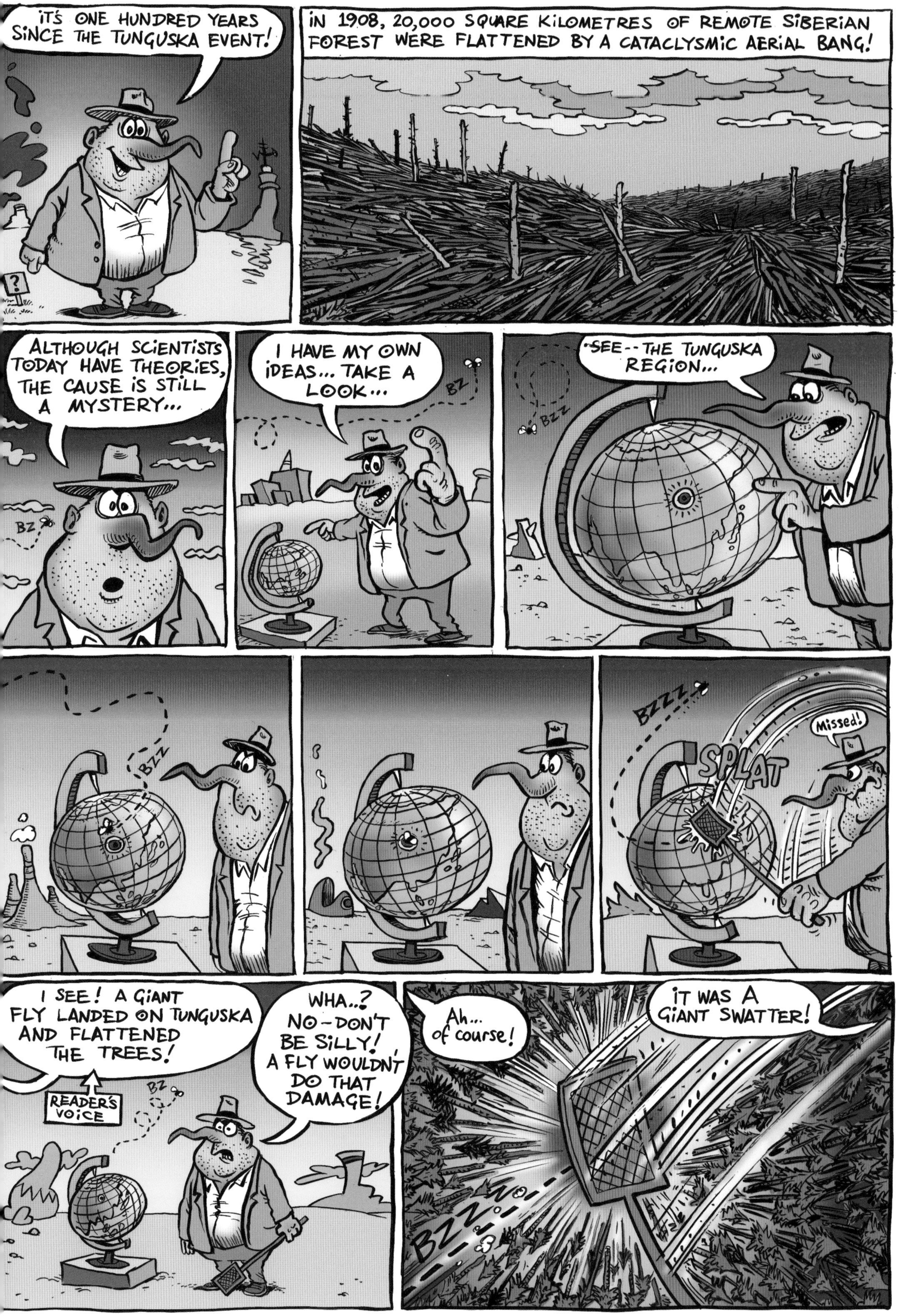

IT'S ONE HUNDRED YEARS SINCE THE TUNGUSKA EVENT!
IN 1908, 20,000 SQUARE KILOMETRES OF REMOTE SIBERIAN FOREST WERE FLATTENED BY A CATACLYSMIC AERIAL BANG!
ALTHOUGH SCIENTISTS TODAY HAVE THEORIES, THE CAUSE IS STILL A MYSTERY...
BZ
I HAVE MY OWN IDEAS... TAKE A LOOK...
BZ
SEE -- THE TUNGUSKA REGION...
BZZ
BZZ
BZZZ
SPLAT
Missed!
I SEE! A GIANT FLY LANDED ON TUNGUSKA AND FLATTENED THE TREES!
READER'S VOICE
BZ
WHA..? NO - DON'T BE SILLY! A FLY WOULDN'T DO THAT DAMAGE!
Ah... of course!
IT WAS A GIANT SWATTER!
BZZ-NO!

UNDER A STONE

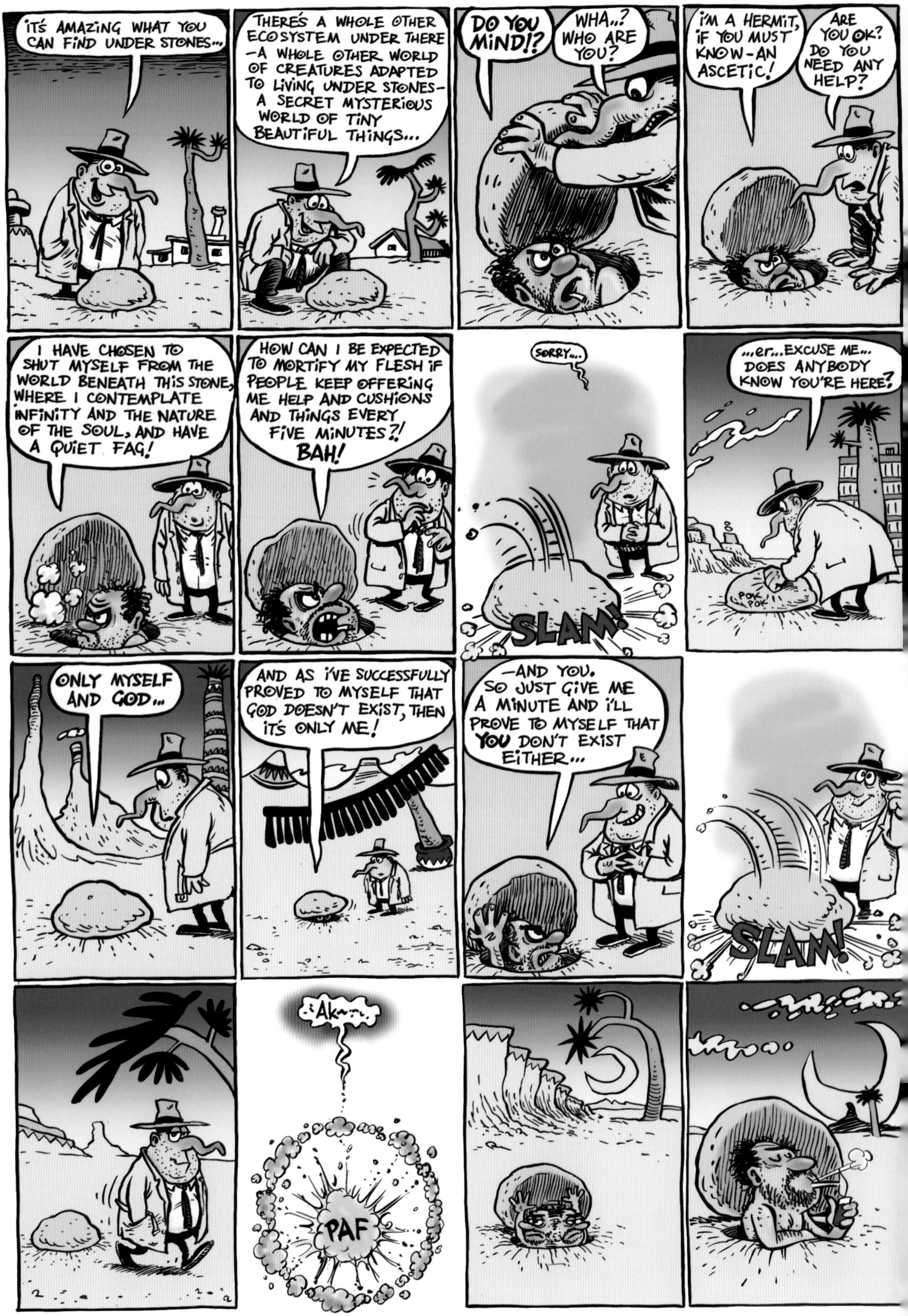

IT'S AMAZING WHAT YOU CAN FIND UNDER STONES...
THERE'S A WHOLE OTHER ECOSYSTEM UNDER THERE —A WHOLE OTHER WORLD OF CREATURES ADAPTED TO LIVING UNDER STONES— A SECRET MYSTERIOUS WORLD OF TINY BEAUTIFUL THINGS...
DO YOU MIND!?
WHA..? WHO ARE YOU?
I'M A HERMIT, IF YOU MUST KNOW—AN ASCETIC!
ARE YOU OK? DO YOU NEED ANY HELP?
I HAVE CHOSEN TO SHUT MYSELF FROM THE WORLD BENEATH THIS STONE, WHERE I CONTEMPLATE INFINITY AND THE NATURE OF THE SOUL, AND HAVE A QUIET FAG!
HOW CAN I BE EXPECTED TO MORTIFY MY FLESH IF PEOPLE KEEP OFFERING ME HELP AND CUSHIONS AND THINGS EVERY FIVE MINUTES?! BAH!
SORRY...
SLAM!
...er...EXCUSE ME... DOES ANYBODY KNOW YOU'RE HERE?
POK POK
ONLY MYSELF AND GOD...
AND AS I'VE SUCCESSFULLY PROVED TO MYSELF THAT GOD DOESN'T EXIST, THEN IT'S ONLY ME!
—AND YOU. SO JUST GIVE ME A MINUTE AND I'LL PROVE TO MYSELF THAT YOU DON'T EXIST EITHER...
SLAM!
Ak~
PAF

UFO PIG

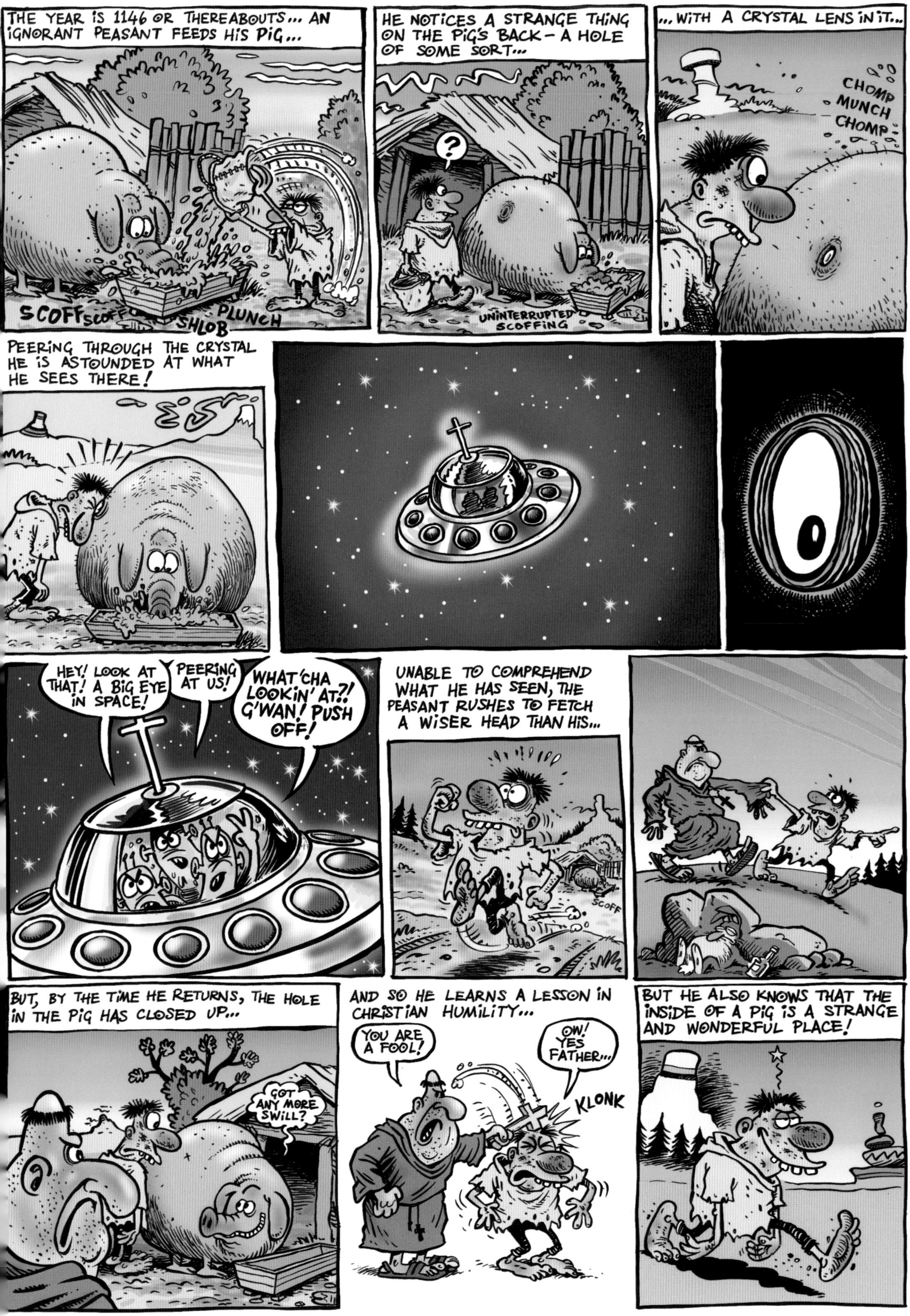

THE YEAR IS 1146 OR THEREABOUTS... AN IGNORANT PEASANT FEEDS HIS PIG...
SCOFF SCOFF
SHLOB
PLUNCH
HE NOTICES A STRANGE THING ON THE PIG'S BACK – A HOLE OF SOME SORT...
?
UNINTERRUPTED SCOFFING
... WITH A CRYSTAL LENS IN IT...
CHOMP
MUNCH
CHOMP
PEERING THROUGH THE CRYSTAL HE IS ASTOUNDED AT WHAT HE SEES THERE!
HEY! LOOK AT THAT! A BIG EYE IN SPACE!
PEERING AT US!
WHAT'CHA LOOKIN' AT?! G'WAN! PUSH OFF!
UNABLE TO COMPREHEND WHAT HE HAS SEEN, THE PEASANT RUSHES TO FETCH A WISER HEAD THAN HIS...
SCOFF
BUT, BY THE TIME HE RETURNS, THE HOLE IN THE PIG HAS CLOSED UP...
GOT ANY MORE SWILL?
AND SO HE LEARNS A LESSON IN CHRISTIAN HUMILITY...
YOU ARE A FOOL!
OW! YES FATHER...
KLONK
BUT HE ALSO KNOWS THAT THE INSIDE OF A PIG IS A STRANGE AND WONDERFUL PLACE!

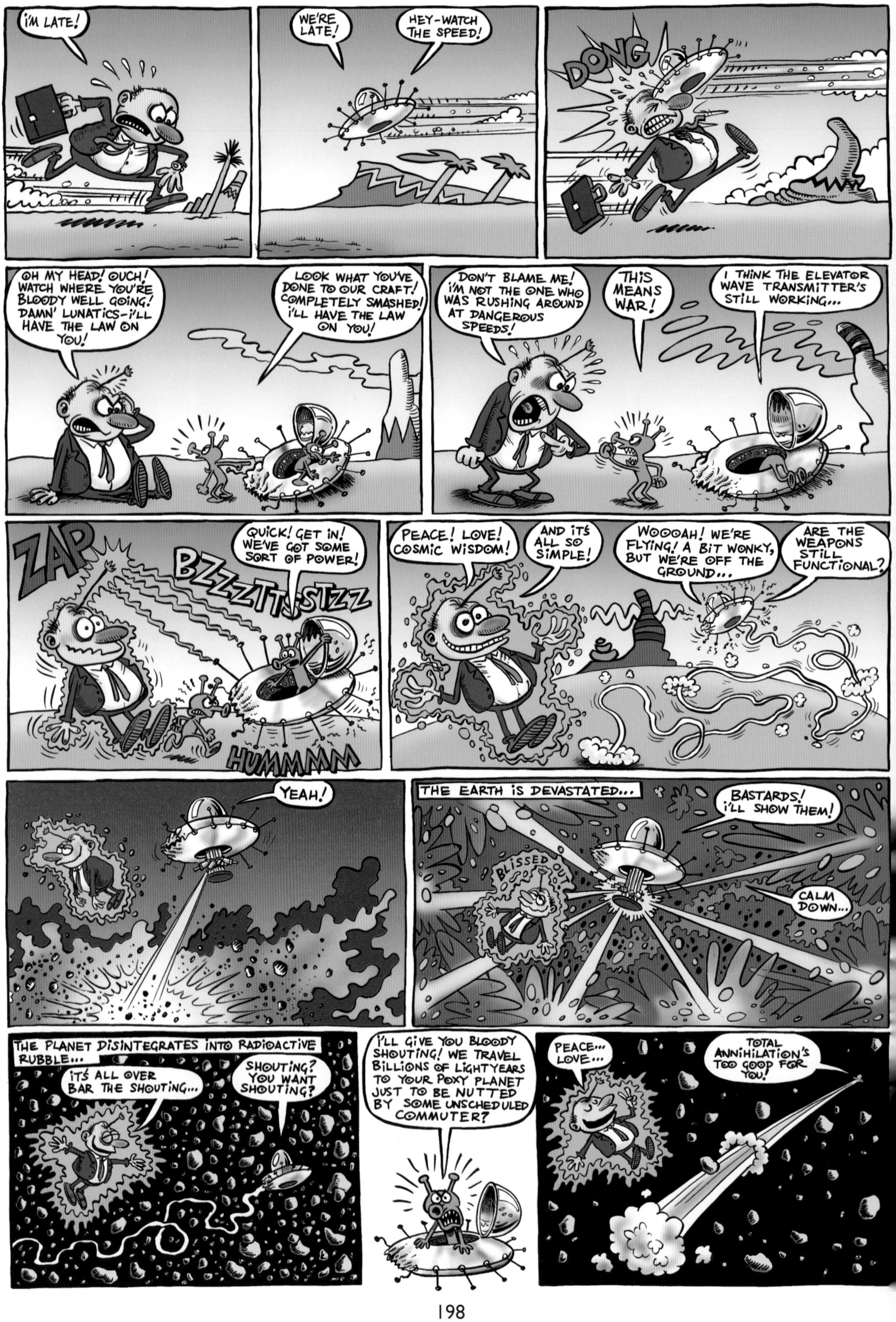
I'M LATE!
WE'RE LATE!
HEY-WATCH THE SPEED!
DONG
OH MY HEAD! OUCH! WATCH WHERE YOU'RE BLOODY WELL GOING! DAMN' LUNATICS-I'LL HAVE THE LAW ON YOU!
LOOK WHAT YOU'VE DONE TO OUR CRAFT! COMPLETELY SMASHED! I'LL HAVE THE LAW ON YOU!
DON'T BLAME ME! I'M NOT THE ONE WHO WAS RUSHING AROUND AT DANGEROUS SPEEDS!
THIS MEANS WAR!
I THINK THE ELEVATOR WAVE TRANSMITTER'S STILL WORKING...
ZAP
QUICK! GET IN! WE'VE GOT SOME SORT OF POWER!
BZZZZTTSSTZZ
HUMMMM
PEACE! LOVE! COSMIC WISDOM!
AND IT'S ALL SO SIMPLE!
WOOOAH! WE'RE FLYING! A BIT WONKY, BUT WE'RE OFF THE GROUND...
ARE THE WEAPONS STILL FUNCTIONAL?
YEAH!
THE EARTH IS DEVASTATED...
BASTARDS! I'LL SHOW THEM!
BLISSED OUT
CALM DOWN...
THE PLANET DISINTEGRATES INTO RADIOACTIVE RUBBLE...
IT'S ALL OVER BAR THE SHOUTING...
SHOUTING? YOU WANT SHOUTING?
I'LL GIVE YOU BLOODY SHOUTING! WE TRAVEL BILLIONS OF LIGHTYEARS TO YOUR POXY PLANET JUST TO BE NUTTED BY SOME UNSCHEDULED COMMUTER?
PEACE... LOVE...
TOTAL ANNIHILATION'S TOO GOOD FOR YOU!

UFO SUBCONTRACTORS

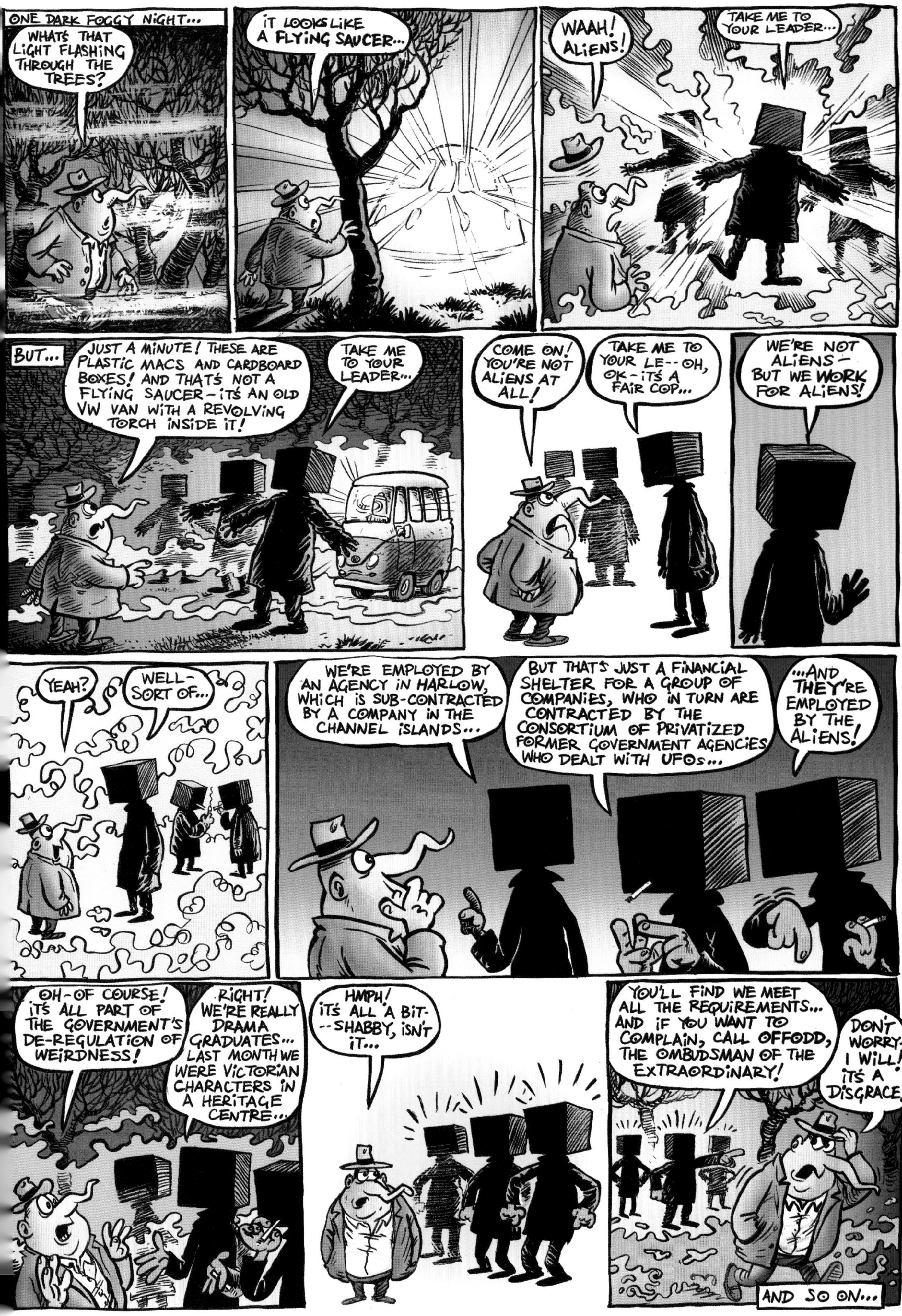

ONE DARK FOGGY NIGHT...
WHATS THAT LIGHT FLASHING THROUGH THE TREES?
IT LOOKS LIKE A FLYING SAUCER...
WAAH! ALIENS!
TAKE ME TO YOUR LEADER...
BUT...
JUST A MINUTE! THESE ARE PLASTIC MACS AND CARDBOARD BOXES! AND THATS NOT A FLYING SAUCER - ITS AN OLD VW VAN WITH A REVOLVING TORCH INSIDE IT!
TAKE ME TO YOUR LEADER...
COME ON! YOU'RE NOT ALIENS AT ALL!
TAKE ME TO YOUR LE-- OH, OK - ITS A FAIR COP...
WE'RE NOT ALIENS - BUT WE WORK FOR ALIENS!
YEAH?
WELL- SORT OF...
WE'RE EMPLOYED BY AN AGENCY IN HARLOW, WHICH IS SUB-CONTRACTED BY A COMPANY IN THE CHANNEL ISLANDS...
BUT THATS JUST A FINANCIAL SHELTER FOR A GROUP OF COMPANIES, WHO IN TURN ARE CONTRACTED BY THE CONSORTIUM OF PRIVATIZED FORMER GOVERNMENT AGENCIES WHO DEALT WITH UFOs...
...AND THEY'RE EMPLOYED BY THE ALIENS!
OH - OF COURSE! ITS ALL PART OF THE GOVERNMENT'S DE-REGULATION OF WEIRDNESS!
RIGHT! WE'RE REALLY DRAMA GRADUATES... LAST MONTH WE WERE VICTORIAN CHARACTERS IN A HERITAGE CENTRE...
HMPH! ITS ALL A BIT - - SHABBY, ISN'T IT...
YOU'LL FIND WE MEET ALL THE REQUIREMENTS... AND IF YOU WANT TO COMPLAIN, CALL OFFODD, THE OMBUDSMAN OF THE EXTRAORDINARY!
DON'T WORRY - I WILL! ITS A DISGRACE!
AND SO ON...

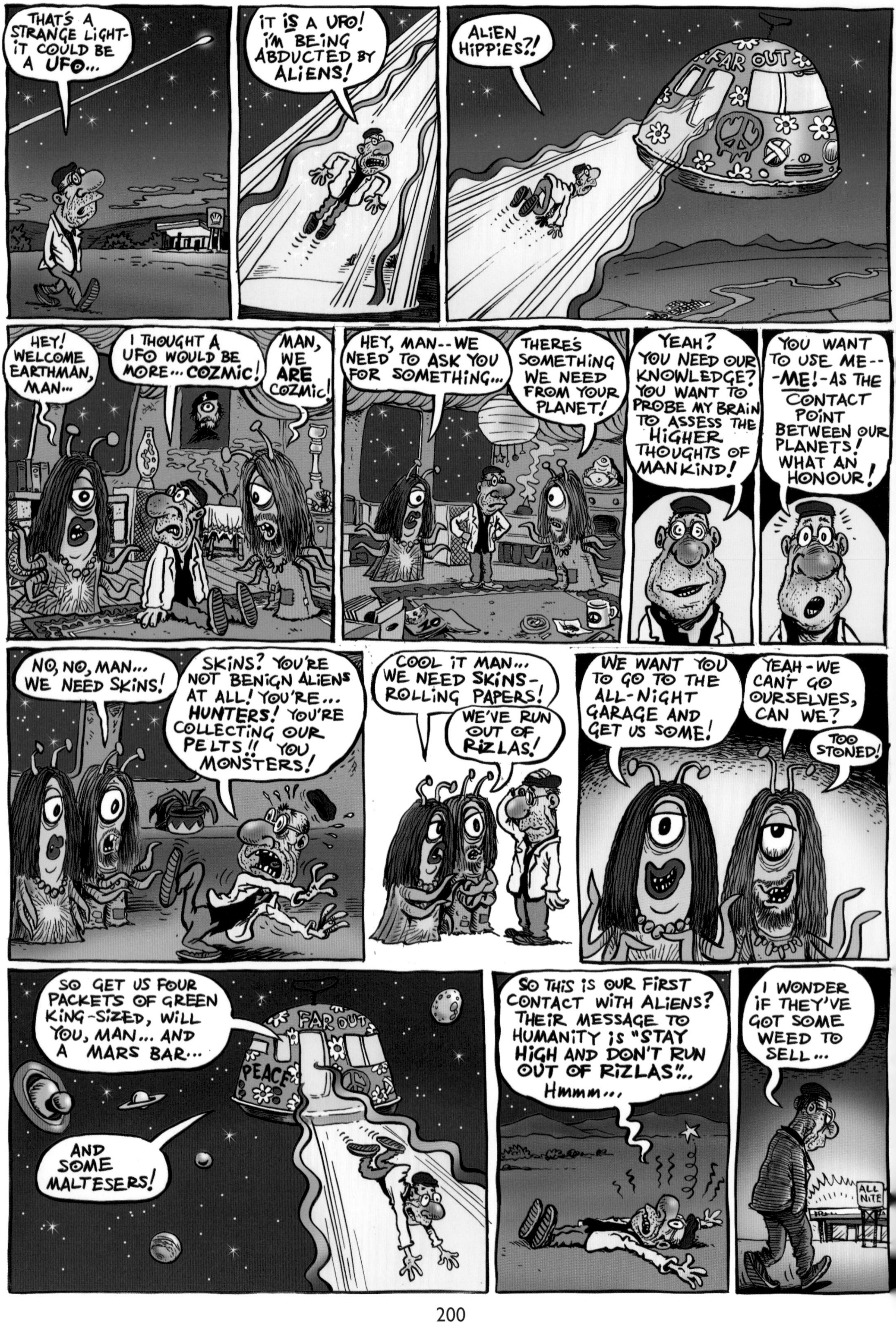
THAT'S A STRANGE LIGHT- IT COULD BE A UFO...
IT IS A UFO! I'M BEING ABDUCTED BY ALIENS!
ALIEN HIPPIES?!
FAR OUT
HEY! WELCOME EARTHMAN, MAN...
I THOUGHT A UFO WOULD BE MORE... COZMIC!
MAN, WE ARE COZMIC!
HEY, MAN-- WE NEED TO ASK YOU FOR SOMETHING...
THERE'S SOMETHING WE NEED FROM YOUR PLANET!
YEAH? YOU NEED OUR KNOWLEDGE? YOU WANT TO PROBE MY BRAIN TO ASSESS THE HIGHER THOUGHTS OF MANKIND!
YOU WANT TO USE ME-- -ME!- AS THE CONTACT POINT BETWEEN OUR PLANETS! WHAT AN HONOUR!
NO, NO, MAN... WE NEED SKINS!
SKINS? YOU'RE NOT BENIGN ALIENS AT ALL! YOU'RE... HUNTERS! YOU'RE COLLECTING OUR PELTS!! YOU MONSTERS!
COOL IT MAN... WE NEED SKINS- ROLLING PAPERS!
WE'VE RUN OUT OF RIZLAS!
WE WANT YOU TO GO TO THE ALL-NIGHT GARAGE AND GET US SOME!
YEAH-WE CAN'T GO OURSELVES, CAN WE?
TOO STONED!
SO GET US FOUR PACKETS OF GREEN KING-SIZED, WILL YOU, MAN... AND A MARS BAR...
FAR OUT
PEACE
AND SOME MALTESERS!
SO THIS IS OUR FIRST CONTACT WITH ALIENS? THEIR MESSAGE TO HUMANITY IS "STAY HIGH AND DON'T RUN OUT OF RIZLAS"... Hmmm...
I WONDER IF THEY'VE GOT SOME WEED TO SELL...
ALL NITE

VAMPIRE RABBIT

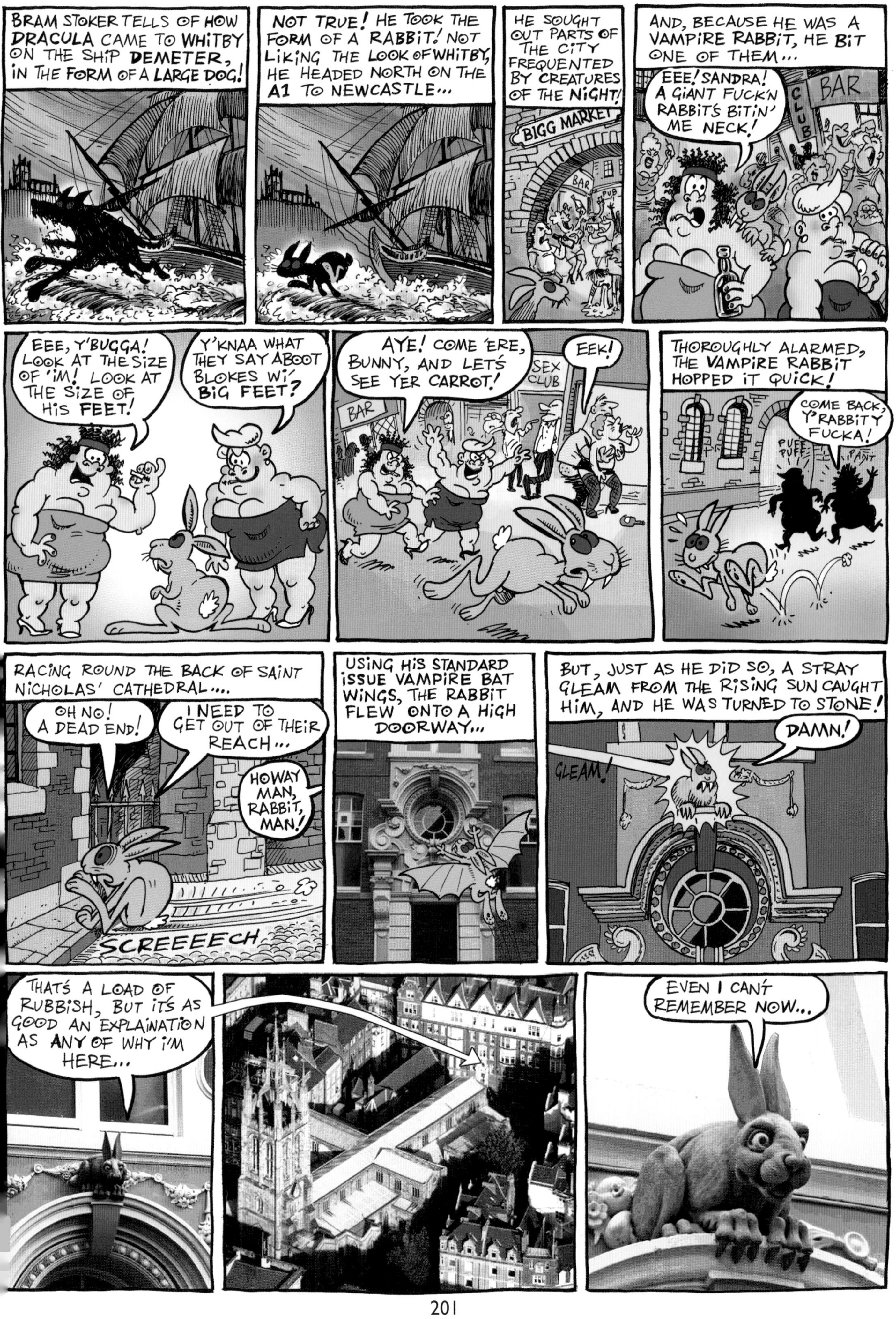
BRAM STOKER TELLS OF HOW DRACULA CAME TO WHITBY ON THE SHIP DEMETER, IN THE FORM OF A LARGE DOG!
NOT TRUE! HE TOOK THE FORM OF A RABBIT! NOT LIKING THE LOOK OF WHITBY, HE HEADED NORTH ON THE A1 TO NEWCASTLE...
HE SOUGHT OUT PARTS OF THE CITY FREQUENTED BY CREATURES OF THE NIGHT!
BIGG MARKET
BAR
PUB
AND, BECAUSE HE WAS A VAMPIRE RABBIT, HE BIT ONE OF THEM...
EEE! SANDRA! A GIANT FUCK'N RABBIT'S BITIN' ME NECK!
CLUB
BAR
EEE, Y'BUGGA! LOOK AT THE SIZE OF 'IM! LOOK AT THE SIZE OF HIS FEET!
Y'KNAA WHAT THEY SAY ABOOT BLOKES WI' BIG FEET?
AYE! COME 'ERE, BUNNY, AND LET'S SEE YER CARROT!
EEK!
SEX CLUB
BAR
THOROUGHLY ALARMED, THE VAMPIRE RABBIT HOPPED IT QUICK!
COME BACK, Y'RABBITY FUCKA!
PUFF PUFF
PANT
RACING ROUND THE BACK OF SAINT NICHOLAS' CATHEDRAL....
OH NO! A DEAD END!
I NEED TO GET OUT OF THEIR REACH...
HOWAY MAN, RABBIT, MAN!
SCREEEECH
USING HIS STANDARD ISSUE VAMPIRE BAT WINGS, THE RABBIT FLEW ONTO A HIGH DOORWAY...
BUT, JUST AS HE DID SO, A STRAY GLEAM FROM THE RISING SUN CAUGHT HIM, AND HE WAS TURNED TO STONE!
DAMN!
GLEAM!
THAT'S A LOAD OF RUBBISH, BUT IT'S AS GOOD AN EXPLAINATION AS ANY OF WHY I'M HERE...
EVEN I CAN'T REMEMBER NOW...

PHANTOM HITCH HIKER

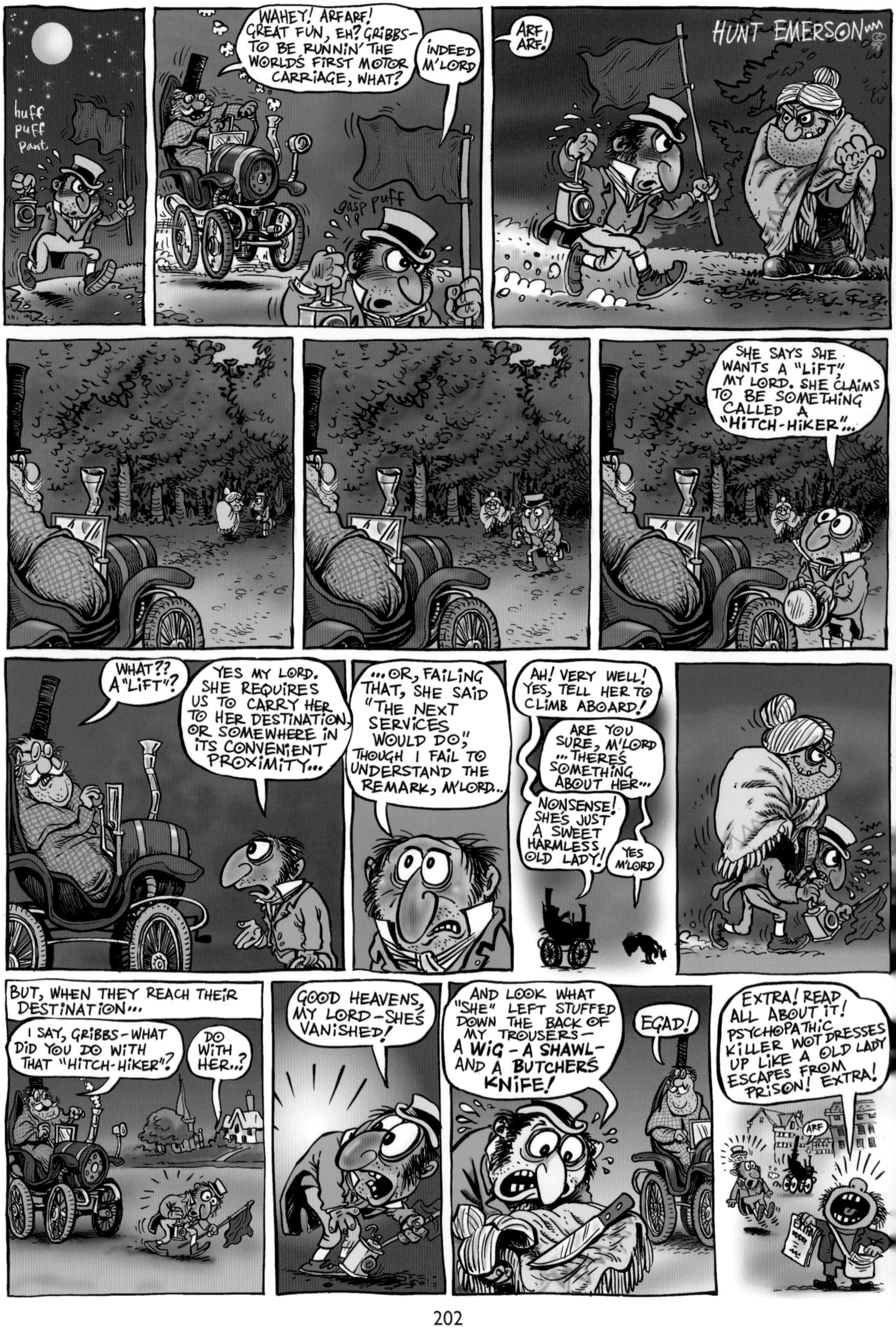

huff puff pant
WAHEY! ARFARF! GREAT FUN, EH? GRIBBS-TO BE RUNNIN' THE WORLD'S FIRST MOTOR CARRIAGE, WHAT?
INDEED M'LORD
gasp puff
ARF ARF!
HUNT EMERSON '98
SHE SAYS SHE WANTS A "LIFT", MY LORD. SHE CLAIMS TO BE SOMETHING CALLED A "HITCH-HIKER"...
WHAT?? A "LIFT"?
YES MY LORD. SHE REQUIRES US TO CARRY HER TO HER DESTINATION, OR SOMEWHERE IN ITS CONVENIENT PROXIMITY...
...OR, FAILING THAT, SHE SAID "THE NEXT SERVICES WOULD DO," THOUGH I FAIL TO UNDERSTAND THE REMARK, M'LORD...
AH! VERY WELL! YES, TELL HER TO CLIMB ABOARD!
ARE YOU SURE, M'LORD ...THERE'S SOMETHING ABOUT HER...
NONSENSE! SHE'S JUST A SWEET HARMLESS OLD LADY!
YES M'LORD
BUT, WHEN THEY REACH THEIR DESTINATION...
I SAY, GRIBBS-WHAT DID YOU DO WITH THAT "HITCH-HIKER"?
DO WITH HER..?
GOOD HEAVENS, MY LORD-SHE'S VANISHED!
AND LOOK WHAT "SHE" LEFT STUFFED DOWN THE BACK OF MY TROUSERS- A WIG - A SHAWL- AND A BUTCHER'S KNIFE!
EGAD!
EXTRA! READ ALL ABOUT IT! PSYCHOPATHIC KILLER WOT DRESSES UP LIKE A OLD LADY ESCAPES FROM PRISON! EXTRA!
ARF

WAR OF THE WORLDS

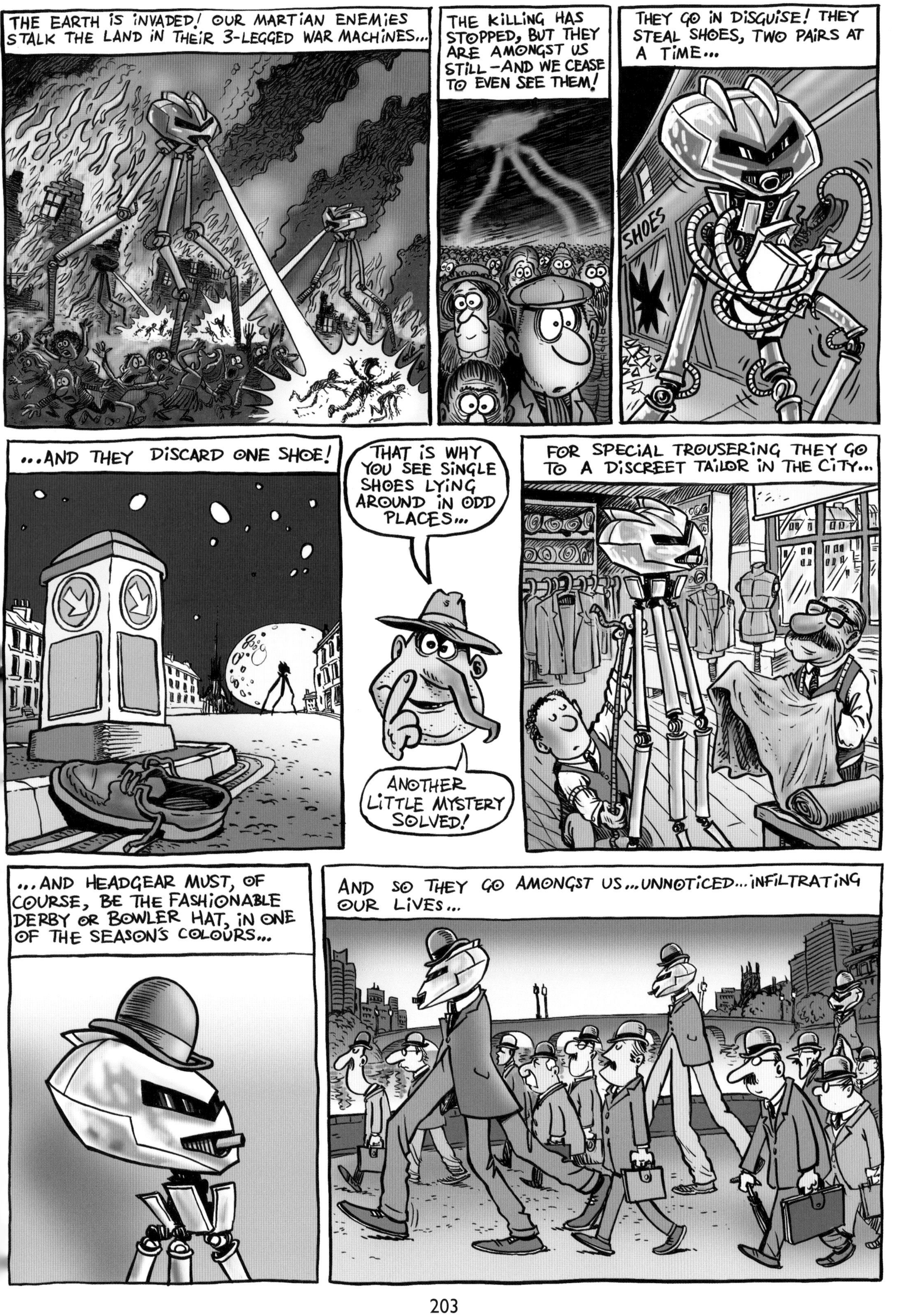
THE EARTH IS INVADED! OUR MARTIAN ENEMIES STALK THE LAND IN THEIR 3-LEGGED WAR MACHINES...
THE KILLING HAS STOPPED, BUT THEY ARE AMONGST US STILL – AND WE CEASE TO EVEN SEE THEM!
THEY GO IN DISGUISE! THEY STEAL SHOES, TWO PAIRS AT A TIME...
SHOES
...AND THEY DISCARD ONE SHOE!
THAT IS WHY YOU SEE SINGLE SHOES LYING AROUND IN ODD PLACES...
ANOTHER LITTLE MYSTERY SOLVED!
FOR SPECIAL TROUSERING THEY GO TO A DISCREET TAILOR IN THE CITY...
...AND HEADGEAR MUST, OF COURSE, BE THE FASHIONABLE DERBY OR BOWLER HAT, IN ONE OF THE SEASON'S COLOURS...
AND SO THEY GO AMONGST US...UNNOTICED...INFILTRATING OUR LIVES...

WEIRD BEAKS

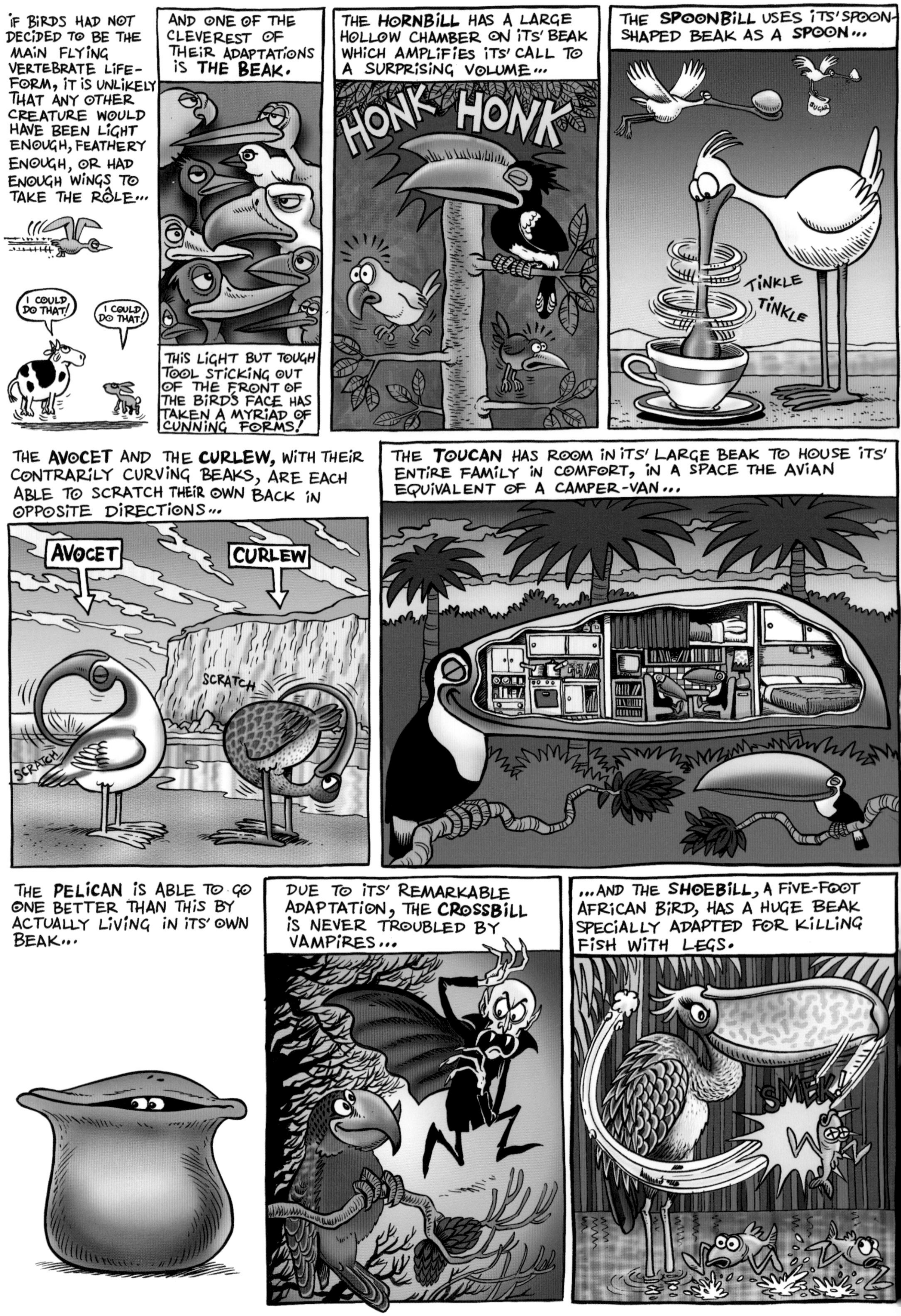
IF BIRDS HAD NOT DECIDED TO BE THE MAIN FLYING VERTEBRATE LIFE-FORM, IT IS UNLIKELY THAT ANY OTHER CREATURE WOULD HAVE BEEN LIGHT ENOUGH, FEATHERY ENOUGH, OR HAD ENOUGH WINGS TO TAKE THE RÔLE...
I COULD DO THAT!
I COULD DO THAT!
AND ONE OF THE CLEVEREST OF THEIR ADAPTATIONS IS THE BEAK.
THIS LIGHT BUT TOUGH TOOL STICKING OUT OF THE FRONT OF THE BIRD'S FACE HAS TAKEN A MYRIAD OF CUNNING FORMS!
THE HORNBILL HAS A LARGE HOLLOW CHAMBER ON ITS' BEAK WHICH AMPLIFIES ITS' CALL TO A SURPRISING VOLUME...
HONK HONK
THE SPOONBILL USES ITS' SPOON-SHAPED BEAK AS A SPOON...
SUGAR
TINKLE
TINKLE
THE AVOCET AND THE CURLEW, WITH THEIR CONTRARILY CURVING BEAKS, ARE EACH ABLE TO SCRATCH THEIR OWN BACK IN OPPOSITE DIRECTIONS...
AVOCET
CURLEW
SCRATCH
SCRATCH
THE TOUCAN HAS ROOM IN ITS' LARGE BEAK TO HOUSE ITS' ENTIRE FAMILY IN COMFORT, IN A SPACE THE AVIAN EQUIVALENT OF A CAMPER-VAN...
THE PELICAN IS ABLE TO GO ONE BETTER THAN THIS BY ACTUALLY LIVING IN ITS' OWN BEAK...
DUE TO ITS' REMARKABLE ADAPTATION, THE CROSSBILL IS NEVER TROUBLED BY VAMPIRES...
...AND THE SHOEBILL, A FIVE-FOOT AFRICAN BIRD, HAS A HUGE BEAK SPECIALLY ADAPTED FOR KILLING FISH WITH LEGS.
SMEK!

WEIRD WEATHER

THINGS ARE VERY QUIET ON THE PHENOMENA SCENE JUST NOW!

YES, VERY QUIET -- NOTHING TO INVESTIGATE FOR WEEKS!

I THINK I'LL CHECK OUT THE WEIRD WEATHER CHANNEL! I DON'T USUALLY DO THIS -- IT'S TOO MUCH LIKE CHEATING -- BUT NEEDS MUST!

CLIK

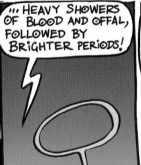

"... HEAVY SHOWERS OF BLOOD AND OFFAL, FOLLOWED BY BRIGHTER PERIODS!

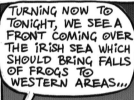

TURNING NOW TO TONIGHT, WE SEE A FRONT COMING OVER THE IRISH SEA WHICH SHOULD BRING FALLS OF FROGS TO WESTERN AREAS...

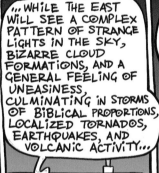

"...WHILE THE EAST WILL SEE A COMPLEX PATTERN OF STRANGE LIGHTS IN THE SKY, BIZARRE CLOUD FORMATIONS, AND A GENERAL FEELING OF UNEASINESS, CULMINATING IN STORMS OF BIBLICAL PROPORTIONS, LOCALIZED TORNADOS, EARTHQUAKES, AND VOLCANIC ACTIVITY...

"...EASING OFF BY MORNING TO GIVE RISE TO A SUNNY DAY. WELL, THAT'S ALL FROM ME - NOW BACK TO TOM IN THE STUDIO!

HMPH!

CLIK

THAT'S ALL VERY WELL, BUT NOTHING'S FALLING OUT OF THE SKY *HERE!* IT'S SO *BORING!*

I SUPPOSE I'D BETTER GET OUT ON THE STREET JUST IN CASE SOMETHING WEIRD *DOES* HAPPEN!

BAH!

SLAM!

CRASH CRASH CRASH CRASH

WERE ACCOUNTANT

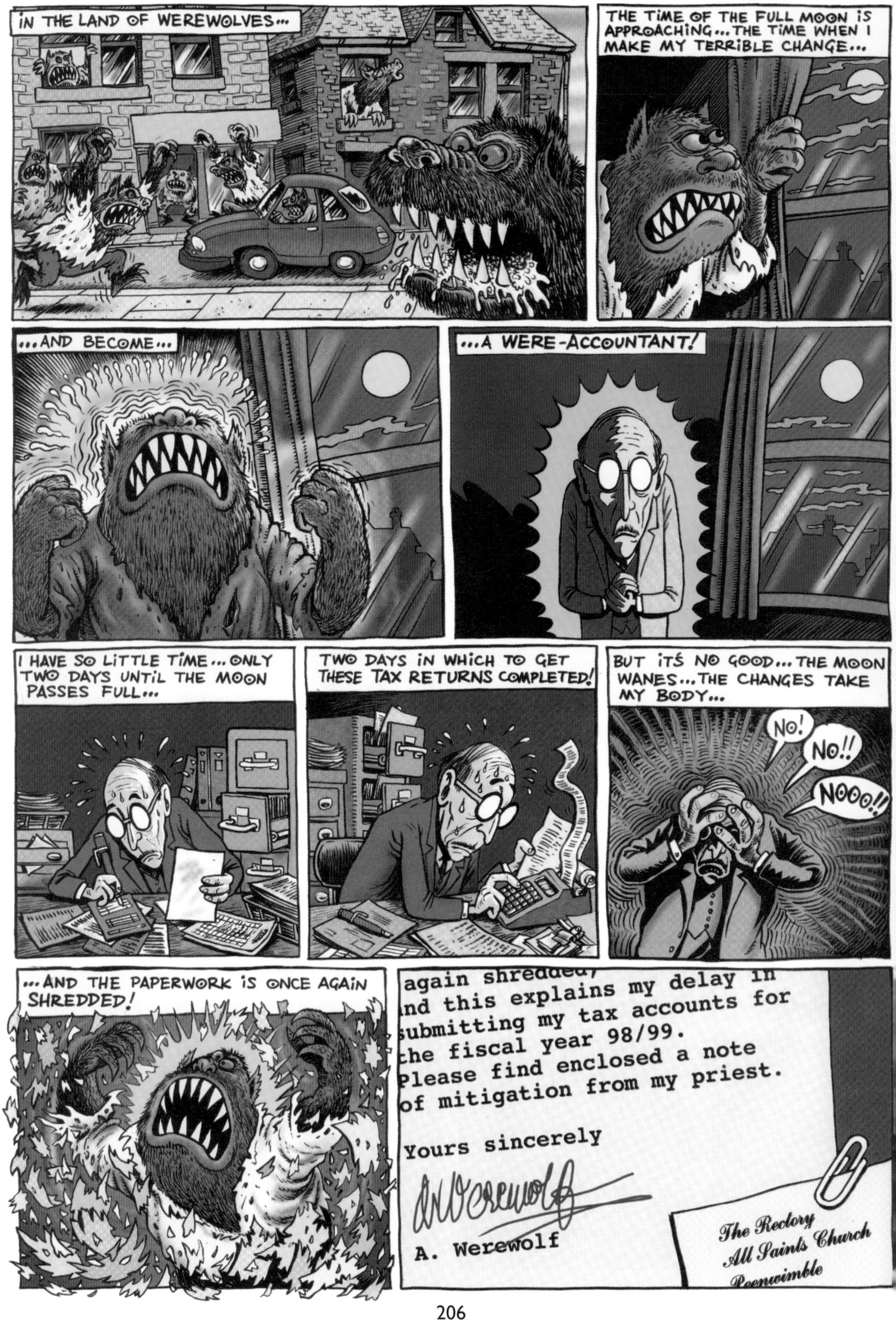
IN THE LAND OF WEREWOLVES...
THE TIME OF THE FULL MOON IS APPROACHING... THE TIME WHEN I MAKE MY TERRIBLE CHANGE...
...AND BECOME...
...A WERE-ACCOUNTANT!
I HAVE SO LITTLE TIME... ONLY TWO DAYS UNTIL THE MOON PASSES FULL...
TWO DAYS IN WHICH TO GET THESE TAX RETURNS COMPLETED!
BUT IT'S NO GOOD... THE MOON WANES... THE CHANGES TAKE MY BODY...
NO!
NO!!
NOOO!!
...AND THE PAPERWORK IS ONCE AGAIN SHREDDED!
again shredded,
nd this explains my delay in
submitting my tax accounts for
the fiscal year 98/99.
Please find enclosed a note
of mitigation from my priest.
Yours sincerely
A. Werewolf
The Rectory
All Saints Church
Peenwimble

WEREWOLF

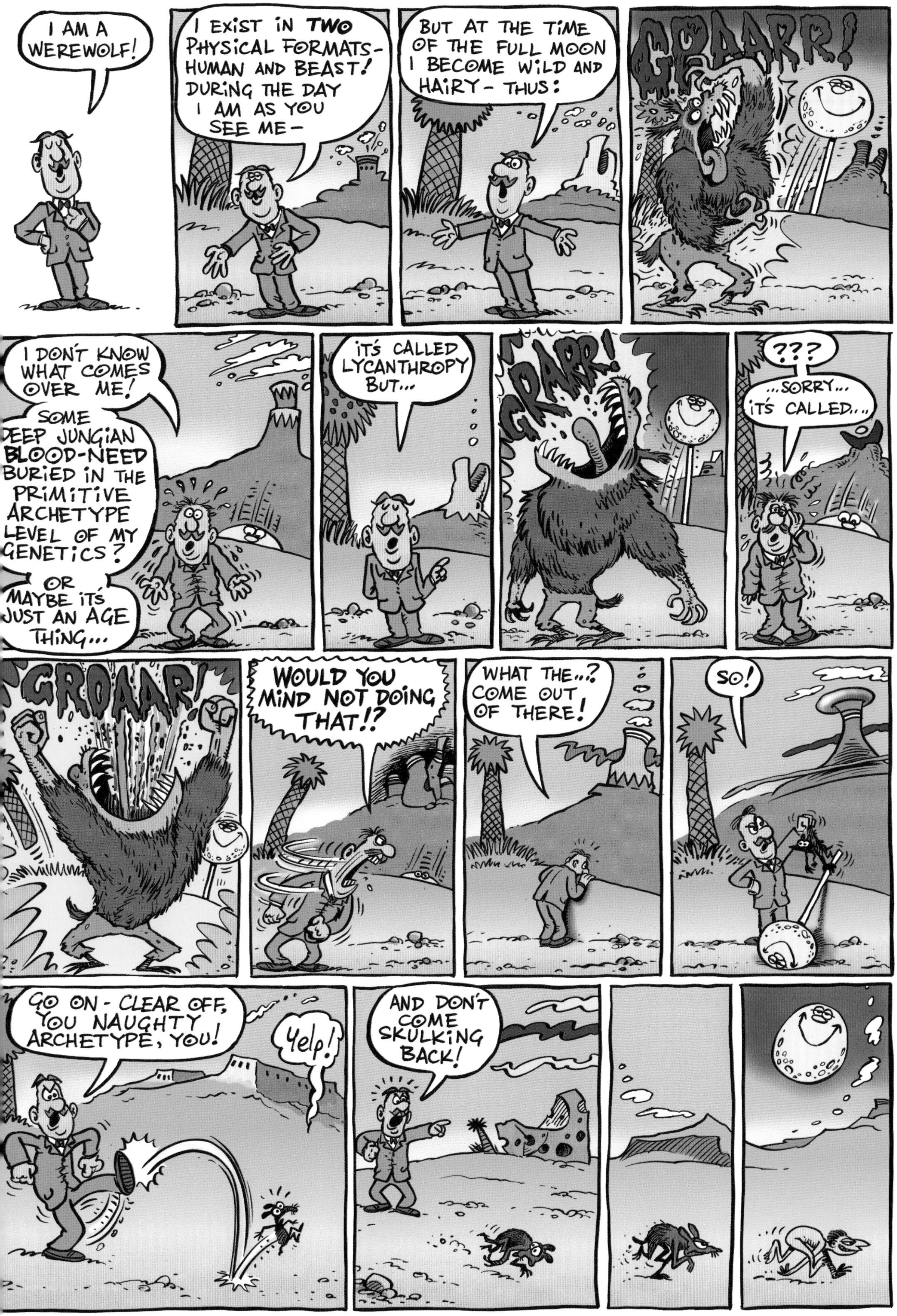

I AM A WEREWOLF!
I EXIST IN TWO PHYSICAL FORMATS-HUMAN AND BEAST! DURING THE DAY I AM AS YOU SEE ME-
BUT AT THE TIME OF THE FULL MOON I BECOME WILD AND HAIRY- THUS:
GRAARR!
I DON'T KNOW WHAT COMES OVER ME!
SOME DEEP JUNGIAN BLOOD-NEED BURIED IN THE PRIMITIVE ARCHETYPE LEVEL OF MY GENETICS?
OR MAYBE IT'S JUST AN AGE THING...
IT'S CALLED LYCANTHROPY BUT...
GRARR!
???
...SORRY... IT'S CALLED...
GROAAR!
WOULD YOU MIND NOT DOING THAT!?
WHAT THE..? COME OUT OF THERE!
SO!
GO ON- CLEAR OFF, YOU NAUGHTY ARCHETYPE, YOU!
Yelp!
AND DON'T COME SKULKING BACK!

WILD WEST WEREWOLF

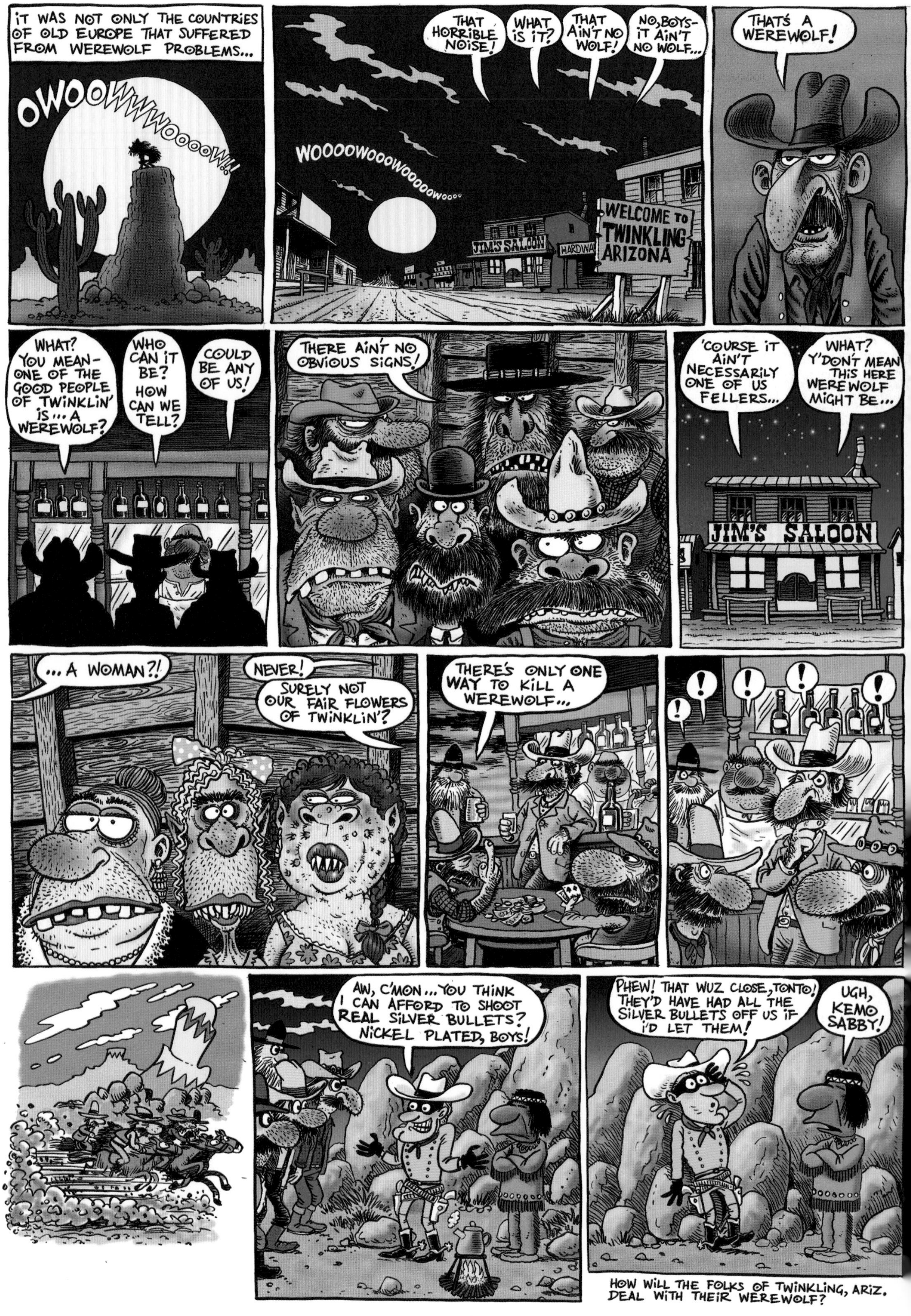
IT WAS NOT ONLY THE COUNTRIES OF OLD EUROPE THAT SUFFERED FROM WEREWOLF PROBLEMS...
OWOOWWWWOOOOW!!
WOOOOWOOOWOOOOOWOOOO
THAT HORRIBLE NOISE!
WHAT IS IT?
THAT AIN'T NO WOLF!
NO, BOYS- IT AIN'T NO WOLF...
JIM'S SALOON
HARDWA
WELCOME TO TWINKLING ARIZONA
THAT'S A WEREWOLF!
WHAT? YOU MEAN- ONE OF THE GOOD PEOPLE OF TWINKLIN' IS... A WEREWOLF?
WHO CAN IT BE? HOW CAN WE TELL?
COULD BE ANY OF US!
THERE AIN'T NO OBVIOUS SIGNS!
'COURSE IT AIN'T NECESSARILY ONE OF US FELLERS...
WHAT? Y'DON'T MEAN THIS HERE WEREWOLF MIGHT BE...
JIM'S SALOON
... A WOMAN?!
NEVER!
SURELY NOT OUR FAIR FLOWERS OF TWINKLIN'?
THERE'S ONLY ONE WAY TO KILL A WEREWOLF...
!
!
!
!
!
AW, C'MON... YOU THINK I CAN AFFORD TO SHOOT REAL SILVER BULLETS? NICKEL PLATED, BOYS!
PHEW! THAT WUZ CLOSE, TONTO! THEY'D HAVE HAD ALL THE SILVER BULLETS OFF US IF I'D LET THEM!
UGH, KEMO SABBY!

HOW WILL THE FOLKS OF TWINKLING, ARIZ. DEAL WITH THEIR WEREWOLF?

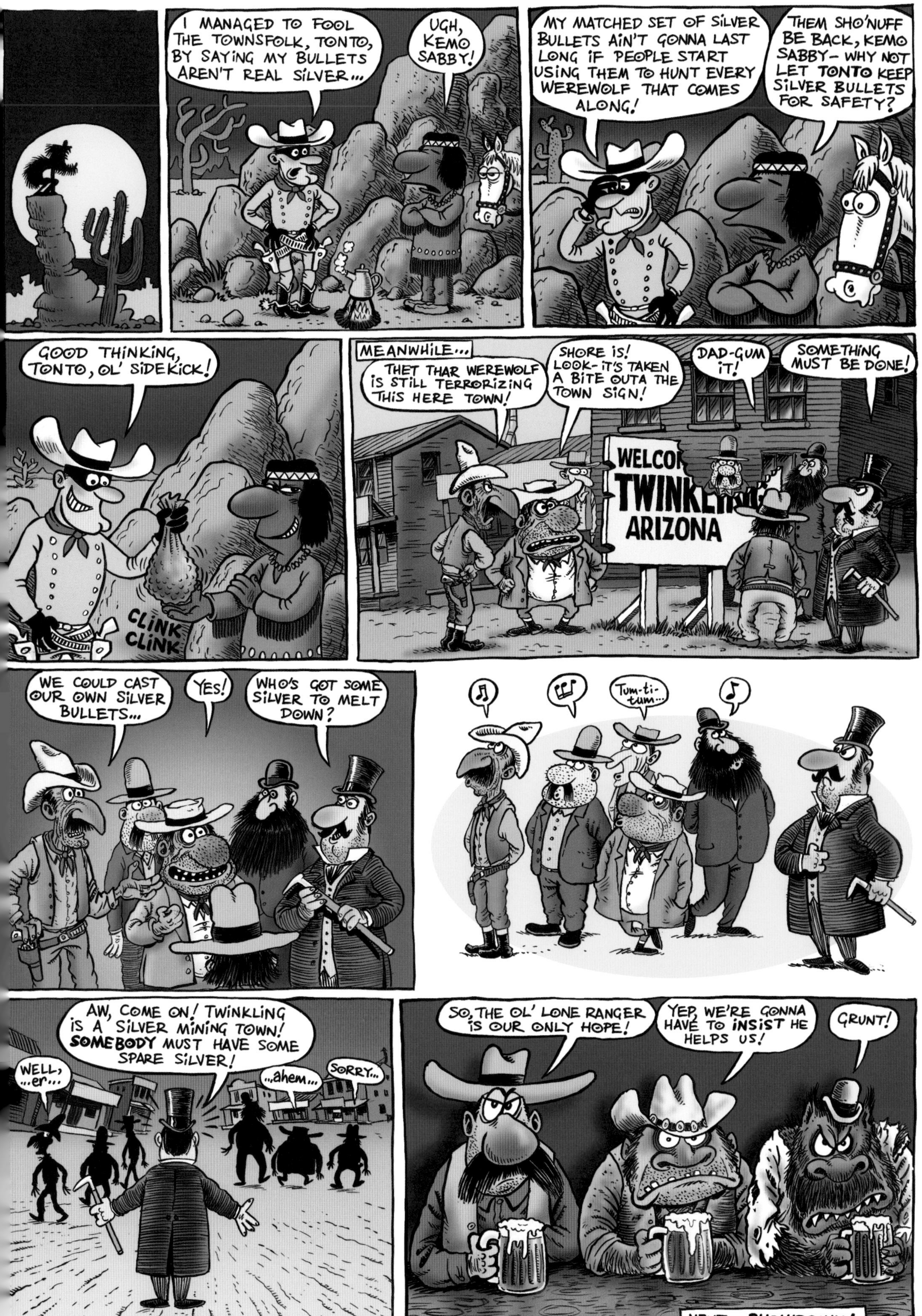
I MANAGED TO FOOL THE TOWNSFOLK, TONTO, BY SAYING MY BULLETS AREN'T REAL SILVER...
UGH, KEMO SABBY!
MY MATCHED SET OF SILVER BULLETS AIN'T GONNA LAST LONG IF PEOPLE START USING THEM TO HUNT EVERY WEREWOLF THAT COMES ALONG!
THEM SHO'NUFF BE BACK, KEMO SABBY– WHY NOT LET TONTO KEEP SILVER BULLETS FOR SAFETY?
GOOD THINKING, TONTO, OL' SIDEKICK!
CLINK CLINK
MEANWHILE...
THET THAR WEREWOLF IS STILL TERRORIZING THIS HERE TOWN!
SHORE IS! LOOK– IT'S TAKEN A BITE OUTA THE TOWN SIGN!
DAD-GUM IT!
SOMETHING MUST BE DONE!
WELCO
TWINKL
ARIZONA
WE COULD CAST OUR OWN SILVER BULLETS...
YES!
WHO'S GOT SOME SILVER TO MELT DOWN?
Tum-ti-tum...
AW, COME ON! TWINKLING IS A SILVER MINING TOWN! SOMEBODY MUST HAVE SOME SPARE SILVER!
WELL, ...er...
...ahem...
SORRY...
SO, THE OL' LONE RANGER IS OUR ONLY HOPE!
YEP, WE'RE GONNA HAVE TO INSIST HE HELPS US!
GRUNT!
NEXT — SHOWDOWN!

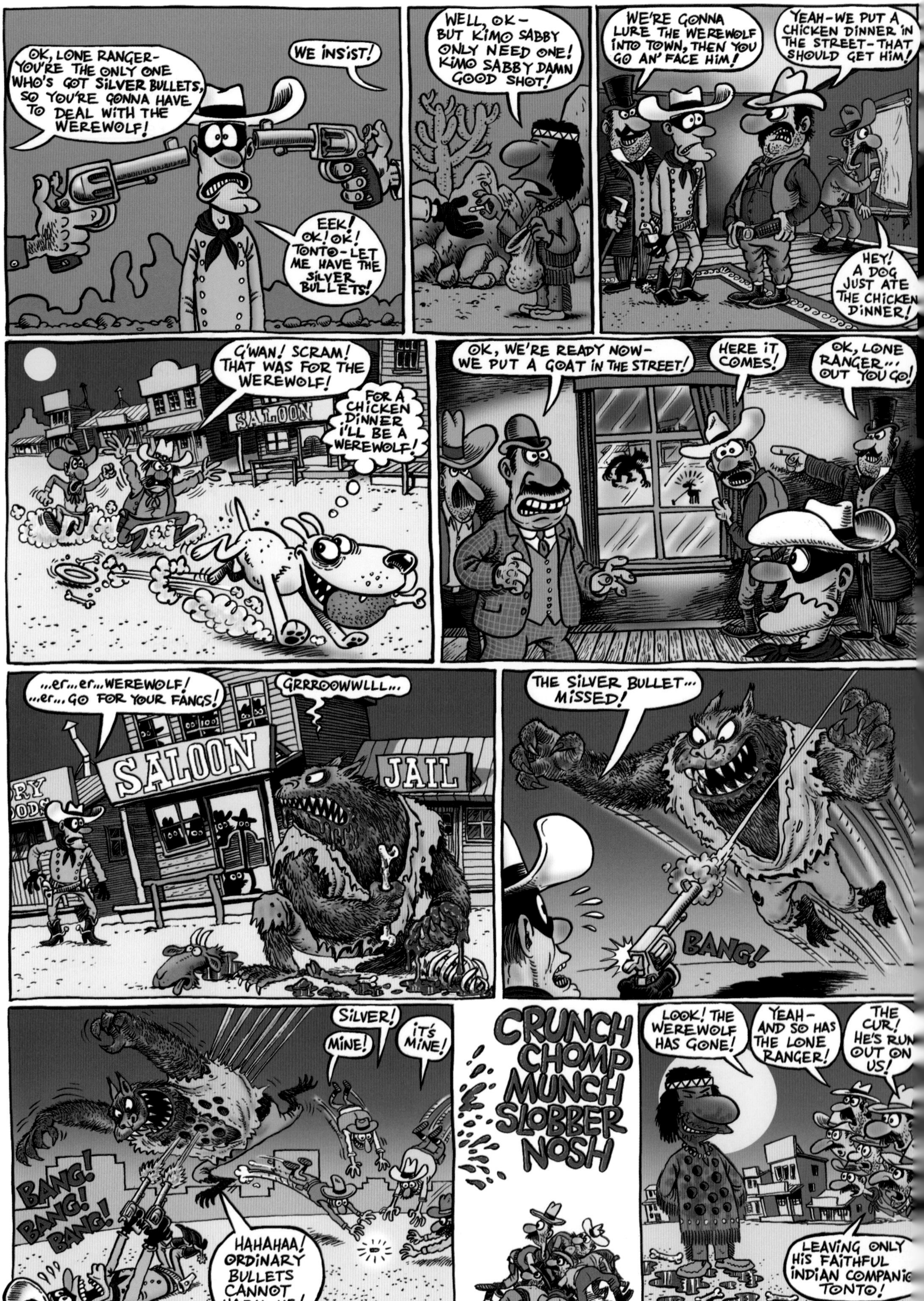
OK, LONE RANGER- YOU'RE THE ONLY ONE WHO'S GOT SILVER BULLETS, SO YOU'RE GONNA HAVE TO DEAL WITH THE WEREWOLF!
WE INSIST!
EEK! OK! OK! TONTO-LET ME HAVE THE SILVER BULLETS!
WELL, OK- BUT KIMO SABBY ONLY NEED ONE! KIMO SABBY DAMN GOOD SHOT!
WE'RE GONNA LURE THE WEREWOLF INTO TOWN, THEN YOU GO AN' FACE HIM!
YEAH-WE PUT A CHICKEN DINNER IN THE STREET-THAT SHOULD GET HIM!
HEY! A DOG JUST ATE THE CHICKEN DINNER!
G'WAN! SCRAM! THAT WAS FOR THE WEREWOLF!
SALOON
FOR A CHICKEN DINNER I'LL BE A WEREWOLF!
OK, WE'RE READY NOW- WE PUT A GOAT IN THE STREET!
HERE IT COMES!
OK, LONE RANGER... OUT YOU GO!
...er...er...WEREWOLF! ...er...GO FOR YOUR FANGS!
GRRROOWWLLL...
SALOON
JAIL
THE SILVER BULLET... MISSED!
BANG!
SILVER!
MINE!
IT'S MINE!
BANG! BANG! BANG!
HAHAHAA! ORDINARY BULLETS CANNOT HARM ME!
CRUNCH CHOMP MUNCH SLOBBER NOSH
LOOK! THE WEREWOLF HAS GONE!
YEAH- AND SO HAS THE LONE RANGER!
THE CUR! HE'S RUN OUT ON US!
LEAVING ONLY HIS FAITHFUL INDIAN COMPANIO TONTO!
OK, THAT'S ALL ABOUT WILD WEST WEREWOLVES

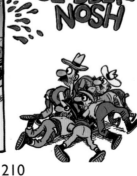

THE WINCHESTER MYSTERY HOUSE

WILLIAM WIRT WINCHESTER INVENTED HIS EPONYMOUS RIFLE IN 1866! WHEN HE DIED IN 1881 HIS WIFE SARAH INHERITED ENORMOUS WEALTH!

SHE VISITED ADAM COONS, A PSYCHIC MEDIUM, WHO TOLD HER...

THE WINCHESTER FAMILY IS HAUNTED BY THE GHOSTS OF ALL THOSE KILLED BY THE RIFLE...

YOU MUST MOVE WEST, AND BUILD!

SHE BOUGHT A PROPERTY IN SAN JOSE, CA. AND CONSTRUCTION WORK COMMENCED! IT CONTINUED NON-STOP FOR THE NEXT 38 YEARS - TO FEND OFF THE MALIGNANT SPIRITS...

IF WE STOP BUILDING, WE ARE DOOMED!

YES, M'AM...

THE HOUSE BECAME BIGGER AND BIGGER - AND EVER MORE STRANGE!

IT HAD DOORS OPENING ONTO BLANK WALLS...

...STAIRCASES THAT LED NOWHERE...

...LABYRINTHINE ROOMS AND CORRIDORS...

HELP! I'M LOST!

ME TOO!

SO AM I!!

HELP!

THE NUMBER 13 RECURRED FREQUENTLY IN THE HOUSE'S DESIGNS...

ROOMS WITH 13 WINDOWS

13 CANDLES IN CHANDELIERS

13 PANES IN WINDOWS

STAIR CASES WITH 13 STEPS

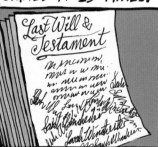

SARAH WAS OBSESSED BY THE NUMBER 13 - HER WILL WAS WRITTEN IN 13 SECTIONS, AND SHE SIGNED IT 13 TIMES!

Last Will & Testament

SARAH LIVED IN THE WINCHESTER MYSTERY HOUSE UNTIL THE 1906 EARTHQUAKE, WHEN SHE WAS TRAPPED IN A BEDROOM FOR SEVERAL HOURS...

13 HOURS, ACTUALLY!

AFTER THAT SHE MOVED OUT, BUT INSISTED THAT CONSTRUCTION BE CONTINUED AS BEFORE...

BUILD MORE AT THE BACK OF THE HOUSE! WE'VE BEEN SPENDING TOO MUCH TIME ON THE FRONT, AND THE SPIRITS ARE ANGRY!

YES M'AM...

WHEN SHE DIED - OF HEART FAILURE, IN HER SLEEP, IN 1922 - THE HOUSE WAS SOLD, AND TURNED INTO A TOURIST ATTRACTION...

IT MUST BE SAID THAT SARAH'S BIOGRAPHER DENIES THAT THE STRANGER STORIES ABOUT HER WERE TRUE - THAT, FOR INSTANCE, THE NEW OWNERS INSTALLED "13" FEATURES IN THE HOUSE IN ORDER TO ENHANCE HER LEGEND!

BUT HER BIOGRAPHER IS A SPOILSPORT!

WE KNOW WHICH VERSION OF SARAH WINCHESTER'S LIFE WE PREFER, DON'T WE, FORTEAN CHUMS!?

WIND

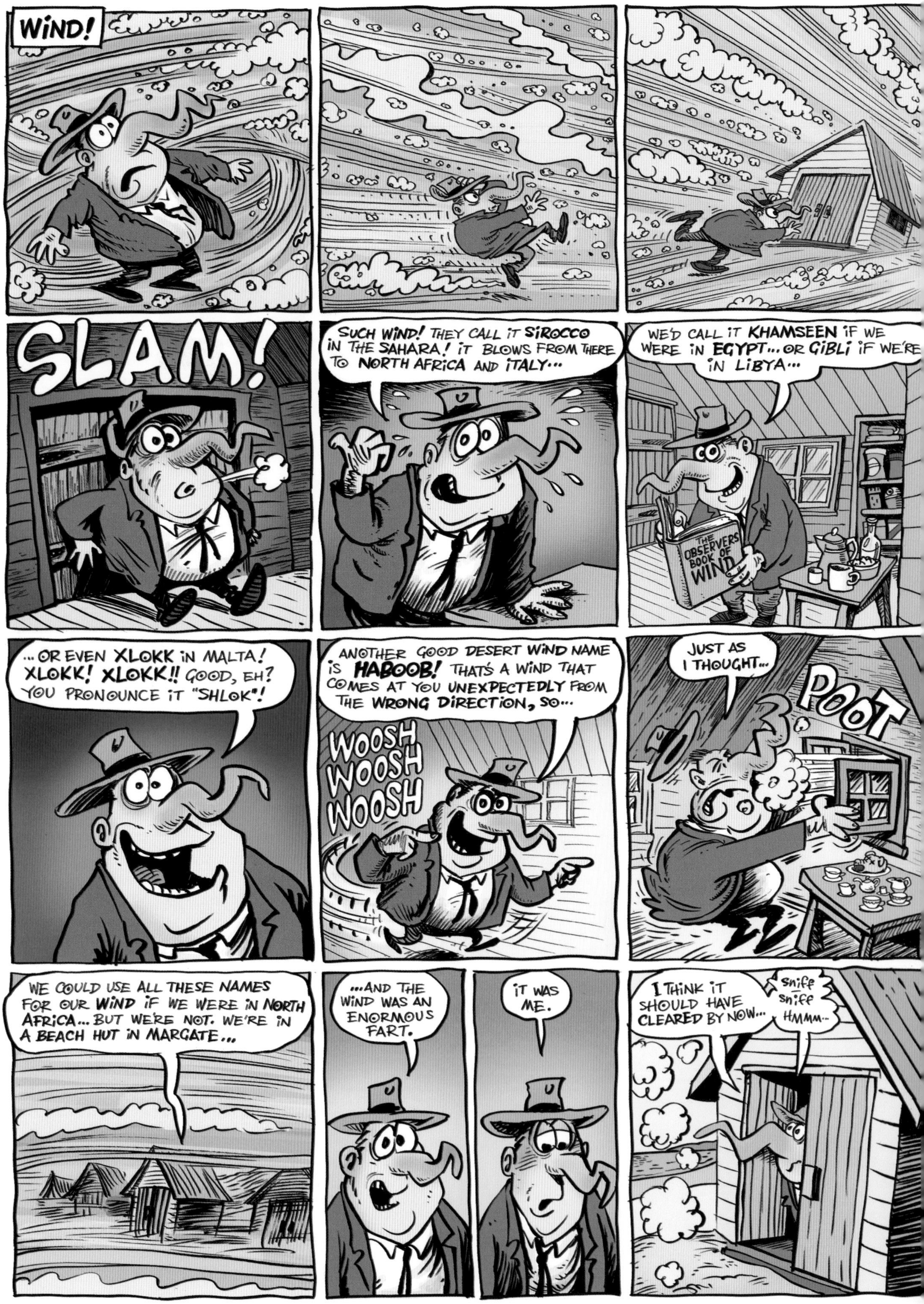
WIND!
SLAM!
SUCH WIND! THEY CALL IT SIROCCO IN THE SAHARA! IT BLOWS FROM THERE TO NORTH AFRICA AND ITALY...
WE'D CALL IT KHAMSEEN IF WE WERE IN EGYPT... OR GIBLI IF WE'RE IN LIBYA...
THE OBSERVERS BOOK OF WIND
...OR EVEN XLOKK IN MALTA! XLOKK! XLOKK!! GOOD, EH? YOU PRONOUNCE IT "SHLOK"!
ANOTHER GOOD DESERT WIND NAME IS HABOOB! THAT'S A WIND THAT COMES AT YOU UNEXPECTEDLY FROM THE WRONG DIRECTION, SO...
WOOSH WOOSH WOOSH
JUST AS I THOUGHT...
POOT
WE COULD USE ALL THESE NAMES FOR OUR WIND IF WE WERE IN NORTH AFRICA... BUT WE'RE NOT. WE'RE IN A BEACH HUT IN MARGATE...
...AND THE WIND WAS AN ENORMOUS FART.
IT WAS ME.
I THINK IT SHOULD HAVE CLEARED BY NOW...
sniff sniff HMMM...

ANCIENT METEORITE

AN ANCIENT PERSON IN AN ANCIENT LAND IS ALONE IN THE DESERT! HE HAS A FRUSTRATING PERSONAL PROBLEM...

AW MAN! I JUST WANNA BE THE BOSS OF EVERYBODY, BUT THEY WON'T TAKE ME SERIOUSLY!

HO-LY SHIT!!

SHLAM!

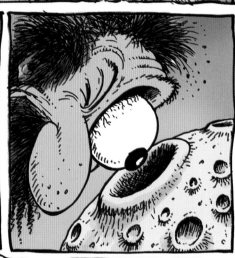

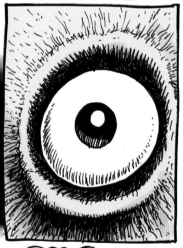

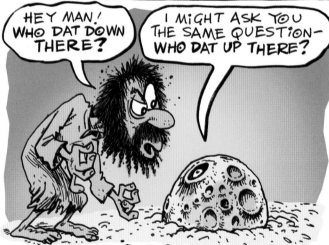

HEY MAN! WHO DAT DOWN THERE?

I MIGHT ASK YOU THE SAME QUESTION— WHO DAT UP THERE?

HMMM! A CONUNDRUM THAT COULD KEEP MY PEOPLE IN SUBJUCATION FOR THOUSANDS OF YEARS!

AND SO, TO THE SOUND OF THE WOODY HERMAN BAND, HISTORY BEGINS...

WHO DAT UP THERE?!!

WHO DAT DOWN THERE?!!

www.youtube.com/watch?v=K0UZzXb_ick&list=RDK0UZzXb_ick&start_radio=1

OK— I WANT A BIG VERSION OF ME— HUGE, RIGHT? FOR ME TO STAND ON!

EEK! OK BOSS!

RIGHT AWAY!

I'LL GET THEM ONTO IT!

THE YAMYAM

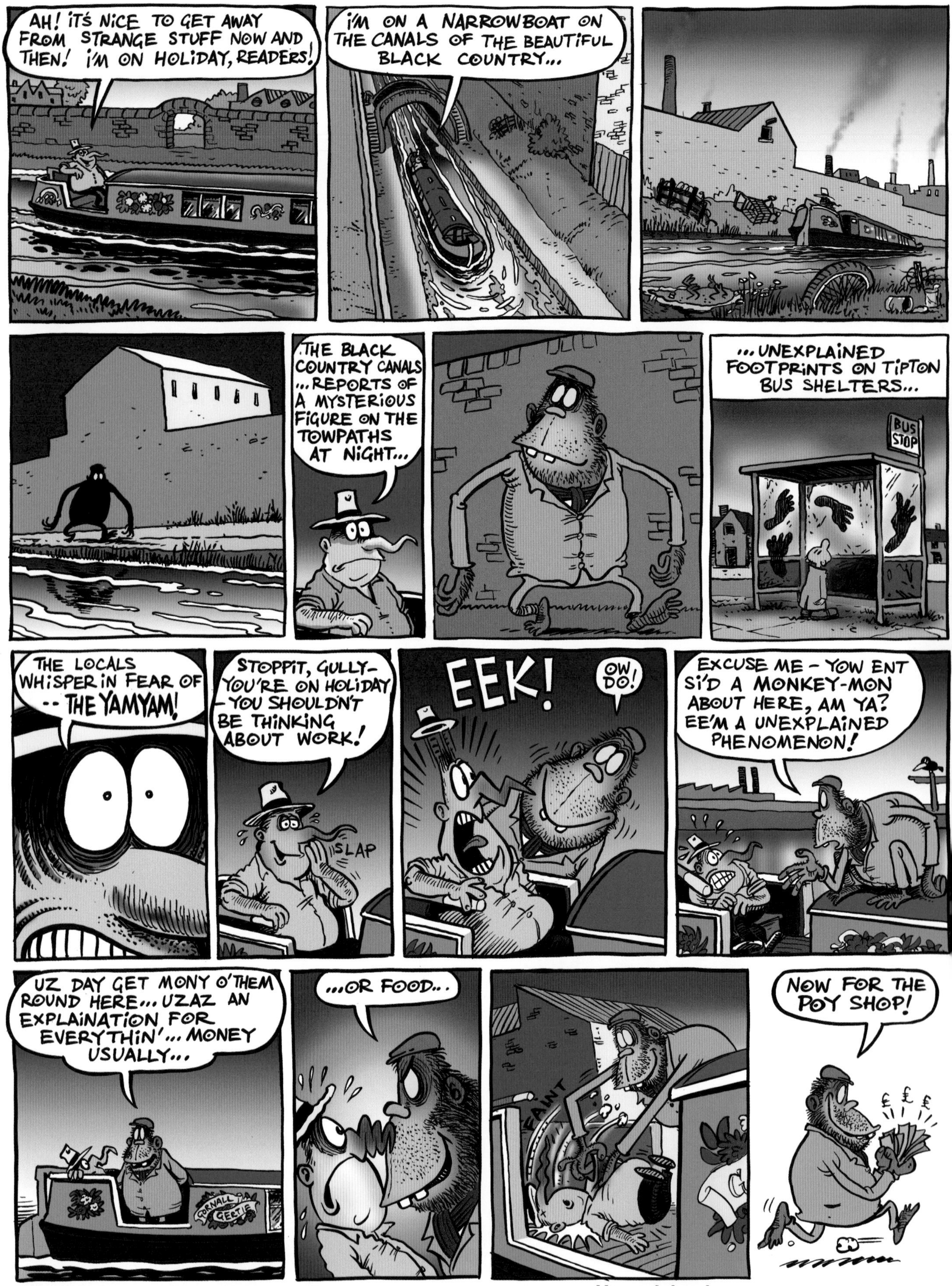

AH! IT'S NICE TO GET AWAY FROM STRANGE STUFF NOW AND THEN! I'M ON HOLIDAY, READERS!
I'M ON A NARROWBOAT ON THE CANALS OF THE BEAUTIFUL BLACK COUNTRY...
THE BLACK COUNTRY CANALS ...REPORTS OF A MYSTERIOUS FIGURE ON THE TOWPATHS AT NIGHT...
...UNEXPLAINED FOOTPRINTS ON TIPTON BUS SHELTERS...
BUS STOP
THE LOCALS WHISPER IN FEAR OF -- THE YAMYAM!
STOPPIT, GULLY- YOU'RE ON HOLIDAY - YOU SHOULDN'T BE THINKING ABOUT WORK!
SLAP
EEK!
OW DO!
EXCUSE ME - YOW ENT SI'D A MONKEY-MON ABOUT HERE, AM YA? EE'M A UNEXPLAINED PHENOMENON!
UZ DAY GET MONY O'THEM ROUND HERE... UZAZ AN EXPLAINATION FOR EVERYTHIN'... MONEY USUALLY...
CORNALL GERTIE
...OR FOOD...
FAINT
NOW FOR THE POY SHOP!
£ £ £

Glossary:

Am ya?	- *Have you?*	**Ent**	- *Haven't*	**Ow do**	- *Hello*	**Unexplained Phenomenon**	- *Oy day know what thissun means.*	**Uz**	- *We*
Day	- *Don't*	**Mon**	- *Man*	**Poy**	- *Pie*			**Uzaz**	- *We have*
Ee'm	- *He's*	**Mony**	- *Many*	**Si'd**	- *Seen*			**Yow**	- *You*

A STRANGE FISH

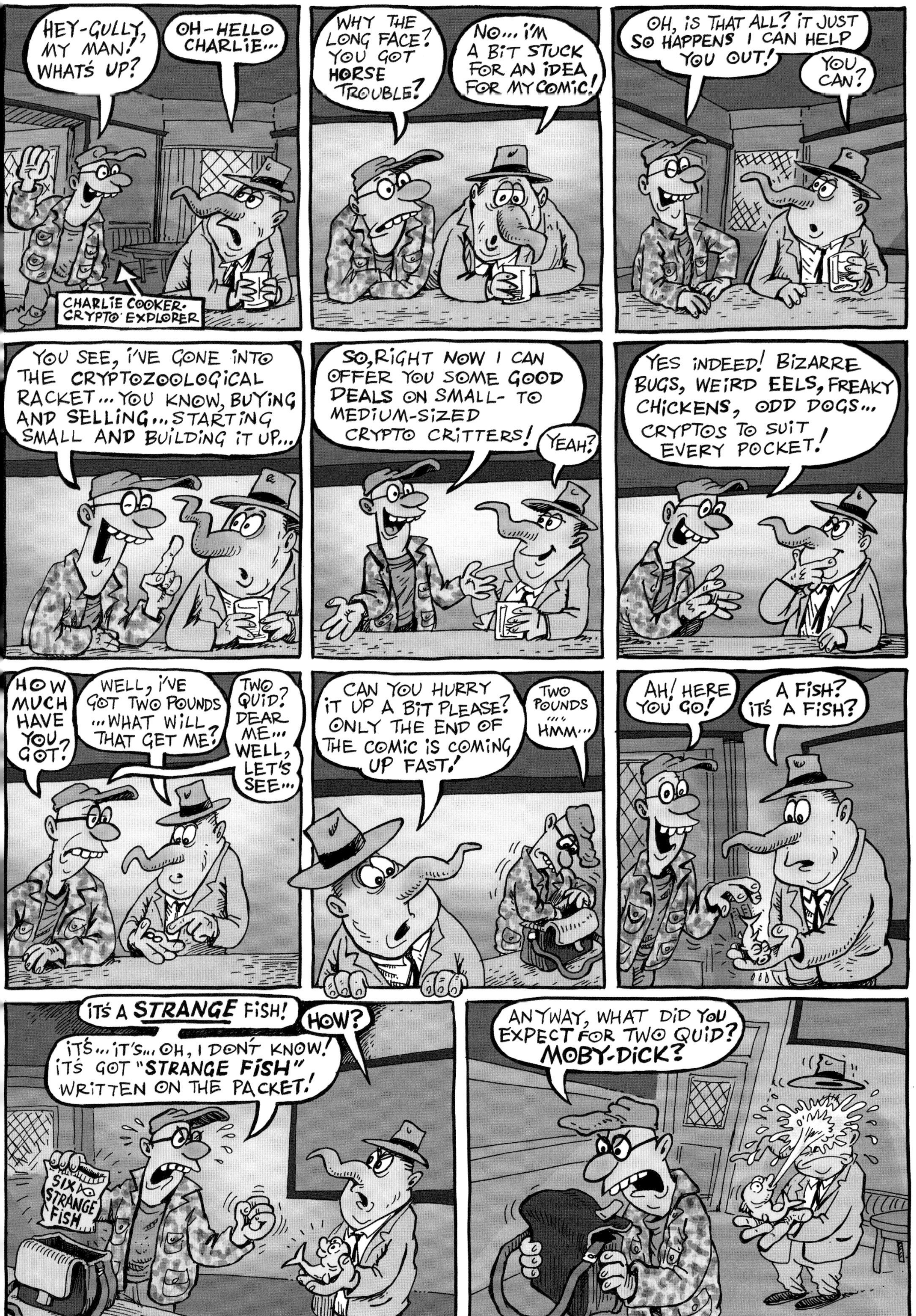
HEY-GULLY, MY MAN! WHAT'S UP?
OH-HELLO CHARLIE...
CHARLIE COOKER. CRYPTO EXPLORER
WHY THE LONG FACE? YOU GOT HORSE TROUBLE?
NO... I'M A BIT STUCK FOR AN IDEA FOR MY COMIC!
OH, IS THAT ALL? IT JUST SO HAPPENS I CAN HELP YOU OUT!
YOU CAN?
YOU SEE, I'VE GONE INTO THE CRYPTOZOOLOGICAL RACKET... YOU KNOW, BUYING AND SELLING... STARTING SMALL AND BUILDING IT UP...
SO, RIGHT NOW I CAN OFFER YOU SOME GOOD DEALS ON SMALL- TO MEDIUM-SIZED CRYPTO CRITTERS!
YEAH?
YES INDEED! BIZARRE BUGS, WEIRD EELS, FREAKY CHICKENS, ODD DOGS... CRYPTOS TO SUIT EVERY POCKET!
HOW MUCH HAVE YOU GOT?
WELL, I'VE GOT TWO POUNDS ...WHAT WILL THAT GET ME?
TWO QUID? DEAR ME... WELL, LET'S SEE...
CAN YOU HURRY IT UP A BIT PLEASE? ONLY THE END OF THE COMIC IS COMING UP FAST!
TWO POUNDS .... HMM...
AH! HERE YOU GO!
A FISH? IT'S A FISH?
IT'S A STRANGE FISH!
HOW?
IT'S... IT'S... OH, I DON'T KNOW! IT'S GOT "STRANGE FISH" WRITTEN ON THE PACKET!
SIX STRANGE FISH
ANYWAY, WHAT DID YOU EXPECT FOR TWO QUID? MOBY-DICK?

THE YODELLING YIPYANG

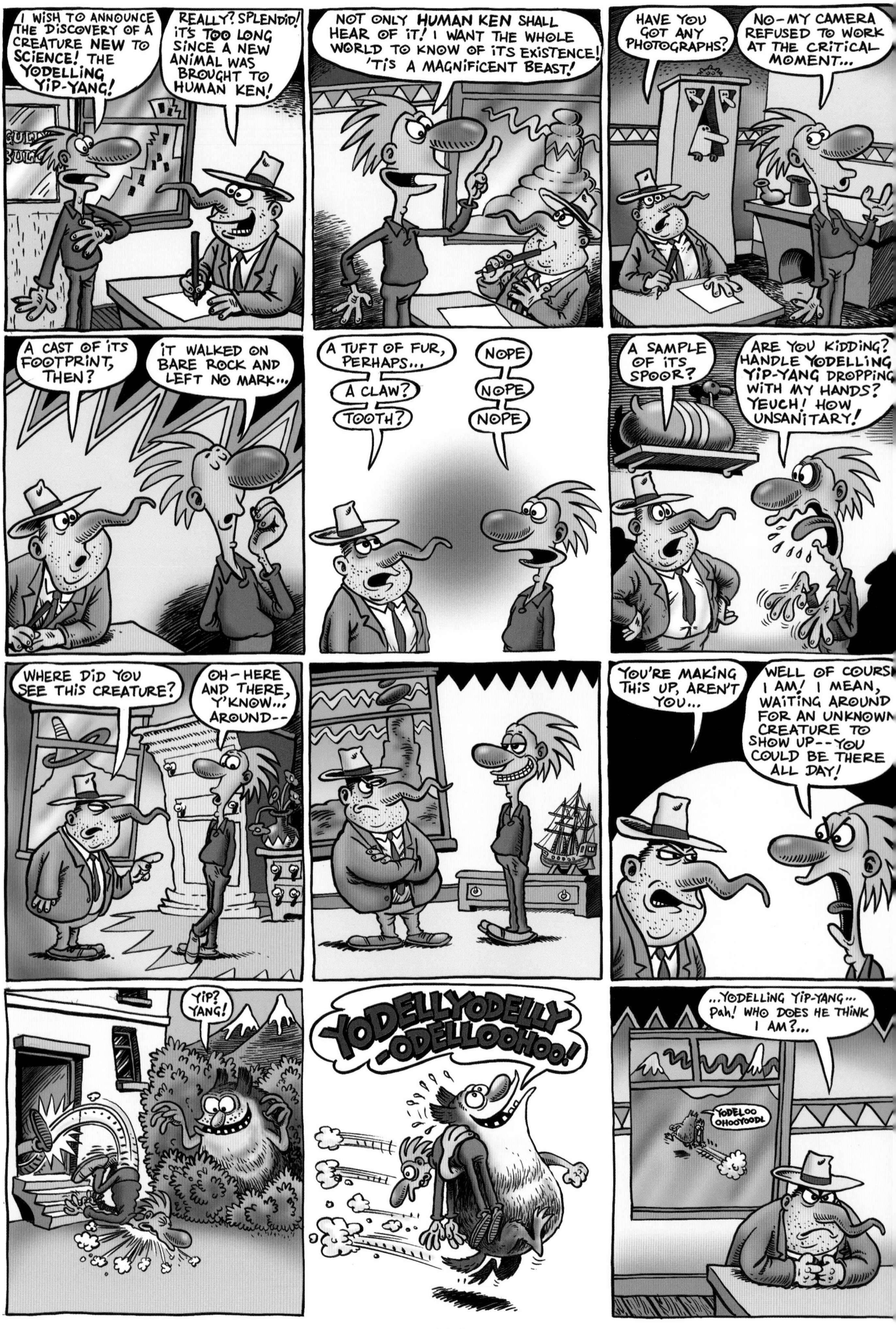
I WISH TO ANNOUNCE THE DISCOVERY OF A CREATURE NEW TO SCIENCE! THE YODELLING YIP-YANG!
REALLY? SPLENDID! IT'S TOO LONG SINCE A NEW ANIMAL WAS BROUGHT TO HUMAN KEN!
NOT ONLY HUMAN KEN SHALL HEAR OF IT! I WANT THE WHOLE WORLD TO KNOW OF ITS EXISTENCE! 'TIS A MAGNIFICENT BEAST!
HAVE YOU GOT ANY PHOTOGRAPHS?
NO-MY CAMERA REFUSED TO WORK AT THE CRITICAL MOMENT...
A CAST OF ITS FOOTPRINT, THEN?
IT WALKED ON BARE ROCK AND LEFT NO MARK...
A TUFT OF FUR, PERHAPS...
NOPE
A CLAW?
NOPE
TOOTH?
NOPE
A SAMPLE OF ITS SPOOR?
ARE YOU KIDDING? HANDLE YODELLING YIP-YANG DROPPING WITH MY HANDS? YEUCH! HOW UNSANITARY!
WHERE DID YOU SEE THIS CREATURE?
OH-HERE AND THERE, Y'KNOW... AROUND--
YOU'RE MAKING THIS UP, AREN'T YOU...
WELL OF COURS I AM! I MEAN, WAITING AROUND FOR AN UNKNOWN CREATURE TO SHOW UP--YOU COULD BE THERE ALL DAY!
YIP? YANG!
YODELLYODELLY-ODELLOOHOO!
...YODELLING YIP-YANG... Pah! WHO DOES HE THINK I AM?...
YODELOO OHOOYOODL

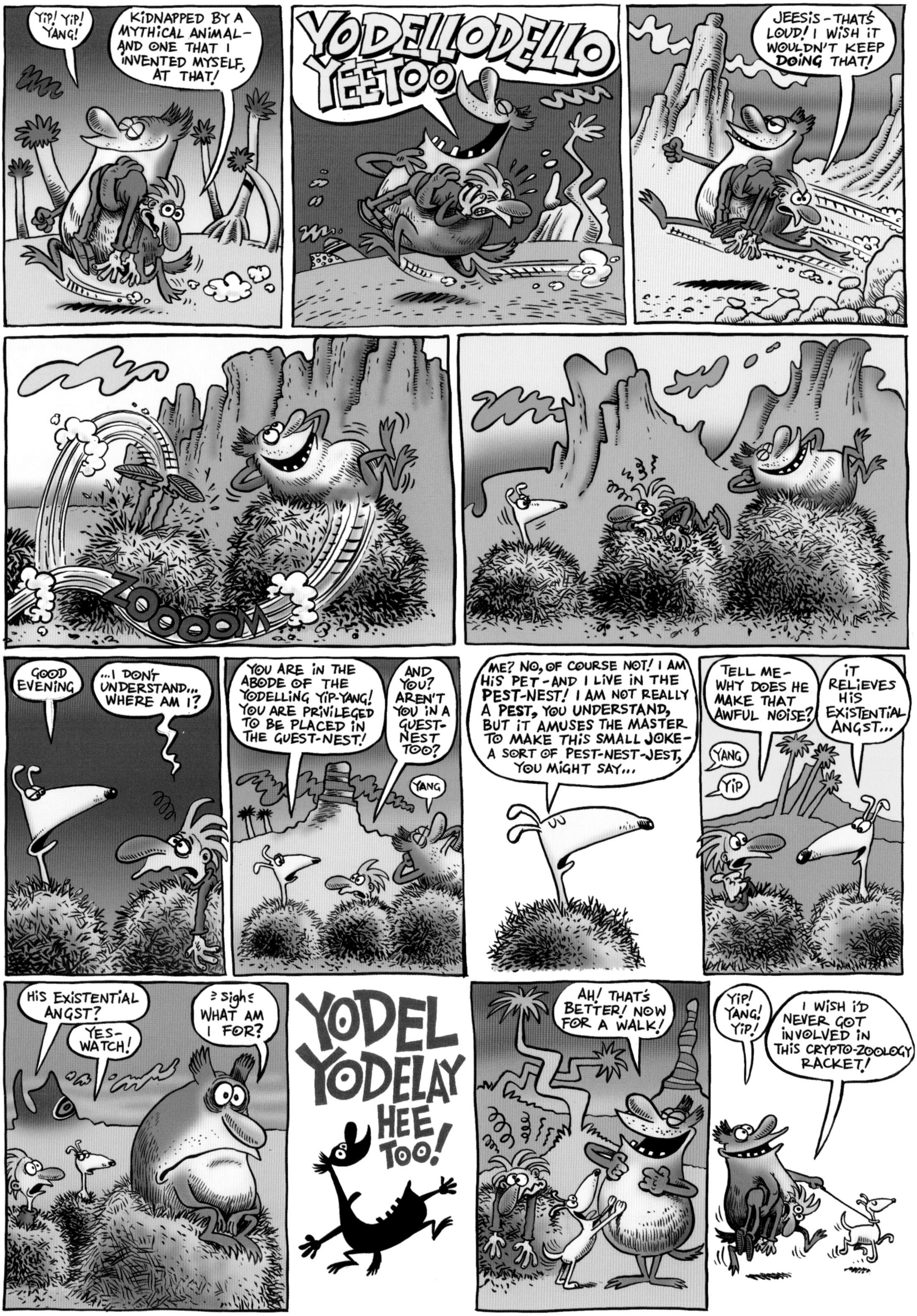

YIP! YIP! YANG!
KIDNAPPED BY A MYTHICAL ANIMAL-AND ONE THAT I INVENTED MYSELF, AT THAT!
YODELLODELLO YEETOO
JEESIS-THAT'S LOUD! I WISH IT WOULDN'T KEEP DOING THAT!
ZOOOOM
GOOD EVENING
...I DON'T UNDERSTAND... WHERE AM I?
YOU ARE IN THE ABODE OF THE YODELLING YIP-YANG! YOU ARE PRIVILEGED TO BE PLACED IN THE GUEST-NEST!
AND YOU? AREN'T YOU IN A GUEST-NEST TOO?
YANG
ME? NO, OF COURSE NOT! I AM HIS PET-AND I LIVE IN THE PEST-NEST! I AM NOT REALLY A PEST, YOU UNDERSTAND, BUT IT AMUSES THE MASTER TO MAKE THIS SMALL JOKE-A SORT OF PEST-NEST-JEST, YOU MIGHT SAY...
TELL ME-WHY DOES HE MAKE THAT AWFUL NOISE?
IT RELIEVES HIS EXISTENTIAL ANGST...
YANG
YIP
HIS EXISTENTIAL ANGST?
YES-WATCH!
≥ SIGH ≤ WHAT AM I FOR?
YODEL YODELAY HEE TOO!
AH! THAT'S BETTER! NOW FOR A WALK!
YIP! YANG! YIP!
I WISH I'D NEVER GOT INVOLVED IN THIS CRYPTO-ZOOLOGY RACKET!

THE YAPOK

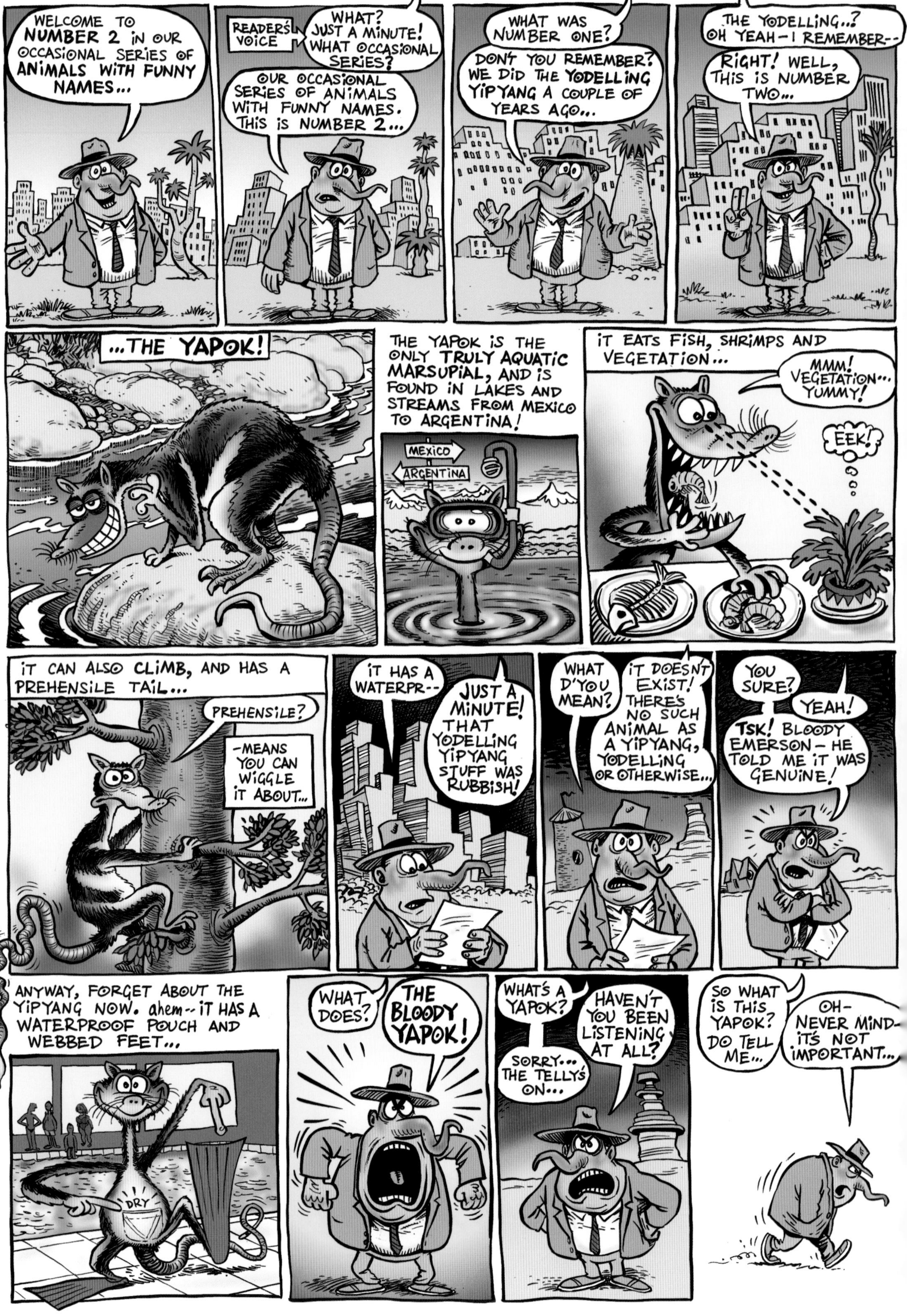

WELCOME TO NUMBER 2 IN OUR OCCASIONAL SERIES OF ANIMALS WITH FUNNY NAMES...
READER'S VOICE
WHAT? JUST A MINUTE! WHAT OCCASIONAL SERIES?
OUR OCCASIONAL SERIES OF ANIMALS WITH FUNNY NAMES. THIS IS NUMBER 2...
WHAT WAS NUMBER ONE?
DON'T YOU REMEMBER? WE DID THE YODELLING YIPYANG A COUPLE OF YEARS AGO...
THE YODELLING..? OH YEAH - I REMEMBER--
RIGHT! WELL, THIS IS NUMBER TWO...
...THE YAPOK!
THE YAPOK IS THE ONLY TRULY AQUATIC MARSUPIAL, AND IS FOUND IN LAKES AND STREAMS FROM MEXICO TO ARGENTINA!
MEXICO
ARGENTINA
IT EATS FISH, SHRIMPS AND VEGETATION...
MMM! VEGETATION... YUMMY!
EEK!
IT CAN ALSO CLIMB, AND HAS A PREHENSILE TAIL...
PREHENSILE?
-MEANS YOU CAN WIGGLE IT ABOUT...
IT HAS A WATERPR--
JUST A MINUTE! THAT YODELLING YIPYANG STUFF WAS RUBBISH!
WHAT D'YOU MEAN?
IT DOESN'T EXIST! THERE'S NO SUCH ANIMAL AS A YIPYANG, YODELLING OR OTHERWISE...
YOU SURE?
YEAH!
TSK! BLOODY EMERSON - HE TOLD ME IT WAS GENUINE!
ANYWAY, FORGET ABOUT THE YIPYANG NOW. ahem -- IT HAS A WATERPROOF POUCH AND WEBBED FEET...
DRY
WHAT DOES?
THE BLOODY YAPOK!
WHAT'S A YAPOK?
HAVEN'T YOU BEEN LISTENING AT ALL?
SORRY... THE TELLY'S ON...
SO WHAT IS THIS YAPOK? DO TELL ME...
OH- NEVER MIND- IT'S NOT IMPORTANT...

THE GROGOCH

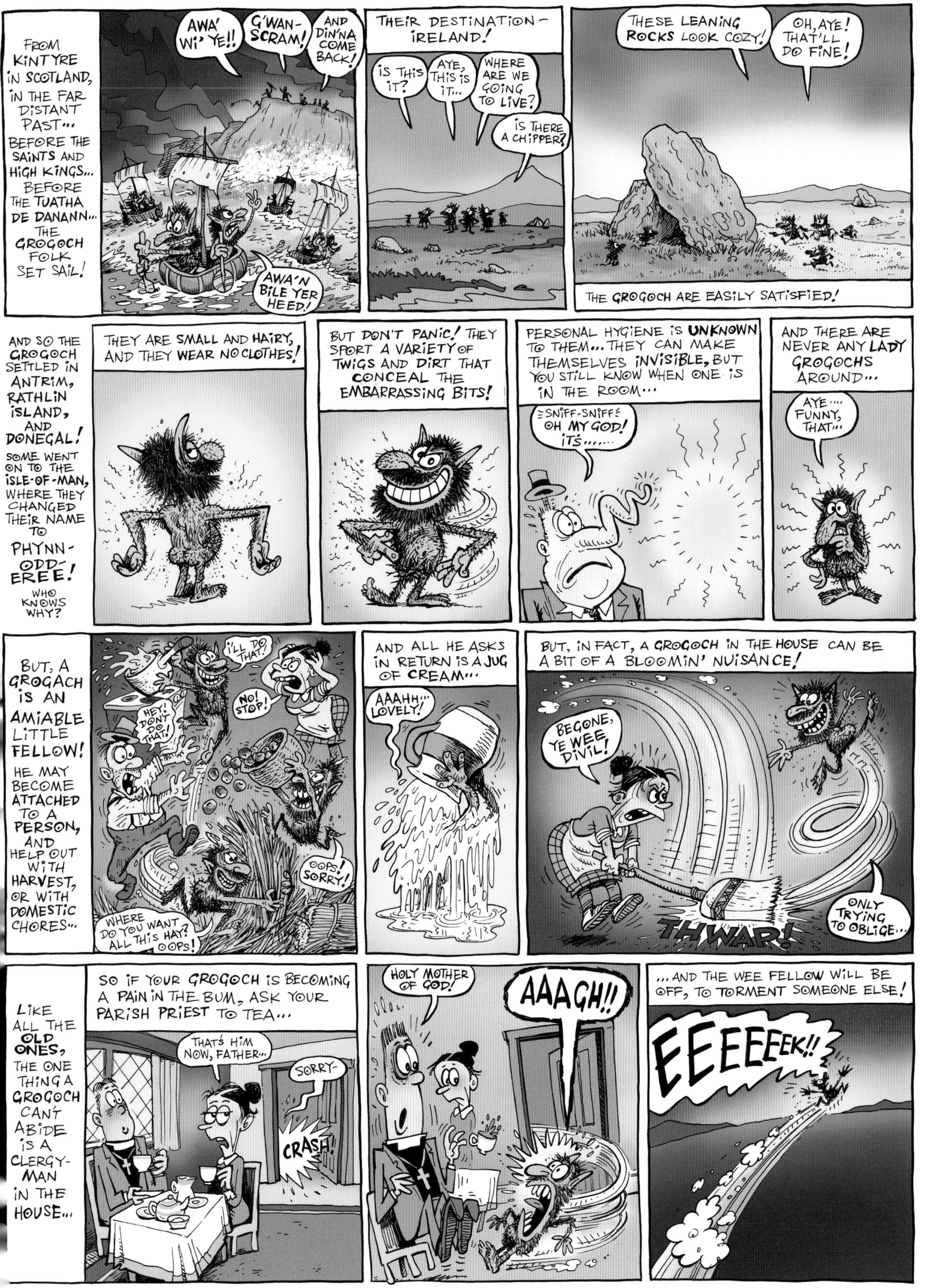

FROM KINTYRE IN SCOTLAND, IN THE FAR DISTANT PAST... BEFORE THE SAINTS AND HIGH KINGS... BEFORE THE TUATHA DE DANANN... THE GROGOCH FOLK SET SAIL!
AWA' WI' YE!!
G'WAN-SCRAM!
AND DIN'NA COME BACK!
AWA'N BILE YER HEED!
THEIR DESTINATION - IRELAND!
IS THIS IT?
AYE, THIS IS IT...
WHERE ARE WE GOING TO LIVE?
IS THERE A CHIPPER?
THESE LEANING ROCKS LOOK COZY!
OH, AYE! THAT'LL DO FINE!
THE GROGOCH ARE EASILY SATISFIED!
AND SO THE GROGOCH SETTLED IN ANTRIM, RATHLIN ISLAND, AND DONEGAL! SOME WENT ON TO THE ISLE-OF-MAN, WHERE THEY CHANGED THEIR NAME TO PHYNN-ODD-EREE! WHO KNOWS WHY?
THEY ARE SMALL AND HAIRY, AND THEY WEAR NO CLOTHES!
BUT DON'T PANIC! THEY SPORT A VARIETY OF TWIGS AND DIRT THAT CONCEAL THE EMBARRASSING BITS!
PERSONAL HYGIENE IS UNKNOWN TO THEM... THEY CAN MAKE THEMSELVES INVISIBLE, BUT YOU STILL KNOW WHEN ONE IS IN THE ROOM...
SNIFF-SNIFF OH MY GOD! IT'S......
AND THERE ARE NEVER ANY LADY GROGOCHS AROUND...
AYE.... FUNNY, THAT...
BUT, A GROGACH IS AN AMIABLE LITTLE FELLOW! HE MAY BECOME ATTACHED TO A PERSON, AND HELP OUT WITH HARVEST, OR WITH DOMESTIC CHORES...
I'LL DO THAT!
NO! STOP!
HEY! DON'T DO THAT!
OOPS! SORRY!
WHERE DO YOU WANT ALL THIS HAY? OOPS!
AND ALL HE ASKS IN RETURN IS A JUG OF CREAM...
AAAHH... LOVELY!
BUT, IN FACT, A GROGOCH IN THE HOUSE CAN BE A BIT OF A BLOOMIN' NUISANCE!
BEGONE, YE WEE DIVIL!
THWAP!
ONLY TRYING TO OBLIGE...
LIKE ALL THE OLD ONES, THE ONE THING A GROGOCH CAN'T ABIDE IS A CLERGY-MAN IN THE HOUSE...
SO IF YOUR GROGOCH IS BECOMING A PAIN IN THE BUM, ASK YOUR PARISH PRIEST TO TEA...
THAT'S HIM NOW, FATHER...
SORRY-
CRASH!
HOLY MOTHER OF GOD!
AAAGH!!
...AND THE WEE FELLOW WILL BE OFF, TO TORMENT SOMEONE ELSE!
EEEEEEEK!!

SPONTANEOUS HUMAN COMBUSTION CLINIC

HOSPITAL
Y RAYS
X-RAYS
EYE EAR NEB
°C
HEAT CLINICS
WARD A-G
OUT
COLD
HOT
FEVERS FLUSHES & PHEWS
SENSATIONS OF BURNING
INTERNAL BURNING of THE ORGANS HEARTBURN SUNBURN CHINESE BURN BURNS NIGHT VICTIMS
EXTERNAL BURNING
PHYSICAL BURNS
PSYCHOLOGICAL BURNS
ACTUAL ONGOING FIRES
RELIGIOUS FIRES
SELF INFLICTED INCINERATION
ACCIDENTAL INCINERATION
SPONTANEOUS HUMAN COMBUSTION CLINIC
SHC CLINIC
WHOLE BODY COMBUSTION
TOTAL INCINERATION
PARTIAL INCINERATION
BURNING HEAD
WITH HYSTERIA
WITH ZENLIKE CALM
TORSO
LIMBS
ARMS
LEGS
HANDS
PINKY
RING
MIDDLE
INDEX
THUMB

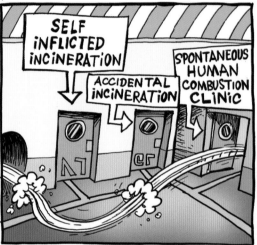

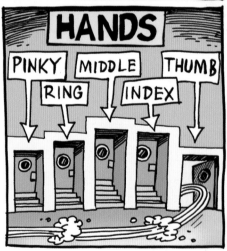

SHAMANISTIC SURGERY

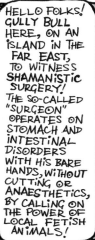

HELLO FOLKS! GULLY BULL HERE, ON AN ISLAND IN THE FAR EAST, TO WITNESS SHAMANISTIC SURGERY! THE SO-CALLED "SURGEON" OPERATES ON STOMACH AND INTESTINAL DISORDERS WITH HIS BARE HANDS, WITHOUT CUTTING OR ANAESTHETICS, BY CALLING ON THE POWER OF LOCAL FETISH ANIMALS!

HE HAS ALREADY GATHERED TRIBUTE FROM THE PATIENT'S FAMILY AND VILLAGE, AND IS NOW ENTERING THE TRANCE STATE THAT WILL ENABLE HIM TO CONDUCT THE OPERATION...

LEAVE TRIBUTE HERE

THE SHAMAN IS KNEADING AND MASSAGING THE PATIENT'S BELLY! I CAN'T QUITE SEE WHAT'S HAPPENING, BUT HIS FINGERS SEEM TO BE PUSHING AND DIGGING INTO THE FLESH OF THE PATIENT... THERE ARE TRACES OF BLOOD AND TISSUE...

GRUNT GRUNT

THE CROWD GATHERED ROUND ARE GASPING AND CHATTERING... AND—YES! I CAN SEE WHAT LOOKS LIKE INTESTINE!

GREAT SCOTT! INTESTINAL TUBE IS SPRINGING AND WRIGGLING FORTH FROM THE PATIENT! IT LOOKS LIKE IT'S OUT OF CONTROL!

SQUEAK SQUEAK SQUEAK

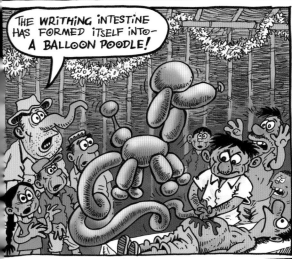

THE WRITHING INTESTINE HAS FORMED ITSELF INTO— A BALLOON POODLE!

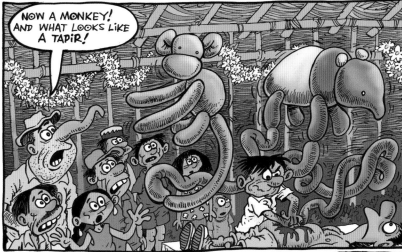

NOW A MONKEY! AND WHAT LOOKS LIKE A TAPIR!

INCREDIBLE! THE DISEASED GUTS HAVE TAKEN THE SHAPES OF THE LOCAL FETISH ANIMALS— AND THE TRIBE ARE GOING WILD!

I'VE MANAGED TO GET NEAR THE PATIENT... TELL ME— HOW DO YOU FEEL?

BURP!

'SCUSE ME... A TOUCH OF WIND!

BIRD SUPERSTITIONS

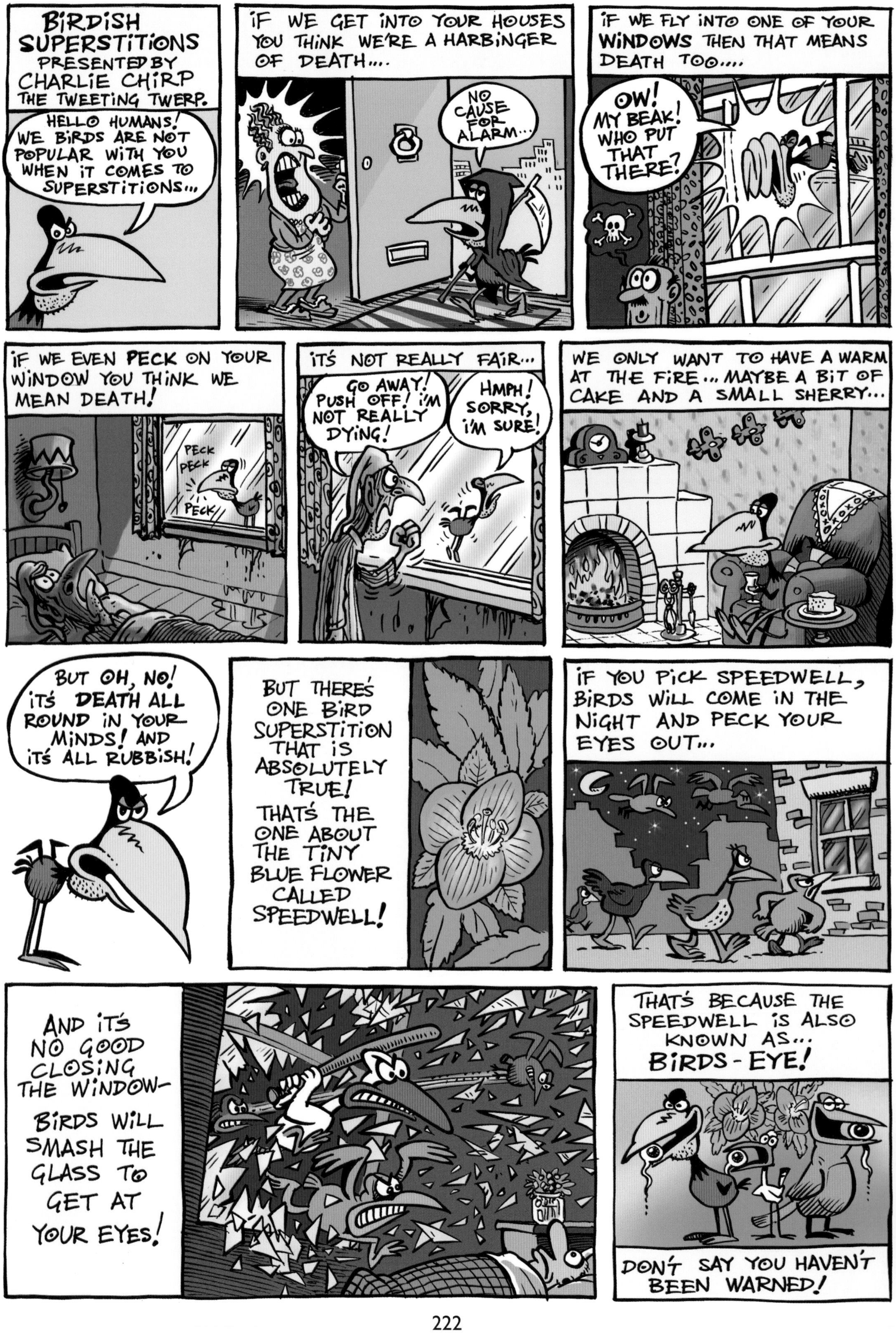
BIRDISH SUPERSTITIONS PRESENTED BY CHARLIE CHIRP THE TWEETING TWERP.
HELLO HUMANS! WE BIRDS ARE NOT POPULAR WITH YOU WHEN IT COMES TO SUPERSTITIONS...
IF WE GET INTO YOUR HOUSES YOU THINK WE'RE A HARBINGER OF DEATH....
NO CAUSE FOR ALARM...
IF WE FLY INTO ONE OF YOUR WINDOWS THEN THAT MEANS DEATH TOO....
OW! MY BEAK! WHO PUT THAT THERE?
IF WE EVEN PECK ON YOUR WINDOW YOU THINK WE MEAN DEATH!
PECK
PECK
PECK
IT'S NOT REALLY FAIR...
GO AWAY! PUSH OFF! I'M NOT REALLY DYING!
HMPH! SORRY, I'M SURE!
WE ONLY WANT TO HAVE A WARM AT THE FIRE... MAYBE A BIT OF CAKE AND A SMALL SHERRY...
BUT OH, NO! IT'S DEATH ALL ROUND IN YOUR MINDS! AND IT'S ALL RUBBISH!
BUT THERE'S ONE BIRD SUPERSTITION THAT IS ABSOLUTELY TRUE! THAT'S THE ONE ABOUT THE TINY BLUE FLOWER CALLED SPEEDWELL!
IF YOU PICK SPEEDWELL, BIRDS WILL COME IN THE NIGHT AND PECK YOUR EYES OUT...
AND IT'S NO GOOD CLOSING THE WINDOW- BIRDS WILL SMASH THE GLASS TO GET AT YOUR EYES!
THAT'S BECAUSE THE SPEEDWELL IS ALSO KNOWN AS... BIRDS-EYE!
DON'T SAY YOU HAVEN'T BEEN WARNED!

ISSUE 400! WHO'D HAVE IMAGINED IT, eh? 400!

woo!

Fortean Times 400!

FOR ISSUE 200 I DEPICTED 200 PHENOMENA IN TWO PAGES!

NO YOU DIDN'T—YOU CHEATED!

I DID NOT!

YOU DID...

DIDN'T!

DID!

DIDN'T!

DID

WELL, I'M NOT GOING THROUGH THAT AGAIN, I CAN TELL YOU! IT NEARLY FINISHED ME OFF!

DID!

NO, THIS TIME I THOUGHT I'D GO BACK TO SOURCE! I'LL LOOK AT PAGE 400 OF THE COMPLETE BOOKS OF CHARLES FORT—(DOVER, 1974)

THE GREEN ONE WITH THE FALL OF FISH ON IT...

THE COMPLETE BOOKS OF CHARLES FORT

LET'S SEE... 400... AH! IT'S IN "NEW LANDS", AND IT SEEMS MR. F IS GOING ON ABOUT UNKNOWN OBJECTS IN THE MORNING SKY THAT APPEAR AND DISAPPEAR CLOSE TO AND AROUND VENUS...

REPORTS OF THESE STRANGE LIGHTS ALWAYS SEEM TO COINCIDE WITH A PERIODIC NEAR APPROACH OF VENUS TO THE EARTH...

...AND THEY GENERALLY TURN OUT TO BE... VENUS ITSELF!

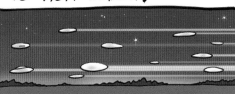

BUT FORT, AS ALWAYS, GIVES EQUAL CREDENCE TO THE AMBIGUOUS! HOW CAN WE DISMISS THE IDEA THAT SPACECRAFT FROM THE PLANET MIGHT TAKE ADVANTAGE OF THE NEAR APPROACH, EVERY 584 DAYS, TO VISIT EARTH?

ON VENUS...

C'MON KIDS— WE'RE GOING TO EARTH FOR THE WEEKEND!

AWW— DO WE HAVE TO?

IT STINKS!

GET IN AND STOP WHINING!

ARE WE NEARLY THERE YET?

FORT GOES ON TO DISCUSS OTHER, MORE EXOTIC VENUS-RELATED AERIAL PHENOMENA, BUT THAT'S NOT ON PAGE 400, SO...

SLAM!

THE SEARCH CONTINUES...

GULLY BULL – FORTEAN INVESTIGATOR!

I KNOW WHAT YOU'RE THINKING: "THE FAMOUS NOSE FOR MYSTERY, SNIFFING OUT A PHENOMENON!"

WELL, YOU'RE WRONG! I'VE NO IDEA WHERE I'M GOING OR WHAT I'M LOOKING FOR!

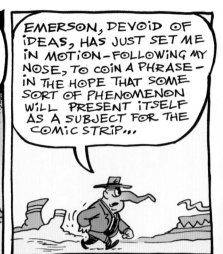

EMERSON, DEVOID OF IDEAS, HAS JUST SET ME IN MOTION – FOLLOWING MY NOSE, TO COIN A PHRASE – IN THE HOPE THAT SOME SORT OF PHENOMENON WILL PRESENT ITSELF AS A SUBJECT FOR THE COMIC STRIP...

SO – I FIND MYSELF **DRAWN** IN THE ACT OF INVESTIGATING, WITH NO NOTION OF **WHAT** I'M INVESTIGATING!

MY NOSE IS NOT VERY HAPPY!

mutter mutter
mutter mutter

IT'S NOT WORKING, IS IT?!

NO... YOU'RE RIGHT...

← Voice of Emerson

MAYBE IF I....

HEY! WHAT'S THIS?

IT'S A **WEIRDNESS ATTRACTOR** OF MY OWN DEVISING!

A TINFOIL HAT?? ARE YOU TRYING TO MAKE ME LOOK STUPID?

IT'S GOT **WIRE COAT HANGERS** IN IT TOO!

NO! I'M NOT HAVING IT... IT'S EMBARRASSING! I'M OFF!

TINKLE

WOW! WAIT, GULLY! COME BACK – QUICK!!

WHAT IS IT?

OH... NOTHING ...NEVER MIND. WE'VE GOT TO THE END OF THE PAGE NOW...